D0941445

Dictionary of Astrology

A COMPLETE

Dictionary of Astrology,

IN WHICH

EVERY TECHNICAL AND ABSTRUSE TERM

Belonging to the science is minutely and correctly explained,

AND THE

VARIOUS SYSTEMS AND OPINIONS

OF

THE MOST APPROVED AUTHORS

CAREFULLY COLLECTED AND ACCURATELY DEFINED.

COMPRISING

The only rational Method of calculating NATIVITIES,
and The Doctrine of HORARY QUESTIONS complete.

DIVESTED OF THEIR EXTRAVAGANCE, CONTRADICTIONS,
AND ABSURDITIES.

WITH AN INTRODUCTORY PREFACE BY

PROF. OLIVER AMES GOOLD.

By JAMES WILSON Esq. *Philomath.*

SAMUEL WEISER, INC.

New York

1969

SAMUEL WEISER, INC.
734 Broadway
New York, N.Y. 10003

Printed in U.S.A. by
NOBLE OFFSET PRINTERS, INC.
NEW YORK 3, N. Y.

PROLEGOMENA.

I assume the task assigned me, with no other purpose or expectation, than to aid such persons as are endeavoring to advance in a knowledge of the principles of planetary science, and their application to every day practice.

In the course of my earlier study of the elementary part of the science (before I had ventured to its practice), I applied to an old and quite learned professor of astrology, and, with candor, asked him some plain and simple questions for information. I received in reply no scrap of knowledge, but met with the discouragement of his assumption that he could do what no one else could, in the application of planetary laws. He appeared anxious to shroud the subject in mystery, and to claim special inspiration neccessary to its understanding and practice. My resolution was then, and there, turned more positively toward the avenues of information, and I reached a determination, with a unanimity of all the forces of my mind, to ever throw the greatest possible light upon the subject, for the benefit of every honest and sincere seeker after its truth, who should follow in my footsteps. In the years that have elapsed since that time, I have ever held that experience in vivid recollection, and have sent no student away hungering or thirsting for information which it was in my power to impart; neither have I ever exacted or received in any instance, pecuniary compensation therefor.

It is with the desire to disseminate the principles which underlie this science, that I am induced to steal some time from the flying hours in the midst of a very active life, in an endeavor to conduct the reader of the following pages to a more lucid understanding of the authors meaning; also to correct some of his honest errors of opinion in some important points and applications of the science.

As an apology for the errors aforenamed, let it not be forgotten by the reader, that the author, in his time, was not a practitioner of astrology as a means of livelihood; hence was never able to make as broad and extensive an application of his observation as many others, whose necessities compelled them to constant and unremitting effort and experiment: thus he omitted to verify many aphorisms and truths of which others (perhaps less learned in general philosophy) had found abundant or convincing proof. I will be somewhat explicit in my statement of what appears to me to be erroneous in his enunciation of the cardinal principles of the ancient writers and commentators on the subject. The reader will observe that the author discards entirely the whole significance of the mansions or houses of the heavens, in the consideration of nativities; likewise the "essential dignity" of the planets; also the Moon's north and south nodes; declaring, that as there is nothing except a point or place, no influence could possibly spring therefrom, unless it could come from nothing.

My own experience and observation have taught me that too much stress should not be placed upon the houses of the heavens, or predictions ventured based entirely upon the house in which a planet is posited, a transit occurs, or a direction falls; but I find a daily application of the usefulness of this division of the zodiac into mansions or houses.

Take, for example, the four angles of the figure, embracing the first, tenth, seventh and fourth houses of the heavens. Almost every person possessing any knowledge of a figure of the heavens, and competent to judge it, to any extent, has found experimental evidence of the fact that the angle of the east, or first house, ever exercises an influence over the personal affairs of the native, and fortunates or afflicts according to its strength or weakness. In the same manner it will be found that the angle of the south or tenth house influences the affairs of business, or profession, honors and reputation of the native; while the seventh house affects the concerns of wives, enemies, or opponents; and the fourth, or angle of the north, gives signification of real estate, of the ultimate of life, and in the language of the learned Mr. Lilly, "ever of the father of the native."

I have substantiated the truth of these in a general way, and with sufficient correspondence of detail to justify me in its promulgation as an astrological axiom. I have ever found in my practice, the Moon's nodes significant in the character to which the ancient teachers have assigned them, viz: the north node, benefic; and the south, malefic in influence. I am of the opinion that any person possessing a figure of the heavens for the time of their birth, can verify the truth of this ancient doctrine of the nodes, by simply observing the time when the Sun, in its annual course through the zodiac, reaches the point or place of the South node in the figure; for, at that time, annoyances, of greater or less degree, will ever mark the period, according to the directions, primary, and secondary, that are in force. This will enable the student in the science, to offer some test of its truth to anyone whose nativity they may possess.

The author, in his most commendable attempt to separate the chaff from the wheat, has given a little too radical blast to the wind of his condemnation; but the many vagaries he has stamped with the seal of his disapproval, renders his work a valuable one to the present generation of students inquiring after truth. The principal lesson that the author has labored to inculcate, by the tenor of his comments, which I most heartily endorse, from whence every student may derive profit, is the wisdom of making general, rather than particular application of planetary influences. In other words, that it is more rational to give a good outline in any case than to attempt uncertain and imperfect detail.

In calculations involving so many and such varied qualities of influence, it is sufficient that a general classification of the forces is accomplished, and the student is never greater in modest self abnegation than when he has the grandeur of mind to say to the overcritical persons, with whom he comes in contact, who propound detailed questions, *I do not know.*

It is neither wise or prudent to make answer or give judgement upon the question so often asked, and urged by many, of the length of human life. No possible benefit can be derived from such an opinion, unless it be given to the family physician of some patient in whose case a prognosis would be made, and who would hold the same in the repository of a faithful heart. The author declares that he should always predict long life to such as were solicitous upon this point. I have given better satisfaction to my own feelings, in cases where such demands are made upon me, by defining at once my position and conclusion, that I am willing and desirous to impart to them all knowledge, within my power, that will shed any ray of light upon the shadowy paths of life, or make its burden easier, without overstepping the boundary line which divides useful and rational knowledge from what belongs to the secret archives of a universal intelligence.

Since the student in astrology will continually meet along the highways of his progress, in study and in practice, individuals who offer every form and color of opposition to the principles of the science, it may be proper for me to furnish him with ammunition with which to repel such noisy, and usually unintelligent foes. The first, and most conspicuous postulate to be offered, by persons possessing a general knowledge of history, literature and science, without having investigated the subject, will be that the discovery of Copernicus, which recognized the solar centre of our system of planets, exploded the whole ancient doctrine of planetary influence, which was originated and promulgated upon the assumption of a mundane centre. Let it be definitely understood that this discovery (or rather verification of the theory advanced by Pythagoras centuries earlier) in no way altered the figure of the heavens, or invalidated the deductions made from the apparent position of the Earth and Sun.

Ancient records of astrological data bearing the musty impress of nearly two thousand (2000) years, furnish conclusive evidence of an accuracy in astronomical mathematics worthy of comparison with the highest modern intelligence, and furnish us with convincing proof, that an eclipse of the Sun, which should occur in 1882, could have been calculated with almost as certain exactness at Alexandria, Egypt, at the beginning of the Christian era as it could have been done at Oxford, Cambridge or Harvard Universities, under the scientific light of the nineteenth century. Let these facts, serve as an answer to this class of critics, who, by their lack of a sufficient investigation, aid in perpetuating a blunder in philosophy and history as well.

The next and most frequent criticism presented by the general skeptic, is one based upon an assumption that the science of astrology would have all persons born at the same time, share the same destiny, and be alike in all particulars. No wise expounder of the science attempts to prove any such theory. It is well known, by the careful observer, that the condition of heredity must be considered in accounting for the differences that exist between two persons born at the same time; but the same position and configuration of the planetary forces will render the times, seasons, and appointments of life correspondent with each other.

I have found in my practice, that, in determining the degree of success that may attend an individual, it is of great value to know the rank and success of two or three preceding generations of the native's ancestry. Families, like all forms of animal and vegetable life, have their period of growth and expansion, and in succession, their time of decline and decay.

Remarkable individuals, in any department of life's accomplishments, usually represent a climax, or the greatest altitude in a family line, from whence the pendulum turns and moves in the opposite direction. Succeding generations show a gradual receding from this maximum of quality, or of power. The student will discover it a valuable supplement to the ordinary data given him, to have a knowledge of the native's ancestry.

With the foregoing understanding of these primary conditions, the student will be able to meet and rebut the most formidable objections which may be urged by intelligent critics.

In conclusion, permit me to say, that no grander or more soul-ennobling theme was ever presented to the human intellect, than the philosophy and language of the starry heavens. It opens to our inspection an endless volume of sublimated grandeur. It comprehends the incomputable in number; the immensity of space; the duration of eternity. Whoever, in the love of celestial mathematics, scans the vault of space, and by the aid of telescopic vision, searches for some new star or satellite, or watches fair Venus in her march across the solar disc, with nothing save the philosophy of distance, time, and motion, to subserve, will find a satisfaction beyond the more material consideration of mundane life; but unto him who reads the language of the heavens, and catches the inspiration of her loftier melodies, there is a charm, and enchantment, that makes every star a divinity, and lights all space with a prophetic vision.

OLIVER AMES GOOLD.

PREFACE

TO THE ORIGINAL EDITION.

———�———

IF I had any motive more prominent than the rest (beyond promoting the cause of truth, which, I trust, will always be the principal) for publishing this work, it was a desire to injure those harpies who gather together scarce books of science, and hide them from the perusal of mankind, merely for the sake of gain, which, after all, can be but trifling: men like these are the enemies of knowledge, and ought to be severely punished in every civilized nation. This treatise will render most of their hoards comparatively useless, for I have been careful to insert the substance of all they contain relating to astrology, whether true or false, adding occasionally some remarks of my own to distinguish the latter as far as I am able, that every student may be enabled to found his own conviction on his own experience.

The system of Directions, both Primary and Secondary, I flatter myself, will be found peculiarly useful, for they are plain, and may be comprehended in a moment. They comprise the entire system of Placidus, not only as relates to Directions, but also to Progressions, Transits, Ingresses, and Lunations.

In this work no system has been wholly rejected on account of its evident falsehood and absurdity, but all are included, investigated, and explained.

The most prominent parts are selected from the works of Ptolemy and Placidus, the former being the founder of most or all the systems at present known, and the latter is universally admitted to have been the most scientific and rational of all Ptolemy's successors. I have, therefore, been careful to include all his opinions, which may be done without great difficulty in small compass, as he was a very circumlocutive author, who often took a page to describe what might have been compressed into half a dozen lines.

His works, however, on the whole, are valuable, particularly his directions, both primary and secondary, which I have here presented to the reader divested of their obscurity and difficulty.

The intention of this work is to render every point in astrology as plain and familiar as possible, that the science may be open to examination and experience, both in its genethliacal and horary departments, and that numbers may have an opportunity of applying themselves to the study of it, which is the only means of demonstrating the truth it contains.

As to the ridiculous idea that it is sinful and presumptuous, none but a very ignorant person will entertain it for a moment. If astral observations were sinful, it would be criminal to foretell an eclipse, a change of weather, the time of high water, or even the time of day by a sun-dial. It is, on the contrary, sinful not to study this and every other thing the Almighty has allotted for instruction, and the ignorance of those who neglect to do this is their only excuse.

There is one great difficulty peculiar to astrological studies which has hitherto retarded their progress considerably, and I fear will continue to do so for ages, namely, the want of proper materials. In all other sciences every thing necessary for practice or experiment can, in general, be readily procured, whereas, proper nativities of persons born with any remarkable defect are seldom to be obtained. A chemist can make a thousand combinations at will, and a thousand experiments on each, whereas, an astrologer might pass the period of his life without being able to make a single experiment in the way he could wish; and he might think himself extremely fortunate if he ever acquired six remarkable nativities that were correctly taken, and the lives of persons annexed to them. The time of a birth is seldom known beyond the hour, and if it be taken to minutes, the minute is almost sure to be incorrect. If a remarkable character be discovered the birth of such a person is nearly as difficult to be obtained as the philosopher's stone. The time of conception cannot be expected, nor the time when the embryo quickened, and yet, doubtless, on these depend many, and perhaps most, of those events, the causes whereof are sought in the radix. Instead, therefore, of wondering why so little is known relative to genethliacal astrology, we might well be surprised that any thing is known. It is not impossible that the nature and fate of an animal are fixed long before it breathes the vital air, and although its separation must occasion considerable alteration, the birth is, in all probability, only a sympathetic event, depending on other antecedent circumstances, and particularly on the position and distance of the luminaries at the time of conception.

In horary questions I have laid down the plain fundamental rules from which an artist should judge, but his own practice will enable him, by an adherence to these, to do this in a way peculiar to himself; for although these rules cannot with safety or propriety be altered, they are capable of many trifling improvements, which the student's practice will suggest to him, and which no one but himself can either feel or describe. He should never employ his art but for his own benefit, or that of his most confidential friends. In this case he will have some additional assistance in his knowledge of their affairs, but in applying this he must be very cautious, and never quit his figure for a moment; if he abandon his science it will abandon him. The knowledge of leading circumstances is only useful to enable him to judge of some abstruse parts of his scheme which otherwise would be unitelligible, but if he prefer his knowledge to his figure, he is an impostor, and will soon feel the effects of his knavery and folly, for foresight will often err, but his figure never; and however prosperous the affairs of the querent may appear in his judgment, if the figure denote evil, that evil will surely arrive, to his disgrace and confusion. In other respects he may be apt to err through a weakness common to human nature, that of believing what we wish, and not seeing what we dread. He must guard against this as much as possible, and give every testimony its full force. It is useless to blink the evil, for if the figure declare it, it will certainly occur, and the more he or his friends are prepared against it the better. Where mischief cannot be avoided, or where the knowledge of impending evil would greatly alarm the party, he should conceal his knowledge, and if any good can be done, rather strengthen them by advice, than terrify them by predictions. Indeed, those are the wisest artists who keep their knowledge to themselves as much as possible; for they may serve their friends more effectually by concealing the source of their information.

I have, under the article "Trignometrical Calculations," enabled every student to find, by trigonometry, his right and oblique ascensions, declinations, longitudes, latitudes, &c., without the help of tables, provided the requisite number of terms be given to find the rest.

I have here to apologize for sometimes using the terms "attraction" and "gravitation," as the reader will soon discover that I believe in neither; but they are terms generally understood, as when we say, the sun rises or sets, although we know that he only appears and disappears by the earth's motion, and under these circumstances we consider such expressions as innocent and convenient absurdities.

All that now remains is, to caution the reader against those shallow characters who think by rule and judge by hearsay. Before he attempts to answer any of their objections, let him give them a date, and bid them to erect a figure to it, and bring up a direction or two. When he finds they know nothing of the matter, as he soon will, his best way will be to adopt the Pythagorean method of cure, and enjoin them silence until they do, and if they comply with this request, it will probably silence them for ever. Should he, however, be of a more mercurial turn, and fond of amusing himself with the absurdities of others, I know not where he could find better game, for, like Yorick, with all their sail, he'll not find them carry an ounce of ballast.

The most ignorant among them will be the most consistent, and consequently the most respectable, for those who have acquired a tolerable share of learning, will be found to have acquired self-sufficiency in an equal ratio, and they will at all times be ready to expose themselves if he hold up his finger. A number of those wiseacres (some of whom, to the disgrace of literature, were permitted to write for an encyclopædia) once took it into their heads, probably at the instigation of some wag, to settle at once the long disputed point, of, whether the moon had any influence on the weather, or not; they had heard somewhere that the lunar influence was most conspicuous at the change or full, and it happening then to be near the change, (which may in some degree account for their folly,) they sallied forth, with an almanac in one hand and a weather-glass in the other, to see what impression would be made on the latter at the moment of conjunction. No doubt they had predetermined to sell their prejudices as dear as possible, and to be convinced at no less price than some of those tremendous convulsions of nature which took place at the demolition of Friar Bacon's brazen head. Alas and a well-a-day for Astrology! the mercury remained stationary—not the smallest difference whatever could be perceived; the moon was non-suited, and the jury returned in triumph, singing "*Io Pœan, Evoe Bacche?*"

I would engage for all I am worth, that any man should pitch

upon the first rustic he met in the street, and, upon explaining
the case to him, if he made any experiment at all, it should be a
more rational one than this. It would be useless to guess at what
ideas such men could have of the manner in which the luminaries act upon the weather, because it is plain they had no ideas at
all. Neither at the moment of conjunction, nor for hours, nor
even a day or two before, can the luminaries affect the atmosphere
in any particular manner relating to such conjunction, and should
a material change of weather happen, it must be owing to other
causes. The luminaries operate on the weather two different
ways; either by crossing or joining their influences. At the
square they cross or impede each other at right angles, and this is
the strongest opposition. As the angle becomes more acute, viz.,
as the Moon approaches the Sun, this opposition declines, and
when they form an angle of 45° it wholly ceases. A little before
this time the change commences. The powers of the luminaries
from being opposed to each other assume an opposite condition,
and become more conjunct. This will naturally cause a great
shock in the atmosphere about the third day after the Moon has
passed her second dichotome, when she forms her last sextile with
the Sun and approaches the semiquadrate; and a manifest change
in consequence will be perceptible. After this, the moon still approaches the Sun, and their conjunctive power increases, but it
increases gradually, and, as its operation is almost uniform until
the third day after the conjunction, the atmosphere can receive no
shock, nor feel any convulsion, except from some different cause,
in no way relating to the conjunction. As to the opposition, it
very seldom produces any remarkable effect on the atmosphere,
which is the more strange, as its effect on the tides is the same.
Until, however, the operation of the luminaries on the water can
be removed, no man, however shallow, or however assuming, will
ever be wholly able to sap the foundation of astrology. It will
maintain its ground in defiance of their puny efforts; and in some
future period, when reason becomes more the order of the day, it
will acquire more popularity than ever.

I cannot conclude this preface without directing the reader's
attention to the announcement of this work in the monthly Magazine for May, 1819, which is accompanied by the following remark:—

"We entreat the authors to reflect, that on the doctrine of
chances any other key will foretell as accurately as the stars, and

that on the mere *chance* that any prognosticated event may happen, depends the entire mystery of every science of prediction."

I certainly should not have suspected this tautological farrago of ill-joined words and sentences to have been the production of the editor of the Monthly Magazine, had he not avowed it as such in a subsequent correspondence with which he has honoured me.

"Chance" follows "chances" with reiterated jar, like the nerve-fretting clank of two cymbals: yet so partial are parents to their own offspring, however homely, that no argument of mine can prevail on the learned editor to allow the word *chances* to remain in its proper place—the errata, where it might have a *chance* of being concealed, but he insists on seeing it dragged, like another Cerberus, into light, where it can serve no other purpose than to sully the few remaining beauties of the paragraph. The metaphor of the "key" too, I took the liberty of offering to his more serious consideration, for I never heard of a key that foretold anything, whatever it might enable its possessor to foretell; besides the proper place of a key is not *on* but in, except the key possess the property of the Cadmean lyre, in which case, being laid *on* the "doctrine of chances," as the other was on the walls of Thebes, it may enable the former to chant forth its oracles in "sweet melodious strains." What the "doctrine of chances" itself is I have yet to learn;—it is, I believe, only to be found in the problems of professor Hoyle, whose works at present I have not time to peruse. Possibly the learned editor may condescend in another paragraph, to describe it himself, without putting me to that inconvience. Is *chance* an effect without a cause, or, one whose cause is unknown? That it can be the former is, I think, an absurdity too great even for the inventor of the new system of Material Phenomena to utter; and if it be the latter, all, or mostly all, the phenomena of nature must be the result of chance, for very few of its effects can be traced to their causes. For my own part, I make it a point to "reason from what I know," and as I perceive some effects which I can trace to their causes, I am naturally led to conclude that all effects arise from causes, and that it is only through our ignorance of those causes (arising partly from our own silly prejudices, which prevent us from searching after them more minutely, but chiefly from our limited powers, which, in numberless cases, must render all research ineffectual,) that we are unable to trace every event to its proper source, and to predict with correctness the nature of such event, and the time when it will happen.

From the nature of the paragraph in question, I was induced to believe that the author had never been able to calculate a direction in his life, and took the liberty to state this as my opinion, but he assures me that at the early age of eighteen he was almost the only one who could bring up directions according to the Placidian system. The age of eighteen, however, is not the age of astrology, and a boy might calculate directions like any other mathematical problems, without knowing or caring about the more intricate parts of the science to which they belong; as he might learn reduction or practice, without any acquaintance with the nature or spirit of trade. At all events, the calculations of nativities seems to have been no part of the learned editor's *forte*, nor will his assertion, "that in perusing his 'Walk to Kew,' I shall perceive that he is no novice in my art," in any way alter my opinion, for I find, on perusing it, that he is a very great novice, not only in "*my art*," but his own theories, for he denies in one part what he affirms in another. The paragraph in question, **if it** means any thing, denounces the whole science of astrology as a falsehood, whereas, in his Walks to Kew he admits "that the planets have been found to foretell some events," and "that every horoscope enabled Partridge to foretell with precision a certain number of events." This is all that astrologers contend for, and more than I would undertake to perform; for I have seen some horoscopes from which little or nothing could be predicted by me at least, owing to the limited knowledge I possess of celestial causes.

In the course of this Walk to Kew we find some light thrown on the famous "doctrine of chances," which, however, will not add lustre to the author's character for acuteness or experience. We are told, that " of any hundred ordinary events of human life, it may be an even chance that sixty of them will or will not happen." If he means eating or sleeping, which are "ordinary events," a slight knowledge of the native's habits may make them nearly all come true; but I will venture to affirm, that of an hundred events, ordinary or extraordinary, that are worth predicting, admitting them all to happen, not one, much less sixty, of them will be likely to happen at the time predicted, except it be done on surer grounds than the mere operation of fancy; if they do, the occurrences must be very ordinary indeed.

Another proof that he is still in his noviciate with respect to astrology, is, his opinion that in nativities the stars are considered as indices, and in horary questions as causes, whereas the very reverse is the fact. The death of her Royal Highness was *caused* not *indicated*, by the Moon acquiring the solar declination in her radix; whereas, in the first horary question, the death of the quesited was *indicated*, not *caused*, by the Moon's opposition to the Sun; for, had this been the cause, the whole world would have been depopulated on that occasion. Another mistake is, his supposition that astrologers must suppose events to govern causes, which is again an evident proof that he never knew much of the science he affects to condemn. The system of Placidus is, indeed, an attempt to trace causes by their effects, but not to govern them. But, if any one thing more than another could demonstrate the learned Editor's ignorance of astrology, it is his assertion, that "the square of Mars and Mercury must operate on the whole earth and its inhabitants alike." In the first place, the square of Mars and Mercury, or the trine of Saturn and Jupiter, are of but small consequence any way, and had he studied even Ptolemy or Placidus, he would have known that the luminaries are the chief moderators. In the second place, he would have learnt that, the aspects of moderators are considered only in respect of their places in each radix, and not as to their general position.

It is a common observation, that "a little learning is a dangerous thing;" but a great deal is fatal to the common sense of the possessor in an equal ratio, as the former may be to his morals;— instead of expanding his mind it contracts it, and imbues him with that overweening arrogance which teaches him to treat every set of opinions but his own with contempt, and to deem himself qualified to comprehend the most abstruse doctrine at a glance, without the trouble of investigation. Hence the learned Editor is induced to consider astrology as the "Daughter of Superstition," (without being able to perceive that many of his own acquirements are the offspring of dogmatic prejudice,) and to declare his opinion that every science of prediction has only chance for its basis, although the greater part of them are only known to him by their names. But, in whatever light he may view *every* science of divination, there are two insurmountable difficulties which I perceive they will always present to him—their *knowledge*, and their *confutation*.

INTRODUCTION.

——*——

THAT the stars have an effect upon the Earth and its inhabitants, is as self-evident a truth as that they have an existence:—the ebbing and flowing of the tides prove this, as well as the periodical returns of heat and cold, light and darkness. These are the most prominent parts of Judicial Astrology, for in these, planetary influence is universally felt and admitted, and its periods are accurately known. Thus far, at least, all men are astrologers, though most of them have not sense sufficient to discover it. Changes of weather, and all the various conditions of the atmosphere proceed from the same causes, namely—the various positions and configurations of the stars, although the manner in which they effect those changes is not wholly known; but an attentive observer will perceive them, more particularly at the lunar dichotomes and sextiles, and not unfrequently at the semisextiles and semiquadrates. Every sublunary event has its origin in planetary influx, and, as Locke justly observes, "the change or removal of any orb, although incomprehensibly distant, would cause things to put on a very different appearance." The dispositions, habits, and fortunes, not only of men, but of every organized being that does or can exist, are derived from the same source; and the infinite variety of action and counteraction arise from the infinite variety of causes operating against each other, in which the less is of course overcome by the greater.

The more immediate of these causes are the planets, owing to their proximity, rapid motion, and frequent combinations with each other, as well as with the fixed stars, which enables them to produce and convey a variety of different influences. Of these the luminaries are the greatest in power,—the Moon by reason of her proximity, and the Sun from his immense magnitude and peculiar conformation. But to give the reader a clearer idea of the nature and power of the planets, it is necessary here to subjoin a short description of them.

The SUN is a globe, apparently of fire, though there is great reason to suppose it to be a body of opake, cool matter, like our own, surrounded by a luminous substance, which, whether it be an atmosphere, as Herschel supposes it to be, or not, is a point not easily decided. Perhaps the sensations of heat and light derived from it, are only the natural consequences of its vivifying power operating on our senses, and, possibly, the inhabitants (if any) of the Moon may experience similar sensations from our Earth, round which they revolve in the same manner as we do round the

Sun. Certain it is, that, apparently, no heat proceeds from the Sun, as is evident from the accumulation of snow on the tops of high mountains, in climates where the sands of the valley would scorch the naked feet like burning embers. Caloric, therefore, must be produced from the Earth, and drawn to its surface by the solar influence. Hence, deep springs are warm in winter, when the Sun has not power to draw the heat from them, and cold in summer. Neither does the air imbibe any warmth from the solar rays, which is a proof they contain none, for the hot surface of the Earth, or any ignited substance, will warm it in an instant.

The Sun is about 1,392,500 times larger than the Earth, its diameter being estimated at 890,000 English miles. It is 1100 times larger than Jupiter, and 2360 times larger than Saturn. Its distance from the Earth is 95,200,000 miles, though some state it at 98,000,000, and others at 100,000,000. Its rotation on its axis from west to east is completed in 25d. 14h. 8m. Its shape, like that of the Earth, is an oblate spheroid. Its mean apparent diameter is 32′ 1$\frac{1}{2}$″. Its heat and light, according to Newton, is 7 times greater at the planet Mercury than with us, consequently that orb must be in many parts red hot, and its water continually boiling. This is a very absurd supposition; there is little reason, as before observed, to suppose that the Sun emits caloric; it only operates upon it where it is found, and there can be very little doubt but that the caloric power of Mercury is suited to the Sun's proximity. The mean daily solar motion is 59′ 8″. The body of the Sun is covered with a variety of shades of light, and appears very rough and uneven. Various spots are seen on it, called *maculæ*, supposed by Herschel to be depressions in the luminous atmosphere; and by others with more probability, to be bodies of opake matter, which in time acquire a degree of ignition, or, rather, they begin to be decomposed, and become luminous like the surrounding matter. These luminous spots are called *faculæ*. Herschel conceives the whole to be a collection of luminous or phosphoric clouds, some of which are brighter than others; and that their distance from the body of the Sun cannot be less than 1843, or more than 2765 miles. The inclination of its axis to its orbit is 82° 44′.

SATURN was formerly considered the most distant planet in the solar system. His mean distance from the Sun is 908, 000,000 miles; his mean diameter, 78,000 miles; he revolves round his axis in 10h. 16m., and round the Sun in 29y. 167d. 5h. His annual motion is 20,800 miles an hour; he is 750 times as large as the Earth, and half as large as Jupiter. He has seven satellites, or moons, and two rings, one of which is considerably larger than the other; the two together are about 39000 miles broad and about 39000 miles distant from Saturn's body. They revolve in the same time as Saturn himself, namely, 10h. 16m. The power of the Sun to Saturn is said to be only one ninetieth of what it is to the Earth. The form of Saturn is the same as that of all other revolving bodies, that of an oblate spheriod. His ascending node is in 22 degrees of Cancer, his mean apparent diameter 18″, and the inclination of his axis to his orbit almost nothing, so that he has no change of season; others state it at 60°.

INTRODUCTORY.

JUPITER is the largest of all the planets belonging to our system, except the Sun, from which he is distant 495,000,000 miles; his period is 11*y*. 314*d*. 12*h*., and he moves at the rate of 30,000 miles an hour. He is 1500 times as large as the Earth, and his diameter is 94000 miles. He revolves on his axis from west to east in 9*h*. 56*m*. His figure is that of an oblate spheroid; his diameter at the equator being to his axis as 13 to 12. The plane of his equator is only one degree 19 minutes different from that of his ecliptic; of course he has no change of seasons. His rotary motion is very rapid, being 30,940 miles, which is quicker than that in his orbit, The Sun has, they suppose, but one forty-eighth part of the power at Jupiter that he has with us, but the quick succession of his day and night, they add, may in some degree make up the deficiency. He has four satellites, and several appearances like belts, which frequently appear and disappear, and are supposed to be vast masses of clouds, caused by periodical winds or monsoons. His ascending node is in 8 degrees and a half of Cancer, and, of course, his descending node is in 8 degrees and a half of Capricorn. Some of his satellites are nearly as large as our Earth. The nearest of them is distant from the body of Jupiter about 266,000 miles, and the fourth is distant 1,189,000 miles. His mean apparent diameter is 39″.

MARS is less than the Earth, his diameter being 5150 miles, whereas ours is 7953 miles. His distance from the Sun is 145,-100,000 miles; he revolves on his own axis in 24*h*. 40*m*., and moves round the Sun in 686*d*. 22*h*. 18*m*. or at the rate of 54,000 miles an hour. He is said to have about half the quantity of our light and heat. It was generally supposed that his ecliptic had nearly the same obliquity to the plane of his equator as ours; others estimate the difference of the axis and orbit to be 59° 22′; but later observers assert that there is no obliquity, and consequently no change of seasons. His light is not so bright as that of Venus, although sometimes he appears as large; but he shines with a dull fiery redness, caused as some suppose, by a thick cloudy atmosphere; though the colours of the planets are probably owing to the nature of their substances which cause them to reflect the solar light differently. He is observed to have a bright part at the south pole, like a polar zone, and something of the kind at the north pole. Maraldi observed the former, with no alteration, for 60 years; the one half of it is brighter than the other. There are spots on his surface, and belts appearing and disappearing occasionally. He is, like the rest, an oblate spheroid, and his diameter at the equator is to his polar diameter as 16 to 15. Dr. Maskelyne, however, could observe no difference in his diameters. His ascending node is in 18 degrees of Taurus, and his mean apparent diameter 27″. The Sun appears to him only half as large as to us.

VENUS is next to the Earth within its orbit, and has generally been considered about the size of our globe, but according to later observation she is supposed to be a third larger, her diameter being 8648 miles; she revolves round her own axis from west to east in 23*h*. 21*m*., at the rate of 12,000 miles an hour, and goes round the Sun in 224*d*. 7*h*., at the rate of 80,000 miles an hour.

Her distance from the Sun is 68,800,000 miles. She seldom transits the Sun's disk above twice in a century. Her two last transits were on the 5th of June, 1761, and 3rd of June, 1769. The next two will happen December 18th, 1874, and December 6th, 1882. When viewed through a telescope she presents all the various phases of the Moon. She is never seen above 47° or 48° distant from the Sun, and when seen to the west of him she is passing to her superior conjunction; but when to the east of him, she is coming to her inferior conjunction between the Sun and the Earth. Casini and others have seen what was undoubtedly a sattellite of Venus, exhibiting the same phases, and about a fourth of her diameter; but it can be seldom seen, because its dark side is towards us when she is in her inferior conjunction, and it only presents its bright side when she comes near to her superior conjunction. She is generally allowed to have an atmosphere like to ours, and Schroeter of Bremen says her mountains are 5 or 6 times as high as ours. Herschel, however, could not see those mountains, nor was he very certain as to the time in which she revolved round her axis. The place of her ascending node is 15° of Gemini. Her mean apparent diameter is 58″. It is thought the obliquity of her ecliptic is much the same as that of our own.

MERCURY is the last planet perceptible between us and the Sun, though doubtless there may be many others. He is seldom seen, being hid by the solar rays; but he emits a very bright white lustre. He is best seen in a right sphere, or near the equinox, for those who live in an oblique sphere, more towards the poles, can hardly perceive him. His distance from the Sun is above 37,000,000 of miles; his diameter is, according to some, about 2600 miles, or, as others assert, 3224 miles; and he passes round the Sun in 87d. 23h., at the rate of 110,000 miles an hour. His light and heat are said to be seven times greater than ours, and he is, therefore, supposed to be either calcined or vitrified, if his substance be not more dense than any with which we are acquainted. This is a very ridiculous notion, and no way warranted on the general principles of nature.

The period in which Mercury revolves round his axis has been but lately known; it is now stated at 24h. 5m. 28s. His ascending node in 16° of Taurus. He never appears above 28 degrees distant from the Sun, and in the different parts of his orbit he displays all the different phases of the Moon. His mean apparent diameter is 10″. The Sun appears 7 times as large to him as to us.

The MOON is the Earth's only satellite; her mean distance is 240,000 miles, though she is sometimes one fourteenth part nearer in her perigee. Her diameter is 2180 miles, and she is one forty-ninth part as large as the Earth. She only reflects one thirteenth part of the quantity of light on the Earth which the Earth reflects on her. The force of gravity on her surface is supposed to be a third of that of the Earth. Her motion on her axis coincides with her periodical revolution round the Earth, so that the same side of her is always next to us. Her periodical revolution in making a complete circle of the globe is 27d. 7h. 43m. 5s., and her synodical revolution from the Sun to the the Sun again, is 29d. 12h. 44m.

3s. 11t.   She flies at the rate of 2290 miles an hour, and her day and night are as long as our lunar month.   Her position, however, is not so steady, for she turns sometimes a small part of her face from us, on one side or the other, which is called her libration; and sometimes she presents a part of one pole or the other.

The surface of the Moon exhibits a number of hills, mountains, caverns, craters, volcanoes, &c.   Some have disputed the existence of a lunar atmosphere, but the ingenious Schroeter, having discovered a twilight in Venus, discovered one shortly after in the the Moon, on the 24th of February, 1792, which of course is a proof that she has an atmosphere.   Her axis inclines to her orbit 88° 17'.   Her mean apparent diameter is 31' 8''.

The planet URANUS was discovered by Herschel, March 13th, 1781.   His distance from the Sun is 1,827,000,000 of miles, his mean diameter is 35,000 miles, and his period 83y. 150d. 18h.   He has six satellites moving round him in a retrograde direction, or from east to west, contrary to all others.   The existence of this planet was partly anticipated before its discovery, by Drs. Halley, Bradley, and others, who observed that Saturn was disturbed in his motion by some force, which they concluded must originate beyond his orbit, as they could not account for it on the known principles of gravitation.   The planet Uranus shines with a fine bluish-white light, between that of Venus and the Moon, and appears the size of a star of the eighth magnitude.   His mean apparent diameter is 3.54''.

NEPTUNE is the most remote planet known to belong to the solar system.   Dr. Galle first observed it in 1846.   Its appearance had previously been predicted both in France and England.   These predictions were based upon certain noticeable irregularities in the motion of the planet Uranus.   Its mean distance from the Sun is 2,746,000,000 miles.   Its diameter nearly 37,000 miles.   It makes its revolution through the signs of the zodiac in about 165 years.   Its volume will be found to be about 100 times as great as the Earth.   Its density about nine-tenths as heavy as water.   Its inclination of orbit to the plane of the ecliptic is 1° 47'.

CERES was discovered January 1st, 1801, by Piazzi, an Italian.   Her mean distance from the Sun is about 260,000,000 of miles, and her revolution round him is performed in 1681d. 12h. 9m.; her diameter, according to Herschel, 163 miles, but Schroeter supposes it to be ten times as much.   Her mean apparent diameter is 1''.

PALLAS was discovered by Dr. Olbers, of Bremen, March 26th, 1802.   Her mean distance from the Sun is 265,000,000 of miles, and her period 170²d. 16h. 48m.   Herschel estimates her diameter at 80 miles, and Schroeter (a very good astronomer) at 2099.   Her mean apparent diameter is 1''.

JUNO was discovered by Harding, a German, in December, 1804.   Her solar distance is 252,000,000 miles, and her period 4y. 129d. 5h.   Her diameter is estimated at 1425 miles, and her mean apparent diameter is 3''.

VESTA was also discovered by Olbers, in 1807.   Her solar distance is 225,000,000 miles, and her period 3y. 60d. 4h.; her diameter is estimated at 238 miles. Her mean apparent diameter is only half a second.

The EARTH we inhabit is distant from the Sun, some say 95, others 98, and others 100 millions of miles; its period is 365d. 5h. 48m. 48s.: and it moves at the rate of 68,856 miles an hour. Its rotation on its axis from west to east is completed in about 24 hours. Hence, the inhabitants of London are moved by the diurnal motion 580 miles, and those of the equator 1042 miles an hour. The difference between the planes of its ecliptic and equator is 23° 28' nearly. Its mean diameter is 7953 miles, but its equatorial diameter is 17 miles more, and its polar 17 less.

COMETS are generally considered as opake bodies, of the same substance as the planets, and only differing from them in the eccentricity of their orbits. They are called Comets from *Coma*, hair, or beams of light, because their rays, in many cases, look as if they were hairy or bearded: but this arises from the appearance of the tail in different positions. It is remarkable that their tails always flow in an opposite direction from the Sun, the cause of which has never been properly explained, although it has been the subject of many conjectures among the learned, who have been equally unfortunate respecting the parabolic curve of their orbits; to solve which, that contradictory doctrine of two forces, the centripetal and centrifugal, (neither of which is founded on either experience or reason,) is called in to their assistance. I know of no one who has exposed this unmeaning paradox with more acuteness than Mr. Brydone, in his Tour to Sicily and Malta, which I would advise the advocates of this system to peruse with attention. However mortifying it may be to human pride to be told that what they are pleased to term "inert matter," is not more inert or less animated than themselves, such, nevertheless, is the fact, and it is time they became acquainted with it. There is no such thing as inert matter; every particle is endowed with life, intelligence, and volition; and its motions, whether circular or parabolic, are the result of choice, and not of blind necessity. Every orb is an animal, moving round its primary, for reasons which, however impenetrable they may be to us, are well known to itself, and turning on its axis as a man would turn on his heel before a fire to warm himself on all sides. Nothing demonstrates the force of prejudice more than the doctrine that—matter has always a tendency to be at rest. The very reverse is the truth; for if matter possesses any quality more prominent than another, it is that of the singular and almost incredible velocity with which it continually moves. There is not an atom on this our globe but moves at the astonishing rate of about 69,900 miles an hour, besides its diurnal motion round its axis; and even this velocity may be almost actual rest compared with its real motion, if, as some have with good reason supposed, the system itself revolves round some other centre.

In ancient times men, deceived by appearances, believed the Earth to be stationary, and that the heavens alone moved; that the Sun and other stars proceeded to the westward by day, and were brought back in the night in some way or other, but by what means they did not know, just as an infant placed in a boat on the river would suppose that the land moved and the boat was fixed. On this optical delusion only was founded the silly notion that matter is inanimate and motionless; and such is the prevalence of habit, that it actually separates knowledge from knowledge, and causes a man to believe that a thing can and cannot exist at the same time. Hence, astronomers believe, because they see and know, that matter and motion are inseparable, and that no particle of it ever was or *can be* at rest; while, at the same time, they belive that it is perfectly inert, dead, averse to motion, and *always* at rest. Such is the strength of prejudice, and the weakness of humanity.

The number of opinions respecting Comets are too numerous to be inserted. Those of Newton seem to confirm the truth of the Shandean opinion, that "it is worth something to have a name." Hevelius and Kepler supposed them to proceed from some gross exhalations of the Sun, and some, very lately, have considered them the embryos of future planets. They are, certainly, different from the planets, although doubtless they are masses of matter reflecting the solar light. Their bodies are changeable, both in magnitude and appearance, and in no way resembling stars of any description. Their colors are sometimes red, sometimes yellow, generally dusky, divided into parts, and sometimes the nucleus wholly disappears, and seems converted into a thin cloudy matter. They appear to be substances positively and highly electrified, and the opinion of Halley and Dr. Hamilton—that their tails are composed of electric fluid—is very probable. This seems fully confirmed by the flashing or shooting of their tails. Whatever warmth they may derive from the abundance of this fluid, added to the heat they acquire from the action of the Sun, (which, probably, after all, is not much,) is all the heat they experience, and this the reader may rest assured is not quite "two thousand times hotter than the heat of red hot iron. It is lamentable that men who have genius should guide it with so loose a rein. The vagaries of Mr. Whiston, too, have been a source of alarm to many, whom I would advise to get rid of their fears as soon as possible. Comets and planets both, know better than to run foul of each other, nor do comets appear to possess those powers assigned to them by astronomers. One of them passed between the satellites of Jupiter, without altering their positions or orbits in any perceptible degree. In other respects, however, they seem sufficiently injurious. They doubtless have a sympathetic power of action, like all other bodies of matter, and cannot fail to disturb the economy of a globe not used to their influence. See the article "Comets."

The nature and substance of the FIXED STARS has hitherto set conjecture at defiance, for although the general supposition is, that they are suns of as many systems, there is but little in their appearance to justify such an opinion. About seven hundred of them are double, in which respect they differ from the only Sun we are acquainted with; and they exhibit various colours, chiefly white, though some are red, blue, and even greenish; and others are dusky; whereas our Sun is a compound of all those colours, and consequently they must differ from it in this particular, except we suppose their rays to pass through certain mediums which transmit only a ray of a particular colour, and absorb the rest. Planets they cannot be, revolving, like us, round a common centre, else we should see still more prominently the suns that light them. All we know of them is, that they must be bodies of some kind of matter, and, as such, possessing each of them a separate influence; but there is much reason to suspect the natures of their influences as nearly or wholly unknown. The only method laid down by Ptolemy is, to class them according to their colours, and judge of their effects according to the nature of such planets they most resemble; thus--the red are considered martial—the pale, saturnine, &c.; but this is a very erroneous method, because many of them resemble no planet in colour, nor is it certain that planets operate by means of their light, for the power of the Moon is as great when her dark side is turned towards us as when she is at full.

The term FIXED is very inapplicable to many of the stars, and probably to them all. Several new stars have appeared, several old ones have disappeared, and a still greater number change their places. One in Cassiopeia, in 1572, appeared as large as Venus at her brightest perigee, and was actually seen in daylight. It continued so for sixteen months, and then gradually disappeared without changing its place. Some think it returns periodically in about 319 years. There is a star in the Whale's Neck that appears and disappears seven times in six years. Another, near the right heel of serpentarius, appeared in 1694, as large as Venus, and totally disappeared in 1605. One star in the Swan's neck appeared and disappeared several times, at very unequal periods, and, in 1715, it settled as a star of the 6th magnitude, and so remains. Another star, near the Swan's Head, appeared and disappeared several times, and is now wholly lost. Another in the Swan, has a period of about 405 days, but not quite regular. A number of other stars have disappeared, and many change their magnitude. Several new stars have appeared in Cassiopeia, and some of them have again been lost. One in her knee disappeared, and two more appeared to the north of its place. Caput Algol is a variable star, and its period is 2*d*. 21*h*. It remains 2*d*. 14*h*, as a star of the 2d magnitude; in about three hours and a half it declines to a star of the 4th magnitude; and in about three hours and a half more it resumes its 2d magnitude, which it retains for 2*d*. 14*h*. as before. *Beta*, in Lyra, likewise has a period of 12*d*. 19*h*, during which time it appears of several magnitudes, from the 3d to the 5th. *Eta*, in Antinus, has a period of 7*d* 4*h*. 38*m*.; and *Delta* in Cepheus, of 5*d*. 8*h*. 37*m*. No doubt all these changes have a manifest effect upon the Earth, and produce some of those strange vicissitudes for which we are at a loss to account, and which baffle all the skill of the astrologer.

The fixed stars differ in their longitudinal positions about fifty seconds and one-third in a year, according to the order of the signs, or from west to east, owing to the receding of the equinoctial points from east to west. It was generally supposed by the ancients that the stars never changed their latitude, but the moderns have discovered this to be an error. Halley found Sirius,

Aldebaran, and Arcturus about half a degree more south, and Betelguese nearly a whole degree; but whether this arises from the proper motion of the star, or from our solar system changing its place, is uncertain.

The immense distance of the fixed stars may be conceived from their having no sensible parallax; and their apparant magnitude not being increased, but, on the contrary, diminished, by the power of a telescope. That they are not lighted by the Sun is supposed to be evident, on account of their distance, though there does not appear any sufficient proof that light, as such, proceeds from the Sun at all, but rather that it is, like heat, created or produced by the Sun's influence on any body of opake matter opposed to it, and that its quantity is more or less according to the capability of such substance to produce it. Were light a luminous emanation from the Sun's body, we should see it not only by day but also by night in its progress through the immensity of space, enclosing the Earth on all sides; whereas, not even a sunbeam can be perceived but from the surfaces of opake atoms that reflect it. We cannot know the boundary of the solar influence, nor is it probable that the light or heat of bodies opposed to it is wholly regulated by their distance, but rather by their fitness to receive and propagate them. We see that Mars is not so bright as Jupiter although nearer to the Sun; nor is it probable that Jupiter or Saturn are colder than Venus or Mercury. The belts of Jupiter and Saturn give us great reason to suppose they have each an atmosphere with clouds floating in it, and we are certain nothing of the kind could exist on our globe with only one nintieth of the Sun's present heat. It is probable, therefore, that the powers of generating light and heat are in all bodies proportional to their distance from the Sun, and this supposition is equally applicable to the fixed stars as to the planets. A much better reason why the fixed stars shine by their own light, or by light derived from other sources than our Sun, is their infinity, (which can hardly be doubted,) and the little probability that such an atom could operate through boundless immensity.

Many very ingenious attempts have been made to ascertain the distance of the nearest of the fixed stars, but, after all, the whole is conjectural. Dr. Bradley thought the nearest would be about 40,000 times as far off as the breadth of the earth's orbit, or 7,600,000,000,000 of miles. Later astronomers have supposed them much nearer; and, really, when we reflect on the short periods in which they alter their magnitudes, as before stated,(even in the course of a few hours,) their velocity must be beyond all human conception, if they are at such distances. Hence some have imagined that in their rotary motion they present various phases, which is the cause of such apparent difference in magnitude.

Those stars which appear to us the largest are supposed to be the nearest, but this is uncertain, as no doubt they differ in magnitude. That they seem to change their position by some means is evident, but whether this appearance is the result of their own proper motion, or that of our system is not quite certain. Most of the phenomena may be accounted for from the latter, but not the whole. Some think the stars never change their relative posi-

tions with each other, as double stars never separate. Motion,
however, is inseparable from matter, and there can be little doubt
that every system is in motion as well as our own; and whether
the fixed stars are or are not suns and centres of other systems,
they probably move with great rapidity through interminable
space.

Astrology is generally supposed to have been invented by the
Chaldeans, but this conjecture is only founded on their early astronomical knowledge, which they probably derived from Hindo-
stan. Its origin was assuredly in the east, where it is now universally practised and believed. The Arabs are generally supposed to have procured it from Egypt, but there can be no doubt
they had a system of their own in common with other oriental
nations long before that period, though, be this as it may, neither
are of much value. What we know of it is chiefly gathered from
the books of Arabian authors, and whatever astrology was originally, the whole appears to have been perverted into a mere system of divination, so as to be unfit for any genethliacal purpose.
The Quadripartite of Ptolemy, however, gives us reason to suppose that in Egypt, at least, it had once been on a more
respectable footing, though the absurdities contained in that
work, mixed up with some important truths, shew that it had
been long neglected, its original meaning almost forgotten. This
may have been owing to the mean selfish policy of the Egyptians,
who, to keep everyone in the dark but themselves, converted all
their knowledge into hieroglyphics, or transcribed it in the sacred
letters, as they were called, which were an alphabet used by the
priesthood only, the key of which being once lost, all their learn-
was lost with it.

This work of Ptolemy is the only standard we possess, and has
served as a foundation for every other. Some speak of it with
much veneration, though very few comprehend its meaning; and
it is evident, from the tenor of many parts, that the author did
not comprehend it himself. It is, however, preferable to the
works of the Arabians, which are the most superstitious mass of
symbolical and allegorical trash that can be conceived. Many
authors have written on the subject in all nations, but they chiefly
adhere to the Ptolemaic doctrines of essential dignities, lunar
nodes, and horoscope, which can have no effect in nativities; and
by misquoting some of his theories, the greater part of them have
contrived to render the science truly ridiculous. But this ought
not to deter others from studying it, for any reflecting person
must perceive, that effects in general being so very disproportion-
ate to their supposed causes, must proceed from something very
different, and this can be no other than astral influence; for on
what else does the whole fabric of the universe depend for its support, and the laws by which it is governed. To ascribe the whole
to the will of providence is merely an equivocation; that all
events depend on the will of providence cannot be doubted; but
we are alluding to secondary causes, under providence, which
always enforces its will by natural means, for we see it uses no
other. Providence would be much more highly honoured if mankind would take the trouble to investigate the ingenious laws and

machinery by which it governs the universe, than when they sit down and idly exclaim, "Oh, it is the will of providence," and think no more about it.

We know the change of season wholly depends on planetary influence, and, doubtless, the changes in the weather do the same; or, at least, on celestial causes of some kind. They are the result of variations in the atmosphere, and although these depend on the condition of the Earth, the latter depends on the state of the heavenly bodies by which it is surrounded and affected. Brutes and insects are early sensible of these vicissitudes; and nervous, sickly, or elderly people are the same: doors or shutters will swell or shrink, metals will contract or expand, watches will lose or gain time, stones and other substances impregnated with saline particles will sweat, and the entire face of nature becomes altered.

These alterations are frequently experienced when the Moon arrives at her quadratures, and particularly when she forms her last sextile with the Sun. Her conjunction with Mars is frequently productive of wet, especially when their latitudes agree. But the atmosphere often is liable to unusual and very lasting impressions. Some seasons are remarkable for dryness, wet, cold, or heat; some are sickly; others, healthy; and by these overwhelming causes even the the lunar aspects are neutralized. They do, indeed, produce certain changes, but such as are weak and of short duration. When particular diseases abound, they are usually ascribed to heat, cold, wet, &c., but a little reflection would shew the incorrectness of such opinions; for at other times when heat, cold, &c., are much more prevalent, such diseases are unknown. The observation of persons that they catch cold they know not how, is extremely just, for though colds are often caught by carelessness, they are more frequently the result of an altered state of the atmosphere from sidereal causes, against which no precaution is available, and many persons who encounter cold and wet without sustaining injury, will catch cold in a room without being exposed to either. Nothing can be a stronger proof of sidereal influence than the strange succession of fortunate and unfortunate events experienced by many individuals. The whole lives of some are a succession of disasters, and all their exertions terminate in disappointment. Injudicious conduct will, no doubt, produce misfortunes, but many to whom no blame can be attached are injured and ruined by a strange coincidence of circum. stances which no human prudence could foresee or prevent. Certain times are peculiarly disastrous to certain people, and in families numbers die nearly together. This is, probably, owing to some resemblance in their horoscopes, a thing very common among relatives.

Many of the more durable changes of the atmosphere may arise from the proximity of comets, a greater number of which approach the Earth than is generally supposed, although they are hidden by the blaze of the Sun. They mostly cause heat and dryness, particularly in the hemisphere where they are posited; and as opposite changes usually succeed each other, they may ultimately cause cold and wet. The luminaries, however, are the more immediate causes of sublunary vicissitudes in their mutual configurations with each other, and with the angles, particularly when posited in the midheaven. There is something remarkable in this angle, even when no planets are in or near it, for all vegetables will point to it by nature, and will dwindle and waste if any substance intervene between them and the zenith. This is the reason why grass will not grow beneath trees; animals decline from the same cause; and those who are confined in houses or mines, or who live in woods, are pale, cadaverous, and unhealthy, however freely the air may be admitted. No portion of matter affects the Earth so much as the Moon, for besides that she by means of her proximity conveys the influences of the celestial bodies to us by her various configurations with them, much depends on her anomaly or eccentricity. Nothing domonstrates the power of the Moon more than the period of gestation being 9 or 7 months, at which time she forms the square or trine of her radical place at the time of conception. Children born at the end of those periods may live; whereas, it is affirmed that, no infant produced in 8 months ever survived.

The medium through which distant portions of matter operate on each other may probably be a very fine fluid, emanating from each through infinite space, and wholly imperceptible except by its effects. This may be denominated sympathy, and to it may be traced whatever is deemed supernatural or miraculous; or, to speak more properly, whatever cannot be accounted for from the known properties, or, rather, the acknowledged properties of matter, for many of its properties are known that are not acknowledged. Locomotion and volition, for instance, by which the planets revolve round their axes, and move through their orbits, and by which every particle gravitates toward the centre of the mass to which it belongs; these are general sympathies, common to all matter with which we are acquainted. But the more particular or occult sympathies are those not common to matter, and apparently, contrary to its general laws; such as the polarity and attraction of the magnet, with numberless other unusual sympathies subsisting between certain bodies. for which we cannot accouut in the usual way. Those marks and accidents communicable to the fœtus in the womb, and the periodical alterations of such impressions according to the season of the fruit, flowers, or other substances from whence they originate, are two of the most common and striking proofs of occult sympathy that can be produced. Second sight, which, however it may be ridiculed, is too well authenticated to be disproved; ominous dreams, and those unaccountable forebodings and depressions of the mind very common in persons of a nervous, weak, or irritable frame, prior to unforeseen calamities, with a number of other instances superfluous to mention, are all incontestible proofs that every thing in nature operates upon the rest, and is operated on by them more or less according to its nature and texture, in a way of which we can form no conception. This occult sympathy was and is the source of every species of divination, which, notwithstanding the silly commonplace gibes of imitative witlings, and the frauds of its knavish professors, is really founded in nature and truth.

The mind, when anxiously and steadily fixed on knowing the result of an undertaking, has, from the tripod to the teacup, always been gratified, if a proper intelligent system were adhered to. Cicero ridiculed the augurs, probably with reason, (for there were many knaves among them) and perhaps without, for he might, after all, be more of an orator than a diviner, although, like the cobbler of Apelles, he could not be persuaded to stick to his last. At all events the Roman general would have shewn more solid judgment in following the line marked out to him by the chickens, than he did in throwing them into the sea, saying, "If they would not eat, they should drink," for he paid the full price of his folly.

Upon these sympathies of nature is founded the entire Science of Astrology, both Genethliacal and Horary. Genethical Astrology rests on the more common and obvious effects of a matter on matter, for the stars cannot affect the globe without inserting their power into every separate portion of matter that it contains.

Horary Astrology depends on that uncertain species of sympathy which, although equally a property of matter with the other, is seen in certain modifications only. Those whose minds are ardent, whose feelings are acute, and whose irritability of frame and consequent anxiety are excessive, are more subject to its operations than others, when their sensibility is excited by any object or event of importance. Thus, husbands sympathize with their wives, mothers with their children, and individuals of every description with those who are peculiarly dear to them, whether they be united or not by the ties of custom or consanguinity. They whose nerves are more indurated, and whose sensations are less acute, although their attachments be equally firm, are strangers to this kind of sympathy, through nervous insensibility, and it is very natural for them to deny the existence of what they never experienced, although placed in the same relative situations with those who do; hence, many disputes originate concerning the truth of those unusual perceptions. But there is nothing untrue or preternatural in them, for it is quite according to the course of nature that animals of a peculiar conformation should have the peculiar perceptions, sensations, and powers adapted to such conformation. This is the great secret of all divination, which was so denominated from the supposition that it was of divine origin, and proceeded from the gods; but it is neither divine nor diabolical, but the natural result of matter operating upon matter, as one planet disturbs another in its orbit, as the Moon disturbs the ocean, as the magnet draws iron, or glass excited by rubbing draws wax, &c.

There is no part of judicial astrology so easily and so perfectly attainable as the power of solving horary questions, where nature (if proper attention be paid to her impulses) will be found to accommodate herself to every emergency; whereas, in nativities, qualities and fate of an animal being regulated by the same fixed, uniform, unerring laws as the other phenomena of nature, the causes are too numerous, too complicated, and too remote ever to be wholly comprehended by any stretch of human intellect. Some of these are, from their nature, imperative; others, subordinate; and the greater must always overcome the less. Thus, as Ptolemy justly observes, the same act that with a man would produce a man, would with a horse produce a horse, although the positions of the stars may be exactly the same; and both the man and horse would be in any climate, or under a particular discipline, very different from what they would have been if produced at the same instant in any other climate, or under any other mode of tuition. Men born with indications of violent death would, in countries where wars and violence are unknown, die like others; whereas, in countries and times where wars predominate, a very slight direction would cause an untimely end. In the former case, however, the dissolu'e lives, hair-breath escapes, and numerous accidents common to such ill-fated and depraved characters clearly demonstrates that from their birth a train was laid for their destruction, which only awaited the concurrence of some other cause, as, for a match to fire it; and should confusion become the order of the day, they would be the first to rush into danger, and to perish in the conflict. Indeed, this is a fact generally known (although the true cause is not suspected), that the most worthless and desperate characters are the most anxious to engage in violent and hazardous enterprises. The effect, therefore, is traced to its cause, which cause is itself only an effect of planetary influence, as every one's reason, were it attended to, must acknowledge; for did no such thing as planetary interposition exist, men's minds and bodies would be perfectly alike, for what should cause them to differ? The answer will be, "the will of Providence." I grant it; and these are the natural means used by Providence to carry its will into effect.

PLATE 1.

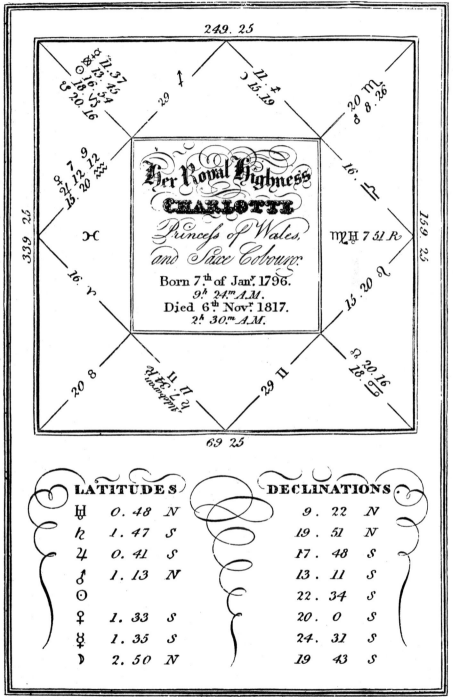

249. 25

249. 25

339 25

159. 25

69 25

Her Royal Highness
CHARLOTTE
Princess of Wales,
and Saxe Cobourg.

Born 7.th of Jan.y 1796.
9.h 24.m A.M.
Died 6.th Nov.r 1817.
2.h 30.m A.M.

LATITUDES			DECLINATIONS		
♅	0 . 48	N	9 . 22	N
♄	1 . 47	S	19 . 51	N
♃	0 . 41	S	17 . 48	S
♂	1 . 13	N	13 . 11	S
☉			22 . 34	S
♀	1 . 33	S	20 . 0	S
☿	1 . 35	S	24 . 31	S
☽	2 . 50	N	19 . 43	S

PLATE 2

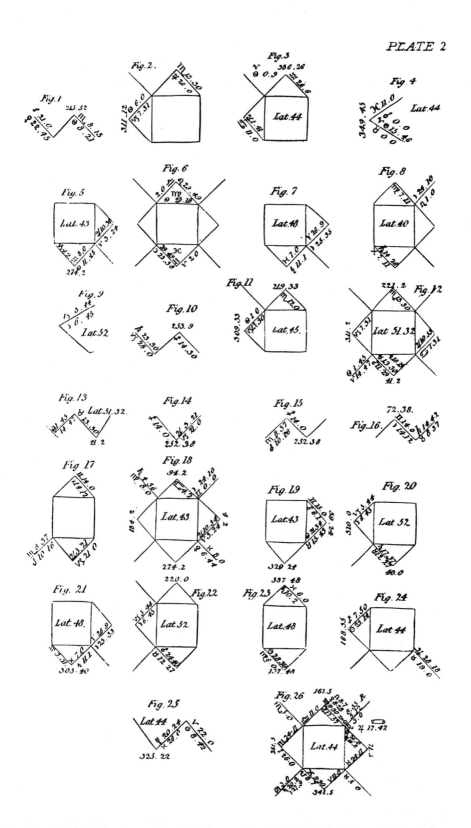

PLATE III

Fig. 1.

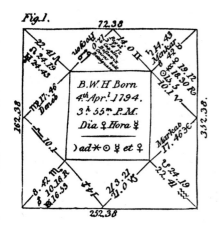

B.W.H Born
4th Apr.l 1794.
3h 55m P.M.
Dia ♀ Hora ☿
☽ ad ✱ ☉ ☿ et ♀

Fig. 2.

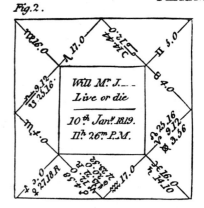

Will Mr J____
Live or die
10th Jan.y 1819.
11h 26m P.M.

Fig. 3.

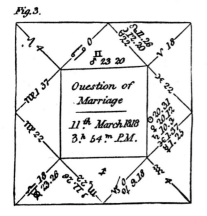

Question of
Marriage
11th March 1818
3h 54m P.M.

Fig. 4.

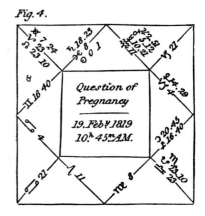

Question of
Pregnancy
19. Feb.y 1819
10h 45m A.M.

Fig. 5.

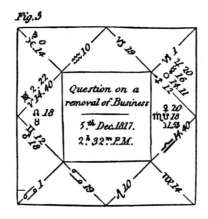

Question on a
removal of Business
5th Dec. 1817.
2h 32m P.M.

Names of the characters used in this Work.

PLANETS.

♄	Saturn	♀	Venus.	⚴	Pallas.
♃	Jupiter.	☿	Mercury.	⚳	Ceres.
♂	Mars.	☾	The Moon.	⚵	Juno.
☉	The Sun.	♅	Uranus.	⚶	Vesta.

SIGNS OF THE ZODIAC.

♈	Aries.	♋	Cancer.	♎	Libra.	♑	Capricorn.
♉	Taurus.	♌	Leo.	♏	Scorpio.	♒	Aquaries.
♊	Gemini.	♍	Virgo.	♐	Sagittarius	♓	Pisces.

□	Square.	✳	Sextile.	𝄐	Opposition.
△	Trine.	☌	Conjunction.		

☊ The Dragon's Head. | ☋ The Dragon's Tail.

⊕ The Part of Fortune.

MARKS OF DISTANCE.

s. Signs. | ° Degrees. | ′ Minutes. | ″ Seconds. | ‴ Thirds.

OF TIME.

y.	Years.	*h.*	Hours.	*s.*	Seconds.
d.	Days.	*m.*	Minutes.	*t.*	Thirds.

A COMPLETE

Dictionary of Astrology.

~~~~~~~~~~~~~~~~~~~~~~~~~

A L M

ABSCISSION, Frustration.

ACRONYCAL RISING, when a star rises exactly as the Sun sets.

ACRONYCAL SETTING, when a star sets with the Sun.

ACTINOBOLIA, the rays of the Hyleg when it is on the east of the Mid-heaven.

ACTIVE VIRTUES, heat and cold.

ACTIVE STARS, those which operate as Promittors, viz:— ♄, ♃, ♂, ♀, and ☿, and also the ☉ and ☾, when they operate as Promittors.

AFFLICTION, when a planet is in Conjunction or Evil Aspect with an Infortune; or having the same parallel, zodiacal or mundane; or being besieged by both the Infortunes.

AIRY SIGNS, ♊, ♎, and ♒.

AIRY TRIPLICITY, that Triplicity composed of the above three Airy Signs.

ALCOHODEN, an Arabic name for the Hyleg.

ALDEBARAN, the Bull's Eye, a violent fixed star in Gemini, of the nature of ♂, which, when in ☌ with ♄ or ♂, or with either of the luminaries, particularly in the ascendant, is said to threaten a violent death.

ALMUTEN, the strongest planet in a figure, in essential or accidental dignities

1

ALTITUDE, the distance of any star above the Earth from the Horizon. *Meridian* ALTITUDE is when a star is on the cusp of the *Medium Cœli.*

ANABIBAZON, the Dragon's Head.

ANARETA, the planet that destroys life.

ANARETIC POINT, or PLACE, the Place of the Anareta at the Nativity. The Anaretic Planets are ♄ and ♂; but as the ☉, ☽ and ☿ are variable from the nature of the planet with which they have familiarity, they also become Anaretas when in aspect with either Saturn or Mars, except one of the Benefics gives testimony, The ☉ likewise is said to be Anaretic when the ☽ is Hyleg, although he be not vitiated by the Infortunes. The west angle also is said to be Anaretic, because when the Hyleg sets, death ensues.

The Hyleg, directed to ☌, □, or ☍ of ♄ or ♂, whether zodiacal or mundane; or to a parallel of their declination, whether of the same kind or opposite; or to their mundane parallel when they are at equal distance from any angle; is said to destroy life, if any secondary direction or revolution coincide; or if any fatal ingress or transit happen at the time: but, it is said, one evil direction seldom kills. The sesquiquadrate is also an evil aspect, although in an inferior degree, and Ptolemy affirms, that either a ✶ or △ of an Infortune will kill, if the sextile be from a sign of long ascension, or the △ from a sign of short ascension, because it then becomes the same as a square. Placidus, however, affirms, that signs of long or short ascensions are the same in point of effect, except so far as they may make a different aspect in the world; and his opinion appears the most rational. It is probable that no aspect of an Infortune is good, as it impregnates the Hyleg with its malignant nature, which is always inimical to life and health. The sextile and trine of an Infortune is said to kill when it comes from signs obedient or beholding, but this must mean the zodiacal parallel, which must always proceed from such signs. When there are two Anaretas, that one will kill of which the position is the strongest in the figure. A planet under the ☉ beams, is is said, cannot kill, but it disposes that luminary so as to kill in its stead. If the native be young, or naturally vigorous and healthy, one evil direction seldom kills: it requires a train of malevolent directions to destroy, aided by secondary causes; but if old, infirm, and of a broken constitution, a slight direction will generally prove fatal.

The manner and quality of death is taken by Ptolemy from that planet which follows the Anareta, either by conjunction or aspect, to the place of the Hyleg; but if none follow, it is taken from that which last preceded: thus, Benefics, although they do not cause death, are as liable to show the nature of it as any other. A Benefic also aspecting the place at the same time, but too weak to save, will shew the nature of the death. It is also said by Ptolemy, that a planet, whether good or bad, being in the Anaretic place, will shew the quality of death; or a planet having dignities therein will do the same; but if there be neither, then the planet which by body or aspect comes first to the place must be taken for that purpose: his meaning, however, is quite uncertain, as there is no sign but what is the house of some planet, which consequently has dignity therein.

♄ denotes death by cold chronic diseases, such as ague, dropsy, flux, consumption, illiac passion, melancholy, fear, epilepsy, hysterics, etc.

♃, by inflamations, swelling, cancers, tumours, quinsey, foul stomach, jaundice, and other diseases denoting foul blood and a decayed system.

♂, by fevers, eresipelas, bruises, falls, stabs, mortification, fire, violent hemorrhage, and all hot diseases.

♀, by diseases arising from putrefaction and rottenness; as flux, poison, syphilis, gleets, tabes dorsalis, atrophy, typhus fever, putrid sore throat, pestilence, and all other epidemic diseases, and such as proceed from too much moisture.

☿, by all diseases of the brain, stomach and nerves: as madness, melancholy, grief, despair, phrenitis, epilepsy, and all diseases proceeding from a dry habit; but as ☿ is convertible to the nature of those planets by which he is aspected, he often produces diseases according as he is situated.

Violent deaths are caused when both the Malefics have dignities in the Anaretic place, or when in □ or ☍ to the luminaries at the time of birth. If ♄ square or oppose the ☉ from a fixed sign, being at the same time oriental, he causes death by suffocation, hanging, or being trodden to death in a tumult; and if when he is occidental and in fixed signs he □ or oppose the ☾ in like manner, he produces the same effects.

If ♄ aspect the luminaries in the above manner from brutal signs, it denotes death by beasts; and if ♀ give testimony, it often happens by female treachery, or poison. If the aspect be from a watery sign, or from ♍, it threatens death by drowning; and if from some part near the constellation Argo, by shipwreck.

If Saturn be joined or in ☍ to the ☉ from cardinal signs, it threatens death by falls. If Mars be joined to him, or aspect the place, it makes the effect more violent and certain.

If Mars be oriental and in □ or ☍ to the ☉ from fixed signs, it threatens the native with murder or suicide, and the same if occidental and so aspecting the ☽. If ♀ be with him, it will be caused by women; and if ☿, by thieves. If in mutilated signs, or with *Caput Medusa*, it threatens the native with beheading. If in ♏ or ♉, it causes death by fire, or some surgical operation. If from the tenth or fourth house, or near Cepheus and Andromeda, it denotes hanging. If from the west angle, it threatens death by fire, except he be in a four-footed sign, when it will be by falls or broken bones. If ♃ be in configuration with them, and evilly affected, so as to be unable to save, it will be by sentence of a judge. If both the Malefics join their influence, the consequences will be more dreadful, and the death more terrible.

If either of the fortunes, according to Ptolemy, cast a ray of any kind to the very Anaretic point, it will save life; but Placidus, although he never contradicts Ptolemy, gives several examples where the Benefics, even with a friendly ray, could not save. His opinion is, that if a Benefic be in the term of a Malefic, it renders it vicious and less able to do good; or if the place of the Anareta be in the term of a Malefic, it is the same. They are also said to be vitiated by being either in the house, exultation, or triplicity of a Malefic; but of all the dignities the term appears to be the most powerful. On the contrary, if a Malefic be in the term of a Benefic, it greatly lessens its malignity; and if the Anaretic point be in the term of a Benific, it contributes to save life.

If a Fortune be alone and not well dignified and strong, either in the zodiac or in the world, it cannot, according to Placidus, effect any permanent good, when the native is threatened by two Infortunes. It may lengthen the life a little, but the Malefics, being more in number and greater in power, will ultimately prevail.

When the Hyleg and Anareta in a ☌ differ much in point of declination, life is often saved. In the zodiac, when the latitude is more than the orb of the planet, though the longitude be the same to a minute, there is little or no effect either good or evil; and if it be somewhat more than half the orb, the effect will be much diminished. In the world, a small portion of latitude will have a great effect in conjunctions, and life has been saved only by the Significator passing the Promittor at one degree distance, when the Anaretic point lay in the term of a Benefic. A severe indisposition, however, attended with the utmost danger, is sure to be the consequence, and it is only owing to a good constitution and the utmost caution, that the patient escapes with his life. If ♃ or ♂, it is said, are but posited within orbs of the Anaretic Point, in an evil direction, ♃ within 12°, and ♀ within 8°, they invariably save life; but, as we before observed, Placidus is quite of a different opinion.

After all, it is necessary to observe, that some of these rules should be received with caution. We must have better authority than that of Ptolemy or Placidus either, to convince us that because a certain constellation has been fancifully called Medusa's Head, or the Ship Argo, they should cause beheading and ship-wreck, or that watery signs (which for any rational cause we know, might have been with equal propriety called fiery, or earthly signs) should cause drowning. In Horary questions, where they operate as symbols, they may probably signify such calamities; but that they can cause them by their position at a Nativity, is wholly repugnant to reason. Neither does it appear reasonable that the term of any planet can produce the effect ascribed to it, and there can be no doubt, that an attention to such silly whims, while the more important parts of the science were neglected, has contributed to bring that disgrace upon Astrology under which it now labours: neither is it rational to suppose that other places, where the planets possess dignities, can have the effects ascribed to them when the planet is not there. They may, like other fixed stars, have a certain influence, but nothing more.

Argol, who, contrary to the rules of Ptolemy, generally considered the Horoscope as Hyleg, when he found himself in a strait, would direct his Hyleg to a □ or ☍ of either of the Benefics as Anaretas: nothing can be more absurd than this, as, if there be any truth in Astrology, the stars operate by their natures, not their aspects; for, as no aspect of the infortunes can save life, neither can any aspect of a Fortune destroy it.

It has now become a favorite system amongst Astrologers, to consider the Eighth House and its Lord as Anaretas, and the Ascendant and its Lord as Hyleg: they therefore direct the Lord of the Ascendant to the Lord of the Eighth, or to the cusp of the Eighth, as the Anaretic Point; or the Lord of the Eighth to the cusp of the Ascendant. A little reflection would demonstrate to them the absurdity of such a system: there is much reason to doubt the effects of Houses, Exaltations, Triplicities, Etc., even when the owners are in them; and it is certain the planet cannot influence the House, nor the House the planet, when they are asunder. In Horary questions, where the stars are consulted as signs, not as causes of events, the Houses and their Lords must be considered as Significators; but in Genethliacal Astrology none but the Horoscope and the Mid-heaven can be considered as of any importance; nor even then in a zodiacal, but merely in a mundane point of view, when planets are either posited in them or directed to them.

Fixed Stars are also considered as Anaretic when joined with the luminaries, or the Hyleg: but for this I shall refer the reader to the article, Fixed Stars. Some have been so silly as to direct the Hyleg to the Dragon's Tail as Anaretic, which is only a character in an almanac, and neither emits any rays nor possesses any substance whatever.

ANGLES, the four Cardinal Points: the first is the East Angle, or the point of the heavens ascending at the time of a nativity, horary question, or any thing which requires a figure to be erected: it is called the First House, Horoscope, or Ascendant, The second is the South Angle, and is that point which culminates in any figure: it is called the *Medium Cœli*, or Mid-heaven. The third is the West Angle, or that point of the heavens setting at the time of a figure being erected: it is called the Descendant, or Seventh House. The fourth is the North Angle, or lowest point of depression in the heavens at the erection of a figure, being directly opposite the Mid-heaven: it is called the *Imum Cœli*, or Lowest Heaven.

Most authors give the preference to the east angle, as being strongest in the figure; or in other words, that a planet there is more powerful than in any other place, but Ptolemy gives the preference to the south angle, and with reason, for the stars are more powerful in their meridian altitude than when rising. The next angle in power is the west, and the north angle is the weakest of the four. For the properties of the Angles, see "Houses."

ANIMODER. See Rectification.

ANTIPATHIES are those unaccountable aversions people are said to feel towards each other when, from some particular cause, their nativities do not sympathize. The principal of these causes may be traced to the luminaries: first, when they are dissociate, being one or five signs distant; as, for example, the ☽ of one being in ♍, and that of the other in ♎ or ♈, they would be injunct, having no aspect to each other; and if this was the case with the Sun also, so as to cause a total want of agreement among the luminaries on both sides, the natives would dislike and shun each other, though probably without being able to assign a sufficient reason. If the luminaries were in evil aspect to each other, a mutual dislike and hatred would be the consequence; and if the ascendants were in opposite signs, as ♈ for the one and ♎ for the other; or one or both of the Infortunes of one nativity in ☌ or evil aspect with the places of the lights in the other, or in square or opposition, or sesquiquadrate to their own places, or to the places of each other, or from opposite cardinal houses, it would cause the most furious disputes between the parties, in proportion to the number of testimonies, and those whose planets were more angular, oriental, or better fortified, would ultimately prevail.

ANTISCIONS. See Parallels.

APHETA, HYLEG, or PROROGATOR; the place or planet that carries with it the life of the native, until it comes to the place or evil aspect of the anareta, when death ensues. See Anareta.

According to Ptolemy, the Aphetic Places are five, viz., the whole space of the 1st 7th, 9th, 10th, and 11th Houses, taken from 5° above the cusp to 25° below it, computed by oblique ascension; from five degrees, therefore, above the cusp of the Ninth, to five degrees above that of the Twelfth, must be Aphetic; but Placidus thinks a planet, when it has passed beyond the five degrees above the cusp of the Horoscope, ought to be one-half of his semidiurnal arc above the cusp of the Horoscope, viz., in the middle of the Eleventh House, before he can be Apheta, The reason why the Eighth and Twelfth are not Aphetic, is because they have no aspect to the Horoscope; and the other Houses are not Aphetic, because they are under the Earth. If by day, the Sun be in an Aphetic place, he becomes Hyleg in preference to all others; but if he be not found in any such place, and the situation of the ☽ will admit of it, she becomes Hyleg. If the ☽ be not in an Aphetic place, that planet must be taken as Hyleg which has most dignitaries by Triplicity, House, Exaltation, Term, or Configuration, in the place where the Sun was at the time of the preceding New Moon; or in the Ascendant; but it must have three dignities in one of them at least, and be in an aphetical place. If there be no such planet, the Horoscope becomes Hyleg.

By night the ☽ is Apheta if in an aphetical place; but if not, the Sun, if in such place, will be Apheta. If neither of the lights be so situated, that planet will be Hyleg which has most dignities in the place of the last Full Moon, or in the place of the Part of Fortune, provided it be in an aphetical place; but it must be dignified three ways at least, If there be no such planet, and a New

Moon preceded the birth, take the Horoscope; but if a Full Moon preceded, take the ⊕, if it be aphetically situated.

When both the luminaries, or a number of planets, are so situated that it seems doubtful which is the Apheta, that must be taken which is found in the strongest aphetical place. The Tenth is the principal, the Horoscope next, the Eleventh ranks next the Horoscope, the Seventh is next in power, and the Ninth is the weakest of all.

It was a favorite opinion with Argol, and a number of others, that the Horoscope was generally Hyleg; and so anxious were they to support this absurd hypothesis, that they not only altered the time of nativities to suit their directions, but actually directed their Hyleg to evil aspects of the Fortunes as Anaretas; on the other hand, Placidus, in his unbounded veneration for Ptolemy, which was often ill placed, would, on certain occasions, hint that the time of birth might be incorrect, when he could not suit the Hyleg to the direction. An example of this we have in the Nativity of Cardinal Peretti, where he sadly wants a quarter of an hour more, to send the Sun into the Twelfth House, that the ☽ might be Hyleg. It is but justice to Placidus to say, he was the most rational of all those who have hitherto written on Astrology, and one who would not sit down quietly and propagate an error, merely because others had done it before him; he would try a number of experiments, and search everywhere for what he thought ample proof, before he committed anything finally to paper. Had every other author been equally industrious, Astrology would not have been so little understood as it is; but the genius of Placidus was not of the first rate, his mind was active, but not profound; and although he would not blindly adopt an opinion, even of Ptolemy, yet he had a strong bias in favor of his system, that often misled him. There is likewise a degree of inaccuracy in his works not easily accounted for, as they do not appear to be errors of the translator. In the Nativity in question, the Pole of the Country is 42 degrees; Oblique Ascension of the Horoscope 285 degrees, 40 minutes; Sun is in 18 degrees, 23 minutes, ♐, which gives his Oblique Ascension 279 degrees, 51 minutes, which subtracted from that of the horoscope, gives the Sun's distance from the horoscope, 5 degrees, 49 minutes; the quarter of an hour could be therefore of no use to him, as according to the precept of Ptolemy the Aphetical Place only extends 5 degrees above the cusp of the angle, and as the Sun was 4 degrees, 49 minutes distant, he was already in the Twelfth House.

The notion that planets which have dignities in the new and

full Moon, Ascendant, and Part of Fortune, are Aphetas, seems wholly irrational. Placidus never gives a single example of it, but passes the whole over in silence, which was generally his way when he could not comprehend any of Ptolemy's dogmas, for he made it a point never to censure him. The zodiacal dignities of the planets savour very strongly of human invention, as we have shown under the article "Dignities;" but allowing them really to exist, it seems extremely absurd to suppose the dignity of a planet can have any effect upon such planet when it is out of it. As to the Horoscope, we have one instance in Placidus where it is Hyleg, which, in the absence of the luminaries, may be the case. We know, however, that in all other cases the aspects of the Sun and Moon are considered as equally powerful, whether above or below the Earth, and it does not clearly appear why they should be more unfit for this purpose than any other; indeed the office of Hyleg appears to require more investigation than it has hitherto received, unbiassed by the opinion of Ptolemy, Placidus, or any one else, and regulated solely by the dictates of reason and experience. The Part of Fortune seems equally à human invention with the rest, and founded on no rational principle. It would be difficult to explain why the Sun should sympathize with the ascending Part of Heaven more than any other planet, and it would not be easy to demonstrate what connexion any of them have with it at all. The Horoscope is wholly a mundane, not a zodiacal position; it respects the Earth and not the Sun, and no aspect but what is mundane can affect it: the Part of Fortune, therefore, if it must be taken at all, should be taken in the World, not in the Zodiac. Placidus has given also one solitary instance wherein the Part of Fortune was Prorogator; but "one Swallow," says the proverb, "does not make Summer," nor does one instance establish a System. I would here be understood, as only denying the operation of the Part of Fortune in nativities as a cause, and not in horary questions as a symbol.

APOGEE, that part in the orbit of a planet where it is at the greatest distance from the Earth.

APORHŒA, a term given to the Moon when she separates from one planet and applies to another.

APPLICATION, is of three kinds, in all of which it means one planet applying to any familiarity with another.

1st. *Direct* APPLICATION, when two planets are direct, and one applies to another, of which the motion is slower than its own, and overtakes it.

2d. *Retrograde* APPLICATION, when two planets are retrograde, and one overtakes the other in a similar manner.

3d. *Mixed* APPLICATION, is when one being direct and the other retrograde they mutually apply to each other.

In horary questions, only the first is deemed good, and the two latter are deemed evil Applications, as the thing sought after will be injurious or of little value when it comes to pass. In all cases Application is stronger than Separation, either for good or evil. Ptolemy mentions none of these kinds of Applications, but merely says, that planets preceeding apply to those that follow; and planets that follow separate from those that preceed; because all his aspects being mundane, a planet preceeding another in the zodiac would apply to it by converse motion, and *vice versa.*

AQUARIES. See Signs.

ARC, or ARCH, the distance between any two places in the heavens; for as the zodiac forms a circle equal to 360 degrees, every distance, whether zodiacal or mundane, must be an Arch, viz., a portion or segment of that circle.

ARC OF DIRECTION, the distance between any two places in a Nativity found by direction. See Direction.

ARIES. See Signs.

ASCENDANT, the Horoscope. See Houses. Some authors call that part of heaven from the *Imum Cœli* eastward to the *Medium Cœli*, the Ascendant, because it is always ascending, but the term is seldom so applied at present.

ASCENDING SIGNS, ♈, ♉, ♊, ♎, ♏, ♐, so called, because when the Sun is in them his declination is increasing.

ASCENDING PART OF HEAVEN, from the Fourth House, eastward to Mid-heaven.

ASCEND TO, to the Sun, is being oriental and Matutine to the Sun; to the Moon, being occidental and vespertine to the Moon; this is what Ptolemy calls the luminaries being guarded.

ASCENSIONS, arcs or parts of the equator, which rise with any planet or part of the ecliptic, See Right and Oblique Ascension.

ASCENSIONAL DIFFERENCE, the difference between the right and oblique ascension of any star or part of the ecliptic. It is found by taking the declination of the star, or place of the ecliptic, and entering the table of Ascensional Difference under the proper pole of the planet, or the country, as occasion may require; and in the common angle of meeting will be found the Ascentional Difference. Example : —

If a star, or any part of the ecliptic, has 19 degrees of declina-

*s*ion in the latitude of 51 degrees, what will be its Ascensional Difference ? Look in the first column for 19 degrees, and in the next column (on the top of which is the pole's elevation, 51 degrees,) will be found 25 degrees, 10 minutes for the Ascensional Difference.

If there be fractional parts, as there generally are, a proportional sum must be taken for each. Example : —

If a star have 19 degrees, 20 minutes declination in the latitude of London 51 degrees, 32 minutes, what will be the Ascentional difference ? In the common angle for 19 degrees and 51 minutes we find as before 25 degrees, 10 minutes; and for the remaining 20 minutes of declination say, " if 60 minutes give 1 degree, 33 minutes (the difference between the declination for 19 degrees and 20 degrees) what will 20 minutes give ? It will give 31 minutes, which add to the 25 degrees, 10 minutes, and it makes 25 degrees, 41 minutes. There yet remains the 32 minutes difference in the poll to be accounted for. We therefore say, if 60 minutes give 59 minutes (the differences between the poles of 51 and 52 degrees) what will 32 minutes give ? It will give 32 minutes, which added to the 25 degrees, 41 minutes makes the Ascensional Difference complete 26 degrees, 13 minutes.

ASPECTS, any degree of familiarity between planets, except the Conjunction. See Familiarities.

ATHAZER, a term given to the Moon when she is in conjunction with the Sun; or at distances from him of 12°, 45°, 90°, 150°, 168°, 180°, 192°, 215°, 270°, or 348°.

AUSTRAL, or Southern Signs, ♎, ♏, ♐, ♑, ♒, ♓.

AZIMENE, or Weak and Lame Degrees, are those parts of signs which, when they ascend at a birth, are said to render the Native lame, blind, etc. See the table of Degrees.

BARREN SIGNS, ♊, ♌, and ♍. See Children.

BENEFICS, the two benevolent planets, ♃ and ♀.

BEASTIAL SIGNS, ♈, ♉, ♌, ♐ and ♑.

BEHOLDING SIGNS, signs having the same declination, being at equal distance from the tropics, as ♈ and ♍, ♉ and ♌, ♊ and ♋, ♎ and ♓, ♏ and ♒, ♐ and ♑.

BESEIGED, a planet inclosed between two others. If between Jupiter and Venus it is good, but if between Saturn and Mars, extremely evil.

BICORPORAL SIGNS, ♊, ♐, and ♓, because each contains two different animals. Some call these double bodied Signs, distinguishing them from the Bicorporal, though the word means the same They say that the Bicorporal are the four common

signs, ♊, ♍, ♐, and ♓, because, lying between a fixed and tropical sign, they partake of both natures: such folly merits no
observation.

BIQUINTILE, an aspect invented by Kepler, in the zodiac it
contains 144°, and in the World it is four-fifths of the whole
diurnal arc of any planet or point in the Heavens. It is reckoned
benevolent, but not so powerful as the sextile, and is admitted to
be such by Placidus.

BITTER SIGNS, are ♈, ♌, and ♐, because they are said to be
hot, fiery, and bitter.

BOREAL SIGNS, the six northern signs, ♈, ♉, ♊, ♋, ♌,
and ♍.

BRETHREN, the places in a Nativity signifying Brothers and
Sisters are, according to Ptolemy, the sign on the Midheaven, and
that which follows it; and to these are added the maternal place,
viz., that of Venus by day and the Moon by night. If these signs
and places be configurated by Benefics, they give increase of
Brethren in proportion to the number of planets by which they
are so aspected; and if these planets are in double-bodied signs,
they double the number. If the Sun be surrounded by good
stars (within 30 degrees of him according to some, but according
to Placidus, in some kind of aspect with him, though I think it
means besieged,) it signifies the same.

If the Malefics are configurated to those places, or surround
the Sun, and overcome the Benefics in number and strength,
there will be few, and those of little value.

If the Fortunes so aspecting be oriental or angular, or, if inferior,
occidental, swift, direct or increasing in motion, the Brethren will
be great and renowned; but if they are occidental, or, if inferior,
oriental, slow, retrograde, cadent or decreasing in motion, they
will be proportionally mean. If both Benefics and Malefics aspect
the places, and the Malefics are stronger or more in number than
the Benefics, they will be sickly and short lived. It is said, that
the Nativity of one brother may be made from that of another,
by placing that planet which hath rule in the place of Brethren
on the Cusp of the Ascendant, and regulating the other Houses
accordingly; but this seems quite absurd. In modern Astrology,
the 3d House and its Lord are considered Significators of Brethren;
and, when any question is proposed concerning them, they make
the 3d House the Ascendant; this may do in horary questions, but
it is wholly useless in Nativities. If those stars denoting brethren, that is, the Moon by night, or Venus by day, be in good configuration with the stars, having dignities in their places, they

will love each other; but, if in evil familiarity, or in signs inconjunct, they will injure and hate each other.

BROKEN SIGNS, ♌, ♏, and ♓; they are also called mutilated or imperfect, because those born under them with bad aspects are deformed in some way or other.

BRUTISH SIGNS, are ♌ and the last part of ♐, and those born under them are said to be savage and coarse in their manners, brutish, intractable, and inhuman.

CACODEMON, the 12th House, because of its evil qualities.

CADENT, falling from an angle, thus the 3d, 6th, 9th, and 12th Houses are Cadent, because the stars pass from the angles into them. Cadent stars are extremely weak in Nativities, and render what is signified by them almost ineffectual. In horary questions, a cadent planet seldom brings any event to pass of which it is the Significator, and if at all, it will be when all hopes are vanished, and when obtained, it is either evil or useless.

CANCER. See Signs.

CAPRICORN. See Signs.

CAPUT DRACONIS, the Dragon's Head.

CARDINAL HOUSES, the 10th, 1st, 7th, and 4th.

CARDINAL SIGNS, ♈, ♋, ♎, and ♑.

CAUDA DRACONIS, the Dragon's Tail.

CAZIMI, in modern Astrology, is when a planet is in what is called the Heart of the Sun, or within 17′ of his body. It is said to fortify the planet as much as combustion debilitates it. This I conceive to be a silly unmeaning distinction; for a planet so situated is undoubtedly in the worst state of combustion.

CHANGEABLE SIGNS, are ♊, ♉, ♌, ♍, ♐, and ♑, because they are said to change their nature according to their position; thus ♊ in the east is hot and dry, and in the west cold and moist: ♉ in the east is rather hot, and in the west cold; ♌ in the east is hot and dry, and in the west hot and moist; ♍ in the east is hottish, and in the west cold and moist; ♐ in the east is cold and moist, and in the west hot and dry; ♑ in the east is cold and dry, and in the west cold and moist: these appear to be very foolish distinctions.

CHILDREN. The Tenth and Eleventh Houses, according to Ptolemy, signify Children, if planets are in them or configurated to them; but if none be there, or in aspect, those must be taken that are in the Fourth and Fifth Houses. The Moon, Jupiter, or Venus, are givers of Children, but Saturn or Mars cause barrenness. Mercury operates according to the stars to which he is configurated: he is, however, said to give Children when oriental, and to cause barrenness when occidental. If the Moon, Jupiter, or Venus, be in one of those Houses by themselves in a watery sign, they are said to give two or three children at a birth; if in double bodied or feminine signs, twins; but in any other, only one child. If they are masculine signs, or configurated to the Sun, they give males; but if in feminine signs, or configurated with the Sun occidentally, females. If in barren signs, or if the Malefics be more powerful by number or strength, they will give Children, but such as are weakly or short lived.

If a Malefic be in either of those Houses in a masculine or barren sign, the native will be always barren, particularly if the Sun be with it. If it be in a feminine or fruitful sign, or if a Benefic cast a ray to the place, there will be Children, but such as are sickly and short lived, or with blemishes. If the Benefics aspect the places from fruitful signs, and are more numerous, or oriental, or angular, or succeedent, than the Malefics, the children will be stronger and more numerous. If the Lords of those signs be oriental, or angular, the Children will be enterprising and fortunate, but if occidental or cadent, more obscure and mean. If they agree in good aspect with the Horoscope and ⊕, there will be harmony between the Parents and Children, but if in bad aspect or inconjunct, they will hate each other, and such Children frequently ruin their Parents, or get themselves disinherited. If they are well configurated among each other, the Children will agree among themselves, and live together in harmony; but if they are in evil aspect and inconjunct, there will be hatred and separation. If there be planets in the 10th, 11th, 4th, or 5th House, the place of such a planet, it is said, may be made the cusp of the Ascendant, and the rest of the Houses regulated accordingly, and it will serve for such Child's Nativity. I have already given an opinion on this method under the article Brethren, and it is therefore useless to repeat it; I have also stated the improbability, that the Lords of Signs can have any efficacy as such, when out of their signs; nor do I conceive it less an absurdity because it has been taught by Ptolemy and believed by Placidus.

In modern Astrology the Significators of Children are the 5th House and its Lord, but this is only proper for horary questions.

CHRONOCRATER, Ruler of Time. It is generally considered as the light of time, viz. the ☉ by day and the ☾ by night. Others divide the life of man into seven parts, and assign the care of the first four years to the ☾, from thence to fourteen to ☿, from fourteen to twenty-two to ♀, &c. and these are called Chronocraters: by Ptolemy.

CIRCLE, the whole Circumference of the Zodiac, containing 360 degrees of 60 minutes each; or, when reduced to time, 12 hours.

CIRCLES OF POSITION, Circles passing through the common intersections of the horizon and meridian, and passing through any part of the ecliptic in their way, or through the centre of any star, so as to shew the position of such star or place. These, however, are not the Circles of Position used by Ptolemy or Placidus, who measure the place and distance of every star by its semi-arc.

CLIMACTERICAL YEARS, every 7th or 9th year in a man's life, answering to the days of the ☾, because she comes to the □ of her own place in the radix about every 7th day, and in △ to it about every 9th day; thus the 7th, 9th, 14th, 18th, 21st, 27th, 28th, 35th, 36th, 42d, 45th, 49th, 54th, 56th, 63d, years, are all Climacterical, and are reckoned, and perhaps truly, to be productive of remarkable events. The most dangerous of them are the 49th and 63d, because they are doubly Climacterical, being 7 X 7 and 7 X 9, and, when evil directions occur, are reckoned generally fatal. The 63d year is called the Grand Climacteric, and a careful observer will find that more people die in their 63d year than in any other year from 50 to 80. Many are of opinion that the 7th Climacterical year is always caused by ♄, because he comes every 7th year or thereabouts to the □, ☍ or ☌, of his place in the radix; this may be the case, but I should rather attribute it to the ☾, whose effects, in all things we know of, are more prominent than those of ♄. In some cases it may be the joint effect of ♄ and the ☾, as their septennial periods nearly agree; one reason, however, against the probable operations of ♄ in the septennial year is, that his period is not strictly septennial, but nearly seven years and a half, and his 2d Climacteric would be fifteen years, whereas the periodical lunation is twenty-seven days, seven hours, 44 minutes, dividing nearly seven for her □ to her place in the radix; besides, as ♃ is larger and nearer than ♄, and his period twelve years within fifty-one days, we should have a more powerful Climateric every fourth year, which is not the case; ♂, too, is reckoned every way as powerful as ♄, and therefore we should have four more Climacterics in every two years; all these considerations almost amount to a demonstration, that every Climaterical Period is Lunar, and regulated, not by a Synodical, but a Periodical Lunation.

CLIMATE, a portion of heaven contained between two parallel circles, whose diurnal arcs are half an hour different from each other. The Globe is divided into 48 climates,—24 northern, and 24 southern. The First Climate begins at the equator, where the diurnal arc is 12 hours, and extends to the next Climate, where the diurnal arc is 11*h*. 30*m*. and so on to the polar elevation, where, at a certain season, the Sun sets not during the 24 hours.

COLLECTION OF LIGHT, is when a planet receives the rays of two others less ponderous than itself, and which are inconjunct with each other. This, in horary questions, signifies, that the business will be completed by the interference of a third person, without whose aid it could not have taken place. It is said, however, that if they do not both receive him in some of their essential dignities, he will feel no interest in the affair, nor will it be prosperous.

COLOURS. Colours, according to Astrologers, are symptoms of the nature of stars; the fixed stars, therefore, of the colour of Jupiter are of the nature of Jupiter; those of Mars, of the nature of Mars; &c. Placidus says, that the yellow or golden colour of the Sun has an active power, and is the sign of radical heat: the white of the Moon has a passive power, and is the sign of radical moisture. Lead colour such as Saturn's is a sign of intemperate cold and dryness; the fiery red of Mars is the result of intemperate heat and dryness; the mixture of blue and yellow found in Jupiter and Venus are signs of heat and moisture united; the blue of Jupiter, he says, shews, that in him heat is predominant; and the yellow of Venus shews excess of moisture; this seems a mistake, for, whatever blue may be the sign of, Venus has more of it than Jupiter.

Beside the colours of the planets, there are others which they are said to signify; thus ♄, signifies black; ♃, red mixed with green; ♂, fiery red; ☉, yellow, or inclined to purple; ♀, white and purple; ☿, light blue, or azure; and ☾, white, or white spotted, or a light mixed colour. The Signs of the Zodiac have also colours assigned to them; ♈, white and red; ♉, red mixed with citron; ♊, red and white mixed; ♋, green or russet; ♌, red or green; ♍, black spotted with blue; ♎, black, or dark crimson, or swarthy; ♏, dark brown; ♐, light green, or olive; ♑, black, or dark brown; ♒, sky-blue; ♓, pure white, or glistening. These colours are said to shew the complexion of any native, signified by such signs, though it would be difficult to find a native who was green or blue; it may, however, in horary questions, signify their dress. If two cocks were to fight, or two horses to race, etc., a figure, it is said, may be erected, and that sign or planet, signifying their colour, which is strongest or posited in the best house of the two, shews which will be victorious.

COMBUSTION. A planet is combust when within 8° 30′ of the body of the Sun; its influence is then said to be burnt up, or destroyed. It is said by Ptolemy, that a planet when combust can neither save nor destroy, but it impregnates the Sun with its power, whether good or evil. To be under the Sun-beams is a degree of combustion, and as the Sun's orb extends 17°, all planets are under its beams within that distance.

Mercury, it is said, does not suffer like other planets from being under the ⊙ beams; but this must relate only to horary questions, when those signified by Mercury would be generally in that state signified by combustion, as he is always near the Sun. In nativities there seems a manifest difference in the genius and propensities of natives according to the distance of their ☿ from the Sun. Those who have him in a state of combustion, evince but a moderate capacity, have little wit or solid judgment, though they will persevere in business, and frequently with good success. A good aspect with the Moon, if she be angular, and increasing in light, will in a great degree remedy this defect, and render them active, judicious, and penetrating. In horary questions, when a planet is combust, it signifies the person to be in great fear and danger from some superior person, who, if there be application to Combustion, will finally overpower or greatly injure him.

COMETS. Comets have ever been considered as effecting great changes in the Earth, the atmosphere, and the affairs of men; to deny this would be as absurd as to deny the effects of any other celestial body, by which we are surrounded, not excepting even the Sun and Moon. They have always been considered as productive of evil, which is certainly probable, as their presence cannot fail to derange the system for a time. The ancients, who, though not so learned as the moderns, were more acute in their observations, considered them as the cause of every calamity that could afflict mankind; and modern observations confirm this opinion. The great comet in 1680, followed by another in 1682, was probably the main spring of all those disastrous events that ended in the rebellion in 1688. To that in 1807, which appeared towards the south in September, just after it had passed its perihelium, may be ascribed the troubles in Spain: the dethroning of its king, and the subsequent usurpation of his son Ferdinand.

The comet in 1811, near the constellation of Ursa Major, was doubtless the precursor of all the troubles in Russia, and the war with America. From its northern position it was probably the cause of that subsequent convulsion that separated some of those vast continents of ice near the pole, which had subsisted for ages: some idea of their duration may be formed from the observations of Kotzebue, who commanded the Russian northern expedition in 1715, and who on his return three years after had found Ice-bergs covered with land, vegetables, and even trees, and one of them contained the body of a mammoth in a state of putrefaction; it had, no doubt been preserved by the frost for ages, and on its progress, after separation, towards a warmer climate the process of putrefaction began.

From these events, some idea may be formed of the duration of the effect of a Comet, which remains long after the cause has been removed. No doubt but Nature is thrown into great convulsions, which, like all agitations of bodies of great magnitude, require a long time before they can finally subside. Their operations are probably most conspicuous in the quarter where they appear, north or south, like those of all other celestial bodies, which are most powerful in those places where they approach the zenith. And they most likely have an effect on certain persons when like eclipses, they happen near the ecliptic, and on the principal places of the radix: but of this I cannot speak from my own observation. Ptolemy says, they cause wars and hot seasons, and countries governed by the sign they are in when they first appear are those that suffer; and those suffer most towards which its tail points.

COMMANDING SIGNS ♈, ♉, ♊, ♋, ♌, ♍, because they are more powerful from being nearer to our zenith; and stars having parallels of north declination. There is also a silly notion that those born under the six northern signs are more fitted to command than those born under the others, and are generally more successful.

COMMON SIGNS are ♊, ♍, ♐, and ♓, because they are not in extremes, but in a medium between fixed and moveable. They are said to produce twins, monsters, hermaphrodites, &c.

CONCEPTION. Ptolemy says, that the sex, as well as the incidents relating to a child, prior to its birth, may be known by the position of the planets at the time of conception. If the luminaries, or the ascendant, or the stars in aspect with them, or with the ascendant, be in feminine signs; or if they are feminine by occidental, the child conceived will be female. If oriental, or in masculine signs a male. If the lights or ascendant, or planet aspecting them be in bicorporal signs, there will be twins or more; and the same if both the lights are in the south angle. If ♄, ♃, and ♂, behold the horoscope or luminaries from bicorporal signs, there will be three males, but if ♀, ☿, and ☾, behold them in like manner, three females. If one feminine and two male planets, there will be two males and a female; but if one male and two feminine planets, two females and a male. If all the configurations are imperfect, the children will be imperfect also; but if some be perfect and others imperfect, the children will be the same. When the Malefics are angular, and the luminaries in the 12th or 6th, monsters are generated, and the same if the place of the last full Moon and its Lord, and the disposer of the luminaries, have no aspect to the horoscope.

If the luminaries, being so posited, are in fourfooted signs, with the Malefics angular, the embryo will be of a beastly form; but if a Benefic give testimony, it will be of human shape, but of a savage disposition. If ☿ be in good familiarity with the ☾, the faculties will be improved, although the body be ill formed; and if the luminaries be in human signs, the shape will be much better. If a Malefic be with the luminaries, the child will be foolish; but if a Fortune be also with them, the Child's intellect will be saved, but it will be an hermaphrodite. If ☿ be with them, it will be dumb, though of good abilities. If one of the luminaries be in an aphetic place, joined to a Malefic, or in □ or ☍ to it, there will be an abortion, and the same if it have a parallel of the Malefics declination; it will either die in the womb, or shortly after birth. If the two Malefics, or only one of them, afflict either ☉ or ☾ by a partile aspect there will be an abortion, and the same if the luminaries are in ☍ to ♄ and ♂ from angles in partile or platic aspect. If the conditionary luminary is separating from a Benefic, and applying to a Malefic, the child will be born alive, but will live only such a number of months, days, or hours, as there are degrees, minutes, and seconds between the luminary who is apheta, and the nearest Malefic. If on the contrary the luminary separates from the Malefic in any way, and applies to a Benefic, the child will be sickly, but will recover and do well. These things, however, must be difficult to ascertain, and it is probable that Ptolemy wrote this more from fancy than experience.

CONDITIONARY ARC, the diurnal arc by day, and the nocturnal by night.

CONDITIONARY LUMINARY, the ☉ by day and the ☾ by night.

CONFIGURATIONS, See Familiarities.

CONJUGATIONS. The planets are said to have four Conjugations, according to where they are situated; the 1st is when they are near the Earth and increasing in light; 2d, when they are near and decreasing in light; 3d, when distant and in their decrease; and 4th, when distant and in their increase.

CONJUNCTION, is when two planets are within half of their orbs of each other with respect either to longitude or latitude. If a planet be within the distance of its own orb to a fixed star it is the same. This configuration is good with good stars and bad with evil ones.

COSIGNIFICATORS are planets and signs that have a kind of rotatory signification: thus Aries is a cosignificator of all ascendants, because though it be not the sign ascending, it is the first sign in the zodiac, as the ascendant is the first house in the world. ♄ is also a cosignificator of the ascendant because he is the first planet in the system, and therefore those who hold this doctrine, say, that if ♄ be in the ascendant at a Nativity well dignified and aspected, he promises a sober disposition and long life, though the very reverse is the fact; thus the 12 signs are cosignificators of the 12 mundane houses in rotation, but as there are not so many planets as houses, some of them are compelled to do double duty. Thus ♄ is cosignificator of both the 1st and 8th houses, ♃ of the 2d and 9th; ♂ of the 3d and 10th, etc. These are silly refinements in astrology and only fit to render the science rediculous.

In horary questions the ☾ is always Cosignificator with the lord of the ascendant, and must be directed as such to any Promittor. In questions relative to marriage the ☾ and ♀ are the Cosignificators of a man, but the ☉ and ♂ are Cosignificators if the querent be a woman. A planet also in ☌ or aspect with the Significator of any thing is called a Cosignificator, because it influences the matter in question.

CONTRA ANTISCIONS. See parallels.

CONVERSE MOTION, when the Significator is moved from east to west by the diurnal motion of the Earth. See Directions in the World.

COSMICAL, Mundane.

COSMICAL RISING, when a star rises exactly with the Sun.

COSMICAL SETTING, when a star sets with the Sun.

CREPUSCLE, Twilight. When the ☉ is in the Crepuscle he must be directed differently from any other planet; and when he is under the Earth in what is called the Obscure Arc beyond the utmost parallel of twilight, the crepusculine arc must be sub-tracted from his seminocturnal arc before he can be directed. See Zodiacal and Mundane Directions.

Crepusculine Tables are published by the author, and the meth-od of using them will be found under the article "Directions."

CRITICAL DAYS, those days on which any accident is calcu-lated by direction to happen. Climacterical days are also called' Critical, and those in fevers and other diseases on which a change is likely to happen, owing to the Moon's position with her radical place when the disease commenced. The 7th and 8th days are the most Critical because on them she comes to a □ of the place she was in when the patient was taken ill. The 4th and 5th days are also Critical, when she comes to her own Sextile, on the 9th or 10th she comes to her △, and on the 14th, to her ☍; on all which days a change may be expected.

CROOKED SIGNS are ♉, ♑ and ♓, and if the ascendant or Moon be in one of these, and afflicted by the Malefics, the Native, it is said, will be crooked, or imperfect. Placidus gives an in-stance of this in the nativity of Doctor Massari, who was born with his feet inverted, owing to the ☾ being in the west angle in ♉, and in □ of ♂ in the world, who was posited in ♓, the sign of the feet, and in mundane ☍ to ♄, who was posited in ♐, the sign of the thighs. I own, however, I should require more proof of the truth of this doctrine than this solitary instance can afford, although backed by the opinion of Placidus; nor do I see any rational cause why ♓ should govern the feet, merely because men have thought proper to make it the last sign or foot of the Zo-diac, and begin their right ascension at the first point of ♈.

CULMINATE, to arrive at the cusp of mid-heaven.

CULMEN CŒLI, the 10th house.

CUSP, the begining or edge of a house.

CYCLE OF THE MOON, 19 years, at the end of which she re-turns to her position with the Sun.

CYCLE OF THE SUN, 28 years.

DAY HOUSE, those houses in which the planets are said to be stronger by day than by night. ♒ is the day house of ♄; ♐ of ♃; ♈ of ♂; ♎ of ♀; and ♊ of ☿. The ☉ and ☾ have but one house each, which serves them both by day and night.

DAY TRIPLICITIES, those triplicities in which a planet is stronger by day than night. ♄ is stronger by day in the airy triplicity. ☉ in the fiery triplicity; ♂ in the watery triplicity, and ♀ in the earth.

DEBILITIES. See Dignities.

DECANT, or DECANATE, the Face; thus every sign has three Decanates.

DECATOM, a dichotome.

DECILE, the Semiquintile, a distance of 36°.

DECLINATION, the distance of any planet or place from the equator, whether north, or south. Thus, every part of the ecliptic, except the beginning of Aries or Libra, has declination, because the plane of the ecliptic is not parallel with that of the equator.

To find the Declination of any star or place:

Enter the table with the longitude as it stands in the column on the left hand, and under the latitude in the common angle of meeting is the declination.

Suppose a planet in 22° 0′ of ♌ with 7° north latitude, what will be its Declination? Enter the column on the left at No. 22, and in the common angle of meeting under No. 7 at the top will be found 20° 50′, which is the Declination. If the longitude and latitude consist of fractional parts, find the nearest whole number as before; then by the Rule of Three find the proportional value of the fractions, and add or subtract them as occasion may require. Example,—

What is the declination of a star in 22° 10′ of Leo with 4° 15′ north lattitude ?

Opposite the 22° of longitude under the column No. 4, north latitude, will be found 18° 0′; for the odd 15′ take the difference between the columns 4 and 5: it amounts to 57′. Thus, say, if 1 degree of latitude gives 57 minutes, what will 15 minutes give ? It gives 14 minutes; which added to the 18° 0′ makes 18° 14′; for the odd 10′ of longitude find the difference between 22 and 23 degrees of longitude: it is 20′ less, because the declination decreases. If 1 degree of longitude gives 20 minutes, what will 10 minutes give ? Answer, 3 minutes; which, as it is less, must be subtracted from the 18 degrees, 14 minutes, and the remainder is the true declination required: 18 degrees, 11 minutes. This mode of finding the value of the fractions by the Golden Rule is greatly preferable to using the Tables of Logarithms. The Rule of Three may at first seem difficult to the unpractised student, but it soon becomes familiar, and like an old beaten track which will never mislead him; in two or three days it will perform every operation in half the time in which it can be selected from the tables, with much less confusion, and with infinitely more accuracy. Care must be taken not to confuse the latitudes by taking the table of south for north latitude and *vice versa,* as is common among young beginners, and if this mistake be avoided there is hardly any other can happen. Each table serves for two signs, one of which begins the longitude at the top, and the other at the bottom, but the common angles of meeting for the latitudes are the same. The junction of the different declinations where the north ends and the south begins, is marked N & S, and should the fractional parts so fall as to be one part north and the other south declination, they must both be added: the sum of these is called the difference, from which find the proportional parts for the minutes, and if they are less than the first angle's declination, subtract them from it. Example,—

What is the declination of a star in 9 deg. 10 min. of Libra, with 40 deg. N latitude? in the common angle of meeting opposite 9° is 0° 6′ N declination, and opposite 10° is 0° 18′ S. declination: these added make 24′ which is called the difference. If 1 deg. of longitude gives the difference 24 min. what will the odd 10 min. give? answer, 4 min., which being less than the first angle's declination 6 min. subtract it from it, and the remainder is the true declination of 0° 2′ north. Had the number found been greater than the first angle's declination the latter must have been subtracted from it: the remainder will be the true declination south. Example,—

Suppose the longitude to be 9 deg. 40 min. of Libra with 4 deg. north latitude what will be its declination?

Proceeding as before described, the fourth term found for the odd 40 min. would be 16 min., which being greater than the 6 min. found in the common angle, the latter must be subtracted from it, and the remainder will be the declination: 0° 10′ south.

From these tables the longitude of a planet may be discovered (though not the sign), by taking the declination and latitude in the common angle, and finding the longitude opposite: thus, 10° 0′ of north declination, arising from 4° north latitude, answers either to 14° 0′ of ♍, or 16° 0′ of ♈.

DECREASING IN LIGHT. All planets decrease in light when they approach the Sun, after having passed the opposition. ♀ and ☿ decrease in light as they go nearer to the ☉, after having reached their greatest elongation. It is a sign of weakness in the thing or office described by such planet.

DECUMBITURE, a horary question or figure, erected for a sick person. It should be made to the time when the patient first perceives his disease; but if this pass unobserved, it may be erected like the figure of any other horary question at the option of the patient.

DEFERENT, an imaginary circle or orb, supposed by Ptolemy (who was ignorant of the Earth's motion) to carry a planet about with it.

DEGREE, the 30th part of a sign, or 360th part of a circle: every degree is divided into 60 minutes.

DEGREES, certain degrees or parts of the Zodiac, supposed to possess certain qualities wholly imaginary: but to render this Dictionary complete, I shall insert the Table of them, which is as follows:

A TABLE

Exhibiting the *Affections* and *Significations* of the *Degrees* in each *Sign* of the *Zodiac*.

Signs	Degrees Masculine	Degrees Feminine	Degrees Light	Degrees Dark	Degrees Smoky	Degrees Void	Pitted or Deep Degrees	Deficient or Azimene Degrees	Degrees increasing Fortune
♈	8 15 30	9 22	8 20 29	3 16	0	24 30	6 11 16 23 29	0	19
♉	11 21 30	5 17 24	7 15 28	3 30	0	12 20	5 12 24 25	6 7 8 9 10	3 15 27
♊	16 26	5 22 30	4 12 22	7 27	0	16 30	2 12 17 26 30	0	11
♋	2 10 23 30	8 12 27	12 28	14	20	18 30	12 17 23 26 30	9 10 11 12 13 14 15	1 2 3 4 15
♌	5 15 30	8 23	30	10	20	25	6 13 15 22 23 28	18 27 28	2 5 7 19
♍	12 30	8 20	8 16	5 30	22	10 17	8 13 16 21 22	0	3 14 20
♎	5 20 30	15 27	5 18 27	10 21	0	30	17 20 30	0	3 15 21
♏	4 17 30	14 25	8 22	3 30	24	14 29	9 10 22 23 27	19 28	7 18 20
♐	2 12 30	5 24	9 19 30	12	23	0	7 12 15 24 27 30	1 7 8 18 19	13 20
♑	11 30	10	10 19	7 22 30	15	25	7 17 22 24 29	26 27 28 29	12 13 14 20
♒	5 21 27	15 25 30	9 21 30	13	4	25	1 12 17 22 24 29	18 19	7 16 17 20
♓	10 23 30	20 28	12 22 28	6 18 30	0	25	4 9 24 27 28	0	13 10

Against ♈ are found 8, 15, and 30 in the masculine column and 9 and 22 in the feminine column: — this shews the first 8 degrees of ♈ to be masculine, the 9th feminine, from thence to the 15th masculine; from the 15th to the 22d feminine, and from thence to the 30th masculine: in like manner the 3 first are dark degrees, from thence to the 8th light degrees, from thence to the 16th dark, and from thence to the 20th light. The 29th is also a light degree, the rest are indifferent. There are no smoky degrees in ♈. The 24th and 30th are void degrees, the 6th, 11th, 16th, 23d, and 29th, are pitted or deep degrees. — There are no azimene degrees, and the 19th degree is fortunate.

If the ascendant or its lord be in any of these degrees in a nativity it is said to denote something in the native's fortune or appearance corresponding; thus, if in a masculine degree he or she will be more masculine: if in a feminine, more feminine. If in a light or dark degree, more fair or dark; and if in a smoky degree more dun and swarthy, with dull intellect. Void degrees render the native empty and void of knowledge. Deep pitted degrees subject the native to deep marks of small pox or scars, etc., or, according to other sapient gentlemen, they cause an impediment in speech, troubles and disputes in which they are sunk as in a deep pit. The azimene degrees make them crooked, lame or deformed, according to the nature of the sign and the part signified by it, and this they say is the invariable rule. The fortunate degrees, if on the cusp of the 2d house, or if the lord of the 2d be in such a degree, or if ♃ be in a fortunate degree, the native will acquire great riches and honour; such nonsense as this deserves no comment.

DEPRESSION of a star, is its distance from the Horizon when under the Earth.

DESCENDANT, the west angle, or 7th house.

DETRIMENT. A planet has its detriment in the sign opposite its house. Planets in detriment are reckoned unfortunate and weak, and it is a symbol of poverty, distress, loss, and subjugation.

DEXTER ASPECTS are those contrary to the order of the signs; thus, a planet in ♈ casts a dexter ✶ to ♒, and a dexter △ to ♐. They are said to be of greater force than sinister aspects, but this must be merely fancy.

DICHOTOME (cut in two,) a term given to the 1st and 3d quarters of the ☾, because she is then acquiring the shape of a half moon, or, as if she were cut in two. In these dichotomes she is oriental.

DIGNITIES are certain situations where a planet is said to

acquire strength, either to do evil or good, according to its nature. We say, to do evil, because, although a malefic is supposed to be better disposed when in its dignities than when peregrine or out of them, yet in the event of a contest between two planets, ♄ and ♃ for instance, in a natal position, or a subsequent direction to the hyleg, or any other significator, if ♄ were dignified above ♃, the evil threatened by the malefic would, it is said, predominate.

Planetary DIGNITIES are said to be of two kinds, Essential and Accidental. Essential Dignities are only five, viz. House, Exaltation, Triplicity, Term and face, all of which will be found under their respective heads, but the accidental dignities are very numerous.

The modern system of applying dignities is to assign a specific value to each, which are as follows:

Essential Dignities.

A planet in its house, or in mutual reception by house, has	5
In Exaltation or mutal reception by Exaltation - -	4
In Triplicity - - - - - -	3
In its Term - - - - - -	2
In Face - - - - - -	1

Accidental Dignities.

In the ascendant or midheaven - - - -	5
Free from combustion - - - - -	5
In Cazimi - - - - - - -	5
Beseiged by ♃ and ♀ - - - - -	6
In partile ☌ of ♃ and ♀ - - - - -	5
In ☌ of Cor Leonis - - - - - -	6
In ☌ of Spica - - - - - -	5
In the 4th, 7th, or 11th, house - - - -	4
Direct - - - - - - -	4
Partile ☌ of Caput Draconis - - - -	4
Partile △ of ♃ and ♀ - - - - -	4
Partile ✶ of ♃ and ♀ - - - - -	3
In the 2d or 5th house - - - - -	3
In the 9th house - - - - - -	2
Swift in motion - - - - - -	2
Increasing in light - - - - - -	2
♄, ♃, or ♂, when oriental, have - - - -	2
♀, ☿, or ☽, occidental, have - - - -	2
In the 3d house - - - - - -	1
In the Hayze - - - - - -	1

Accidental Dignities, continued.

In the term of ♃ or ♀   -   -   -   -   -   1

There are also a corresponding number of debilities both essential and accidental, as follows:

Essential Debilities.

In Detriment - - - - - -	5
In Fall - - - - - - -	4
Peregrine - - - - - -	5

Accidental Debilities.

Beseiged by ♄ and ♂ - - - - -	6
In partile conjunction of ♄ and ♂ - - - -	5
In conjunction with Caput Algol (it threatens beheading if joined to the hyleg,) - - - - -	6
Combust - - - - - - -	5
Retrograde - - - - - -	5
In the 12th house - - - - - -	5
Under the Sunbeams (from 8° 30′ to 17°, distant from him	4
In the 6th or 8th house - - - - -	4
Partile conjunction of the Dragon's Tail - - -	4
In partile opposition of ♄ or ♂ - - - -	4
In partile □ of ♄ or ♂ - - • - -	3
Decreasing in light - - - - - -	2
Decreasing in motion or slow - - - -	2
♄, ♃, or ♂, occidental - - - - -	2
♀, ☿, or ☾, oriental - - - - -	2
In the term of ♄ or ♂ - - - - -	1

The Part of Fortune, although in some situations it is dignified or debilitated like the planets, has also certain dignities and debilities peculiar to itself.

Dignities of the Part of Fortune.

In conjunction of Cor Leonis - - - -	6
In the ascendant or midheaven - - - -	5
In partile conjunction of ♃ or ♀ - - - -	5
In conjunction of Spica - - - - -	5
Not combust - - - - - -	5
In Taurus or Pisces - - - - - -	5
Beseiged by ♃ or ♀ - - - - -	6
In ♋, ♌, ♎, or ♐ - - - - - -	4
In the 7th, 4th, or 11th, house - - - -	4

Dignities of the Part of Fortune, continued.

In partile △ of ♃ or ♀ - - - - -	4
In partile ☌ of ☟ - - - - - -	4
In Gemini - - - - - - -	3
In the 2d or 5th house - - - - -	3
In partile sextile of ♃ or ♀ - - - ,	3
In Virgo - - - - - - -	2
In the 9th house - - - - - -	2
In the 3d house - - - - - -	1
In the term of ♃ or ♀ - - - - -	1

Debilities of the Part of Fortune.

In conjunction with Caput Algol - - - -	6
Beseiged by ♄ and ♂ - - - - -	6
In the 12th house - - - - -	5
In ♏, ♑, or ♒ - - - - - -	5
Combust - - - - - - -	5
In partile ☌ of the ♄ or ♂ - - - -	5
In the 6th or 8th house - - - - -	4
In ☍ of ♃ or ♂ - - - - - -	4
In partile ☌ of the ☟ - - - - -	4
In Aries - - - - - - -	3
In partile □ of ♄ or ♂ - - - - -	3
In the term of ♄ or ♂ - - - - -	1

A fixed star is in ☌ when not above 5° distant from a planet.

The state of every planet is to be considered according to this table, and its dignities and debilities collected together; the one is to be subtracted from the other, and the remainder is the criterion whereby the strength or weakness of a planet is ascertained. Many objections may be made to this rule; doubtless planets are stronger or weaker according to their positions; but I have no opinion of dignities conferred by house, exaltation, or triplicity, or of debilities caused by detriment, fall, or peregrination. Placidus partly believed in their efficacy, and had particular confidence in the nature of the term where a planet was situated, more than probably it merited. It would not be easy to demonstrate, why the motion of a planet, whether swift or slow, direct or retrograde, should alter its influence, which must wholly proceed from attraction; nor is it rational to suppose any planet was ever affected by the ☌ with the lunar nodes, which can have no relation to any thing but the moon to whom they belong. The power of any star is probably increased by being angular, or in perigee, or when it is far advanced in our hemisphere and its rays become more vertical; and proportionally diminished in those situations where its rays are more oblique.

If I comprehend Ptolemy rightly, he considered those zodiacal dignities of house, exaltation, triplicity and term, not as strengthening its power, but only as disposing it to create certain propensities in the mind of the native, whom it was supposed to govern. He says, "planets are strong in the world when they are oriental, swift in motion, direct, and increasing in light; and strong in respect of the geniture when angular or succeedent, and particulaly in the south or east angles." There is nothing here said about the strength of essential dignities.

DIRECT is when a planet moves on according to the order of the signs: as from ♈ to ♉, &c, It is the reverse of retrograde.

DIRECT MOTION in mundane directions, is when the significator (or rather its place) being immoveable in the horary circle, the promittor by converse motion forms a conjunction or aspect with it. Example:—

If the ☉ be posited on the cusp of the 10th, and a promittor comes by direction to the cusp of the 8th, it will form a mundane Sextile to the ☉ by what is called direct motion, though for what reason I am not aware, for the significator remains immoveable, and the promittor is moved conversely.

DIRECTIONS are of two kinds, primary and secondary, for the last of which see Secondary Direction.

Primary directions are arithmetical calculations of the time of events caused by the significator forming conjunctions, or aspects, with the places of promittors, and they are of two kinds; zodiacal and mundane. Zodiacal directions are founded upon the familiarities of the stars among each other in the zodiac, subsequent to the time of nativity, and consist of a series of rules, or problems, for calculating the distance of the place of a significator in a nativity from the place he must arrive at before he can form the aspect, which distance is called the arc of direction. It must here be observed, that in directions the place of a planet in a nativity is called the planet itself, as they are supposed to impress their natures on the places where they are found at the moment of their birth as strongly as if they were continually present in that spot, although they may be no longer there when the significator arrives; thus, if we direct the ☉ to the ☌ of ♃, we mean to the radical position of ♃, which always possesses his efficacy.

When the arc of direction is found, the Sun's right ascension must be added to it, and the sum will be the right ascension (without latitude) of that place in the zodiac, at which, when the ☉ arrives, the direction is complete. For every day of the ☉'s approach to this point, a year must be added, and so on in proportion, viz. for every 2 hours a month, &c. thus the time when the event is likely to happen is pointed out; but those primary directions are seldom supposed to produce any event of importance, unless some secondary direction, revolution, transit &c. agree: but where a nativity is weak, or the constitution broken by age, disease, &c. the primary direction alone will kill, if it be inimical to the hyleg: and misfortune will happen if the positions of the planets at the hour of birth are unfortunate, without the coincidence of any secondary direction.

Before an attempt be made to calculate any direction, a complete speculum should be formed, the nature of which will be seen under the article Speculum. This will save the operator infinite trouble and confusion, as every thing will be ready to his hand and he may bring up the whole directions of a nativity with ease in two or three hours.

ZODIACAL DIRECTIONS.

Problem 1st.—To direct the Sun when not more than 2° distant from the cusp of the mid-heaven to any conjunction or aspect:

Subtract the right ascension of the Sun from the right ascension (without latitude) of the place of the conjunction or aspect, the remainder will be the arc of direction.

Example:—Suppose the ☉ posited near the cusp of the 10th, with ♀ in the 12th house, (as in plate 2d, figure 1st): I would direct the ☉ to the ☌ of ♀.

Right ascension of ♀ without latitude, - - - -	262°	6'
Right ascension of the ☉, - - - - - - - -	215	58
Arc of Direction	46	8

Note, if the latitude of the promittor be greater than the orb, the direction will have little or no effect.

Problem 2d.—To direct the ☉, when not more than 3° distant from the cusp of the 1st or 7th house, to any conjunction or aspect.

If the ☉ be in the ascendant, subtract his oblique ascension, taken under the pole of the country, from the oblique ascension of the place of the conjunction or aspect, taken under the same pole, but without latitude as before: the remainder will be the arc of direction. If the Sun be in the 7th house, his oblique descension must be taken in like manner from that of the place required.

It may also be done by subtracting the oblique ascension of the
☉'s opposite place from that of the ascendant, which was a favorite system with Placidus, instead of using the descensions, though
it is difficult to tell why.

Example:—Suppose the ☉ in the latitude of London, posited
near the cusp of, the ascendant, and ♃ in 26° of ♍ (as in plate 2d,
fig. 2d,) I would direct the ☉ to the sextile of ♃: it falls in 26°
of ♑.

Oblique Ascension of 26° of ♑, under the pole of London,	326°	56'
Oblique Ascension of the ☉ under the same pole,	309	32
Arc of Direction,	17	24

The latitude of the promittor in this as in the former problem
should be less than its orb.

Problem 3d.—To direct the ☉, when above the Earth, and more
than 3 degrees distant from the cusp of a cardinal house, to any
conjunction or aspect.

1st. Find both their right distances from the mid-heaven, and
call that of the aspect, the primary distance.

2d. Say, "as the ☉'s semidiurnal arc is to his right distance
from the mid-heaven, so is the promittor's semidiurnal arc to the
secondary distance of the aspect.

3d. If the primary and secondary distances of the place of the
aspect be on the ascending or descending part of heaven, subtract
the less from the greater, the remainder will be the arc of direction; but if one be in the ascending and the other in the descending part of heaven, add them, and their sum will be the arc of
direction.

Note, the ascending part of heaven is from the 4th eastward, to
the 10th; and the descending part, from the 10th westward to
the 4th.

Example:—Suppose the cusp of the 10th to have 24° 6' of ♒,
the ☉ in the 11th house in 0° 9' of ♈, and ♃ in 1° 41' of ♋, I
would direct the ☉ to the quintile of ♃ in the zodiac (see plate 2d,
fig. 3d.); it falls in 19° 41' of ♈.

☉'s Right Ascension,	0°	8'
Add for subtraction,	360	0
	360	8
Right Ascension of the Mid-heaven,	326	26
☉'s Right distance from the Mid-heaven,	33	42

Right Ascension of the Aspect, 19° 41′ of ♈,   18ᶜ   9′
Add for subtraction,   360   0

                          378   9
Right Ascension of the Midheaven,   326   26

Right distance of the Aspect, 51   43 Primary Distance.

As the ☉'s semidiurnal arc, 6*h.* 0*m*, is to the ☉'s right distance, 33° 42′, so is the semidiurnal arc of the aspect (viz. 19° 41′ ♈) 6*h.* 30*m.* to the secondary distance, 36° 30′

Both these distances being in the ascending part of heaven, subtract the less from the greater.

Primary Distance,   51° 43′
Secondary Distance,   36   30

Arc of Direction,   15   13

Problem 4th. To direct the ☉, when under the Earth in the space of the crepuscle or twilight, to any conjunction or aspect:

Subtract the oblique ascension of the ☉ from that of the aspect, the remainder would be the arc of direction, but as the ☉ is in the crepuscle, it is a false arc.

2d. Find the ☉'s primary distance from the horoscope, taken in the pole of the horoscope (viz. the latitude of the country), and with it enter the table of twilight for that latitude, as near as possible to the degree the ☉ is in, and in the left hand column marked *Pa* (parallel), will be found the degree or parallel of the ☉'s depression.

Note, the highest number of these degrees is 18, so that if the Sun's primary distance leads to a higher number than 18 he is not in the crepuscle, but is in the obscure arc, and must be directed as in problem 5th.

3d, Opposite this parallel of the ☉'s depression, take the place of the aspect's sign and degree, and this will be the secondary distance.

4th, Subtract from this the primary distance, obtained in the same way; the remainder is the ortive difference, which subtract from the false arc, and it will give the true arc of direction. If the primary distance be greater than the secondary, the ortive difference must be added to the false arc.

Example:—Suppose the cusp of the horoscope to be 11° of ♓;
♂ in 0° 0′ of ♈, and ☉ in 15° 46′ of ♈, (see plate 2d, fig. 4th):
I would direct the ☉ to the □ of ♂: it falls of course in 0° 0′ of
♋

Oblique Ascension of the Aspect 0° 0′ of ♋, taken in the Horoscope,	65°	10′
☉'s Oblique Ascension in the Pole of the Horoscope,	8	28
False Arc of Direction,	56	42

Oblique Ascension of the Sun taken in the Horoscope,	8°	28′
Add for subtraction, the circle	360	0
	368	28
Oblique Ascension of the Horoscope,	349	45
The Sun's primary distance,	18	43

The pole of the horoscope is 44°, I enter therefore the table of
twilight for the latitude of 44° with this primary distance, supposing the Sun's place in Aries to be 16°, for the sake of whole
numbers, which is near enough: under the column 10 of Aries I
look for 18° 43′, and the nearest I find to it is 18° 32′, which I set
down: there yet remains 6° of Aries to be accounted for. The
column 20 of Aries is 19° 1′, making a difference from the column
of 10 of Aries, 29′. This difference is for 10 degrees, and the proportion of it for the 6 degrees not yet accounted for, is 17 minutes,
which I add to the 18° 32′, and it makes 18° 49′, which must be
taken for the primary distance in the room of 18° 43′. Opposite
to these numbers, in the column of parallels on the left hand, is
No. 13, which is the parallel of twilight where the sun is: called
the Sun's depression.

Opposite this parallel of the Sun's depression, 13 deg. under 0
deg. of Cancer, I find 24 deg. 45 min. for the □ of Mars: this is
the secondary distance.

Subtract from this the primary distance.

Secondary distance,	24°	45′
Primary distance,	18	49
Ortive difference,	5	56

This ortive difference must be subtracted from the false arc because the secondary distance is the greater; but had this primary been the greater it must have been added.

$$\begin{array}{lrr}\text{False arc of direction,} & 56° & 42' \\ \text{Ortive difference,} & 5 & 56 \\ \hline \text{True arc of direction} & 50 & 46 \end{array}$$

Should the Sun be in the evening instead of the morning crepuscle, he must be directed to the aspect by oblique descension, or by the oblique ascension of their opposite places. The only remaining difference will be reversing the distances. If the secondary difference be the greater the ortive difference must be added; and *vice versa*.

Problem 5th. To direct the Sun when found in the space of the obscure arc to any conjunction or aspect.

When the Sun's distance from the horoscope is so great as to be below the 18th parallel of twilight as marked in the table he is then in the obscure arc.

1st, Subtract the whole crepusculine arc of the Sun from his seminocturnal arc; the remainder is his obscure arc.

Note. The whole crepusculine arc is the highest number found opposite to the parallel 18° in the table, under the sign and degree the Sun is in, taken proportionally as before, which may be turned into hours und minutes should the seminocturnal arc be the same.

2d, Subtract the whole crepusculine arc of the Sun which he will have in the place of the aspect (taken as before) from the seminocturnal arc of the said place, the remainder will be his obscure arc in that place.

3d, Find the distance of the place of the aspect from the 4th house, and call it the primary distance.

4th, Find the secondary distance by the Rule of Three: thus, As the Sun's obscure arc is to his distance from the 4th, so is the aspect's obscure arc to the secondary distance.

5th, If both these distances are in the ascending or descending hemisphere; subtract one from the other; but if one be in the ascending and the other in the descending part, add them, and the result will be the true arc of direction.

Example: Suppose in the latitude of 43 deg., 4° 2' of Capricorn on the cusp of the 4th, the Sun in 11 deg. 45 m. of Aquarius, Jupiter in 10 deg. 34 m. of Aries; I would direct the Sun to a parallel of Jupiter's declination: as Jupiter has 1° 20' south latitude, his declination is 2° 57' north (see plate 2d, fig. 5.)

The nearest table of twilight is to the latitude of 44°, where
11° 45′ of Aquarius taken proportionally would give about 26° 10′
opposite to the 18th parallel; but under the pole of 43° it would
be about 25° 45′ or 1*h*, 43*m*.

⊙'s seminocturnal arc	7*h*.	7*m*.
⊙'s whole crepusculine arc	1	43
⊙'s obscure arc	5	24

When the Sun comes to 22° 35′ of Pisces, he will acquire a declination of 2° 57′ south, the same as Jupiter has north, which is
coming to his parallel.

Seminocturnal arc of 22° 35′ of Pisces	6*h*.	11*m*.
Whole crepusculine arc of ⊙ in that place,	1	39
⊙'s obscure arc in 22° 35′ of Pisces,	4	32

Right ascension of 22° 35′ of Pisces,	353°	12′
Right ascension of the 4th house,	274	2
Distance of the aspect from the 4th	79	10 Primary Dist.

Right ascension of the ⊙,	314°	13′
Right ascension of the 4th house,	274	2
⊙'s distance from the 4th house,	40	11

As the Sun's obscure arc, 5*h*. 24*m*., is to his distance from the
4th house, 40° 11′, so is the aspect's obscure arc, 4*h*. 32*m*., to the
secondary distance, 33° 44′.

Both these distances being in one hemisphere, namely, the descending hemisphere, subtract the one from the other,

Primary distance,	79°	10′
Secondary distance,	33	44
Arc of direction,	45	26

Problem 6th. To direct the Sun, wherever he may be, to the
parallels in the zodiac.

If the planet has latitude, the Sun will meet his parallel in a
different part of the zodiac, because the Sun has never any lati-

tude; the point, therefore, must be sought in the table where the Sun meets the proposed declination.

Subtract the Sun's oblique ascension taken under his pole, from the oblique ascension of the point where he meets the parallel, taken under the same pole, the remainder will be the arc of direction.

Example:—Suppose 29° 49′ of Leo on the cusp of the 10th, 2° 0′ of Libra on that of the 11th, the Sun 29° 19′ in Virgo intercepted in the 10th, and the Moon in 23° 38′ of Aquarius with 16° 35′ south declination: I would direct the Sun to a parallel of the Moon's declination (see pl. 2 fig. 6.)

The point where the Sun has this declination is in 15° 40′ Scorpio.

The pole of the Sun is 16° 0′.

Oblique ascension of 15° 40′ of Scorpio under the Sun's pole of 16°,	228° 4′
Oblique ascension of the Sun under his own pole,	179 18
Arc of direction,	48 46

It must be here noted, that accidents arising from directions to parallels always happen before the time a little, owing, as Placidus thinks, to the magnitude of the luminaries, whereby their bodies are affected before their center can arrive at the point of direction: whatever be the cause, this very inaccuracy in point of time is a proof of the truth of parallel directions in the zodiac.

Problem 7th. To direct a significator with latitude to any conjunction or aspect.

The point must be found where the significator will form the aspect, according to the latitude it will have in that place: the latitude of the promittor must be wholly omitted, except it be greater than its orb, as before stated.

Find the right ascension of the significator, or its oblique ascension or descension with latitude, under its pole, according to its position, and subtract it from the same ascension or descension of the place of the aspect; the remainder will be the arc of direction.

Example:---Suppose 26° 9′ of Aries on the cusp of the 7th. the Moon in 25° 35′ of Aries, Saturn, 11° 1′ of Pisces: I would direct the Moon to the Square of Saturn (See plate 2 Fig. 7.)

The square of Saturn falls of course in 11° 1′ of Gemini.

The pole of the Moon is 46° 0′.

Oblique descension of the aspect 11° 1′ of Gemini
taken under the Moon's pole, with 3° 21′ S. latitude,
which she will have there,   -   -   -   -   -   90° 37′

Oblique descension of the Moon under her pole,
with 5° south latitude, and 5° 16′ north declination,   30   59
                                                          _____

                        Arc of direction   59   38

This is the way in which I should perform the operation, as it
is the easiest and most natural to work by oblique descension,
when the planets happen to be so situated, but the method adopted
by Placidus is as follows:

Oblique ascension of the opposite place of the aspect, viz. 11° 1′ of Sagittary taken under the Moon's
pole, with opposite latitude of 3° 21′ north,   -   270° 37′

Oblique ascension of the Moon's opposite place un-
der her pole, with opposite latitude,   -   -   -   210   59
                                                        _____

                        Arc of direction,   59   38

For what reason he could prefer taking an opposite place in
preference to the place itself, and working with opposite latitude
(which may confuse a young artist, and cannot benefit an old one)
is difficult to imagine, except it was for the sublime gratification
of working by ascension instead of descension.

Should any one, however, be disposed to imitate him, they may
save themselves the trouble of working by contrary latitude, as
when they have found the descension, they may get the ascension
of the opposite place by adding 180° to it.

Problem 8th, To direct a significator with latitude to parallels
of declination.

The point must be found where the significator acquires the
declination of the promittor, according to the latitude the former
will have in that place.

Subtract its oblique ascension or descension, with latitude
under its pole, from the oblique ascension or descension of the
place where it will meet the aspect taken under the same pole;
the remainder will be the arc of direction.

Example:—Suppose 7° 11′ of Virgo on the cusp of the 10th,
1° 0′ of Leo on the cusp of the 9th, the Moon in 24° 10′ of Leo,
Saturn in the 4th house in 14° 26′ of Pisces, with 7° 47′ south de-

clination (see plate 2, fig. 8): I would direct the Moon to the zodiacal parallel of Saturn.

She will acquire this declination at 21° of Virgo, where she will have 4° 23′ north latitude. (The readiest way of finding the declination required of any planet with latitude is by inspecting an Ephemeris for the year.)

The pole of the Moon is 5°.

Oblique descension of 21° of Virgo taken under the Moon's pole, with 4° 23′ north latitude, which she will have there, - - - - - - 174° 9′

Oblique descension of the Moon under her pole with 2° 51′ north latitude, and 16° 12′ north declination, - - - - - - - - 148 56

Arc of direction, 25 13

Placidus works this question as usual by opposite ascensions.

It should here be observed, that paralells of declination in the zodiac are of two kinds; northern and commanding, or southern and obeying: So that if two planets have the same declination as to degrees and minutes, but one north and the other south, that which is north will be stronger than the other; but where a significator is concerned, whether its declination be north or south, it is equally fatal if the promittor be an infortune, particularly if the significator be hyleg.

In finding parallels of declination it should be observed, that if the significator is leaving either of the tropics, its declination decreases, and it will of course fall upon the parallels of stars of which the declinations are less than its own; but when separating from equinoctial signs its declination increases, and it will fall in in such parallels as have declinations greater than its own.

Problem 9th. To direct any significator to its own rays in the zodiac.

Subtract the right or oblique ascension or descension of the significator, with latitude, if it have any, taken under its pole, from the ascension or descension of the aspect, with the latitude (if any) the significator will have when it arrives there, taken under the same pole; the remainder is the arc of direction.

Example: Suppose the Moon ascending in 6 deg. 45 m. of Capricorn, under the pole of 52 deg., with 2 deg. 4 m. of south latitude, and 25° 24′ south declination, I would direct her to her own square in the zodiac.

The place of aspect is of course 6 deg. 45 m. of Aries, where, on
her arrival, she will acquire 4 deg. 32 m. south latitude (see plate
2, fig. 9.)

Oblique ascension of 6 deg. 45 m. of Aries under
   the ☾'s pole of 52 deg., with 4 deg. 32 min.
   south latitude, - . - - - - - - 9° 52′
Add for subtraction,   - - - - -   360   0
                                              ―――――
                                        369 52
Oblique ascension of the ☾ under her pole with
   latitude, - - - - - - - - 314 52
                                            ―――――
               Arc of direction,   - - - 55   0

As the ☉ never has any latitude, nothing more is required than
to subtract his ascension or descension under his pole from that
of the aspect taken under the same pole, the remainder will be the
arc of direction.

MUNDANE DIRECTIONS.

Mundane directions differ from zodiacal in this, that they are
wholly independent of the zodiac, as much as if such a circle had
never existed, and only operate in respect of the world; for
instance, the Sun in Sagittary, on the cusp of the 11th house,
would be in mundane sextile to Capricorn, on the cusp of the
ascendant: whereas, in respect to the zodiac he would have no
aspect to that point at all. In this, therefore, they differ. The
zodiacal aspects are measured by the signs and degrees of the
zodiac, and the mundane aspects are wholly measured by the arcs
or semi-arcs of the planets; hence it is necessary, in calculating
mundane aspects, that the latitude of both significator and promittor should be taken, that their true distance may be ascertained.

Placidus was the inventor of them, and so bigoted was he to
this system, that he once, as he says, rejected the doctrine of zodiacal aspects *in toto*; but, it appears, he soon discovered his error;
as he makes abundant use of them in his "Thirty Nativities."
How far the doctrine of mundane directions is consistent with
truth, experience alone can determine. No doubt the planets
operate on the Earth according to their mundane position: this
every day's observation will confirm; but that they have equal
efficacy in directions is an hypothesis that rests upon little more

than the assertion of Placidus himself, for his examples are not (in my opinion at least) satisfactory; indeed, the doctrine of directions altogether seems to want correcting. There is something not quite agreeable to reason in the idea of the influence of a planet being transferred to his place in the radix, although it certainly seems true in parallels of declination. As to mundane parallels, those who consult the Nativities of Placidus will not find them quite infallible.

There are three ways of directing in the world; first, by what is called direct motion, when the promittor by moving conversely forms any conjunction or aspect with the place of the significator. Secondly, when the significator by converse motion forms any similar configuration with the place of the promittor. Thirdly, when both are carried away by the motion of the *Primum Mobile*, (as Placidus calls it, in imitation of Ptolemy, who was ignorant of the Earth's diurnal motion on its own axis); this is called rapt motion, but it forms no aspect, but parallels from angles.

Problem 1st.

To direct the mid-heaven to the conjunction of a star.

Subtract the right ascension of the mid-heaven from the star's right ascension with latitude, the remainder will be the arc of direction.

Example:—Suppose ♄ in 23° 30′ of ♑, with 0° 6′ north latitude, and 14° 30′ of ♐, on the cusp of the mid-heaven, (see plate 2 fig. 10.) I would direct the planet ♄ to the cusp of the mid-heaven.

Right ascension of ♄ with 0° 6′ north latitude,	295°	23′
Right ascension of the mid-heaven,	253	9
Arc of direction,	42	14

Problem 2d.

To direct the mid-heaven to the sextile of a star.

1st, If the sextile be from the cusp of the 8th, add ⅔ of the star's semidiurnal arc to its right ascension with latitude; but if from the cusp of the 12th, subtract it.

2d, From the sum or remainder subtract the right ascension of the mid-heaven, the remainder will be the arc of direction.

Example: Suppose the ☉ in 1° 0′ of ♑. with 12° 0′ of ♏ on the

cusp of the mid heaven (see plate 2. fig. 11.), I would direct the
mid-heaven to the Sextile of the Sun.

☉'s right ascension (he has no latitude),	271°	5′
Being from the 12th; subtract ⅔ of his		
semidiurnal arc,	42	48
	228	17
Right ascension of the mid-heaven,	219	33
Arc of direction,	8	44

Problem 3d.

To direct the mid-heaven to the square of a star.

1st. If the square be from the cusp of the 7th, add the star's
semidiurnal arc to its right ascension with latitude; but if from
the cusp of the ascendant, subtract it.

2d, Subtract from this sum or remainder the right ascension
of the mid-heaven, the remainder will be the arc of direction.

Example:—Suppose 13° 30′ of ♏ on the cusp of the 10th, the ☉
in 1° 45′ of ♈, in the latitude of London, 51° 32′. I would direct
the ☉ to the □ of the mid-heaven (see plate 2, fig. 12.)

☉'s right ascension (he has no latitude),	1°	6′
Add for subtraction,	360	0
	361	6
Subtract the ☉'s semidiurnal arc,	90	53
	270	13
Subtract the right ascension of the mid-heaven,	221	2
Arc of direction,	49	11

It may also be done by bringing it by oblique ascension to the
cusp of the ascendant, from whence it casts the square to the midheaven.

Problem 4th.

To direct the mid-heaven to the trine of a star

1st, If the trine be from the cusp of the 6th, subtract ⅔ of the
star's seminocturnal arc from its right ascension with latitude;
but if from the cusp of the 2d, add it.

2d, From the sum or remainder subtract the right ascension of the *Imum Cœli*; the remainder will be the arc of direction.

Example:—Suppose 13° 30′ of ♉ on the cusp of the 4th, the ☉ in ♈ 1° 45′ latitude of London 51° 32′; I would direct the ☉ to the trine of the mid-heaven (see plate 2, fig. 13.)

☉'s right ascension,	1°	36′
Add ⅔ of the ☉'s seminocturnal arc,	59	25
	61	1
Subtract the right ascension of the 4th,	41	2
Arc of direction,	19	59

This is the sextile to the 4th house, which is the trine to the mid-heaven.

Problem 5th.

To direct the mid-heaven to the opposition of a star. (This is done by bringing it to the cusp of the 4th.)

Subtract the right ascension of the Imum Cœli from that of the star with latitude (if it has any); the remainder will be the arc of direction.

Example: Suppose 14° 0′ of ♐, on the cusp of the lower heaven ♃ in 3° 21′ of ♑, with 0° 24′ north latitude; I would direct the midheaven to the ☍ of ♃ (see plate 2, fig. 14.)

Right ascension of ♃ with 0° 24′ north latitude,	273°	39′
Right ascension of the Imum Cœli,	252	38
Arc of direction,	21	1

Problem 6th.

To direct the midheaven to the quintile of a star.

1st. If the quintile be in the descending part of heaven, viz. in the 8th house, add four-fifths of the star's semidiurnal arc to its right ascension, with latitude, but if in the ascending part, viz. the 12th, subtract it.

2d, Subtract the right ascension of the midheaven from the sum or remainder, and it will give the arc of direction.

Example: Suppose the ☉ and midheaven situated as in problem 2d: I would direct the midheaven to the quintile of the ☉ (see plate 2, fig, 11.)

☉'s right ascension	271° 5
Being in the ascending part of heaven, subtract four-fifths of the ☉,s semidiurnal arc,	51 22
	219 43
Subtract the right ascension of the midheaven,	219 33
Arc of direction,	0 10

Problem 7th.

To direct the midheaven to the sesquiquadrate of a star;

1st, If the sesquiquadrate be in the descending part of heaven viz. the 5th house, subtract ½ the seminocturnal arc of the star from its right ascension, with latitude, if it has any; but if in the ascending part, viz. the 2d house, add them.

2d, From the sum or remainder, subtract the right ascension of the 4th house; it will give the arc of direction.

Example:—Suppose the ☉ and cusp of the 4th, as in problem 4th, I would direct the midheaven to the sesquiquadrate of the ☉ (see plate 2, fig. 13.)

☉'s right ascension,	1°	6'
As the ☉ is ascending in the 3d house, add ½ his seminocturnal arc,	44	5
	45	11
Subtract the right ascension of the 4th house,	41	2
Arc of direction,	4	9

Problem 8th.

To direct the midheaven to the biquintile of a star:

1st, If the biquintile be in the descending part of heaven, viz. in the 5th house, subtract two-fifths of the seminocturnal arc of the star from its right ascension, with latitude, if it has any; but if it be in the ascending part, the 2d house, add them.

2d, From the sum or remainder subtract the right ascension of the 4th, and it will give the arc of direction.

Example:—Suppose 14 ° 0' of ♐ on the cusp of the 4th, with ♂ in 10° 16' of ♏, with 1° 49' north latitude; I would direct the midheaven to the biquintile of ♂.

Right ascension of ♂ with 1° 49′ north latitude,	218°	26′
Two-fifths of his seminocturnal arc added, as he is ascending,	42	51
	261	17
Right ascension of the lower heaven,	252	38
Arc of direction,	8	39

N. B. I have not added problems for the semiquadrate, semisextile, &c. because Placidus denies their efficacy: but those who choose to direct to them, may do it in the same way by adding or subtracting the proportional part of their semiarcs to or from their right ascension with latitude.

Problem 9th.

To direct the horoscope to the conjunction of a star.

The manner of doing this by right ascension has been shewn in problem 3d of mundane directions; it now remains to shew, how it may be done by oblique ascension.

Subtract the oblique ascension of the horoscope from the oblique ascension of the star, with latitude, taken in the pole of the horoscope, the remainder is the arc of direction.

Example:—From the diagram of problem 3d (plate 2, fig. 12.) I would direct the ☉ to the cusp of the horoscope.

Oblique ascension of the ☉ under the pole of the horoscope,	0°	13′
Add for subtraction,	360	0
	360	13
Oblique ascension of the horoscope, under its pole	311	2
Arc of direction,	49	11

Problem 10th.

To direct the horoscope to the sextile of a star.

1st, If the sextile be from the 11th house, add ⅔ of the star's semidiurnal arc to its oblique ascension, with latitude, taken under the pole of the horoscope: if it be from the 3d house, subtract ⅔ of the star's seminocturnal arc from its oblique ascension.

2d. From the sum or remainder subtract the oblique ascension of the horoscope, the remainder will be the arc of direction.

Example:—From the diagram in problem 3d, I would direct the horoscope to the ✶ of ♂.

Oblique ascension of ♂ with 0° 25′ north latitude taken in the pole of the horoscope, 51° 32′,	18°	12′
Add for subtraction,	360	0
	378	12
⅔ of the seminocturnal arc of ♂, being from the 3d house,	46	12
	332	0
Oblique ascension of the horoscope,	311	2
Arc of direction,	20	58

Problem 11th.

To direct the horoscope to the square of a star.

Bring it by right ascension to the cusp of the 10th, or 4th house according to its position above or below the Earth, as directed in problems 1st and 5th.

Problem 12th.

To direct the horoscope to the trine of a star.

1st, If the trine be from the 9th house, add four-thirds of the star's semidiurnal arc to its oblique ascension with latitude, but if from the 5th house subtract four-thirds of its seminocturnal arc.

2d, From the sum or remainder subtract the oblique ascension of the horoscope, the remainder will be the arc of direction.

Example:—Suppose ♃ posited near the cusp of the 7th, in 10° 55′ of ♋, as in problem 10th (plate 2, fig. 12.): I would direct ♃ to the △ of the horoscope.

Oblique ascension of ♃ with 0° 19′ north latitude, taken in the pole of the horoscope,	70°	0′
Add for subtraction,	360	0
	430	0
Being directed to the cusp of the 5th, subtract four-thirds of his seminocturnal arc,	76	0
	354	0
Oblique ascension of the horoscope,	311	2
Arc of direction,	42	58

To direct the horoscope to the quintile of a star.

1st, If the place of the quintile be above the Earth, add four-fifths of the star's semidiurnal arc to its oblique ascension with latitude taken in the horoscope; but if the place of the quintile be under the Earth subtract four-fifths of its seminocturnal arc.

2d, From the sum or remainder subtract the oblique ascension of the horoscope, the remainder will be the arc of direction.

Example:—From the diagram in problem 3d I would direct ♂ to the quintile of the horoscope (plate 2, fig 12.)

Oblique ascension of ♂ with 0° 25′ north latitude, taken in the pole of the horoscope	18°	12′
Add for subtraction,	360	0
	378	12
Being under the Earth subtract four-fifths of his seminocturnal arc,	55	26
	322	46
Oblique ascension of the horoscope,	311	2
Arc of direction,	11	44

Problem 14th.

To direct the horoscope to the sesquiquadrate of a star.

1st, If the place of the sesquiquadrate be above the Earth, add ¾ of the star's whole diurnal arc to its oblique ascension; or if under the Earth, subtract ¾ of its whole nocturnal arc.

2d, From the sum or remainder subtract the oblique ascension of the horoscope, the remainder will be the arc of direction.

Example:—From the diagram in problem 12th I would direct ♃ to the sesquiquadrate of the horoscope (see plate 2, fig. 12.)

Oblique ascension of ♃ with latitude as before,	70°	0′
Add for subtraction,	360	0
	430	0
The aspect being under the Earth, subtract ¾ of its whole nocturnal arc,	85	30
	344	30
Oblique ascension of the horoscope,	311	2
Arc of direction,	33	28

Problem 15*th*.

To direct the ascendant to the biquintile of a star,

1st, If the place of the biquintile be above the Earth, add four-fifths of the star's whole diurnal arc to its oblique ascension; but if under the Earth, subtract four-fifths of its whole nocturnal arc.

2d, From the sum or remainder subtract the oblique ascension of the horoscope; the remainder will be the arc of direction.

Example:—From the diagram of the last problem (see plate 2, fig. 12) I would direct the horoscope to the biquintile of ♃.

Oblique ascension of ♃	70°	0′
Add for subtraction,	360	0
	430	0
The aspect being under the Earth, subtract four-fifths of ♃'s whole nocturnal arc,	91	0
	339	0
Oblique ascension of the horoscope,	311	2
Arc of direction,	27	58

Problem 16*th*.

To direct the horoscope to the opposition of a star.

Bring it to the square of the midheaven by right ascension, as directed in problem 3.

Problem 17*th*.

To bring a star to the cusp of any house by right or oblique ascension.

If by right ascension, and the star is to be brought to the cusp of the ascendant, subtract its semidiurnal arc from its right ascension. If to the cusp of the 12th, subtract $\frac{2}{3}$ of its semidiurnal arc; if to the cusp of the 11th, subtract $\frac{1}{3}$; if to the cusp of the 10th, neither add nor subtract; if to the cusp of the 9th, add $\frac{1}{3}$ of the said semi-arc; if to the 8th, add $\frac{2}{3}$; if to the 7th, add the whole semidiurnal arc.

Subtract from this sum or remainder the right ascension of the mid-heaven, the remainder will be the arc of direction to the cusp required.

If the star be below the Earth, and is to be brought to the cusp of the sixth, subtract $\frac{2}{3}$ of its seminocturnal arc from its right ascension; if to the 5th, subtract $\frac{1}{3}$; if to the 4th, neither add nor subtract; if to the 3d, add $\frac{1}{3}$ of the seminocturnal arc; and if to the 2d, add $\frac{2}{3}$.

Subtract from this sum or remainder the right ascension of the *Imum Cœli*, the remainder will be the arc of direction to the cusp required.

If by oblique ascension, and the star is to be brought to the cusp of the 4th, subtract the seminocturnal arc of the star from its oblique ascension; if to the cusp of the 3d, subtract $\frac{2}{3}$; if to the 2d, $\frac{1}{3}$; if to the horoscope, neither add nor subtract; if to the 12th add $\frac{1}{3}$ of its semidiurnal arc; if to to the cusp of the 11th, add $\frac{2}{3}$; and if to the mid-heaven, add the whole semidiurnal arc.

Subtract from the sum or remainder the oblique ascension of the horoscope, the remainder will be the arc of direction to the cusp required.

From the midheaven to the *Imum Cœli* the distance from any cusp may be wrought by oblique descension: thus, if the star is to be brought to the cusp of the 9th; subtract $\frac{2}{3}$ of its semidiurnal arc from its oblique descension; if to the cusp of the 8th, $\frac{1}{3}$; if to the descendant, neither add nor subtract; if to the 6th, add $\frac{1}{3}$ of its seminocturnal arc; if to the 5th, add $\frac{2}{3}$; and if to the 4th, add the whole of its seminocturnal arc.

Subtract from this sum or remainder the oblique descension of the 7th, the remainder will be the arc of direction to the cusp required.

Example:—I would direct the midheaven to the $\triangle$ of the $\odot$ by oblique ascension instead of right ascension, as performed by problem 4th: this is done by bringing it to the cusp of the 2d, which is the trine to the midheaven.

Oblique ascension of the $\odot$,	0°	43′
Add for subtraction,	360	0
	360	43
One third of the $\odot$'s seminocturnal arc subtracted, as the trine is from the cusp of the 2d house,	29	42
	331	1
Subtract the oblique ascension of the horoscope,	311	2
Arc of direction,	19	51

Again:—I would direct the horoscope to the trine of Jupiter by right ascension instead of oblique as performed by problem 11th: this is done by bringing it to the cusp of the 5th house, whence it casts the trine to the horoscope.

Oblique descension of ♃,	136°	0′
Being from the 5th, add two-thirds of ♃'s seminocturnal arc,	38	0
	174	0
Oblique descension of the descendant,	131	2
Arc of direction,	42	58

Thus right and oblique ascensions operate mutually, as proofs of each other; and I would recommend to the artist to bring up a direction both ways, that he may be sure his calculations are correct. The student will also perceive, that the rule for subtracting the semi-arc or its parts, is when the star by converse motion approaches the angle from whence the direction is taken. Thus, when a star is passing from the 4th towards the 10th, and the direction is calculated from the 10th by right ascension, the arc or its parts must be subtracted from the right ascension of the star, because it approaches the 10th; but when it recedes from the 10th towards the 4th, the arc or its parts must be added. The rule is the same in the ascendant, or any other angle. Subtraction of the arc or its parts must be made from its oblique ascension or descension, as it approaches the angle from whence the direction is taken; and when it recedes, they must be added.

Problem 18th.

To find any arc of direction from another given arc.

This is done by adding or subtracting the proportional part of an arc or semi-arc to or from the given arc: thus, if the arc of direction to the square be given, the arc of direction to the sextile will be found by subtracting ⅓ of the planet's semi-arc, or to the trine by adding ⅓ of its semi-arc, and thus one arc of direction of a planet in the world may be made to produce all the rest of that kind, whether direct or converse, by means of addition or subtraction.

Example:—Suppose the arc of direction to □ of the mid-heaven was 47° 0′, and the semidiurnal arc of the star 66° 0′: subtract ⅓ of the semidiurnal arc which is 22° 0′ from the 47° 0′; it will give the arc of direction to the sextile, 25° 0′. The trine is under the Earth, and of course ⅓ of the seminocturnal arc must be added

and it will make the arc of direction to the trine 85° 0'. In all
directions, care must be taken not to confound the two arcs by
taking the diurnal for the nocturnal, and *vice versa*, as in all cases
the diurnal must be used when a planet is above the Earth, and
the nocturnal when below it.

Problem 19th.

To direct a significator, when within 3° of the cusp of the midheaven, to the conjunction of a promittor, by direct, or converse
motion.

This is called directing the significator, but it will also answer
for directing the promittor: for when the significator is directed
to a conjunction with a promittor, or, to speak more properly, to
the place of the promittor, the latter must be to the west of the
mid-heaven; and this is called converse motion, because the significator moves by its diurnal motion conversely, while the place
of the promittor must remain fixed. When the promittor is
eastward of the mid-heaven, it is called direct motion (a term not
very intelligible, as neither of them moves direct; the promittor
only moving conversely, while the place of the significator remains fixed.)

If by direct motion, subtract the right ascension of the significator, with latitude, from that of the promittor, with latitude, the
remainder is the arc of direction.

Example:—Direct the ☉ to the conjunction of ♀, direct motion.
See Zodiacal Directions, problem 1st. (plate 2d. fig. 1.). Supposing the latitude of ♀ to be 3° 36' south.

Right ascension of ♀, with 3° 36' south latitude, 261° 52'
Right ascension of the ☉ (he has no latitude,) 215 58

Arc of direction, 45 54

By converse motion: Suppose 14° 0' of ♊ on the cusp of the
mid-heaven, the ☽ in 14° 12' of ♊; ♄ in 14° 42' of ♉; I would
direct the ☽ to the ☌ of ♄, converse motion; (see plate 2. fig. 16)
☽'s latitude 4° 52' south, ♄'s latitude 2° 3' south.

Subtract the right ascension of the promittor from that of the
significator (both with latitude,) the remainder is the arc of direction.

Right ascension of the ☽, with 4° 52' south latiiude, 73° 26'
Right ascension of ♄, with 2° 3' south latitude, 42 51

Arc of direction, 30 35

NOTE, *In all mundane directions the ascensions or descensions must be taken with latitude, if either the significator or promittor has any.*

Problem 20th.

To direct a planet within 3° of the cusp of the mid-heaven to the mundane opposition of a star, direct or converse.

If direct, subtract the right ascension of the significator from that of the opposite place of the promittor (both with latitude,) the remainder will be the arc of direction.

Example:—Suppose 14° 0′ of ♊ on the cusp of the 10th, the ☾ in 14° 12′ of ♊; ♃ in the 4th house in 3° 21′ of ♑; I would direct the ☾ to the ☍ of ♃ in the world, direct motion (see plate 2, fig. 17.)

NOTE, *The opposite place of ♃ is obtained by adding 180° 0′ to his right ascension with latitude.*

♃'s right ascension with latitude,	273°	39′
Add for the opposite place,	180	0
	453	39
Being more than the circle, subtract	360	0
	93	39
☾'s right ascension with latitude,	73	26
Arc of direction,	20	13

If by converse motion, subtract the right ascension of the opposite place of the promittor from that of the significator (both with latitude;) the remainder will be the arc of direction.

Example:—Suppose from the figure of the above operation that ♂ be found in ♏, 10° 16′; I would direct the ☾ to his opposition by converse motion; (see the same figure.)

Right ascension of the ☾ with latitude,	73°	26′
Right ascension of ♂, 218° 26′, add 180°, it makes 398° 26′		
Subtract the circle, it gives 38° 26′,	38	26
Arc of direction,	35	0

This is the method laid down by Placidus, but it would not be correct, except the planet was on the very cusp of the mid-heaven. If it be not so situated, the most regular way is to proceed as directed in the following problem.

Problem 21st.

To direct a significator or promittor, wherever it be, to any mundane ✶, ☐, or △, direct or converse.

NOTE, *The planet that forms the aspect by moving conversely must be directed, whether it be significator or promittor.*

1st, Observe the star to whose place or aspect the direction is to be made, and take its distance from the cusp either of the preceding or succeeding house; find also the distance of the star to be directed, from the cusp of that house that forms the required configuration with the cusp of the other house from whence the first distance was taken, and call this last the primary distance.

2d, Say, as the horary time of the planet to whose configuration the other is to be directed, is to its distance from the cusp of the house from whence its distance is taken, so is the horary time of the planet to be directed to its secondary distance. If this secondary distance be on the same side of the cusp from whence the primary distance is taken, subtract the one from the other, and the remainder will be the arc of direction; but if the primary and secondary distance be on opposite sides, add them, and their sum will be the arc required.

Example:—Suppose 4° 2′ of ♋ on the cusp of the 10th, 0° 0′ of ♊ on the cusp of the 9th; 8° 0′ of ♍ on the cusp of the 12th; 3° 24′ of ♈ on the cusp of the 7th, 8° 0′ of ♓ on the cusp of the 6th; the ☽ in 24° 10′ of ♊ with 0° 31′ N. Lat.; ♄ in 4° 56′ of ♍ with 1° 54′ N. Lat., ♃ in 10° 34′ of ♈ with 1° 20′ S Lat.; and ♀ in 6° 44° of ♓ with 1° 16′ S. Lat; pole of the country 43° (see plate 2, fig- 18): I would direct the Moon to the sextile of Saturn, square of Jupiter, and trine of Venus, in the world.

Right ascension of the 10th,	94°	2′
Right ascension of the Moon with 0° 31′ N. Lat.	83	38
Distance of the Moon from the midheaven,	10	24

To direct the Moon to the Sextile of Saturn.

Here Saturn must move conversely to form the sextile, as he is more than that distance from the Moon, and of course must be directed; but had it been to the square, the Moon must have been directed. The distance of Saturn must be taken from the 12th house, because it forms the sextile with the 10th, from which the distance of the moon was taken.

Oblique ascension of the 12th house found by adding 60° to the right ascension of the midheaven,	154°	2'
Oblique ascension of Saturn with latitude taken under the pole of the 12th house, 32°,	150	10
Saturn's primary distance from the 12th house,	3	52

We must now find what his distance should be from the 12th house to make the aspect exact, and this when found will be the secondary or true distance.

As the ☾'s diurnal horary time, 19° 5', is to her distance from the midheaven, 10° 24', so is Saturn's diurnal horary time, 16° 50', to his secondary distance, 9° 10'.

This is the distance he should be from the 12th house when the aspect is formed; but as we find he is already by his primary distance, 7° 29' distant from it, this must be subtracted from the secondary distance, and the remainder will be the arc of direction which he has to perform.

Secondary distance,	9°	10'
Primary distance,	3	52
Arc of Direction,	5	18

To direct the Moon to the Square of Jupiter.

Here ♃ must also move conversely before he can come to the □ and is therefore the proper planet to be directed. As the ☾'s distance is taken from the 10th, the distance of ♃ must be taken from the 7th, because the 7th forms the □ with the 10th.

Oblique ascension of ♃ with his latitude 1° 20' south taken in the pole of the horoscope	13°	1'
Oblique decension of the descendant under the same pole,	4	2
Primary distance of ♃ from the west angle,	8	59

As the ☾'s diurnal horary time 19° 5' is to her distance from the midheaven, 10° 24', so is ♃'s nocturnal horary time, 14° 32', to his secondary distance from the west angle, 7° 55'.

This is the distance he must have from the cusp of the west

angle before he can arrive at the square of the ☾'s place; and as his primary distance was 8° 59′ short of the west angle, and of course on the opposite side of the secondary distance, both distances must be added together, and their sum will be the arc of direction.

Primary distance.	8° 59′
Secondary distance,	7 55
Arc of direction,	16 54

To direct the Moon to the Trine of Venus:

This is done in the same way as the preceding direction; ♀ moves conversely to form the trine. Her primary distance from the 6th, which forms the trine to the 10th, is 1° 34′; as the Moon's diurnal horary time 19° 5′ is to her distance from the 10th, 10° 24′, so is the nocturnal horary time of ♀, 16° 37′, to her secondary distance from the 6th 9° 3′; both distances are on the same side of the 6th; and therefore the primary must be subtracted from the secondary, leaving the arc of direction, 7° 29′.

All these directions are by direct motion, because the promittor is directed to the significator; it may therefore be as well to direct the Moon to the square of Venus, to give a specimen of converse direction; there the significator is directed to the aspect of the promittor, for the Moon must move conversely before she can come to the square of Venus; but the method is the same in directing the significator to the promittor as in directing the promittor to the significator, except that the secondary distance of the significator must be found instead of that of the promittor.

To direct the Moon to the Square of Venus.

Oblique descension of the 6th house, by adding 60 degrees to the right ascension of the 4th house,	334° 2′
Oblique descension of Venus under the pole of the 6th house, 32°, with 1° 16′ S. Lat.,	332 28
Distance of Venus from the cusp of the 6th house,	1 34
Oblique descension of the Moon under the pole of the 9th house 18° with 0° 31′ north latitude,	91° 55′

Oblique descension of the 9th house, obtained by
   subtracting 30° from the right ascension of the
   midheaven,   64   2

Primary distance of the Moon from the cusp of the
   9th house,   27   53

As the nocturnal horary time of Venus, 16° 37′ is to her distance from the cusp of the 6th house, 1° 34′, so is the Moon's diurnal horary time, 19° 5′ to her secondary distance from the cusp
of the 9th house, 1° 48′.

This is where the Moon must arrive, beyond the cusp of the 9th
house, before the aspect is completed: and as the primary distance is on the one side of the cusp of the 9th, and the secondary
on the other side, both must be added together, which will give
the arc of direction.

                 Primary distance,   27° 53′
                 Secondary distance,   1 48
                                                 _____

Arc of direction to the square of Venus,   29 41

Problem 22d.

To find the arcs of direction to the inferior aspects; as the
quintile, sesquiquadrate, and biquintile; from any other given arc
of direction.

The rules laid down by Placidus in his 33d canon for this, are
extremely loose and unsatisfactory; he seems eager to rid himself
of a task which he was unable to perform as it should be, and to
avoid an explanation on a subject the fundamental principle of
which he appear not to have properly understood.

In forming any configuration of two stars from any other configuration, the aspect of the star so directed should be distinguished according as it is dexter or sinister.

A *dexter* aspect is that which is formed towards the right of the
star directed, contrary to the order of the signs, and here the longest aspects are first formed; as for instance, from the opposition,
the biquintile is first formed, then the sesquiquadrate, the trine,
the square, the quintile, the sextile, and last of all the conjunction;
it is therefore evident, that in forming a short aspect from a long
one, the arc of direction will increase as the aspect becomes
shorter, and therefore the difference must be added: as supposing

the semi-arc of the star directed be 90°, 36° must be added to the opposition before it can be brought to the biquintile, 9° more, to bring it to the sesquiquadrate, 15° more to bring it the trine, &c. Such star, therefore, directed to another with a *dexter* aspect, supposing its arc of direction to the trine to be 16° 12′, would have an arc of direction to the square of 46° 12′, because the square would be formed after the trine, and 30° distant from it; but if the trine were to be found from the square the 30° must be subtracted from the arc of direction to the square, 46° 12′, and the trine would be 16° 12′.

A star directed and casting a *sinister* aspect towards the left, or according to the order of signs, forms the shortest configurations: first by passing from the conjunction, to the $\ast$, quintile, square, trine, sesquiquadrate, biquintile, and lastly, to the opposition. In forming, therefore, the longer configuration, the arc of direction will be increased as the aspects lengthen, and consequently if the semi-arc of the star directed be 90°, and the arc of direction to the $\square$ be 16° 12′, that to the $\triangle$ would be 46° 12′.

In *dexter* aspects, therefore, the directions to the shorter aspects from the longer must be found by addition, and *vice versa*: and in *sinister* aspects, by subtraction, and *vice versa*.

Example in a Sinister Aspect.

From the arc of direction in problem 20th of the $\triangle$ of $\venus$ to the $\leftmoon$, I would direct her to the sesquiquadrate.

The difference of the sesquiquadrate to the $\triangle$ is $\frac{1}{6}$ of the $\triangle$, or one-sixth of a semi-arc, viz the planet's horary time.

Nocturnal horary time of $\venus$ (being under the Earth)	16°	37′
Arc of direction to the $\triangle$,	7	29
Arc of direction to the sesquiquadrate,	24	6

The difference is here added, because the aspect is sinister, and the planet is directed to a longer aspect; but had the arc of direction to the sesquiquadrate been known, and the arc to the $\triangle$ been required, the difference must have been subtracted, as being from a longer to a shorter aspect, as follows;—

Arc of direction to the sesquiquadrate,	24°	6′
Subtract the one-sixth of her seminocturnal arc for the difference of the $\triangle$,	16	37
Arc of direction to the $\triangle$,	7	29

Example in a Dexter Aspect

From the arc of direction in problem 20th of the □ of the ☾ to ♀, I would direct her to the quintile.

The difference of the quintile from the square is one-fifth of the square, or semi-arc, and as the ☾'s semidiurnal arc is 114° 30′, one-fifth amounts to 22° 54′.

Arc of direction to the □ of ♀,	29° 41′
One-fifth of the ☾'s semidiurnal arc (being above the Earth.)	22 54
Arc of direction to the quintile of ♀,	52 35

The difference is here added, because the aspect is *dexter*, and the planet directed to a shorter aspect; but had the arc of direction to the quintile been known, and the arc to the □ required, the difference must have been subtracted, as being from a shorter to a longer aspect as follows:

Arc of direction to the quintile,	52° 35′
Subtract one-fifth of the ☾'s semidiurnal arc,	22 54
Arc of direction to the square,	29 41

The inferior or new configurations may be all taken in the same way from the superior or original configurations, by being careful not to confound the diurnal with the nocturnal arcs, or the *dexter* with the *sinister* aspects. The distances from one aspect to another must be all measured by the arc or semi-arc of the star directed, according as it is posited.

The quintile may be found from the ✳ or from the square, as it is one-fifth of the ✳ more than the ✳ either way, and one-fifth of the □ less than the □, either way. Thus, if the ✳ be 60° the quintile will be 72°, which is one-fifth more; and if the □ be 90° the quintile will be 72°, which is one-fifth less,

The sesquiquadrate may be taken either from the △ or from the ☍, because it is one-sixth of a semi-arc more than the △, and one-half of a semi-arc less than the ☍. Thus, if the semi-arc where the planet to be directed is posited, be 90°, the sesquiquadrate will be 15° beyond the △, because 15° is one-sixth of 90°; again, if the semi-arc be 90° the sesquiquadrate will be 45° less than the ☍, because 45° is ½ of 90°.

The biquintile may be found likewise from the △ or the ☍ ; it is two-fifths of the ✶ of that semi-arc where the planet is posited more than the △, and three-fifths of the same ✶ less than the ☍. Thus, if the semi-arc be 90°, the difference of the biquintile beyond the △ any way, will be 24°, which is two-fifths of 60°, the ✶ of 60°, and it will also be 36° less than the ☍, which is three-fifths of the same ✶ of 60°.

If the planet have to pass over part of two different semi-arcs to form any of these aspects, take the original aspect beyond it, and bring it from that to the aspect required.

Example:—Having found, in problem 20th, the arc of direction of ♃'s square to the ☾, I would find his arc of direction to her quintile. The aspect is sinister, and as the direction is made to a shorter configuration, the difference should be subtracted; but as this would pass over part of two different semi-arcs, as ♃'s secondary distance is in one, and his primary in the other, I must bring him to the ✶ on the other side, and find the quintile from the ✶. To do this, I take his distance from the ☾, and by subtracting it from ⅔ of his semidiurnal arc, the remainder will be the arc of direction to his ✶.

♃'s ✶, or ⅔ of his semidiurnal arc, is 61° 52′.

The distance of ♃ from the ☾ is found by subtracting his oblique descension from that or the ☾ (both taken under her pole) which is 4°.

Oblique descension of the ☾, taken under her pole,	85° 25′
Oblique descension of ♃, taken under the same pole,	10 26
Distance of ♃ from the ☾,	74 59

This cannot be subtracted from ♃'s ✶, 61° 52′, which shews that he had already passed the ✶ before the time of birth. We must now add one-fifth of this ✶ to form the quintile.

♃'s sextile	61° 55′
Add one-fifth for the quintile,	12 22
Distance of ♃'s quintile,	74 14

We cannot take 74° 59′ from 74° 14′, which shews likewise that he had just passed the quintile before birth; had it, however, been otherwise, and a remainder left, that remainder would have been the arc of direction to the quintile of ♃.

These are the only aspects approved of by Placidus, but those who wish to calculate the arcs of direction to the other aspects, may find them all in the same manner by using the proportional part as before. These are as follows:

The Vigintile, which is one-fifth of a semi-arc.

The Quindecile is two-fifths of a Sextile.

The Semisextile is $\frac{1}{3}$ of a semi-arc.

The Semiquintile, called by some the Decile, is three-fifths of a sextile.

The Semiquadrate is $\frac{1}{2}$ of a semi-arc.

The Sesquiquintile is a semi-arc and a vigintile.

The Quadrasextile is a semi-arc and a sextile.

Problem 23d.

To direct a star when above 3° from the mid-heaven to the conjunction or opposition.

Subtract the oblique ascension or descension of the point of direction, from that of the star directed (both taken under the pole of the former) the remainder will be the arc of direction.

Example:—Suppose 5° 44' of ♑ on the cusp of the ascendant; the ☾ in 6° 45' of ♑; 12° 27' of ♉ on the cusp of the 4th, ♄ in 17° 37' of ♉ : I would direct the ☾ to the mundane ☍ of ♄, converse motion. (see plate 2, fig. 20.)

♄'s lat. 2° 0' south. Pole of ♄ 6° 0', ☾'s lat. 2° 4' south.

I find the oblique descension of ♄ under his pole of 6° 0' to be 47° 21', to which I add 180° for the half circle or opposition, which makes the oblique ascension of his opposition 227° 21'.

Oblique ascension of the ☾ (taken under the pole of ♄, 6° 0') with 2° 4' south latitude,	280° 19'
Oblique ascension of ♄'s opposition under his pole,	227 21
Arc of direction,	52 58

It is the same with the conjunction; for had the point to which we have just been directing been the place of ♄'s body, instead of his opposition, the arc of direction would have been the same

Problem 24th.

To direct the luminaries to their own rays.

This is done by making the proportional part of their semi-arcs the arc of direction; as ⅔ for the ✳, four-fifths for the quintile, and the whole semi-arc for the square.

Example:—Suppose the Sun's semi-arc to be 109° 27′, I would direct him to his own ✳.

⅔ of this semi-arc is 72° 58′, which will be the arc of direction.

The only care required, is to be sure there is room for the direction under the present arc of the luminary, so that it does not include a part of two arcs, as we have already seen in other directions; and the way to discover this, when it is doubtful, is to find the star's distance from the horizon by oblique ascension or descension. Thus, in the present instance, suppose the ☉'s oblique descension to be 147° 1′, and that of the west angle 71° 5′, the distance would be 75° 56′, near 3° more than the aspect.

When the direction falls within two different semi-arcs by including a part of two hemispheres, the diurnal and nocturnal, it must be performed by the Rule of Three, as in other aspects.

Example:—I would direct the Sun, so situated, to his own mundane □.

☉'s distance from the 10th house, 33° 31′.

Primary distance from the 7th house, 75° 56′.

As the ☉'s semidiurnal arc, 109° 27′, is to his distance from the mid-heaven, 33° 31′, so is his seminocturnal arc, 70° 33′, to his secondary distance from the 7th house (which is the □ to the mid-heaven,) 19° 4′.

As the primary and secondary distances are on different sides of the cusp of the 7th, add them.

Primary distance,	75° 56′
Secondary distance,	19 4
Arc of direction of the ☉ to his own □	95 0

Of Mundane Parallels.

These are of three kinds, viz. direct, converse, and rapt. Direct and converse parallels are directed to like other direct and converse aspects.

Problem 25th.

To direct a significator to any mundane parallel, direct or converse.

1st, Find the distance of both significator and promittor from the cusp of the angle on which the parallel is formed, and call that distance of the star to be directed to the others parallel, the primary distance.

2d, As the semi-arc of the star to whose parallel the other is to be directed is to its distance from the said angle, so is the semi-arc of the star to be directed to its secondary distance.

3d, If the primary and secondary distances are on different sides of the angle add them; if on the same side, subtract one from the other, for the arc of direction.

Example:—Suppose 15° 0′ of ♊ on the cusp of the 8th, ♂ in 6° 1′ of ♊, 15° 43′ of ♉ on the cusp of the 7th, ☉ in 21° 34′ of ♉ (see plate 2, fig. 19,),I would direct the ☉ to a parallel of ♂, direct motion. (Here ♂ moves conversely until he forms a parallel with the Sun's place on the west angle.)

Oblique descension of the ☉ under the pole of the horoscope,	66° 58′
Oblique descension of the west angle,	59 24

☉'s distance from the west angle,	7 34
Oblique descension of ♂ under the pole of the horoscope,	85° 34′
Oblique descension of the west angle,	59 24

Primary distance of ♂ (the star to be directed) from the west,	26 10

As the ☉'s semidiurnal arc, 7h. 12 m. is to his distance from the west angle, 7° 34′, so is the seminocturnal arc of ♂, 4h. 34m., to his secondary distance from the west angle, 4° 47′.

As the primary and secondary distances are on opposite sides of the west angle, add them for the arc of direction.

Primary distance,	26° 10′
Secondary distance,	4 47

Arc of direction,	30 57

Again, I would direct the Sun to the parallel of Mars converse motion, (Here the Sun passes conversely until he forms a parallel with the place of Mars on the west angle.)

We have already got the distance of both from the west angle, and that of the ☉ becomes now the primary distance.

As the semidiurnal arc of Mars, 7h. 26m., is to his distance from the west, 26° 10′, so is the ☉'s seminocturnal arc, 4*h*. 48*m*., to his secondary distance from the west 16° 54′

The primary and secondary distances being on different sides of the angle, add them for the arc of direction.

☉'s primary distance,	7° 34′
Secondary distance	16 54
Arc of direction,	24 28

Rapt parallels are always formed by right ascension from the midheaven or lower heaven, let them belong to whatsoever angle they will. If they belong to either of those two angles, the angle is a true one; but if they belong either to the ascendant or descendant, the angle on which they are formed may be called a false one, merely for the sake of a term; for two stars in a parallel from any angle are really in a parallel with every angle in the figure.

Parallels are called rapt when two stars by moving conversely together (or, as Placidus calls it, being rapt or carried away by the motion of the *Primum Mobile*,) form parallels from angles without having any respect to their radical places in the figure.

Problem 26th,

To direct two stars moving together conversely to rapt parallels.

1st, Add their semi-arcs together, which semi-arcs will be diurnal or nocturnal, according as the parallel is formed above or below the Earth.

2d, Find the difference between their right ascensions.

3d, Find the distance of the star that applies to the angle (when the parallel is formed) from the said angle, and call it the primary distance.

4th, As the sum of their semi-arcs is to the semiarc of the planet applying to the angle, so is the difference of their right ascensions to the secondary distance of the said planet.

If both distances are on the same side of the angle, subtract one from the other, but if on different sides, add them.

Example:—Suppose 26° 9′ of Aries on the cusp of the 7th, the Moon in 25° 35° of Aries, 7° 0′ of Pisces on the cusp of the 5th, Saturn in 11° 1′ of Pisces; right ascension of the Imum Cœli, 305° 40′; I would direct the Moon to the rapt parallel of Saturn.

The parallel will be formed on the Imum Cœli, to which, when the parallel is formed, the Moon will apply (see pl. 2, fig. 21.)

As the parallel is formed below the Earth, the seminocturnal arcs must be used.

Seminocturnal arc of the Moon,	5h. 37m.	
Seminocturnal arc of Saturn,	6 41	
Sum of their arcs,	12 18	

Right ascension of the Moon, with 5° 0′ south latitude,	25ᶜ 33′	
Add for subtraction,	360 0	
	385 33	
Right ascension of Saturn, with 1° 55′ S. lat.	343 14	
Difference of their right ascensions,	42 19	

Right ascension of the Moon, with the circle added as before,	385° 33′	
Right ascension of the lower heaven,	305 40	
Primary distance of the Moon,	79 53	

As the sum of their seminocturnal arcs 12h. 18m., is to the Moon's seminocturnal arc, 5h. 37m., (because she will apply to the Imum Cœli when the parallel is formed,) so is their difference in right ascension, 42° 19′ to the Moon's secondary distance from the 4th, 19° 19′

As both distances are on the same side of the Imum Cœli, subtract the secondary for the arc of direction.

The Moon's primary distance,	79° 53′	
Secondary distance,	19 19	
Arc of direction,	60 34	

Observe, had Saturn been in the Moon's place, and the Moon in in his, Saturn would have been the applying planet when the aspect was formed, and consequently his seminocturnal arc would have been used as the secondary term instead of that of the Moon.

When a parallel is to be formed on the east angle, take the opposite place of the succeeding star, and work with it as if it were there and approaching to form a parallel on the south angle, which in this case may be called the false angle. When its opposite place forms a parallel with the other star on the south angle, then will the real parallel be formed at equal distances from the horoscope.

Example:—Suppose 5° 44′ of ♑ on the horoscope, the ☾ in 6° 45′ of ♑, 12° 27′ of ♉ on the *Imum Cœli*, with ♂ in 20° 40′ of Taurus (see plate 2, fig. 22.) I would direct the ☾ to the rapt parallel of ♐, which he will form with her from the ascendant. Here ♂ is the succeeding planet, for he follows the Moon, I therefore take him as if he was in his opposite place, and direct him to a parallel of the Moon from the south angle. As the parallel is formed on the mid-heaven, the semidiurnal arcs must be used; and although Mars is the planet that applies to the true angle when the parallel is formed, yet, considered in his opposite place, he is the receding planet from the false angle, and the Moon applies so that her semidiurnal arc must be used for the second term.

Semidiurnal arc of the opposite place of ♂,	62°	27′
Semidiurnal arc of the ☾,	52	33
Sum of their arcs,	115	0
Right ascension of the ☾, with latitude,	277°	28′
Right ascension of ♂, with opposite latitude,	232	3,
Difference between their right ascensions,	45	25
Right ascension of the Moon,	277°	28′
Right ascension of the mid-heaven,	220	0
☾'s primary distance,	57	28

As the sum of the semidiurnal arcs, 115° 0′, is to the semidiurnal arc of the ☾, 52° 33′, (the applying planet to the midheaven,) so is the difference between the right ascension, 45° 25′, to the ☾'s secondary distance from the midheaven, 20° 45′

As both the primary and secondary distances are on the midheaven, subtract the secondary.

Primary distance,	57°	28′
Secondary distance,	20	45
Arc of direction,	36	43

I shall give one more example from the positions in problem 25th, of a rapt parallel formed on the west angle.

We here take the opposite place of the succeeding star, which is ♂, and make the *Imum Cœli* the false angle.

Seminocturnal arc of the opposition of ♂,	7h.	26m.
Seminocturnal arc of the Sun,	4	48
Sum of their arcs,	12	14

Right ascension of the ☉ with the circle added,	409°	7′
Right ascension of ♂'s opposition with latitude,	244	7
Difference in right ascension,	165	0
Right ascension of the ☉ with the circle added,	409°	7′
Right ascension of the lower heaven,	329	24
☉'s primary distance from the north angle,	79	43

As the sum of the seminocturnal arcs, 12h. 14m., is to the seminocturnal arc of the ☉, 4h, 48m., (because he applies to the false angle,) so is the difference in right ascension, 165° 0′, to the ☉'s secondary distance from the false angle, 64° 44′.

As they are both on the same side of the angle, subtract the secondary from the primary.

Primary distance,	79°	43′
Secondary distance,	64	44
Arc of direction,	14	59

Before I close the subject of parallels, it may not be amiss to give an example of a converse parallel from opposite angles, as a star equidistant from opposite angles has the same effect as when equidistant from the same angle: this is called a *contra* parallel, and is the same in the world as the *contra* antiscion is in the zodiac.

Suppose 6° 0′ of ♓ on the cusp of the 10th, ♄ in 10° 2′ of ♓, the ☉ in the 4th house in 28°.39′ of ♍; I would direct him to a *contra* parallel of ♄, by converse motion (see plate 2, fig. 23.)

The operation is the same as if ♄ had been in 10° 2′ of ♍, with opposite latitude.

Right ascension of ♄ with 2° 10′ south latitude,	342°	44′
Right ascension of the midheaven,	337	48
Distance of ♄ from the midheaven,	4	56

| Right ascension of the ☉, | 178° 46′ |
| Right ascension of the *Imum Cæli*, | 157 48 |

| Primary distance of the ☉ from the lower heaven, | 20 58 |

As the semidiurnal arc of ♄, 5*h*. 16*m*., is to his distance from the midheaven, 4° 56′, so is the seminocturnal arc of the ☉ to his secondary distance from the lowest heaven, 5° 35′.

As the primary and secondary distances are on opposite sides of the lowest heaven, add them.

☉'s Primary distance,	20° 58′
Secondary distance,	5 35
Arc of direction,	26 33

Problem 27th.

To direct the ☉, when under the Earth in the space of the crepuscle, to any mundane aspect.

1st, Find the common arc of direction, according to the rules laid down in former problems, and call it the false arc of direction.

2d, Add this false arc to the oblique ascension of the Sun taken under his own pole.

3d, In the table of crepuscles for the pole of the country find the ☉ s crepusculine circle for that degree of the zodiac in which he is posited, and this will be obtained by taking the number opposite to his primary distance. This number, when found, is the degree of the ☉'s depression.

4th, Opposite this crepusculine degree of the ☉'s depression the secondary distance will be found under that degree of the zodiac which answers to the sum of the false arc and the ☉'s oblique ascension added together.

5th, As the ☉'s horary time is to his secondary distance, so is the horary time of the promittor to his secondary distance. Add or subtract this according to the rules hitherto laid down, and it will give the arc of direction.

Example:—Suppose 7° 50′ of ♐ on the cusp of the horoscope, the ☉ in 25° 14′ of ♐, 19° 0′ of ♉ on the cusp of the 6th, and ♃ in 28° 18′ of ♉ : I would direct the ☉ to the mundane △ of ♃, direct motion (see plate 2, fig. 24.)

I first find the common arc of direction as follows :

| Oblique ascension of the ☉ taken in the pole of the horoscope, | 289° 32′ |

Oblique ascension of the horoscope,	268	35
Primary distance of the ☉ from the horoscope,	20	57
Oblique ascension of ♃'s opposition with opposite latitude (his real latitude is 1° 18′ south) taken under the pole of the 11th house, which is 18° 0′,	242°	38′
Oblique ascension of the 11th house under its pole 18° 0′	208	35
Primary distance of ♃ from the 5th house,	34	3

(I have followed the whim of Placidus in taking ♃'s opposite place, but his primary distance may more easily be found in his own place by oblique descension.)

As the nocturnal horary time of the ☉, 19° 7′, is to his primary distance from the horoscope, 20° 57′, so is the nocturnal horary time of ♃, 11° 51′, to his secondary distance from the 5th 12° 59′.

As both ♃,s distances are on the same side of the cusp of the 5th, subtract, and it gives the arc of direction (which, as I before observed, is the false arc,) 21° 4′

Oblique ascension of the ☉ under his own pole of 38° 0′,	284°	35′
Add the false arc,	21	4
It gives,	305	39

which is the oblique ascension of 15° 20′ of ♑.

I now look in the Crepusculine Table for the circle belonging to the ☉'s distance from the horoscope, 20° 57′, under 25° of ♐, which is the Sun's place in the zodiac, as the minutes are not regarded. The latitude of the country is 44°: so I take the table for that latitude, and look for 25° of ♐, but there is no such thing; I therefore take the nearest number, which is the column of 20° of Sagittary. Neither is there such a number as the Sun's distance, 20° 57′, but the nearest I can find to it in the column of 20° of Sagittary is 20° 12′; opposite to this, on the left, is the crepusculine parallel, 13°. I have now to find for the remaining 5° of Sagittary, which will be half the difference between the columns 20° and 30° of Sagittary; this difference is 5′, the half of which is 2′, which added to the 20° 12′ gives 20° 14′ out of the 20° 57′ leaving 43′ yet to be accounted for: to do this, we must take the proportional part of the difference between the circles 13 and 14: 20° 12′ taken from 21° 41′ gives a difference of 1° 29′ so that, if 1° 29′ be equal to 1° of crepusculine parallel, 43′ will be equal to 28′ which shews the true crepusculine circle or parallel to be 13° 28′.

Opposite this crepusculine circle of 13° 28′ I look for 15° of ♑ (to which the false arc added to the ☉'s oblique ascension answered): the nearest column is 10° of ♑, in which, opposite 13° of crepusculine circle, will be found 20° 12′. I have now to find for the remaining 5° of ♑; the difference between the columns 10° and 20° of ♑ is 16′ less, the half of which is 8′ which subtracted from 20° 12′ leaves 20° 4′. The remaining 28′ of the crepusculine circle will be found by the rule of proportion to give 42′ more, which added to the 20° 4′ we already possess, makes the ☉'s secondary distance 20° 46′.

As the ☉'s nocturnal horary time, 19° 7′ is to his secondary distance from the horoscope, 20° 46′, so is the nocturnal horary time of ♃, 11° 51′, to ♃'s secondary distance from the 5th house, 12° 52′.

Both distances are on the same side of the cusp of the 5th, and therefore subtraction must be made.

♃'s primary distance,	34°	3′
Secondary distance,	12	52
True arc of direction,	21	11

Problem 28th.

To direct the Sun when under the Earth in the obscure arc to any mundane aspect.

1st, Find the false arc of direction, in the same manner as in the last problem.

2d, Add the false arc to his oblique ascension taken under his pole, as before, and mark the degree of the zodiac to which it answers.

3d, Subtract the whole crepusculine arc from his seminocturnal arc, and the remainder will be his obscure arc.

4th, Subtract the whole crepusculine arc of the part of the zodiac to which the false arc added to the Sun's oblique ascension answers, from its seminocturnal arc, and the remainder will be its obscure arc,

5th, Find the Sun's right distance from the 4th house, and call it the primary distance.

6th, As the ☉'s obscure arc is to his primary distance from the 4th house, so is the obscure arc of that place to which his oblique ascension and false arc answers, to his secondary distance from the 4th house.

7th, As the ☉'s horary time is to his secondary distance, so is the horary time of the promittor to its secondary distance from its given house, which must be added to or subtracted from the primary distance as usual,

Example:—Suppose 26° 0′ of ♓ on the cusp of the 5th, ☿ in 20° 24′ of ♓, 22° 0′ of ♈ on the cusp of the 6th house, the ☉ in 8° 42′ of ♈ (see pl. 2, fig. 25): I would direct the ☉ to the mundane ⚹ of ☿, direct motion,

Oblique descension of the ☉ under the pole of the 5th, 18°,	9°	7′
Add for subtraction,	360	0
	369	7
Oblique descension of the 5th under its pole of 18°,	355	22
Distance of the Sun from the cusp of the 5th,	13	45
Oblique ascension of ☿ under the pole of the 3d, 18°,	354°	13′
Oblique ascension of the 3d house under its pole, 18°,	295	22
Primary distance of ☿ from the cusp of the 3d,	58	51

As the Sun's nocturnal horary time, 14° 26′, is to his distance from the 5th, 13° 45′, so is ☿'s nocturnal horary time, 16° 0′, to to his secondary distance from the 3d, 15° 15′.

Both distances being on the same side of the 3d house, subtract for the arc of direction,

Primary distance,	58°	51′
Secondary distance,	15	15
False arc of direction,	43	36
Oblique descension of the Sun under his own pole of 25°.	9°	35′
Add the false arc of direction,	43	36
Their sum,	53	11

which answers in oblique ascension to, 17° 30′ of Taurus.

I now look for the whole crepusculine arc of those two places viz. 8° 42′ of Aries, (where the sun is) and 17° 30′ of Taurus. The whole crepusculine arc is always that which is opposite the 18th parallel, at the bottom of the left-hand column.

The nearest to 8° 42′ of Aries is the column 10° of Aries, in that table of which the pole is 44°; here, opposite the circle 18 at the bottom, I find 26° 3′, which, when brought into hours and minutes (to suit the Sun's seminocturnal arc, which is also in hours and minutes,) makes 1h. 44m. It is true, the Sun's place is only 8° 42′ of Aries, and we have calculated it for 10° of Aries; but in dividing by 15 to bring it to time, we have left a remainder of 3′, which will make up for the difference.

Seminocturnal arc of the ☉,	5h.	46m.
Whole crepusculine arc of the ☉,	1	44
Obscure arc of the ☉,	4	2

I now find the whole crepusculine arc for 17° 30′ of ♉, as follows:—

Under 10 degrees of Taurus, in the same table, opposite to the last parallel of 18°, I find 29° 38′; the difference between the columns 10° and 20° of Taurus is 1° 52′ more: so that, if 10° give 1° 52′, 7° 30′ will give 1° 17′ which added to the 29° 38′ already obtained, makes 30° 55′, or, when turned into time, 2h. 4m.

Seminocturnal arc of 17° 30′ of Taurus,	4h.	50m,
Its whole crepusculine arc,	2	4
Its obscure arc,	2	46

I now seek for the Sun's primary distance from the 4th.

Right ascension of the Sun,	8°	0′
Add the circle for subtraction,	360	0
	368	0
Right ascension of the 4th,	325	22
☉'s primary distance from the 4th,	42	38

As the Sun's obscure arc, 4h. 2m., is to his primary distance from the 4th house, 42 deg. 38 min., so is the obscure arc of 17

deg. 3 min. of Taurus, 2*h*. 46*m*., to his secondary distance from
the 4th, 29 deg. 15 min.   This is more than a house distant from
the 4th, for the Sun's double nocturnal horary time (the space of
his house) is 28 deg. 52 min., which subtracted from 29 deg. 15
min., makes his secondary distance 0 deg, 23 min. beyond the
cusp of the 5th; this, owing to the subtraction of the crepusculine
arc, is his real position, where alone he can receive the ✶ of ☿,
we must, therefore, find to what point the secondary distance of ☿
should extend for that purpose.

As the Sun's horary time, 14 deg. 26 min,, is to his secondary
distance from the 5th, 0 deg. 23 min., so is the horary time of ☿,
16 deg. 0 min., to his secondary distance from the 3d, 0 deg.
26 min.

Both the distances being on the same side of the cusp of the 3d,
subtract for the arc of direction.

Primary distance of ☿ from the 5th,	58°	51'
Secondary distance,	0	26
True arc of direction,	58	25

Problem 29*th*.

To direct a significator to the west. (Ptolemy entertained an
opinion (which, if rightly understood, was very erroneous,) that
if no malignant direction destroyed life before the hyleg arrived
by direction at the western horizon, life must certainly terminate
when that period arrived.   The time, however, was either diminished or protracted, according to the aspects of other planets,
which reached the angle before it.   Argol denied the truth of this
system *in toto;* but Placidus affirms it to be true, and had he accompanied this declaration by an example in point, it might have
merited some attention; but every example he quotes only serves
to confirm the opinion of Argol, that it is *vain and useless.*   The
direction to the west in Cardinal Gymnasius's Nativity agrees
with the time of death, but the ☉, who was apheta, came at the
same time to a parallel of ♄'s declination, a direction sufficiently
malignant to destroy a man above 87 years old.   In Pope Urban's
Nativity, which Placidus quotes as another instance in his " Celestial Philosophy," the hyleg met with the square of Mars; and the
Duchess of Sfortia died from the effect of a parallel of the declination of Mars; the direction to the west, therefore, could not have
any visible effect in either of those nativities, and I know not that
he mentions any other.)

1st, Find the hyleg's arc of direction to the west.

2d, Find the arc of direction of every fortune that forms a good configuration with the west angle, and of every infortune that forms an evil configuration with it.

3d, Add the arcs of the fortunes together and divide them by 12, and do the same by the arcs of their infortunes.

4th, Add the quotient of the fortunes to the arc of direction of the hyleg, and subtract the quotient of the infortunes from it, the remainder will be the true arc of direction.

Example:—From the radix in plate 2, fig. 26, I would direct the ☉, who is hyleg, to the west.

Oblique descension of the ☉ in the pole of the horoscope,	147° 1′
Oblique descension of the west angle,	71 5
☉'s arc of direction to the west,	75 56

I now find, on inspection, that ♃ will arrive at the west before the ☉, and as the ☌ is a good configuration, I find his arc of direction.

Oblique descension of ♃ in the pole of the horoscope (he had no latitude,)	132° 35′
Oblique descension of the west angle,	71 5
♃'s arc of direction to the west,	61 30

I likewise find that ♀ comes both to a quintile and a ✳ to the west before the ☉ reaches it.

Right ascension of ♀ with 1° 42′ north lat.	160° 46′
Right ascension of the midheaven,	161 5
Distance of ♀ from the midheaven,	0 19

Her double horary time, or space of her house, is 33 deg. 16 min, from which subtract the 19 min. she differs from the 10th, and her arc of direction to the ✳ will be 32 deg. 57 min. Her sextile, or space of two houses, is 66 deg. 32 min., one-fifth of which subtracted from her arc of direction to the ✳ will give her arc of direction to the quintile as follows:

Arc of direction to the ✳,   32° 57′

One-fifth of her ✶,   13   18

Arc of direction to her quintile   19   39

♂ interposes the square.

Right ascension of ♂, with 0 deg. 17 min. north lat.	168° 59′
Right ascension of the mid-heaven, whence he casts the □,	161 5
Arc of direction to the square,	7 54

He also forms the quintile and sextile, but these have no effect either way, being good aspects of an evil planet.

♄ also interposes the sesquiquadrate.

Right ascension of the Imum Cœli,	341° 5′
Right ascension of ♄ with 1 deg. 14 min. south lat.	322 51
Distance of ♄ from the 4th.	18 14

This subtracted from his double horary time or space of his house, 35 deg. 22 min., leaves a remainder, 17 deg. 8 min., which is what he wants to complete the trine. The sesquiquadrate is his horary time, or half a house farther, viz. 17 deg. 41 min., which added to the 17 deg. 8 min. makes his arc of direction to the sesquiquadrate, 34 deg. 49 min.

Placidus, who is not remarkable for brevity in any of his operations, finds all these parts by the Rule of Proportion, viz. as the whole arc, whether diurnal or nocturnal, is to the horary time of the planet, so is its arc of direction to the number required. This is a very circumlocutive method, for the proportion of a whole arc to its horary time is as 12 to 1; or in other words, to divide the arc of direction by 12: the shortest method, therefore, is to add all the arcs of the infortunes together, divide them by 12, and subtract the quotient from the hyleg's arc of direction to the west; then add together the arcs of the fortunes in like manner, divide them by 12, and add the quotient to the remainder of the arc of direction. This will give the ultimate arc of direction more complete than can be done by the bungling method of Placidus, who would often lose a degree of his arc in fractions.

☌ of ♃,	61° 30′
✶ of ♀,	32 57
Quintile of ♀,	19 39
	12)114 6(9° 30′, fortunate.

$\square$ of δ,   7° 54'

Sesquiquadrate of ♄   34   49

12)42   43(3° 34', unfortunate.

Hyleg's arc of direction to the west,	75°	56'
Subtract the unfortunate,	3	34
Remainder,	72	22
Add the fortunate,	9	30
True arc of direction,	81	52

It would have been difficult for Placidus to assign a reason why the ☾ should here have been excluded, she is evidently an infortune, from her ☌ with ♄, and should have been directed to the sesquiquadrate as well as ♄ himself. If the ☾ can operate as anareta when in evil aspect with the infortunes, surely her rays to the west must be equally anaretic. In the Nativity of Pope Urban, Placidus allows that ☿ would possess an influence were he not of a mixed nature, and as the luminaries are supposed to be equally convertible with ☿ to the nature of such planets as they are familiar with, and as they are allowed by all parties to be equal to fortunes or infortunes, according to their condition, there can be no doubt, that their arcs are equally efficacious and admissible.

Those who are doubtful of the efficacy of planetary configurations, according to the space of time measured by arcs of direction, would do well to peruse the *Primum Mobile* of Placidus which presents such a mass of evidence as I think, cannot easily be invalidated. It is true, that events do not always follow their apparent causes, but this is owing to the influence of certain stars, with whose effects we are not acquainted, some of which have been discovered since the time of Placidus, and others, which will probably never be known. The lately discovered planet Ouranos no doubt has some kind of influence hitherto undiscovered, and if there be any truth in the doctrine of colours, its influence must be evil and somewhat resembling that ♄. Pallas, Ceres, Vesta, &c, must all have an influence of some kind, and the only objection that can be made to this theory is, their small magnitude and vast distance: this, however, has not been considered as having any weight in the case of the rest. ♄, although above twice the distance of ♃ from the Earth, and much smaller, is always supposed to have had as powerful an effect upon it; whereas, if magnitude or proximity could make any difference, ♃ must greatly preponderate. As to ♂, he is but a speck in the heavens compared to ♃, yet his power is held to be equally great: this doctrine, no doubt, may appear absurd, that magnitude and distance are of small consideration in planetary influence, but experience shews it in certain cases to be true. Of this we have daily proof: the Moon raises the tides about three times as high as the Sun, this astronomers say, is the result of her proximity. The Sun operates on the aggregate of the globe infinitely more powerfully than the Moon, for the globe revolves round it, and this they attribute to his magnitude, which involves a contradiction. The Sun gives heat, light and life to all existence: the Moon gives no heat whatever, and no light but what is caused by reflection. That every planet operates in a similar way, according to its own nature, may be fairly concluded from analogy, nor is it any proof of the non-existence of such a power, to say it is not so perceptible as that of the Sun or Moon. If magnitude were the source of influence, the Sun alone would raise the tides; and were proximity to the Earth its source, the Earth would revolve round the Moon. It is evident, therefore, that all heavenly bodies possess qualities peculiarly their own: the Moon has an effect on moisture, the Sun on the whole substance of the globe, and every other planet operates in a similar way according to its nature, although, probably, its properties are not yet understood.

As to the new aspects invented by Kepler, I own I have not so much confidence in their efficacy as that astronomer had, but experience alone can decide this question. Placidus only approved of the quintile, biquintile, and sesquiquadrate. I have more opinion of the efficacy of the ⚹ than of the △, because the greatest changes happen when the ☾ forms her last ⚹ to the Sun, previous to the conjunction. The effect of the square is evident, as the tides are always lowest when the ☾ is in □ to the ☉: for this reason, I conceive a □ of ♄ and ♂ to each other in a figure as a good position, because they must lessen each others influence. I likewise suspect the □ of ♃ to be an evil aspect, as thereby his influence is lessened, for it is evident, from the effect of the ☉ and ☾ on each other, that planets oppose each others power most at right angles. I suspect the opposition of a friendly planet to be a good configuration and equal to a conjunction, as we find the luminaries operate together the same at an ☍ as at the conjunction. Of all configurations, I have most confidence in a zodiacal parallel; but I do not think so highly of a mundane parallel, nor of any mundane aspect. All these opinions, however, require the sanction of experience.

It was a doctrine of Ptolemy, that no converse direction can kill, but that of the hyleg to the west. Here, however, Placidus must differ from him, for he mentions several converse directions that kill; and what is the direction of the horoscope (when it is hyleg) to the anareta but a fatal converse direction.

Another doctrine of Ptolemy, and to which Placidus adheres, is that the angles can only be directed in mundo and not in the zodiac; this, if not founded in error, seems at least not founded in reason. If the horoscope be hyleg, why should not a zodiacal aspect have the same effect on that as any other hyleg. I remember reading an instance in the Nativity of an Artist in the Science, wherein he says, 0° 27′ of ♍ were on the cusp of his ascendant, and ♄ was in 2° 10′ of ♊, when the horoscope came to 2° 10′ of ♍, the zodiacal □ of ♄, he broke his leg at the age of two years and eight months: this might or might not be the cause of the accident, but I would sooner rely on such a circumstance than on all the wild theories of Ptolemy.

As to the foolish system of directing the lord of the ascendant to the anareta, or to the lord of the 8th to the hyleg, nothing can more ridiculous. The planets operate as substances, not as symbols.

I shall here add another problem for directing the ascendant or midheaven to the zodiacal aspect of a star, for although both Placidus and Ptolemy deny the efficacy of zodiacal directions to the angles, I have much more confidence in them than in any mundane direction, and would advise the student to give them a fair trial.

Problem 30th.

To direct the ascendant and midheaven to any zodiacal aspect of a star.

Bring the angle to the place of the aspect by ascension or descension.

Example:—Suppose, according to the circumstance just quoted, 0° 27′ of ♍ on the cusp of the ascendant, with ♄ in 2° 10′ of ♊: I would direct the horoscope to the zodiacal □ of ♄, this, of course, falls in 2° 10′ of ♍; therefore direct this to the cusp of the horoscope. We will suppose the pole of the horoscope, that of London, 51° 32′.

Oblique ascension of 2° 10′ of ♍ under the pole of
the horoscope,   140° 21′
Oblique ascension of the horoscope,   137 54

Arc of direction,   2 27

If the direction be made to the 10th it must be made by right ascension.

If the conjunction of either house, it must be brought to its cusp without latitude, because, as we have before seen in the zodiacal directions, the latitude of a promittor is never taken in the zodiac, and the angle being significator has no latitude. For the trine o the ascendant, when under the Earth, bring it to the ✶ of the 7th by oblique descension, or if above the Earth, bring its trine to the cusp of the horoscope; and if to the trine of the 10th, bring it by right ascension to the ✶ of the *Imum Cœli.*

DISEASES. Diseases and blemishes are said by Ptolemy to belong to the 7th house, the 6th, and the ascendant. A malefic, either in the east or west angle, or in □ to them, will produce a blemish or disease in that part signified by the sign in which it is posited. If either of the lights are in one of those angles, or in the 6th, in ☌ or evil aspect with the malefic, there will, it is said, be a disease or blemish in the part signified by the sign where the malefic is posited. Placidus gives an instance of this in the Nativity of Doctor Massari, whose ☾ was in the west angle in □ to ♂, and ☍ to ♄; ♂ was in ♓, the sign of the feet; and ♄ in ♐, the sign of the thighs; the consequence of which was, that he was born with his feet inverted: such examples, I think, should be received with caution, It was also an opinion of Placidus, that the lord or lady of the ascendant in the 1st, 7th, or 6th, in evil aspect of the infortunes, would have a similar effect. Of this he gives an instance in the Nativity of the Duchess of Sfortia, whose lady of the ascendant, ♀, was posited in the 6th, in a parallel of ♄'s declination, who was posited in the sign ♎ in the horoscope, which governs the kidneys: she died of a retention of urine. He also adds, that ♀ was in mundane □ to the ☾, who was then an infortune, being under the parallel of ♂'s declination: either the mundane square was of no effect, or the Moon did not operate as an infortune, for she was in the sign ♊, but her disease did not affect her arms and shoulders.

☿ in a nativity in a parallel of the declination of an infortune, or in square to the Moon from the east or west angles, causes the head to be very much diseased, and if both malefics concur, is apt to cause apoplexy. The ☾ being in a parallel of an infortune's declination will cause a disease or humor in the head; and if ☿ likewise be afflicted by an infortune, the disease will be very severe.

The ☾ in exact ☌, ☍, or ◻, to the ☉, when she is in the east or west angle, or if she be angular in ☌ of ♄, or ♂, or with any nebulous cluster of stars, it is said to cause the loss of an eye.

If both the malefics are in ☌ or ☍ to both the luminaries, and especially if those that afflict the ☉ be oriental, and those that afflict the ☾ occidental, it will cause total blindness. ♂ will cause blindness by fire, wounds, bruises, lightning, small-pox, &c. and if with ♀, it will happen at play or some amusement, or by some vile artifice or private injury. ♄ causes blindness by colds, cataracts, specks, gutta serena, &c. If ☿ be with him, it will proceed from reading, study, or mental exertion.

When Melefics are oriental, and in evil configuration with the luminaries, they cause blemishes; but if they are occidental they produce diseases.

Planets being retrograde have a general tendency to cause diseases.

If one or both the luminaries are in an angle, particularly the east or west angles, or in the 6th house in conjunction with ♄, ♂, and ♀, the native will have no children, and if a female, will be liable to abortion.

If the ☾ be in the east angle, with ♄, and ☿, particularly if ♂ gives testimony, the native will be an hermaphrodite, or perhaps have but one passage.

If the ☉ be joined to ☿, and applying to conjunction, opposition, or declination of both the infortunes, and angular, particularly in ♈, ♌, ♏, ♑, or ♒, the native will be wholly unfit for generation.

If the ☉ and ☾ are configurated together, and both in masculine signs, both of them having configuration with ♂, and ♀ in any way, males then born will have excessive virile members, and women will be quite or nearly hermaphrodites. If ♂ and ♀ be also in masculine signs, men will have a mixture of sex, and females will be violently libidinous. If ♀ only be in a masculine sign, they will be more discreet and conceal their desires.

If the luminaries are configurated together in feminine signs, with ♂ and ♀, females will be of a masculine turn, and very salacious, but the men effeminate. If ♀ be in a feminine sign, the native, if a male will be nearly impotent, but if a female, very lustful. If ♂ be feminine, and ♀ masculine, males will have more strength and vigour. ♂ and ♀ being so configurated, when oriental and diurnal, make men more robust, but if occidental and vespertine, they are more debilitated. If ♄ be configurated with them all, they are more prone to violent and unnatural desires. ☿ adds to their lust, and makes them fond of variety of contrivances; but if ♃ be configurated also, he moderates their desires, and renders them more circumspect.

If the ☉ be in the east or west angles, in ☌ with ♄ and ☿, and particularly in the west in evil aspect with the ☾, the native will have an impediment in his speech, particularly if ☿ be in one of the mute signs, ♋, ♏, or ♓.

If ☿ and the ☾ are in conjunction either with each other or with the horoscope, and in bad configuration with ♄ or ♂ from angles, particularly with ♄ by day and ♂ by night, they will be liable to fits; but if with ♂ by day or ♄ by night, they are apt to be melancholy or frantic.

If ♂ be in evil configuration of the ☾ at the full, or ♄ at the change, in ♐ or ♓, it causes lunacy.

If the benefics are oriental or angular, and have any configuration to the ☾, those diseases will be curable. If ♃, these will be cured by medicine, but if ♀, they will cure themselves.

If the benefics be cadent or occidental, and the malefics oriental, they will be wholly incurable.

If the malefics are angular, in ☌ or ☍ of the luminaries, and the ☾ in her node, in what are called hurtful signs, viz. Aries, Taurus, Cancer, Scorpio, or Capricorn, the native will be lame or distorted. If the malefics are joined to the lights, the defect will be from the birth; but if in ☍ to them or if they have a □ to them from the 10th, it will be by blows, falls, stabs, &c.

The Moon, it is said, gives blemishes when she is in tropical or equinoctial signs.

When the Moon is in any of the three vernal signs, she causes eruptions in the face; in summer signs, she causes ring-worms, tetters, shingles, &c.; in autumnal signs, she causes scurvy; and in winter signs, she gives boils and pimples.

When the malefics are oriental to the Sun, or occidental to the Moon, they cause diseases; and Mercury with them increases the evil.

If the Malefics are angular and occidental to the Moon, or oriental to the Sun, and in Cancer, Capricorn or Pisces, they cause scurvy or scrofula. If in ♊ or ♐, they do injury by falls, or the falling sickness. If they are in the last degree of these signs, they cause gout, cramp, and rheumatism. If the benefics are with the malefics, or oriental or angular, and cast any ray to the luminaries, they will be cured: the rapidity and certainty of the cure will be proportionate to their strength. If the benefics do not assist, or are very weak, they will be incurable. The more angular or oriental a planet is, the more powerful will its effects be, whether benefic or malefic. This is the doctrine of Ptolemy respecting diseases, and I would advise the student to receive it with the utmost caution, until its truth becomes obvious by repeated experience: where so many conflicting testimonies are to be duly weighed, it is difficult for the soundest judgment to in many cases to arrive at the truth, as nothing but incessant practice and experience can enable any one to judge with correctness. He must not blindly subscribe to any authority, however respectable, until he acquires conviction by repeated proofs, and this will be obtained by exertion. Many of these dogmas of Ptolemy and Placidus are very absurd and ridiculous, but they contain in the aggregate some truth. Those who are afflicted from the birth by strange and incurable complaints, as blindness, deformity, and a continual flow of humors from the head, generally evince a strangeness of disposition sufficient to remove any doubt that the whole is the result of malefic influence. I have generally observed that those who have a copious flow of humors from the head, are remarkable for dishonesty and shallowness of intellect; and others who have scars in or near the eyes, or who lose an eye, are extremely vicious and irascible. The cause why the ascendant operates upon the human constitution is unknown, but experience proves it has some effect. It does not so clearly appear that the west angle has any such influence, and still less that the 6th house can be the place from whence we can judge of diseases. It was easy for Ptolemy, or any one, to ascribe the effect of the horoscope to the 7th house, as all evil aspects are common to both, but the reason why he prognosticates diseases from the 6th, is because it is inconjunct with the ascendant. If that were the cause, the 2d, 8th, and 12th, would also be houses of disease, for they are all inconjunct. The lord of the ascendant can have no effect whatever when out of the ascendant, and therefore the notion of Placidus, that ♀, lady of the ascendant, being afflicted in the 6th, was the cause of the death of the Duchess of Sfortia, is extremely ridiculous. The position of Saturn in the ascendant, and the Moon, who is hyleg, having the declination of ♂, is quite sufficient to account for it, and had it not been for the zodiacal and cosmical △ of ♃, concurring with both places, the native would not have lived to the age of 64 years. See Life and Health.

DISSOCIATE SIGNS, those that by being 1 or 5 signs distant, have no aspect to each other: thus, ♈ is dissociate with ♓, ♉, ♍, and ♏.

DISPOSE. A planet disposes of any other which is in its house: thus, if ♄ were in ♐ he would be disposed of by ♃. In horary questions, it is a sign that the thing or person signified by the planet so disposed of, is in the power or interest of the planet (or those whom it signifies) that disposes of it. If several planets dispose in succession, the event is generally governed by the last that disposes, if it be one of the significators: thus, if ♂ be disposed of by ♄, and ♄ by ♀, and ♀ by ♃, who is lord of the ascendant, it is a favourable symptom. Planets also dispose by exaltation and term; the former is seldom attended to, but Placidus has great faith in the term, supposing it alters the nature of any planet nearly to that of the term wherein it is posited.

DISPOSITION. See Mind.

DISPOSITOR, that planet which disposes of another.

DISTANCE. The distance of any place is found by subtracting the ascension of the preceding part, or its descension from that of the succeeding part. If subtraction cannot be made, which will sometimes happen, the circle, or 360°, must be added. Example: if 18° of ♒, whose right ascension is 320° 30′, were to be taken from 15° of ♈, whose right ascension is 13° 48′, it cannot be done until 360° be added, when its distance will be found, 53° 18′, See Right and Oblique Distances, &c.

DIURNAL, by day. Planets also are called diurnal that contain more active than passive qualities: those, on the contrary, which contain more passive than active qualities are called nocturnal. Thus, ♃ being more hot than moist, ♄ more cold than dry, and the ☉ more hot than dry, they are called diurnal, because heat and cold are the active qualities; but ♂ being more dry than hot, ♀ more moist than hot, and the ☾ more moist than cold, they are called nocturnal, because dryness and moisture are passive qualities. ☿ is diurnal when oriental, and nocturnal when occidental: this is said by some to be contrived with a view to moderate the effects of the malefics. ♄ being made diurnal that the heat of the day may moderate his coldness; and ♂ nocturnal, that the moisture of night might moderate his dryness: their meaning is, that they are not so malignant at these times, A planet is also called diurnal, when in the same hemisphere with the Sun, viz. above the Earth by day, and under it at night, and *vice versa*. Thus, by the whims of those wiseacres, a planet may be both diurnal and nocturnal at the same time. Signs also are divided into diurnal and nocturnal: those of the fiery and airy triplicities are diurnal, and those of the earthy and watery triplicities, nocturnal. Here they are again involved in a contradiction by adding heat to heat and cold to cold. It cannot be on account of the predominance of their active qualities, for in all signs the active and passive qualities are equally mixed; it, therefore, originates in another foolish whim, that everything masculine must be diurnal, and that those being masculine signs must be diurnal signs likewise. A sign is said to be diurnal when by its warmth it resembles the day, and nocturnal, when by its cold it resembles the night. Here the active qualities, or one of them at least, are applied in a different sense from that in the case of the planets, and shew the whole is nothing but a mass of contradiction, not worth attending to. That the day may have some small effect in moderating the cold of ♄, and the night in moderating the heat of ♂, is possible, but it certainly does not deprive them of their anaretic qualities, which are equally destructive to life whether the infortune be diurnal or nocturnal.

DIURNAL ARC, the arc or distance which a star passes over from its rising to its setting,

DIURNAL HOUSES. Every planet but the ☉ and ☾ have two houses assigned them, one for the day and the other for the night. The day house of ♄ is ♒, of ♃, ♐; of ♂, ♈; of ♀, ♎; and of ☿, ♊; because those signs are called diurnal. The night house of ♄ is ♑; of ♃, ♓; of ♂, ♏; of ♀, ♉; and of ☿, ♍; because these signs are considered nocturnal. They are supposed to be stronger in a day house by day, and in a night house by night, but the opinion is absurd and unworthy of further notice.

DIURNAL TRIPLICITIES. The fiery triplicity is diurnal for the ☉ and nocturnal for ♃; the earthy triplicity is diurnal for ♀ and nocturnal for the ☾; the airy triplicity is diurnal for ♄ and nocturnal for ☿; and the watery triplicity is both diurnal and nocturnal for ♂. By some a planet by day in its nocturnal triplicity, or by night in its diurnal, would, if it had no other dignity, be considered peregrine; but others would allow them their triplicity, although they consider them much weaker: the whole is absurd and imaginary.

DOG. The little dog Procyon is a star of the first magnitude, in the 23d degree of ♋, of the nature of ♂ and ☿, and of course violent. It denotes activity and sudden preferment by exertion, but generally causes evil in the end. For the great dog see Sirius.

DOMAL DIGNITY, when a planet is in its own house.

DOMICILIATED, a planet is so called when in its own house.

DOUBLE BODIED SIGNS, ♊, ♓, ♐, because they are formed of two distinct animals.

DRAGON'S HEAD, the ☾'s north node or point where she crosses the ecliptic to the northward. The Dragon's Tail is her south node, where she croses it to the southward. They were so called from a notion common among eastern nations, that a great dragon, an enemy of mankind, was continually watching an opportunity to devour the Sun and Moon; by dint of threats or entreaties he was eventually prevented from swallowing them, but they were always eclipsed while he had them in his mouth. As the Moon in those points has no latitude, and the ☉ never has any, they are the only places where eclipses can happen. The place of Dragon's Head is considered of great efficacy both by Ptolemy and Placidus, from the latter of whom one would at least expect something more rational. When the ☾ travels out of the ecliptic, owing to her latitude, there is a certain point where she must again return, as her latitude diminishes, and recross it: for this reason an account is kept in the ephemeris of her progress marked by the character ☊, which is called the Dragon's Head, and is carried on retrograde at the rate of about 3′ per day, and when it exactly corresponds in longitude with her longitude, or with the longitude of her opposition, she is at that instant crossing the ecliptic; yet this character, which is only used as an astronomical mark, is supposed (by those who, professing to be guided by reason, ought to have known better,) to possess the same power as the planets themselves. The Dragon's Head, ☊, is said to be equal to ♃ or ♀ in benefic influence, while the tail, ☋, resembles ♄ or ♂ in malignity. The ☊ is also supposed to strengthen any planet it is joined with to do good or evil according to its nature, and the ☋ renders them weaker in proportion, both benefics and malefics: that they must have such an effect on the ☾ herself is evident, because, as she passes through the Dragon's Head to the northward, her strength must evidently increase as her rays become more direct; and it decreases of course in the same proportion, and from the opposite cause, as she passes to the south by the Dragon's Tail; but nothing can be more ridiculous than to suppose it can have any such effect on another planet no way connected with it, and which may according to its own peculiar latitude be actually passing to the southward through the ☾'s north node, or *vice versa*.

Every other planet, except the ☉, has its nodes in the same way as the ☾, where it crosses and recrosses the ecliptic, and where no doubt it is equally increased or diminished in power according as its rays become more direct or diagonal. Nothing, however, in these observations can apply to horary questions, because the nature of them is not operative but purely symbolical, and consequently, every symbol has its established meaning.

DRAGON'S TAIL, the reverse of the Dragon's Head in every thing. Some are simple enough to direct it to the horoscope as anareta, and Gadbury says, he knew three instances where it destroyed life; a moment's reflection would have convinced him, that it could do nothing of the kind, being a mere non entity.

DUMB SIGNS, ♋, ♏, and ♓ : they are sometimes called mute signs, and it is said, if one of them ascend, and ☿ be afflicted, or if ☿ be afflicted by a malefic posited in one of them, the native will be dumb, or have a great impediment in his speech.

DYSIS, the west angle.

EAGLE, some call it the Vulture, but the bright star in it is called Attair; it is of the 2d, magnitude, of the nature of ♄ and ☿, in 29° of ♑, and its effects are said to be evil, causing disgrace, ruin, and great affliction.

EARTHY SIGNS, those that form the earthy triplicity.

EARTHY TRIPLICITY, ♉, ♍, and ♑ : it is cold and dry.

ECCENTRIC, one of the imaginary circles invented by Ptolemy to account for the apparent motion of a planet in its orbit.

ECLIPTIC, the Sun's orbit or path round the Globe, or rather the Earth's orbit round the Sun ; it is also called *Via Solis*, or the Sun's way, because the sun never moves out of it. All the rest of the planets, by reason of their latitude, move out of it except when they cross it in their nodes. It forms an angle of 23° 28′ with the plane of the equator, but at the time when the astronomical calculations of Placidus were made, it was supposed to form an angle of 23° 32′. It is called the Ecliptic because all Eclipses happen therein.

ECLIPSES. The duration of the effects of an eclipse is said to be a year for every hour the Sun is eclipsed, and a month for every hour the ☽ is eclipsed : the nature of the events are calculated by erecting a figure to the moment the eclipse commences, and those countries represented by the sign ascending, and by those signs containing the planets, will be situated exactly according to the state of those planets, whether strong or weak. The houses, too, are also considered, and such accidents are said to happen as the nature of such houses must produce : the whole of this doctrine is childish and visionary, as every year's experience manifests.

Doubtless eclipses have an effect, particularly those of the Sun, and countries where the shadow is greatest, feel it the most: what those effects are, can be but little known in the present infant state of astrology, though we may naturally conclude them to be productive of vast changes in the Earth and atmosphere.

Eclipses are said to have a powerful influence on those individuals in whose radix they occupy the places of the ascendant, or luminaries, or the square, or opposition. If they occupy the places of the malefics, they renew and increase their original influence, whether it relate to trouble, sickness, or death: and some say, they are the cause of good, when they fall on the places of benefics, or in good aspect to the luminaries; but it is not likely an eclipse, happen when it will, can be productive of much good, though the evil effects ascribed to them are very probable.

ELECTIONS. See Radical Elections.

ELEVATED. There are several opinions concerning the meaning of one planet being elevated above another, as laid down in the doctrine of Ptolemy: in his time, it was no doubt a technical term, and well understood; but we have at present no perfect clue to guide us to a certainty of its real signification. Some suppose it to be when a planet is nearer the cusp of the 10th, it being then more elevated than another at a greater distance. Others conceive it to mean, being in its apogee, or nearer to it than another planet, in which case it would be as it were higher above the Earth, and so more elevated. Others think it relates to its essential dignities, or accidental dignities, and some add the whole of these advantages together and recommend them to be collected and compared, and that planet which had most testimonies in its favour would be elevated above the other. The opinion of Placidus, which seems the most rational, is, that it merely relates to their strength in the geniture or figure: thus, a planet succeedent will be elevated above another that is cadent, and a planet angular will be elevated above another that is succeedent; a planet in the 10th will be elevated above all the rest; one in the 1st, above every other except those in the 10th; and one in the 7th, above another in the 4th, &c. Elevation in one planet depresses or destroys the effect of the other above which it is elevated; an infortune elevated above the luminaries, denotes misfortunes, sickness, and death; and where it is anareta, it causes a violent death; if it be elevated above a benefic, that benefic connot save; but if the benefic be elevated above the malefic, it will moderate or destroy its anaretic tendency: if the luminaries be elevated above the malefics, it greatly lessens the injurious effects

ELEVATION OF THE POLE. This term in its common acceptation signifies the latitude of the country, because as we advance from the equator north or south, those poles appear elevated: and were we to reach the pole of the Earth, the celestial pole would be elevated to our zenith. The elevation of the pole at London is 51° 32′ north.

The poles of the celestial houses increase as they recede from the mid and lowest heaven, which have no pole, unto the horizon, the pole of which is always the latitude of the country: thus, in our latitude of London, which is 51° 32′, the pole of the 3d, 5th, 9th, and 11th, is 23° 27′, because they are all equidistant from the mid-heaven and Imum Cœli. which have no pole. The 2d, 6th, 8th, and 12th, have likewise equal distance from the same angles, and their pole is 40° 48′. The ascendant and descendant are likewise at equal distances from the said angles, and on the verge of the horizon; their pole is therefore that of the country, 51° 32′; thus, all houses opposite to each other, or that are equidistant from the north and south angles, have the same pole, under which pole their oblique ascension must be taken, and the oblique ascension or descension of every planet, which is directed to the cusp or opposition of any house, or of which the distance is required from the cusp of any house, must be taken under the pole of that house. To the 10th or 4th houses, which have no pole, they are directed by right ascension. See the Table:

CIRCLES of POSITIONS of the 11th, 3d, 12th, and 2d HOUSES, from 31° to 60° of Latitude.

Ascendant.	11th & 3d Houses.	12th & 2d Houses.	Ascendant.	11th & 3d Houses.	12th & 2d Houses.
Degrees.	Deg. Min.	Deg. Min.	Degrees.	Deg. Min.	Deg. Min.
31	11 25	21 58	46	19 28	35 9
32	11 52	22 47	47	20 7	36 8
33	12 19	23 35	48	20 49	37 8
34	12 48	24 24	49	21 33	38 10
35	13 17	25 13	50	22 17	39 11
36	13 48	26 4	51	23 4	40 16
37	14 17	26 55	52	23 51	41 20
38	14 49	27 46	53	24 40	42 26
39	15 20	28 38	54	25 34	43 32
40	15 52	29 32	55	26 29	44 41
41	16 25	30 25	56	27 25	45 51
42	16 59	31 22	57	28 24	47 0
43	17 36	32 16	58	29 26	48 13
44	18 13	33 13	59	30 30	49 26
45	18 50	34 11	60	31 39	50 42

The pole of the 7th is of course the same as the 1st, namely, the latitude of the place of birth.

The pole of a planet or star to which another is directed, must also be ascertained; and the oblique ascension or descension of every planet, directed to its body or opposition, must be taken under the pole of the planet or star to which it is directed.

The pole of a star is found as follows:

1st, Find its distance from either of the cusps between which it is posited, by right or oblique ascension or descension.

2d, Find the difference between the poles of the cusps between which it is posited.

3d, As its double horary time is to the difference of the two poles, so is its distance from the said cusp to the difference between its pole and that of the said cusp.

Example: Suppose the latitude of the country to be 48°, right ascension of the midheaven 337° 48'; the ☾ in the 9th house, with 2° 30' of N. lat.; her right ascension 328° 50'; the polar elevation of the cusp of the 9th, 21°; her double horary time 26° 14'.

Right ascension of the midheaven,	337° 48
Right ascension of the ☾ with 2° 30' N. lat.,	328 50
The ☾'s distance from the cusp of the 10th,	8 58

Pole of the cusp of the 9th (between which and the cusp of the 10th the ☾ is posited,)	21° 0'
Pole of the midheaven,	0 0
Difference between them,	21 0

As the Moon's double horary time, 26° 14', is to the difference between the poles of the 9th and 10th, 21°; so is her distance from the 10th, 8° 58' to her pole, 7°.

It will here be observed, that the pole of a house or planet is generally taken in whole numbers, as the odd minutes are of little consequence, and it renders the operation of working with it more easy. Those, however, who are inclined to be more exact, may include the odd minutes; though I think it will be quite sufficient to work to the half degree, by adding a .5 decimally: this would be nearer than the method adopted by Placidus, who works with nothing less than a degree, adding a degree if the fractional minutes be more than 30, and rejecting them if less.

If the ☾ had been in the 8th house, her distance must have

been found from the cusp of the 9th, in like manner by subtracting her oblique descensien under the pole of the 9th, from the
oblique descension of the 9th. Then, in the same manner as before,
as her double horary time, 26° 14′, would have been to the difference of the poles of the 8th and 9th, so would her distance from
the 9th have been to her polar distance from the 9th, which, if we
suppose it, for example's sake, to have been 4°, would have been
4° more than the pole of the 9th, 21°, and, therefore, when added
to it, would have made the pole of the ☾ 25°.

Or it might have been done by taking the oblique descension of
the Moon under the pole of the 8th house, and subtracting the
oblique descension of the 8th house from it, which would have
given the ☾'s distance from the 8th. Then, as the Moon's double
horary time would have been to the difference of the poles of the
8th and 9th, so would her distance from the 8th house have been
to her polar distance from the 8th; this subtracted from the pole
of the 8th would have made her pole the same 25°.

I shall give an example of the latter, as follows: Suppose in
the same latitude 48°, the oblique descension of the 7th house to
be 35° 40′, oblique descension of the Moon with latitude taken
under the pole of the horoscope (she being in the 7th house, which
has the same pole) 31° 25′, (or we may take the round-about way of
Placidus, and take the oblique ascension of the horoscope, 215° 40′,
and the oblique ascension of the Moon with latitude under the
pole of the horoscope, 211° 25′, it all comes to the same thing,)
the difference between the two will be 4° 15′, which is the ☾'s
distance from the cusp of the 7th. Suppose her double horary
time to be 28° 0′, and the difference between the poles of the 6th
and the 7th, 11°.

As the ☾'s double horary time, 28°, is to the difference of the
poles of the 6th and 7th, 11°, so is her distance from the 7th, 4°
15′, to her polar distance from the 7th, 2°: thus she has less pole
by 2° than the 7th house, which is that of the country, 48°: and
therefore her difference of pole, 2°, subtracted from 48° gives her
true pole; 46°.

The polar distances, however, are not proportionate to the
houses, as will be seen by inspecting the table: for the pole of the
11th is greater in progression than that of the 12th, which in its
turn is greater in its progress than that of the horoscope; in different latitudes it alters accordingly, but in ours the pole of the
11th is 23° 27′, and that of the 12, 40° 48′, so that a star in its progress from the 10th to the 9th would gain a pole of 23° 27′,
whereas in its further progress to the cusp of the 8th, an equal dis-

tance in oblique descension, it would gain but 17° 21′, amounting
to 40° 49′; and in its further progress to the horizon it would gain
but 10° 44′, making in all the pole of the country, 51° 32′. It is
clear, therefore, the nearer we come to the horizon the less does
the polar distance increase; so that a star in the midst of a house
will have a greater polar elevation than the half of the pole of
such house: as, for instance, the half of the pole of the 9th, 23° 27′,
would be 11° 43′; but the star would have gained above 12°, by
having passed over that half of the house where the pole increases
more rapidly. It will be more correct, therefore, when a star is
near the middle of a house, to add nearly a degree to that pole
which is found for it, by the Rule of Proportion, but if near the
cusp, the difference will be but trifling.

ELONGATION, the greatest distance a planet can appear to
have from the Sun. It is a term chiefly applied to ♀ and ☿,
because when ☿ acquires a distance of 28, and ♀ of 48 degrees,
we perceive them return; so that they never appear at any greater
distance from the ⊙, and these are called their greatest elongation. Some authors, however, smong whom is the learned Mr.
Sibly, give them (as Commodore Trunnion would call it) a greater length of cable, and talk as freely about the effects of their
squares, trines, and oppositions to the ⊙, as if they were superior
planets; although neither of them yet ever attained to a zodiacal ✶.

EMBOLISMIC, intercalatory. In every year there are 12
moons of 29 days and a half each, and 11 days over, and when
these odd days amount to 30, they make an additional or Emboli-
mic Lunation. Placidus calls every lunation of 29 days and a
half, an Embolismic Lunation; for he says "the ☽ finisheth 12
Embolismic Lunations in 11 days less than a year." From these
Lunations the progression or process is formed, as every lunation
answers to a year of the native's life. See Progression.

EMERSION, a star coming from under the Sunbeams so as
to be seen. It is a term chiefly used in eclipses, and occultations.

ENEMIES. We must here class enmity and friendship together, because they, according to Ptolemy, proceed from the same
places. These places of friendship and enmity are the ascendant,
with the places of the Sun, Moon, and Part of Fortune; if these
are all together, it is a token of long and sincere friendship, provided none of them are above 17° distant.

If they are in ☍, or inconjunct with each other, it is a proof of
bitter and lasting enmity.

If in ✶ or △, it shews a slight friendship.

If in □ to each other, it causes slight enmities.

When the malefics transit any of these configurations, friendships will cease for a time; and when they are past, the friendships will be renewed.

When the benefics transit an evil configuration, the enmity ceases; but when the transit is over, it will be renewed.

If the luminaries only are in good configuration with each other, the native's attachment will be natural and involuntary, without any particular motive, except good will, and as such they will be lasting.

If the configuration be evil, the hatred will be equally involuntary, and from natural aversion. The former class are what we call agreeable characters, the latter, naturally ill-conditioned and forbidding.

If the ⊕ join either of these configurations, the attachment or aversion will originate in motives of gain.

If the luminaries are in good aspect with the ascendant, friendship will arise from the mirth and good temper of the native; but if the configuration be evil, he will have enemies through his own morose temper.

All trivial and slight friendships and enmities arise from the mutual position of these significators in two different nativities when the natives meet, and these also produce lasting friends and enemies. When they come to the same points in each others genitures, friendship will take place, but will last no longer than until they separate, and the same of enmities.

♄ and ♃ coming to each others places, in different nativities, cause an intimacy, by meeting in company, agricultural pursuits, or joint inheritance.

♄ and ♂ cause quarrels, fraud, and villainy.

♄ and ♀ cause friendship through the medium of kindred, but it will not be lasting.

♄ and ☿ cause intimacy by conversation, partnership in trade, scientific associations, &c.

♃ and ♂ produce political enmity, quarrels arising from honours ill bestowed, government enemies, &c.

♃ and ♀ cause intimacy with females, churchmen, teachers, &c.

♃ and ☿ form attachments by means of literary or scientific associations.

♂ and ♀ cause those intimacies that arise from lust, intemperance, debauchery, and all kind of dissipation.

♂ and ☿ produce enmity by interests clashing together, fraud overeaching, rivalship in trade, science, &c.

♀ and ☿ cause friendship by learnieg, epistolary correspondence, &c. and sometimes enmity by female jealousy.

When significators of good or evil apply to the luminaries from angles, the friendship or enmity will be more open and increase; but if the significators are cadent, the friendship and emnity will be more slight and secret.

The friendship or emnity of servants, and its consequence, is taken from the 12th house, its lord and the stars posited there, or that have configuration with it, according as they aspect the places of the luminaries, Part of Fortune, or the ascendant.

According to others, the 7th house is the place of open enemies, and the 12th house of secret enemies; and from those a judgement must be formed.

Planets in the 7th, or in ☍ to the luminaries from angles or succeedents, are all open enemies.

Planets in the 12th, or in ☍ to the lights from cadent houses, are secret enemies.

Planets also in ☍ to the lord of the ascendant are considered to represent enemies.

If the lord of the ascendant be in the 7th or 12th, or either of their lords in the ascendant, there are many enemies.

If the lord of the ascendant disposes of the significators of enmity, or if he be more strong or angular than they, he will overcome his enemies; but if they are stronger than he, they will ruin him. This doctrine of lords of houses is only fit for horary questions, and cannot imply any such thing in nativities.

If stars, signifying enemies, are cadent, peregrine, retrograde or combust, they are mean rascally characters; but if they are angular and well dignified, they are people of some importance.

Infortunes in the 12th, or angular, shew many enemies. Many planets in mutual reception shew many friends.

The luminaries, or the fortunes in the 11th, well fortified, shew good friends, particularly when in △, ✶, or ☌ with the lord of the ascendant. The ☋ in the 3d, or 11th, false friends. Fortunes in the 1st, 7th, 5th, 9th and 11th, houses, give many friends.

If the lord of the 11th be stronger than the lord of the 7th, friends will be more powerful than enemies. The lord of the ascendant, or 3d, in good aspect or reception, shews the friendship of neighbors and kindred, and *vice versa*. ♄ and ♂ peregrine in the 3d, or the ☋ there, denotes continual disputes with them.

All this may have its proper signification in horary questions, but every thing relating to lords of houses, or the 11th or 3d houses, or ☋, can have nothing to do with nativities: they are merely symbolical.

Much of the doctrine of Ptolemy on this head if not false, is very suspicious, and should not be received without being well confirmed by experience. No doubt, there is a great similiarity in nativities, and much friendship and enmity is produced by the the positions of the luminaries in each, so far as they regard each other: but I have no opinion of the conjunctions of the other planets with each other being productive of the effects ascribed to them. Whatever may be their influence in this way, repeated experience will not fail to discover: but this arrangement seems too methodical to be true.

ENNEATICAL, the ninth. Every ninth year of a person's life, which being climacterical, is thought to bring with it a change of fortune. It also signifies the ninth day of a disease, when a change may be expected.

EPHEMERIS, a kind of an almanac, containing the places of the planets. The best should shew the position of every planet for every day at noon, with their respective latitudes and declinations for every 7th day: it is indispensably necessary in erecting a figure, to those who cannot work by tables, and much easier to those who can.

EPICYCLE, a little circle (according to Ptolemy, who knew nothing about the Earth's motion), in the centre of which the deferent of a planet was said to be fixed and carried about with its motion, and yet with its own motion it carried the planet fixed to it round it own centre: all but the ☉ had one of these, for as he was never retrograde, he had no occasion for an epicycle to account for it.

EQUAL POWER. Beholding signs are signs of equal power, because they have equal distances from tropical signs , or equal declination.

EQUATION OF TIME. After any arc of direction is found, it must be equated to time by adding the Sun's right ascension to the arc: their sum will be the right ascension of that part of the zodiac which when the Sun reaches (which will be seen on inspecting the ephemeris for the year of birth) the direction is formed, and the time must be equated, by allowing a year for every day he takes in coming to that place: a month for every two hours, &c.

Example: Suppose the arc of direction of the zodiacal △ of ♃ to the ascendant be 40° 55′; the ☉'s right ascension 1° 36′.

Arc of direction,	40° 55′
Right ascension of the ☉,	1 36
Their sum is	42 31

which is the right ascension of 15° 0 of ♉.

On inspecting the ephemeris for the year of birth, which was 1765, I find the Sun arrives at 15° 0′ of Taurus in 44 days, 5 hours, and 20 minutes from the time of birth, viz. the 21st of March, 14*h*. 40*m*. p. m,: this is equal to 44 years and three months nearly, wanting about 9 or 10 days: so that the event would happen about the 11th or 12th of June, 1809.

Authors have various ways of equating directions: some divide the arc by the Sun's mean motion for a year; others by the motion he had at the time of birth; and some measure it by degrees of the equator: but the most rational way is that of Placidus, for when the Sun arrives at the end of the arc, the direction must be finished, and the true time he takes in doing this is the time required. See Measure of Time.

EQUATOR, an imaginary circle dividing the globe into two equal parts north and south.

EQUATORIAL, of the equator.

EQUINOX, equal night; that time, or place in the ecliptic where the days and nights are equal, which happens twice a year; when the Sun enters ♈ and ♎ .

EQUINOCTIAL SIGNS, ♈ and ♎.

ERRATICS, or ERRATIC STARS, the wandering stars, viz. the planets, so called in contradistinction to the fixed stars, because the erratics are always wandering or changing places.

ESSENTIAL DIGNITIES. See Dignities.

EUDEMON, the good demon, the 11th house, so called because it is the source of as many good things as the 12th house is of evil.

EXALTATION, an essential dignity of 4 degrees. The ☉ has his exaltation in ♈, the ☽ in ♉, ♄ in ♎, ♃ in ♋, ♂ in ♑, ♀ in ♓, and ☿ in ♍.

Whence this supposed dignity had its origin is uncertain, but it seems a part of the Arabian system. Almansor in his aphorisms says, that ♄ and the ☉ have their exaltations opposite, because one loves darkness and the other light; ♃ and ♂ are opposite, because one is a lover of justice and the other of misrule; and ☿ and ♀ have opposite places, because one loves learning and science, and the other sensual pleasures, which are mutual

enemies to each other; this is silly enough, and the reasons
assigned by Ptolemy are equally so. The ☉, he says, is exalted
in ♈, because he is then proceeding to the northward, the days
lengthen, and his heating power increases: but this is equally
true when he is in ♑, ♒, ♓, &c. It may be said, he has more
power and north declination in ♈, but by the same rule he has
still more in ♉ and ♊, yet neither of them is his exaltation; on
the contrary he is peregrine in both. The only reason why ♄
has his exaltation in ♎ is because the ☉ has his in Aries, that
they may be opposite in dignity as in nature, and because Ptolemy made the wonderful discovery that "where heat is increased
cold is diminished, and where cold is increased heat is diminished." The ☾, he says, is exalted in ♉, because when she forms
a ☌ with the ☉ in Aries, she first appears in her increase in ♉, a
sign of her triplicity: but where should her exaltation be when
the ☌ is not in Aries? ♃, he says, is the cause of northern and
fruitful winds, and therefore is exalted in ♋, because it is the
most northern point of the zodiac. Northern winds may be
fruitful in Egypt, where they cause the Nile to overflow: but had
Ptolemy been a European instead of an African, he would have
found nothing less fruitful than a north wind. ♂, he says, is
most heating in ♑, and therefore he has his exaltation in that
sign. The Egyptians dreaded the hot south winds, and therefore
gave ♂ his exaltation in Capricorn, as being the centre of mischief. ♀ had hers in ♓, because her nature was moist; and in
Pisces, says Ptolemy, the beginning of a moist air is perceived:
in England he would have found the beginning of a very moist
air in ♐, which the ☉ enters in November, ☿, being rather dry
has his exaltation in ♍, where, Ptolemy says, dryness first appears when autumn commences: he seems to have thought the
planets created for the use of none but the Egyptians.

The original meaning of the planets' exaltations seems to have
been unknown in the time of Ptolemy, who in his usual style of
dogmatical allegoric mystery, endeavored to account for them in
his own way. Conjectures are almost useless in such cases, but if
I were to hazard one, it would be this: that the ☉ was considered
as commencing his exaltation when he arrived at the equator in
his progress northward, and that this exaltation continued, increasing and afterwards diminishing until he arrived again at the
ecliptic at the autumnal equinox, where he was considered in his
fall, which increased and diminished in the same proportion until
he again reached the vernal equinox. The ☾ was exalted in
Taurus upon the same principle. ♃ was exalted in ♋, because

there the rays of all the planets are more direct and powerful in northern latitudes; and as ♃ is the greater fortune, he was there enabled to become more beneficial. As, no doubt, the term exaltation implied some position that increased the power of good planets and diminished that of all evil ones, ♄ was exalted in ♎, because as he passed to the south his power of doing evil was abated by his rays becoming more oblique, and having less force; and ♂, for the same reason, was exalted in Capricorn, where his heat was diminished by his distance. Having thus disposed of of the superior and more powerful planets, ☿ was exalted in ♍, because it is in △ to Taurus, the exaltation of the ☾, from whence ☿ derives his power chiefly, and although the ☾ might not be there, it was a very common notion, that the dignity of a planet retained its nature although the owner was absent. ♀, being of the same nature as ♃, was placed in Pisces, in trine to ♋, his exaltation, that she might be strengthened by his assistance.

However this may have been, it is certain that if power may be deemed exaltation, all planets must be exalted when they arrive at their northern nodes, and advance towards our zenith. The ☉ and ☾, therefore, and the two fortunes, must be rendered more beneficial by such a position, and the infortunes more malignant.

The opinion of Ptolemy concerning exaltation, or house, was not that a planet acquired strength from it, for he mentions but two kinds of strength; that in the geniture and that in the world, —such as being oriental, angular, &c. The effects arising from the essential dignities were considered by him as merely productive of certain qualities of the mind, which were evil when a planet was ill dignified, and good when well dignified. A planet in its detriment, fall, or peregrine, was thought to be equally powerful to do evil, as when exalted or domiciliated, and infinitely more injurious.

The Dragon's Head and Tail, too, have their exaltations assigned them, the former in ♊, the latter in ♐. Modern astronomers have limited the exaltations of the planets to certain degrees, and do not consider the ☉ in his exaltation until he arrives at 19° of ♈; the ☾ is exalted in 3° of ♉; ♄ in 21° of ♎; ♃ in 15° of ♋; ♂ in 28° of ♑: ♀ in 27° of ♓; ☿ in 15° of ♍; and the Dragon's Head and Tail in 3° of ♊ and ♐. Ptolemy, however, assigns no exaltations for the Moon's nodes, nor does he limit the planets to any particular number of degrees.

In horary questions a planet in its exaltation denotes success and prosperity to the person or thing of which it is significator; the person whom it represents is in great esteem, possessing influence, and will not easily be overcome; and, particularly if it be angular, it denotes a person of consequence and some property, very proud and assuming, and one who thinks himself greater than he really is.

FACE, a planet is in its face when it is at the same distance from the ☉ or ☾ as its house is from their houses, and in the same succession of signs; thus, ☿, when one sign to the west of the ☉, or one sign to the east of the ☾, is in his face; because ♍, his house, is one sign to the west of ♌, the house of the ☉; and ♊. his other house, one sign to the east of ♋, the house of the Moon. So ♀ is in her face two signs west of the ☉, and two signs east of the ☾; ♃ four signs, and ♄ five signs; this is the doctrine of Ptolemy, and apparently without any foundation; but modern astrologers have improved upon this absurdity, and invented a new set of faces, which they have inserted in their table of essential dignities. Every sign is divided into three faces of 10° each, commencing at ♈, and proceeding thence in the order of the signs and planets.

The 1st face is the face of ♂, and denotes, courage, strength, and magnanimity.

The 2d, to 20° of ♈, is that of the ☉, denoting, grandeur, power, fame, candour, generosity and true greatness of soul.

The 3d, to 30° of ♈, is the face of ♀, signifying effeminacy, mirth, wantonness and delight.

The 4th, to 10° of ♉, is that of ☿, the face of arts, sciences, wit, oratory, mechanics, agriculture, and every species of learning and knowledge.

The 5th face, to 20° of ♉, belongs to the ☾, and denotes ambition, authority, violence, and arbitrary sway.

The 6th, that of ♄, to 30° of ♉, is the face of cruelty, oppression, slavery, poverty, and wretchedness.

The 7th, that of ♃, to 10 ° of ♊, is the face of arithmetic, algebra, sculpture, cyphers, and hieroglyphics.

The 8th, to 20° of ♊. is that of ♂, and denotes deep study, labour, and perseverence, rewarded with grief, trouble and anxiety.

The 9th, to 30° of ♊, is the face of the ☉, and denotes boldness, contempt, insolence, brutality, idleness, forgetfulness, and illbreeding.

The 10th, that of ♀, to 10° of ♋, shews good sense, wit, mirth, kindness, love, and cheerfulness.

The 11th, that of ☿. to 20° of ♋, denotes wealth, honor, preferment, fruitfulness, and great success in business.

The 12th is that of the ☾, and extends to 30° of ♋, it denotes success in law, arms, and travelling; much exertion, strength and power to overcome all opposition.

The 13th is the face of ♄, to 10° of ♌, and denotes violence, rage, cruelty, lust, tyranny, and wickedness.

The 14th, the face of ♃, extends to 20° of ♌, and signifies esteem, friendship, public spirit, and conquest.

The 15th, that of ♂, to 30° of ♌, denotes contention, enmity, violence, murder, battle, and destruction,

The 16th, that of the ☉, to 10° of ♍, denotes wealth, industry, and prosperity.

The 17th, extending to 20° of ♍, the face of ♀, shews avarice, covetousness, and parsimony.

The 18th is that of ☿, and extends to 30° of ♍, it denotes old age, infirmity, weakness, decay, and dissolution.

The 19th, that of the ☽, extending to 10° of ♎, denotes justice, mercy, truth, kindness, and liberality.

The 20th, that of ♄, extends to 20° of ♎, and signifies gain, advantage, and success, with labour, vigilance, and cunning.

The 21st, the face of ♃, to 30° of ♎, signifies lasciviousness, luxury, licentiousness, dissipation, drunkenness, and depravity.

The 22d, that of ♂, to 10° of ♏, denotes strife, violence, robbery, and murder,

The 23d, that of the ☉, to 20° of ♏, denotes envy, deceit, malice, discord, and detraction.

The 24th, that of ♀, to 30° of ♏, denotes adultery, fornication, lewdness of every kind, flattery, and deceit.

The 25th, that of ☿, to 10° of ♐, denotes intrepidity and strength, openness, mirth, and festivity,

The 26th, that of the ☽, to 20° of ♐, shews sorrow and affliction, great distress of mind, suspicion, mistrust, and woe.

The 27th, the face of ♄, to 30° of ♐, denotes obduracy, tyranny, obstinacy, cruelty, and wickedness.

The 28th, the face of ♃, to 10° of ♑, is that of benevolence, honesty, mirth, hospitality, and happiness.

The 29th, that of ♂, to 20° of ♑, shews intemperate lust, unbridled passions, disappointment, discontent, and peevishness.

The 30th, that of the ☉, to 30° of ♑, denotes wisdom, sound intellect, honour sobriety, and integrity.

The 31st, that of ♀, to 10° of ♒, gives covetousness, labour and vigilance, loss and disappointment.

The 32d, that of ☿, to 20° of ♒, denotes good nature, mildness, modesty, and complacency.

The 33d, that of the ☾, to 30° of ♒, denotes discontent, envy, anxiety, jealousy, and ingratitude.

The 34th, that of ♄, to 10° of ♓, denotes temperance, reflection, attention, reputation, and success in trade.

The 35th, that of ♃, to 20° of ♓, denotes austerity, haughtinets, ambition, and vain glory.

The 36th, that of ♂, to 30° of ♓, denotes lust, profligacy, and every kind of lewdness.

It is said, that in a nativity, the native's disposition will strongly partake of the quality of that face which is upon the cusp of of the ascendant, subject, however, to the nature of other aspects. It will also partake of the quality of such faces as the lord of the ascendant, the ☾, or planets aspecting the ascendant are in; this, so far as respects nativities, is extremely vain and ridiculous, but it might be useful in horary questions to distinguish the dispositions of the querent and quesited, were it reduced to anything like method; but there are so many significators, all, perhaps, in different and opposite faces, beside the different signification of the signs, the planets in them, their various aspects and strength, that the whole has become a complete mass of confusion; every artist should select such parts of it as may best suit his own judgement or fancy, and be guided by no other; for as the science of horary questions is purely symbolical, every one may use what symbols he thinks most proper and convenient, so as he adheres to them uniformly, to avoid confusion and intricacy. The faces here laid down are, I think, not the most proper on many accounts: they do not seem quite agreeable to the nature of the signs and planets, and are too much in extremes to suit the general bent of of human nature.

The faces, as laid down by Ptolemy, are merely a species of accidental dignity, but wholly as groundless as the others, because they depend on the domal dignities of the planets, which certainly do not exist.

A planet in its face, having no other dignity, denotes a person of whom it is the significator (in a horary question) to be but indifferently situated, and in danger, distress, and anxiety; or, as Moxon says, like a man ready to be turned out of doors, and who has much difficulty in supporting his sinking credit: it can hardly be called a dignity, as it is the next state to peregrine, or beggary and meanness. The person so signified has much to do to live, and in genealogies it denotes a family quite decayed, and scarcely able to support itself.

FALL. A planet has its fall in the opposite sign to that where

it has his exaltation; thus the ☉ has his fall in ♎, the ☾ in ♏,
♄ in ♈, ♃ in ♑, ♂ in ♋, ♀ in ♍, and ☿ in ♓; the ☊, to complete the absurdity, has its fall in ♐, and the ☋ in ♊: it is a
debility of 4°.

In horary questions, a planet in its fall denotes a person unfortunate, despised, and degraded; mean, insolvent, or helpless; and
the thing signified by it is in a hopeless state, except some good
aspect by application, or some translation of light, happen, which
will retrieve it quite unexpectedly.

FALSE ANGLE. See Directions.

FALSE ARC. See Directions.

FAMILIARITIES, called also configurations, or aspects, were
but six in number, according to Ptolemy, viz. the conjunction,
marked ☌; the sextile, marked ✶; the quintile or square, marked
□; the trine marked △; the opposition, marked ☍; and the
antiscion or zodiacal parallel: to these Kepler added eleven more,
viz. the Vigintile, marked *Vig.*; the quindecile, marked *Qdle.*;
the semisextile, marked *Ss.*; the decile, or semiquintile, marked
Dec.; the semiquadrate, octile, or sesquadrate, marked *Sq.*; the
quintile, marked *Q.*; the tredicile, or sesquiquintile, marked *Td.*;
the sesquiquadrate, marked *Sqq.*; the biquintile, marked *B.*; and
the quincunx, or quadrasextile, marked *Qx.*; of these Placidus only
admits the quintile, sesquiquadrate, and biquintile; but he invented a method of calculating them in the world as well as in the
zodiac, by which means they are supposed to operate at different
distances from each other from what they do in the zodiac, being
wholly measured by their semi-arcs instead of ecliptical degrees.
If we add to these, his mundane parallel, or equal distance from
angles, which is certainly wholly different from a zodiacal antiscion, the aspects admitted by Placidus are ten in all. Many authors,
however, deny the conjunction to be an aspect, because the stars
do not behold each other, but their influence is on the Earth,
which they behold with a conjunct aspect.

The ☌ is when two or more planets are in the same sign and
degree.

The ✶, when in the same degree, but two signs distant.

The □, when three signs distant.

The △, when four signs distant.

The ☍, when in the same degree of an opposite sign: thus, the
4th degree of Aries is in ✶ to the 4th degree of ♒ and ♊, in □
to the 4th of ♑ and ♋, in △ to the 4th of ♐ and ♌, and in ☍ to
the 4th degree of ♎.

The antiscion or zodiacal parallel is when two stars have the same or opposite declination; thus, a star in 4 degrees of Aries, without latitude, will have the same declination as a star in 26° of Pisces, without latitude, and the same opposite declination as another in 25° of ♍; but when a star has latitude, its declination is proportionally increased or diminished. (See Parallels.) These are the only aspects mentioned by Ptolemy: it is evident, therefore, that the distance of the ✳ is 60°, the □ 90°, the △ 120° and the ☍ 180°.

Their distances in the world are wholly independent of the measure in the zodiac, and depend on the length of the semi-arcs of each planet. If the semi-arc be 90°, their distance will be the same as in the zodiac, viz. 60°, for the ✳, 90° for the □, &c; but if the semi-arc be but 60°, the ✳ will be but 40,° the □ 60°, and the △ 80°. The mundane parallel is when two stars have equal distances from any angle, no matter how great or how little.

The new aspects invented by Kepler are mostly produced by subdividing the others.

The Vigintile is a zodiacal distances of 18°, the circle being divided by 20.

The Quindecile, a distance of 24°, is the circle divided by 15.

The Semisextile is a distance of 30°, or the ✳ divided by 2.

The Decile, a distance of 36°, is the circle divided by 10.

The Semiquadrate, of 45°, is the □ divided by 2.

The Quintile, of 72°, is a circle divided by 5.

The Tredecile, of 108°, is a quintile and half, or three deciles.

The Sesquiquadrate, of 135°, is a square and half.

The Biquintile is two quintiles, or 144°.

The Quincunx, of 150° is 5 signs distant.

Those arising from a division of the square were thought by Kepler to be evil, and those arising from a division of the △ or ✳ by 5, were good; thus, the vigintile, being the ¼ of a quintile, is good; the quindecile, being one-fifth of the △, is good; the semisextile, or half sextile, is good; the decile, being half a quintile, is good; the quintile, being formed of a sextile and one-fifth of a sextile, is good: the tredecile, being a quintile and a half, is good; and the biquintile, or double quintile, is good. Those, on the contrary, produced by a subdivision of the □, were evil; but of these there are but two, the semiquadrate or half square, and the sesquiquadrate or a square and half, both of which were evil. As Kepler entertained a very high opinion of the number 5, he supposes the quincunx or distance of 5 signs to be a good aspect, because it is a △ and ½ of a ✳; but the ancient opinion was, that a planet, being five signs distant from any moderator or significator, was inconjunct, and had no effect on it whatever: in many cases, therefore, this position is deemed evil, as, when the luminaries are inconjunct with ♃, or with the horoscope, &c. The semi-sextile was likewise considered as an inconjunct position. How far their effects correspond with the opinion of Kepler, repeated trials and long practice alone can determine, but my opinion of Kepler is, that he relied more upon the imaginary charm of numbers, than upon the conviction arising from experiment. The square operates by its own position alone, through the planetary influences crossing each other at right angles, and its effect is manifest in the state of the tides when the luminaries are in this position; but that the semiquadrate or sesquiquadrate should have any such effect merely because they contain parts of an aspect, which at that time does not exist between them, and when they form angles more resembling the trine or sextile than the square, seems very unreasonable, and requires more practical confirmation than, I believe, it has hitherto received. It seems strange, that Placidus should reject the semiquadrate, when he acknowledged the sesquiquadrate, as they are both equally distant from an inconjunct position: he thinks a luminary cannot operate as hyleg until it is the semiquadrate or half the semidiurnal arc distant from the horoscope, and this opinion seems highly rational, as its rays become more direct than oblique; but the same objection will apply to the place of the sesquiquadrate, for if the hylegiacal influence commence in the middle of the 11th house, it must cease in the middle of tne 9th.

Familiarities are, as I have before observed, taken two ways: 1st, in the zodiac; and 2d, in the world.

Zodiacal aspects are such as we have just been describing, with their distance measured in the zodiac by signs and degrees.

Mundane, or worldly aspects, are formed from the distance between the angles, and are longer or shorter as the quarters are more or less unequally divided. Thus, if 8° of Capricorn be on the cusp of the horoscope, and 14° of ♉ on the cusp of the Imum Cœli, in this case, if ♃ were on the cusp of the Imum Cœli, he would be in mundane square to the horoscope, although in a zodiacal trine. Again, if the cusp of the 3d house were 17° of ♈, and ♄ there, he would be in mundane sextile to the horoscope, although in a zodiacal square.

There are two kinds of approximation in familiarities: partile and platic.

Partile, is when the familiarity falls in the same degree and minute; as, if ♄ were in 6° 4′ of ♈ he would be in partile trine to ♃ in 6° 4′ of ♐.

Platic, is when the familiarity is within half the distance of the orbs of both planets added together: thus, ♄ in 16° of ♑ would be in platic △ of ♀ in 25° of ♉, because the orb of ♄ is 12°, and that of ♀ 8°, which added together make 20°, the half of which is 10°, and they are only 9° distant from a partile △.

Aspects are either *dexter*, or *sinister*, as they lie to the right or left hand in the order of the signs: thus, Saturn in Capricorn would cast a dexter square to Jupiter in Libra, who on his part would cast a sinister square to Saturn. In this case the dexter aspect, or that which is contrary to the order of the signs, operates with the greater force.

Conjunctions are good with good planets, and bad with evil. A conjunction of Saturn and Mars is particularly evil, and threatens the most serious consequences. A conjunction of Jupiter and Venus is equally good, and denotes the most perfect and durable happiness. The conjunction of Saturn and Jupiter, although the latter be a fortune, is generally evil; it causes sickness and bad weather, and in nativities is generally the sign of some great disaster. In horary questions, where every planet is distinguished as a significator, it is different: the person signified by ♃ would be much injured by ♄, and it would denote his disposition to be cowardly, mean and suspicious, and himself very unfortunate. But if ♄ were significator, the presence of ♃ would denote good, and the disposition, though grave and austere, would be noble-minded, just and respectable, and the native tolerably fortunate. The ☌ of ♀ is not so good; she denotes treachery, and a long train of consequent evils, and if with ♂, lewdness and infamy.

Antiscions, or parallels, are like conjunctions: good with good planets, and evil with evil ones.

Trines are reckoned good, and sextiles the same, but in an inferior degree.

Oppositions are considered evil, and squares the same, but in an inferior degree. For the more particular effects of the familiarities, see Horary Questions.

FEMININE. See Masculine.

FEMININE SIGNS, ♉, ♋, ♍, ♏. ♑, ♓; they are supposed to be weak and feminine on account of their active and passive qualities, coldness and moisture, and are supposed to render those they govern the same.

FERAL, brutish, like a wild beast; such is said to be the dispopositions of those whose ascendant is ♌, or the last half of ♐;

or if the luminaries be in either of them and the malefics in angles, it renders them fierce, cruel, and brutish, the ☾ is also said to be feral, when she is void of course, having separated from a planet, and applying to no other while she is in that sign. There does not appear to be any ground for such an opinion; but this will be best decided by experience.

FIERY SIGNS, ♈, ♌, and ♐.

FIERY TRIPLICITY, the triplicity formed by the three fiery signs.

FIGURE, a draught or scheme of the heavens at any particular time, such as the time of a nativity, disease, revolution, ingress, horary question, &c. &c.

The circle of the heavens must be divided into 12 parts, called houses, but authors differ much in opinion concerning the method of dividing it. Ptolemy is understood by some to have divided it by circles of position, drawn at equal distances through the poles of the ecliptic, 30° from each other, which, if so, would place the 12 signs exactly in the twelve houses, with the same degree and minute on the cusp of each, but I believe very few understand Ptolemy in this way.

Alcabitius recommended those circles of position to be drawn through the poles of the world, so as to intersect the equator in the same manner as the others did the ecliptic, at equal distances of 30° each, so that the ecliptical degree answering to every 30° of the equator (as the circle passes through both) shall be on the cusp of each house.

Campanus divided the prime vertical circle into 12 parts of 30° each, by circles of position, and placed that degree of the ecliptic on the cusp of each house that the circle of position passed through in the same manner.

Regiomontanus, in what is called the rational way, divided the ecliptic by the circles of position passing through the equator, and dividing the ecliptic in that manner by every 30° of the equator; this, though far from deserving the name of rational, comes nearer the truth than the others.

The true method of dividing the heavens is by oblique ascension, and this was evidently the method recommended by Ptolemy and observed by Placidus: thus, supposing the globe so fixed as to have 0° 29′ of ♋ on the cusp of the horoscope, in our latitude 25° 0′ of ♒ will be found to culminate, and of course must occupy the cusp of the midheaven, the right ascension of which is 327° 18′: add to this, 30° 0′, it will give the oblique ascension of the cusp of the 11th, 357° 18′, or about 26° of Pisces; again, add 30°

more and it will give the oblique ascension of the 12th, 27° 18°, or about 14° of Taurus; again, add 30°, and it will give the oblique ascension of the horoscope, 57° 18′, or 0° 29′ of Cancer: this is the real method of Ptolemy, whose aim was to mark the mundane distances of the stars from the angles so as to distinguish which were angular, succedent, or cadent.

The first of these systems, falsely ascribed to Ptolemy, is merely an equal division of the zodiac into 12 parts, and cannot in any way relate to a figure of the heavens, as may be decided by the globe in a minute, where, if 0° 29′ of Cancer be brought to the eastern horizon, the sign Aquaries will be found in the midheaven; whereas, the pretended Ptolemaic division would place the cusps of the houses as follows:

Cusp of the ascendant, 0° 29′ ♋, of the 10th, 0° 29′ ♈.
    of the 2d, 0 29 ♌   11th, 0 29 ♉.
          3d, 0 29 ♍,   12th, 0 29 ♊.

The cusp of the 10th could not be the cusp of the midheaven, nor does the scheme appear calculated to answer any purpose whatever.

The plan of Alcabitius is equally ridiculous, and would stand as follows:

Cusp of the ascendant, 0° 29′ ♋, of the 10th, 0° 29′ ♈,
            2d, 28, 29 ♋,   11th, 2 29 ♉,
            3d, 28, 29 ♌   12th, 2 29 ♊.

Here the same objection holds good as before, that the cusp of of the 10th is not that of the midheaven,

The method of Campanus comes much nearer to the truth, as the positions of the angles at least are correct.

Cusp of the ascendant, 0° 29′ ♋, of the 10th, 25° 0′ ♒,
            2d, 28 0 ♋,   11th, 12 0 ♓,
           3d, 12 0 ♌,   12th, 22 0 ♈.

The *modus rationalis* of Regiomontanus is still more correct, but with the exception of the angles, his houses will seldom answer to the oblique ascension under their respective poles.

Cusp of the ascendant, 0° 29′ ♋, of the 10th, 25° 0′ ♒,
           2d, 21 25 ♋,   11th, 25 57 ♓,
           3d, 7   5 ♌,   12th, 20 22 ♉,

This system, although evidently erroneous, except in its angles, is still adhered to by most artists; if, however, they are correct in their oblique ascensions, the exactness of the figure itself is but of little consequence.

By the Placidian method, which was undoubtedly that of Ptolemy, the cusps will be as follows:

Cusp of the ascendant, 0° 29′ ♋, of the 10th, 25° 0′ ♒,

2d, 16　0 ♋,　　　　11th, 26　0 ♓,

3d, 4　0 ♌,　　　　12th, 14　0 ♉.

This is taken in whole numbers, which is quite near enough for any purpose whatever, and will save the artist much trouble in correcting the cusps of the houses to a minute by oblique ascension; only the cusp of the 10th need be perfectly correct, because when its right ascension is known, the ascension or descension of every cusp in the figure will, as before observed, be found by adding 30° for each house, according to its distance.

The most demonstrative way, is to erect the figure by a globe: but for those who do not understand its use, the usual method is to erect it by a table of houses.

(It would have been improper for me to have enhanced the price of this work by adding to it a table of this kind, which some might possess already, and others not think proper to use; I have, therefore, added it to the rest of the tables in a separate volume. It is calculated for the latitude of London, not according to the system of Regiomontanus, but by oblique ascension, according to the doctrines of Ptolemy and Placidus.)

The first thing to be done, is to find the Sun's place at noon on that day for which the figure is erected, which may be found in an Ephemeris for the year. Thus, supposing a native to be born, or a horary question to be asked on the 4th of April, 1794, at 3 hours, 35 minutes, in the afternoon: I find, on inspecting the Ephemeris for that year, that the ☉ was on that day at noon in 14° 55′ 40″ of ♈, which may be called 15° of Aries, as it is nearer 15° than 14°. Enter that table of houses which is marked over the top, 'Sun in Aries,' and opposite to 15 (in the column headed $\frac{10}{\text{♈}}$) will be found on the left, 0h. 55m. 14s., this was the Sun's right ascension in time on that day at noon; add to this, the time he had passed since noon when the birth took place, namely, 3h. 55m., and it makes 4h. 50m. 14s., which is the right ascension in time of the midheaven at the time of birth, if the giv-

en time be exact. This must be sought for in the table of houses
(in the column headed 'time from noon'): the nearest number to
it, namely, 4*h*. 50*m*. 32*s*., will be found opposite to 14° of ♊,
which must be placed accordingly on the cusp of the 10th house.
On the right hand will be found (in the column headed, $\frac{11}{\text{♋}}$), 21
which is 21° of Cancer, and must be put on the cusp of the 11th
house. To the right of this, again, will be found (in the column
marked, $\frac{12}{\text{♌}}$), 22, which is 22° of Leo, and must be placed on the
cusp of the 12th house. On the right of this will be found, in the
same manner, 17° 46′ of ♍, for the cusp of the ascendant: 10° of
♎, for the cusp of the 2d, (for although the column is marked
$\frac{2}{\text{♍}}$, yet, in looking down it, ♎ will be found to have succeeded ♍),
and 9° of ♏, for the cusp of the 3d; the cusps of these six houses
being found, the cusps of the other six follow of course, being
the same degrees of the opposite signs. Thus, the cusp of the 4th
is 14° of ♐; of the 5th, 21° of ♑; the 6th, 22° of ♒; the 7th, 17°
46′ of ♓; the 8th, 10° of ♈, and the 9th, 9° of ♉. The 4*h*. 50*m*.
32*s*. should then be multiplied by 15, which will give 72° 38′ for
the right ascension of the midheaven in distance, and this should
be written over the angle, as the data from whence the oblique
ascensions are to be taken. The oblique ascension of the ascendant, 162° 38′, formed by adding 90° to the right ascension of the
midheaven; the right ascension of the 4th, 252° 38′ found by adding
180° to the said right ascension; and the oblique descension of the
7th, found by adding 180° to the oblique ascension of the horoscope,
should all be placed in like manner, over their respective angles,
when the figure will stand as shown on following page.

The cusp of these houses, with the exception of the angles, are
not exactly the same as in the true figure, because I there reduced
them to exact minutes, to coincide with their oblique ascensions,
but this is all mere formality and wholly superfluous and useless.

It is here necessary to observe, that although this is the usual
mode of erecting a figure, the right ascension of the midheaven is
not quite correct: it should be recollected, that the Sun's place at
noon on that day, was only in 14° 55′ 40″ of ♈, although we
called it 15°, which makes an error of 4° 20′, or about 16*s*. in the
time of the right ascension more than it really is. Again, the
right ascension in time of the midheaven was 4*h*. 50*m*. 14*s*.,
whereas the nearest sum we could find to it was 4*h*. 50*m*. 32*s*.,
making a second error in time of 18*s*., or 4′ 30″ in distance, more:

so that the two errors make the right ascension of the south angle about 8′ or 9′ more than it should be, which would, in a direction to any of the angles, make a difference of about two months in the time of the event.

72° 38′

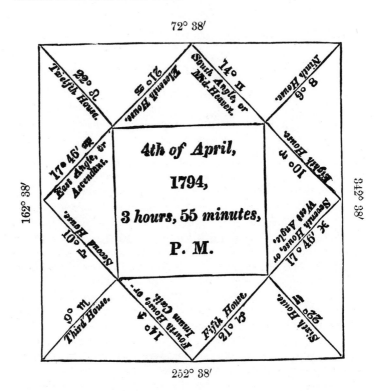

162° 38′

342° 38′

252° 38′

I merely make this remark, to shew how correct every operation ought to be, to be true; but, after all, this error is too trifling to deserve notice, though where it is much greater, it ought to be attended to. The whole is not much above half a minute in time and it is very probable, the given time of birth may be wrong many minutes: few watches, or even clocks, are right to 5 minutes, and it is customary with most people to count their time by 5 minutes, so that, if it had been from 53 to 57 minutes past three, the time would have been called probably 55 minutes: the clock, too, on this day, was nearly three minutes faster than the Sun, which I have not taken into the account, so that allowing directions to angles to have an effect, the time of their events must be very uncertain. The zodiacal aspect cannot be materially altered by such a mistake: it can have no effect on any planet but the Moon, which moves only at the rate of about a minute in two minutes of time, whereas the ascendant in a sign of short ascension would gain above a degree in the same space of time.

We must next consider the method of placing the planets in the figure, and this ought to be done with the greatest exactness. In the Ephemeris their places are calculated for every day at noon, and to this the proportional distance they have gone since that period must be added: thus, I find ♄ at noon in 14° 41′ of ♉, and on the next day at noon in 14° 48′ of ♉, which indicates his motion to be 7′ in 24 hours. The birth was nearly 4 hours afternoon, which is one sixth of 24, and I therefore add one sixth of his course, which is 1′, and place him in 14° 42′ of ♉. ♃ only moves half a minute in the time, which of course makes no difference in his position, which is 3° 21′ of ♋. The places of the rest are found in the same way, and therefore it is superfluous to calculate them here. Except the ☾, which being the most difficult to place, on account of the rapidity of her motion, I shall here calculate her position as an example:

At noon on the 4th, she is in 12° 0′ of ♊, and at noon on the 5th, in 25° 28′ of ♊, which shews her motion to have been 13° 28′ in 24 hours. I therefore say, by the Rule of Three, "If 24h. give 808 minutes, what will one hour give?" it gives nearly 34′, and therefore 4 hours will give 2° 16′; but the time of birth was only 3 hours, 55 minutes, afternoon and therefore her course for 5 minutes must be deducted from the 4 hours: if, therefore, she moves 34′ in an hour, she will in 5 minutes move 3′; subtract this from the 2° 16′, and the remainder will be 2° 13′, or rather 2° 12′, when we allow for casual fractions; add this to her place at noon, 12° 0′ of ♊, and her true place, at the estimate-time of birth will be in 14° 12′ of ♊.

The next points are those of the Dragon's Head and Tail, in the top of the right hand page of the Ephemeris, next to Saturn's latitude, is the place of the Moon's node; this is her north node, or what is called the Dragon's Head, and it is there calculated for every six days, which is quite often enough, considering its value. On the 1st of April, I find the Dragon's Head at noon in 24° 28′ of ♌; and on the 7th, it is in 24° 9′ for, it always moves retrograde: in 6 days, therefore, it has changed its place 19′, or about 3′ a day, and as the day of birth was 3 days after the 1st of April, I deduct 9′ for those 3 days, and its place will be in 24° 19′ of Leo. The

Tail is always opposite to the Head, and of course in 24° 19′ of ♒.

We have yet the Part of Fortune to fix, which, according to the usual way, is done as follows: Add the ascendant to the Moon's place, and from their sum subtract the Sun's place, the remainder is the place of ⊕.

Example :—

The ascendant is in 17° 46′ of ♍, or	5 *signs,*	17°	46′
The Moon's place in 14° 12′ of ♊, or	2	14	12
Their sum	8	1	58
The Sun's place is in 15° 5′ of ♈, or	0	15	5
Place of the Part of Fortune,	7	16	53

which signifies 7 signs, 16° 53′, or in 16° 53′ of ♏. When subtraction cannot be made, 12 signs must be added.

Those who wish to place the Part of Fortune by the method of Negusantius, will find ample directions under the article, Part of Fortune.

The last operation is that of placing the Fixed Stars. This can only be necessary when they are joined to the luminaries, or to planets aspecting the ascendant or midheaven: or where they are within a few degrees of the cusps of those angles. Most artists, however, insert them when they are within 5° of the cusp of any house, but this is useless, for the houses in themselves have no effect, except in horary questions as symbols. I think, if they have any real power (which some have disputed), they must operate in a zodiacal parallel, and therefore their declination ought to be attended to, when it agrees with those of the luminaries.

In looking over the longitudes of the fixed stars, I find Deneb about 18° of ♍, and accordingly place it near the cusp of the horoscope, by writing. "Deneb;" Rigel is about 14° of ♊, culminating with the ☽, and therefore I write the name close to her; Bellatrix must also be inserted, as it is not 5 degrees from the Moon, being in 18° of Gemini; the ⊕ is between the two Scales; ♄ is near Menkar, a star of his own nature; Markab is near the cusp of the 7th, &c.; when all this is done, the figure is complete in itself, but the latitudes and declinations of the planets should be inserted at the bottom for the purpose of calculation. It is also customary to collect the principal aspects in the centre of a figure as for instance; ☽ *ad* ✶, ☉, ☿, and ♀, signifying that the ☽ is applying to the ✶ of the ☉, ☿, and ♀. It is also usual to insert the planetary hour, but this is wholly useless and unmeaning.

A figure may be erected by ascensions, without having recourse
to a table of houses. Thus, if the Sun's place be found, as before,
in 15° of Aries, look at the table of the Sun's right ascension in
the Ephemeris, opposite 15° of ♈, where will be found 0h. 55m.
14s.; to this must be added the time from noon, 3h. 55m., making
as before, 4h. 50m. 14s., for the right ascension of the midheaven,
which, in the same table of the ☉'s right ascension, will be found
nearly to agree with 14° of ♊, whose right ascension in the Ephemeris is 4h. 50m. 34s., which, by the bye, is more correct by 2s.
than that in the table of houses. Place, therefore, 14° of Gemini
on the cusp of the midheaven, and find its right ascension in
degrees, which will be the same as before, 72° 38', as the 2s. make
only half a minute difference. Add 30° to this right ascension and
it will give the oblique ascension of the 11th house under its pole
of 23° (for the poles of houses are to save trouble), generally taken
in round numbers, namely, 102° 38': now, the right ascension of
21° of Cancer is 112° 43', and its ascensional difference under the
pole of 23° is 9° 53', which, subtracted from the right ascension
(as its declination is north), leaves the oblique ascension, 102° 50',
which is near enough, and consequently 21° of Cancer must be
put on the cusp of the 11th. Add 30° more, for the oblique ascension of the 12th house, which will be 132° 38', and under the pole
of the 12th house, which is 41°, working as before, it will be found
to answer nearly to 22° of Leo. Add 30° more for the oblique ascension of the ascendant, it will give 162° 38', which in the tables
of oblique ascension for the latitude of London will answer to 17°
46' ♍, for the minutes of an angle should always be taken. Add
30° more for the oblique ascension of the 2d house, which has the
same pole as the 12th, and under this pole it will be found to
agree with 10° of Libra, and 30° more being added for the oblique
ascension of the 3d house, which has the same pole as the 11th, it
will answer to 9° of ♏.

By this means a figure may be erected to any latitude by ascensions, as for instance, had this birth been in the latitude of 32°,
with the same longitude, the midheaven would have been the
same, and the right and oblique ascensions the same; but the
poles of the houses would have been different: that of the 11th
and 3d would have been 12°, and that of the 12th and 2d, 23° of
course the oblique ascension of 102° 38', when found by the pole
of 12° instead of 23°, would have placed 16° of Cancer on the cusp
of the 11th, and the oblique ascension of the 12th, 132° 38', would
uuder the pole of 23°, place 17° of Leo on the cusp of the 12th,
and the rest of the houses would have been altered in a similar

proportion.   When, in consequence of those numerous additions of
30°, the ascensions should exceed 360°, that sum must be subtracted, and the remainder will be the oblique ascension.

Having finished the figure (see plate 3, fig. 1.), supposing it to
be a Nativity, we next proceed to Judgement.

♍ ascending, gives a tall, spare body, but compact and well
made, with darkish hair, a round face, rather ruddy, and a small
shrill voice; an ingenious active mind, inclined to cunning, and
well calculated for business of any kind.

The ☾ is particularly fortunate, having no aspect whatever
either to ♄ or ♂ (both of whom are also cadent,) and posited in
the south angle almost on the cusp, in ✶ to ☉, ♀, and ☿, and
joined to Rigel and Bellatrix, two eminent fixed stars.   There can
scarcely be a more fortunate position than this, except she had
received also the △ or ✶ of ♃, but to him also she has no aspect.
Her condition denotes the greatest good fortune, and immense
riches, success in almost every undertaking, and a commanding influence wherever he goes during life.   She, however,
approaches within 3° of ♄'s declination, which renders the native
rather nervous, fearful and peevish, and gives disorders in the
head and stomach.   Her ✶ to ☿, endows the native with tolerably good abilities, which would be excellent were it not for the
condition of ☿, who is combust, and fills the native with a propensity to visionary speculations and pursuits, and no great inclination for learning, although it wonderfully qualifies him for business.   It also renders him active, diligent, and enterprising.   As
she has no aspect to ♂, the native will be deficient in that kind of
acute sharpness, which fits a man for the world, and also in courage, more particularly as she has at the same time an approach to
the declination of ♄.   This declination, however, renders him
more sedate, cautious, careful, and domestic.   Her application to
three planets, gives, it is said, a plurality of wives, and causes
him to form a number of attachments, several of which are of
little value, as both ☿ and ♀ are combust, and the former is retrograde

The ☉ is in his exaltation, but of this I think nothing, and also
succedent, of which I think as little.   Ptolemy says, when the
satellites of the ☉ are angular (by which, according to Placidus,
he means those he aspects,) it gives great dignities, but here the
☾ is the only planet with whom he has any aspect, for I hardly
think that the □ of ♃, being so far from partile, is of any importance: the ☾ cannot well be more powerfully situated.   The midheaven contains a vast number of eminent fixed stars which are

certainly very propitious to a native, and the Lion's Tail, Deneb, occupies the cusp of the ascendant: all of these are signs of fortune, friends, and riches, and serve in a great degree to nullify the ill effects of ☿'s combustion. Indeed, the ☾ angular with Rigel, is one of the most fortunate, favourable, and commanding positions, that can be, and in my opinion more favourable than even the ☌ of Arista, as there are more eminent fixed stars near it.

♄ and ♂ are both cadent. Some think it more propitious for all the planets to be angular, whether infortunes or fortunes, but I should not choose an infortune to be angular: if they give advantages, they are more than over balanced by their evil effects.

♂ and ☿ are both retrograde, which, according to Placidus, is a mark of sickness.

♃ and the ☾ are both angular, although ♃ is in his fall: this weakens ♃ considerably; not because of his fall, but because of his extreme south declination rendering his rays so oblique as scarcely to produce any effect, except one of the luminaries had acquired a similar declination. As to the power of ♄, I own, I cannot consider it in the least diminished, although cadent. Constant experience demonstrates, that the effects of both the luminaries are more evident when they are posited in the 9th than when in the south angles, and I know not why that of ♄ should not be the same. Most of the aspects of the superior planets are good: ♃ is in ⚹ to ♂ and in △ to ♄. There is, indeed, an evil ☍ of ♂ and ♄, which inclines the native to quarrels, and subjects him to disappointments, but as they are not angular, those evils cannot be very severe, or of long duration. ♄ is joined to the Whale's Jaw, Menkar, but it is said to be a star of his own nature, and, as such, of little importance.

The ⊕ with ♂ retrograde and cadent, would be supposed by many, with Ptolemy and Placidus at their head, to be a most direful omen of loss by thieves and swindlers, and, in short, eventual ruin, and the most abject poverty, more especially as it has the ☍ of ♄, but the whole of this doctrine is absurdity and nonsense.

The ☾ being angular, and the luminaries nearly free from affliction, denotes a strength of constitution, and a power in the ☾ to resist an evil direction, and shews the native to be tolerably healthy, with the trifling exceptions above mentioned.

We come now to calculate the directions for the good and evil of the life of the native, and the time of accidents according to the rules already laid down. (See the article "Directions.")

The first thing to be done is to rectify the figure according to the rules laid down (see Rectification.) This may easily be done by bringing the ☾ to the cusp of the 10th (as she is but 12° distant, which makes not the difference of a minute in time,) and regulating the other cusps accordingly; the horoscope would be then 17° 54′ of ♍. A speculum must be likewise made, containing the declinations, latitudes, right and oblique ascensions, semi-arcs, poles ascensional differences, or anything belonging to the planets that the student thinks he may frequently have occasion to refer to (see "Speculum,") after which he will have nothing to do but to calculate the directions.

The first direction in this figure, supposing it to be taken as it stands, without rectifying, would be the ☾ to the cusp of the midheaven, but as this is but a few minutes, and would happen before the infant was a year old, it is of no importance

The next direction is the ☉ to ☌ of ☿, viz. when the ☉ comes to 18° 29′ of ♈.

Right ascension of the midheaven,	72°	38′
Right ascension of 18° 29′ of ♈,	17	2

Right distance of the aspect from the midheaven,	55	36	**Primary** distance.

Right ascension of the midheaven,	72°	38′
Right ascension of the ☉,	13	53

Right distance of the ☉ from the midheaven	58	45

As the Sun's semidiurnal arc, 97° 32′, is to his right distance from the midheaven, 58° 45′, so is the semidiurnal arc of the ☌ (viz. 18° 29′ of Aries.) 99° 23′, to the secondary

distance of the ☌,	59°	52′
Primary distance of the aspect,	55	36

Arc of direction,	4	16
To equate it to time, add the ☉'s right ascension,	13	53

It gives	18	9

which look for in the tables of right ascension, and it will be found to answer to 19° 41′ of Aries, at which the Sun will be found in the ephemeris to arrive in 4 days and about 16 hours, equal to four years, 8 months, about December, 1798.

The ☉ to the ☌ of ♀, it falls in 19° 12′ of ♈.

Right ascension of the midheaven,	72° 38′	
Right ascension of 19° 12′ of ♈,	17 42	

Right distance of 19° 12′ of ♈,	54 56	Primary distance.

Right ascension of the midheaven,	72 38
Right ascension of the ☉,	13 53

☉'s right distance	58 45

As the Semidiurnal arc of the Sun, 97° 32′, is to his right distance, 58° 45′, so is the Semidiurnal arc of the ☌, 99° 46′, to the secondary distance   60° 6′
Subtract the primary distance,   54 56

Arc of direction,	5 10

amounting, when equated, to about 5 years, 5 months, or to September, 1799.

Auriga's left shoulder, Capella, to the midheaven.

Right ascension of Capella,	75° 18′
Right ascension of the midheaven,	72 38

Arc of direction,	2 40

Orion's Foot, Rigel, to the midheaven.

Right ascension of Rigel,	76° 7′
Right ascension of the midheaven,	72 38

Arc of direction,	3 29

Orion's right shoulder, Betelguese, to the midheaven.

Right ascension of Betelguese,	82° 36′
Right ascension of the midheaven,	72 38

Arc of direction,	9 58,

equal to about 11 years, all but a month, March, 1805.

All those directions happen during the youth of the native, when their effects are said to be transferred to the parents or guardians, who have the care of the native, provided the fortune of the latter be affected by any change in their circumstances. I have no opinion of the effects of these stars being directed to the cusp of the midheaven: in the present figure, they are in the midheaven already, and their approach to its cusp is gradual, and cannot well be productive of any sudden change in the life or affairs of the native, though they may probably operate, as they culminate by slow and almost indistinct progression. The ✶ of the ☉ to the cusp of the 10th, gives only 6° 16′ for an arc of direction, so that the native could not be above 7 years old at the time.

The first aspect of importance is the mundane ✶ of ♀ to the midheaven, which Placidus thinks is an aspect of much consequence in improving the native's condition. It is taken as follows:

Right ascension of ♀,	18°	6′
Add ⅔ of the semidiurnal ascension,	65	29
	83	35
Subtract the right ascension of the midheaven,	72	38
Arc of direction,	10	57

This direction coincides with 12 years exactly, April, 1806.

Mundane ✶ of ☿ to the midheaven.

Right ascension of ☿,	16°	0′
Add ⅔ of his semidiurnal ascension,	68	14
	84	14
Subtract the right ascension of the midheaven,	72	38
Arc of direction,	11	36

answering to 12 years, and nearly 8 months, end of December, 1806.

This direction could be of little benefit, as ☿ is combust and retrograde.

The ☾ to the zodiacal quintile of the ☉: it falls in 27° 5′ of Gemini, where the Moon will have 4° 22′ south lat.

Oblique ascension of 27° 5′ Gemini, under the Moon's pole of

0° 29′, with 4° 22′ south lat., which she will have there, 87° 6′
Oblique arcension of the ☽ under her pole, with
   her original latitude, 73 17

                 Arc of direction, 13 49
Add the ☉'s right ascension for equation, 13 53

           It gives the right ascension of 27 42,
which answers to 29° 48′ of ♈, at which the ☉ arrives in 15 days,
and about an hour, equal to 15 years and about a fortnight, in
April, 1809.

The ☽ to the zodiacal quintile of ☿ : it falls in 0° 30′ of ♋,
where she will have 4° 12′ south latitude.
Oblique ascension of 0° 30′ of Cancer, under the
   Moon's pole, with 4° 12′ south lat. 90° 43′
Oblique ascension of the ☽ as before, 73 17

           Arc of direction, 17 26,
which when equated as before, answers to 3° 33′ of ♉, at which
the ☉ arrives in 18 days, 21 hours, equal to 18 years and nearly
11 months, about the end of February, 1813.

The ☽ to the zodiacal quintile of ♀ : it falls in 1° 12′ of Cancer, where she will have 4° 8′ south latitude.
Oblique ascension of 1° 12′ of ♋, with 4° 8′
   south lat. 91° 27′
Oblique ascension of the ☽ as before, 73 17

           Arc of direction, 18 10,
answering to 19 years, 8 months, December, 1813.
   These three quintiles are very different in their effects: the first,
of the ☉, is the most beneficial, as he is wholly free from affliction; and it causes some remarkable change in the affairs of the
native, and generally raises him to dignity and happiness. The
quintile of ☿ is of little value. as he is combust and retrograde, if
the latter quality be an evil, of which I often doubt. ♀ is also
combust, and consequently cannot be of much service.

The ☉ to the quintile of the midheaven.
   To direct the ☉ to the quintile, we may as well first direct it to
the ✶ mentioned before.

Right ascension of the ☉,   13° 53′
Add ⅔ of his semidiurnal arc,   65   1

                                                             78 54
Subtract the right ascension of the midheaven,   72 38

Arc of direction to the ✳,   6 16
Add one-fifth of the Sun's ✳ for the quintile,   13   0

                Arc of direction to the quintile,   19 16
answering to 20 years, and nearly 11 months, about the end of
February, 1815.

This is supposed by Placidus to be a very fortunate direction
both for honours and riches.

The ☾ to the ☍ of ♃ in the zodiac: it falls in 3° 21′ of Cancer,
where she has 4° 2′ south lat.
Oblique ascension of the aspect under the ☾'s
  pole, with her latitude there,   93° 24′
Oblique ascension of the ☾ with her own lati-
  tude taken under her pole,   73 17

                        Arc of direction,   20   7
answering, when equated, to 21 years, 9 months, January, 1816.

It is generally supposed, that evil aspects with good planets, or
good aspects of evil planets, have no effect, as the aspect and the
planet, being of opposite tendency, completely neutralize each
other: this doctrine cannot be rational, for when a planet receives
the influence of another, some effect must be produced, the nature
of which is at present unknown, for want of proper investigation.
I have little doubt the ☍ of ♃ is productive of slight evil of some
kind, though not so tremendous in its effects as if it proceeded
from ♄ or ♂.

The ☾ to the mundane ☍ of ♃.
Right ascension of ♃ with latitude,   273° 39′
Add for the opposition,   180   0

                                                             453 39
Being more than the circle, subtract   360   0

                                                             93   39
Right ascension of the ☾, with latitude,   73   26

                        Arc of direction,   20 13
equal to 21 years, 10 months, February, 1816.

The horoscope to the mundane □ of ♃.

Oblique ascension of ♃, with latitude,	306°	5′
Seminocturnal arc of ♃,	122	26
	183	39
Oblique ascension of the horoscope,	162	38
Arc of direction,	21	1

We may as well, while we are at it, find his mundane quintile and ✶ to the horoscope, as follows:

Arc of direction to the □,	21°	1′
Add ⅓ of the seminocturnal arc of ♃,	40	38
Arc of direction to the ✶,	61	39
Subtract ⅓ of the sextile,	16	19
Arc of direction to the quintile,	45	20

This is making short work of them, and serves as an example how easily one mundane aspect may be taken from another. The □ answers to 22 years, 8 months; the quintile to 47 years, 8 months; and the ✶ to 63 years, 8 months: the two last are said to be good, but I have not the same opinion of them as Placidus had. They answer to the same month, December, in the years 1816, 1841, and 1857.

The three following aspects are more likely to be depended on, though I cannot be certain as to their effects.

The horoscope to the zodiacal □ of ♃.

Oblique ascension of 3° 21′ of ♎,	184°	45′
Oblique ascension of the horoscope,	162	38
Arc of direction,	22	7,

equal to 23 years, 10 months, February, 1818.

The horoscope to the zodiacal quintile of ♃: it falls of course, (by adding 18°, the difference between the □ and quintile), in 21° 21′ of ♎.

Oblique ascension of 21° 21′ of ♎,	210°	22′
Oblique ascension of the horoscope,	162	38
Arc of direction,	47	44

equal to 50 years, and a few days, April, 1844.

The horoscope to the ✳ of ♃.

Oblique ascension of 3° 21' of ♏,	227° 33'
Oblique ascension of the horoscope,	162 38
Arc of direction,	64 55

equal to 66 years, 10 months February, 1860.

These last two directions, if they operate, will be favourable.

It will be superfluous to direct the other planets to the mundane aspects to the midheaven, as they may be easily calculated. The following is an example:

The midheaven to the mundance ✳ of ♀.

Right ascension of ♀,	18° 6'
Add ⅜ of her semidiurnal arc,	65 29
	83 35
Right ascension of the midheaven,	72 38
Arc of direction,	10 57
Add one-fifth of her sextile,	13 6
Arc of direction to her quintile,	24 3
Add one-fifth of her semidiurnal arc to make the □,	19 39
Arc of direction to the □,	43 42

The mundane directions to the horoscope are made in the same way, using oblique instead of right ascension.

The ☽ to the mundane parallel of ♃, converse motion.

Right ascension of the ☽,	73° 26'
Right ascension of the midheaven,	72 38

Distance of the ☽ from the midheaven, 0 48, primary distance.

Right ascension of ♃,	273° 39'
Right ascension of the Imum Cœli,	252 38

Distance of ♃ from the Imum Cœli, 21 1

As the seminocturnal arc of ♃, 122° 26', is to his distance from the Imum Cœli, 21° 1', so is the semidiurnal arc of the Moon, 113° 35', to her secondary distance from the midheaven, 19° 28'.

As one is from the ascending and the other from the descending side of the midheaven, add their primary and secondary distances together.

Primary distance of the Moon from the midheaven,   0° 48′
Secondary dist. of the Moon from the midheaven,   19   28

Arc of direction,   20   16

answering to 21 years, 11 months, March, 1816.

This is one of Placidus's good directions, but there is little reason to suppose it has any efficacy.

The Moon to a parallel of the declination of ♃.

When the Moon comes to 8° 28′ of ♋, she acquires 19° 26′ of north declination, but this she never exceeds on this occasion, owing to her great south latitude, which is 3° 46′; of course her declination falls short of that of ♃ by 3° 36′.

Oblique ascension of 8° 28′ of ♋, taken under the
    pole of the ☾, with 3° 46′, south latitude,   98° 49
Oblique ascension of the ☾ under her pole,   73   17

Arc of direction,   25   32,

answering to 27 years, 6 months, October, 1821.

This, had it been complete, would have been an eminent direction for health and prosperity, but it is weak in proportion to its deficiency. It helps to relieve the malignant effects of the radical declination of ♄. Its good effects will endure until the native is turned of 40 years, after which it manifestly declines until the ☾ again falls back upon the declination of ♄.

The ☾ to the zodiacal △ of ♂: it falls of course in 10° 16′ of ♋, where she has 3° 48′ south latitude.

Oblique ascension of 10° 16′ of ♋, under the
    ☾'s pole, with 3° 48′ south latitude,   100° 40′
Oblique ascension of the ☾, with her own
    latitude,   73   17

Arc of direction,   27   23

equal to 29 years, and above 4 months, August, 1823.

This is said to cause military honours and preferment, but, like all aspects of evil planets, it generally leads to dangers and difficulties. As we are upon this subject, I shall insert the △ of ♂ to the midheaven, which is said to be a sure presage of military preferment and victory. But ♂, being retrograde and cadent, would threaten defeat, or, they say, damp the native's courage.

Right ascension of ♂,   218° 26′
⅔ of his seminocturnal ascension,   71 25

                                                         289 51
Right ascension of the Imum Cœli,   252 38
                                                         ─────
            Arc of direction,   37 13

This gives the ✳ to the 4th house, which is the △ to the midheaven. It answers to 39 years, 6 months, Oct. 1833.
I have not much faith in this direction.

The ☾ to the mundane ☌ of ♄, converse motion.
Right ascension of the ☾ with latitude,   73° 26′
Right ascension of ♄ with latitude,   42 51
                                                         ─────
            Arc of direction,   30 35
equal to 32 years, and above 8 months, December, 1826.
   This, according to Placidus, would be a fatal direction, as the
☾ is hyleg: but I should in point of time first have directed the
☉ to the ☌ of ♄ *in mundo*.

The ☉ to the mundane ☌ of ♄, direct motion.
Oblique descension of ♄, under the pole of the
   ☉, with latitude,   45° 52′
Oblique descension of the ☉, under his own pole,   18 13
                                                         ─────
            Arc of direction,   27 39
It answers to 29 years, and 8 months, December, 1823.
   This direction would, according to Placidus, cause great sickness or disgrace, though as the ☉ is not hyleg, it would not affect
life, unless united with some other fatal direction: however, it is
but a mundane direction.

The ☉ to the zodiacal ☍ of ♂ : it falls in 10° 16′ of ♉.
Right ascension of the midheaven,   72° 38′
Right ascension of the ☍ of ♂, with contrary
   latitude,   38 26
                                                         ─────
Primary distance of ♂ from the midheaven,   34 12

Right ascension of the midheaven,   72 38
Right ascension of the ☉,   13 53
                                                         ─────
Distance of the ☉ from the midheaven,   58 45

As the Sun's semidiurnal arc, 6*h*. 30*m*., is to his right distance, 58° 45′, so is the semidiurnal ascension of the opposition of ♂, 7*h*. 9*m*., to his secondary distance,   64° 37′
                    Primary distance,   34 12
                                                         ————
                    Arc of direction,   30 25,
answering to 32 years, 7 months, November, 1826.

This would be a dangerous time to the native through sickness or some accident which would probably have a lasting effect, as it is followed by the ☌ of ♄. Very fortunately it is not the ☾, or the consequence might be fatal. Mars, however, has some north latitude, which would relieve the evil considerably, and, if the lunation that precedes it be not evil, the danger is considerably lessened.

              The ☉ to the zodiacal ☌ of ♄.
Right ascension of the midheaven,   72° 38′
Right ascension of ♄,   42 51
                                                ————
Primary distance of ♄ from the midheaven,   29 47

Right ascension of the midheaven,   72 38
Right ascension of the ☉,   13 53
                                                ————
Distance of the ☉ from the midheaven,   58 45

As the ☉'s semidiurnal arc, 97° 32′, is to his right distance, 58° 45′, so is the semidiurnal arc of ♄, 108° 43′, to his secondary distance,   64° 23′
            Primary distance,   29 47
                                                 ————
                    Arc of direction,   34 36
amounting to 37 years, 9 months, nearly, January, 1831.

This is also an evil direction, and would be dangerous were the ☉ hyleg, It threatens disease, loss, trouble, and disappointment, but the great south latitude of ♄ will do away much of the evil, though much depends, as before, on the preceding lunation.

The ☾ to the zodiacal □ of the ☉; it falls of course in 15° 6′ of Cancer, where she will have 3° 20′ south latitude.
Oblique ascension of 15° 6′ of Cancer, under the ☾'s pole, with her latitude there,   105° 49′
Oblique ascension of the ☾, under her pole, with original latitude,   73 17
                                                 ————
            Arc of direction,   32 32

answering to 34 years, and nearly 9 months, December, 1828.

This is a very evil and perilous direction, threatening sickness and much danger; also loss of property or disgrace. The ☾, however, approaches the declination of ♃, which is some assistance, and being originally strong, and the native young, it is not likely to be fatal; much, however, depends on the preceding lunation.

The ☾ to the zodiacal □ of ☿ : in 18° 29′ of ♋, where she has 3° 5′, south latitude.

Oblique ascension of 18° 29′ of Cancer, under the
    Moon's pole, as before,   109° 23′
Oblique ascension of the Moon,   73 17

                  Arc of direction,   36   6,
equal to 38 years, and about 5 months, September, 1832.

This also is an evil direction, and threatens much disorder in the head and stomach. She still, however, hovers near the declination of ♃, which affords some assistance, but the native about this time would be very sickly and unfortunate.

The □ of ♀ follows in about a year after, which, although not dangerous to health, in some degree prolongs the troubles of the native.

The ☾ to the zodiacal △ of the horoscope.
Oblique ascension of 14° 12′ of ♎, the △ of the Moon, 200° 9′
Oblique ascension of the horoscope,   162 38

                  Arc of direction,   37 31,
equal to 39 years, 10 months, February, 1834.

The Moon to the mundane trine of the horoscope.
Oblique ascension of the Moon under the pole of the horoscope
    with latitude,   49° 51′
Four-thirds of the Moon's semidiurnal arc,   151 27

                                       201 18
Oblique ascension of the horoscope,   162 38

                  Arc of direction,   38 40
equal to 41 years, April, 1835,

These directions, if they take place are good ones. Of the mundane △ I have less opinion; the zodiacal △ is more likely to be depended on; but I am uncertain of the efficacy of any direction of the horoscope, except to conjunctions. These trines are said to denote good health and prosperity.

The Moon to the biquintile of ♃ in the zodiac; it falls in 9° 21′ of ♌, where she will have 1° 27′ south latitude.

Oblique ascension of 9° 21′ of ♌ (with latitude.) under the Moon's pole,   131° 16′

Oblique ascension of the Moon under her pole, with original latitude,   73 17

Arc of direction,   57 59,

equal to 60 years, 2 months, June, 1854.

This is a good direction, denoting recovery from sickness, or good health and fortune.

The Moon to the zodiacal □ of ♂ : in 10° 16′ of Leo, where she will have 1° 22′ south latitude.

Oblique ascension of 10° 16′ of Leo, under the Moon's pole with latitude,   132° 12′

Oblique ascension of the Moon,   73 17

Arc of direction,   58 55,

equal to 57 years, April, 1851.

This is a dangerous direction, as the Moon has no assistance from the benefics except the separating biquintile of ♃, and should it be preceded by an evil lunation, the consequences would be fatal.

The Moon to the square of ♄ in the zodiac: in 14° 42′ of Leo, where she will have 1° 3′ south latitude.

Oblique ascension of 14° 42′ of Leo,   136° 44′

Oblique ascension of the Moon,   73 17

Arc of Direction,   63 27,

equal to 61 years, 5 months, September, 1855.

This is a more dangerous direction than the last, as the Moon is hastening fast to the declination of ♄. She is, indeed, hastening to a △ of the ☉, which happens about 5 months after, but I am not certain that the opinions of those are correct, who assert that the ☉ will operate as a benefic from being joined to ♀.

The ☾ to the declination of ♄.

She meets the parallel of ♄'s declination in 20° 24′ of Leo, where she will have 0° 27′, south latitude, and 14° 17′ north declination.

Oblique ascension of 20° 24′ of Leo, under the ☾'s pole,	142° 34′
Oblique ascension of the ☾,	73 17
Arc of direction,	73 18

answering to 23° 43′ of ♊, at which the ☉ arrives in 71 days, 1 hour, equal to about 71 years, viz. in April, 1865. This is the *terminus vitæ*, as the parallel of the declinatien of ♂ immediately follows.

Those who choose to direct the Part of Fortune, must first place it according to the rule of Negusantius, as follows:

Oblique ascension of the horoscope,	162° 38′
Oblique ascension of the ☉, in the pole of the horoscope,	6 21
	156 17
Right ascension of the ☾,	73 26
Right ascension of the ⊕,	229 43
Ascensional difference,	23 35
Oblique ascension,	206 8

The ⊕ to the mundane ☌ of ♂, direct motion.

As the horary time of the ⊕, 11° 4′, is to its distance from the imum cœli, 22° 55′, so is the horary time of ♂ to his secondary distance, 36° 58′. Subtract his primary distance, 34° 12′ from this, and it leaves the arc of direction, 2deg. 46min.

The ⊕ to the mundane ☍ of ♄, direct motion.

As the horary time of the ⊕, 11deg. 4min., is to its distance from the imum cœli, 22deg. 55min., so is the horary time of ♄, 18deg. 7min., to his secondary distance from the midheaven, 35deg 0min. Subtract from this his primary distance, 29deg. 47min., it leaves the arc of direction, 5deg. 13min.

These are very evil directions to those who believe in the efficacy of the ⊕, and as they happen in the youth of a native they are supposed to injure him through the medium of his parents, by destroying their property and reputation.

According to Negusantius, the Part of Fortune always remains fixed in its horary circle, waiting for the coming of the aspects, and, therefore, he thinks it cannot be directed conversely; neither can it be directed zodiacally, because it has nothing to do with the zodiac.

These are most of the principal directions, and from these the student will easily perceive the method of calculating the rest. One principal direction, however, I have omitted, which is the ☽ to the zodiacal sesquiquadrate of ♂: it falls in 25deg. 16min. of ♊, where the ☽ has 4deg. 28min. south latitude.

Oblique ascension of 25 deg, 16min. of ♊,
    under the ☽'s pole,   84° 49
Oblique ascension of the ☽,   73 17

                    Arc of direction,   11 32

equal to 12 years, 6 months, Nov. 1806. It denotes some accident by a blow, cut, stab, or fever, that may endanger life.

The body of ♂ to the horoscope may be calculated zodiacally, as follows:

Oblique ascension of ♂ in the pole of the horoscope, 235° 34′
Oblique ascension of the horoscope,   162 38

                    Arc of direction,   72 56,

which answers, within a few months, to the *terminus vitæ*, and renders that event still more certain.

I have repeatedly reminded the reader, that the result of these directions depends greatly on the nature of the preceding quadrate lunations, and that their effects may be considerably accelerated or retarded by a long succession of these lunations, as the ☽ happens to be in the ☌, □, or ☍, to the ☉, in the good or evil parts of the figure. It is likewise probable, that the power of these lunations will be greater or less in proportion to the proximity of the Moon to her nodes, not from any power in the nodes themselves, but because the Moon in those places receives the rays of the ☉ more powerfully. This is the foundation of Ptolemy's doctrine of Eclipses, which he considered as having such eminent influence in the affairs of men and things, in all places where they were seen, because at those places the ☌ and ☍ is most partile, whereas in those parts of the globe where the eclipse did not take place, the increased latitude diminished the effects of the lunation. It should, however, be observed, that Ptolemy is not sufficiently explicit in this doctrine, for whether the eclipse be visible or not, its effects will be the same to those who live under the same horary circle in which it is visible, for the interposition of the Earth does not hinder the effect of the luminaries, as is evident in the flux and reflux of the tide, which are as great when the luminaries are in their nadir as when they are in their zenith.

I am, however, fully persuaded, that the doctrine of primary directions has many defects, which will require much application and deep research to eradicate. I have often found them to fail: and as to mundane directions, except to the angles, they can have no foundation in nature. What Placidus could be about when he rejected the zodiacal aspects in favour of the mundane I cannot imagine: he soon found out his error, for he uses them abundantly in his *Primum Mobile*. The parallel of declination is, in my opinion, an unobjectionable aspect: I have always found its effects coincide, and I would advise every student, not to reject it without the clearest proof of its inefficacy. The error relating to that unmeaning point, the ⊕, was, I imagine, chiefly founded on the known and obvious effects of the lunar declination, at least, this was the groundwork of the doctrine of Negusantius, which Placidus adopted. Those who peruse the Thirty Nativities of Placidus will not fail to perceive a strange and remarkable coincidence in their fatal periods with the times of the declination of the luminaries. To these I shall add a more modern example, of an event which must, in my opinion, at least, be wholly owing to an anaretic power operating upon a lunar parallel of declination.

Nativity of Her Royal Highness the Princess Charlotte of Wales and Saxe Cobourg.

(See the Frontispiece.)

The position of ♃ in ♒, near the cusp of the horoscope, and nearly conjoined with ♀, is indicative of the best disposition, and the purest mind; for with the exception of ♎, there is no sign gives more perfection of body and mind than ♒. The ⚹ of ☿ with ♂, gives spirit and acuteness, but as the aspect is good, the temper, though probably hasty, is neither malignant nor irascible. The zodiacal parallel of the ☾ with ♄, denotes great irratibility of nerve, with a strong disposition to disease, and as the ☾ is hyleg, it also denotes the disease to have a tendency towards premature dissolution: so close a parallel as this, wanting only 8 minutes of a partile aspect, must have destroyed life shortly after the birth, had it not been for the zodiacal parallel of ♀ concurring within 9′ with that of ♄, but the position of the latter was northern and commanding, which, from his nearer approximation to our zenith, rendered him more powerful than ♀, she had, however, weakened his power in every respect, for although the radical ☾ was within orb of ♄'s ☍, she had the ⚹ of ♀ at the same time, and also the additional ⚹ of ♃, who was more angular than ♄, and only inferior from his southern position. The native's life was therefore preserved for a time, but there was no aspect sufficiently powerful to counteract the declination of ♄, whose malignity was wonderfully increased by the presence of Aldebaran, nor indeed is it probable that so close a parallel can ever be wholly neutralized: its effects are extreme nervous debility, affecting occasionally the whole frame, but mostly perceptible in the head and stomach, and its diseases are grief, agitation, lowness of spirits, a propensity to retirement and solitude, and a system so reduced as to be unequal to support any shock it may receive from a subsequent malevolent direction.

The ☾ is hyleg both according to Ptolemy and to reason (a distinction that should always be made), and being in the chief angle, becomes a very powerful significator of life. In 21 years and about 10 months she comes nearly to a parallel of the ☉'s declination in 6° 45' of ♑, where she has 1° 5' of north latitude, and acquires about 22° 13' of south declination: this is not the full declination of the ☉, which is 22° 24', but owing to her north latitude, she does not acquire more than 22° 13' or 14', before her declination begins to diminish. The calculation is as follows:

The semidiurnal arc of the ☾ is 63° 12', which gives 21° 4' for the space of her house, or double horary time.

The polar elevation of the 11th house, for the latitude of London, is 23° 27'.

Right ascension of the Moon,	254° 22'
Right ascension of the midheaven,	249 25
	—— ——
Distance of the Moon from the midheaven,	4 57

As the Moon's double horary time, 21° 4', is to the polar difference of the 10th and 11th houses, 23° 27' so is the Moon's distance from the 10th, 4° 57', to her pole 6°.

The oblique ascension of 6° 45' of ♑, under the pole of 6°, with 1° 5' of north latitude, which the Moon has there, is	279° 46'
Oblique ascension of the Moon under her pole of 6°, with her radical latitude of 2° 50' north, is	256 34
	—— ——
Arc of direction,	23 12
Add the Sun's right ascension,	288 22
	—— ——
	311 34

This is the right ascension of 9° 7′ of ♒, at which the ☉ arrives in about 21 days, 20 hours, equal to 21 years, 10 months, the exact time of the native's death. This time is too exact to be correct, for the luminaries always operate in zodiacal parallel before the direction is complete, owing, as Placidus thinks, to the magnitude of their bodies, which produces the effect before their centers have time to arrive at the true point of declination, and of this he gives several instances: but I have already observed, that the Moon in this geniture never acquires the full declination of the ☉ within 9 or 10 minutes, which was near enough to produce the fatal catastrophe, and had she kept on declining to the southward the native would have died at the same time, before the completion of the aspect.

The secondary direction is as follows:

Had the native lived 22 years, 22 days must have been added to the nativity, but as it was only 21 years, 10 months, 4 hours must be deducted for the odd 2 months, which will bring the time of the secondary direction to the 29th of January, 1796, at 5h. 26m, A. M. (for I have allowed 2 minutes for the few odd hours) when the places of the planets were as follows:

	♅ ♍	♄ ♊	♃ ♒	♂ ♏	☉ ♒	♀ ♓	☿ ♒	☽ ♎
	° ′	° ′	° ′	° ′	° ′	° ′	° ′	° ′
Lon.	7 12R	6 48R	17 19	20 54	9 8	4 21	18 21	9 16
Lat.	N. 0 48	S. 1 41	S. 0 42	N. 1 7		S. 1 30	S. 1 55	N. 5 7
Decln.	N. 9 36	S. 19 47	S. 16 4	N. 15 43	S. 17 51	S. 11 25	S. 17 29	N. 1 4

On the 6th of November, the time of death, the places of the planets were as follows:

	♅ ♐	♄ ♒	♃ ♐	♂ ♊	☉ ♏	♀ ♎	☿ ♎	☽ ♎
	° ′	° ′	° ′	° ′	° ′	° ′	° ′	° ′
Lon.	13 33	29 22	13 25	25 54	13 21	13 10	29 8	1 46
Lat.	N. 0 1	S. 1 45	N. 0 23	N. 0 54		N. 1 42	N. 1 45	N. 3 49
Decln.	S. 22 27	S. 13 21	S. 22 4	N. 24 18	S. 15 52	S. 3 38	S. 9 32	N. 2 48

In the secondary direction there appears to be little cause for the dire catastrophe which followed. The Moon, indeed, was applying to the radical Square of Mercury, and afterwards of the Sun, but she also applied to the △ of ♃, and was separating from the △ of ♀, within orb: this therefore could have no material effect, neither does there appear on the day of death any fatal transit or ingress, so that we must refer to the lunations that more immediately precede it. The first of these was a full moon on the 23d of October, in 1° 19′ of Gemini, where she had 21° 32′ of N. declination, by which means she partook of the radical declinations both of the ☉ and ♄, for she lay between them. The ☉ also at the same time had the radical declination both of ♄ and the ☾, so that there was a mutual and fatal interchange of declination between them.

The ☾ formed her last quadrature with the ☉, four days before the day of death, when the ☉ was in 9° 39′ of ♏, very near the radical place of ♂, and consequently a most malignant position, and, what is particularly deserving of attention, the ☾ had at that instant the same declination exactly as she had at the full, viz, 21° 30′ north, still moving between the radical declination of the ☉ and ♄, and being at the same time within 1° 31′ of the radical □ of ♂, she being in 9° 39′ of ♌; and the Sun having at that moment nearly the declination of ♂ in the radix, viz. 14° 40′ south, and the declination of ♄ on the day of death.

I have not an Ephemeris handy to calculate the Moon's process, nor would it be worth the trouble, after such a singular chain of circumstances as these, sufficiently powerful in themselves to render any progressive position, whether good or bad, entirely unavailing.

The absurdity and fallacy of the doctrine of terms, may be fully seen in this instance: for the ☉ and ♄ in the radix were both in the terms of ♃, a circumstance that would have had much weight with Placidus; though it is of no importance in the operations of nature.

It is worth observing, that both in the secondary direction and the time of death, the ☾ was in ♎, applying to a □ of the anaretic place as well as of ☿ and the ☉ in the radix: but I do not mention this as having had any particular effect, but wherever there is anything like a striking coincidence, it should always be noticed, as we thereby are often enabled to make discoveries.

The hour of death was probably regulated wholly by the mundane position of the ☉, who generally causes an important crisis when he is elongated ⅓ of his semi-arc either beyond the north or south angles, namely, about 2 in the morning or afternoon.

Why the ☉ should in the primary direction operate as anareta by his parallel is not, perhaps, so easily explained, and I confess I at one time suspected the ☉ not to be anaretic, though Placidus is of a different opinion, and this nativity seems to confirm it. He, however, would lay great stress upon the sign the Sun was in being the house of ♄ and exaltation of ♂, and that it in a great measure derived its anaretic quality from these circumstances. These pretended causes have no foundation in nature, and if ever the Sun operated as anareta, it was likely to do so in this nativity, for with the exception of the declination of ♀, it had no kind of connexion with the fortunes in any way; and even this was fully balanced by the zodiacal parallel of ♄ to the ☾, if what is observed by authors in general be true, that the lights acquire the nature of those planets they are in aspect with, the Sun must have partaken wholly of the nature of ♄ and ♂, for he was within orbs of the zodiacal □ of ♂ and sesquiquadrate of ♄ : but the Sun probably operates upon the ☾ more by his own proper influence than from any secondary cause, and it is very probable that his dry and heating nature may have a similar effect to that of ♂, when the ☾ is principally hyleg, as she undoubtedly is, when posited in the midheaven.

The marriage of Her Royal Highness took place on the direction of ♃ to the ✳ of the midheaven.

Right ascension of ♃,	314°	52′
Subtract from this ⅔ of his semidiurnal arc,	44	8
	270	44
Right ascension of the midheaven,	249	25
Arc of direction,	21	19
Add the Sun's right ascension,	288	22
	309	41

which is equal to the right ascension of 7° 16′ of ♒, at which the Sun arrives in 20 days from the time or birth, answering to 20 years of the native's life, viz. January, 1816. The marriage took place on the 2d of May, that year, and had the given time of birth been given for only a minute sooner, which is a very small difference, it would have brought the time of direction 3 months later, which shews how correctly the time of birth was taken, as a minute of time either way may be lost or gained in the course of calculation.

The ✳ of ♀ to the midheaven preceded that of ♃ about 2 years and a half, at which time probably she may have had an offer of marriage, but the ✳ of ♀ was too imperfect in many respects to effect any thing: she had already passed the zodiacal ✳ of the midheaven, and had separated above her whole orb from the ✳ of the ☾, so that she was deprived of the lunar testimony (which is of the utmost consequence in all cases) and she was more cadent than ♃.

♃ on the contrary was in zodiacal ✳ to the very cusp almost of the midheaven, and had only separated from that of the ☾ about 3 degrees, a very material circumstance, for it is always observed that promittors having a lunar testimony, are always strong in directions (particularly if the ☾ be angular,) whether good or evil.

Of all directions, I have been most divided in opinion respecting those of the angles, because they are seldom verified by their events. I, however, suspect this to be owing to the incorrectness of time, for when we consider that the midheaven will by a mistake of only 4 minutes differ a whole year in direction, we need not wonder, considering how inaccurately times of births are taken, that directions to angles are so seldom correct to time. Those of the horoscope differ still more widely, but where the time, as in the present instance, is very correct, there can be little doubt of their effect, it also shews that a promittor should not be blindly depended upon, merely as such, but its strength and fitness to cause events should be well weighed and considered, and particularly its connexion with the ☾. In cases of marriage, the youth of the party ought to be considered, for in the foregoing directions that of ♀, had she been stronger, was less likely to produce such an event than that of ♃, because the native was not arrived at such a degree of maturity. But she disposed the native to agree with the ✳ of ♃, so that the second direction was in all respects the most fit to be depended on. The exactness of the directions in this nativity shew the necessity of taking the most illustrious births as examples, when they can be procured. Those who are in attendance on those occasions are in no want of the means of being correct as to the time, and this is everything.

FIRST MOVER, the *Primum Mobile*, or Firmament.

FIXED SIGNS, Taurus, Leo, Scorpio, and Aquaries, because the seasons, according to some, and the weather, according to others, become more fixed when the Sun enters those signs. The temper of those born under them is said to be more fixed, and any thing over which they preside has more stability: thus, a tree planted, a house built, or a city founded, when a fixed sign ascends, and the luminaries are in fixed signs, will be more durable. Significators of events in fixed signs forward events more slowly than when in a tropical or common sign, but render their effects more lasting: their effects, however, relate chiefly to horary questions.

FIXED STARS, All stars, except the planets, are called fixed, because they appear to remain stationary, and have no periodical revolution around the Sun. They are said, in astrology, to cast no rays: the meaning of which is, that they do not operate on the planets by ✳, ☐, △, or any other way, except when in conjunction. In this position they increase, diminish, or alter their influence, according to their nature. Stars of the first magnitude are said to have great power, those of the second magnitude less, and they seldom operate beyond the fourth magnitude, except when in a nebulous cluster, as the Pleiades, Præspe, &c. They are mor powerful in angles, and, like the planets, very weak when cadent. They are also most powerful with north latitude and declination, and, very weak when much to the southward. They are said not to be so injurious with a planet of their own nature, but will be productive of good although the star and planet be evil, as if ♂ be with Aldebaran, a star of his own nature, he will cause great good fortune to the native: this seems rather absurd. When they are within 5° of the cusp of a cardinal house, or a body of a planet, their names should be inserted in every figure, whether of a nativity or horary question, and, to enable the student to find their places, I here subjoin a table of the longitude and latitude of those that are most remarkable among them, calculated to the year 1820. Their places, although they may not be exact to a minute, will be fully sufficient for every astrological purpose.

From these longitudes and latitudes, their ascensions, descensions, and declinations, may be found in the tables, like those of the planets. The only difference between them is, that the latitudes of the fixed stars are greater, and beyond the reach of a table which only extends to 9° of latitude north or south: but their proportions are the same, and therefore the common difference of a degree of latitude may be multiplied to any extent the latitude of the star requires. Thus, the latitude of Caput Algol is 22° 24', north; longitude, 23° 40' of ♉ : in the table of declination north latitude, I find 23° 40' of ♉ gives about 18° 45' north declination without latitude: I likewise find, that every degree of north latitude gives about 58' more declination; I therefore multiply 58' by 22, the number of its degrees in north latitude; it gives 21° 16' and the odd 24' of latitude gives 23' more, making, in all, 21° 39' of declination, which, when added to the 18° 45', already obtained, gives, on the whole, 40° 25' for the star's declination north, which

Names.	Signs.	Longitude.	Latitude.	Magnitude.	Nature.
		° ′	° ′		
South end of the Whale,	♈	0 58	20 46 *S.*	2	♄
Andromeda's Head,	♈	11 54	25 40 *N.*	2	♃ ♀
Whale's Belly,	♈	15 31	25 0 *S.*	4	♄
Andromeda's Girdle, Mirach,	♈	27 55	25 57 *N.*	2	♀
Ram's following Horn,	♉	5 8	9 57 *N.*	2	♄ ♂
Andromeda's left Foot, Almach,	♉	11 40	27 41 *N.*	2	♀
Whale's Jaw, Menkar,	♉	11 47	12 35 *S.*	2	♄
Medusa's Head, Caput Algol,	♉	23 40	22 24 *N.*	2	♄ ♃
The Pleiades,	♉	26 42	4 31 *N.*	5	♂ ☾
Brightest of the Seven Stars,	♉	27 37	4 2 *N.*	3	♂ ☾
Bull's North Eye, Occulus Taurus,	♊	5 58	2 36 *S.*	3	♀
Bull's South Eye, Aldebaran,	♊	7 18	5 29 *S.*	1	♂
Orion's left Foot, Rigel,	♊	14 18	31 7 *S.*	1	♃ ♄
Orion's left Shoulder, Bellatrix,	♊	18 26	16 51 *S.*	2	♂ ☿
Auriga's left Shoulder, Capella,	♊	19 20	22 51 *N.*	1	☿ ♂
Bull's North Horn,	♊	20 4	5 22 *N.*	2	♂
1st in Orion's Belt,	♊	21 44	23 33 *S.*	2	♃ ♄
Highest in Orion's Head,	♊	21 20	13 26 *S.*	4	♃ ♄
Zeta in the Bull's Horn,	♊	22 17	2 14 *S.*	3	♂
2d in Orion's Belt,	♊	22 48	24 38 *S.*	2	♃ ♄
Orion's Right Shoulder, Betelguese	♊	26 14	16 3 *S.*	1	♂ ☿
Propus,	♊	28 24	0 13 *S.*	4	♂
Auriga's Right Shoulder,	♊	28 54	21 27 *N.*	2	♂ ☿
Bright Foot of Gemini,	♋	6 33	6 48 *S.*	2	☿ ♀
Sirius,	♋	11 35	40 13 *S.*	1	♃ ♂
Castor,	♋	17 35	10 4 *N.*	1	♂ ♀ ♄
Pollux,	♋	20 46	6 40 *N.*	2	♂
Little Dog, Procyon,	♋	22 54	16 1 *S.*	1	☿ ♂
The Crab's Claw, Præspe,	♌	4 48	1 14 *N.*	*Neb*	♂ ☾
North Assellus,	♌	4 32	3 10 *N.*	4	♂ ☉
South Assellus,	♌	6 13	0 4 *N.*	4	♂ ☉
Hydra's Heart, Alphard,	♌	19 30	7 32 *S.*	2	♄ ♀
Lion's Heart, Regulus,	♌	27 20	0 27 *N.*	1	♂
Vindemiatrix,	♍	7 25	10 15 S.	3	♄ ♀ ☿
Lion's Back,	♍	8 43	14 20 *N.*	2	♄ ♀
Lion's Tail, Deneb,	♍	19 4	12 21 *N.*	2	♄ ♀ ☿
Crater, the Cup,	♍	21 0	33 0 *S.*	4	♀ ☿
Arcturus in Bootes,	♎	21 43	30 53 *N.*	1	♃ ♂
Virgin's Spica, Arista,	♎	21 20	2 2 *S.*	1	♀ ♂
South Scale,	♏	12 35	0 22 *N.*	2	♄ ♀
North Scale,	♏	16 47	8 46 *N.*	2	♃ ♂
Left Hand of Ophiucus,	♏	29 48	17 19 *N.*	3	♂ ♄
Frons Scorpio,	♐	0 41	1 2 *N.*	2	♄ ♀
Left Knee of Ophiucus,	♐	6 42	11 30 *N.*	3	♂ ♃
Scorpion's Heart, Antares,	♐	7 16	4 32 *S.*	1	☿ ♂
Right Knee of Ophiacus,	♐	15 28	7 18 *N.*	3	♄ ♀
Eagle, or Vulture, Attair,	♑	29 14	17 21 *N.*	2	♄ ☿
Capricorn's Tail,	♒	21 2	2 33 *S.*	3	♄
South Fish, Fomahaut,	♓	1 19	21 6 *S.*	1	♀ ☿
Wing of Pegasus, Markab,	♓	20 58	19 24 *N.*	2	♂ ☿
Scheat Pegasi,	♓	26 16	1 7 *N.*	2	♄

will be found correct within about 10 minutes, and sufficiently so
to answer every purpose required.

The right ascension and declination of most of these stars are
to be found in the Ephemeris with the annual difference to each,
which annual difference will regulate their places for any number
of years.

The latitude of a fixed star never differs much, but the longitude increases at about 50″ every year, so that their longitude
being once known their places may be found for any number of
years, by allowing at the rate 50⅓″ increase, for each. Some
would insert a table for this purpose, but it is so plain that it
requires none. Those who wish to find the longitude, latitude, or
declination, more correctly, may refer to the article, "Trignometrical Calculations."

Fixed stars are said to operate by position when they are joined
to a planet, or near the cusp of a house; and by direction, when a
planet or house comes to their places by direction: in both cases
their effects are the same.

The Sun joined with Caput Algol, Aldebaran, Hercules, Bellatrix, Regulus, Antares, or any eminent star of the nature of Mars,
threatens a violent death, or extreme sickness. They are also
said to endow the native with riches, honour, and preferment,
chiefly military, but the whole will end in disgrace, poverty and
ruin. Caput Algol, according to Ptolemy, when joined to the
hyleg in an angle, threatens beheading, and Placidus, in endeavouring to support this superstitious error, has made himself some
what ridiculous. Cardan was beheaded, and in his nativity he
places Medusa's Head with the Moon on the cusp of the seventh,
which is 14° 39′ of Gemini, whereas it had not in his time arrived
even at 23° of Taurus, and there is 26° of Taurus on the cusp of
the 6th, so that to use his own words to Algol, " I know not how
this could be taken." This was one of the silly whims of Ptolemy,
who supposed, that because Medusa had been beheaded by Perseus, nobody's head could be safe whose prorogator was near her:
but to proceed.

The Sun, joined to the Pleiades, Hyades, Castor, Pollux,
Præspe, or the Asselli, is indicative of an evil disposition, and
danger of the native's being a murderer, or of being murdered,
particularly when the Sun is with Præspe. They threaten death
by blows, stabs, shooting, beheading, or shipwreck. Being near
Argo, also, is said to denote shipwreck: this is another foolish
whim, because Argo was a ship that carried the Argonauts. The
Asselli denote death by fire, fevers, hanging, beheading, or some

violent catastrophe, and frequently disgrace and utter ruin. Deneb gives riches, and honours, but they are but of short duration and end in trouble and disgrace. The stars in the Lion's Neck, back and wing, the South Scale, the Knee and Right Leg of Ophiucus, the Goat's Back, and the Left Shoulder and Right Arm of Aquaries, are all productive of trouble and disgrace. The Jaw of the Whale, the Knee of Castor and Pollux, and the Little Bear, Cynosura, cause much sickness, trouble, loss of fortune, disgrace, and great affliction. The Right Leg of Aquaries, Orion's Belt, North Scale, Armpit of Sagittary, and the Goat's South Horn, cause good fortune and lasting happiness. Arista gives the most eminent and permanent good fortune, and if she culminate, unbounded honour and riches. Rigel is nearly the same.

All eminent fixed stars, with the $\odot$ in an angle, give good fortune and success, but those of the nature of $\mathcal{J}$, cause a violent death, or ultimate ruin, by the pride, folly, or rashness of the native, and generally destroy the good they produce, and those of the nature of Saturn bring disgrace, ruin, and great calamity. Caput Algol is reckoned the worst of the whole, and if in an angle, or with the hyleg, or if $\mathcal{J}$ be there, or elevated above the luminaries, when Caput Algol is angular, it is said to denote a murderer who will come to an untimely end. The bright star in the Eagle, or Fomalhaut, or the last star in Capricorn's Back with the $\odot$ or $\mathcal{J}$, are said to cause the native to be bitten by venemous animals, but this appears ridiculous. The Pleiades, or Præspe, with the $\odot$, give bad eyes, and if in an angle blindness.

The $\mathbb{C}$ with Caput Algol, Aldebaran, Pollux, or Bellatrix, denotes a violent death. With the Pleiades, Præspe, Antares, or Deneb, blindness or injuries to the eyes. With Orion's Belt, blindness of one eye at least. When joined to the Pleiades, and Saturn or $\mathcal{J}$ be joined to Regulus, it generally causes total blindness, especially if the $\mathbb{C}$ be combust. With Antares in $\mathcal{S}$ to Saturn with Aldebaran, a violent death, generally by hanging. If $\mathcal{J}$ be with Aldebaran, the native will die by a stab, blow, or fall, particularly if the $\mathcal{S}$ be from angles. If with Hercules, or Arcturus, with Mars, it threatens death by suffocation. With Cor Hydra, in $\mathcal{d}$, $\square$, or $\mathcal{S}$ of $\mathcal{J}$, or $\hbar$, death by drowning or poison, particularly if Mars be angular. With Sirius and Saturn, or with Markab and Mars, death by wild beasts or soldiers. With Orion's Belt and Saturn, or with Caput Hercules, or Antares, danger of drowning or assassination. With Aldebaran or Antares in the first or 10th, gives honour and preferment, with many dangers and calamities.

If Aldebaran, Regulus, Hercules, Arista, Antares, or the North Scale, culminate, they give great honour and preferment. It is said to be nearly the same when they ascend. Fomahaut, or Rigel, ascending or culminating, give great and lasting honours. Orion's Shoulder does the same.

Those stars of the nature of ♂, ☉, ☿, or ☾, are said to give great glory and renown when ascending or culminating. Those of the nature of ♃ and Venus, give much honour and riches. Those of the nature of Saturn are always evil. All fixed stars in angles are said to give honours and preferment, if they be of the first magnitude, but if they are of the nature of Mars it will be lost again, or held with much danger and trouble, and if of the nature of Saturn, it will end in dreadful disgrace and ruin. Stars of the 1st magnitude near the cusp of the 7th give, it is said, a good rich wife. It may signify this in a horary question of marriage, but nowhere else. If Mars be with the Pleiades, and Saturn with Regulus, it denotes a violent death. Eminent fixed stars, near the ecliptic, have great power when the planets are with them.

It is common to consider the second house, or its lord, or the ⊕ and its lord, according to the stars they are with, as significators of riches; but this is wholly absurd and unmeaning, at least in nativities, but in horary questions I should certainly consider whether any fixed star of importance was near the cusp of the house to which the question belonged, or to its lord, and judge accordingly.

In directions, the qualities of the fixed stars are supposed to operate in a similar way, according to their respective natures.

The ascendant is supposed to operate on the body, the 10th on the fortune of the native, and the luminaries on both, according to the nature of the stars to which they are directed.

The Pleiades, Hyades, Præspe, Castor, Pollux, and the Asselli, are remarkable, when directed to the ascendant or luminaries, for causing blindness or bad eyes, hurts in the face, sickness, wounds, stabs, disgrace, imprisonment, and every evil that can befall humanity. The Asselli cause violent fevers.

Aldebaran, Regulus, Frons Scorpio, Antares, the Shoulders of Orion and Deneb, give riches and preferment, but attended with danger, violence, trouble and sickness; and the benefits they confer are seldom lasting.

The Whale's Jaw, Cynosura, and the Twins, give sometimes, it is said, legacies and inheritances but such as are attended with much evil.

The stars in the Lion, the Right Side of Aquaries, the last in

Capricorn's Back, Deneb, and the Left arm and Shoulder of Aquaries, are all reckoned unfortunate.

Arista, Rigel, and the North Scale, are very fortunate, and give lasting honours, riches and happiness. Some think Rigel unfortunate, because Ptolemy says he is of the nature of $\hbar$ and $\mathcal{U}$, but others affirm him to be of the nature of $\mathcal{U}$ and $\mathcal{J}$.

The midheaven directed to the Nebulous Stars, Præspe, the Pleiades, Shoulders of Orion, the Hyades. and the Twins, is said to be the cause of disgrace and ruin, and often a violent death; and the Asselli, Caput Hercules, Markab, Auriga's Right Shoulder, and Medusa's Head, are the same.

The Sun directed to Præspe, threatens the native with murder; to the Pleiades, death by pestilential disease; and to all the nebulous clusters, Castor and Pollux, threatens blindness, dreadful diseases, quarrels, murders, rapes, &c. both committed by, and on the native, violent fevers, decapitation, banishment and wretchedness. To the Asselli, threatens the native with burning alive, violent fevers, hanging, beheading, &c. To Aldebaran, Regulus, Deneb, Antares, Betelguese, Bellatrix, and Frons Scorpio, honours and preferment, which will end in ultimate ruin; disease, putrid fevers, and all hot distempers. To Arista, great and lasting preferment, especially if they culminate in the radix. Also Rigel, Orion's Belt, the North Scale, Goat's South Horn, and Armpit of Sagittary, give great good fortune. To the Jaw of the Whale, Cynosura, and the Twins, much evil. The stars in the Lion, the South Scale, Knee and Right Leg of Ophiucus, Goat's Back, Left Shoulder and Right Arm of Aquaries. cause sickness, disgrace, ruin, and every evil. To Capella, martial honours and wealth. To Markab, Occulus Taurus, and the Right Foot of Gemini, great martial honour, but danger of losing them again.

The $\mathbb{C}$ directed to the Pleiades, Hyades, Præspe, or the Twins, brings disgrace, sickness, trouble, blindness, or hurts in the eyes. To the Asselli, inflammatory fevers, pains in the head, and blindness. To Markab, Bull's North Eye, or the Right Foot of Gemini, good health, honour, and riches. To Orion's Belt, North Scale, Sagittary's Armpit, Goat's South Horn, and Right Leg of Aquaries, great and new friends, love of respectable women, and valuable gifts. To Aldebaran, Regulus, Frons Scorpio, Antares, Bellatrix or Betelguese, great power, honour, and wealth. To Deneb, honour among the vulgar, but ultimate disgrace and ruin. To the Whale's Jaw, Knees of Castor and Pollux, Belly of the Twins, or Cynosura, causes hatred of the vulgar, ill will of some women, danger by thieves, and many evils. To the Back, Neck, or Wing of the Lion, South Scale, Right Leg of Ophiucus, Deneb, Goat's Back, or the Left Shoulder and Right Arm of Aquaries, ruin and disgrace, and diseases in the parts of the body signified by the signs in which those stars are posited. A direction to Capella is reckoned good for preferment, but the native generally ruins himself by his vices, and connections with infamous women; and is also in danger of losing his life by blows or stabs.

For further particulars respecting the Fixed Stars, see the article "Promittor."

When any planet comes to a fixed star of its own nature, however evil both may be, it generally denotes some present good, and if to a star of an opposite quality, the reverse; though this is an opinion that should be received with great caution, as indeed should all the foregoing doctrine of the fixed stars. For my own part, I can see no reason why they should not operate by aspect like the planets, if the planets really do operate by certain aspects, for with the exception of the luminaries, I have often doubted the effects of some of them to the extent generally imagined: indeed, the zodiacal parallel seems the chief aspect that can be relied on, and the ☌ or ☍ apparently derive their greatest force from the parallel of the star's declination, from which, at such times, they cannot be very far distant. I would, therefore, advise that the zodiacal parallel of all the fixed stars be taken both in nativities and directions of nativities, and would recommend the student to pay strict attention to them. In horary questions they may doubtless be made equally symbolical with the planets, but this is entirely at the option of the professor, who should always have a clear and distinct notion of what he is about, and suffer nothing to interfere in one part of his system, that may cause confusion in another.

I have only to repeat, that whatever is said here respecting fixed stars should be received with great caution, as it contains some absurdity mixed up with much truth, which can only be elicited by practice and observation.

FOMAHAUT, a star of the 1st magnitude, in the Mouth of the South Fish, in the 2d degree of ♓, of the nature of ♀ and ☿. Some say it is moderately beneficial, but others say it threatens bites of venemous creatures when joined to ♂ : this is ridiculous, for it is too far south to be joined to any planet, or to do much evil or good in our hemisphere.

FORM OF THE BODY, this, according to Ptolemy, proceeds from the ascendant, its lord, the planets posited there, the Sun and Moon, and the Moon's aspects. I have, however, no opinion of any judgment taken from the lord of the ascendant in nativities.

If the sign ascending, or those where the luminaries are posited, belong to the spring quarter, viz: Aries, Taurus, Gemini, the native will be of a sanguine complexion and good stature, abounding with heat and moisture. If those signs belong to the summer quarter, viz: Cancer, Leo, Virgo, they make the body strong, vigorous, healthy, and well proportioned, but indifferent complexion, and a constitution abounding with heat and dryness. If the signs be autumnal, viz: Libra, Scorpio, Saggittary, the constitution is inclined to be cold and dry, weak and sickly, and the body slender and lean. Winter signs, viz: Capricorn, Aquaries, and Pisces, give a cold moist constitution, dark complexion, moderate stature but square and strong make, and tolerably healthy.

There certainly is a contradiction between this and other doctrines of Ptolemy, where every sign is supposed to communicate its own nature, whether hot and dry, cold and moist, &c.: neither is it agreeable to reason, that signs can have a wintry effect in summer, merely because they contain the Sun in winter.

I have no doubt, in my own mind, that every sign has a distinct influence of its own, which it impresses both on the body and mind, at all times, when it ascends in a nativity. (See "Signs.") No doubt, the position of the luminaries, their aspects, and the planets that possess, or aspect the ascendant, are productive of sensible changes, but upon the whole, the sign ascending will mark the disposition. For the blemishes and diseases of the body, see "Diseases" and "Life and Health."

The ☾, also, is said to make the constitution more moist, from the change to her first dichotome; from thence to the full, she makes it hot, from the full to her second dichotome she causes dryness, and from thence to the conjunction, cold.

There is also an opinion (whether correct or not repeated trial alone can determine), that planets aspecting the ascendant, impress certain qualities upon the body and mind according to the nature of the signs in which they are posited. The rule is, to take that planet which is strongest and in most partile aspect to the horoscope, and judge from it as follows:

The Effects of Saturn.

♄ in ♈ gives a ruddy complexion, large bones, but square body, full face, little beard, dark hair, and deep voice; a boasting, conceited, empty character, very quarrelsome and ill-natured.

♄ in ♉, causes a dark complexion and hair, rough skin, a

middle stature; very uncomely person, awkward, dull and heavy; of a rugged, uneven, vicious, sordid disposition; one who is very mean and unfortunate.

♄ in ♊, makes the complexion dark, though sanguine; the body tall and well proportioned; the face oval and the hair dark brown or black; the mind ingenious, but crafty and perverse and selfish, and mostly unfortunate.

♄ in ♋, makes the body weak, infirm and crooked, or ill made; a thin pale face, sad brown hair, languid eyes, that seem dull and heavy; a morose disposition, envious, jealous and vicious.

♄ in ♌, produces a moderately large size, with broad round shoulders, wide chest, large bones and muscles, rather lean; bending forward, hollow eyed, light brown hair, and surly aspect; tolerably good in disposition, not very courageous, apparently of a noble, generous temper, but prone to anger and revenge.

♄ in ♍, the native is tall and thin: swarthy, with dark brown or black hair, and much of it; long face, grave countenance; inclined to melancholy, and to retain malice; very studious, reserved and subtle; often engaged in useless speculations, very indirect in his dealings, and often given to pilfering.

♄ in ♎, tall and rather handsome, but not beautiful; brown hair, oval face with a tolerably clear complexion, large forehead and nose; fond of expense and prodigality, and entertaining notions above his sphere in life; inclined to controversy, and tolerably well qualified for argument.

♄ in ♏, middling stature, square, short and thick, strong well set body, broad shoulders, with black or dark hair; very evil disposed, quarrelsome, violent, and devoted to mischief.

♄ in ♐, good size, well proportioned, brown hair, with a tolerably good complexion; honest and upright; a good friend and merciful enemy; very obliging though not courteous; rather choleric but not vicious; profuse in promises through excess of good nature.

♄ in ♑, rather short than otherwise, lean and raw boned; sallow complexion, long face and little eyes, generally of a middle stature every way, dark brown or black hair and rough coarse skin; very bad gait, melancholy, peevish, covetous, and discontented with every thing; very fearful, grave, silent, and apt to bear malice; fond of the Earth and all its productions.

♄ in ♒, large stature, big head and face, corpulent; clear complexion, dark brown hair; sober and grave in deportment, affable, graceful, and courteous; possessing much ingenuity and research, and often becomes a good proficient in arts and sciences.

♄ in ♓, middle stature, pale with dark hair, large head and eyes, and ill-placed or rotten teeth, and generally very ugly; one who is full of contention, malice and deceit, and always active to do evil; not loquacious, but rather deliberative, fickle minded and treacherous, though often with a good outside. It is said the disposition mends as the native grows older. Saturn always gives bad teeth.

The Effects of Jupiter.

♃ in ♈, gives a middle sized body, but lean; light brown or flaxen hair, ruddy complexion, quick piercing eyes, oval face, high nose, and often pimples in the face; of a free, generous, obliging disposition, with becoming pride, but courteous and polite.

♃ in Taurus, middle stature, well set, stout, but not handsome, strong and compact; swarthy complexion, with brown rugged hair, inclined to curl or rather frizzle; of a tolerably good disposition and sound judgement; well behaved in general, good natured and humane, but very fond of women.

♃ in Gemini, a decent made compact body, rather tall, sanguine, but dusky complexion, brown hair, full handsome eyes; very affable, gentle, mild, and obliging; one who is learned, but often addicted to women: but if ♃ be near some of the violent fixed stars in Gemini, the native will be rash, unstable, and very disagreeable.

♃ in ♋, gives middle stature, fleshy body but disproportioned, with a pale unwholesome, sickly complexion, dark brown hair and oval face; a busy, loquacious, conceited character; fond of women; much attached to the water, and very fortunate thereon. The native will have but very little courage, except ♂ cast a good aspect to Jupiter.

♃ in ♌, makes the native strong, tall, and well made, with light brown or yellowish curling hair, full eyes, ruddy countenance, and rather comely; a noble minded courageous person, ambitious, warlike, and very enterprising.

♃ in Virgo, gives a full sized person, well made and handsome, with brown or blackish hair, ruddy but not fair; of a choleric and ambitious turn, and given to boasting; obstinate and rash, yet covetous, and often studious.

♃ in ♎, makes the native tall and handsome, slender and upright, with an oval face, light brown hair, full eye and fair complexion, but sometimes pimpled; the temper is mild and winning, extremely obliging, and much respected; they are generally fond of amusement.

♃ in Scorpio, makes the body compact and stout, middle sized and fleshy, full face, dull complexion and dark hair; a lofty, ambitious, resolute character, eager to grasp at power, subtle, ill-natured, covetous, and selfish.

♃ in ♐, gives a fine, tall, upright, well made body, ruddy countenance, fine eye, oval face, chestnut hair, and thick beard; of a courteous, affable disposition, graceful, just, humane, and highly accomplished; they are said to be fond of horses.

♃ in ♑ gives a mean stature, small and weakly, little head and thin beard, which is generally lighter than the hair, brown hair and pale countenance; they are generally harmless, peevish, helpless, indolent, weak and poor, and mostly unfortunate.

♃ in ♒, gives a middle stature, but compact and corpulent, fair complexion, and brown hair; of a cheerful, affable temper, very obliging and kind, humane and attentive; laborious and not extravagant.

♃ in ♓, causes a middling stature, full fleshy body, dark complexion, but light brown hair; one who is studious, and possesses abilities; friendly, kind and inoffensive; they are said to be fortunate on water, if the ☾ be not in □ or ☍.

♃ always gives good teeth, but it is said, that in a watery sign in □ or ☍ of ☿ the native will have an impediment in his speech.

The effects of Mars.

♂ in ♈, causes a middle stature, well set body, large bones, swarthy complexion, with light or red curling hair. If ♂ be occidental, the native will be more ruddy and smooth, but if oriental, tall and less swarthy, and more manly and courageous; in either case, he is bold, choleric, proud and confident; ambitious, warlike, and often gains preferment.

♂ in Taurus, makes the native rather short, but corpulent and compact, brown or black rugged hair, broad face, wide mouth, sometimes ruddy but never fair, and frequently there is a mark in the face; of a vicious, profligate disposition, debauched, ill-natured, and unfortunate; a gamester, drunkard, and whoremaster. If ♂ be posited near the Pleiades, it is extremely unfortunate.

♂ in Gemini, gives a tall person, well made, sanguine complexion, black or dark brown hair, but if ♂ be in the beginning of the sign it will be light brown; of a very unsettled, restless disposition, ingenious but unfortunate, and one who generally lives by his wits in a mean dishonest way.

♂ in ♋, gives a short, ill made and generally crooked body, with thick brown hair; the disposition is dull, sottish, mean, servile, and unfortunate.

♂ in Leo, gives a large, tall, strong body, stout limbs, great eyes, a sunburnt complexion; the hair is generally flaxen; the temper is choleric and violent, but the mind is generous and free, and the native is much attached to all violent pursuits, as war, riding, hunting, shooting, &c.

♂ in ♍, makes a middle sized well proportioned body, with dark brown or black hair, and swarthy complexion, and generally, it is said, with a scar or blemish in the face; the temper is angry and spiteful, revengeful and implacable; one who is pleased with nothing, very conceited, and unfortunate.

Mars in ♎, gives a well proportioned, tall body, oval face, sanguine complexion, and light brown hair; the disposition is brisk and cheerful, but fond of boasting, and very conceited; one who is fond of dress, and much attached to women, by whom he is equally beloved, and often ruined.

Mars in ♏, gives a well set middling stature, but corpulent, with a broad face, swarthy complexion, and black curled hair; the temper is unsociable, quarrelsome, revengeful, ungrateful, and wholly wicked, yet the genius is good, and generally capable of what he undertakes.

Mars in ♐, gives a tall, compact, well made body, oval face, brown hair, and sanguine complexion, with a very quick eye; the disposition is jovial, cheerful, and active, yet high-minded, choleric, and hasty, very courageous, fond of talking, and ambitious of praise, but by no means a bad character.

Mars in ♑, gives a small, thin stature, lean body, thin face, little head, black lank hair, and bad complexion, but one who is witty, penetrating, and successful in most undertakings.

Mars in ♒, makes a body well set, and rather tall and corpulent (though others say, it is but middle sized), fair complexion, and sandy hair; the disposition is turbulent, and fond of controversy, and the native seldom fortunate.

Mars in ♓, gives a mean, short, fleshy body, with a bad complexion, and generally ugly; the mind is dull and stupid, (though others say, sly and artful), deceitful, idle, and worthless, sottish, debauched, and much addicted to lustful depravities.

Mars is the giver of courage and resolution, which if he be weak is always defective. If he be in □, ☍, or ☌, of ♄, the disposition is extremely evil, especially if in an angle, and some say he is rendered more evil by being with the ☊. In airy signs the disposition is best, in watery signs more dull and stupid, in earthy signs more sullen and evil conditioned, and in fiery signs more choleric, and in these the native is observed to have a falling in of the cheeks.

The Effects of the Sun.

☉ in ♈, gives a good stature, strong and well made, with a good but not fair complexion; the hair is yellow, or flaxen, the native is very courageous, and famous for victory.

☉ in ♉, makes the native short and well set but rather ugly, dark complexion, wide mouth, broad face, and large nose; one who is strong, bold, proud, fond of opposition, and often victorious.

☉ in Gemini, gives a well proportioned, tall body, sanguine complexion and brown hair; of a good, affable, kind disposition, but not very fortunate, being too meek to resist the imposition of others.

☉ in Cancer, gives a mean, ill made body, with an unhealthy countenance, and deformed face; the disposition is harmless and cheerful, but indolent, and much addicted to women, dancing, and other amusements.

☉ in ♌, gives a strong, well made body, light brown or yellow hair, sanguine complexion, with large eyes, a full face, and sometimes a mark or scar in it; very honourable and upright in all his dealings, but ambitious and fond of dissipation.

☉ in Virgo, makes the body tall and slender, but well proportioned, with much brown hair, and a good complexion; the mind is ingenious, cheerful and agreeable, but too fond of recreations and conviviality.

Sun in Libra, gives a straight, tall, upright body, full eyes, light hair, and pimples in the face; the disposition is good, but the native is unfortunate, especially in war, and in all ambitious pursuits.

Sun in ♏, gives a square, fleshy body, broad face, cloudy, sun burnt complexion and brown hair; the native is ingenious, but ambitious and overbearing, of a rugged temper, and very disagreeable; they are said to be fortunate as sailors or surgeons.

Sun in ♐, gives a tall, well proportioned body, a comely person oval face, sanguine complexion, light brown hair; disposition lofty, proud and austere, bold, and calculated for great undertakings.

Sun in ♑, gives a mean stature, and not well made, oval face, pale, sickly complexion, and lank brown hair; the native is just and upright in principle, and generally good natured, though sometimes hasty, and too fond of women.

Sun in ♒, gives a middle stature, corpulent but well made, round full face, light brown hair, and fair complexion. The native is proud, vain and ambitious, but with these exceptions, tolerably good, and wholly free from malice or treachery.

☉ in ♓, gives a short fleshy body, round face, and good complexion, with light brown or flaxen hair; one who is harmless to others, but ruining himself by gaming, intemperance, and debauchery, prodigality, and extravagance.

The Effects of Venus.

♀ in ♈, gives a middle stature, but slender, light hair, good complexion, with a mark or scar in the face; one who is pensive, and unfortunate, both to himself and others.

♀ in ♉, gives a comely person, though the stature is mean, the body is fleshy, but well made, a ruddy but not clear complexion, and brown hair; the temper is mild, kind and humane; the native is much respected and generally fortunate.

♀ in ♊, gives a tall, slender, well made person, rather fair, with brown hair; one who is loving, affectionate, just, humane, and charitable.

♀ in ♋, gives a short, thick body, round face, sickly complexion, and light hair; one who is slothful, fond of low pleasure, and very fickle minded.

♀ in ♌, gives a body tall and well made, clear complexion, round face, full eye, light flaxen or red hair, and freckled face; soon angry and soon pleased, but sociable and good tempered, with much decent pride, generosity and kindness; one who is often indisposed, but not seriously.

♀ in ♍, gives a tall, well proportioned body, dark complexion, with sad brown or dark hair, and oval face; one who is eloquent, ingenious, active and subtle, but generally unfortunate.

♀ in ♎, gives a tall, upright, elegant person, oval face, and rather beautiful, sanguine complexion, often freckled, brown hair, and beautiful dimples; one who is kind, affectionate, and generally beloved.

♀ in ♏, gives a stout, corpulent, well set body, broad face, sad brown hair, and dusky complexion; an envious, contentious and debauched character.

♀ in ♐, rather tall and well made, fair, sanguine complexion, oval face and brown hair; one who is rather proud, and passionate, but generous and noble, kind, and for the most part inoffensive; generally fortunate.

♀ in ♑, gives a mean, short stature, pale, thin, sickly visage, dark or black hair; the disposition is not very good, too much addicted to pleasure and fond of women; the native is generally unfortunate, apt to meet with sudden and strange catastrophes in his affairs, and often change his station in life.

♀ in ♒, gives a person handsome, rather corpulent but well made, fair, with light brown or flaxen hair; the temper excellent, kind, affable, quiet, humane and courteous to all; fortunate and much admired.

♀ in ♓, gives a middle size, but rather plump and fleshy; moderate good complexion, round face, brown hair, sometimes flaxen, with a dimple in the chin; one who is good humoured, just and kind, mild and peaceable, though rather changeable, and quite fortunate.

The Effects of Mercury.

☿ in ♈, gives a thin, mean stature, oval face, light brown curley hair, and no clear complexion; an ill-disposed person, addicted to theft, and other kinds of villainy.

☿ in ♉, gives a middle stature, corpulent, but well set; swarthy sunburnt complexion, short, thick brown hair; a slothful, idle glutton, and one who ruins himself by women.

☿ in ♊, gives a person tall, upright, and well made, with brown hair and good complexion; an ingenious person, and frequently an orator, lawyer, or bookseller; one who is always awake to his own interest, and generally an overmatch for the most cunning knave.

☿ in ♋, gives a short squab figure, bad complexion, sad brown hair, thin face, sharp nose, and small eyes; a dishonest, ill-natured, deceitful wretch, and one who is generally given to drinking.

☿ in ♌, gives a large body, swarthy complexion, light brown hair, round face, full eye, and high nose; one who is hasty and proud, a boasting, ambitious, troublesome character.

☿ in ♍, makes the body tall, slender, and well proportioned; bad complexion, dark brown or black hair, long face, and austere look; one who is witty, ingenious and profound, and, if ☿ be free from affliction, capable of any undertaking that requires capacity.

☿ in ♎, gives a tall handsome person, but not thin; smooth light brown hair, sanguine complexion; a just and virtuous character, addicted to learning, and every way accomplished.

☿ in ♏, gives a mean stature, but well set and broad shouldered, swarthy complexion, brown curling hair, and ill made; one who is subtle and careful of his own interest, fond of company and women, but not on the whole disagreeable.

☿ in ♐, tall and well shaped, but rather spare and large boned; large nose, brown hair, oval face and ruddy; hasty tempered, but soon reconciled; rash, yet well disposed, but not very fortunate.

☿ in ♑, gives a mean figure, bow legged, thin face, often crooked; dusky complexion and brown hair; one who is helpless, sickly, and dejected, peevish and unfortunate.

☿ in ♒, gives a middling size, rather fleshy, full face, clear complexion, and brown hair; an ingenious, witty, kind, humane character, posessing great invention.

☿ in ♓, gives a short squab figure, though others say, rather thin; a pale, sickly face, but hairy body; always repining and peevish, yet addicted to women and drinking, and very foppish and effeminate.

The Effects of the Moon.

☾ in ♈, gives a middle stature, but rather plump; round face, light brown or flaxen hair, tolerably good complexion; the mind rash, changeable, ambitious, and seldom fortunate.

☾ in ♉, gives a strong, corpulent, well set person, of the middle size, or rather short; bad complexion, brown or black hair; one who is gentle in manners, sober and kind, generally respectable and fortunate.

☾ in ♊, makes the native tall and well formed, very comely and upright; brown hair and good complexion; one who is subtle, crafty and ingenious, not very well disposed, and generally unfortunate.

☾ in ♋, gives a middle sized, well proportioned, fleshy body; round full face, brown hair, pale dusky complexion; of a pleasant, merry, easy disposition; very harmless, and free from passion; one who is fortunate and much respected, but very unstable in mind and fond of change.

☾ in ♌, makes the native strong, large boned, and rather tall; large eyes, full face, sanguine complexion, and light brown hair;

high-minded, very ambitious, and above servitude or dependence, and generally unfortunate.

☽ in ♍, gives a tall person, rather ruddy, oval face, dark brown or black hair; an ingenious, reserved, covetous, melancholy person, seldom well disposed, and generally unfortunate.

☽ in ♎, gives a tall, well made person; with smooth light brown hair, fine red and white complexion, and handsome face; one who is pleasant and merry, and very fond of amusement. They are generally much beloved; but if the native be a woman, she is said to be unfortunate, except the dispositor of ♀ be strong and free from affliction.

☽ in ♏, gives an ill made, short, thick, fleshy body; dark brown or black hair, and dark complexion; one who is ill-disposed, treacherous, malicious, brutish, and sottish. If a woman, she is generally infamous.

☽ in ♐, gives a handsome person, oval face, sanguine complexion and bright brown hair; disposition open and generous, rather hasty and ambitious, but honest and kind, one who is fortunate and much respected.

☽ in ♑, gives a mean, small, weak figure, thin body and face; the native is never strong, and particularly weak in the knees; bad complexion, brown or black hair; one who is imbecile, idle, dull and mean, and generally a very debauched character.

☽ in ♒, gives a middle sized, corpulent person, but well formed; brown hair, clear sanguine complexion; ingenious, affable, kind, and inoffensive; one who possesses an active fancy and good genius.

☽ in ♓, gives a short mean stature, but plump, or fat; pale countenance, and bright brown hair; one who is idle and dull, evil disposed, and unfortunate.

Those positions seem more fit for horary questions (to determine the qualities and appearance of those denoted by certain significators) than for nativities. If every aspect were supposed to convey the qualities of the sign from whence it proceeded in any eminent degree, there would be no end to the confusion it would create in most nativities, where all the planets aspect the horoscope in one way or other, from signs of opposite or very different qualities, with various degrees of strength, dignity, orientality, &c. No doubt they have all their effects according to their nature and strength in the world and the geniture, but the signs they are in, can have little or no effect, except they occupy the cusp of the horoscope. The effects of the signs alone are said to be as follows.

♈ gives a spare, dry, moderate-sized, strong body, with red or sandy hair, and swarthy or sallow complexion, and a piercing eye.

♉ gives a short, or middle-sized, thick, strong body, thick lips, broad forehead, with dark curled hair.

♊ makes the native fair, tall and straight, of a dark sanguine complexion, long arms and legs, but short fleshy hands and feet; though others say, the fingers are long, which seems nearer the truth; dark hazel eyes, dark brown hair, quick sight, with a look that denotes smartness and activity.

♋ gives a short stature, the lower part of the body small, but the upper part rounder, pale round face, brown hair, gray eyes, weak voice, and dull effeminate constitution. If the native be a woman she is generally prolific.

♌ gives a large, strong body, broad shoulders, great bones, large eyes, and ruddy countenance, light or yellow hair, and a masculine rough voice.

♍ gives a well made body, tall and slender, but well proportioned and compact, dark ruddy complexion, dark brown or black hair, roundish face, and small shrill voice.

♎ gives a form tall and elegant, beautiful round face, blue eyes, light yellow or flaxen hair, and ruddy complexion in youth, but inclined to pimples when old.

♏ gives a strong corpulent body, of a middle size, but very robust, dark complexion, brown curling hair, hairy body, and thick short neck and legs.

♐ gives a well formed tall body, ruddy and handsome, chestnut coloured hair, but liable to fall off, oval face, fine clear eyes, and stout athletic frame.

♑ gives a small body, rather slender, long neck, narrow chin and breast, weak knees and inclined to be ricketty or crooked, long thin face, little beard, and dark hair.

♒ makes the native well set, robust, strong and healthy, sometimes corpulent, long face, delicate clear complexion, though some say, rather pale, with sandy or fair hair, and hazel eyes.

♓ makes the native pale, sickly, short, fleshy, crooked or stooping, round shouldered, with brown hair and dull appearance.

It is a general opinion, that those signs containing the luminaries are to be considered equally with that on the cusp of the ascendant, but there is no good reason why it should be so. No doubt, the horoscope is affected by all the planets, according to their various strengths and positions, which accounts for the variety of forms and features of different persons, no two of whom are exactly alike; beside which there is generally a sympathetic resemblance between parents and their offspring, all of which causes, and no doubt many more with which we are totally unacquainted, must render this part of the science wholly unattainable (to a degree of correctness) by any exertion of the human intellect. That the position of the heavens has such an effect is abundantly manifest, from the resemblance of children born nearly together, whereas the offspring of the same parents, born at a distant period under a different constitution of the heavens, are essentially and sometimes wholly unlike both in body and mind. Now, if either climate or parentage were the sole cause of the formation of the body, or if education and example could entirely form the disposition, all children born of the same parents in the same place would be alike in appearance, and if subjected to the same tuition their sentiments and propensities would be the same. This, therefore, is an incontrovertible proof, that however accidental circumstances may operate in effecting a change, the leading features both of body and mind are constitutional, and that this constitution is the result of the constitution of heaven at the moment of birth. So true is the observation of Locke, whose opinion, even if it stood alone, unsupported by proof, must ever be paramount to the silly notions of superficial minds, who are ready to deny what they have neither industry nor capacity to examine, who repeat like children the common place sayings of their companions, and who would have been strenuous advocates for the most absurd system of astrology, had everyone about them been the same.

"We are wrong to think," says Locke, "that things contain those qualities that appear in them to us. Did we understand them rightly, we ought, perhaps, to look for them beyond the fixed stars. We see certain motions and operations in things about us, but know not whence the streams come that cause them; perhaps things would with us put on a different face did some great star or body incomprehensibly remote from us alter or cease to be."

According to Ptolemy, that planet which has the greatest power in forming the body is the lord of the ascendant and next to him the Moon. The ascending fixed stars, also, he supposes have a considerable effect. If the lord of the ascendant be Saturn and oriental, viz: between the 1st and midheaven, or between the 7th and Imum Cœli, he causes a swarthy complexion, black hair, curly head, broad breast, great eyes, middle stature, cold and moist; if occidental, they are small, thin, and of a dark complexion, little or no hair on the body, black eyes, and good shape, cold and dry.

♃ ruling and oriental, gives a white fair complexion, good colour, great eyes, and fine stature, hot and moist; if occidental, fair but not like the other, long hair, bald, middle stature, and moist constitution.

♂ oriental, makes the native ruddy, well made, good habit and size, hairy, hot and dry; occidental, a red complexion, middle stature, small eyes, no hair on the body, yellow lank hair, and dry constitution.

♀ gives the same appearance as Jupiter, but more delicate, soft, and sweet, with fine blue eyes, and very beautiful.

☿ oriental, gives a swarthy complexion, good stature and make, small eyes, and hot constitution; if occidental, fair complexion, but not good colour, long black hair, lean, thin, squinting, and reddish colour, with a dry constitution.

When the Sun is configurated with the lord of the ascendant, the person is more comely and the habit better. The Moon has different effects in her different quarters, but he does not not particularly describe them. Again, oriental planets in their first orientality, cause large stout bodies; in their 2d, smaller and weaker; when occidental, the native is cowardly and mean spirited, but when oriental, more apt to resent an injury.

Modern astrologers make a sad confusion in describing the form of any person, and although their rules can evidently extend no farther than horary questions, with which doctrine they have confounded that of nativities, yet even in that symbolical way their doctrines are too intricate to admit of clear definition, and too contradictory to be easily reconciled. The sign on the cusp of the horoscope, and the sign intercepted, if there be one, their lords, the planets, in the horoscope, or any way aspecting it, the fixed stars near the cusp, and to these some add the luminaries and the stars that aspect them; all these are significators of the form of the body as well as the mind. This may be so in horary questions and with the exception of the lords of the ascendant in nativities also, but I am certain no human intellect, however acute, can form a correct judgment of any one's appearance from so many conflicting testimonies.

♈, ♉, ♎, and ♏, describe a body moderate in stature, but rather long.

♌, ♍, and ♐, rather tall.

♋, ♑, and ♓, rather short.

♊, indifferent.

♒, moderately proportioned.

This doctrine cannot be correct, for no two signs are more different than ♏, and ♎, the former being thick, fleshy, broad shouldered, strong and heavy; whereas ♎ gives an elegant proportion, almost the reverse of the former. Taurus also gives a body not greatly unlike what is produced by ♏.

Northern signs, and also ♐ and ♓, are said to give a good colour; and winter signs, and those signs that are houses of ♄ or ♂, a bad colour. Now, ♈ is the house of ♂, and also a northern sign, so that its colour must be both good and bad; and Pisces, which is said to give a good colour, gives also a bad one from its being a winter sign.◦ These distinctions must therefore be laid aside; there is no difference between northern and southern signs, merely as such, nor have the zodiacal constellations any more effect in forming the body than any other constellation. When we say Libra gives a certain form, and Scorpio another, we mean the effect arising from the whole ambient that ascends with these points of the ecliptic; nor can any one know whether it most depends upon the ascending or culminating stars, but the probability is, that the whole have a joint influence, varying according to the varied position of the ambient.

The quarters of the year are also said to have considerable effect in a nativity and with truth; for assuredly children born in March particularly, and in the spring generally, are stronger in constitution, and longer lived, on an average, than those born in winter.

♉, ♋, ♏, ♑, ♓, and the last part of ♌ and ♈, are said to cause deformity.

♄, ♂, and ☊, ascending, shew a mark or blemish in the face, though the latter can have no effect in a nativity, unless the Moon be there.

The ☉ and ☾, ascending and not afflicted, make the native fair, but the Sun never causes beauty, though he may give a good complexion.

♃ and ♀ give handsome faces.

The ☉ and Moon, ascending, impedited of ♄ or ♂, give blindness, bad eyes, or marks or scars in them. If they are both impedited in any parts of the figure, it hurts them.

♄ and ♂, joined any where, but particulaly if angular, cause deformity, scrofula, lameness, &c. especially if in their own nodes, and others say, in the lunar nodes.

♄, ♃, or ♂, in fall or detriment, and retrograde, denote rather a short stature, but if they are not retrograde, their fall or detriment cause no alteration.

♀ or ☿, domiciliated or exalted, and aspecting the horoscope, cause tallness, but if in detriment or fall, shortness.

If no planet aspect the lord of the ascendant with a partile configuration, he must alone be considered independent of the sign he is in, if he be direct. If he be in his fall and retrograde, judge not from him but from the sign which he is in.

☿ ascending, gives a stature according to the nature of the lord of the ascendant. The lights ascending, judge wholly from the quality of the sign they are in.

♈, ♉, or ♌, the first part makes the body more fat, the latter parts more lean.

♊ or ♏, the first parts cause thinness, the latter parts fatness.

Cancer and Capricorn, the first parts more fleshy than the latter parts.

♐, the first part of this sign makes a spare body, the last part fleshy.

♍, ♎, ♒, and ♓, give a moderate proportion, but the latter part of Aquarius causes the body to be rather spare and thin.

FORTITUDE, strength. See Dignities.

FORTUNES, ♃ and ♀. The Sun also when in good aspect, with one or both of these, and without affliction, is considered equal to one of the fortunes. The Moon and Mercury are likewise esteemed as fortunes when well aspected by ♃ and ♀, and free from affliction.

FORTUNATE SIGNS, ♈, ♊, ♌, ♎, ♐, ♒. When either of these ascend in a nativity, the native is supposed more likely to be fortunate in his undertakings.

FOURFOOTED SIGNS, ♈, ♉, ♌, ♐, ♑. Those born when they ascend are said to have the qualities of such animals: as being bold as the lion, lustful as the goat, &c.

FRIENDS   See Enemies.

FRIENDLY PLANETS. There are different opinions on this subject: as some affirm, that those who have house, exaltation, or triplicity in each others signs, are friendly, and this seems to be the opinion of Ptolemy. Others, however, arrange them as follows: ♄ is only friendly with the Sun, Jupiter and Mercury. Jupiter with all but Mars. Mars is only friendly with Venus. The Sun is friendly with all but Saturn. Venus is friendly to all but Saturn. Mercury is friendly to all but Mars. The Moon is at enmity with ♄ and Mars only. Some say Mars is friendly to all but the ☾. The whole is nonsense, so far as relates to nativities, and the confusion and contradiction will prevent it being useful even in horary questions.

FRUITFUL SIGNS. Cancer, Scorpio, and Pisces. In horary questions, the ascendant, the Moon, or lord of the ascendant in one of these signs, and strong, are symbols of children. Some consider this to be the case in nativities, and that the 5th, or its lord being in a fruitful sign, is a symbol of children.

FRUSTRATION, a term solely applicable to horary questions. It is when one planet is applying to, and within orbs of, an aspect with another planet; but before the aspect is complete, another, either swifter or nearer, forms an aspect with the latter, which is supposed to destroy or frustrate that which was promised by the first aspect. See Horary Questions. Thus, if ♃ were in 8° of Gemini, and Mercury in 6° of Aries, applying to his Sextile, and the Moon in 3° of Aries, applying also to the Sextile, the Moon would form her Sextile before Mercury, and of course frustrate that intended by the aspect of Mercury.

GEMINATED, double. Thus, geminated horary time, is double horary time.

GEMINI. See signs. Castor and Pollux, two violent stars of the 2d magnitude, in the 18th and 21st degrees of Cancer. Castor is of the nature of Mars, Venus, and Saturn, and Pollux of Mars. They are reckoned extremely evil, denoting disgrace, ruin, death, and every calamity. The stars in their feet, knees, &c. are all considered equally injurious.

GENESIS. See Geniture.

GENETHLIACAL, belonging to the Geniture, or the doctrine of nativities.

GENITURE, the Birth, the radical figure, the plan of a nativity.

GEOCENTRIC, having the earth for its centre, or the same centre as the earth. All astrological positions are geocentric, because they relate wholly to the earth.

GIVER OF LIFE, the hyleg.

HAYZ. When a masculine diurnal plant is above the Earth in the day, or when a feminine nocturnal planet is under it in the night it is a kind of dignity of one degree, and is reckoned fortunate in horary questions. The Arabians did not conceive it a perfect Hayz, except when the masculine planet, was in a masculine sign, or the feminine planet was in a feminine sign. When a masculine planet was in a masculine sign, but under the Earth by day, he was said to be in his light only. The person denoted by it in a horary question is in a state of contentment.

HEALTH. See Life and Health.

HEART OF THE SUN, in Cazimi.

HEART OF THE HYDRA, Alphard or Cor Hydra, a fixed star of the 2d magnitude in the 5th degree of ♍, of the nature of ♄

and ♀. It is said to cause drowning or death by poison when joined to ♂ and in evil aspect with the luminaries.

HELIACAL RISING, is when a star that was hidden by the Sun's rays becomes visible to the east or west of him, by getting clear of his rays.

HELIACAL SETTING, is when a star that before was visible is overtaken by the Sun and lost in his rays. The Moon is said to rise or set heliacally when 17° distant from the Sun, but other stars when a whole sign distant.

HELIOCENTRIC, having the Sun for a center.

HEMISPHERE, half the sphere or circle. The visible hemisphere is that which is always in our view, the obscure hemisphere is that beneath us, which is hidden. The oriental or eastern hemisphere is that part of the circle ascending from the cusp of the Imum Cœli to the midheaven; the western hemisphere, called the occidental, is that descending or going down from the cusp of the midheaven, to that of the Imum Cœli.

HERMAPHRODITES. See Form of the Body.

HEXAGON, the Sextile.

HIRCUS, the Goat, called Capella, an eminent fixed star of the first magnitude, in the 20th degree of Gemini. It is of the nature of Mars and Mercury, and is said to give martial honours and riches when culminating, for it is too far north to be with the lights, or to rise or set.

HOARSE SIGNS, Aries, Taurus, Leo, and Capricorn. Those born under them are said to have a kind of roughness, or hoarseness in the voice, and those under ♑ are weak and feminine, and speak with a kind of whistling sound.

HONOURS. According to Ptolemy, if the luminaries are angular, in masculine signs, and attended by the other five planets, all of them being oriental to the ☉, and occidental to the ☾, the native's power and riches will be unbounded.

If the planets be angular, or configurated above the Earth to the ascendant or midheaven, the ☉ being in a masculine, or the ☾ in a feminine sign, and particularly if the configuration to the angles be by dexter aspects, the native will be eminently rich and powerful.

If the lights be thus situated, although none of the planets be angular, or in testimony to the angles, the native will be rich and honourable, but not in the extreme.

If the five planets be angular, or configurated to the angles, above the Earth, although the lights be not angular, it will be nearly the same.

If neither of the lights be angular, nor posited in a masculine sign, nor in aspect with the angles, nor any of the five planets angular, or configurated to angles, nor the luminaries having friendly aspect with the fortunes, the whole life of the native will be a succession of contempt, poverty, and misery: thus far Ptolemy.

Others take the midheaven and its lord, with the lords of the ascendant and of the signs containing the luminaries, as significators of honour. I should never consider the lords of any houses or signs as significators in nativities, but the midheaven may certainly be taken as the angle of honours and happiness, when planets are posited therein.

These significators of honour are said to confer riches and dignity, when they are in their houses, exaltations, mutual reception, or ☌ with each other.

The ☉, ☾, ♃, or ♀ in the midheaven, essentially dignified, are said to have the same effect.

The ☉ and ☾, in their exaltations, are said to be signs of great preferment.

The light of time, culminating and in ⚹ or △ with the other luminary, or with ♃ or ♀, confers great dignity.

The lord of the ascendant, or the dispositors of the luminaries, angular and essentially fortified, cause the native, it is said, to acquire great honour.

The ☉ culminating in a fiery sign; the lights in mutual reception, ⚹ or △; the light of time in conjunction with Aldebaran, Regulus, Arista, Antares, Rigel, the Pleiades, Hircus, Cor Hydra, Arcturus, Fomahaut, or Markab, particularly when culminating are all said to be signs of honour. Such honours, however, would soon prove the greatest calamities, except those derived from Arista or Rigel.

The ☉ in △ or reception with ♂, is said to produce great military honours, if they are both in fiery signs.

The ☉, ☾, and ♃, in △ to each other; or the ☾ in partile △, or ☌, particularly from angles; ♃ and ♀ joined in any angle with the Dragon's Head, particularly in the midheaven, are all said to be signs of eminent preferment.

♃ and the ☉ joined in ♋, with the ☾ in ♏; or if ♃ be in △ to them both from ♓; the ☾ ascending in the horoscope near the full; or with ♃ or ♀ there, or in good aspect with them or the ☉; or joined with fixed stars of their nature; either of the lights with Regulus or Arista, or in △ to ♃, ♂ or ♀; the lords of the ascendant and midheaven with the Dragon's Head, each essentially dignified and applying to each other by good aspect and oriental, are all said to be signs of honour and preferment.

The lord of the ascendant in ✶ or △ with the ☉, or the lord of the midheaven, will, it is said, give the native favour with the great, if the lord of the ascendant be oriental.

The lord of the ascendant in his own dignities, if he apply to a planet in an angle that is exalted, is said to give the native honour by his own exertions. If to ♄, it will be by inheritance or legacies. If to ♃, by virtue, learning, religion, justice, or wealth. If to ♂, by physic, surgery, chemistry or war. If to ♀ by courtship, cheerfulness, good nature, or women. If to ☿, by wit, oratory, genius, arts, &c., but in this, they say, the nature of the house where the promittor is must be considered, as the means or source from whence the honour is to be derived.

If no planet aspect the luminaries, they direct us to consider the planet in the midheaven, and if many be there, the strongest is to be taken. If none be there, the lord of the 10th, the planet that disposes of the light of time, and the strongest luminary, is to be taken, if it be above the Earth. If all these significators are strong, and free from affliction, the native's honours, they say, will be lasting.

If the malefics cast an evil ray to, or are in ☌ with either of the significators of honour, it will not be lasting. ♂ in detriment in ♎ to the horoscope, shews disgrace and misfortune. If he be in the 10th, it shews scandal and infamy, and ♄ in the 10th brings sudden disgrace and irretrievable ruin.

A fiery sign ascending, and the lord of the ascendant in the 10th, shew, they say, the native to be aiming at things beyond his birth, fortune, or attainment.

Honours caused by inferior planets, are said to be but of short duration.

Amidst this vast heap of incongruities, I would advise the student to confine himself chiefly to the rules laid down by Ptolemy, which are by far the most rational.

The lords of houses in nativities can have no power as significators. Their dignities and receptions are nothing. The Dragon's Head is of no more value than his Tail. And the dispositors can dispose of nothing but themselves.

The midheaven however ought to be considered, when any planets are there: it is the principal position from whence the strongest rays proceed, and consequently a star so situated must have great power in sublunary matters. The position of Saturn there deranged all the plans of the late Premier, Mr. Pitt, and brought him eventually to disgrace and ruin

HORARY CIRCLES, the arcs or circles in which the stars move round the Earth. They are either diurnal or nocturnal.

HORARY TIME, is the one-twelfth of the diurnal or nocturnal arc of a star, or one-sixth of its semidiurnal or seminocturnal arc. It is called the horary time, because the star passes over it in the one-twelfth part of a day, or night, or in the space of an astronomical or planetary hour, which is longer or shorter as the day or night is longer or shorter. Thus, if the day be 16 hours long, the night will be 8 hours. The diurnal horary time, or hours, will be 80 minutes or 20°, and the nocturnal horary time will be 40 minutes or 10°. It is therefore half the space of a house, and of course, the double horary time is the space of a whole house, or $\frac{1}{3}$ of a semi-arc.

The horary time, when the days and nights are even, is 60 minutes, or 15°, both diurnal and nocturnal. They may always be obtained by dividing the semi-arc, whether diurnal or nocturnal, by 6.

Example :—Suppose the ⊙'s semidiurnal arc to be 104° 45', what is his horary time ?

$$6)104° 45°(17° 27' 30''.$$

They may also be found by multiplying the semi arc when it is in hours and minutes by $2\frac{1}{2}$.

Example :—Suppose the semidiurnal arc of ♃ to be 7h. 9m., what will be his horary time in degrees?

$$
\begin{array}{r}
7h.\ 9m. \\
2\tfrac{1}{2} \\
\hline
14\ 18 \\
\text{The half,}\qquad 3\ 34 \\
\hline
17°\ 52'
\end{array}
$$

If one horary time be known, the other may be found by subtracting that which is known from 30°, if in distance or from 2h. if in time. Thus, if the horary time diurnal be 20°, subtract this from 30°, it gives the nocturnal horary time 10°; or if it be 1h. 20m. it being subtracted from 2h, leaves the nocturnal time, 40m.

HORARY QUESTIONS, questions asked at a certain hour; when a person feels his mind seriously agitated concerning the result of any undertaking or impending event, he may, if he be not an artist himself, apply to one who is, and request an answer to such question or questions as he may propose. A figure is then erected for the minute in which the question was asked, and if the artist be skillful, and the querent sincere, and really anxious respecting the result, there is little reason to doubt but the answer will in general be true and satisfactory, not in those minute particulars which some pretend to discover, but in the real and essential circumstances which ought alone to be the end and design of such a question; namely, the final conclusion of the business and its ultimate consequences. The figure for a horary question is erected in the same manner as for a nativity, at the same instant of time, because, as they say, the question is the birth of the mind, as the nativity is the birth of the body; these are words without meaning, for the mind always exists; the whole is the effect of that sympathy which pervades all nature, and which is the fundamental principle of all divination under whatever form practised, where the querent and the artist are sincere. There is nothing in it either celestial or diabolical, meritorious or criminal, good or evil; a person is equally justifiable in making an inquiry into one thing as another, and to propose a horary question is an act as indifferent in itself as to ask what it is o'clock; it contains nothing supernatural, for it is nature itself, operating in its usual way. It is the same kind of sympathy which causes the magnet and iron to approach each other; a detached portion of earth to return towards the common centre; the water to approach the luminaries; the child to approach the nipple; the planets to revolve round the Sun; the needle to point to the pole; the husband to suffer the pain of gestation alternately with his wife, and to have milk in his breasts at the time of parturition; the mother to feel the draught flow into her breasts some seconds before the child awakes; the marks imprinted on a child in the womb by the mother's wants or fears; the increasing or diminishing colour of a fruit-mark as the fruit it represents is in or out of season; the turbulence of wine at vintage time; the responsive sound of one musical instrument untouched to another that is struck, and a thousand more instances, superfluous to mention. All instinct is sympathy, and the same common affinity between various parts of matter, which induces rats to forsake a falling house; ants to quit their nests carrying their young with them before an innundation; and dogs to foretell disasters, will enable a human being to propose a horary question at the instant of time when the heavens are favourably disposed to give a solution. Only one rational objection can be made to this, namely, why this kind of divination is not more correct, or, in fact why it is not infallible; for this many reasons may be given. Much depends on the artist; for in this science, the most extensive practice must be united with sound judgment, quick penetration, and a strong memory; he must be a person of cool habits, no ambition, unlimited patience, and one who will rigidly adhere only to the truth; few possess those qualities. The object too often is gain or vanity, which prompts them to have recourse to indirect methods, such as urging a person to partly tell their own story, that they may be able to guess the remainder, or, predicting a number of the common events in life, most of which probably will happen, or at least a sufficient number to preserve their credit.

In some cases, also, where the artist is sincere, the fault may lie in the querent. If anyone come out of curiosity or from very superficial motives, no prediction can be made, because the mind having no impulse, no sympathy can be excited. The only person likely to receive an answer, is one in deep distress, or great anxiety of mind, or at least strongly bent upon knowing the final consequence of some affair of importance. It may, however, happen that even in this case the question may not be what is called radical, or one from which anything can be predicted. Every person certainly does not contain an equal portion of sympathy, as may be evidently seen in all the various instances above mentioned.

Even animals differ in this way considerably, and among dogs the greatest part of them are entirely without any singular degree of sagacity beyond what is necessary to their preservation, and only here and there one can be found possessing an unusual degree of sympathy, or, as naturalists term it, instinct. If human beings differ in a similar way, those figures will be most radical whose owners are most sympathic. Of this, however, little can be known, as the science is yet in its infancy. On account of the world's "dread laugh" few venture to profess it, and of these few the greatest part are either ignorant pretenders, or gross impostors, who practise for gain, and are so far from understanding astrology, that they do not believe in it themselves.

As to the common place objections against horary questions (which every witling who has acquired a sufficient stock of them from others is proud of retailing to shew his sagacity,) they are too superficial to be worth a moment's attention, much less to deter an active mind from pursuing its researches. A small degree of penetration in a student will soon enable him to perceive that his adversaries are men of little knowledge, or great prejudice, with very limited capacities, and almost incapable of reflection, without any original thoughts, or indeed any thoughts at all but what they have borrowed, and such as have made few observations of their own respecting themselves or the universe in general. Men that are either absorbed in other speculations than those of nature, or who think only by permission; that would believe the legend, and deny the existence of the antipodes if others about them did the same. With them the *vox populi* is truly the *vox Dei*; the only argument capable of convincing them is a great shew of hands, and any absurd hypothesis, having the major part of the world on its side (a thing not very uncommon,) would soon add them to the number of its disciples. I know that in answer to this, the opinions of learned men may be quoted; but learning is not always united with discernment nor real knowledge, any more than the words of a talking bird are united with ideas. Learning is a mechanical acquirement, and may be possessed by a very silly person, and of this we have numberless instances. With such men reason is useless; they would oppose custom to reason, and authorities to facts. I had once an argument with one of these, a person of extensive learning and uniform dullness, except when relieved at intervals by a most unaccountable persevering obstinacy. We were speaking of the Moon, which he denied had any influence on the weather. I pointed out to him and even predicted several instances wherein a change of weather would take place, which were most or all of them verified, and I won some trifling wagers from him on this score: but though still vanquished, as Goldsmith says, he would still argue, and with as much obstinacy as if he had never been proved to be in the wrong. I then began to appeal to his reason, and asked him, if the Moon could move a fluid of such gravity as water, why it might not more easily affect the atmosphere, which was more light and elastic? He denied that I could prove that it did affect the water. Surely, said I, the tides prove that: this, too, he denied. He admitted, that it was a strange coincidence of periods, but contended that the tides might have been as they are, had the Moon never existed. I had some inclination to make him affirm (which I easily could have done) that day and night might have been as they are, had the Sun never existed, but I was weary of his folly.

Many disputes have arisen about the proper time for the figure of a horary question to be erected to. Some think, the moment when the querent is first seen by the artist, others when he salutes

him, others when he enquires for him, &c.: the true time is the
moment when a question is asked; or, if the artist cast his own
figure, it should be the moment when he determined on doing it,
whether he did it at that time or not, because it might not be done
for want of convenience. Bonatus thought no artist could judge
from his own figure, because he must judge partially, but of this
he must be careful, and certainly no one ought to be so good a
judge of his own feelings and the proper sympathetic sensation
requisite to constitute a true figure as an artist. Some affirm,
that the moment in which the querent experiences such a sensation is the time for erecting the figure, but if the querent be not
aware of this the time cannot be directly known, and therefore the
moment of his proposing the question is the true time, however
long he may have been in the journey: for nature and sympathy
will amply provide for all this, and adapt the time to the circumstances. Thus, in case of a letter to such an effect being received
by an artist, however long it may have remained in his hands un-
opened, the moment in which he comprehends its contents is the
moment to which the figure must be erected. Should, however,
any querent be aware of these things, and direct a figure to be
made to any particular time, to that time must the figure be
erected,

Reception in a horary question is generally allowed in all essential dignities, house, exaltation, triplicity, term or face. That by
house is of course the strongest, and that by face the weakest, yet
still it is a degree of reception. In this case the triplicities must
be attended to, as ♃ can have no triplicity by day, nor the ☉ by
night, &c.

It is always a good symbol, when a sign ascends in the horary
question or part of a sign that contained ♃ or ♀ in the radix,
and unfortunate if any part ascend that contained ♄ or ♂. The
signs also that contained the luminaries, if they were not afflicted,
are fortunate; or the parts that receive their ⚹ or △. The
same horoscope, if it be not afflicted, is also good, but otherwise
it is evil.

When a thing is denoted by any approaching aspect, the proper
day to undertake the business is on the day when the aspect is
formed, which may be found in the Ephemeris.

The general opinion is, that no figure should be erected when
the radix can be had and referred to, but this is ridiculous; for
although the radix may point out the leading events of a person's
life, there are many subordinate circumstances to which it can
only have a general and not a particular reference, Those, how-

ever, who use the radical figure, draw it out into a speculum, bring up the secondary directions, with the process, the revolution for the year, the ingress and the transits, which, allowing it to answer the intended purpose, as I believe it does not, must create ten times the trouble required in a horary question.

When the time of birth is not known, or the querent would prefer a figure for the present time, it should be erected to the minute when the question is asked. The sign ascending and its lords are significators of the querent, and to these the Moon is added as a consignificator and to be considered equally with the lord of the ascendant. The house to which the thing properly belongs that is enquired after and its lord are significators of that thing or person, and every other house and its lord are to be considered according to their respective significations, as such and such houses, so as to point out the means and persons by which events are accelerated or retarded, &c. A kind of speculum should also be drawn not like those in nativities, but merely showing the good and evil aspects, applications, separations, translations of light, and, in short, of all of the leading particulars. The declination should also be had, for it must be recollected, that declination is an aspect, though it is seldom considered in horary questions.

The Time of Events.

This is regulated by signs and angles. The significator of the event, whether good or evil, in a moveable sign and an angle, will bring it to pass in the same number of days as there are degrees between the significator's aspect and the star to which it is directed, if the aspect be by application, for if it be by separation the thing will not happen at all. Thus, if the lord of the ascendant be in 22° of ♎ in the ascendant, and the question be concerning money, the lord of the 2d is its significator, who being posited in the 10th in 17° of ♋, the querent would receive it in about five days, but with much trouble, as the application is to a square. If it be a common sign, in an angle, every degree will be a week. If in a fixed sign, a degree is a month.

In a succeedent house, moveable signs give months; common signs, years; and fixed signs bring about the event when all hopes of it are past.

Significators in cadent houses seldom do any thing, and should they bring about an event, it is when every hope is past, and attended with much trouble and vexation.

Degrees and minutes of latitude, if it be south, should, it is said, be added to the time, but if north, subtracted from it; as north latitude shortens the time of an event, and south latitude lengthens it, but I have not much opinion of this.

The Cause of Events.

The house of which the assisting or impeding planet is lord, is the relation which the person or thing has to the querent. The house where he is posited is the matter in question, and the house where the translation, frustration, or prohibition happens, is the cause or reason.

Of the Sincerity of the Querent, &c.

Questions improperly put, or incorrectly stated, or proposed by an impostor with a view to disgrace the professor, are said to be known as follows:

1st, If the very beginning or extreme end of a sign ascend, the querent is a knave, and the question not fit to be answered.

2d, If the question be not radical: by radical is meant agreeing with the radical figure, for it is supposed, that when the birth be not known, the horary figure will represent it, and the querent will have the same marks on his body as the heavens represent at the time of the question.

The sign ascending shews a mark on the part signified by that sign.

The sign on the cusp of the house where the lord of the ascendant is posited, will give another.

The sign on the cusp of the 6th will do the same.

The sign in which the lord of the 6th is posited will give another, and there will also be a mark according to the sign in which the Moon is posited.

If ♄ give the mark, it will be black or dark. If ♃, purple or bluish. If ♂, red; but if he be in a fiery sign it will be a scar or dent. If the ☉, it will be olive or chestnut coloured. If ♀, the mark will be yellow. If ☿, a pale lead colour. If it proceed from the ☾, it will be whitish, or partly of the colour of the planet she aspects.

The infortunes also mark according to their positions. If one be in the ascendant a mole or scar will be in the face; if in the 2d, in the neck or throat; if in the 3d, the arm or shoulder, &c.

If the Moon be exactly at the new or full, and in evil aspect with ♂, there will be a blemish in or near the eye.

If the sign and planet be masculine, the mark will be on the right side or member, but if feminine, on the left.

If the sign or planet be above the Earth, the mark will be before, but if under the Earth, behind.

If the first part of a sign ascend or descend, or if the planets be posited in the first degrees of a sign, the mark will be on the upper part of the member or part. If the last degrees be on the cusp of the 1st or 6th, or if planets be so posited, the mark will be in the lower part. If the middle degrees, it will be in the middle.

3d, If the Moon be in square or opposition to the lord of the 7th;

4th, If the Moon be void of course, or combust;

5th, If the lord of the ascendant be combust, or retrograde;

6th, If ♄ be in the ascendant, impedited or afflicted; and

7th, If the sign ascending and planet in it do not in a great degree describe the querent's person; in all these cases, it shews the question to be put for some knavish purpose, or, at all events, it is improper and not fit to be meddled with. For my own part, having never made a trade of astrology, I can say nothing to all this, but must leave it to the student's experience. For further particulars, see Radical.

Of the Signification and Qualities of the Houses.

The first, or ascendant, has its extent to 5° above the cusp or horizon, and 25° below it; though others say, in signs of short ascension it extends to 5° above and 50° below the cusp, and in signs of long ascension it only extends to $2\frac{1}{2}$° above the cusp, and 13° below it.

It signifies the nature, life, and health, of the native, either in nativities or horary questions, and in the latter it relates to all questions of life, health, and appearance; namely, stature, colour, shape and size, and also sickness and accidents. It is also said to shew what part of life will be most prosperous, by aspects directed to it. By being made the ascendant of any other person, it will shew the same to them as if the figure had been erected at their own request. It also shews the events of journeys, voyages. &c. with respect to the life and health of the querent while engaged in them, and in all cases where life and health are to be considered it becomes the significator. In state questions, comets, eclipses, great conjunctions, and annual ingresses into ♈, it signifies the health and prosperity of the kingdom where it is erected, namely, the common people, or general mass of the inhabitants.

♄ and ♈ are said to be its consignificators, but this is all nonsense. It is also said, that ♄ being there, and well dignified and fortified by good aspects, gives a sober constitution and long life, but I should not choose an infortune in my ascendant however well dignified. ☿ ascending, well dignified and aspected, shews a great orator; and in horary questions it signifies the same, if he be lord of the ascendant and well dignified, It is a masculine house, and is a significator of the head and face.

Signs of short life are when one or both malefics ascend, or the light of time be eclipsed or afflicted, or the birth be exactly at the new or full moon.

The ☾ in ☌ or evil aspect of an infortune in the 4th, 6th, 8th, or 12th house, or besieged by ♄ and ♂.

The lord of the ascendant being combust, retrograde or peregrine. The cause will be shewn by the house that the afflicting planet is lord of, and in which he is posited.

Signs of long life are when the ascendant, its lord, and the planets there, be well dignified, free from affliction, well posited, and increasing in light and motion. The colour is white. ♄ here gives melancholy and much sorrow, and if near the cusp, short life; ♃ gives long life and happiness; ♂, short life, quarrels, wounds and scars in the head and face, small pox, measles, &c.; the ☉, honour, riches and long life; ♀, health, but lust, and injury by women; ☿, great abilities, according to his condition, learning, oratory, &c.; the ☾, travels, fortune, power, and favour of the great; the ☊ gives honesty; the ☋, knavery; the ⊕, riches, and the native makes his own fortune. The meaning of the colour is, that a native signified by it will have a white dress, and if the significator of any native be there, it is said to denote the same. If a planet denoting white be there, the person signified by such planet will be very pale, and the significator of cattle being found there, denotes the colour to be light.

The 2d house; it signifies the fortune and property of the querent, denotes loss and gain, moveable goods, personal property, loans, speculations, business, riches and poverty, friends and assistants in law-suits, and in a duel the querent's second. In state questions it denotes the prosperity or adversity of a nation. At the vernal ingress, it denotes warlike officers, allies, and pecuniary resources. ♃ and ♉ are its consignificators. ♃ being there, signifies a rapid fortune; ♂ and the ☉, shew waste and ruin.

The cusp being free from affliction, having a benefic or its good aspect there; the ⊕ in the second, or the lord of the second in the second, or in any other good house, strong and free from affliction, or in ☌ or good aspect of the fortunes, or with good fixed stars of the first magnitude, are all symptoms of great wealth, and the reverse of poverty and ruin. Its colour is green. ♄ being here causes loss and ruin; ♃, great gain; ♂, poverty and great distress; the ☉, continual riches and continual waste; ♀, riches or poverty by women, according to her dignity or debility; ☿, gain or loss by learning, books, &c. according to his strength or weakness; the ☾, an unsettled fortune; the ☊, a good estate; the ☋, great loss and poverty; the ⊕, great riches. It is a feminine house, and signifies the neck and back part of it down to the shoulders.

The 3d house is that of brethren, sisters, and cousins, neighbors, short inland journeys, letters, messages, rumours, messengers, and removal of trade and manufactories. Its consignificators are ♂ and ♊, which they foolishly say is the cause why ♂ is not so bad here as elsewhere, like ♄ in the ascendant. The ☾ here shews an unsettled life and perpetual restlessness. If the ☾ have good aspect to the cusp and its lord, it shews pleasant fortunate journeys. If the lord of the 3d be in evil aspect with the ☾, or in the 7th or 8th house, it denotes robbery, and perhaps murder in travelling. Its colour is yellow, red, or sorrel. ♄ being here gives hatred of brethren and neighbors, and danger in journeys; ♃, quite the reverse; ♂, spiteful bretheren and neighbors, want of religion, evil journeys and robbery; the ☉, good brethren and journeys, and shews the native busy about religion; ♀, good journeys, brethren, and pious neighbors; ☿ gives crafty brethren and neighbors, swift journeys, and success, as he is dignified; the ☾, incessant travelling, with good or ill success, according to her condition; the ☊, the same as ♃; the ☋, the same as ♂; the ⊕ great gain by journeys, brethren, or neighbors. It is a maseuline house, and denotes the shoulders, arms, hands, and fingers.

The 4th house is the weakest of the angles, and shews the end of all things, and of the native among the rest, his fall, decay, and death. His end will be according to the planets therein, and the sign denotes the part of the body where the complaint lies. In horary questions it denotes the querent's father, and all his affairs relative to lands, houses, estates, towns, castles, cities, and entrenchments, hidden treasures, and all things belonging to or under the Earth, old houses, gardens, fields, orchards, vineyards, cornfields, &c. The ☉ and ♋ are called its consignificators, and if the ☉ be there, it shews the father, it is said, to be great, noble and generous.

Good planets or aspects there shew an inheritance, but if they are evil, there either is none, or it will be lost. It is a feminine house and denotes the breast and lungs. Its colour is red. ♄ being here, destroys the parents before the native, and ruins the inheritance; ♃ gives inheritance and lands, a happy life and a good end; ♂ gives a short life to the father, quarrels between him and the native, and destroys the inheritance; the ☉ gives a good inheritance; and honour in old age; ♀ gives the same; ☿ gains an inheritance by learning, or cunning; the ☾ gives land by travelling; the ☊ gives a good estate; the ☋ ruins the estate; the ⊕ improves the estate, and makes it profitable. In sieges, the sign denotes the town, and its lord the governor.

The 5th house is the house of children and women, those in particular that are pregnant; also of pleasure, amusement, and gaming; taverns, alehouses, playhouses, banquets, and merrymaking. It denotes the father's property, real or personal; children's health and welfare, wherever they be. In states it denotes ambassadors or messengers, or the strength or weakness of any besieged place. ♀ and ♌ are called its cosignificators. ♄ or ♂ being there denote evil children. The cusp and its lord, being strong, or in fruitful signs, or if many planets, especially fortunes, be there, or in translation or reception with its lord, or if the lord of the ascendant be there, or the ☊, all give many children. ♄, ♂, the ☉, or the ☋ being there, or if a barren sign be on its cusp and the ☾ be in a barren sign, or if the lord of the 1st and 5th be in evil aspect to each other, or with ♄ or ♂, all cause barrenness. Its colour is mixed black and white, or sanguine. ♄, being here, gives few or no children, and such as are sickly and disobedient; ♃ gives many virtuous children; ♂, spiteful, wicked, sickly, short lived children, if any, but he generally causes barrenness; the ☉, few children, but those high minded and virtuous; ♀, many children, handsome and virtuous; ☿, ingenious children; the ☾, many children, well or ill disposed, according to her aspects; the ☊, happy, virtuous, long lived children; the ☋, wicked, malicious children; the ⊕, causes the native to gain by his children. It is a masculine house, and denotes the stomach, liver, heart, sides, and back.

The 6th house is that of servants and dependents, uncles and aunts, and all kindred by the father's side; small cattle, rabbits, hares, sheep, goats and hogs; tenants, stewards, farmers, shepherds, and also sickness. Its consignificators are ☿ and ♍. ♂ and ♃, or ♀ being here, in ☌, denote a good physician. The lords of the 1st and 6th being in each others houses, or afflicting each other; or if the lord of the 1st be disposed of by the lord of the 6th, or be in □ or ☍ of ♄ or ♂, or be combust in the 6th, 7th, or 12th, the native will be sickly, and his servants dishonest. Its colour is dark or black. ♄ being in the 6th, gives dishonest servants, sickness, and loss by cattle; ♃, gives the reverse; ♂, fevers, knavish servants, and destruction among cattle; the ☉ causes mental diseases, and proud, wasteful servants; ♀, venereal complaints, but good servants, and gain by cattle; ☿, knavish servants, disordered brain, and bad breath; the ☾, diseases of the head, good servants, and gain by small cattle, but this is according to her condition; the Dragon's Head, the same as ♃; the Dragon's Tail, the same as ♄; the ⊕, faithful servants and gain by cattle. It is a feminine house, and denotes the lower belly, intestines and rectum.

The 7th house is that of marriage, love questions, contracts, or speculations in business, war, or travelling about business; of dealings with friends, strangers and women, and their honesty or knavery; encounters with thieves and their success; law-suits, public enemies, and all kinds of litigation. It is also the ascendant of thieves, and describes their persons; in astrology it denotes the artist; in an ingress it shews if there will be peace or war, or in a battle who will gain the victory; it denotes outlaws and runaways, and the place to which any one will remove when he changes his residence or situation. Its consignificators are the ☾ and ♎. ♄ or ♂ being here shew great misery in marriage. If there be translation, reception, or good aspect between the lords of the 1st and 7th, from fruitful signs, the querent will marry.

Many planets being in the 7th, and in good aspect with ♀ or the ☾, or the lord of the 1st or 7th, the native will marry more than once. If the lord of the 1st be stronger or less afflicted than the lord of the 7th, the querent will overcome his enemies, but if the lord of the 7th be strongest, they will overpower him. Good aspects, translation, reception, &c. between them, shew harmony between man and wife. Its colour is blue, brown, or black. It is a masculine house, and rules the naval and haunches. ♄ being here gives a bad wife, many enemies, and short life; ♃, an excellent wife; ♂, quarrels, law-suits, public enemies, a bad wife whoredom, and sickness; the ☉, sickness, but a good wife and honourable enemies; ♀, a good wife, and few enemies; ☿, a good wife, but a great propensity to quarrels, law-suits, and litigation; the ☾, an honourable marriage; the ☊, a good wife; the ☋, an evil wife, and a prostitute; the ⊕, great gain by marriage, and fortunate law-suits.

The 8th house is the house of death, denoting the manner and

time of it. It relates also to wills, legacies, portions, and dowers.
In a duel it is the adversary's second.   In law-suits it is his
friends, means, and success.   It also denotes the property and
security of the querent's partner, and the strength of public enemies.

The lord of the 1st in good aspect with, or stronger than the
lord of the 8th, or planets therein; or if the fortunes be lords of
the 8th, or posited there; or if there be translation by good aspect,
the native will die a natural death: but if it be a violent sign, or
the luminaries or lord of the 8th be in one, or if the lord of the
8th, or planets there, be strong, or in evil aspect to the ascendant
or its lord, from violent signs, or to the luminaries, there is danger of a violent death.   Fixed stars of the 1st or 2d magnitude, or
the fortunes, or luminaries, or if the ☊, or the ⊕ be there, or the
lord of the 8th strong and well aspected, give a good dower with
the wife, but if the reverse, there is nothing.   Its colours are gray
and black.   Its consignificators are ♄ and ♏.   ♄ being here destroys the wife's dower or property, and renders legacies unprofitable, threatens a violent death, but also denotes the poverty of enemies; ♃ gives legacies, a rich wife, long life, and a natural
death; ♂ gives a violent death, poverty and ruin; the ☉ gives a
rich wife, but danger of a violent death; ♀, a good dower with a
wife, and a natural death; ☿, estates by legacy, death by consumption; the ☾, long life but danger of drowning; the Dragon's
Head the same as ♃; the Dragon's Tail the same as ♄; the ⊕,
great profit by a wife and legacies.   It is a feminine house, and
denotes the genitals.

The 9th house is the house of religion, learning, books and science, voyages and travels abroad, and all church preferments,
clergymen of all degrees, dreams, visions, and kindred on the
wife's side, (or on the husband's side, if the wife be the querent.)
♃ being there shews a pious good character; ♄, ♂, or the Dragon's Tail being there shews an atheist.   The consignificators are
♃ and ♐.   It is a masculine house, and denotes the fundament,
hips and thighs.

The lords of the 1st and 9th, being in good agreement, make
the native a great traveller, merchant and scholar; and if ♃, ♀,
☿, the ☾ or the ☊ be there, or in good aspect with the lord of
the 9th, the native will be truly religious and fortunate; if ♄,
♂, the ☋ or the lord of an evil house be there, the native will be
reprobate and atheistical, evil and unfortunate; and if the lord of
the 9th be weak, retrograde or combust, it denotes great evil,
The colours are green and white.   ♄ makes an atheist and causes

loss by sea; ♃ gives good voyages, piety and church preferment; ♂, atheism or apostacy, loss at sea by pirates, lightning, &c.; the ☉, fortunate voyages, true religion, and church preferment; ♀, the same as ♃, but her condition must be good; the native generally marries in his travels; ☿ gives great science, invention, and it is said, makes the native an adept at occult sciences, he generally travels as an artist or scientific man, and is fortunate or otherwise, as ☿ is strong or weak; the ☊, the same as ♃; the ☋, the same as ♄; the ⊕ gives riches by voyages or the church; the ☾ causes many voyages, and great inconstancy in religion.

The 10th house is the house of honour, authority, preferment, trade, situation and profession, and also of disgrace. It denotes the native's mother, kings, nobility, places, pensions, sinecures, and in state questions, empires, kingdoms, provinces, &c.; ♃ or the ☉ being there, give the greatest honours, but ♄ or the ☋, is disgrace and ruin to great men, and great distress in trade and employment to the lower orders. The consignificators are ♂ and ♑. It is a feminine house, and denotes the knees and hams.

When the lords of the 1st and 10th are strong, and in reception, translation, good application or position, or with the fortunes or the ☊, or in good aspect with any planet but the two infortunes, or with the ⊕ in the 10th or 11th house, all these are signs of honour and prosperity. If the significators be ill disposed, or if there be evil planets in the 10th, it denotes disgrace and often a violent death. The colours are red and white. ♄ being here gives a sudden fall and inevitable ruin to great men, and either disgrace, imprisonment, ignominious death, cr infamy, with loss of trade to all; ♃ is the reverse of ♄; ♂ gives great trouble from magistrates, with martial honours, which will end in misery, it also causes sickness and short life to the mother and much evil; the ☉ gives glory and power beyond the native's birth, from great persons; ♀ gives honour and preferment by great women; ☿ gives preferment, and the native is honoured by learning, and is often secretary to some embassy; the ☾ gives profit and honour by sea, trade, or great women; the Dragon's Head renders honours durable; the Dragon's Tail destroys them; the ⊕ ensures riches by trade, and preferment.

The 11th house is that of friends, connexions, counsellors, advisers, favourites, minions, and flatterers, and denotes all our wishes, expectations, attachments and earnest desires. The ☉ and ♒ are its consignificators. The lord of the 11th being there shews many powerful friends; and the usual harmonies between the lords of 1st and 11th shew good and valuable friends. If the lord of the

12th be there, they are pretended friends and private enemies. Its colours are saffron or deep yellow. ♄ being here gives false friends, despair, and death of children; ♃, true friends, riches and happiness; ♂, false friends, ruin, and wicked children; the ☉, great and noble friends, and great happiness; ♀, honourable faithful friends, particularly women; ☿, inconstant friends, but much depends on his condition; the ☾, the friendship of great women, but her condition is every thing; the Dragon's Head is the same as ♃; the Dragon's Tail is the same as ♂; the ⊕ gives great riches by friendship. It denotes the legs, and is a significator in state questions of the king's riches, treasure, ammunition and soldiery. It is a masculine house.

The 12th house is that of affliction, misery, and suffering, distress of every kind, grief, persecution, malice, secret enmity, anxiety, envy, imprisonment, treason, sedition, assassination, and suicide. It is also the house of great cattle, and kindred by the mother's side. Its consignificators are ♀ and ♓. It is said to be the joy of ♄, because he is the parent of malignity. It is a feminine house and denotes the feet.

If no planet be there, and its lord have no aspect with the ascendant or its lord, there will be few private enemies. If the lord of the ascendant have a good aspect with the lord of the 12th from bad houses, his enemies will injure him under false pretences. If the aspects be evil, especially if the rays of infortunes concur, he will have many enemies, much trouble and imprisonment. If the lord of the 1st be in the 12th, or the lord of the 12th in the 1st, it denotes imprisonment and much anguish. The colour is green. Saturn being here gives every evil except death, that can afflict mankind; ♃ gives few enemies or troubles, and victory over them all; ♂ is the same as ♄, but the enemies will be more courageous and daring; the ☉ makes enemies powerful; ♀ gives great profit by cattle, and few private enemies, and those weak, but her condition must be considered; ☿ gives very knavish enemies, but this will be according to his condition which will make much difference; the ☾, it is said, makes the lower order of people enemies, her condition must be particularly observed; the Dragon's Head is the same as ♃, and the Dragon's Tail the same as Saturn, some say the Dragon's Head strengthens private enemies, and that the Dragon's Tail weakens them; the ⊕ shews great loss and ruin by repeated diasters, enmity, &c. Lilly says, that the 12th is the house of witchcraft, and all enquirers concerning witches.

The description of the 12 houses, as here laid down, has lately been adopted in nativities as well as in horary questions, but I have no opinion of it in nativities whatever, although I have seen several instances in which it has been verifieo : reason is against it, and the effects of the houses, except the 1st and 10th can only be admitted in horary questions. They seem to have their influence assigned them through a misconception of the system of Ptolemy, who certainly did not mean anything of the kind; yet Placidus talks with much confidence of evil aspects from the 8th house, as the house of death, which he says "is terrible " It might be so to him, but I should think it of very little consequence. I have, however, copied the system correctly, and the artist may put it to what use he pleases, but I would advise him to have nothing to do with lords of houses, Dragon's Head or Tail, or *Pars Fortuna*, in nativities; they are merely symbols, and only calculated for horary questions.

The lords of the different houses are also supposed to have a certain effect in their dominative capacity, as follows:

The Lord of the 1st.

In the 1st, Denotes a fortunate life and power over enemies.

2d, Riches by the native's own industry.

3d, Many voluntary journeys.

4th, Lands and inheritance.

5th, Propensity to pleasure, and many children.

6th, Much sickness.

7th, Many public enemies, and he may add himself to the number.

8th, Legacies, or riches by a wife, suicide.

9th, He is religious, learned, and a traveller.

10th, Great honour, and preferment by real merit.

11th, Friends, and he is his own friend.

12th, Danger of imprisonment, and much unhappiness.

The Lord of the 2d.

In the 1st, The native is born to riches, and a good fortune.

2d, Much wealth.

3d, Wealth by brethren, neighbours, and travelling.

4th, Wealth by the father.

5th, Wealth by gaming, or by children.

6th, By dealing in cattle.

7th, By women and marriage.

8th, By legacies or by marriage.

In the 9th, By religion, learning, or foreign journeys.

10th, By preferment, trade and merchandise.

11th, By friends.

12th, By great cattle, also loss of wealth.

The Lord of the 3d.

In the 1st, Pleasure and profit in travelling.

2d, Riches by travelling.

3d, Good brethren and journeys.

4th, Travelling to take possession of an estate.

5th, Travelling for pleasure.

6th, Sickness in journeys.

7th, The native gets a wife, or meets with thieves in his journeys.

8th, He dies on a journey.

9th, Missionary journeys, or as an itinerant preacher.

10th, Journeys for trade or preferment.

11th, Travelling for improvement.

12th, Imprisonment and great misfortunes in journeys.

The Lord of the 4th.

In the 1st, A good inheritance.

2d, An estate by purchase.

3d, Inheritance by brethren.

4th, A healthy long lived father, or good estate.

5th, The estate will pass to his children.

6th, An estate gained by physic, or wasted by sickness.

7th, Estates by a wife.

8th, Estates by wives, legacies or gifts.

9th, By voyages, religion or science.

10th, By some office or dignity.

11th, By friendship.

12th, By dealing in black cattle, or loss by treachery.

The Lord of the 5th.

In the 1st, Affectionate dutiful children.

2d, The riches increased or diminished by children.

3d, Journeys on account of children.

4th, Estates divided among children, or given to them by their grandfather.

In the 5th, Children prudent, healthy, fortunate and happy.

    6th, Disagreement with children, causing sickness, and affliction.

    7th, Open enmity between the native and his children.

    8th, Many evils from children, so as to shorten life.

    9th, Children that will assist their father in learning, and travelling.

    10th, Great honour or disgrace by children.

    11th, Great attachment between the native and his children.

    12th, His children are his private enemies, and the sources of much uneasiness, and often ruin.

In considering the affairs and fortunes of the native's children, the 5th house must be considered as an ascendant, and the lords be directed for it as for a separate nativity.

The Lord of the 6th.

In the 1st, Causes much sickness by the native's irregularity.

    2d, Waste of property by sickness, or by servants.

    3d, Sickness by journeys.

    4th, Sickness from vexation at losses of inheritance.

    5th, From bad children and a profligate love of pleasure.

    6th, Good servants, but severe sickness.

    7th, Sickness by quarrels, fighting, and women.

    8th, Dangerous sickness, and danger of some untimely death.

    9th, Sickness abroad or at sea.

    10th, Sickness from shame and disgrace.

    11th, Sickness on account of friends or ill treatment.

    12th, Sickness by imprisonment and deep vexation.

The Lord of 7th.

In the 1st, Gives a very good saving wife, or loss by enemies.

    2d, Riches or poverty by marriage.

    3d, Quarrels with brethren or neighbors.

    4th, Inheritance or lands by marriage.

    5th, A pleasing wife and many children, also enmity with children.

    6th, An ill disposed wife, the cause of sickness and affliction.

    7th, A very creditable wife with property.

    8th, A rich or poor wife, as he is well or ill dignified.

In the 9th, One who will be separated from her husband by the
    sea.
    10th, Great honour and profit, or digrace and loss, by wives
    or enemies.
    11th, A friendly loving wife or enemies among friends.
    12th, Great misery by marriage, quarrels, law-suits, &c.

The Lord of the 8th

In the 1st, Death by irregularity or suicide.
    2d, Much riches by legacies.
    3d, Dangers from short journeys of being murdered.
    4th, Death through vexation and loss of property.
    5th, Death by drinking and debauchery, or by bad children.
    6th, Incurable sickness.
    7th, Death by suicide, quarrels, thieves, or violent passion.
    8th, A rich wife and a natural death.
    9th, Death by drowning.
    10th, Death by sentence of a judge.
    11th, Legacies by friends.
    12th, Death in prison.

The Lord of the 9th.

In the 1st, Shews piety, learning, and a great traveller.
    2d, Riches by the sea, the church, or by learning.
    3d, The native will be a sectarian or dissenter.
    4th, Church inheritances and lands.
    5th, A free liver and little piety.
    6th, Church preferment, but ill health in foreign countries.
    7th, Enemies in the church and at sea.
    8th, Death or persecution for religion, or abroad.
    9th, A traveller, churchman, or a great scholar.
    10th, Church preferment, or great honours abroad.
    11th, Many friends and fortunate voyages.
    12th, Great vexation and persecution in religion or travel-
    ling.

The Lord of the 10th.

In the 1st, Gives honour and prosperity.
    2d, Purchased honours, riches by trade.
    3d, The native is fortunate and much respected.

4th, Lands and inheritances.
5th, Honourable pursuits and creditable children.
6th, Sickness by aiming at greatness.
7th, An honourable wife, and increase of trade by property.
8th, Gain by a wife, sometimes a violent death.
9th, Honour in the church, and by learning or by voyages.
10th, Great success and renown.
11th, Noble friends.
12th, Disgrace, ruin, and imprisonment.

The Lord of the 11th.

In the 1st, Gives a real friend.
2d, Riches by friends.
3d, Friendship among kindred, fortunate journeys.
4th, Love of the father, good inheritance.
5th, Loving children and an honourable life.
6th, Faithful servants, little sickness.
7th, A loving wife, and few enemies, &c.
8th, An easy death.
9th, Great fortune in voyages, learning, &c.
10th, Great honour, and preferment by the great.
11th, Valuable friends, and great happiness.
12th, Deceitful friends, and much suffering,

The Lord of the 12th.

In the 1st, Gives disgrace and ruin, folly, and consequent misery.
2d, Poverty and ruin.
3d, False kindred, and great disappointment.
4th, An envious father, loss of estates.
5th, Infamous children, and the native is very profligate.
6th, Vile servants, diseases among cattle, much sickness.
7th, Vile enemies, law-suits, an ill wife, and much injury from enemies of every description.
8th, A miserable death, after great misfortunes.
9th, Shipwreck, imprisonment, loss, ignorance, and ruin.
10th, Sad disgrace and ruin by envy, an untimely end.
11th, Deceitful friends, and great disappointments.
12th, Powerful enemies, who overcome in the end.

These positions require some explanation; they have little or no meaning as they stand, and when compared with the descrip_

tion of the houses, involve a great contradiction. Because ♂ might be lord of the 2d, which being in the first would denote riches and good fortune, whereas, in reality, being a malefic he would denote sudden death, or great sickness and danger. ♄ might be the lord of the 2d, which in the 10th denotes great wealth and success in trade, whereas he would denote inevitable disgrace and ultimate ruin. The whole, therefore, is decided by the nature of the question, as, if it related to riches and how they were likely to be obtained, the lord of the 2d posited in the 1st, would denote that the native must gain them by his own industry and that by exertion he could not fail. Again, if the question related to the circumstance of a clergyman being promoted to a benefice, if ♄ were the lord of the 9th, and posited in the 10th, he would be sure to have it. I do not, however, think that an infortune, being significator of a thing desired, is much in its favour, although artists in general make no distinction, but this must be left to every one's experience: my only aim is caution, to guard the student against carelessness and too much deference to old opinions, many of which I can affirm, of my own knowledge, are very erroneous. Care must likewise be taken not to receive anything here laid down in an unlimited sense.

The lord of the 1st in the 2d is said to cause riches by the native's own industry but nothing could be more absurd than this doctrine in certain cases. If the ☾, for instance, were lady of the ascendant and posited in the 2d in square or opposition to ♂ and ♀ or the ☉, it would denote the querent to be a profligate character, who instead of realizing a fortune by his own industry would shortly work his own ruin by his extravagance, with the assistance of his dissolute connexions and his own unsettled disposition, which would prevent him from adhering to any thing good long enough to be serviceable. If posited in the 10th house, he would work his own downfall in the same manner; and if ♂ were at that time in opposition to the luminaries, his end would be violent and untimely; and if either of them were posited in the 10th, or in evil aspect to it or its lord, or to ♃, he would probably be publicly executed. Thus the artist will see, that it is not by a blind adherence to the rules here laid down that correct judgments can be formed; in fact, they are from their present imperfect state worse than useless, for they lead many astray, and should not have been inserted, could the work have been perfect without them. Nevertheless, they have their uses, because they will teach the student, after a few failures, to rely on his own experience and observation, and not on those of others.

The familiarities of planets have a powerful effect both in nativities and in horary questions. In horary questions every planet is deemed a significator of something, and therefore the aspect he receives must be considered accordingly; but in nativities there can be rationally no other significators but the moderators, of which Ptolemy and Placidus reckon 5, viz: the horoscope, the midheaven, the Sun, the Moon, and the Part of Fortune, and this last, the lunar horoscope, I shrewdly suspect to have no influence whatever; nor do I think any moderator can be relied on but the luminaries. To these may be added, ☿ in common with the ☾, as the significator of intellect and disposition.

The following are said to be the effects of the familiarites.

The ☌ of ♄ and ♃, if ♄ be significator, gives the native possessions and inheritances, and profits arising from agriculture, particularly from corn, as ♃ is said to rule the fruits of the Earth. The disposition will be grave, sober, honest, slow, and laborious, if ♃ be well dignified, but if not, he will be dull, vain, superstitious, obstinate and unfortunate.

If ♃ be significator and ♄ well dignified, the native will be cowardly and suspicious, grave, austere and unsociable, inclined to covetuousness, and by this and perseverance often makes a fortune. The most prosperous undertaking he can embark in, is any thing connected with mines and quarries, or in digging and cultivating the Earth. If ♄ be ill dignified, the native is treacherous and base, dull, but sly, full of low cunning, and hypocrisy, a religious bigot, superstitious and selfish, generally hated and despised and of course very unfortunate.

The conjuction of ♄ with ♂, if ♄ be significator and ♂ well dignified, makes the native rash, and unruly, quarrelsome, obdurate and cruel. He may gain preferment in a warlike capacity, but by some means, probably by cowardice or caution, and sometimes by ill timed rashness, or austerity, he will be rendered unfit for it, and be cashiered, or disgraced. If ♂ be ill dignified, he will be treacherous, malignant, a murderer and an assassin probably a footpad, and always a thief when he has an opportunity.

If ♂ be significator, and ♄ well dignified, the native will be cowardly, yet seemingly rash and daring, cruel, hardened and obdurate, and incapable of forgiving. He generally succeeds to his father's estate, and may gain property by labour, knavery, or rapacity, but it is accompanied with cares, vexation and anxiety, and generally chequered with repeated losses, arising chiefly from attempts to over-reach others. If ♄ be ill dignified, the native will be a malignant, cowardly assassin, hypocritical, treacherous and desperately wicked; always in trouble and difficulty, frequently in prison, incessantly in danger, forward in every species of outrage and wickedness, yet often escape by betraying his companions, and generally finish his career by a violent or miserable death.

The ☌ of ♄ with the ☉, if ♄ be significator and the ☉ be well dignified, denotes much evil. It is said, it causes great loss from fire, except good aspects of the fortunes intervene. The native is proud, lofty, and very unfortunate, and has his pride often mortified by his superiors. His condition is often mean, servile, and disagreeable, liable to oppression and insult, and extremely apt to deserve it. He is dull, bewildered, knavish, and base, and always unhappy. If the ☉ be ill dignified, the disposition and fortune are of the same character, but much worse, his disasters more frequent, he lives unhappy and dies miserably, and often comes to an untimely end. If the ☉ be significator, and ♄ be well dignified, he is proud, mean, treacherous, wasteful, and careless, loses his inheritance or destroys it by his prodigality, except a good benefic ray intervene, and often breaks his limbs, or loses his life by falls. If ♄ be ill dignified, his disposition is base and infamous, his fortune bad, and his life extremely miserable, he is a mixture of pride, meanness, covetousness, prodigality, cowardice and rashness, poverty and beggarly pride. He has often a mark or blemish in his face, some of his limbs broken or distorted by falls, or other accidents, sometimes blind or with sore eyes, and often dies a violent death.

The ☌ of ♄ with ♀, if ♄ be significator, and well dignified, makes the native libidinous, and much attached to women, by whom, nevertheless, he may make his fortune. His disposition, though grave, is mild and quiet, yet much addicted to pleasure. He is tolerably fortunate, and gains, mostly by dealing in finery, female dresses, toys. &c. or as a musician or teacher of dancing. If ♀ be ill dignified he is mean, effeminate, selfish and treacherous, and either ruins himself by infamous women or marries one who is poor, or of bad character, or of a different disposition from his own, which renders him permanently miserable.

If ♀ be significator and ♄ well dignified, the native will be cowardly, but wise and careful, always unfortunate in his undertakings, but often retrieves or avoids loss by superior caution and prudence; moderate in his desires, grave, steady, but austere, slow, and one of few words. If ♄ be ill dignified, the native is savage and beastly, malignant and cruel, full of cowardice, dissimulation and treachery, ignorant, stubborn and envious, his fortune is bad, and his life an entire series of misconduct and its consequent train of anxiety and sufferings.

The conjunction of ♄ with ☿, if ♄ be significator, and ☿ well dignified, makes the native subtle and crafty, but with sound judgment, deep learning and good elocution, one ready to acquire knowledge and able to retain it; in any profession connected with literature he is usually successful, his manners are not always the most amiable, as he is inclined to be supercilious and pedantic.

If ☿ be ill dignified, the native is weak minded, conceited, idle, talkative and ignorant; and, if in bad aspect with the ☾, has generally an impediment in speech, he is extremely dishonest, artful, treacherous and base, frequently a sly thief or swindler, and always unfortunate, mean and infamous.

If ☿ be significator and ♄ well dignified, the native is fearful, suspicious, grave and reserved, of some knowledge, but slow parts, cool, secret, cautious, calculating, and very covetous, and frequently makes a fortune thereby; fond of scheming, which he often turns to good account, but selfish, unsociable and worthless.

If ♄ be ill dignified, he is treacherous, base, and malignant, without abilities, and envious of those possessed by others; of shallow judgment, cowardly and suspicious, base and dishonest, and deeply revengeful; always ignorant, obstinate and intractable, often wholly stupid, and if the ☾ be in ☌, □, or ☍, to the place, frequently dumb or silly, and always unfortunate.

The ☌ of ♄ with the ☾, if ♄ be significator and the ☾ well dignified, makes the native tolerably acute, and of sound judgment, provided ☿ be free from affliction, but often unfortunate, except in his dealings with women, or the common or lower order of mankind: very unsettled, restless, and fond of change, which frequently deranges his circumstances, although he in general profits by it in the end. If the ☾ be ill dignified, it denotes great misfortunes and losses, and reduces the native to beggary, by his own folly, instability, and fondness of low company and the dregs of mankind; he is always poor, obscure, mean, and infamous, wretched and shameless; the dupe of infamous women, and an associate of the vilest prostitutes, and if ☿ cast a square or opposite ray to the conjunction, and the ☉ be ill dignified, or in his fall, he will, however high-born, be a beggar and thief by nature, and quit his lofty station to mingle with wretches and vagabonds; and if ♂ give an evil aspect, he will come to an untimely end.

If the ☾ be significator, and ♄ well dignified, the native will be timorous, and suspicious, austere, morose and reserved, covetous and fond of gain, and careful of what he acquires; of slow parts, but sound judgment, laborious and not very aspiring, coarse in manners, and generally makes a fortune by his own exertions.

If ♄ be ill dignified, he is cruel, malicious, brutish and gross in his ideas, without natural affection, suspicious, and deeply malignant, fond of secret revenge, cowardly and implacable, very avaricious, yet changeable, and often wasting his means without end or design, generally hated and avoided, and extremely unfortunate.

It must here be observed, that these effects are only when the conjunction operates independently of any aspects from other planets. If ♃ irradiate the conjunction in any way, it will mitigate its evil effects: for an opposition of Jupiter is held to be better than a trine of ♄ or ♂. If ♂ irradiate the place of the conjunction, even by ⚹ or △, it seldom mends the disposition, but by rendering it more bold, active, and enterprising, generally renders it more mischievous, especially if he be ill dignified. If the aspect be a □, ☍, or ☌, it renders the native more cruel and ferocious, makes him prone to robbery and murder, increases his danger and threatens dissolution by blows, stabs, and fire. If the ☉ cast a good aspect, it denotes riches, favour from the great, and always mends the native's fortune, if he be well dignified; but if not, it will be of short duration and end in nothing. If he be in close conjunction, he adds to the evil by threatening blindness, burning alive, or loss by fire, and violent death, often by the sentence of a judge, besides continual oppression and misery. If he be in square or opposition, he threatens great misery, and a violent or ignominious death. If ♀ irradiate the place by a good aspect, and be well dignified, her effects are equal to those of Jupiter, but if ill dignified, or cadent, the good she gives is but trifling and of short duration. If she irradiate the place by an evil aspect, her effects differ from those of Jupiter, for she rather increases than mitigates the evil. She adds treachery to cowardice, threatens diseases, ruin and death, by means of bad women; injures the native's fortune by inclining him to lust and dissipation, and destroys his wealth and reputation. However, her □ or ☍ will often save life, if the ☾ be hyleg, and afflicted by ♄ or ♂. ☿ partakes of the nature of those with whom he has familiarity. So that if he be well dignified himself, and cast a good aspect to the point of the ☌, he is equal to one of the fortunes; but if in ☌, or □, or ☍, he increases the evil in the manner of the planets by whom he is aspected. The ☾ is like ☿, according to the nature of the planets by which she is aspected. Her ✳ or △ is good, particularly if she be well dignified and free from affliction, but her conjunction where there is an infortune is evil.

The conjunction of ♃ with ♂, if ♃ be significator and ♂ well dignified, makes the native bold, choleric, proud, lofty, magnanimous and daring, very fortunate in war, or a good chemist, surgeon, or physician, and tolerably fortunate, but generally irrascible, and fond of fighting and duelling. If ♂ be ill-dignified, his ill humour is intolerable, and if cadent, he is generally a coward, and in all cases an ill-conditioned, idle, unprincipled, dissipated fellow, fond of broils and strife, with mean abilities, and liable to accidents, wounds, and death, the consequence of his folly.

If ♂ be significator, and ♃ well dignified, the native is noble, just, and beneficent, a man of piety, and often gets church preferment, or rises to eminence in the law, and is fortunate in most of his undertakings. If ♃ be ill dignified, he possesses the same qualities in a very moderate degree, is weak and credulous in matters of religion, and becomes an easy dupe to a hypocrite.

The conjunction of ♃ with the ☉, if the Sun be well dignified, and Jupiter significator, is at best but an evil familiarity. It denotes sickness, oppression and ruin by men in power, or bad parents, but if the native survive until ♃ free himself from the Sunbeams he will recover. If the ☉ be ill dignified, he will be a vain, silly character, and extremely unfortunate, generally sickly in his youth, liable to melancholy, religious despair and madness, especially if ☿ or the ☾ be afflicted.

If the ☉ be significator, whether ♃ be well or ill dignified, he is, they say, so debilitated by the Sunbeams, that the native is but little affected by him, except being rather more religious.

The conjunction of ♃ and ♀ is the most happy familiarity that can possibly be, and promises every good to the native that can fall to the lot of humanity. The better they are dignified the more amiable and happy they will be, and if ♀ be significator the native will be superlatively beautiful. If any thing can add to their felicity, it is when the conjunction happens in ♓, the house of ♃, and exaltation of ♀; but, wherever it happens, it denotes virtue, honour, piety, and tranquility, riches and love. If ♀, however, be ill dignified, the native will be subject to loose desires, but never infamous.

The ☌ of ♃ and ☿, if ♃ be significator, and ☿ well dignified and free from affliction, makes the native virtuous, pious, and of good capacity and extensive information, very eloquent and an excellent scholar and divine. In short, if they are angular, there are no bounds to his capacity. He is generally handsome and elegantly formed, very fortunate, and seems endowed with a kind of magic power, which defeats or overawes all opponents, and obviates every difficulty.

If ☿ be ill dignified, or afflicted, it makes a striking difference. If ill dignified, he is weak, superficial, conceited, very forward in youth, and seemingly sharp, but his mind does not improve progressively, but rather seems to decline as he arrives at manhood. The strength or weakness of the ☾, however, and her aspect to the place of conjunction, makes a very sensible difference in the abilities of the native. If ☿ be afflicted he will communicate the disposition of those planets that afflicted him; if by ♄, the native will be cowardly and base; if by ♂, desperate, passionate, and dishonest; and if combust of the ☉, ignorant, mean and stupid.

If ☿ be significator, and ♃ well dignified, provided ☿ be not combust, the native is mild, gentle, and amiable; a man of abilities and feeling, and a friend to all mankind. His knowledge will always procure him respect, and ensure him riches, honours, good fortune, patronage and protection, according to his station in life. If ♃ be ill dignified, the disposition is equally good, but the native is more credulous and more easily imposed on; nor will he possess that sound judgment and depth of research, as if ♃ were stronger. He will be moderately fortunate, and, if not admired, generally beloved, although his patrons or friends are not so powerful.

The ☌ of ♃ with the ☾, if ♃ be significator, and the ☾ well dignified, is the aspect of harmless good nature, yet of acuteness sufficient to answer all the purposes of self-preservation. The native will be changeable, restless and fond of travelling, and might always be rich, prosperous, and happy, provided he could settle. If the ☾ be increasing in light, his good fortune will be unbounded, and he will probably be united to a lady much above his own condition; but if decreasing, he will meet with some reverses of fortune, though nothing that will injure him materially. If at the new or full, he will suffer occassionally by great men. His greatest fortune will be on the water and among ladies of respectability; and his travels will be beyond the sea.

If the ☾ be ill dignified, he will be good natured, but unsteady in temper, rather pettish, but soon reconciled, extremely changeable, and never satisfied any where. If angular, it is better; but if in a cadent house, he will be generally unfortunate, and suffer much by means of low company, to which he will be too much addicted, except the Sun behold the conjunction with good aspect, and probably may ruin himself by some infamous women, if ♂ aspect the place of the conjunction.

If the ☾ be significator and ♃ well dignified, the native will be highly honoured and respected, and extremely fortunate, and likely to gain considerably by ecclesiastical people or concerns. The disposition is noble, magnanimous, and generous, kind, humane, and hospitable.

If ♃ be ill dignified, the native will possess all those properties in a moderate degree, though his unsuspecting good nature may occasionally make him the prey of the hypocritical and designing, especially in religious matters.

The conjunction of ♂ with the ☉, whether well or ill dignified generally cuts life short by fevers, phrensy, fire, or lightning. If the native escape until ♂ clear himself from combustion, he will be more healthy, but never fortunate. If the conjunction be not near enough for ♂ to be combust, the native will be proud, lofty, arrogant and empty; a daring, boasting, troublesome fellow, always in broils and paying continually the penalty of some outrageous folly. He may gain martial honours, and riches, but they will be held with difficulty amid strife and violence, and finally come to nothing.

If the ☉ be significator, and ♂ well dignified and not near enough to be combust, the native will be violent, headstrong and rash, high in command, and generally victorious; but almost uniformly end his days in battle, or in a duel or dreadful quarrel, or come off terribly wounded.

If ♂ be ill dignified, the native is treacherous, rash and bloody minded, probably a soldier, housebreaker, or foot-pad, and murderer; always in danger, and generally ends his days by a violent and, probably, ignominious death.

The ☌ of ♂ with ♀, if ♂ be significator, and ♀ well dignified, makes the native of a hasty temper, but on the whole good-natured, very forgiving, much addicted to women, but maintains his respectability; is generally fortunate, admired and respected. If ♀ be ill dignified, the pursuits of the native will be low and dishonourable, and seldom attended with success except to accomplish his ruin. His chief companions are prostitutes, which seldom fail to render him prodigal, dissipated and diseased.

If ♀ be significator, and ♂ well dignified, the native will be proud, quarrelsome, and very lustful, and although brave and fortunate in war, generally end his days by some quarrel; he will often, however, make a good surgeon or chemist, and generally meet with success in his undertakings, and, when his passions are out of the question, evince considerable abilities and ingenuity. If ♂ be ill dignified, it renders the native wholly debauched and deeply wicked, a companion of prostitutes, proud, empty, quarrelsome, hardened, cruel and sottish, a thief or thieftaker, the bully of a brothel, or midnight assassin, particularly if ☿ be with them, or in evil aspect.

The ☌ of ♂ with ☿, if ♂ be significator, and ☿ well dignified and free from affliction, gives the native great learning and acuteness, and, when his passions are not concerned, of tolerably sound judgement, one that will excel in anything that requires presence of mind, ready-wit, brilliant imagination, or quick penetration, a good lawyer, orator or politician, ambassador, messenger, or spy upon occasion, and if the ☌ be in an angle, a man of never-failing resources, wonderfully successful, and almost invincible. If ☿ be ill dignified, or afflicted, he will be a chattering, ill-natured, pragmatical pedant, with little learning, and less honesty. frequently a pettifogging attorney, an ignorant pedagogue, a thief, traitor, spy, or common informer, resembling chiefly in disposition those planets by which ☿ is most powerfully aspected or afflicted.

If ☿ be significator, and ♂ well dignified, he makes a great, acute, and powerful commander; and if the ☉ or ♃ are angular and in good aspect, may rise to the highest honour in the army or navy, owing to his great presence of mind, acute perception, and invincible courage.

If ♂ be ill dignified, the native is treacherous, felonious, and blood-thirsty; and if the configuration be in an angle, will possess the power of doing an immense deal of mischief. Idle, dissipated and drunken; capable of any degree of infamy, a thief, house-breaker, footpad, or assassin, a traitor, rebel, informer, impostor, and renegade, a pettifogging lawyer, gambler, or swindler.

The conjunction of ♂ with the ☾, if ♂ be significator, and the ☾ well dignified, makes the native very changeable, but bold and enterprising, not easily disconcerted, and generally marries some lady much above his own sphere of life; one much addicted to women, yet seldom suffers by them.

If the ☾ be ill dignified, the native is naturally vulgar, base and mean, be his birth and connexions what they will; one who delights to associate with the meanest of mankind, vulgar, despicable, and contemptible; in disposition, changeable and silly, of shallow abilities; always poor and unfortunate, drunken and dissipated; often a wanderer, beggar, and frequently a thief; and if a woman, generally a prostitute; they generally through distress or banishment end their days abroad.

If the ☾ be significator, and ♂ well dignified, the native is bold, rash, and unruly; of no great abilities, but possessing much courage and enterprise; well calculated for a warrior, surgeon, chemist, or physician; is fond of travelling and exploring foreign countries, where he generally falls a prey to assassins, or dies of some hot, moist, putrid distemper, though generally fortunate in other respects. If ♂ be ill dignified, the native will be of a violent, furious, temper; malignant, treacherous and cruel; an incendiary, murderer, robber, rebel, and traitor, who seldom lives long, especially if the ☾ be hyleg, and generally comes to an untimely end. Those persons are generally marked with a scar in the eye or face.

The ☌ of the ☉ with ♀, if the ☉ be significator, and ♀ well dignified, makes the native soft and effeminate, yet above any thing mean; some say he is ambitious and fond of glory, but his chief glory will be found to consist in his victories over the fair sex, and his greatest ambition is to be seen in their company. If ♀ be near enough to be combust, much of her power will be destroyed, though enough will be left to give the native a turn for extravagance, and an attachment for persons whose affairs are always in a deranged or ruinous state, and his property will be continually wasted in retrieving them. If ♀ be ill dignified, he will keep company with none but low and infamous women, who will speedily bring him to ruin.

If ♀ be significatrix, the native will be proud, and prodigal; and if the ☉ be ill dignified, extremely mean and poor withal, generally short lived, liable to consumption, and hectic fever; and full of crosses and vexations. If, however, the native live until she separate from the Sun, he will be more healthy, but seldom fortunate.

The ☌ of the ☉ and ☿, if the ☉ be significator, and ☿ well dignified, is said to give great wit, learning and ingenuity. It is the general opinion, that ☿ does not suffer like the other planets by combustion, but is rather strengthened by it; experience, however, does not warrant this conclusion. The native will seldom have much propensity to learning, although he may have no inconsiderable proportion of low cunning. One of this description may probably turn out pettifogger, thief-taker, bailiff, or some other worthless character. If ☿ be significator, the effects will be nearly the same, as ☿ imbibes the nature of the planet he is joined with. He will be addicted to boasting and lying through want of common sense, very deceitful, and always endeavoring to appear what he is not. If the ☉ be well dignified, it is said he will acquire either riches, promotion, or favour with the great; however this may be, he is generally sickly in youth, liable to fevers, burns, or scalds, and latent diseases not easily cured. If in good aspect with ♃, he will be more healthy, and if the ☾ be in good aspect with him, his intellects will be much improved, though he will seldom be remarkable for learning.

The ☌ of the ☉ with the ☾, if the ☉ be significator, and the ☾ well dignified, is said to give profit by travelling. No doubt the ☾, from her proximity, is stronger under the Sun-beams than any other planet, though her influence must suffer a material change. If the ☾ be ill dignified, the native will be very unsteady, fond of travelling, and never very rich or respectable, and will probably be very sickly in youth, though if he live until the Moon get from under the Sun-beams, he may do well. If the ☾ be significator, it denotes blindness or very bad eyes, and if the condition of ☿ be such as to indicate a love of learning, he may probably blind himself, or acquire the Myopia or near-sightedness, by reading. If the ☾ be in close conjunction, the native will be very short lived, or if applying to close conjunction, the same. If coming from under the Sun-beams, and the native survive, he may be very healthy after a while, but something will ail his eyes, and he will probably have a scar in one of them or in the face. He will be proud, aiming at high things, but will seldom attain them; unstable in his resolves, and encounter a great variety of new situations.

The ☌ of ♀ with ☿, if ♀ be significator and ☿ well dignified and free from affliction, makes the native handsome and well shaped, ingenious, witty and eloquent; well disposed and kind to every one. Such a one generally acquires a fortune by some literary undertaking, and is always fortunate. If ☿ be weak, or combust, it shews the native to be mean and artful, arising from oppression, and a broken spirit.

If ☿ be significator, and ♀ well dignified, it is the aspect of elegance and beauty, sound wisdom and goodness of heart, love, beneficence, tenderness, delicacy, compassion, meekness, modesty, truth, and innocence. If ♀ be ill dignified, the native, although eminently beautiful, will be artful and too much given to the company of the opposite sex, which will ultimately prove his ruin. They are generally good proficients in music.

The ☌ of ♀ and the ☾, if ♀ be significator, and the ☾ well dignified, makes the native unstable, but always fortunate, very good natured and of an easy temper, yet fully conscious of his own dignity and importance, and generally admired by the multitude. If the ☾ be ill dignified, he will be unstable and foolish, very talkative, boasting, and full of promises, without either a wish or ability to fulfil them; always changing place, and liable to many disappointments.

If the ☾ be significator, and ♀ well dignified, the native will be effeminate but pleasing, very handsome and of good understanding; a great proficient in the fine arts, of elegant manners, fond of company, always presenting to himself the best side of things, and seldom laying any thing to heart, indeed, he has little reason so to do, for he is generally admired and respected. If ♀ be ill dignified, it makes the native lustful, thoughtless, and abandoned, profligate, foolish and careless, but this depends much on the other aspects of the ☾.

The ☌ of ☿ and the ☾, if ☿ be significator, and the ☾ well dignified and both of them free from affliction, makes the native of sound understanding; and if ☿ be at good distance from the ☉, fond of learning, endowed with great abilities, and much admired by the lower orders. He will be changeable and unsteady, fond of travelling, and very judicious and aspiring in his acquaintance and connexions. One who is much favoured by women of a higher order, and generally prosperous in all undertakings.

If the ☾ be significator, and ☿ well dignified, their effects are nearly the same, except that the native has more abilities and less instability; is generally slight made and handsome, learned, ingenious and profound, and one who often produces some new invention, but the disposition in both these cases depends on the nature of the various planets configurated with the ☾ and ☿.

Of the Sextile and Trine.

The ⚹ or △ of ♃, if ♄ be significator, makes the native wise, sober, discreet, grave and pious; gives him favour among the great, and sometimes church preferment, or riches by agriculture.

The ⚹ or △ of ♂ adds a degree of courage to the natural timidity of the native, and is a sign of military preferment; it renders him generous though choleric, more bold, active and enterprising, open and confident.

The ⚹ or △ of the ☉ makes the native more noble, and highminded, but, it is said, with but little courage, especially if the ☉ be weak or ill dignified. He is generous, but very revengeful and austere. He is large-boned, round-shouldered and stooping, not very prepossessing in appearance, but if the ☉ be strong, he wil. acquire riches, and be tolerably fortunate and honourable.

The ⚹ or △ of ♀ gives the native a comely appearance, brown hair and gray eyes; fondness of women, and every degree of extravagance connected with them. If ♀ be strong, he may marry to advantage, and rather gain than lose by women; but, if weak, they will generally lead him to dissipation and ruin.

The ⚹ or △ of ☿ makes the native ingenious, but without sterling merit or sound judgment, except ☿ be strong and well aspected. He is very curious, artful, fond of new whims that seldom amount to any thing, and very grave, subtle and reserved.

The ⚹ or △ of the ☾ makes him very changeable, fearful and suspicious: but if the ☾ be well dignified, he will be tolerably fortunate, much admired by the vulgar, and generally gain considerably by the favour of, or by marriage with, some lady of consequence.

If ♃ be significator, the ⚹ or △ of ♄ makes him cautious, fearful, melancholy or very grave; fond of agricultural pursuits, and embarking in concerns relative to mines, quarries, or anything that relates to digging in the Earth, by which he may gain considerably, if ♄ be well dignified. He is rather above the middle stature, inclining to baldness; and if ♄ be weak, is very covetous, and not always fortunate, though he often gains by purchasing land or houses, and frequently by legacies or by his father, or by the favour of old men.

The ⚹ or △ of ♂ makes the native bold, but noble and generous, somewhat choleric and very ambitious; he is fortunate in war, ingenious in chemistry, and skilful in surgery. If ♂ be weak, he will be more subtle, and though he may acquire martial preferment, it may not be great or lasting.

The ⚹ or △ of the ☉ makes the native of good stature, well made and ruddy; very lofty and courageous, especially if the ☉ be strong; always fortunate, and highly respected by the great and men in power. If the ☉ be weak, he will possess the same qualities and fortune, though in a more moderate degree, but if Mars afflict the ☉, he will die a violent death, or meet with some dreadful injury.

The ⚹ or △ of ♀ makes the native superlatively beautiful, tall and elegant, fine blue eyes and brown hair, kind, loving, and every way amiable; always beloved and of course fortunate, rich and honourable. If ♀, however, be weak, the native will be ɑnprudent, and too fond of pleasure.

The ✶ or △ of ☿ makes the native good and virtuous, and gives him refined wit and solid judgment. It is the aspect of ingenuity, eloquence, sound learning, and great abilities. It bestows kindness and affability, yet with sufficient acuteness, and uninterrnpted good fortune, except ☿ be much afflicted. If he be weak, the endowments and fortune of the native will be in some small degree diminished.

The ✶ or △ of the ☾ makes the native very mutable and easily persuaded to change his situation, attachment or profession; and he may be a traveller by sea if the Moon be posited in a watery sign, in which case he will be extremely fortunate, if the ☾ be free from affliction. He is generally a great favorite with women and beloved by the lower orders of mankind, and if belonging to the higher class, is generally a favorite with the queen, or some great lady of quality, and mostly marries to advantage. If the ☾ be weak, he will be loquacious and conceited, and if there be good familiarity between ☿ and the ☾, his fortune will be greater than his abilities.

If ♂ be significator, the ✶ or △ of ♄ makes the native grave and far from headstrong; for ♄ always gives caution approaching to cowardice. He, however, if ♂ be strong, may be tolerably obstinate, and probably a bigot, if he be religious. If ♄ be strong, he may gain by legacies, or by insinuating himself into the good graces of some elderly person, who will most likely suffer by him; but if ♄ be weak, or afflicted, it will occasion some trouble, and probably not be lasting.

The ✶ or △ of ♃ makes the native bold, high minded, and rather ambitious, but truly honourable and respectable. He is enterprising, but strictly just, and above a mean action. If ♃ be weak, he will be conceited, and perhaps a little enthusiastic in religion, yet tolerably fortunate.

The ✶ or △ of the ☉ gives the native great preferment and favour, and, if the ☉ be strong, he will rise almost from obscurity to great eminence by favour of great and powerful men. People of this description rise rapidly in the army, navy, or at court, or in any employ where they have dealings with the great; or if connected with money matters and such as have the handling of gold, they are sure to get rich. At all times they are sure of being fortunate and honourable, except ♄ be joined with the ☉, or posited in the south angle, which is sure to destroy all.

The ✶ or △ of ♀ is, according to modern astrologers, a very bad aspect; but this is an opinion not founded in truth, or justified by experience. The native will, doubtless, be a libertine in love

matters, and, if ♀ be ill dignified, a person of loose character; but
if ♀ be strong, he will generally be respectable in his connexions,
rather wild than wicked, and by no means of an evil disposition,
but kind, generous, and tractable, except where women or pleasures intervene; not so prudent as might be wished, but active,
acute, insinuating, handsome, elegant, and one of very prepossessing manners and appearance; bright penetrating eyes, and tolerably fortunate, though he seldom makes the most of it; much
admired and courted by women, whose rank and condition of life
may be known by the dignity or debility of Venus, and by observing whether she be angular or cadent.

The ✶ or △ of ☿ gives the native good abilities, makes him
ingenious, eloquent and learned; unites his valour with prudence,
and renders him acute and penetrating, particularly if ☿ be well
dignified, in good aspect with the ☾, and free from affliction.
If he be weak, combust, or cadent, the native will be more
dull and superficial, which defects he will endeavour to remedy
by craft and subtlety, boasting and perhaps, lying, swindling, or
gaming. His fortune will be proportionate to the strength or
weakness of ☿.

The ✶ or △ of the ☾ makes the native very talkative and
changeable, a restless, unsettled traveller, and one who by subtlety gains by the lower classes. He will most likely be in some
military or naval capacity, probably the latter, if the ☾ be in a
watery sign; often angry, but soon pleased, and if the ☾ be well
dignified, tolerably fortunate and respectable; but if she be weak,
he will gain little by his travels, and probably be much injured by
his intimacy with low women. If ♂ himself be strong, he will
captivate every woman he comes near.

If the ☉ be significator, the ✶ or △ of ♄ will make the native
covetous, fearful and inclined to meanness, yet given to boasting,
and very conceited and obstinate, though, except ♄ be very ill
dignified, he is not malicious. If ♄ be weak, he will be weak
minded and prodigal, and seldom fortunate. It, however, shews
a good understanding to exist between the native and his father,
and that he will ultimately inherit what the latter possesses.

The ✶ or △ of ♃, if they are both strong, is the aspect of honour, glory, and riches. The native is high-minded, noble, just,
generous, and strictly honourable, and happy in all his undertakings. It is, however, said, that his generosity amounts to prodigality, and that from an unbounded spirit of liberality, his treasures, although immense, are frequently exhausted.

The ✶ or △ of ♂ is the aspect of valour and victory, unbounded honour, and rapid preferment. The native is of a hot, dry, constitution, strong and vigorous, noble, and possessing exalted notions of his own pre-eminence; very ambitious, fortunate, powerful, and of an overwhelming mind, that nothing can resist; great and magnanimous, a true friend, and a generous enemy. If ♂, however, be ill dignified, it lessens those qualities in a very remarkable degree, and if the ☉ be weak also, the native's character, although the same in appearance, will be merely superficial, and his fortune be neither great nor lasting. If ♄ aspect ♂ in any way, it greatly lessens the native's courage.

The ⚹ or △ of ♀ and of ☿ to the ☉ may be found in some systems of astrology, and also their squares and oppositions, but as no such aspects can ever be formed, it must be a difficult task to describe their effects. Ptolemy, indeed, mentions the sextile of ♀, but by this he must mean a mundane sextile, for ♀ is never above 48° distant from the Sun, and of course can form no aspect in the zodiac beyond the semiquadrate.

The ⚹ or △ of the ☾ makes the native famous and fortunate, especially among the lower orders of mankind, and if both the luminaries be well dignified, among the great likewise. The native is kind and cheerful, fond of variety, and much addicted to travelling or rambling about, but if the ☾ be afflicted, it hurts the native's fortune.

If ♀ be significator, the ⚹ or △ of ♄ makes the native comely, rather pale, affable and quiet, yet somewhat artful, and not very courageous; not fond of debate or strife, but more grave and retired; very shy and modest, and if ♄ be well dignified, is very liable to gain by legacies, and by old people, who generally take a fancy to the native. It is said, they never marry until 30 years old. If ♄ be weak, or ill dignified, they seldom gain much by this aspect, unless other good aspects assist it.

The ⚹ or △ of ♃ makes the native eminently beautiful, noble, virtuous, just, generous and honourable. If ♃ be strong, it gives great fortune, preferment, and felicity, particularly in agricultural and ecclesiastical professions. If ♃ be weak or ill dignified, the native is more credulous and unguarded, but in all cases it is an excellent aspect.

The ⚹ or △ of ♂ makes the native handsome and fresh coloured, but proud and artful, and very libidinous, much inclined to anger and rashness, and fond of embarking in hazardous adventures, in which if ♂ be well dignified they often succeed, but if weak, they generally suffer by their folly. If ♂ and ♀ are both ill dignified, they are very lewd and unprincipled.

The ⚹ of ☿ (for they never form a trine) makes the native well shaped and elegant, and if well dignified, very handsome, except ☿ be too near the ☉. They often gain much by arts or sciences, and are generally learned and polite, but there is no aspect more uncertain than this, as it wholly depends on those planets, with which ☿ is configurated.

The ⚹ or △ of the ☾ gives great honour and fortune in proportion as the ☾ is dignified and free from affliction. The native is always extremely popular, though unstable and eccentric, and often gains much by women; they are generally neat, comely, and prepossessing. If the ☾ be ill dignified, they are seldom capable of any great action, but fond of novelty and unprofitable speculations.

If ☿ be significator, the ⚹ or △ of ♄ makes the native very studious, subtle and reserved, and if well dignified, gives him a cold calculating judgment tolerably correct; but he is mean and insinuating, selfish, and one who generally gets into the good graces of old men, and often gains considerably by them, if their horoscopes correspond with his own. If ♄ be ill dignified, these advantages seldom remain with him for any length of time, he is full of conceits and plans that are vain and futile.

The ⚹ or △ of ♃ makes the native a just, upright and virtuous character, with great wit and solid sense; majestic, noble, ingenious, learned and eloquent; very fortunate and universally respected. If Mercury, however, be debilitated or combust, or in evil aspect of the ☾, it greatly impairs the native's understanding, and consequently his good fortune.

The ⚹ or △ of ♂ gives great ability and confidence, subtlety, ingenuity and learning, but the native is extremely proud and conceited, and not too remarkable for honour or integrity. If ♂ be well dignified, and ☿ free from combustion, he generally gains a fortune either by the army, surgery, medicine, chemistry, or the fabrication of iron, or working at the fire. If ♂ be ill dignified, it makes the native rash, fond of gaming, or any indirect way of gaining money, and too much addicted to company, drinking, and other unprofitable pursuits.

The ⚹ of ♀ depends much on her dignity: if she be well dignified, the native is a pattern of elegance, both in body and mind; gentle, kind, soft and pleasing, and if a male, highly favoured by the ladies. If she be ill dignified, the form of the native will be equally elegant, but the mind less pure; too much addicted to bad company, loose desires, and prodigality. There is no planet, however, so convertible as ☿, and any bad aspect of an infortune will wholly counteract the good effects of ♃ or ♀, or ieduce them to a nullity, by making the native a strange mixture of good and evil, wisdom and folly, and inconsistency.

The ✳ or △ of the ☾ is the aspect of sound abilities, as nothing strengthens the mind so much as good agreement between ☿ and the ☾, especially if she be angular, and well dignified, the native will be ingenious and witty, yet strong in judgment and quick in penetration, and (if ☿ and the ☾ be free from combustion and affliction) capable of any undertaking. If the ☾ be weak, they will be very changeable, fond of novelty, often busy in unprofitable speculations, and not very sincere in their professions or attachments. The disposition, however, in all cases, may chiefly be known by the nature of those planets in configuration with both ☿ and the ☾.

Of the Square and Opposition.

The □ or ☍ of ♃, if ♄ be significator, causes great troubles and sufferings to the native, persecution by the clergy, and much injury arising from the native's own baseness, selfishness, or folly.

The □ or ☍ of ♂ is the aspect of cruelty and murder. The native is treacherous, proud, angry, base, ungrateful, and deeply wicked.

The □ or ☍ of the ☉ is the aspect of infamy and contempt. The native is proud, prodigal, ambitious, revengeful, and insolent, yet not courageous, always unfortunate and disappointed, and frequently meets a violent death, by falls, suicide, or a public execution.

The □ or ☍ of ♀ shews lust, vice, and infamy. The native is base, vicious, sometimes mean and sometimes prodigal, connected with the most infamous strumpets, and in the high road to eventual ruin.

The □ or ☍ of ☿ makes the native a thief, cheat, or swindler, with just abilities sufficient to enable him to be a villian, yet of more cunning than resolution. The native is frequently dumb, or with great impediment in his speech, ignorant, dull, and averse to learning.

The □ or ☍ of the ☾ makes the native a wanderer and vagabond, often crooked, and always badly made and ugly; frequently lame, or with one leg shorter than the other. The disposition is mean, base, sordid and vulgar, which makes him despised and detested by all; destitute of any qualifications but for wickedness.

often in danger of a violent death by mobs, riots, falls, hanging, drowning, &c.

If ♃ be significator, the □ or ☍ of ♄ is the aspect of unceasing misery and suffering, disgrace and ruin. The native is always unfortunate and afflicted, and this naturally renders him dull, peevish, too often idle, wretched and beggarly.

The □ or ☍ of ♂ makes the native very angry and furious, ill-natured, subtle, ungrateful, very ambitious, bold, fond of war and quarreling, and he often meets a violent death by wounds, blows, or resistance to robbers.

The □ or ☍ of the ☉ makes the native excessively proud and arrogant, vain-glorious, prodigal, and wholly wasteful of his substance; addicted to riot, intemperance, drinking, gaming, or any species of folly to look great in the eyes of others. Unfortunate, despised, and finally ruined.

The □ or ☍ of ♀ makes the native prone to intemperate lust of all kinds, particularly if ♃ be disposed of by ♀. His company generally devoted to strumpets, high or low, according as ♀ is dignified, and these connexions inevitable bring him to ruin. In other respects, his disposition is not radically bad, if we except a total want of principle arising from gaiety, thoughtlessness, distress, and dissipation. Generally handsome, but with a countenance indicative of intemperance and debauchery.

The □ or ☍ of ☿ makes the native prone to strife and contention, and torments him with law-suits, frauds, and numerous vexations from people of high or low condition, according to the dignity or debility of ☿. The native is generally but of weak understanding, whimsical, unstable, rash, and foolish; for, it is said, his mind is filled with wrong impressions, arising from the bad aspect of ☿. There can be no doubt, however, that the understanding of every one depends much on the strength and distance of ☿ from the ☉, his being to the west of that luminary, increasing in light and motion, and above all, his good aspect with the ☾.

The □ or ☍ of the ☾ makes the native silly, loquacious, changeable and irresolute, and he is, it is said, generally injured or ruined by the common people, and hated by powerful women.

If ♂ be significator, the □ or ☍ of ♄ makes the native deeply malicious or wicked; a treacherous lurking assassin. The natural consequence of such propensities is continual danger and suffering, especially if ♄ be stronger than ♂. He generally meets death or severe injuries from falls, blows, poison, or by suicide, if either of them be in the ascendant, or, if ♄ be in the midheaven, by coming to an untimely end.

The □ or ☍ of ♃, it is said, makes the native an atheist or infidel, impudent, proud, daring, and obstinate; a scoffer at all piety, common decency, and moral honesty; a companion of the wicked, the terror of the good, and the ruin of himself. If ♃ be stronger than ♂, the native will not be so infamous but very unfortunate, and always at enmity with ecclesiastical or other great men.

The □ or ☍ of the ☉ threatens death by fever, phrensy, fire, or the sentence of a judge. The native is furious, proud, rash, prodigal, wicked and desperate, and, it is said, if the ☉ be lord of the 7th, he will be murdered by enemies or robbers, and if of the 10th, he will be executed.

The □ or ☍ of ♀ makes the native lustful, abominable, and every way depraved; a gamester, glutton, and drunkard, malignant, treacherous, and if a female, a prostitute, or if a male, married to one, or becomes a bully to, or keeper of, a brothel.

The □ or ☍ of ☿ makes the native a thief, swindler, in short, one who continually lives by the most infamous practices. He is daringly wicked, yet artful, knowing, and deeply versed in every species of infamy. His affairs are always in an unsettled and desperate state, and he is destitute of every just and moral principle; a sly atheist or infidel, slanderer, felon, footpad, turnkey to a prison, bully in a brothel, hangman, pettifogger, street-keeper, low police-officer, in short, he is always injuring and cheating mankind.

The □ or ☍ of the ☾ makes the native a low, vulgar, unprincipled, despicable wretch, and one who, were he born a prince, would delight in being a beggar and a thief; a bitter-tongued, abusive vagabond; wretched, filthy, envious, stupid, servile, base, despised, insulted, and wholly unfortunate.

If the ☉ be significator, the □ or ☍ of ♄ makes the native cowardly, treacherous, spiteful and malicious to every one, and wholly insensible to friendship or kindness. He is proud, boasting, covetous and prodigal by turns; very impudent, ignorant, obstinate and brutish; in great danger of violent death by falls, blows, or hanging, particularly if either of them be in the 10th. If in the ascendant, he will be diseased and short-lived, except an aspect of ♃ intervene, which may save after a severe illness, if ♃ be angular.

The □ or ☍ of ♃ makes the native proud, lofty, and dissipated; a scornful arrogant man; careless of his property, at enmity with religion, and its professors, and one who eventually ruins himself by waste, pride, and prodigality.

The □ or ☍ of ♂ makes the native mad and furious, rash, prodigal, noisy, and desperate. It threatens fevers, phrensy, loss of an eye, and a violent death.

The □ or ☍ of the ☾ makes the native proud, vain, changeable and mean, and if the ☾ be ill dignified, very vulgar; one who is only calculated for low company, and lives as a sailor, soldier, or beggarly wandering vagabond, at enmity with the common order of people, and much injured by low women, careless, ignorant, and unsteady. If the opposition be close, and the ☾ hyleg, the native will be short lived, if not, he will be diseased, and perhaps blind, or liable to lose an eye.

The square or opposition of ♄, if ♀ be significator, makes the native deformed in body and mind; base, poor, cowardly, sordid, beastly, unnatural, and despicable, fortunate in nothing, and he ultimately comes to ruin.

The square or opposition of ♃ makes the native proud, superficial; a stranger to piety and decency; prodigal, lustful, and intemperate.

The square or opposition of ♂ makes the native extremely base, felonious, and deeply wicked; given up to every species of lust and intemperance; fond of brothels, prostitution, inebriety, quarrels, midnight broils, and every species of infamy.

The square or opposition of the ☾ makes the native vulgar, brawling and contentious; ill conditioned, idle, mean, and beggarly; silly, unstable, conceited, ignorant, and stupid; and if the ☾ be strong, they will always be a prey to their enemies. If the native be a male, he will be extremely unfortunate in marriage.

If ♀ be significator, the square or opposition of ♃ makes the native, dull, poor, cowardly, ignorant, covetous, envious and malicious; dejected, spiteful, slanderous, often a secret thief or murderer, and fit for nothing good.

The square or opposition of ♃ disposes the native to strife, contention, lawsuits, disgrace and vexation, the consequence of his own imprudence; makes him foolish, absurd, always prone to do wrong, and then fretting and repenting of his folly.

The square or opposition of ♂ is the aspect of felony and murder, highway or footpad robbery, housebreaking, and every species of the deepest villainy. The native is bold, furious, and desperate; cruel, malignant, bloodthirsty, hardened, obdurate and inexorable, and if ♀ be with either of them he will probably murder his wife or sweetheart, if either of the luminaries be in bad aspect, or ☌, or if ♄ or ♂ or ☿ be in the 10th, he will be led to public execution, or if the square or opposition be in the ascendant, he will probably die by his own hand to prevent it.

The □ or ☍ of the ☾ makes the native foolish, idle, unsteady, vulgar, slow of speech, stupid, stammering, proud, ignorant, and fit for nothing. They are generally poor and disagreeable in their ways, obnoxious to decent women, and always unsettled, roving, low minded, unprincipled vagabonds.

If the ☾ be significator, the □ or ☍ of ♄ makes the native vulgar, grovelling and beastly; crooked in body and mind; cowardly, artful, covetous, envious, malicious, jealous, treacherous, debauched, sly, and deeply wicked. Always in trouble and affliction, dejected and melancholy, secret and concealed in all his ways, pinched by poverty, bad health, and extreme misery. He frequently meets with a violent death, and, it is said, generally hastens the death of his mother by his evil ways.

The □ or ☍ of ♃ causes many afflictions and sufferings, unstable fortune, false friends, and powerful, unfeeling enemies. The native is often persecuted for religious opinions, to which he generally adheres with a degree of pride and obstinacy that often accelerates his ruin.

The □ or ☍ of ♂ makes the native proud, desperate, mischievous and cruel, furious, bitter, treacherous, and blood-thirsty; often a felon or murderer; very prodigal, and extremely wretched in every one's eyes but his own. He seldom escapes a violent death, either at the gallows or by blows or stabbing, often in the field of battle, or by such characters as himself. If the ☾ be hyleg, he is sure to be short lived.

The square or opposition of the ☉ makes the native proud and prodigal, very ambitious, but always mortified and disappointed, wasting his substance in pursuit of foolish phantoms, which he will never attain, and which, if he did, would be vain and useless. If there be a close opposition, the native will not attain the age of maturity, and the same if the ☾ be near and hastening to the opposition; but if it be past, he may live, but will generally be sickly, marked in the face, and generally blind or diseased in the eyes. There is also danger of the native being burnt or scalded, or losing his life by fire, or some malignant fever, especially if ♂ aspect the ☉ in any way.

The □ or ☍ of ♀ makes the native lustful, lewd, and infamous, and if ♀ be ill dignified, a mean, selfish, vulgar, deceitful, debauched vagabond; prostituted, unfortunate and despicable.

The □ or ☍ of ☿ gives the native a defect in speech, renders

him destitute of ability, except that species of low cunning which
alone serves the purpose of dishonesty. The peculiar turn of the
disposition is better known by observing how ☿ is aspected by
the other planets, which makes a material difference.

A good planet, strong, and casting a friendly ray to the place of
a ☌ or to any significator, however badly aspected, would materially alter the disposition and fortune for the better, in a
manner peculiar to its own nature. If ♃ were strong and in △
to ☿ when in ☍ to ♂, the native would, in a great degree, resemble Socrates, who, although (as he affirmed himself to be)
extremely wicked, was enabled to conquer his vicious inclinations
by the divine aid of philosophy. The native would feel violent,
strong compunction within him when about to plunge into guilt
or danger, which would often arrest him in his progress, and perhaps he might repent, or amend from religious motives. If the ☾
cast a good aspect to ☿ being herself in good configuration with
the fortunes, he might extricate himself by means of sound judgment, fortitude and discernment; or if ♀ were strong and in △
to Mercury he might be united to some respectable female, who
might wholly reclaim him.

If, on the contrary, ♄ cast a malignant ray to the ☌ of Venus
and ♃, the native will be sly, covetous, treacherous, and mean,
without any apparent reason or necessity for being so. If ☿,
afflicted by ♂, were in ☍, the native although surrounded by
affluence, would be a thief, and steal everything he could get at.
And if ♂ were in □ or ☍ he would be fond of war, quarrels, and
contention, until he brought himself to an untimely end, or got so
miserably maimed as to render him wretched for life.

It is necessary here to observe, that neither ♄, ♃, ♂, ♀, or ☿,
can be significators as lords of the ascendant, except in horary
questions. In nativities only the luminaries and the horoscope
can govern the disposition, except in what relates to the strength
or weakness of the intellects, which are governed by ☿ and the ☾.
We must likewise be cautious in nativities of entering into the
more minute particulars of these aspects; they are chiefly calculated for horary questions, when any one's disposition and situation are required to be known. In that case the ascendant and
its lord, or the house relative to the thing and its lord, are always
taken as significators, and judgment formed as above.

To judge properly of the various effects of these aspects is the
most difficult thing either in horary questions or nativities. It
requires acute genius, uncommon penetration, sound judgment and
almost unbounded experience; and it is only owing to a want of

these that predictions have so often failed. When we consider the various qualities of stars aspecting the same place, their strength or weakness, and take into the account the influence of climate, habit, disposition, education, mode of living, strength or weakness of constitution, &c. all of which have the power of increasing the effects of some stars and diminishing or neutralizing those of others; it is almost presumption to expect a correct judgment in many cases; none but an impudent or ignorant impostor would pretend to give it. To this we may add, what I suspect is the case, that the effect of some of the aspects are misunderstood. I have more opinion of the $\ast$ than the $\triangle$, and I suspect the $\square$ to be stronger than the $\mathcal{8}$. The $\mathbb{C}$ generally produces remarkable changes of weather in her $\ast$ with the $\odot$, either way; whereas, such effects are seldom the result of a $\triangle$. Her $\mathcal{8}$ and δ are mostly alike in their effects; whereas, her $\square$ is manifestly different from either. It is chiefly from the effects of the luminaries on each other, that a knowledge of the nature of aspects can be derived, because their influence is more powerful than that of the other planets, and comes more within the reach of our observation.

That planets operate in nativities according to the nature of the signs they are in, as, feral, bicorporal, human, watery, fiery, &c.; or, that in particular signs they govern particular parts of the body, seems rather improbable, but this must be left to the test of experience.

Some allowance ought to be made for the platic distance of aspects, both in longitude and latitude. Those most partile are most powerful, and I conceive that their influence gradually diminishes as they are distant from that partile position, and not (as the general opinion is) that they remain in force the extent of their orb, and not a degree beyond it. Neither do I think any good reason can be given why planets may not have a platic familiarity, although their signs do not correspond. Thus I should conceive $\mathcal{2\!\!\!\downarrow}$ in the 28th degree of $\mathcal{H}$ to be in platic δ with $\hbar$ in the 1st degree of $\mathcal{\gamma}$, although in different signs; nor do I think the $\mathbb{C}$ being void of course, a matter of any importance in nativities, although I would always allow the usual system in horary questions.

When a question is asked, the artist must take it for granted, that no more is meant than is asked, and not frame questions and answers of his own. This would not agree or sympathise with the mind of the querent, and would consequently be a false prediction. Everything, however, that is required, may be answered by the same figure. In other respects the artist is more at liberty and may form his own system, according to his own experience. He ought also to consider himself as much influenced by sympathy as the querent. The latter has wholly the task of producing the question, and the former the choice of which method he pleases to adopt in resolving it. He should nevertheless be steady in his system, when he has once adopted a method on a full conviction of its propriety, that is right to him, however wrong it might be to others.

I would strenuously recommend to every student, to have nothing to do with the questions of strangers. They are generally the result of knavery or folly, and seldom answer any end but to render him ridiculous. Neither should he meddle with anything even of his own, that springs from curiosity alone, or from a desire to try experiments.

Hitherto it has been customary only to predict by zodiacal aspects, but he may adopt the mundane, if he think proper and feel himself convinced of their efficacy; for the whole is symbolical, and he may use what symbols he please. In doing this, however, he must avoid all contradictions, and all rules which are difficult to reconcile to each other; for a system that contradicts itself cannot be productive of truth, and he will find difficulties enough in the plainest system, without creating any additional ones of his own. I need not add, that he should always be perfectly sober, and if his drink be wholly water it will enhance his reputation.

Above all things, let him be careful of entering too minutely into particulars; the science will not admit of it, and the artist is sure to be disgraced. Those who lay down such examples are generally impostors, and, at all events, gross enthusiasts. When an artist has calculated a number of events, he generally acquires some after knowledge of their issue; this he ought carefully to collect, and compare each with its figure, which will shew him how far he ought to go in future; but this cannot be relied on until by a considerable number of instances, without a single failure, the fact be fully established. It must, however, be admitted, that some artists can judge with greater correctness and more minutely than others, which can alone be accounted for from sympathy, and in my opinion (though I cannot speak from experience) there may be cases where an antipathy may subsist between the querent and the quesited, owing to the figures of their genitures not being in unison, which may in many cases contribute to render a question not radical, or so confused by opposite testimonies, that no positive answer can be given. It would be much better could every one solve their own questions, and the design of this book is to enable them to do it. They would have the great advantage of knowing their own affairs, and thereby perceiving the drift of many things at once, all of which an artist has carefully to pick out of the figure at the hazard of his reputation. One evil, however, would often arise in the querent being biased by his own wishes, which, without great care, would often mislead him.

QUESTION 1*st*. — *Of the Length or Shortness of Life.*

This judgment is formed from the ascendant, its lord, the ☉, and ☾. If they, or the greatest part of them, be strong and free from affliction, and near no violent fixed stars, neither combust, nor retrograde, nor impeded by the lords of the 4th, 6th, 8th, or 12th, or in either of those houses, or besieged by the malefics, or possessing their declination, or if the question be not asked exactly at a new or full moon; all these are signs of long life. The Light of Time, it is said, should always be taken in preference to the other luminary; but I should always prefer the ☾. If the lord of the 1st, or the ☾, be in the term of ♃ or ♀, it is said to denote long life.

If all or most of these are reversed, it denotes short life, or great danger.

Signs of Short Life.

The Light of Time besieged by ♄ and ♂, cadent, afflicted by the lords of the 8th or 6th, or fixed stars of their nature.

The ☾ exactly at the change, or full except she have great latitude.

The Malefics ascending.

♄ causes death by cold chronic diseases, phthisis, flux, agues, dropsies, melancholy, and many others.

♂ causes hot diseases, particularly small pox and measles, scarlet fever, erysipelas, typhus fever, &c,

♂ afflicting the luminaries from angles, particularly the Light of Time, denotes a violent death.

The Light of Time near violent fixed stars, or having their declination, if afflicted at the same time by ♄ or ♂, causes violent death, or great danger, if the fortunes do not interfere.

The ☉ or ☾ joined with ♂ cause the same diseases as if he were in the ascendant.

The ☾ hyleg and in evil aspect with ♄ or ♂ and ☿, threatens madness and death.

Many planets retrograde, and the luminaries afflicted, denote severe sickness that will end in death.

♄, ♂, or the ☋, in the 1st or 7th, peregrine, or retrograde, or violent fixed stars in either of these angles, or the lord of the ascendant going to a ☌ of the lord of the 4th.

If there be signs of a violent death in the figure, and one of the malefics be posited in the 10th, squaring or opposing the luminaries, it denotes ignominious death.

♄ squaring the ascendant from the midheaven, if the Light of Time be afflicted, threatens death by falls or blows.

♂ in a similar situation, causes death by stabbing, blows or bruises.

The lord of the ascendant in ill aspect with the infortunes, or in opposition to the ☉, or in ☌, □, or ☍ to the lord of the 8th, or in the 8th, or combust, or retrograde, threatens death, especially if the luminaries be afflicted, for in horary questions the lord of the ascendant signifies the native.

The ascendant receiving the evil aspects of the malefics, or having violent fixed stars near its cusp, threatens death, because the evil stars must assail it from angles, and all angular aspects are extremely dangerous. The danger will be greater the nearer the aspect is to its cusp. In all cases, however, the luminaries being afflicted increases the danger, and particularly the Light of Time and the Hyleg. Some are of opinion, and with reason, that the ascendant and both luminaries are at all times significators of life, and that even if the hyleg be free from affliction, yet if the other two are afflicted it denotes short life, both in nativities and horary questions.

In all these cases the benefics must be considered; for if they cast a ray of any kind, whether evil or good, to the anaretic point life will be saved, if they are not out-numbered by the malefics; but if two malefics be opposed to one benefic, there is little hope, except the latter be very strong in an angle, and both malefics cadent. The ☉ is reckoned a fortune, if he have aspect with the fortunes, and none with the malefics; but in whatever condition he may be, his ☌ always increases the evil. When he is in any kind of aspect with the malefics, he acquires their nature, and many say this is the case when he occupies their houses or terms. Both Ptolemy and Placidus were of this opinion. In this condition he operates every way as a malefic, and must be considered as such.

The terms of the planets are said to have greai influence: for if the anaretic point fall in the term of a malefic, it greatly adds to the danger; but if in the term of a benefic, almost any aspect of a benefic will save life. There has been much dispute about the real situation of those terms; some preferring the Egyptian and others those of Ptolemy: for my own part, I never had any great opinion of the Egyptian astrology, and should, therefore, with Placidus prefer the latter, were I once quite convinced that either could be relied on; but I have no confidence in essential dignities of any kind, so far as relates to nativities. In horary questions they are equally symbolical with the rest.

When planets are combust, they are said to lose their power, which, whether good or evil, is then transferred to the ☉, to whom in that case the direction for time should be made, and his aspect in all respects taken instead of the aspect of that planet which he covers. This may alter the effect materially; for if ♂, for instance, were within 10° of the ☉, it would alter the anaretic point 10°. In this case, if the Sun were nearest, it would cause death, although ♂ were beyond the reach of the aspect; and in other cases where ♂ would really cause death by his position, yet being deprived of his influence by the ☉, he could do no evil, and the ☉ being 10° further, would have no aspect to the place. It is the same with the benefics. If ♃ were combust, the ☉ alone could save life, and he would operate like any other star, according to his distance. This, I think, wants confirming by practice.

The ☾ and ☿ are likewise considered as fortunes when similarly situated; but I should not consider them as having power equal to ♃ or ♀ as benefics; they govern the faculties, and in this case operate as they are affected; they may also aid a benefic or a malefic in their operations, but I should never consider them as capable alone either to save or destroy, though I know Placidus and most others were of a different opinion. Neither have I that confidence in the ☉'s operation in this way to the extent generally imagined, but this can only be decided by extensive practice.

In horary questions, the ☊ and ☋ are said to have great efficacy: the ☊ will save life by ☌, and the ☋ will destroy. Others affirm that their effect is merely to strengthen or weaken planets, and that the ☊ will strengthen a malefic to destroy as readily as a benefic to save, and that the ☋ will weaken both parties in a similar degree by being joined to them. I wish these silly points had never been heard of: they have no other effect, in my opinion, but to cause contradiction and mistake, even Placidus himself appears to have been ashamed of them, though he disliked to own it, and for my own part, I deem them too unmeaning to be used even as symbols.

When symptoms of death are perceived in a figure, the time may be ascertained by taking the intervening degrees between the two significators and equating them by the method laid down in the beginning of this article. In nativities this is done by direction (see Directions); but in horary questions, where the whole is symbolical, the time is pointed out by a degree for a day, month, or year, according to the quality of the sign where the anareta is posited.

It should always be carefully represented to the querent or native, that notwithstanding the threatening aspects either in radical figures or horary questions, life may be generally preserved by their own care and exertion, except in certain cases of disease. This was the opinion of both Ptolemy and Placidus, and is strictly true. It is, however, truly astonishing to observe the strong propensity of people at those periods to do wrong and involve themselves in destruction, and how firmly they will refuse to take the most simple and easy methods and medicines to promote their recovery.

QUESTION 2d.—*Of Sickness and Health.*

The same significators are used in this question as in the last, but the 6th house and its lord are added, being the natural significators of sickness, and some add the 12th house and its lord, as being the significators of all kinds of anguish and suffering, among which of course sickness is included. To these others add the lord of the 4th house, but I cannot see in what way he can denote sickness, although he certainly signifies death, as the 4th denotes the grave, and the end of all things.

It is usual to erect a figure, called a Decumbiture, for the hour when any person is seized with a distemper, but there are few instances wherein any one can tell the hour when a disease commences. When, however, a decumbiture can be erected, it should be compared with the radical figure and the revolution, and considered as to the transits and ingresses: this is seldom done, and when a decumbiture is erected it is generally considered in the light of a horary question, which is quite absurd. If any particular position of the planets occasion disease, it must be in those where the geniture is affected by such position, and it will be proper to compare them together, if the radix can be had; if it cannot, the question is horary, and may be asked at any time, whether the disease commenced at that time or not.

When the question is horary, the 1st and 6th houses, the luminaries and dispositors of the luminaries are to be taken.

An infortune or the ☊ in the ascendant denotes the disease to be in the head, and in that part of the body signified by the sign ascending.

If an infortune afflict the lord of the ascendant or the ☾, the body is alone afflicted, and the part is that which is ruled by that sign of which the afflicting planet is lord, when the question is asked, viz: by day or night.

If the ascendant, its lord, and either of the luminaries be afflicted, both body and mind are diseased.

If ♄ afflict the ascendant, the ☾ and dispositors of the luminaries, the disease is chiefly in the mind (for the 1st house and the dispositors of the ☉ and ☾ signify the mind,) and it is said to denote the cause to be about some loss in business or estate, and the same if the ☾ square or oppose the lord of the 1st.

If ♃ afflict, which he may do when he is lord of an evil house, the disease is caused by religion.

If ♀ afflict in a similar way, it springs from love.

If ♂ or ☿ are the afflicting planets, it is said to arise from too intense an application to those things they represent.

I have no opinion of those causes; whatever the cause may be, the disease exists, and the part where it is located is but too well known to the patient, or those about him, already. Horary questions are not intended to discover what is known, but what is unknown, and what the querent is anxious to discover.

Of the Duration of the Disease.

Signs of long chronic distempers are fixed signs on the cusp of the 6th, or in the ☾'s place. It is said to be the same if the lord of the 6th be an infortune, and in the 6th. If the lord of the ascendant, or 6th, or the Moon, be in ☌, □, or ☍ of ♄ or ♂, the disease will be lasting.

The ☾ in a common sign, or a common sign on the cusp of the 6th, or the lord of the 6th, being a fortune and in the 6th: or if the lord of the ascendant or 6th or the ☾ be in ☌, ✶, or △ with a benefic, or with the lord of the 10th, it will not be of long duration, and the same if the last degree of a sign be on the cusp of the 6th.

The ☾, or the cusp of the 6th, in a moveable sign, terminates the disease very quick, either in recovery or death.

The lord of the 6th stronger than the lord of the 1st, the disease will increase, and *vice versa.* ♄ lord of the 6th, shews a long disease. A moveable sign, or ♓ on the cusp of the 6th, denotes it to be short. If the ☾ square or oppose the lord of the 1st, the disease is increasing; but much of this depends on application or separation. The ☾ in the 6th, in ill aspect with ♀, the patient is disorderly, and the cause of the disease; and if ♀ be in ♏, it denotes siphilis, fluor albus, or menses. The lord of the 6th, applying to the □ or ☍ of the lord of the 1st, the distemper will increase, and the same if the lord of the 6th be in the 8th, or 12th.

An infortune removing from the 6th, the disease will remove shortly after, in so many days, weeks, or months, according to the nature of the sign. The lord of the 6th, retrograde, combust, in ☌, □, or ☍ with ♄, or ♂, or the lord of the 4th, or 8th, there will be much sickness and great danger. The lord of the 6th in the 8th, or lord of the 8th in the 6th, beholding each other by ⚹, or △, denotes recovery. The lord of the 1st in an azimene degree, afflicted by the lord of the 6th, the disease is incurable. The lord of the 1st in the 6th, and of the 6th in the 1st, the disease will continue till one of them quits the sign he is in, and then if he meet the □ or ☍ of ♄, ♂, or the lords of the 4th or 8th, it is a symbol of death. The lord of the 1st in the 4th or 8th, is not according to some a mark of death if he be not afflicted. All the significators in fixed signs make the disease long and *vice versa.* It is the same if they are slow in motion. ♏ ascending, shews the disease arose from the querent's own folly, anger, &c. The ☾ separating from the ☍ of the ☉, the next planet she applies to decides the event of the disease. The ☾ in a fixed sign, denotes a long disease, and in a moveable sign, a short one.

Of the Termination of the Disease.

SIGNS of recovery are, when the ☾ separates from the infortunes and applies to benefics, without frustration, or prohibition. The lord of the ascendant or of the 6th in good aspect, or reception, with the luminaries, or with one of them, or if wholly free from affliction. The ☾ increasing in light, in a good house, and applying to a good aspect with the lord of the ascendant, and in this case his being a malefic makes no difference. If the ☾ be well dignified, or in the ascendant, or in ⚹ or △ to it; or if the ☾ apply to the fortunes by good aspect, or to the ☉.

Signs of death are the lord of the ascendant, or the ☾ combust, though, it is said, there are great hopes of recovering if in this case the ☾ or lord of the ascendant dispose of the ☉. I cannot speak as to this; but, in my opinion, much depends on the position of the significator. If they separate from the Sun, it certainly affords great hope of recovery, particularly if they are 2 or 3 degrees distant; but if they apply, I fear there can be little hope of recovery, except they apply at the same time to good aspect of a strong benefic, and even then the danger will be imminent. If the lord of the ascendant or the ☾ be in ☌ with the lord of the 8th. If the lord of the 8th be in an angle, and the lord of the 1st cadent or afflicted. If the lord of the ascendant or the ☾ apply by evil aspect to the lord of the 8th, and if the latter be an infortune, they consider death to be certain. Antares or Caput Algol ascending is fatal. It is said, the lord of the 1st in the 8th, or the lord of the 8th in the 1st, renders death inevitable. An infortune in the 6th; the lord of the 8th in the 10th, or the lord of the 1st in the 4th, 6th, or 7th; the lord of the ascendant or the ☾, with violent fixed stars, give little hope of recovery, or the lord of the 8th angular and the lord of the 1st cadent. I should not, however, in the most desperate positions with the lord of the 8th, reject application to good aspects as symptoms of recovery, though certainly an evil application to the lord of the 8th is a fatal symptom.

Declinations are seldom regarded in horary questions, and, perhaps, it is as well; for as every thing here is symbolical, too many testimonies only serve to increase difficulties and create confusion. Those, however, who choose to admit of parallels of declination in their judgments, will find them answer, provided the practice be uniform, so as not to use them at one time and reject them at another.

According to some, ♂ lord of the 6th, and in the 6th, shews a good physician; others say, that any benefic in the 6th shews the same. This is of little consequence either way.

The nature of diseases is said to be known from the signs containing the lords of the 1st and 6th, and the ☾. If fiery signs, they arise from choler; causing fever, inflammation, &c. If in airy signs, from corrupt blood; as gout, leprosy, &c. Earthy signs cause melancholy diseases; as agues, consumption, &c., and all chronic diseases. Watery signs cause phlegm; as colds, catarrhs, hydrocephalus, dropsy, &c. All this seems very absurd and useless; as the duration and end of a disease are the chief objects of enquiry.

The Sun is, in my opinion, a powerful anareta, and when in ☌

or ☍ to the ☾ by application, certainly denotes death. If the anareta be in the 4th, death is certain, and I believe the lords of 4th and 6th in reception, or the lords of the 8th and 6th the same, denotes death. Neither of the fortunes will save life if lords of the 8th or 6th, are in evil aspect; and ☿ joined to the anareta causes great anguish and delirium. The lord of the 1st and 8th being the same planet, I think, denotes death, and that the patient has been by intemperance, or some other means, the cause of it himself. There will, however, generally be a number of these fatal testimonies, when the disease is to terminate fatally.

QUESTION 3d.—*Of the Good or Evil of the Querent's Life.*

This is taken from the figure in general. When the benefics or luminaries possess the principal places of the figure, and the malefics the secondary places; when there are no evil aspects and none of the planets are combust or retrograde, and when no violent fixed stars occupy the cusps or are joined with the luminaries; these are all symptoms of a fortunate and happy life, and *vice versa.* In short, where a nativity cannot be had, a horary question of this description will answer all its purposes, and if asked in a proper way, with strong anxiety to know the result, a figure may be erected, which may be considered as the querent's nativity. It may be judged by the same rules as a nativity, and its directions calculated in the usual way.

QUESTION 4th.—*What part of Life will be most Fortunate?*

This is discovered from the position of the fortunes, by allowing if the hyleg be weak, 5 years for every sign's distance between the east angle and the fortunes. If the significator of life be moderately strong, allow 6 years for a sign; and if very strong, 7 years. Thus, if a fortune be in the 1st, 12th, or 11th houses, it will be in the youth of the querent, from the 1st year to the 15th, 18th, or 21st. If between the cusps of the 11th and 8th, to the 30th, 36th, or 42d year. If in the 7th, 6th, or 5th, to the 45th, 54th, or 63d year; and from thence to the 60th, 72d, or 84th year. A due proportion upon this scale must be allowed for every portion of a sign, and if the fortune be strong the effects will be more prominent; but if weak, of little effect. The places of the malefics are also to be taken in the same way for the evil of life, and this doctrine, it is said, will also hold good in nativities, where the place of a planet will when calculated in this way, answer every purpose of a direction. The most general way is to average 6 years for each house. Some allow only that period of life to be happy where the fortunes are found, as if one be found in the 10th, the period of life from the 10th to the 15th year will be happy, and they begin at the 12th house instead of the ascendant. The evil or good also that had preceded, is denoted by the planets from which the lord of the ascendant and the ☾ separate; their next application denotes what will happen first; and the time is measured according to the rule already laid down.

QUESTION 5th.—*At what Time is a Change in the Querent's Fortune to be expected?*

Erect a figure, and direct the significators to promittors as in a nativity, if in a matter of great consequence. In ordinary cases the number of degrees between the significators and promittors will point out the time sufficiently correct by taking a degree for a year. If violent fixed stars occupy the cusp of the 1st, 10th, or place of the ☾, some sudden mischief is near; but if their nature be good it denotes some sudden benefit.

Many answer this question as directed in the last, because, if there be a period of good or ill fortune in a person's life, that is the time when a change may be expected.

QUESTION 6th.—*In what Part of the World will the Querent be most Fortunate?*

When this question is asked in a general sense, it is proper to direct them to that part of the world where ♃, ♀, the ☾, or the ⊕ are posited; or, if they be not together, where the greatest number of them are collected, but they must be strong and free from affliction, or nothing can be done that is good. It is better, therefore, to take the direction of that which is most dignified and fortified, than of two or three that are weak.

If any particular purpose or pursuit be stated, they should follow the significator of such purpose; as, for instance, if health be the object, they must follow the lord of the ascendant and the ☾; if they want riches, they must follow the lord of the 2d and the ⊕; if they seek for honour, let them go in the direction of the lord of the 10th and the ☉; and the same in all other cases. If they lie in different places, that must be followed which is strongest and best dignified. If neither of them be in good condition, or the malefics in any way afflict them, the pursuit must be abandoned, for it will come to nothing. If violent fixed stars be near them, the querent will probably lose his life in the pursuit; or if a malefic be there, or the ☉ or ☾ afflicted, he will have such diseases as they signify; and if ♂ oppose either of the luminaries, he will probably come to an untimely end. The places where the malefics are found are always to be avoided, both in horary questions and nativities. The places of direction are as follows:

The horoscope, full east; 12th, east by south; 11th, south by east; 10th, south; 9th, south by west; 8th, west by south; 7th, west; 6th, west by north; 5th, north by west; 4th, north; 3d, north by east; 2d, east by north. A proportional difference should be made, if it can be done, for the part of the quadrant the significator is in; as if he be in the midst of the quadrant, for instance, say, the middle of the 11th, the querent should go exactly south east, if possible, and the same with the rest. Some use a different method, by taking the sign the significator is in as one direction, and the quarter of heaven where it is posited as the other. Thus, if the lord of the ascendant were posited in ♈, in the 9th house and fortunate, the querent would do well to travel south east; for ♈ is an eastern sign, and the 9th house is in the southern part of the figure. The journey should be made to those countries subject to ♈ and to the south east parts of those countries. The signs containing those planets to which the ☾ applies are taken in a similar way.

QUESTION 7th.—Of Riches or Gain.

The significators of riches are the 2d house, its lord, the planets therein, the Part of Fortune, and its dispositor. The native will be rich as these are strong, dignified, free from affliction, well aspected by the fortunes, or in reception with them. The house containing the ☊ is always the cause of loss and poverty, whether much or little.

Signs of riches are the lords of the 1st and 2d, in reception or good aspect; the lord of the 1st in the 2d, or the lord of the 2d in the 1st, or strong in their own houses. The ☾ in the 2d house, or in ☌ with its lord, or if the two lords be in ☌ with each other, or if any translation of light be between them. ♃, ♀, or the ☋, strong and free from affliction, and posited in the 2d, or if in good aspect with it or its lord, or strong, well dignified, and free from evil aspect with the infortunes, or with each other. The ⊕ angular and free from affliction, particularly in the 1st or 10th, is a good symptom, or if it be succeedent and in good aspect with the for-

tunes, particularly in the 2d, or with the lord of the 1st, or with
♃, ♀, or the ☊. The dispositor of the ⊕, strong, well aspected
and free from affliction, are signs of riches, and if translation of
light happen between any of the significators, it is a favourable
symbol. When the significators of riches are small, light planets,
or swift in motion, wealth will come quickly: but if they are ponderous planets, or slow in motion, wealth will come but slowly.
If few or none of these symptoms appear, the native will be poor
all his life; and if ♄, ♂, or the ☋, be in the 2d, or with its lord,
or with the ⊕, or in evil aspect to them, or in evil aspect to ♃,
or ♀, poverty and distress is approaching. The ⊙ in the 2d, or
with its lord, or the ⊕, is not good, except he be very strong and
well dignified, as he generally denotes poverty occasioned by dissipation and extravagance. His good aspects, however, are equal
to those of the fortunes, except he be afflicted.

Many predict the sources whence riches or poverty will arise
according to the houses where the significators of riches are posited. In this case there should be but one significator, else the
whole will become a mass of confusion. For my own part, I
always avoid such minute predictions; but every artist ought to
be the best judge of his own qualifications and sympathies, though
I am well convinced that where artists descend to particulars,
they are on the verge of error, and disgrace, and must be very
careful, and fortunate, if they escape them.

If the ⊕ be in the 1st house, the querent will generally acquire
property by his own exertion, or by saving it when he gets it. If
in the 10th, he will gain it in trade, and if in the 11th by friends
and a constant succession of good fortune, provided its condition
be good; but, if evil, he will lose it by extravagance, idleness
or carelessness, by trade, or by a continued succession of ill fortune.

When the significators of substance apply to each other by □
or ☍, if they are in mutual reception, the querent will acquire
riches, but with great difficulty. The time is known by the distance in degrees between the lord of the 1st, or the ☾, and the
significators of substance to whom they apply according to the
sign the latter is in, whether moveable, common, or fixed.

The best sign of great and durable riches is the lords of the 1st
and 2d and ♃, joined together in the 2d, 1st, 10th, 7th, 4th, or
11th. The next best testimony is their application to ✶ or △,
with reception. Reception in this question is one of the best symbols; for if they apply to □ or ☍, if they have reception, it
denotes riches, though attended by much labour and difficulty.

Infortunes, being lords of good houses, or in them, and in good aspect, are equal to the fortunes; and ♃ or ♀, if they be lords of evil houses, or afflicted, denote obstruction as much as infortunes, because the whole is symbolical. The house containing the ☋ generally shews the cause of the querent's poverty or his losses.

If it be in the 1st, it arises from his own folly; if in the 2d, he cannot turn himself for want of money; if in the 3d, by beggarly or worthless relations, or bad neighbours; &c. The ☊ will give a probable cause whence riches will arise in a similar way. All the planets angular, or succeedent and swift in motion, is a good symbol. All of them direct, in good houses, and each having some essential dignity, is good.

The means by which riches will be obtained, are, if the lord of of the 2d have a good application to the ☾, the house she governs, and the house she is in; both promise riches. The lords of the 1st and 2d, in good aspect, the querent will make his own fortune by industry; or if a poor man he will thrive by labour, or by some invention. The lords of the 2d and 3d in good aspect, he will benefit either by relations, neighbours, or short journeys. The lord of the 4th gives wealth by the father, or by lands or houses purchased, or by money lent by his kindred. The lord of the 5th gives gain by gaming or amusement, carrying letters or messages, keeping ale-houses, or places of recreation, match-making, &c. The lord of the 6th, by good servants, if the sign be human, by faithful stewards, active bailiffs, agents, &c.; dealing in small cattle, turning physician if he be capable, &c. The lord of the 7th by women, wives, bargains, law-suits, war or commerce. If the lord of the 8th cast the aspect, it will come by a legacy, wife's portion, or by travelling to some country where he will settle and become rich unexpectedly. The lord of the 9th gives riches by voyages, wife's relations, or some neighbour where she lived when he married her, or by religious profession, or learning. If a watery sign be on its cusp, the querent will gain by voyages, but if an earthy sign be there, he should remove to those countries denoted by that sign, and by dealing in the commodities of such country, he will probably realize a fortune. The lord of the 10th gives riches by those trades denoted by the sign on the cusp of that house, and its lord, by offices, by being in the service of kings or great men, or by any mechanical profession. The lord of the 11th brings riches by recommendation of friends, great men, and unexpected good fortune. The lord of the 12th increases the querent's substance by horses, great cattle; by keeping prisons, sponging houses; or by thief-taking, if the sign be human; if earthy, by cattle, except ♍, which denotes corn; and if the sign be ♈, by grazing sheep. The manner in which these things are denoted is by the lords of these several houses, or planets therein, casting a good aspect to the lords of the 1st or 2d, or the cusps of these houses, the ☉ or the ☽.

If the figure deny riches, the evil arises from the planet or planets which obstruct the cusps of the 1st and 2d, their lords, the ☉ or the ☽, or the dispositor of the ⊕. If the lord of the 1st do this, the querent is his own ruin; if the lord of the 2d, he is poor and cannot help himself; if the lord of the 3d, he will be kept poor by rascally relations, or by some neighbour injuring or under-selling him, &c. In all questions concerning loans, the lord of the 1st and the ☽ denote the querent, the 2d and its lord his property, the 7th and its lord the borrower, or lender, and the 8th, his property, except it be wages or money for offices of state, which are denoted by the 10th and its lord.

Question 8th—*Of Marriage.*

The lord of the first is the querent's significator, whether man or woman; and if a man, the ☽ and ♀ are his consignificators, but if a woman the ☉ and ♂.

If (supposing the querent to be a male) the ☽ or lord of the ascendant be in good aspect with the ☉ or one of the fortunes, he he is likely to marry.

If the lord of the 1st, the ☽ or ♀ be in the 7th, and the lord of the 7th in the 1st, or in ✳ or △ to its lord, the Moon or ♀, he is sure to marry.

The major part of the significators in fruitful signs, or in good agreement with each other, or with the significators of the opposite sex, viz. the ☉ and ♂, are very likely to marry.

If there be translation of light, or frustration of aspect, the planet causing it is the person who promotes or prevents the match, and the house and sign they are in shews who they are.

If all the significators are in barren signs, or in □ or ☍ to the 7th, or its lord, the party has an aversion to marriage.

When the question is general, the time is judged by the significators of the querent, applying as before, and being posited in the 1st, 12th, 11th, or 10th, house, which shews the querent will be married suddenly. If they are between the cusps of the 10th and 7th, some time will elapse, and if between the cusps of the 7th and 4th, it will be very late in life. Between the 4th and the 1st the native will probably never marry, or when very old, and when all hope is past. All the significators above the Earth, and swift in motion, hasten marriage considerably, and retard it in the same proportion if they are under the Earth and slow.

When a treaty of marriage is going forward, and the particular time is required, the difference in degrees must be taken between the lords of the ascendant and the 7th, or between the aspects of either of the consignificators and those of the opposite party, that apply to each other by aspect, as before directed, viz. for moveable signs, weeks, or days; for common signs, weeks or months; and fixed signs, months, or years, according to the houses being angular or succeedent; or as others say, accordingly as the significator applying is quick or slow in motion. If the respective significators are inconjunct, the quesited likes some one better than the querent. If the lord of the 7th be in the 7th they have no desire to marry.

If a □ or ☍ happen between the significators or consignificators of each party, without reception, the match, however near being concluded, will be broken off.

If an infortune interpose an evil ray, or according to others, if any planet oppose an evil aspect before the significators form theirs, it will frustrate the intention of the party, and the match will be prevented by the person signified by that planet which frustrates. If there be good translation of light, without aspect, the person denoted by the planet that translates will bring the parties together.

The person whom the querent will marry is said to be described by the planet which the lord of the ascendant or the ☽ (or the ☉ if it be a woman) is nearest in aspect with, and the sign such planet is in; and they will be noble or mean as such planet is well or ill-dignified. For my own part, I should prefer the ☽ or the ☉ to the lord of the ascendant in this case, and I have every reason to believe that the aspects should be made by application. No one will marry that person from whom all their significators separate.

But if the aspect be evil, or good, provided there be application, the parties may marry. The happiness or misery of the parties may be denoted by the aspects of the significators or consignificators of each party. If the application be friendly, the parties will agree; but if evil, to a □ or ☍, there will be contention and unhappiness; and the same if ♄, ♂, or the ☋, be along with any significator, or in the 1st or 7th house. If in the 1st, the querent is of an evil temper; and if in the 7th, the person they intend to marry will be the same. In questions relative to conjugal happiness, there can be no better symbol than mutual reception.

If the querent's significators are in double bodied signs, they will marry more than once; and the same if they are joined with, or apply to, many planets, particularly from the 5th, 7th, or 11th houses. Many planets in the 7th, or in good aspect with the lord of the 1st, or the luminaries, are all signs of repeated marriage.

If the significators are in fixed signs, or in aspect to only one planet, the querent will only marry once. In this case, I should always prefer the ☾ for a man, or the ☉ for a woman, to the lord of the ascendant, and I fully believe, if the luminary have no application, or but one, the querent will never marry, or but once, let the lord of the 1st be situated how he will.

If the lord of the 8th be in good condition and free from affliction, the querent will marry a person of some property, and it is a good sign if ♃, ♀, or the ☊, be in the 8th. A fortune, lord of the 8th, and disposing of the ⊕ in the 8th; the lords of the 8th and 2d, in each others houses, or in friendly aspect with reception, are all signs of acquiring property by the marriage.

If the lords of the 8th and 2d be in □ or ☍, or if the lord of the 8th be combust or retrograde, or if ♄, ♂, or the ☋ be there, it is a sign of poverty and future distress, and if it be a man he will either marry a beggar, or be cheated out of her property.

Refranation is the most certain symptom of a breach between the parties, and if all the significators are in separating aspects, it is nearly the same.

Retrograde application is an evil symbol, and the party so applying is worthless.

QUESTION 9th.—*Shall the Querent have Children?*

If the lord of the 5th be in the 1st, or the lord of the 1st or the Moon be in the 5th, if the lords of the 1st and 5th be in ☌; a fruitful sign on the cusp of the 5th, or 1st, or their lords, or the ☾ be in a fruitful sign; or if a fortune be in the 1st, 3d, 5th, 11th, or 9th house; all these are signs of children. It is said, that ♀ being lady of the 1st, and in the 5th, in a fruitful sign, gives three children; and if this sign be ♓, she will give six children; should the Moon be with her, there will be nine children; others say eighteen children: this is, indeed, counting with a vengeance. A fortune in △ to a good configuration, will give in addition three children, or if in ✶, two. I would advise the artist to let numbers alone, and merely confine himself to the question whether the querent will have children or not, all who go beyond this are knaves or fools. Translation of light between the lords of the 1st and 5th, particularly if made by the Moon, is a good symptom. The ☉ in the 5th, causes barrenness, except it be a watery sign, and even then it is doubtful.

If the 1st and 5th are occupied by barren signs, without their significators being in reception, good aspect or translation, the party will not conceive. If the testimonies be favourable, and the evil ray of a malefic fall on the place, there will be children, but such as are short lived, or sickly; ♄ or the ☋ in the 5th, or ♄ or ♂ in evil aspect to the 5th, or its lord; or if the significators are all in barren signs, or the fortunes in barren signs, there will probably be no children, or if any they will not live.

There are various ways of reckoning the time of conception, should the rest prove favourable. Some say, if the lord of the 5th be in the 1st, it will be in the first year; in the 2d, the second year; in the 10th the third year; in the 7th, the fourth year; in the 4th, the fifth year; and so on, according to the pre-eminence of the houses. Others, with more propriety, measure the time by the application of the lord of the ascendant or the ☾ to the lord of the 5th, ♃, or ♀, reckoning by degrees, according to the nature of the sign the applying planet is in, as before. The lord of the 1st, angular, with reception, denotes children. The ☾, very unfortunate, is a very evil sign, as is also ♃, or more particularly ♀, being afflicted.

It is possible the querent may be with child at the moment of enquiry, of which the following are said to be the symbols. If translation of light have passed between the lords of the 1st and 5th, or if the ☾ be just separating from the latter in a fruitful sign, or in the 5th, 11th, or 7th houses; or the lords of the 1st and 5th, or the ☾ in reception with a planet that is angular; or if the ☾ and the lord of that triplicity she is in be both in fruitful signs; or if ♃ and ♀ be both angular and free from affliction.

If at the time any of these symptoms appear, ♃ be cadent or afflicted, or if ♄, ♂, or the ☋ be present at the place of the aspect, or on the cusp of the 5th, there is either no conception or there will be an abortion. It is the same if they afflict the ☾, ♀, or the lord of the 1st or 5th.

To know how long the querent has conceived, it is usual to take the ☾, the lord of the ascendant, and the lord of the hour. That one of the three which is nearest to the separating aspect of any planet is said to shew the time. If it be from a ☌ she has conceived a month; if a ⚹, 2 or 6 months; if a □, 4 months; if a △, 3 or 5 months; and if from an ☍, 7 months. This, I think, so far as relates to round numbers, will be found tolerably correct.

If the 1st or 5th, their lords, the ☾ and planet to which she applies, be all or most of them in masculine signs, or in aspect with masculine planets, or with stars of a masculine nature, the child will be a male, and *vice versa*.   ☿ is masculine or feminine as he is aspected; he is also masculine when oriental of the ☉, and feminine when occidental.

If the 1st or 5th, or their lords, be in bicorporal signs, or the most of them, she will have twins.

♃, ♀, or the ☋ in a fruitful sign, on the cusp of the 1st or 5th, she may have three, if the ☾ have good aspect.

If the ☉, ☾, and cusps of the 1st and 5th, be in fixed or moveable signs, there will be but one.

When a person who is pregnant wishes to know the time of birth, it is usual to direct the lord of the ascendant or the Moon to the cusp of the 5th by oblique ascension, according to which of the two is nearest, and to allow a day for every degree in the arc of direction. Another way is to observe on what day the planets ♃, or ♀, will transit the cusp of the 5th, and prognosticate the birth to happen that day. I would advise the artist to study all these things minutely, but have nothing to do with them in the way of predictions if he value his own character. No horary question can tell to a day or a week when a birth will happen, nor when conception will or has taken place: there is no sympathy in nature to account for such things, because the mind of the querent can never be wound up to such a pitch of anxiety on those matters as will produce a radical figure. Predictions like these are the tricks of impostors, who acquire such information by indirect means, and palm it on the querent as the inevitable result of science.

Perhaps the sex of the child may be discovered, because this is a point on which some people feel much anxiety; but no prediction ought to be hazarded, unless all the testimonies, or nearly all of them, agree. Where there are a number of testimonies on both sides of any question, although one side may predominate, the question, owing to some cause or other, can never be radical, and no artist should hazard his credit upon it. There is either something concealed or improperly stated, or the querent is actuated by some foolish or knavish impulse, or is nearly indifferent about the result, or in fear and confusion, or prompted by curiosity alone. In any of these cases, the figure will appear as unmeaning as the question, and ought not to be meddled with.

It is said, that if the dispositor of the ☾, and the lord of the hour, be angular, or ♂ in the 7th, the party has just conceived. If ♄ be in the 7th, she has quickened. ♃ in the 7th, shews a male. ♐ or ♓ in the 7th, shews a female: but these are not strong testimonies in themselves, but just serve to turn the scale when it is nearly even. According to Lilly, a planet is always angular in its own house, succeedent in the next to it, and cadent in the next to that, let it be in what place of the figure it will: but this I believe to be nonsense, and only fit to cause confusion. The ☋ in the 5th denotes abortion, and in the 1st (if the woman ask the question) great danger of it. A fortune in cazimi is a a sign of pregnancy; and an infortune, of abortion. The last application of the ☾, before she leaves the sign she is in, denotes the state of the mother. The lord of the 5th, peregrine, in the 8th, denotes the child's death. A child born at the instant of a full moon, dies, it is said, at the next new moon.

Question 10th.—Of the Welfare of an Absent Person.

If the person be a relation it is usual to erect the figure as for the querent, and take the house belonging to such relation for their ascendant, and judge of it as an horary question erected for such relation. Thus, the 3d house would be the ascendant of a brother, the 4th for a father, the 5th for a child, &c. If the party be no relation, the figure should be erected as if the party inquired after were the querent, and judged accordingly.

This may also be done, if it be a relation, and, in my opinion, is most proper to prevent confusion. Whichever way it be, the lord of either the assumed or real ascendant, and the ☾ are significators of the absent party. If he be applying to the ☌, or evil aspect of the lord of his 8th, or in his 8th, he is near death, and if no good aspects interfere there is no hope of his recovery. If the aspect be past without the assistance of any benefic ray that could save, he has ceased to exist for so many days, months, &c. as there are degrees between the significators. Others say, no evil aspect of the lord of the 8th denotes death, except it be from the 6th or 12th house, but only great danger.

If the lord of the ascendant be in the 4th, and the ☾ in square to him, it denotes death or excessive danger. An infortune translating the light of the lord of the 8th to him, is a symbol of death. The ☾ or lord of the 1st in ☌ with the lord of the 8th in the 8th or 4th, he is dead, or if in the 6th, he will die. The lord of the 1st, or the ☾ in the 8th, combust, or in the 4th, the party is dead. If in their fall, he is at the point of death, and the same if retrograde. If the lord of the 1st or the ☾ separate from the lord of the 6th, he has been in great danger, and if to no aspect of the fortunes he will long remain so; but if to a good aspect of the fortunes he will soon recover. It is the same if he separate from the lord of the 8th, if the planet casting the aspect were stronger than the latter, and the aspect were nearly partile. If he be separating from the lord of the 12th, he has been in prison, or in great trouble. In all other respects, his past, present, or future situation, may be known by considering the figure according to the rules laid down for every other department of horary questions.

Combustion or retrogradation, in conjunction of a malefic, is certain death. If he be in his 9th, he is either travelling or gone to a more distant country. If in his 10th, he is situated according to the aspects he has with fortunes or infortunes. If in his 2d, he is doing very well. And if in the 11th, he is with some friends.

QUESTION 11th.—Concerning a Ship at Sea.

The ascendant and the ☾ are significators of the ship and cargo, the lord of the ascendant signifies the crew, and her stores are denoted by ☿ and the ⊕.

The lord of the 8th in the 1st, or the lord of the 1st in the 8th, in evil aspect with its lord, or the lord of the 1st in the 4th, in evil aspect with its lord, or with the lord of the 8th, if the aspect be by separation, the ship is probably lost; and if the ☾ also be evilly affected, the cargo has shared the same fate. If it be by application her destruction is at hand. And if the lords of the 4th are infortunes, the danger is still more imminent. Good planets, aspecting the place, give great hope that the danger may be escaped. If the lord of the ascendant or the ☾ be combust, she is either lost or desperately situated; or if they are in the 6th or 12th house, and in evil aspect with their lords, it denotes sickness or great calamities. If the ascendant and the ☾ be fortunate, and the lord of the ascendant unfortunate, the ship is safe, but the crew sickly, and, if he be in the 12th, they are probably made prisoners. If they are in the 7th house, they are taken by an enemy, and particularly if the lord of the 7th be stronger or more angular or succeedent than the lord of the 1st. If the ☾ be besieged in the 8th house, or 7th, by the infortunes, or joined to the lord of the 7th, it is the same. If the lord of the 7th be strong and disposing of ☿, the ☾, the ⊕, and the lord of the 1st, they are all in the enemy's power; or if the ☾ and ⊕ are in the 8th house, or disposed of by the lord of the 8th; if in this state of things the ☾ and lord of the 1st are in fiery signs, it denotes an engagement having taken place, and the same if the ☉ or ☾ have separated from an ☍ of ♂ in a fiery sign.

In all questions relating to shipping, the angles chiefly are considered, and if the significators and ♃ and ♀ be more angular or succeedent than the lords of evil houses, or ♄ and ♂, it denotes her prosperity and safety. If the malefics are either of them angular or succeedent, she will, it is said, meet with some accident in that part which such a sign denotes, and which, according to Haly, are as follows:

♈, her breast.	♎, the parts above the breast.
♉, the part under her breast, next the water.	♏, the sailor's habitation.
	♐, the seamen.
♊, her helm.	♑, both her ends.
♋, her bottom.	♒, the captain.
♌, her sides above water.	♓, her oars.
♍, her belly.	

I think these are silly distinctions, and are too particular to contain much truth.

♄ afflicting the ascendant and the ☾, it is said, causeth shipwreck; and ♂ denotes they will be captured, if no good aspects of the fortunes intervene. If the lord of the 1st, in this case, be free from affliction and strong, the crew will escape. If the lords of the angles be free from affliction, and the lord of the ascendant and the dispositor of the Moon, the most part of the cargo and crew will be saved. If the lords of the angles and dispositor of the Moon be afflicted by ♂, they are said to be in danger of pirates, or enemies. If the infortunes are in ♏, ♐, or ♒, it is said to denote mutiny (but this is quite ridiculous,) and if ♂ be the infortune, it denotes murder, but if ♄, there will be no bloodshed. ♂ in a fiery sign on the cusp of the 10th, near violent fixed stars, threatens burning by lightning, but if in a human sign, it will be by some person, probably an enemy, and the fire will begin in that place denoted by the sign. If ♄ be in the 10th it denotes shipwreck, and the stronger the afflicting planet is, the greater will be the accident.

The lord of the ascendant only in the 8th, or in evil aspect with its lord, shews the death of some principal officer.

A malefic in the 2d, or with its lord, or with the Part of Fortune, or its lord, denotes loss in disposing of the cargo, and, *vice versa*, much gain.

The lord of the ascendant and dispositor of the Moon, slow in motion, the voyage will be tedious; but if quick, the reverse. An earthy sign on the cusp of the ascendant shews the ship to be a dull sailor.

The lord of the 1st, and the dispositor of the ☾, in evil aspect with each other, without reception, shews discord in the ship; and if the dispositor of the ☾ be the stronger of the two, the captain will get the better, but if the lord of the ascendant be the stronger, the crew will succeed.

The lord of the 2d, peregrine, and having no aspect with the ☾, and the lord of the ⊕ being inconjunct with it, and peregrine, or cadent, or in evil aspect with it, shews want of provisions; and if these lords are in watery signs, it denotes want of fresh water.

I would advise the student to confine himself, in such a maritime question, to general observations, until he be well assured by practice how far he can proceed consistently with truth, and not to hazard a prediction on such precarious evidences as the major part of these appear to be. For my own part I should merely take the ascendant, its lord, and the ☾, as significators, with the 2d, its lord, and the ⊕ for the gain or loss which might happen, and judge of it as of the health and property of any individual. If the lord of the ascendant be under the Earth, it is an evil symptom, and if in the 4th, it generally denotes the ship to have sunk.

QUESTION 12th.—Of the Recovery of Debts.

The 1st, its lord, and the ☾, signify the querent; the 7th and its lord, the debtor; and the 8th, which is the debtor's 2d and its lord, his means of paying it.

If the lord of the ascendant or the ☾ be in ☌ or good aspect with the lord of the 8th, or with a planet in the 8th, the debt will be paid, except the two latter be infortunes, in which case there is great doubt of payment, unless there be reception as well as good aspect. If the lord of the 8th be a fortune, and in the 1st or 2d house, in good aspect by application to the lord of the 1st, or the ☾, it will be paid; but if the lord of the 8th be a malefic, and in no reception of the lord of the 1st or 2d, it is a sure sign that the money will be lost, and the same if the lord of the 7th be there without reception. A fortune having dignity by house or exaltation in the 1st, and joined to the lord of the 1st or the ☾, is a good symptom; but if he be a malefic, it is an evil sign, unless there be reception. The lord of the 1st, or the ☾, joined to a fortune in an angle, especially by application, is a good sign.   The lord of the 7th or 8th, retrograde, combust, cadent, or peregrine, with no good familiarity with the fortunes, shews the debtor to be a cheat, or a miserable wretch, from whom little good can be expected, particularly if he be ♂ or ☿, ill dignified.   If he apply by evil aspect to the lord of the 2d, or the ⊕, or its dispositor, his design is to defraud;   and if the evil application be to the lord of the 1st or the ☾, he owes the creditor ill will, and is determined if possible not to pay him.   The best criterion to judge from is the application of the ☾, or lord of the 1st, to benefics by good aspect;   for if the benefics are strong, the debt will be paid;   but if the application be to malefics and by evil aspect, the money will certainly be lost.   It is said, a malefic interposing an evil ray, shews the cause or person from whom the impediment arises, by the house such planet is lord of by day or night, according to the time of the question.

For the recovery of wages or pensions the same rule is to be observed, only the 10th and 11th houses are taken as significators, instead of the 7th and 8th.

QUESTION 13*th.*—*Of Agreement between Brethren or Neighbours.*

When a person has some difference with his neighbour or kindred, and wishes to enquire into the state of their minds, and to discover the true state and cause of the quarrel, and how it will terminate, take the ascendant, its lord, and the ☾, for the querent, and the 3d house and its lord for the quesited.

If a fortune be in the 1st, or the lord of the 1st be a fortune and applying to the 3d, or its lord by good aspect, the querent is desirous of a reconciliation, but if ♄, ♂, or the ☋ be there, or lord of the ascendant, and apply by evil aspect, he is the cause of the dissension.

It is the same with the quesited;   for whichever of the two significators applies to the other by good or evil aspect, the good or ill intention lies there.

♄ shews an obstinate, covetous person, cool and malignant, and ♂ shews insolence, treachery and desperate revenge, and the worse either of them are dignified the more they denote evil.

If the ☾ or lord of the 1st be a fortune, and in the 3d, or with a fortune there, or in good aspect to its lord, or with reception, or the lord of the 3d be a fortune, and in the 1st, or apply by good aspect to it, or its lord, there will soon be a reconciliation.   If there be translation of light, the planet which gives it will be the peacemaker; or if it frustrates, that person will be at the bottom of the evil, whose house it governs by day or night, according to the time of the question. If good aspects are separating it is no good sign; for application alone denotes reconciliation. If either of the significators apply by evil aspect to an infortune, it will cause that party much evil, and if the lord of the 2d be afflicted, the querent will suffer loss by it; but if the 4th, or its lord, be afflicted, the adversary will suffer in pocket, and the affair will terminate very badly for the querent: for the 4th house is the end of all things. If the ☾ be opposed by ♂, from angles, and near violent fixed stars, it may end in the querent being murdered, except the aspect be separating, and if ♄ be in the querent's 10th, he will be brought by it to disgrace and ruin, though in this as in all other cases, good aspects mitigate much of the evil. If the ☾ apply by ill aspect to the lord of the 12th, the querent will suffer great anxiety and misery, or probably get into prison before the dispute be ended, and the same if the lord of the 1st be in the 12th, or the lord of the 12th in the 1st, particularly if he be an infortune. If the lord of the 1st be in the 6th, or the lord of the 6th in the 1st, being a malefic, it will occasion the querent much sickness, and if the lord of the 1st be in the 8th, and the ☾ in evil aspect to the lord of the 8th, by application without reception, he most likely will die of a broken heart, and the same if the lord of the 8th be an infortune and in the 1st.

If the quarrel or dispute be with a stranger, or one who is neither relation nor neighbour, the 7th house and its lord must be taken instead of the 3d, but the judgment, with this exception, will be the same. If the dispute be with a son or daughter, take the 5th, or with a master, commander, or any superior, take the 10th.

QUESTION 14th.—Of inland and short Journeys.

The lord of the 1st and the Moon signify the querent; the 3d and its lord, the journey. If these significators are in good familiarity or reception; if the lord of the 1st, the Moon, or the lord of the 3d be in the 3d, or if the latter be a fortune in the 1st, or if the lord of the 1st, or the Moon, apply by good aspect to a planet in the 3d, or to the fortunes, or if ♃, ♀, or the ☊, be in the 3d, the journey will be prosperous. ♀ being in the 3d, or lady of it, in good aspect, makes it very pleasant if she be well dignified.

The reverse of all these denotes evil. If ♄ be in the 3d, it shews great melancholy and disappointment; if ♂ be there or the

♋, it denotes that he will be robbed, and if in a fiery sign that he
will be hurt. If the lord of the ascendant be retrograde, he will
return before he reach the place. If the lord of the 6th afflict
him, he will fall sick, and if the lord of the 12th afflict him, he
will meet with much trouble. If the lord of the ascendant and
the ☾ be afflicted by the infortunes from angles, or going into
combustion or evil aspect with the lord of the 8th, especially if the
latter be an infortune, it denotes death or extreme danger.

QUESTION 15th.—*Of Reports, whether True or False?*

The ☾ is significator of a report, and if she be strong, angular,
or succeedent, in a fixed sign, and well aspected by the fortunes,
it is true. If she be every way, or chiefly, unfortunate, it is not
true. If she be afflicted by ♄ or ♂, although she be strong otherwise, it is not true. If the angles be in fixed signs and the ☾ not
unfortunate, it is true. If the ☾ be in a fixed sign in the 10th or
4th, in reception with her dispositor, it is true. ☿ is in some
degree also a significator, and if he be retrograde, combust, or
afflicted or if he or the ☾ apply to a planet that is afflicted, it is
not true. If ☿ or the ☾ be under the Sun-beams, the truth will
be difficult to discover, being kept secret by men in power. If the
Moon be void of course, or in evil aspect to ☿ and neither in ✳ or
△ to the 1st, it is false.

QUESTION 16th.—*Of Advice, whether Good or Evil.*

The 10th house is the significator of advice, and if a fortune be
found there, or if it be in good aspect of the fortunes, or if a fixed
star of the nature of ♃ be near its cusp, the advice is good.   If
an infortune be there, or casting an evil aspect to it, or a violent
fixed star near its cusp, or the lord of the 12th there, the advice is
evil, and either given through ignorance or malice.   If nothing
striking appear in the figure relative to the 10th house, the advice
is indifferent, and of little consequence.   As advice is generally a
matter of opinion, of which everyone ought to be competent to
judge without having recourse to a horary question, the advice
here alluded to must be of a more serious nature, and partly connected with a certain degree of information, which the querent is
desirous of acting upon, and if it is productive of much anxiety it
will admit of horary prediction.   The 10th house alone is given
as a significator, but I should be very unwilling to adopt such

advice, if either the lord of the 10th or the ☽ were much afflicted or ill conditioned.

QUESTION 17*th.—Purchase of Houses or Estates.*

The ascendant and its lord and the ☽ signify the querent, the 4th and its lord the estate: though others take for the querent that planet from which the ☽ has last separated, instead of the ☽, and take the ☽ with the 7th and its lord for the other party, and the 4th house for the thing purchased; but where the ☽ is not given to the querent, it generally is consignificator with the 4th house. The 10th house is the price, and if the 10th and its lord be stronger than the 4th and its lord, the price is too much; but if the 4th and its lord be strongest, the estate is worth more than the money. If the lord of the 7th apply to the lord of the 1st, the seller is more anxious than the buyer, and *vice versa.*

A fortune in the 4th, dignified or not, or the ☊ there, or the fortunes casting good aspect to the cusp, or the lord of the 4th in an angle or a good house, or in good aspect or reception with the lord of the 2d, it will be profitable.

If ♄ or ♂ be in the 4th, dignified or not, or if the lord of the 4th be combust, retrograde, or cadent, or in the 12th house, it is a bad bargain; and if an infortune be in the 4th, combust, or retrograde, it should be abandoned directly, as it will certainly lead to ruin.

The quality of the land is said to be ascertained by the signs on the cusp of the 4th. If it be a fiery sign, the estate will be hilly, hard, and dry; if earthy, it is good; if airy, but of middling quality; and if watery, it is wet or marshy.

Those who assign the ☽ to the querent, consider her in every respect the same as the lord of the ascendant: and those who assign her to the quesited, consider her the same as the lord of the 7th. If she be assigned to the purchase, she is the same as the lord of the 4th.

The best method is to render every operation as simple and free from confusion as possible. The planet from which the ☽ separates has nothing to do in the business, nor is the 10th house connected with it in any way. The ☽ undoubtedly belongs to the querent, whose question it is, and who ought to have the usual significators. The lord of the 7th is quite sufficient for the quesited. The nature of the land, in my opinion, cannot easily be ascertained, because there is no necessity for it; everyone may and ought to know the nature of land before he purchases it, and can therefore feel no anxiety about the matter. Trifles like these are matters of idle curiosity and beneath the dignity of horary questions. Everyone, however, is at liberty to form his own system, but I would caution him against being too particular. It is extreme folly for anyone to purchase land who does not understand it either himself, or by a proxy on whom he can rely. Should anyone, however, determine to speculate, and being conscious of his own ignorance, wish for information, he may no doubt have it by a horary question.

A figure should then be erected as follows: the ascendant and its lord are the tenants or occupiers, and if evil planets be there, or its lord evilly posited, they will be worthless. The 10th signifies the trees or timber, and if good planets be there, or the lord well posited, it is good and plentiful; if a fortune be there, retrograde, there are many trees but little timber; if an infortune be there, there is little of either; if the lord of the 10th be inconjunct with the 10th, it is the same. The angle of the west shews the state of the herbage, grass, corn, &c. The 4th and its lord denote the nature of the ground: fiery signs shew it to be hilly, hard and dry; earthy signs, plain, good ground; airy signs, a mixture of good and bad; watery signs, plenty of water, but if an infortune be there, it is marshy, boggy, and liable to be overflowed. ♄ there, in a fiery sign, it is naturally barren; and in an earthy sign, it is good, but neglected; the lord of the 10th strong, it is too dear; but if weak, or afflicted, it is very cheap.

QUESTION 18th.—Of Removals.

THE 1st, and its lord signify the querent, the 4th and its lord the place where he is, and the 7th and its lord the place to which he is going. That place of the two which with its lord is the strongest and best aspected every way, is the fittest for the querent to be in. If it be the 4th, let him remain where he is; but if it be the 7th, let him remove. Unless there be great advantage on the side of the 7th house, he had better remain, and the preference should be rather given to that which agrees with the lord of the ascendant by house, exaltation, and triplicity. Much depends on the ☾; if she separates from a fortune, the querent should remain, for he is leaving what is good; if she apply, let him remove; and with the infortunes, the reverse. If the lord of the 4th be with good planets, or strong, or the lord of the 7th be with infortunes, or weak, it is best to remain, and *vice versa*. Good planets in the 4th or 1st, it is good to remain; but if in the 7th, or strong in the 8th, it is better to remove. The lord of the 1st, peregrine in the second, or afflicted, he will always be poor where he is, and the same if the lord of the 2nd be afflicted. The ⊕ in the 12th, 8th, or 6th, he had better remove.

QUESTION 19th. — Of Succeeding to Property.

The 1st, its lord, and the ☾, signify the querent; the house belonging to the person leaving the property and its lord, must be chosen as their significator; as the 4th for a father, the 10th for a mother, the 11th for a friend, &c. The houses succeeding them, denote the property, because they are their seconds, as the 5th for a father, the 11th for a mother, the 12th for a friend, &c. If the lords of the querent's and quesited's seconds be in each other's place, or in reception, or applying by good aspect, the querent will inherit the expected property. If the lord of both the seconds be the same planet, or the lord of the quesited's second dispose of the querent's Part of Fortune in the 1st or 2nd; or if the lord of the querent's 1st or 2nd dispose of the quesited's lord of the 2nd, or the quesited's Part of Fortune, which may be calculated for that purpose; or if a benefic be in the 2nd of the quesited, in good aspect of the lord of the ascendant, or the ☾, or the querent's 2nd, or its lord, or if there be translation of light between the lord of the querent's 1st or 2nd and the quesited's respective lords, and proceeding from the latter to the former; all these are signs that the querent will inherit, and *vice versa*.

If the lord of the querent's 2nd be combust, or retrograde, it will do him little good, and if the lord of the quesited's 2nd be so, there is not much property, if any. If they apply by evil aspect, provided there are other good testimonies, they may inherit, but it will be with difficulty. If they are separating from good aspects, it is to be feared the legacy will be left elsewhere, or that the querent's hopes are ill-founded.

It is said, if the lord of the hour be in evil aspect with an infortune, or with the quesited's lord, the person will part with nothing during his life; but if the lords of both the seconds apply to ☌, ✶, or △ by one being retrograde, the person will give something before death.

QUESTION 20th. — Of Dealing in Cattle.

THIS question is said to belong to the 6th house, if the animals dealt in are not above the size of a sheep or a hog. If they are above that size, as cows or horses, they belong to the 12th house.

The querent's significators are the 1st, its lord and the Moon; the quesited's, the 6th, (or as I before observed, the 12th, which is judged exactly in the same way) and its lord.

The lord of the 6th in good aspect, position, or reception, with the querent's 1st or 2nd, or their lords, or with the ☾, or the ⊕, or being a fortune and in the querent's 2nd, or joined to any fortune which is in good aspect to the querent's significators, particularly the lord of the 2nd or the ⊕, he will be a great gainer, and the same if there be translation of light from the lord of the 6th, or planet in the 6th, to the lord of the 1st, 2nd, or the Part of Fortune. It is much better for the lord of the 6th to be a fortune, than an infortune, for although the ✱, △, reception, or translation, by good aspect, be the same, the ☌, or position, in the querent's 2nd or 1st, renders the issue of the undertaking very doubtful. Indeed, in all cases, the presence of an infortune is to be suspected, let him be lord of what house he will; and I should, for my own part, directly abandon any undertaking where such a symbol occurred. If the lord of the ascendant be an infortune, it is nothing in the querent's favour; it shews him to be of an untoward disposition, and people may be injured by themselves as well as others.

If the lord of the 6th be afflicted, or in evil aspect with the lord of the 1st, 2nd, the ⊕ or its dispositor, or the ☾, or retrograde, cadent, peregrine, or combust, all this denotes the querent to be a loser by the speculation.

If ♄ be the afflicting planet, they will die of disease; and if ♂ or ☿, he will be robbed, or cheated, or lose them by his own carelessness and stupidity.

The ☋ in ☌ with the lord of the 6th, or in the 6th, is a very bad symptom.

QUESTION 21st.—Of Partnership.

The 1st, its lord, and the Moon, signify the querent: the 7th and its lord the partner.

If the lords of the 1st and 7th are friendly by nature (see Friendly Planets) it is said to be a good omen; but on this I should place no reliance. Others say, if the lord of the 1st be the most weighty planet, he will be the greater gainer of the two, and *vice versa;* but this is equally frivolous. Others say, that ♂ or ☿, being lord of the 2d, and afflicting the lord of the 8th, the querent will defraud his partner, and *vice versa.* Of this every artist must judge for himself; but it is certain, that if there be any advantage, those whose significators are strongest and best dignified, will have it.

If the significators are friendly, or applying by good aspect to each other, or the lord of the 7th apply by △ to the ascendant, or 2d, or the ⊕, or if both lords are in reception, or if light be translated by good aspect from the lord of the 7th to the lord of the first (except it be by ♂, which denotes enmity and villainy), it is good. Translation by ☿ is evil, if he be very ill dignified, or only in aspect with ♂. Retrograde application is very evil if the retrograde planet be lord of the 7th: his affairs are desperate, and he wishes to retrieve them.

If the lord of the 7th be retrograde, or combust, have nothing to do with him. It is an ill sign, if he be peregrine, or in the 6th, except there be application between him and ♃. ♀, well situated, will also do much in his favour; but if she be ill conditioned, it is evil, except ♃ assist. If an infortune or the ☒ be in the 8th, he is either poor or improvident; and if either of them be in the 7th, he is an ill disposed character. If the lord of the 7th be an infortune, it is not a favourable omen, and if such infortune be in the 1st or 2d, 7th or 8th, or joined to the lord of the 1st, the Moon, or the Part of Fortune, or to the lord of the 2d, the result cannot be good; but if he be a fortune, it is a good symbol.

QUESTION 22d.—Law-Suits.

The 1st, its lord and the Moon, signify the querent; the 7th and and its lord, the adversary; the 10th, the judge.

Those which are most angular and best dignified, will have the best chance of success, and those that have the best and strongest aspect of the fortunes.

Justice is seldom obtained without money, and therefore the longest purse will probably carry the day; and the adversary's means may be known from the situation of the 8th house, its lord, and the adversary's Part of Fortune (which may be calculated for that purpose by considering the 7th house as the ascendant). If these are stronger than the querent's the adversary will probably get the better, and vice versa.

He whose lord is most afflicted, will generally be in the end the greatest loser; and if both are afflicted, it will be a bad undertaking to both.

If there be application by friendly aspect between the lords of the 1st and 7th, he who makes it is the person most desirous of reconciliation; and if there be retrograde application, the planet which is retrograde, is compelled by distress to offer terms.

He to whom ☿ is best affected, has the most honest attorney, and if he be either in the querent's or adversary's 1st or 2d, he will injure and rob that party. If there be translation of light between the two lords, some person is endeavouring to reconcile them, and they that do not embrace this opportunity will be their own enemies. If there be frustration, the person whose house the planet frustrating belongs to, will prevent a reconciliation. If there be a refranation, that party refraining has changed his mind, and if he has been retrograde and become direct, and the application was good, he has found some fresh reason or means to continue the law-suit.

The best symbol for either party is their significators having application to good aspect with the fortunes, and if the other have separation from them at the same time, or application to the malefics, it will most likely terminate in their ruin.

QUESTION 23d.—*Of Warlike Expeditions.*

The 1st, its lord, and the ☽, are significators of the querent; the 7th and its lord, of the enemy. If the figure be erected for a relation, the house of such relative may be taken as before directed for the ascendant, and the opposite house, which is his 7th, for the enemy; or it may be erected at the will of the querent, for a relation as for any other person, by giving them the real ascendant.

If ♂ be weak in the figure, the querent will be fearful and probably be disgraced, and the same if ♄ be in the ascendant or 10th. The ☋ in the 1st or 10th is said to have a similar effect.

The lord of the 1st combust, retrograde, peregrine, or cadent, are all disastrous tokens.

♄ in ☌ with the lord of the ascendant shews fear and great misfortune.

The □ or opposition of infortunes denote much evil; ♄ shews defeat, and ♂ wounds, and if he oppose either of the luminaries there is danger of a violent death, and if it be by application and nearly partile, he will be killed on the spot.

♂ in the ascendant, particularly if ill dignified, shews he will be dangerously wounded, and if he be in □ or ☍ to the ☽, it is certain death.

The lord of the 7th stronger than the lord of the 1st, and in ☍ to him or the ☽ shews defeat, and if he be an infortune, denotes great danger.

The lord of the ascendant or the ☾, separating from the infortunes and applying to the fortunes, is an undoubted sign of victory and safety,

♂ well dignified in the 10th, or in △ to the lord of the ascendant, or the ☾, denotes victory; but if he square or oppose the Sun or ☾, there is great danger.

The lord of the 1st joined to the ☊, denotes courage and strength.

In all aspects between the lord of the 7th and 1st, that which is the strongest will be most victorious.

If the lord of the 1st and the ☾ be wholly free from affliction, the querent will return safe.

QUESTION 24th.—*Of Besieged Places.*

When it is required to be known whether a place besieged will be compelled to surrender, the 4th house must be the significator of the place besieged; the lord of the 4th is the governor, and the 5th house its means of defence in every respect.

If the lord of the 1st be stronger than the lord of the 4th and joined with him in the 1st or 10th, or in reception with the ☾, or in his own house and disposing of the lord of the 4th, he will take the fortress; and the same if the lord of the 4th be combust, retrograde, or in no aspect to the 4th, except he be well dignified in the 5th.

The lord of the 4th in reception with the lord of the 1st, the governor is treacherous and will surrender it.

If the lord of the 4th be stronger than the lord of the 1st, free from the malefics, &c. supported by benefics, angular, in good aspect with ♂ or the ☉ well dignified, or if the lord of the ascendant be unfortunate, afflicted, combust, retrograde, in the 4th house, or cadent and peregrine, it will not be taken.

♄ in the 1st or 10th will defeat and disgrace the besiegers, and if in ☐ or ☍ to either of the luminaries, or to the lord of the 1st, the commander of the expedition, or the querent, if he be one of the besiegers, will be killed or desperately wounded.

QUESTION 25th.—*Of Stray Cattle or Fugitives.*

There seems to be much confusion in this question as it is usually arranged. The 7th and its lord are said by some to be alone the significators of stray cattle, but others join to them the ☾ and ☿, as being the natural significators of strays and fugitives. In horary questions it is best to have as few significators as possible, to prevent confusion, and although ☿ be the significator of fugitives, he generally signifies runaways, or deserters, and not cattle. ☿ is a critically situated planet, and for my own part, I should never take him for a significator, either of man or beast, except he be lord of the 7th; but if that which is lost be a human being, who has deserted or absconded, he may be made a consignificator. As to the ☾, she belongs alone to the querent as his consignificator.

If the lord of the 7th be retrograde, the person or beast will return before it goes far. If the lord of the 7th or the ☾ apply by good aspect to the lord of the 1st, it is the same; but if the lord of the 1st, apply in like manner to the ☾ or lord of the 7th, it may be found by enquiry.

If they apply by evil aspect either way, or if the lord of the 7th be in the 7th, it will never be recovered.

If the ☾ translate light from the lord of the 7th to the lord of the 1st, it will return, and some say, it will return if she translate the light of ☿. A fortune in the ascendant, or in good aspect with it or its lord, or receiving the application of the ☾, or, others say, ☿, it is the same; and the lord of the 7th or 6th, in the 2d, 5th, or 11th, in good aspect with the ☉, ♃, or ♀, equally denote its recovery.

The lord of the 7th, or ☿ combust, or in the 12th, it is pounded, or imprisoned; and the same if the lord of the 6th or 12th is in his own house or in the 9th or 12th.

If a planet separate from the lord of the 2d, it is sold. If the ☾ or lord of the 7th be in the 8th, or apply to its lord by evil aspect, or to an evil aspect of an infortune in the 4th, or if the ☾'s dispositor be in the 8th, it is dead.

If the ☾ or the lord of the 7th be in the 1st, or in a fiery sign, they are gone eastward; if in the 10th, or in an earthy sign, southward; if in the 4th, or a watery sign, northward; and if in the 7th, or an airy sign, westward. If the ☾ be not above a sign distant from the lord of the 1st, they are not far off; but if three signs distant, they are a great way off. To this some add, that if the ☾ be only one degree from the fugitive's significator and in a moveable sign, they are about two miles off; if in a common sign, one mile off; and in a fixed sign, somewhere close by.

I have never seen a question of this kind, but the chief part of it seems very ridiculous. The 7th house can have no connexion with cattle or strays either, except they be stolen, and the question properly belongs to the 6th house; or, if it be any thing larger than a sheep or hog, to the 12th house. A servant of any description belongs also to the 6th house, including clerks and apprentices who may abscond; though if the party be very young, he may very properly have ☿ for his significator. A son or daughter belongs to the 5th, and a wife or partner to the 7th. A deserter will be signified by ♂, if he be peregrine, but if not, by the planet that last separated from ♂, or if there be none such, by the Moon. The place and distance cannot be known, nor any of those minute particulars described by knavish pretenders or their dupes; though if it be of any service to the querent, he may probably tell the direction it has taken by the quarter where the significator is posited. The chief point of information is, whether it will ultimately be recovered or not; and if it be a human being, some opinion may be formed of its future conduct and duration from its condition and application.

If it apply by good aspect to the querent's significator, or there be translation of light between them, or if the ☾ agree it will probably be recovered; but if the Moon agree more with the significator of the fugitive than with that of the querent, it will not be recovered. Every artist, however, will best be able to judge from his own observations, but he must not be too hasty in his conclusions, nor too much inclined to descend to particulars, at least until he have weighed them well.

QUESTION 26th.—Of Things Lost or Mislaid.

This is a question that can seldom occur; for horary questions cannot be resorted to on every trivial occasion with any prospect of success. A person losing a thimble must not think to find it by erecting a figure, nor expect to receive any information relative to it whatever, though Lilly, not much to his credit, has asserted that he often found a glove or book by erecting a figure purely out of sport.

When, however, the loss is of that magnitude to create serious uneasiness and real anxiety to know the result, the question may be asked with propriety. It cannot be found by this means, whatever some may take upon themselves to assert, but the final conclusion of the business, namely, whether it shall ever be recovered or not, may be assuredly ascertained.

The lord of the 1st or 2d house in good aspect with the fortunes; the dispositor of the ⊕ in the 2d; a fortune ascending having dignity in the 2d; the Moon in the 2d in good aspect to the lord of of the 1st, or in the 10th in △ to a planet in the 2d, or in the 2d and in △ to its lord or to the lord of the 1st; the lord of the 1st in the 2d; the luminaries in △ to each other, or to the cusp of the 2d; the lord of the 2d in the 11th, or 4th; the lord of the 8th in the 1st, or joined to its lord; ♃, ♀, or the ☊, in the 11th or 2d; the lord of the 4th in good aspect with the lord of the 1st or 2d, or in the 4th well dignified, or a fortune there, or the luminaries, or ♃, or ♀, in good aspect to the cusp of the 4th; are all signs that it will be recovered.

If the lord of the 7th, or ☿, or ♂, peregrine, separate from the ⊕, it has been stolen; and if the Moon have familiarity by good aspect with either of them, it will not be recovered. If ☿ or ♂ be peregrine in the 2d, or in an angle, there is a thief concerned in the business, who will steal more, and is probably unsuspected.

The ☾, the ⊕, or the lord of the 2d, in the 8th; ♄, ♂, or ☿, peregrine in the 2d, or the ☋ there; the lord of the 2d combust, or in evil aspect with the lord of the 8th or 4th, or peregrine in the 4th, or in conjunct with the 4th or its lord; or the lords of the 7th and 8th in ☌ with each other; or the lord of the 2d inconjunct with the 1st or its lord; or the luminaries inconjunct with each other or the ⊕; there is reason to suppose the thing irrecoverably lost.

The luminaries under the Earth, even in good aspect, will make it long before it be recovered; and it will be the same if the lord of the 2d, although in a good position, be afflicted. Much depends on the 4th house when other testimonies are doubtful, because that and its lord signify the end of all things.

The parts of a house or country where the things stolen or strayed, may be found, are said to be denoted by the signs, as follows:

♈, east; ♉, south by east; ♊, west by south; ♋, north; ♌, east by north; ♍, south by west; ♎, west; ♏, north by east; ♐, east by south; ♑, south; ♒, west by north; and ♓, north by west. Airy signs, high above ground, or hanging upon a line or tree; fiery, near a wall, fire-place, or partition; earthy, on or under the ground; watery, near a moist place in the room, or in a dairy or wash-house, or somewhere near water. If the significator be going out of a sign, the thing is behind something; or fallen down between two rooms or places, or at the joining of two rooms. The lord of the 2d angular, it is not out of the house; if in the 1st, it is where he has put it in some place he most frequents; if in the 10th, it is in his shop, hall, or dining room, or the room he makes most use of; if in the 7th, it is in his wife's or maid-servant's room, or where they usually are; and if in the 4th, it is where his father, or some old man, did, or does, most frequent. The significators are the 1st and its lord, the 2d and its lord, the 4th and its lord; the signs these lords, the ☾, and the ⊕, are most in, must be considered, and the greatest number of testimonies taken. Some judge wholly by the lord of the hour and the quadrant he is in, but this is not generally the practice.

QUESTION 27th.—Of Theft.

The lord of the 7th is the proper significator of a thief, but if a planet be found peregrine in an angle, it generally is supposed to denote the thief, because being peregrine, it shews him to be wretched and despicable, and only strong to do mischief. If there be no such planet, it is usual to take the lord of the hour instead of the lord of the 7th, but I should prefer the latter, and should even add him to the peregrine angular planet.

The usual method of describing their sex, is to consider the planets, whether they be masculine or feminine. Thus, ♄, ♃, ♂, and the ☉, denote the thief to be a male; ♀, or the ☾, a female; and ☿ accordingly as he is most in familiarity with male or female planets. Some consider Mercury male or female as he is in a masculine or feminine sign. The personal appearance of the thief is taken from the planet which is its significator, and the sign it is in, according to the rules laid down in the article "Form of the Body."

An artist, however, ought to be careful how he excites suspicion of any person upon no better authority than this, which I am certain is not to be relied on. Some descend to very minute particulars: as, whether they are relations, acquaintances, inmates, or strangers; young or old; the colour of the dress; their profession, &c.: much of this is imposition. I have no doubt that horary questions are calculated to answer every reasonable and necessary purpose, to which end a knowledge of some of these circumstances is particularly essential, but it is painful to observe the frauds practised by impostors, and the consequent disgrace which the art has sustained. Men pretending to a knowledge of Prognostic Astronomy (who were at the same time so grossly ignorant as to suppose ☿ and ♀ were often in opposition to the Sun) and erecting figures with pretended judgments attached to them where stolen goods might be traced even to a certain stone they were hidden under near the sea-side. Such pretenders are only calculated to mislead the unwary, and bring them and their prognostications to inevitable disgrace. The principal end of a horary question respecting theft, is to satisfy the querent whether he shall recover what is lost or not, and this may undoubtedly be known. To discover and punish the criminal is no doubt equally necessary, but owing to the knavery of these pretended artists, the whole system has been thrown into confusion, and I fear the minuter parts are very imperfectly known. Nothing can restore them but the joint operations of a number of judicious artists, who have penetration sufficient to perceive the true tendency of the various aspects, and caution enough to compare the result of their discoveries, until by repeated observation they can found a system on the basis of experience that may be depended upon.

When the significator is once fixed upon, whether it be the lord of the hour, or of the 7th, or a peregrine angular planet (for it must not be both, as some foolishly assert), or a planet in □ or ☍ to the 2d, or to the lord of the 2d, or to the ⊕ or its dispositor, it is usual to discover, if possible, the sex and age of the thief.

If ♄ be significator, it is a man, and very old, except he be quite at the beginning of a sign, which shews him to be about 40. If ♃, ♂, or the ☉, it is a man about the age of 30; and if ♀ or ☿, thief is very young. Others judge their age by that of the ☾. It is said, that if the planet be masculine and in a masculine sign, it is a man; but if feminine and in a feminine sign, a woman; but these wiseacres have not informed us what it is when masculine and in a feminine sign, or feminine in a masculine sign — perhaps of the *epicene* gender! This is the way they create confusion. The above distinction can only apply to ☿, who is male or female according to the number of his aspects with male or female planets and the sign he is in, or as he is oriental or occidental, as the number of testimonies predominate. ♄, ♃, ♂, and the ☉, shew males, let them be posited as they will, and ♀ and the ☾, females. If the ☾ be in the 1st quarter, and significator, she is very young; if in the 2d quarter, between 20 and 30; if after the full, between 30 and 45; and if she have passed her last quadrature, between 45 and 60. If many planets afflict the 2d, its lord, the ⊕, or its dispositor, there are more than one. If the significator of the thief be in ⚹, △, or ☌, with other planets, there are more than one, although only one afflict the significators of property.

If the angles of the figure are in fixed signs, or the significator of the thief in a fixed sign, in no aspect with any planet, except the significators of property, only one is concerned.

If the luminaries aspect the ascendant or its lord; if the lords of the ascendant and 7th are joined in the 1st; if the luminaries are in their own houses, or disposed of by the lord of the 1st, or in his triplicity, the thief is well known by the loser.

If the significator of the thief be strong in the ascendant, he is said to be a brother or kinsman, and of this there need be little doubt, should he be lord of the 3d. He might, however, in the latter case, I think, be a very intimate neighbour.

If the lord of the 7th be in the 7th, he is said to be one of the family.

The lord of the ascendant in the 3d or 4th, shews him, it is said, to be a servant in the family: but I should like to know why.

If the significator of the thief be in his own house (except it be the 7th,) or in the 3d or 9th, or if the lord of the 1st and he be not of the same triplicity, he is a stranger.

If either ♂ or ☿ be significator, he is a common thief, except they are lords of the house of some relation, in which case they point out who it is.

When the thief is discovered to belong to the family connexion, it is usual to distinguish the party as follows:

The ☉ denotes it to be a father or master.

The ☾, a mother or mistress.

♄, a servant or person coming by chance.

♂, a son, brother, or kinsman.

♃, a chaplain, tutor, toad-eater, or some superior servant.

♀, a wife, housekeeper, or waiting-woman.

☿, a youth, familiar, or friend.

Signs of recovery are when the lord of the 2d is in the ascendant, or the dispositor of the Part of Fortune: the luminaries, both in aspect to the ascendant; the lord of the 1st or 2d, or the dispositor of the ⊕, increasing in light and motion, angular, or well dignified, applying by good aspect to the fortunes or to each other, or in ☌ with a fortune; a fortune in the 1st or 2d, having good aspect with either of the luminaries; the significator of the thief applying by good aspect to either of the significators; the lords of the 1st or 2d, strong and disposing of the significator of the thief, if they be in mutual reception, the matter will be compounded; and if there be signs of violent death in the figure, and the significator of the thief be implicated in it, he will probably be executed. If the significator of the thief be in the 6th, which is his 12th, he will be transported or imprisoned.

The luminaries afflicted, the lord of the 1st, 2d, or the ☾ combust, or either of the two former retrograde, or peregrine and cadent; the significator of the thief stronger than the lord of the 2d or 1st, or in evil aspect to the ☾, or in evil aspect to the 1st or 2d, or their lords, or the ⊕ or its dispositor, or the lords of the 1st and 2d in ☌, ☐, or ☍, to a malefic, the property will never be recovered.

Some say, the ☉ is the significator of gold, and if any of that metal be lost, he is to be alone considered significator of the property; but this is a very unmeaning distinction. The lord of the term the ☾ is in is the significator of the thing stolen, the 4th and its lord the place where it is laid. Others say, the 2d and its lord and the ☾ denote the thing stolen; but every one may form his own system as he pleases.

The following are the most striking aphorisms laid down for knowing a thief: —

If the ☉ and ☾ be both in house, or in opposition to the horoscope, or the lord of the 7th in the 1st, the thief is one of the family. If the ☉ or ☾ behold the horoscope, he is one well known, very intimate and not suspected. If the ☉ be in the 7th, or the lord of the 7th in ⚹, or △ to the horoscope, he is an opposite neighbour. If the lights be both in the lord of the ascendant's triplicity, he is a neighbour; in his term, a very familiar acquaintance. If both the lights aspect the lord of the 1st, but not the 1st, the owner knows him well. The ☉ and ☾ in ☍, he is a kinsman; lord of the 1st, in the 3d or 4th, it is said to be a servant.

The lord of the 7th in the 1st, it is one of the family, and where there is cause to suspect the owner himself, it is him. In the 2d it is his wife, sweetheart, or maid-servant. In the 3d, a brother, sister, cousin, companion, or favorite servant. In the 4th, his father or some old man, or a father's relation, lodger, or inmate, or an agricultural servant of the querent, or labourer in agriculture, mines, or buildings. In the 5th, a child of him or of his cousin or nephew, his kept mistress or companion. In the 6th, some servant or labourer, uncle or aunt by the father's side, or some sickly or melancholy person. In the 7th, some enemy who owes him a spite, or some vile prostitute. In the 8th, some person in the habit of coming to the house occasionally to labour, kill cattle, nurse, char, &c. In the 9th, some vagrant, or one pretending to religion, some needy author, sailor, or man of learning reduced to distress. In the 10th, some great person of consequence, who is not necessitated to turn thief. In the 11th, some friend, or person in trust, or one that has done the querent a service. In the 12th, some rascally vagabond, beggar, or miserable wretch, some envious person, or one who lives by theft.

The thief in the end of a sign, or separating from combustion, or applying to a planet in the 9th or 3d, he is making off with the property; and the same if the ☾ and lord of the 1st be in different quadrants.

If the thief be in a fixed sign, take three miles for every house he is distant from the lord of the 1st. If in a common sign, one mile; if in a moveable sign, he is so many doors distant.

If the Moon be angular, he is at home; if succeedant, about home; cadent, a good way off. The lord of the 7th in the 1st, the thief will be at his house before him. The lord of the 1st with the significator of the thief, denotes they are together. The lord of the 7th in the 7th, he is hid at home.

In a fiery sign, he is eastward; in a watery, northward; in an airy sign, west; and in an earthy southward.

Some take the quadrant for the place of the thief; others the place of the ☾, if she be angular, or if she be not, they take the place of her dispositor.

The thief's door is said to be described by the ☾; as, if she be in a fixed sign, there is but one door; in a moveable sign, the door-stand raised above the ground; if ♄ aspect the place, it is a very old door; if ♂ aspect it, it carries marks of fire; if ♄ and ♂ aspect it, the door is iron, or very strong; if the Moon have but little light, it is a back door; if the Moon be afflicted, it is a broken door; in common signs, there is more than one door.

The nature of the place where the stolen property is, is denoted by those places governed by the sign of the 4th.

The significator in fruitful or bicorporal signs, or many peregrine planets angular, denote many thieves; fixed signs on the angles or the significators in barren signs, there is but one.

The person is strong, if oriental and in ♌, ♏, or ♐; but weak, if occidental and in ♋, or ♓.

♄ denotes one of a pale, swarthy, dark complexion, hard rough skin, hairy body, small eyes, jaundiced look, lean, crooked, beetle browed, thin beard, thick lips, bow legged, one who strikes his knees or legs against each other, down looking, seldom free from a cough, and often has bad breath. Crafty, revengeful and malicious, dirty, a great eater, covetous, and seldom rich.

♃ denotes a full face, white and red mixed, full eyes, good make, light beard, though this is according to the sign he is in; thick hair, good teeth, but some imperfection in the two front teeth, moderate curling hair; fat, if in a moist sign; strong, in an airy sign; and large, in an earthy sign, and one of a good moral character.

♂ denotes a full face red or sunburnt, fierce countenance, sharp, ferocious eyes rather yellow, hair and beard reddish, but this is according to the sign, except he be with fixed stars of his own nature; in watery signs, more light and flaxen; in earthy, sad brown. A mark or scar in his face, strong, broad shouldered, proud, scornful, drunken and debauched.

The ☉ denotes a sanguine complexion, round full face, short chin, curling hair, fair, comely, sometimes swarthy; bold, ambitious, vain, slow of speech, outwardly decent, but secretly lascivious and vicious.

♀ denotes a fair round face, full or large eyes, red lips, the lower thicker or larger than the upper, black eyelids, soft smooth brown hair, well shaped, rather short than tall.

☿, middling complexion, sad brown or dark hair, long face, high forehead, black or gray eyes, thin beard, often none at all, slender small legs, quick in walking, and full of business and talk.

The ☾, a round face, more white than red; in watery signs, freckled, not handsome, and generally vulgar and dull.

The colours of the clothes are said to be according to the mixture of the planets, and the signs and the terms they are in, as follows:—

♄, black.

♃, green, spotted, or ash coloured.

♂, red.

☉, saffron or sandy colour.

♀, white or bluish.

☿, gray or dove colour.

☾, white, cream coloured, or pale green.

♄ and ♃, dark black green.

♄ and ♂, dark brown.

♄ & ☉, dark yellow, bronze colour.

♄ and ♀, whitish gray.

♄ and ☿, dark gray, or blue.

♄ and ☾, deep gray, or russet.

♃ and ♂, tawney, with light spots.

♃ and ☉, very deep shining red.

♃ and ♀, greenish gray.

♃ and ☿, spotted green.

♃ and ☾, bright fine green.

♂ and ☉, deep shining red.

♂ and ♀, light red or crimson.

♂ and ☿, red tawney.

♂ and ☾, light red.

☉ and ♀, olive colour.

☉ and ☿, light gray.

☉ and ☾, light yellow or green.

♀ and ☿, purple or light mixture.

♀ and   , light blue or bluish white.

☿ & ☾, buff or fawn colour.

The meaning of this is, that when a planet is in the house of another planet you are to judge of him as mixed with that planet; thus, ♄ in ♌, the house of the ☉, would denote the dress of the thief to be either dark yellow or bronze colour.   The term is by some taken instead of the house, and others take it with the house and mix all three together. If there are two or more significators of theft, the mixture is generally taken from the lord of the triplicity, but for what reason, I cannot say. Every artist may form his system as he thinks best, and, where the sympathy is very strong, no doubt, some information may be obtained respecting the colour of the dress, if the artist thoroughly understands his own system: but in general this does not happen.

Some lay down rules to discover the name of the thief, as follows:

Whatever planet be taken as significator of the thief, see if he be in any kind of aspect with another planet, if he be not, that planet whose house he is in, is the planet that forms the name.

Significator.	*Aspect or House.*	*Name.*
♄	with ☉	George, Elizabeth, or Julia.
♄	♀	William
♄	☾ & ♀	Joan.
♃	♄	Thomas.
♃	alone	Rachel.
♃	with ☉	John or Richard.
♂	☉	Robert or Peter.
♂	alone	Anthony.
♂	with ☿	Catherine.
☉	alone	Roger, Philip, James, Stephen, or Ann.
☉	with ♃	Lawrence, or Lucy.
☉	♄	Andrew.
☉	♀	Alice, Maud, or Matilda.
☉	☿	Benjamin, Margaret, or Editha.
♀	♄	Isabella.
♀	☿	Agnes.
☿	♂	Mathew.
☿	♂ & ☉	Christiana.
☿	☉	Clement.
☾	♄	Nicholas.
☾	♂ & ☉	Mary.
☾	♀	Ellen.
☾	alone	Eleanor.
☾	☿	Simon.

If these are not the right names, they are said to contain the same number of letters as the true name. ♃, the ☉ and ♂ denote short names if they are angular, and if near the midheaven, the name begins with A, or E. ♄ or ♀ give longer names, and some say, if the querent's name be short, the thief's name will be short likewise: this is very ridiculous, and requires no comment.

QUESTION 28th.—*Of Voyages and Travels abroad.*

When a querent wishes to know the result of a voyage or journey to some foreign land, the lord of the 1st, the ☾, and the ascendant, are his significators, and the 9th and its lord are the significators of the voyage.

The lords of the 1st and 9th in each others houses, or in reception, or applying to good aspect with each other, or with the ☾, or with translation by good aspect, or either of them or the luminaries in the 11th, or in good aspect with the fortunes, or the fortunes angular, or strong in the 1st or 9th, or the ☊ in the 9th; all are signs of a prosperous voyage.

If the lords of the 1st and 9th, or the ☾ be oriental in respect of the Sun, or swift, or in moveable signs, the voyage will be quick, but slower if occidental, slow, or in fixed signs.

If the lord of the 1st be retrograde, or if the Moon apply to a retrograde planet, no good will come of the undertaking, and the querent will most probably turn back before he reaches the place.

If the lord of the 1st or the Moon be in the 6th, 8th, or 12th, the querent will suffer much sickness or distress, and the same if combust, peregrine, or in ☌ or evil aspect of a malefic.

If the luminaries, or either of them be afflicted, and the Moon or lord of the 1st be near violent fixed stars, or a malefic, or violent stars ascending, he will be in danger of an untimely death.

If ♄ afflict the significators, it denotes sickness and loss, but if the afflicting planet be ♂, it denotes battles, mutiny, pirates, fire, lightning, or massacre.

If the lords of the 1st, 9th, or the Moon, are inconjunct with each other, or with the ascendant, or in evil aspect either with each other or with the malefics, without either reception or translation, the voyage will be wholly inauspicious.

The 9th house, its lord, or either of the luminaries, being afflicted, denotes sickness and disasters.

QUESTION 29th.—*Of Trade or Profession.*

When a querent is desirous of knowing what trade is best to be chosen either for himself or another, the lords of the ascendant and the ☾ are the proper significators of the person, and the lord of the 10th, ♂, or ♀, of the trade.

If these, or the greatest part of them, be in watery signs, they are said to do best as brewers, distillers, publicans, or any trade that makes or deals in liquids.

If in fiery signs, he will do best as a chemist, apothecary, surgeon, physician, smith, cutler, glassblower, or any trade that works by fire. In airy signs, a lawyer, accomptant, surveyor, clerk, astronomer, painter, milliner, draper, printer, bookseller, or any light, clean, airy business, not too sedentary, and chiefly in a retail way. In earthly signs, an agriculturist, gardener, grazier, coachmaker, carpenter, bricklayer, or any one who deals with the earth, or substances produced from it.

If the trade be fixed upon, observe the lords of the 1st, 10th, and the ☾, for if they agree well among themselves, and with the luminaries and fortunes, the querent will prosper, and be an adept in what he has undertaken : but if the opposite testimonies occur, he will be dull, unpromising, and unfortunate.

If the question relate to arts and sciences, rather than common professions, the lord of the 9th, ☿, and the ☾ must be taken instead of the lord of the 10th.

If these and the lord of the 1st be in ☌ or in good aspect from angles or succeedents, or in good aspect of the fortunes, or fortunes in the 1st or 9th, or the lord of the 1st or 9th in the 11th, or with reception, and above all if ☿ be joined to, or in good aspect with the ☾, and free from affliction or combustion, the person will make great progress in anything abstruse or scientific.

If they disagree among themselves, but above all things if ☿ and the ☾ be inconjunct, or afflicted, or combust, or retrograde, it is an evil symptom, and the pursuit should be abandoned.

The ☋ in the 1st or 9th, or the lord of the 9th being an infortune, are both bad omens.

If the ☉ be inconjunct with these significators, or if they are all cadent, it will greatly lessen their profit and fame.

QUESTION 30th.—Of Ecclesiastical Preferment.

The 1st, its lord, and the Moon, denote the querent; the 9th house and ♃, the living.

The lords of the 1st and 9th in each others houses, or in good aspect with each other by application, or with the ☾ or ♃, there is no doubt that it will be obtained, and that with the utmost ease, if there be reception likewise.

If they apply by ☐, or ☍, with reception, it will be obtained, but with difficulty. The lord of the 9th being an infortune, is no good symbol, as it certainly detracts from its value. Good aspects in this case will do much, but if it be by evil aspect, it will be attained with much difficulty, and when obtained prove the source of much vexation.

When there is translation between the lords of the 1st and the 9th, it will be procured by the agency of some person whom the translating planet represents.

The lord of the 1st retrograde or combust, or he or the ☾ in evil aspect with the infortunes, it will come to nothing. If cadent or in evil familiarity with the lord of the 9th, there is little room for hope, unless some aspect of a benefic make up for the deficiency.

If an infortune be in the 9th, or its lord be combust or retrograde, it will be a source of continual uneasiness.

Malefics in the 1st or 9th, afflicting the lords of these places, or the ☾, denote much trouble, which will end in disappointment.

It is said, the cause of his rejection may be known from the house of the afflicting planet at the time the figure is erected, whether by day or night. If he be lord of the 3d, it is through a neighbour or kinsman. If of the 11th, a pretended friend. Of the 12th, some secret enemy. If of the 10th his patron dislikes him. If of the 9th, his interest is not strong enough, or the parishioners, or the bishop dislikes him on account of some articles of his creed,   If of the 7th or 5th, he is thought contentious, immoral, or some way improper. If of the 2d, he either wants generosity or the means.   If of the 6th, he will lose it through ill health, want of activity, or some unforeseen misfortune.

QUESTION 31st.—*Of Secular Offices or Dignities.*

The significators of the querent are the 1st, its lord, and the ☾ ; of the office, the 10th, its lord, and the ☉.

If they are well situated with each other, either in familiarity, reception, or translation, or posited in each others places and well dignified, the situation will be obtained, and be both honourable and profitable.

If an infortune be lord of the 1st, it is not good; for if joined to the ☉, or in the midheaven, he denotes evil. The lord of the 10th being a malefic, is very unpromising; for if he be posited either in the 10th or 1st (which, were he a benefic, would be good,) it would denote much trouble and disgrace; and whatever

honours ♂ confers, will be ultimately destroyed. As to ♄, he is
wholly the significator of disgrace and ruin.

QUESTION 32d.—*Of Expected Disgrace.*

When a person holds an office or preferment of any kind, which
he expects will shortly be taken from him, let him observe the
positions of the lords of the 1st and 10th, and the ☾. (If it be
ecclesiastical, the lord of the 9th must be taken in place of the lord
of the 10th.)

In this question application has great weight, for if the lords
of the 1st and 10th apply to each other by good aspect, he is
secure. Mutual reception between the two significators is equally
good, and will preserve the situation even if the aspect be evil.
If the lord of the first be in the 10th, or that of the 10th be in the
first it is a good symbol. Translation by good aspect is favourable, and shews he has a friend who interests himself in his
behalf.

Separation in this question is, perhaps, the worst of all symbols; for if either of the lords separate from each other, or the ☾
separate from the lord of the 10th, and apply to no benefic, he
will either lose the place or be suspended. If they also apply to
the malefics, the place is certainly gone, and the same if the
lord of the 1st be combust, or retrograde.   The ☾ combust by
application, is fatal.

The lord of the 1st or the ☾ in □ or ☍ to the lord of the 10th
or the ☉, shews the situation to be in great danger, and if they
at the same time separate from good planets and apply to bad
ones without reception or translation, the place is certainly lost.

The lord of the 1st or the ☾ having evil aspect with the lord
of the 10th, or none at all, and applying to evil aspect with other
planets who are in ☌, ✶, or △ with the lord of the 10th, shews
such people as the houses of these planets represent, by day or
night, according to when the figure is erected, are conspiring to
effect his ruin, and will do it.

QUESTION 33d.—*Of the Sincerity of Friends.*

When persons would ascertain the true disposition of their
friends towards them, they must consider the 11th and its lord.

Where the lords of the 1st and 11th are in good aspect or reception, or if there be translation between them by goo l aspect, or if
there be the same between the lord of the 1st and the dispositor of

the lord of the 11th, their friends are sincere. If they occupy each others places, or if both are in good aspect of the fortunes, it is a mark of reciprocal sincere affection. If, however, either be an infortune, the connexion will be less agreeable.

An infortune in the 11th shews much reliance is not to be placed in them, and if the ☋ be there or with its lord, or the lord of the 11th be joined to an infortune, or near violent fixed stars, they are both perfidious, disagreeable and dangerous.

If they square or oppose each other from angles or fixed signs, they will never be good for any thing.

If the lord of the 11th, its dispositor, or the benefics, be in the 1st or in good aspect to it, they are faithful; but if in evil aspect to it, their friendship is all pretence and delusion.

The ☋ in the 11th is a great mark of deceit, as the ☊ there, is a proof of sincerity.

Fortunes and infortunes make much difference in a question of this kind: malefics always cause that which is disagreeable, however well posited; and benefics, however ill disposed, never denote a very great degree of malignity.

Application signifies reconciliation, if the aspect be good, or a renewing of enmity if evil. Separation shews a falling off in attachment, if the aspect was good; or if it had been evil, it shews contempt and indifference, and if no good aspect follow with a benefic, the connexion will be dissolved for ever.

QUESTION 34th.—Of Private Enemies.

When persons know, or suspect, they have private enemies, and fear the effects of their malice, they must consult the 12th house and its lord.

If the lord of the 12th be a superior planet, or any way dignified, they are more powerful, and consequently dangerous.

If, however, the 1st house, its lord, or the ☽, be well posited in the figure, with no evil rays of the malefics, and good ones of the benefics, he has no private enemies, and his suspicions are ill founded; but if the lords of the 1st and 12th, or the ☽, are in evil aspect, or if the lord of any other house have evil aspect with the lord of the 1st, or the ☽, from the 12th, 6th, 8th, or 4th house, he has many private enemies.

If the lord of the 12th afflict the lord of the 1st, or the ☽, from the 3d, they are kinsmen or neighbours, especially if the lord of the 3d afflict likewise. If from the 4th, it is his father; if in the 5th, his children, or some visitor or companion; in the 6th, his servants, or perhaps an uncle; in the 7th, his wife or patron, &c.

He may likewise expect evil from that quarter where the ☋ is posited, especially if its dispositor be in evil aspect with either the lord of the first or the ☾.

If the lord of the 1st be more angular or better dignified, or better supported by the benefics than the lord of the 12th, he will overcome his enemies and *vice versa*.

If the lord of the 12th be lord of the 1st also, and in evil aspect with the Moon, he is chiefly the cause of the evil by his own indiscretion; and if an evil planet be in the 12th, he has formed an ill connexion, and will reap discontent as the fruit of his own folly.

QUESTION 35th.—*Of Imprisonment.*

The lord of the 1st and the ☾ signify the querent.

If the lord of the 1st, or the ☾ be swift in motion, and not applying to any evil aspect; or if they are in reception or good aspect with the lord of the 3d or 9th, or planets there; or if the lord of the 1st or the ☾ are stronger than the lord of the 12th; or if they separate from any evil aspect with him or his dispositor and apply to good aspect with the fortunes, particularly in moveable signs; if the lord of the ascendant or the ☾ separate from the lord of the 4th and apply to a fortune; if moveable or common signs ascend; or if the lord of the hour, when he was taken be a fortune: all these are signs of short imprisonment.

A fixed sign ascending, and the lord of the 12th a superior planet and angular; or if the lord of the 1st be slow in motion, or the ☾ be so; or if the ☾ be in ♏ or ♒, and the lord of the 1st cadent; or the lord of the hour when he was taken being an infortune and angular; all these are signs of long imprisonment.

If the lord of the 1st be in the 4th, 6th, 8th, or 12th, or combust, or retrograde, the imprisonment will be long and dreadful.

If the lord of the 1st or the ☾ apply to evil aspects of ♄ or ♂, particularly if the infortune be lord of the 8th, or going into combustion without any good aspect of a benefic, or if ♂ or ♄ be in ☍ to the luminaries, or the ☾ or lord of the 1st be near any violent fixed stars, particularly Caput Algol, it denotes that the whole will end in a violent death, or at least that he will die in prison.

The lord of the 1st being lord of the 12th, likewise is a symbol of severe and lasting misfortunes, and an evil life.

If the lords of the 1st and 12th apply to a ☌ with each other, and the latter be the stronger and an infortune, it denotes lasting and fatal imprisonment.

The time of release, it is said, may be known by the degrees between the querent's significator and the benefic planet to which it applies, according to the sign it is in, as before described, whether it be common, fixed, or moveable.

QUESTION 36th—*Of Hidden Treasures.*

This seems a very silly question, and one that will never do the artist any credit.   When treasure is suspected to be hidden any where, the best way is to look for it, for this must be done after all.   Instead of doing this, we are directed to cast a figure of the heavens, and take the 4th and its lord for the treasure and the place where it is hidden.   If the lords of the 1st and 4th have good application, reception or translation, or if joined in an angle, or in a fixed sign, or in any good place of the figure; if a luminary be in the 1st, or in good aspect with it; or the ⊕ in the 1st, aspected by the benefics; or if a fortune be lord of the 4th or in it: there is, they say, treasure, and it will be found.

If any planet be dignified in the 4th, or the major part of the planets in the figure be in their own essential dignities in any house, and free from affliction, it is said to be a proof that there is treasure hidden somewhere.

If an infortune be ill dignified in the 4th, or either of the luminaries there be weak, there has either been none, or it has been removed.   If the lord of the 1st or the ☾ separate from good aspects, it has been taken away.

The lord of the 1st or the ☾, having no good aspect with the 4th or its lord, or being inconjunct, and having no reception or translation, or being cadent or peregrine, or retrograde, or combust, and above all, the luminaries being weak or afflicted, or the lord of the hour an infortune, shews there is no treasure.

QUESTION 37th.—*Of the Time of the Querent's Death.*

This is a very improper question and ought never to be answered by an artist.   It is true, he might often gain credit by it, for however wrong he might be, the terror consequent on such a prediction would sometimes realize it.   Were a querent to apply to me on such a subject, I should always predict long life, whatever might be the planetary position, for the blood of no person should rest on my head.

The most proper way of discovering the time of death is by directing the hyleg to the anareta (see Directions,) and this can only be done where the true time of birth is known. Some, indeed, affirm, that where not the smallest chance remains of discovering the true time of birth, a figure may be erected, at the strong desire of the querent, to any time, which will answer every purpose of a genethliacal figure. In neither of those cases, however. ought an artist to predict the death of anyone, except for his own private use and practice. Some querents, in great anxiety, for their friends, frequently apply to know if they are in danger, with fervent promises not to divulge the prediction; but, beside the possibility that the artist may be in error, it would only increase the suffering of the querent, and if it should by any means reach the ear of the patient, which is more than probable, the consequence might be fatal.

Those artists who cannot calculate a direction (and there are many such) have recourse to the following method : they consider the lord of the 1st and the ☾ as hylegs, and the 8th house with its lord and the planets therein as anaretas, and judge according to the number of the testimonies. The ☋ and both the malefics are all considered anaretic.

If the lord of the 1st, and the ☾, therefore, are no way afflicted, and no infortune, nor the lord of the 8th, nor the ☋ in the ascendant, it is considered as a mark of long life; and the same if either of those two significators are in ☌ or good aspect of a fortune, or a fortune in the ascendant. In this case, they take the number of degrees between the lords of the 1st and 8th, and allow the same number of years for the length of the querent's life. The body, however, of the ☉ is considered anaretic, and, therefore, if the lord of the 1st become combust before he reach the lord of the 8th, they reckon according to the degrees between him and the Sun.

When the significators are afflicted by infortunes or by the lords of the 12th, 8th, 6th, or 4th, or joined to the ☋, it denotes short life, according to the degrees of affliction. The degrees between the significator and the chief afflicting planet, are said to denote the weeks, months, or years, of the querent's life, as the promittor may be in moveable, common, or fixed signs.

I have never tried this last method, and can say little about it; but I very much doubt its correctness. I have no opinion of directing, even symbolically, to a benefic as anareta, merely because he is lord of the 8th.

The manner of death is said to be known from the nature of the planet causing it.   If it be a benefic the dissolution will be gentle, and with little suffering, if the anareta be not near violent fixed stars.   ♄ denotes death by agues, dropsies, consumptions, &c. ♂, by fevers, or some hot or epidemic disease, wounds, falls, &c. The ☉, by pleurisy, or some obstruction in the viscera.   ☿, by phthisis, lethargy, frenzy, &c.   And the ☾, by cold, moist diseases, or drowning.   Fixed stars of the nature of ♂, denote sudden fevers, accidents, murders, &c.   If of the nature of ♄, falls, palsies, agues, and cold diseases.   Of ☿, consumptions, madness, melancholy.   If of the nature of the ☉, blindness, fevers, &c.   Of the ☾, cold watery diseases, cholic, drowning, &c.   Of ♀, siphilis, injury by women.   And if fixed stars of the nature of ♃ be joined to the anareta, it denotes the injury to arise from some one in power, or from religion.   There is, however, little room to suspect that fixed stars of the nature of ♃ or ♀, except they be mixed with that of ♄ or ♂, can do much evil.

The time is not easy to calculate, nor would I venture it except the testimonies were nearly all for death and remarkably strong. Nor have I any idea of calculating time from a square aspect, because there must be a mixture of signs, and often of houses, which must cause confusion.   Neither do I think a square aspect positively denotes death.   Where the evil proceeds from a ☌ or ☍, the signs and houses, both of the significator and anareta, are then alike, and it is usual to allow years for fixed signs, months for common, and weeks for moveable; but here the most correct way is to observe the positions of the angles, and allow days for angles and moveable signs, weeks for common, and months for fixed; weeks for moveable succeedents, months for common, and years for fixed; and months for moveable cadents, years for common, and an indefinite time for fixed, as the event may possibly never happen as predicted.   If it be to a significator, the distance between that and the anareta must be taken: if in the 1st or 7th, the degrees must be taken between the anareta and the cusp, if it apply, but if it separate, there are hopes of recovery. The worst position may not be desperate, if a good aspect of ♃ or ♀ be cast to the very point, before the fatal ☌ or opposition take place, even if it be application to combustion.

QUESTION 38th,—Of the Success of a Message.

This question is extremely different in different cases, many of which are attended with circumstances and expectations quite foreign to others, and therefore the rules here laid down will be, in most situations, partly inapplicable.

The 1st and its lord denote the sender; the lord of the 5th, the messenger; the ☾ is the message; and the 7th and its lord, the place and person to whom it is sent.

In domestic journeys, a fortune in the 3d denotes safe travelling, and an infortune the reverse. In foreign journeys, a fortune or infortune in the 9th, denotes the same. ♄ causes great sufferings, privations, and calamities. ♂ denotes wounds, blows, falls, fevers, robbery, murder, &c. The ☋ has more the effect of ♂ than of ♄. The luminaries operate as they are afflicted or otherwise. Where there is reason to apprehend danger, the lord of the 5th being in opposition to an infortune and near violent fixed stars or either of the luminaries in the same situation, are very bad symbols.

The lord of the 5th, being a fortune, or in reception or good aspect with the lord of the 1st or the ☾, or well configurated with the ascendant, or free from the rays of the malefics, and having some familiarity with a benefic, or translation of light between him and the 1st or its lord, the messenger is honest, and may be depended upon; but if combust, retrograde, or in evil aspect or inconjunct, with the lord of the 1st and the ☾, without reception or translation, there is much reason to suspect either his integrity or ability; at all events, they are very evil symbols.

If he separate from the lord of the 7th and apply to the lord of the 1st, he has done his business and is returning; and if the separation be from the lord of the 8th, it is said, he brings money. If he apply to an infortune by evil aspect before he separate from the lord of the 7th, he has been much impeded by those to whom he was sent, but if he apply to such infortune after separation, he will meet with some accident on his return.

If he separate from good planets, his tidings are good, and if from evil ones, he has met with calamities or performed his task but badly.

If the ☾ alone be afflicted, the message will meet with a bad reception, and if it be by application, will wholly fail. If she be slow in motion, there will be great delay. If she apply to a benefic or be strong and free from affliction, the message will meet with a good reception, and ultimate success.

If there be good aspect between the lords of the 5th and 7th, or reception, the messenger will be well received; and if the lord of the 5th or ☿ translate the light of the lord of the 7th to the lord of the 1st, it denotes a happy termination of the business.

QUESTION 39th.—*Of Servants.*

THERE is seldom any occasion for this question, as persons must be very careless and inattentive to their own affairs, or of very shallow understanding, who cannot form some tolerable idea of the qualities of their servants, and if such a question be asked upon mere impertinent suspicious curiosity, it would receive no proper answer, for it would not be radical. Should, however, any weighty occasion occur, it may be judged as follows:

If the lord of the 6th be in good aspect with the lord of the 1st or the ☾, or in reception, or if his light be transferred to the lord of the 1st by the ☾, or in good aspect to the ascendant; or if the ☊ be in the 6th or good planets there; or the lord of the 6th joined to or in aspect with good planets, or disposed of by the lord of the 1st or by benefics, or if he be a benefic himself and with the ☊ or free from affliction, or if he be well dignified and free from evil aspects; it is a mark of the servant's honesty.

The ☉ in the 6th, ill dignified, is a mark of waste and profligacy; and it is said, if the lord of the 6th be in the 2d, in zodiacal square to the ☾ in the 6th, the servant is a great pilferer.

If there be neither good aspect, reception, nor translation, between the lord of the 1st and 6th, or if the latter be posited in the 8th or 12th, and inconjunct with the lord of the 1st, or joined to an infortune, or in ☐, or ☍, to the ascendant or its lord, or to the ☾, or with the ☋, or combust, or retrograde, none of these testimonies are much in his favour.

☿ is said to be a natural significator of servants, and if he be in the dignities of an infortune, or in evil aspect to the 1st or 2d, or their lords, or with an infortune, or the ☋, it is a bad symbol. If ☿ be inconjunct with the ☾ or combust, or retrograde, the servant's intellects are shallow, and his principles not good.

QUESTION 40th— *Shall a Man or his Wife die first?*

THE best way to answer this question is by a reference to their respective nativities; but it is impossible, even in this way, to give judgment with any certainty, owing to the number of considerations it involves. The age, constitution, and habit of the natives render them more or less able to resist the power of fatal directions; beside which, revolutions, transits, &c. have great power in accelerating or averting the evil. An artist, who is unacquainted with the stamina of the querent, would be very silly in attempting to answer such a question; at all events, should he erect a figure and find any violent directions, it is his duty to conceal them, and do no harm if he can do no good.

Those who have recourse to a horary question sometimes decide by the strength and position of the different significators, taking the lord of the 1st and the ☽ for the man, and the lord of the 7th and the ☉ for the woman; others measure the distance in degrees between the lord of the 7th and 1st, and the lord of the 8th, and predict that the person whose significator is nearest, will die first. This is a very uncertain method, to say the best of it, and as to the question itself, it is generally ridiculous, and either originates in idle curiosity or some worse motive. It can seldom be propounded with seriousness and anxiety, and of course, can seldom be radical.

QUESTION 41st.—*Of Secret Wishes.*

When persons apply to an artist to know if a certain wish or desire they have (the nature of which they are unwilling to explain) shall be fulfilled, it belongs to the 11th house, which is the general significator of all desires and their success.

The lord of the 1st and the ☽ having good aspect with the lord of the 11th, or being posited there, or in reception, or with translation of light from the lord of the 11th to the lord of the 1st, or the lord of the 11th in the 1st, or in △ or ✶ to the 1st, or in the 11th, or with benefics, or applying in good aspect to benefics, or with the ☊, or the lord of the 1st with benefics, or applying to them by good aspect, or benefics in the 1st or 11th: are all signs that the wish will be obtained.

If the reception happen in angles, or in fixed signs, it will be complete ; but if in common signs, not so perfect; and in moveable signs, it will be but trifling.

If the reverse of all these positions happen, or the lord of the 1st or 11th be combust, or retrograde, or the ☽ be new or at the full, it either will not happen or will be productive of much evil, particularly when the significators are combust, retrograde, or with violent fixed stars, or in ☍ to ♄ or ♂.

If the significator of the thing be a fortune and apply to the lord of the 1st by evil aspect, it will be obtained, but with much difficulty : and if the significator be an infortune, the wish whenever obtained will have something in it disagreeable.

QUESTION 42d.—*Of finding a Person at Home.*

If the person be not related he is the lord of the 7th, but if he or she be a relation, they are signified by the lord of the house that signifies such relation.

If this said lord be in an angle, the person is at home; if succeedent, not far off, and easy to be found; and if cadent, they will not be found.

If the lord of the 1st have friendly aspect with him, or if there be translation of light between them, he may be met with or heard of by accident; the planet transferring such light will denote by its sex the person from whom the information will be received, whether a male or female.

I know a person, who declared he never found this to fail; but, for my own part, I think it too trivial for a horary question, and therefore never tried it. It may, however, have its use to some who feel much anxiety on slight occasions. If more than one person be wanted, that person will be found who lives in the direction of the sign containing the lord of the 7th and the quadrant, where that sign is posited. If the application be to the lords of the exaltation and house both, two of them will be found; if also to the lord of the triplicity, three of them will be found, &c.

These are the fundamental principles of the doctrine of horary questions as laid down by the most approved authors, and although they contain some apparent absurdities, even those merit the attention of an artist before they are finally rejected. To enable the student to do this with more ease, I have uniformly studied to avoid confusion, and where that could not well be done (a circumstance which has not frequently occurred,) I have pointed out the contradiction, and shewn how it may be avoided. Nothing now remains to be done but that the reader should collect as many as possible of those questions about which the querents are really anxious and sincere, and judge of them by the rules laid down. As the events occur, let him set down every minute particular of each under its respective figure, and compare them together at his leisure. He will soon find it a pleasing and instructive amusement, and, whatever fools may say about superstition and weakness, or impiety and presumption, he will be more innocently and usefully employed in doing this than in wasting his time in an ale-house, tavern, or any other place of dissipation and intemperance. Moreover, although it will not enable him to raise the devil, as some blockheads foolishly imagine, he will thereby raise his own character and reputation, and be enabled to read the heavens with more correctness, perhaps, than the major part of those who may attempt to ridicule him can read their primer.

If a figure, on inspection, does not appear interesting, or if it be much confused with either weak or contradictory testimonies, he may be sure the question is not radical, but has probably been asked out of idle curiosity, or without any very energetic feeling as to the result, or merely to pass away time. It is superfluous, I hope, to advise him to avoid all strangers, and, above all things, not to do any thing of the kind for gain. I cannot speak with certainty, but there is much cause to suspect, that those who do such things for profit, lose their divining faculty, and can foretell nothing. The cord of sympathy is very fine and may be easily broken when the mind is attentive to a different object. Perhaps this is one reason why they so often meet with the punishment they deserve: at all events, it is a proof they are somehow or other miserably deficient. No respectable artist need set a price upon his services, for, if really useful, he would find more difficulty in avoiding favours than in aquiring them, and instead of publishing his name to the world, he would perceive the necessity of concealing it as much as possible. Next to disinterestedness, modesty is the most valuable quality in an artist: for a man who is diffident, cautious, and mistrustful of himself and the science, must ultimately succeed; while the hasty, credulous professor, who is eager to believe, and ambitious to display his powers, will constantly commit himself, and be continually entangled in his own absurdities.

Before we entirely quit the subject of horary questions, it will be necessary to give some examples, though I am compelled to own, that few are worse qualified than myself for such a task, as, from a culpable negligence, I have, after having satisfied myself as to the result, seldom preserved the figure of any horary question. I am therefore only able to present two or three, which will just serve to give the reader some idea of the mode of forming a judgment of this nature. Probably some illiberal critics will remark, that the smallness of the number is a proof how seldom such predictions are verified, and that I have only chosen from a great variety the few that best suited my purpose. I can, however, assure them, my wish is to discover, not to conceal the truth, and a moment's reflection will convince them, that I could easily erect figures and invent questions to suit them, in imitation of a late pretended artist, were I so inclined.

The first example is a question which I erected in great anxiety of mind, on the decumbiture of a much respected friend, who was taken extremely ill with shortness of breath and a considerable tendency to fever. He had been subject to the same complaint during many successive winters, but perfectly recovered his health on the return of spring, and I had no doubt whatever that the complaint was asthmatic, and that no danger was to be apprehended. The physicians, however, declared him in the utmost danger, and affirmed the cause of the distemper to be an approaching dropsy in the chest. I had no confidence whatever in this opinion, but upon finding they persevered in it, a sudden and deep anxiety seized me, and I perceived that this was the moment to know the result. I accordingly erected the figure which will be found in plate 3d, figure 2d: a more fatal one I have never seen and my sensations at that moment may more easily be imagined than described.

The ☾ is hyleg, as possessing the south angle, (but she is always hyleg in a decumbiture in common with the lord of the ascendant) and is hastening to an ☍ of the ☉ from angles and cardinal signs: this is a most fatal direction. The ☉ is here the anareta, and being posited in the 4th house, denoting the grave and the end of all things, too plainly demonstrated the sad catastrophe that ensued.

♃ is lord of the 6th, and of course significator of the disease and its result, and, being joined to the ☉, who is anareta, fully denotes the disease will end in death, the more so, as the ☌ is in the 4th house, denoting the grave. It is also remarkable that the ☉ had exactly the declination of ♃.

♄, lord of the fatal 4th denoting the grave, is posited near the cusp of the 6th, another testimony that the sickness will lead to the grave; and ♄ and ♃, the lords of the disease and the end of all things, are in mutual reception, a strong and fatal testimony, signifying on one hand, that the disease will terminate existence and on the other, that death will be the result of the disease.

♀, lady of the ascendant, is also lady of the 8th, another evil symbol, and what many artists consider as a proof that the deceased has contributed to his own injury by some intemperance in the early part of life; but this, whether true or not, is of little moment, as it cannot be remedied, and is unconnected with the question entirely. The lady of the ascendant is also retrograde, another fatal symbol.

The ☾ is almost in partile ☍ of ☿, a sign that the head is deeply affected, and the ☋ in the ascendant is said to denote the same.

This was amply verified; for the patient was almost constantly delirious. This ☍ of ☿ was of itself sufficient to cause death, and therefore he could not fail to add greatly to the malignity of the ☉. It is also worthy of remark, that ☿ was lord of the 12th, an evil house, and in the term of ♃, lord of the 6th; the ☉ is in the term of ♀, lady of the 8th; and ♃ is in the term of ♄, lord of the 4th: all terms belonging to the lordships of fatal houses. I always use the Egyptian terms because they are less confused than those of Ptolemy.

The ☾ posited in ♋, a watery sign, and a watery sign on the cusp of the 6th, denote a watery disease; and being in ♋, the sign of the breast and stomach, shews the disease to lie there, and that it is a dropsy of the chest, which proved in fact to be the distemper. The dispositors, also, of the luminaries in watery signs, denote the same; for ♄, who disposes of the ☉, is in ♓, and the ☾, who disposes of herself, is in ♋.

The last thing to be considered is the time of the event, and as the fatal direction is the ☾ to the ☍ of the ☉, we take their distance which is 5° 16′, answering to 5 days and a quarter, because the ☾ is in a moveable sign and angular, which gives a day for a degree. She, however, has near 5° north latitude, for which, according to the common rule, there should be subtracted at the rate of a degree for a day, though I know not for what reason, for it makes but a small difference in the right ascension. For my own part, I never allow above a degree for latitude, however great it may be; nor do I allow even that, if it do not amount to two-thirds of a degree; I therefore subtracted a day from the five, and there remained 4 days and a quarter. The figure was cast between 11 and 12 o'clock on Sunday evening, and the time of the event answered to Friday morning.

No language can express my astonishment and regret at this unexpected discovery, and had not the testimonies been so strong, numerous, and unequivocal, I should have doubted the radicality of the figure: so unwilling are we to believe what we dread. My most difficult task was to preserve a countenance before his relatives, as it was useless to give them unnecessary pain. I told them a material change would, I had reason to suppose, take place on the following Friday. Upon being questioned as to the nature of that change, I added, that there was every reason to hope for the best; for I always evade a direct reply on these occasions. However, my countenance, perhaps, too clearly expressed the real truth, for his niece, an affectionate young lady, wished to heaven, on the Thursday evening, that Friday might never arrive. He expired on Friday morning, exactly at 5 o'clock, being within half an hour of the time the figure had predicted.

REMARKS.

I have seldom seen a horary question so perfectly unequivocal as this, nor could it well be otherwise, in consequence of the eagerness and anxiety of mind under which I erected it. None of the testimonies could be misconstrued: they all denoted a fatal termination. Only one good aspect could be found in the figure, which was the △ of ♄ and the ☾, but the △ of ♄ or ♂ is never of much value when lord of an evil house, though, as ♄ was lord of the 4th, or the end, it might denote an easy departure, for he expired almost without a struggle.

I would not, however, recommend generally so close an adherence to the figure as I have shewn in the present example: it was made under a strong sympathetic impulse, as I before observed, and was therefore more likely to be radical in all its parts, but there are many particulars in this figure that would not merit depending on in every case where the impulse is neither so strong nor sudden.

First, the disease cannot always be ascertained, nor is it in most cases necessary, as it is generally but too well known. Here, however, the nature of the disease really formed part of my question, and, indeed, I may say, the substance of it; for had I known what the disease was, I should have been fully aware of the result: it was, therefore, clearly demonstrated.

I always, when I seek to know this, which is seldom the case, take the sign in which the ☾ is, for the nature and place of the disease. Next follows the sign on the cusp of the 6th, and next to it the signs containing the dispositors of the luminaries: when all or nearly all of them agree, there can be no doubt of the nature of the disease; but where they all disagree, it is a proof that the querent has no particular anxiety about that part of the question, and therefore it should be abandoned. This only respects the nature of the disease, but the seat of it can alone be taken from the sign the ☾ is in, at least, this is my opinion.

As to the mutual position of ♄ and ♃, and their reception, it would be in other cases but a slight testimony, not to be wholly relied upon, except corroborated by other strong testimonies, and where this is the case it is very powerful.

The lord of the 4th is not a strong testimony, except when, as in this case, he becomes a leading significator by disposing of the anareta, or being posited near the cusp of the 6th, and even these symbols should be corroborated by other strong testimonies.

With respect to time, I would always advise the artist to be cautious. It is generally foretold through vanity, which is no very praiseworthy motive, and can seldom be beneficial either way, but if there be any particular and useful reason why it should be known, and the querent feel an interest sufficiently deep to excite a strong sympathy, he will seldom be deceived. When the result is fatal, both that and the time ought to be carefully concealed, as in all probability it cannot be of much, if any, service, and may do incalculable mischief. In the present instance, I had no doubt as to the time, all the testimonies being so strong and decided, and instead of the truth I told a gross falsehood, with the exception of the day, which I mentioned that they might be duly prepared for a change of some kind or other, the nature of which, by the bye, was somewhat too fully explained by the physician.

The next question is one relative to marriage, and is by no means so radical as the foregoing: the querent had for some time paid his addresses to a lady, and I believe the time was fixed for their nuptials, so that this formed no part of the question, which was one rather of curiosity than of deep anxiety, although it was accompanied with a considerable degree of eagerness to know the result, and the disposition of the person in particular. I therefore erected the figure (plate 3d, figure 3d)

The querent's significator is ☿, who is lord both of his 1st and 2d houses, and also of the 10th. Some artists would have made a wonderful story out of this, which, according to them, would have denoted his being a book-seller, (which in fact he was) and, being lord of the 2d and 10th also, that his gains and profession were both clearly signified to belong to letters and books, but I never could place any confidence in this doctrine, because it could be of no service to signify such particulars to those who knew them already.

☿, the querent's significator, being almost on the cusp of the 7th, denoted the wedding to be close at hand, and it happened in less than a month after. ♀, the consignificator of the man, is also applying to a partile conjunction with the ☉, the lady's consignificator, which is a strong symbol of marriage.

♀ in the 7th house: a fruitful sign on the cusp of the 7th: ♀, the ☉, and the lord of the ascendant in a fruitful sign; the ☾ in ⚹ with ☿, ♀ and the ☉, and translating the light of ☿ to ♀ and the ☉ by ⚹, and having no evil aspect with any planet in the figure, are all sure signs of marriage.

♃, lord of the 7th, posited in the 5th, the house of pleasure and illicit love, or (to speak more plainly) of a mistress; and ♄, the lord of the said 5th, in the 7th, in mutual reception with the ☾

separating from both, viz: from the △ of ♃ and ⚹ of ♄, after having translated that light from ☿ to ♄, which she was now translating to ♀, intimated that some intimacy not of the most platonic kind had subsisted between the querent and some other lady under hopes of marriage, and was then disolving rapidly and making room for the approaching union denoted by the ⚹ of the ☾ to ♀ in the 7th house: this was the fact. The ☾ being lady of the 11th, and translating the light of ☿, lord of the 1st, to ♀, posited in the 7th, denoted the attachment to be transferred to another by means of some friend, and the ☾ being disposed of by ♀, signified that the connexion would not be dissolved, but that the querent would certainly marry the quesited. ♀ disposing of the ⊕, denoted that the querent would get money by the marriage, but the ⊕ being in a cadent house was a symbol that it would not be so much as he might expect. ♀, being exalted in both the 7th and 8th houses, also denoted the lady to have some property, and her being angular, signified the same. The lord of the ascendant and 2d, being in his fall, denoted a want of money, which would be in some degree supplied by the lady in question, as he was just entering her exaltation and approaching her ☌. ♀ being combust, was a testimony that she was much oppressed, probably by sickness, because the ☉ was lord of the 12th house of the figure, which when reckoned from the 7th becomes its 6th. The ☾ being near the ☊, and both being in the dignities of ♀, who was lady of the 10th house, the house of trade and credit, was a symbol that both would be improved by the marriage, though the ☾ being cadent in the 9th, rather diminished the strength of this testimony. The □ of ♂ from the 10th house denoted, that the querent would very shortly be robbed of some article in trade, as the square fell near the cusp of the querent's 2d, and, being disposed of by the querent's significator, was a sign that he knew the thief. This actually happened about a fortnight after, for he lost some goods from his door, which were stolen, as he afterwards discovered, by a person he knew, and exactly answered the description of a person described by ♂ in ♊. ♂ being peregrine in an angle always denotes a thief. It also was a symbol that the bride's expected dower would fall short of what was expected, and that some dispute respecting this circumstance would arise through ♂, who was lord of the 4th, which is the 10th or maternal place of the 7th. It would be improper to explain the particulars.

The disposition is taken from ♀ in ♓, to whom the ☾ applies; for if the ☾ be not void of course, the planet to whom she applies should always be the symbol of the temper and qualities of the quesited. I knew the lady, and can affirm that no description could be more exact so far as related to the mind; but the personal appearance differed in this particular, that the face was long instead of round. It is usual to take in those cases the planet with whom the ☽ is nearest in aspect, whether she apply or separate, but a separating aspect, however near, should never be preferred to an application, provided she form the aspect before she quit the signs.

REMARKS.

I must here again observe, that only the strength of the testimonies can justify those critical judgments. I have been more minute than I would recommend any other artist to be, until he is certain of his own system. Many positions relate to events of which the artist is not aware, and he consequently attributes them to others which never take place. The quitting an old connexion for a new one, signified by the separation of the ☽ from the aspect of ♄ and ♃, was a very hazardous prediction; but the testimonies were numerous and strong, and I could not tell to what else they could possibly apply. I at last, however, gave it only as a slight opinion, it happened to be true: but, after all, it might be the effect of chance, and have no connexion with the question, or if it had, the allusion might be very different. Many querents cannot, and others will not, explain the whole of their wishes, yet their sympathies are the same, and therefore the artist often perceives testimonies for the tendency of which he cannot account. This might be the case with ♂, in the south angle. ♂ so posited and peregrine, always denotes a thief, yet I do not see how this could be connected with a question of marraige, and although there were some subsequent family disagreements, they could hardly amount to the testimony of so strong a position. The certainty of this marriage, and the disposition of the bride, I firmly predicted, but I mentioned the others with great diffidence, as things only which might be. They were realized: nevertheless, I should again predict with uncertainty, if a similiar case occurred.

The next was erected at the request of a gentleman, who had reason to suppose his wife was pregnant. He had acquainted me with some of the symptoms, all of which, except one, had the decided marks of pregnancy. I told him, there could be little doubt that she was so, and that it did not require a figure to be erected; though he might as well, I thought, inquire of her mother concerning the symptoms, for as they had been but lately married, she could not judge for herself. He said that had been done, and that she had also the opinion of a lady in the house, the mother of five children, and both of them were fully of the opinion that she was pregnant, and that the symptom alluded to, was merely the effect of weakness. I replied, that was all he could well require. He however expressed much anxiety to have a figure erected, as it was her ardent wish to have a child, and she was very anxious to know the result. I accordingly erected the figure, plate 3d, figure 4, and I never saw one wherein the testimonies were more decided, or less equivocal.

The barren sign, ♊, ascending, denotes the querent's constitution and habit to be inclined to barrenness; the barren sign ♍ occupies the cusp of the 5th; the significator of children, and the house to which the question belongs. Both these symbols denote that there is at present no hopes of her being pregnant. The barren sign, ♌, occupies the 4th house, which signifies the end of all things, and denotes that there is little reason to hope she ever will have children. The cold barren planet, ♄, occupies the 11th house, the house of wishes and expectation, a sign that she will be disappointed in her desire; the ☽ has separated from his □ and is void of course, which is another testimony, if another had been requisite, that the quesited was neither pregnant nor likely to be so. ♄ being lord of the 8th, denoted that her life had been lately in danger on this account, and in fact she had but a short time before miscarried.

When I saw the person on the following day, I owned I had been deceived by the symptom, for I had found by the figure that she was neither pregnant nor likely to be so. He smiled, and said all was right enough. She had been to an old lady, who was reputed for her great experience in those matters, and she told her there was not the least doubt of her pregnancy, that she was about two months gone, and the little irregularity of which she complained was only the result of weakness, I told him that my figure was of that positive nature, that nothing could shake my confidence in it. The disease I suspected was rather the effect of nervous irritability, which had greatly disorded the stomach, and that three or four cups of a strong infusion of Ginseng taken every day, for a week, would soon remove most of her complaints. This I persuaded him to give her, and in a few days the whole of the symptoms disappeared.

REMARKS.

The peculiarity of this figure, on such an occasion, is astonishing. There are but three barren signs in the zodiac, and they occupied the cusps of the three houses that had the chief signification of the question. There is but one barren planet, and he occupied the 11th house, the seat of the querent's wishes. The ☾, the chief significator of children, had just separated from his baleful □, and was void of course. Numerous and strong testimonies like these prove the radicality of the question and admit of no dispute.

The ⊙ had just entered by one minute the fruitful sign ♓; a strange phœnomenon in a figure of this kind, and certainly denoted something which I have not the acuteness to penetrate, but the ⊙ is not the significator of pregnancy, except when he agrees with the ☾ in a particular manner. The ☾, being in the 7th house, in a double bodied sign, is a small testimony, and the only one in the figure, that is favourable; but ♐ is not a fruitful sign, and the □ of ♄, and the ☾ being void of course, renders it wholly nugatory and unavailing.

I can find no more of these examples, but I shall add a figure, which was not erected by me, but only sent for my opinion, (see plate 3, figure 5,) I give it exactly as I had it. The querent was desirous of removing his business to another house, and wished to know the result.

The querent's significator, ♂, being almost peregrine in the 2d, denoted that his circumstances were none of the best, which was farther demonstrated by the ⊕ being in the 12th, the house of difficulties and vexation. He is, however, just entering his term, which shews he is not without resources. The ⊕ disposed of by ♂, denotes that all the querent's property has been acquired by his own exertions. He is also lord of the 7th, which is the place he is going to, and disposes of the lady of the 7th, ♀, and the ☾, which is an excellent symbol. The ☾ is passing to a ☌ with ♀ in the 7th house, where they are both angular and in their triplicity, a sign that he will be eminently successful, though not without encountering great difficulties, as the ☋ is near ♀, and must be passed by the ☾. The ☊, however, is in the 1st, which gives him power to overcome them. ♂, the querent's significator, is passing to an ☍ of ♃, lord of the 12th, an evil symbol, denoting extreme disappointment and anxiety, and at the same time ☿, lord of the querent's second house, or property, is going to his opposition, and to the ☌ of ♃, his enemy, and both of these are combust. The ☉, also, follows to the ☍, and both of them are disposed of by ♃. The ☉ is the lord of the 5th, which is the 2d, or property of the 4th, the place where the querent is before his removal, and denotes some dispute about the property of that house. This dispute was likely to be durable in its effects, as ♂ is void of course after passing the ☍ of ♃.

The whole of the prediction was amply realized. The querent removed, and prospered well in his new situation, though he had many difficulties to surmount, for his very friends, alarmed at the magnitude of his undertaking, refused to lend him any assistance, though after he had struggled through every difficulty by his own exertion and industry, they were profuse enough of their offers, when their assistance was no longer wanted. At the time of removal, a dispute occurred between him and the original landlord, respecting some fixtures, which the young man was compelled in the first instance to purchase of an under landlord, and which the other contended he had no right to sell or remove. This he would and could have disputed, had not want of money compelled him to relinquish his claim to what was undoubtedly his right, and to let the house to any one that would take it, and the future tenant afterwards injured him much in his business, by setting up in the same line, and carrying away a part of his connexion.

I would particularly recommend querents not to erect three or four figures for a question where one may serve. Nothing is more common than for many who can erect their own figures, to be often dissatisfied with them. If they do not understand the first or approve of its prediction, they will erect a 2d, 3d, and so on, until it come right, as they call it, that is until it coincide with their expectations or wishes. This is very irrational and absurd, and can only end in self-delusion. It would be quite as correct, and much easier, to wait for a favourable position and call that their figure. No question should be cast a second time, for the first is the answer, whether it be good or bad. If, indeed, the principal testimonies are so confused or equal, that nothing can be drawn from it, a second figure may be erected at some future time, but this must be the querent's fault for not waiting until an impulse is felt sufficiently strong to render the question radical, or for asking questions from light frivolous motives, arising more from busy curiosity than anxiety. The first figure is alone the true one, or it ought to be so, and if it cannot be easily understood, it must still be adhered to, and considered until it is. One means of rendering questions radical, is to answer questions for no one but themselves, or for others whose welfare they feel an interest in, and whose affairs are in some degree their own. This would prevent the idle silly curiosity of fools, who, even allowing them to be sincere, often ask questions without any particular impulse, but merely to have something to amuse an idle moment, and furnish a theme to talk of and laugh at. I need not add, that nothing so produced can be symbolical or radical.

HORIMEA, the rays of the hyleg when it has passed the mid-heaven.

HORIZON, the circle which separates the visible hemisphere from the invisible. It is distinguished into the sensible and rational horizon. The sensible horizon is that which terminates our view, and where the Sun and stars appear and disappear. The rational is parallel to the Earth's center, and is represented by the wooden horizon on the artificial globe.

HORIZONTAL ASPECTS, mundane aspects.

HOROSCOPE, the ascendant or east angle. It also is used sometimes to signify a figure or scheme of the heavens.

HOURS, in astronomy are of two kinds, natural and artificial. A natural hour is the 24th part of the time the Earth takes in revolving upon its axis, an artificial hour is the 12th part of the time from the Sun's rising to his setting; or from his setting to his rising, and, except at the equinoxes, they are either shorter or longer by day than by night. Thus, at the equinox, when the Sun's duration above the Earth is exactly 12 hours, they are of the same length as a natural hour, which is 60 minutes; but if the Sun's duration above the horizon be but 10 hours, the diurnal hour would be only 50 minutes, and the nocturnal 70, and so in proportion.

The chief reason why they are called planetary hours, is because there is a very silly but very old and generally received notion, that the seven planets rule them in rotation. The absurdity of such an opinion must be manifest (even to those who will neither hear nor understand any other reason) from the late discovery of an eighth planet (allowing the four small ones to be excluded,) which, by having a rule in common with the rest, shews the rotation and of course the system to be entirely erroneous. Its distance cannot be an argument for its exclusion in favour of the rest, any more than the distance of ♄ has hitherto excluded him in respect to others which are much nearer. But the planets operate not by rotation, but by position, and the consequent attraction inseparable from such position; and this may be seen from the action of the luminaries, which will neither dispense light nor heat, nor operate on fluids, according to horary succession, but according to position alone.

The method of finding the true length of a planetary hour, is to divide the time from Sun-rising to noon by 6, the quotient is the length of a planetary hour by day. Thus, if the Sun rise at 14 minutes before 5 o'clock in the morning, his time till noon will be 7 hours, 14 minutes, this divided by 6 will give 1 hour, 12 minutes, and 20 seconds, for his planetary hour by day. The planetary hour by night is found by subtracting the diurnal hour from two natural hours, the remainder will be the length of the planetary hour by night. Thus, if 1 hour, 22 minutes, 20 seconds, be taken from 2 hours, or 120 minutes, it will give the length of the Sun's planetary hour by night, 47 minutes and 40 seconds.

The solar hour is alone used in planetary rotation. Thus, supposing the Sun's planetary hour to be 1*h.* 12*m.* 20*s.* by day, ♄ would take the first hour from midnight on a Saturday, which hour, being nocturnal, would be 47*m.* 40*s.*; ♃ would take the next hour, making 1*h.* 35*m.* 20*s.*; ♂ would govern the third hour, making 2*h.* 23*m.*; the ☉ would rule the fourth; ♀, the fifth; and ☿, the sixth, which would be Sun-rise, when each hour would become as above, 1*h.* 12*m,* 20*s.* long. The ☾ would govern the first of these, (making seven in all,) and ♄ would govern the 8th, 15th, and 22d; ♃, the 23d; ♂, the 24th; and the ☉ would govern the first hour on Sunday, commencing at midnight. The ☾ would begin with Monday in like manner; ♂, with Tuesday; ☿, with Wednesday; ♃, with Thursday; ♀, with Friday; and ♄ again with Saturday. This system is not so much in repute now as formerly, and most of those who adhere to it, reckon by natural hours, which will suit their purpose quite as well, and be much more easily calculated. Some call the horary time of every planet its planetary hour, but the term is seldom taken in this sense.

HOUSES. There are two kinds of houses in astrology, mundane and planetary. Mundane houses are each a 12th part of a figure, and begin their numbers at the east angle, which is the first house, and proceed according to the order of the signs. The 2d house is the left, under the Earth, and is what they call succeedent, because it succeeds to the angle. The 3d house is to the left of the 2d, and is called cadent, because it falls from the angle of the 4th. The 4th is the north angle, or imum cœli. The 5th succeeds the 4th as the 2d does the 1st. The 6th is cadent from the west angle. The 7th is the angle of the west, or descendant. The 8th succeeds the 7th. The 9th is cadent from the midheaven.

The 10th is the midheaven, or medium cœli, or south angle. The 11th succeeds the 10th. And the 12th is cadent from the 1st, or east angle (see the figure, pg. 108.)

The order of the houses in dignity and strength, or rather of the planets when in them, is as follows: the 10th, 1st, 7th, 4th, 11th, 5th, 9th, 3d, 2d, 8th, 6th, and 12th. Modern astrologers place the ascendant before the 10th, but Ptolemy was perfectly right when he considered a planet in the midheaven stronger than in any other part of the figure, and this is every day demonstrated in the power of the solar and lunar influences. There seems, however, much room for amendment in the precedence of houses, and this involves two considerations: because the effects of planets are to be taken two ways, simple and combined. The simple effect of a planet is that which it produces in any position; the combined is this joined with what it already has produced. Thus, the Sun in the beginning. of ♋ is more powerful in his simple operation than any where else, because most vertical; but his effects are more evident when in the middle of ♌, when his power is actually on the decline, because this power is combined with the effect of what he before produced when in ♋. The tides, also, are higher two hours after the luminaries have passed their meridian than when they are actually in the meridian, because their present influence is combined with the effect of what is past. Of course, the effects of a planet will appear more prominent when cadent in the 9th, than when angular in the 10th. Their power, however, in nativities should always be considered in relation to their simple effects, and it will always be found, that those who have the luminaries in their midheaven near the cusp will, allowing for other casualities, be found more active and eminent according to their station in life than those who have them posited in the 9th. The next in power to the 10th is certainly the 11th, whatever authors may say of the east angle, and I suspect the 9th is next to the 11th, but of this I am not quite certain.

Planetary houses are those assigned to the planets as the chief of their essential dignities, but this doctrine, although sanctioned by Ptolemy, is extremely erroneous and absurd. The ☉ and ☾ being the two principal, the former has ♌ assigned him for his house because he there produces the greatest heat, the cause of which has already been shown. The ☾ has her house in ♋ as being nearest to our vertex. She like every other planet, must have power in proportion as her rays are more direct. They should, however, have known that the Sun has the same simple power there as the ☾, and that the ☾ must have her combined

power increased in ♌ as well as the Sun. ♄, being at the greatest distance from the ☉, is lodged as far off as possible, and
accommodated in ♑ and ♒, the former being in ☍ to the house of
the ☾, as the latter is to that of the ☉, and both being inconjunct
with the houses they do not oppose. ♃'s two houses are ♐ and
♓, the former of which is in △ to that of the ☉, and the other to
the house of the ☾ ; they are also inconjunct with the others, the
same as those of ♄, which is rather improper for the houses of a
greater fortune.   ♂, being the next, has ♈ and ♏ for his two
houses, because they are in □ to those of the luminaries, but they
forget they are also in △ to them, although ♂ is the lesser infortune.   ♀ has ♉ and ♎ assigned to her, which by the bye, notwithstanding her being a fortune, sets her more at variance with
the houses of the luminaries than ♂ himself; for her houses are,
like his, in □ to those of the ☉ and ☾, whereas she only beholds
them by a ✶, while ♂ beholds them by a △.   ☿, because he is
never but one sign distant from the ☉, nor that either, is domiciliated in ♍, which is next to ♌, and because they had then only
one sign left, which is ♊, they gave him that for his other house,
which is one sign distant from the ☾, because Ptolemy says, his
sphere lies near that of the ☾ ; an observation that has no meaning whatever. His reason for assigning ♈ and ♏ to ♂, is because
they have an evil aspect to the houses of the luminaries, but he
never mentions those of ♀, which have the same. Had there been
14 signs, the luminaries would have had two as well as the rest,
but there being but 12, they have but one each. The planet Herschel (Uranus) was then unknown, else he would have dislodged
some of them by a writ of ejectment.   Few seem to have been
more aware of this absurdity than Placidus, but, not wishing to
contradict Ptolemy, he preserves an almost profound silence
respecting exaltations and domal dignities. He speaks largely of
the terms, but appears to consider ♄ or ♂ equally anaretic and
powerful, without any regard to their other essential dignities,
although he frequently mentions, their being angular, oriental,
&c.

It is with regret I am obliged to confess that the chief part of
Ptolemy's system is founded on this ridiculous, cabalistic nonsense
of the domal dignities of the planets, a mere human invention and
arrangement, and one of the worst that ever was known, being
neither agreeable to nature, nor reason, nor consistent even with
itself. The existence of an eighth planet unveils the absurdity at
once; but allowing there were but seven, and even admitting for
argument sake, that the planets really possessed such domal dig-

nity and strength in certain signs, they could have no effect in such places when not posited there. How then can they have that "rule and dominion" of which Ptolemy so frequently makes mention, which governs the disposition, regulates the fortune, and even disposes of the life of the native, merely because they would have had dignities in the ascendant, midheaven, or in the places of the new or full moon, had they been there. Instead of considering the heavenly bodies as ponderous masses of matter, operating by their sympathetic attraction on each other, they are represented like school-boys always quarreling and fighting about their playthings; or like the good and evil spirits of the magi, keeping the world in perpetual confusion to gratify their own malice and folly.

Modern astrologers divide these houses into diurnal and nocturnal, so that, although each planet (the luminaries excepted) has two houses, he is not alike strong in each at all times, but prefers one by day and the other by night. The day house of ♄ is ♒, and his night house ♑. The day house of ♃ is ♐ and his night house ♓. The day house of ♂ is ♈ and his night house ♏. The day house of ♀ is ♎ and her night house ♉. And the day house of ☿ is ♊ and his night house ♍. This is founded upon their aspects to the ☉ and ☽, and their being diurnal or nocturnal.

♄ is diurnal, and therefore must have ♒ for his day house, that he may oppose the ☉'s house from it.

♃ is diurnal, and therefore has ♐ by day, that he may cast a friendly △ to the house of the ☉.

♂ is nocturnal, and works all night, he therefore chooses ♏ for his night house, that he may cast a □ to ♌.

♀ is nocturnal and has ♉ for her night house, that she may favour the ☽ by her ✶, for she is too modest to have any dealings with the ☉.

☿ is either diurnal or nocturnal as best suits his purpose, and therefore has ♊ for his day house to be in ✶ to the ☉, or ♍ for his night house, where he is in ✶ to the ☽.

In horary questions, a planet in his house denotes security and prosperity to the person or thing it represents, and is equal to five essential dignities.

For the signification of houses "see Horary Questions."

A planet in his own house denotes one who is well endowed with the good things of this life, independent and master of his own property or estate, and he is also very happy and secure, if the planet be free from affliction.

HUMAN SIGNS, ♊, ♍, ♒, and the first half of ♐. They are said by Ptolemy to give the native a humane disposition when the lord of the geniture or the ascendant is in one, otherwise he will be brutish and savage. He also says that the lord of an eclipse being in any human sign, its evil effects will fall on mankind.

HURTFUL SIGNS, ♈, ♉, ♋, ♏, and ♑. Those born under them are said to be more liable to blows, falls, wounds and other injuries.

HYADES, seven stars in the Bull's Head, near Aldebaran. They are supposed to cause rain when they rise or set heliacally. Their influence in other respects is the same as that of the Pleiades.

HYLEG. See Apheta.

HYLEGIACAL PLACES, the 10th, 1st, 11th, 7th, and 9th houses. They begin, according to Ptolemy, from 5° above the eastern horizon and extend to 25° below it. The ✳ dexter of these 30°, which, of course, is the 11th house from 5° above its cusp to 25° below it; the 10th, the 9th, and the 7th, are all taken in the same way. Placidus thinks nothing hylegiacal can commence below the middle of the 11th, except the horoscope; but there is no such doctrine in Ptolemy. (see "Apheta.") Lilly calls the horoscope, the midheaven, and the places of the ☉, ☾ and ⊕, the five hylegiacal places; but he meant the places of the moderators, not knowing the meaning of the word.

HYPOGEON, under the Earth: a Greek name for the imum cœli, or 4th house.

ILLUMINATION, that period of the ☾ when she may be seen, which is 26 days and about 12 hours.

IMPEDED or IMPEDITED, a term applied chiefly to the luminaries, though sometimes to the other planets, and denotes affliction by an infortune. The ☾ is impeded when in ☌, □, or ☍ of ☉, ♄, or ♂. If in ☌ or ☍, the impediment lasts four days, viz: two before and two after. If in □, one day before and one after. When she is impeded by the ☉ in a nativity, she causes a blemish in or near the eye.

IMPERFECT SIGNS, ♌, ♏, ♓. See Broken Signs.

IMUM CŒLI, the lowest heaven. The 4th house or north angle.

INCLINATION, the motion of a planet towards any place.

INCONJUNCT, when a planet, house, or sign has no aspect or familiarity with another. Thus, ♈ is inconjunct with ♉, ♍, ♏, and ♓, consequently a planet in either of these would be inconjunct with planets in Aries, according to the old aspects of Ptolemy, though the new ones of Kepler make some difference if they are adhered to. Houses also are inconjunct; as the 1st with the 2d, 6th, 8th, and 12th. Planets, therefore, in these would be considered inconjunct with the 1st in respect to mundane familiarity, although they might behold each other in the zodiac. Planets are also inconjunct in any signs when more than the length of their orbs distant from any familiarity.

INCREASING IN LIGHT. When a planet is clearing itself from the Sun-beams it begins to increase in light until it reaches the opposition, after which its light decreases. It is considered as a favourable omen both in nativities and horary questions.

INCREASING IN MOTION, when a planet moves faster every succeeding day.

INCREASING IN NUMBER, the same as swift in motion.

INFERIOR PLANETS, ♀, ☿, an l the ☾.

INFORTUNES, ♄ and ♂.

INGRESSES. (See Secondary Directions.) Annual ingresses.

INTERCEPTED, a sign is intercepted between two houses, when it lies between them without occupying the cusp of either.

JOYS OF THE PLANETS. The joys of the planets, as described by Ptolemy, are very different from what have been considered as such by his successors. "It is said," says Ptolemy, "that they are in their joy when, although the surrounding signs have no familiarity with them, they have it with others of a similar nature, and although this is very distant, yet they have it communicated to them by sympathy." Thus, if a planet be peregrine, or in detriment, or fall, he is said to feel a sympathetic joy when another with whom he has any connexion by dignity enjoys such dignity, which is called having a familiarity with the surrounding signs, because a planet in its triplicity is in familiarity with two other signs of the same triplicity; a benefic in house or exaltation has a familiarity with the solar and lunar dignities; and a malefic has a □ or ☍ to them, which is that kind of familiarity in which it is supposed to delight. ♄ therefore, although peregrine, is supposed by Ptolemy to feel a sympathetic joy when ♂ is in his exaltation, because he is exalted in ♑, which is his house, and in ☍ to ♋ the house of the ☾. He also feels a joy when ☿ is in his triplicity, because they are both of the same triplicity, and likewise when ♀ is in either of her houses, because they are in △ to his houses, and one of them, ♎, is in his triplicity. ♃ is in his joy when the ☉ is in his house, exaltation, or triplicity; when the ☾ is in her house or exaltation; and when ♂ is in his house or triplicity. ♂ joys when the ☉ is exalted, when the ☾ is in her house, and ♄ is in ♑. In short, every planet, according to Ptolemy, is in his joy when another is dignified in any of his dignities.

Doctor Whalley, who undertook to explain Ptolemy, was remarkably silent on this subject, which, it is plain, he did not comprehend, and modern authors have contented themselves with inserting what Ptolemy calls the thrones of the planets for their joys, as follows, ♒ for ♄, ♐ for ♃, ♏ for ♂, ♌ for the ☉, ♉ for ♀, ♍ for ☿, and ♋ for the ☾. The whole, however, is extremely absurd, and not worth anyone's attention; as it rests solely on the credit attached to imaginary dignities, which never had any foundation in nature.

They are also said in modern astrology to have their joys in certain houses according to their nature, whether good or evil, thus ♄ joys in the 12th, ♃ in the 11th, ♂ in the 6th, the ☉ in the 10th, ♀ in the 5th, ☿ in the 1st, and the ☾ in the 3d. It is also said, that the ☉ and ♃ joy in each others houses, as do ♄ and ☿ and also ♀ and the ☾.

JUPITER. See Planets.

KACOTYCHE, ill fortune: a Greek name for the 6th house.

KATABABAZON, the Dragon's Tail.

LATITUDE, the distance of a star from the ecliptic, north or south, towards either of its poles. The ancients thought that no planet could have at any time above 6° of latitude, but the eccentricity of ♂ and ♀ sometimes extends to 9°. The fixed stars have latitude according to their position, extending in some instances to the pole itself, 90°. The ☉ never moves out of the ecliptic, and of course never has any latitude.

Stars having north latitude affect us most as being nearer to our own zenith, and therefore that idea is a foolish one, that stars operate with greater power the nearer they are to the ecliptic. Reason and experience both shew, that the more vertical a planet is the more powerful must be its effects. In all cases, where there is a ☌, the latitude ought to be well considered, as it diminishes the strength of such a familiarity so materially, that, if we may believe some authors, life has been saved by a difference so small as a degree and a half. In this case alone the proximity of a planet to the ecliptic can increase its power, as, if the ☌ be made to the ☉ or to the ☾ in her node, the nearer the promittor is to the ecliptic the more eminent will be its effects, Hence, when any direction is calculated to a ☌ or zodiacal parallel, the latitude of the significator must be taken at the point where the conjunction or parallel is formed, which alone can give its true distance.

LEO. See Signs.

LIBRA. See Signs.

LIFE and HEALTH. The ascendant and luminaries free from affliction is always considered a mark of long life and good health.

Ptolemy judges from the 1st and 7th houses, chiefly the latter, and the 6th house because it is inconjunct with the ascendant. There are however other houses inconjunct with the horoscope as well as the 6th. Malefics in either of these angles, or near the cusps of the other angles, cause diseases and blemishes, which are the more severe if either of the lights be angular. The signs on the cusps of these angles shew the part of the body, and the planet the cause and nature of the disease. They also in some degree shew the part, for ♄, he says, governs the right ear, spleen, bladder, bones, and humours. ♃, the hand, lungs, arteries, and semen. ♂, the left ear, kidneys, reins, and genitals. The ☉, the eyes, brain, nerves, heart, and all the right side. ♀, the flesh, liver, and olfactory nerves. ☿, the tongue and mental faculties, the gall and bile. The ☾ the swallow, stomach. belly, womb, and all the right side.

Modern astrologers have determined to render the whole as ridiculous as possible, by directing the luminaries to the lords of the 6th, 7th, 8th, 12th, and sometimes to the lord of the 4th, whether benefics or malefics as the cause of diseases. When the lights cannot be so directed, they direct the lord of the ascendant in a similar way. This latter part of the system I have given under the article " Horary Questions," for it is fit for no other. The system of Ptolemy is more fully explained in the article " Diseases."

LIGHT COLLECTOR, a ponderous planet, having the aspects of any two significators, who receive him in some of their essential dignities. They must both be lighter planets than himself. It denotes a mediator who will interest himself in the affairs of both the parties, and bring any matter to a favourable issue which could not be perfected without him. It is a favourable position for reconciling of differences, quarrels, lawsuits, bringing about of marriages, &c.

LIGHTS, the luminaries.

LIGHT OF TIME, the ☉ by day and the ☾ by night.

LIGHT PLANETS, the ☾, ☿, and ♀, because they are smaller than the others.

LION'S HEART, REGULUS, or COR LEONIS, a violent fixed star of the nature of ♂, in the 28th degree of ♌. It is said to cause great martial honours, but they eventually end in ruin and a violent death, particularly if it be joined to either of the luminaries.

LION'S TAIL, DENEB, or CAUDA LEONIS, gives, it is said, riches and honours, which will end in trouble and disgrace. It is a star of the second magnitude, in 19° of ♍.

LOGARITHMS, artificial numbers formed by progression, and used by artists, particularly the idle part of them, to supply the place of the Rule of Three, that they may work by addition instead of multiplication, and by subtraction instead of division. After all, they, like others of the same description, take the most pains, for any one used to the Golden Rule, would answer the question while they are looking in the table for their corresponding numbers. In matters of importance, where numbers are immense, in extraction of roots, and in mathematical operations, logarithms, are eminently useful: but in astrology, where the operations are all simple, they can be of no utility whatever, except where the operator works by the rules of Trigonometry. (See Trignometrical Calculations.)

LONGITUDE, a part of the ecliptic reckoned from the beginning of ♈. Thus, 45° of longitude is 45 degrees from that equinnoctial point, or 15° of ♉. The longitude is altered by latitude, as will be seen in the Tables.

LORD. That planet is called the lord of a sign whose house it is: as, ♄ is lord of ♑ and ♒; ♃, of ♐ and ♓; &c. The lord of a house is that planet of which the sign or domal dignity is in the cusp of such house. Thus if ♑ or ♒ were on the cusp of the ascendant, ♄ would be lord of the ascendant. &c. The lord of the geniture is that planet which has most dignities in a figure, whether essential or accidental. The lord of the hour is the planet supposed to govern the planetary hour at the moment of a nativity, or at the time of asking a horary question. (See Hours.) The lord of the year is that planet which has most dignities, or is strongest in a revolutional figure.

As to the lord of the hour, the whole system has such a ridiculous appearance, that even Morinus rejected the doctrine, although he adhered to others quite as ill-founded.

The lord of the geniture is, by those who believe in him, supposed to rule the disposition and propensities of the native; but there have been many disputes about what planet is entitled to such a distinction. Julius Firmicus says it is the lord of that sign into which the ☾ enters next after birth, except it be one of the luminaries, which cannot be taken as being universal significators. Others are of the opinion, that it should be that planet, (not being a luminary) that has most dignities in the places of the lights, the ascendant, the midheaven, and the Part of Fortune. It is not worth a dispute, for the essential dignities are all nonsense and absurdity.

LUCIFER, a giver of light; a name given to ♀ when matutine and rising before the ☉. Among the eastern nations all the planets, not excepting even the ☾, were considered as masculine, and therefore the prophet calls her "Son of the Morning."

LUMINARIES, the ☉ and ☾.

LUNA, the Moon. See "Planets."

LUNAR SEMICIRCLE, from ♒ to ♋, both included.

LUNATION, a lunar period. From the time of the ☾ separating from any given point until she arrive there again. Thus, if the ☾ was at birth in 8° 12′ of ♈, a lunation would be accomplished when it arrived at 8° 12′ of ♈ again. This is called a periodical lunation, and is performed in 27 days, 7 hours, 41 minutes. A synodical lunation is from the time she quits the Sun until she overtakes him again, and is performed in 29 days, 12 hours, 44 minutes. This is also called an embolismic lunation; there are twelve of them in a year, and 11 days over. The quarters are also called lunations, when the ☾ comes to the ☌, □, or ☍ of the ☉, at all times, and if at these times she also forms a ☌, □, or ☍, with the radical infortunes, the native at those periods is generally unfortunate. These are called quadrate lunations.

LUXURIOUS SIGN. ♈ is called a luxurious sign, because it is said to endow the native with a propensity to luxury and intemperance.

MALEFICS, doers of evil: ♄ and ♂.

MARRIAGE. The first thing to be considered, according to Ptolemy, is the luminaries: the ☾ for a man and the ☉ for a woman. If the ☾ be in her 1st or 3d quarter, the native will either marry young, or when old to a young wife. If the ☾ be in these quadrants under the Sunbeams, or configurated with ♄, it causes men not to marry at all. If she be in a sign of one form, and apply to only one planet, the man will marry but once. If she be in a bicorporeal or double-bodied sign, or apply to many stars, (which, Cardan says, should be all in the same sign) he will marry often. If these stars are benefics, his wives will be good; if malefics, evil. If she apply to ♄ the wife will be laborious, but austere and evil; to ♃, she will be modest, grave, retired and domestic; if to ♂, bold, refractory, and vicious; if to ♀, cheerful and merry; if to ☿, wise and active, but this will be according to his condition; ♀, too, is affected by the presence of a superior, for it is said, that if she be with either ♄, ♃, or ☿, she gives good wives, and such as are attached to their husbands and families: but if with ♂, they will be passionate, loose, and thoughtless; if the ☾ be in her 2d or last quarter, he will marry old, or when young to an old woman.

For women the Sun is to be taken; if he be between the east and south angles, or between the west and north angles, the native will marry young, or when old to a young man; if between the 10th and 7th, or the 4th and ascendant, she will either marry when old, or when young to an old man; if he be in a sign of one form, or configurated to one oriental planet, she will marry but once; but if in a double bodied sign, or configurated to many oriental stars, she will have a plurality of husbands. As to oriental planets, he makes no such distinction in the case of the ☾'s application, nor do I think it matters much whether those planets receiving the application be oriental or occidental. If ♄ be configurated with the ☉, the man will be laborious, modest and rich, says Ptolemy: but why he should be rich is difficult to tell. His modesty will be the effect of a dull, cold constitution, but he will certainly be austere and disagreeable. If the ☉ apply to ♃, he will be a kind, steady, honest husband; if to ♂, cruel, angry and vicious; if to ♀, handsome and merry; and if to ☿, a man of business, but this will be as he is situated, for if he be combust, retrograde, or afflicted, he will be very worthless; if ♀ be with ♄ he will be more dull and timid; if with ♃, he will be every way an excellent character; if with ♂, he will be active and very lustful, inconstant and dissipated; and if with ☿, Ptolemy says, he will have unnatural propensities.

It would be best for those who marry to choose those, if they could, in whose nativities the lights were in ⚹ or △ to their own, (Ptolemy says with mutual reception, but that is nothing) for in those cases they will agree by sympathy, and have a much greater chance of being happy. In such cases, all agreements of the planets have their effects, but the best of all is when the ☾ of the male agrees with the ☉ of the female. If on the contrary they are inconjunct, there will be no affection, and if they are in □ or ☍ it portends the most fatal evils, particularly if the aspect be by application. If a benefic give good testimony to good aspects, they will be supremely happy: if the testimony be evil, as a □ or

☍, they will have some trifling differences, and it will be the same if the luminaries behold each other by a □ or ☍, provided the benefics have an agreeing aspect to either. If the ☉ and ☽ be in good aspect with each other, and the malefics afflict either, there will be at times serious dissentions; but if all the aspects be evil, it generally shews a separation or extreme misery. Ptolemy says, if ♀ be with the malefic, the separation will be for adultery or sorcery; by sorcery he probably meant poisoning, an art for which eastern nations have ever been famous.

Thus far the observations of Ptolemy are very rational, as indeed they always are when he keeps clear of lordships and essential dignities. His succeeding observations are mixed with many absurdities, but I shall give them to the reader as they are.

The illegal connexions between the sexes are taken from ♀ for both male and female. If ♀ be in good aspect with ♄ and behold the Moon of a man, or the ☉ of a woman, they will live with their near relations or kindred, and the same if she agree with ♂ in a similiar way, only with ♄ the person will be old but with ♂ young; the reason of this is foolish enough, because her houses are in △ to those of ♄, and her exaltation in △ to the house of ♂, and the exaltation of ♂ in △ to her house. If she be found in promiscuous signs with ♄ or ♂, she causes women to cohabit with brothers or relations, and if a man have ♀ joined to the Moon he will cohabit with two sisters. In women if ♀ be with the ☉ or ♃ she will cohabit with two brothers or kinsmen. If ♀ be found with ♄ they will be constant and live happy; if ☿ join the configuration they will gain by each other, but if ♂ have familiarity, they will be incontinent, jealous, and vicious; if ♀ be in the oriental quadrants, they will unite with young men or women, but if in the occidental quadrants with those that are older than themselves; if ♀ be in ♑ and ♄ in ♎, and one of them in the east or south angles, and the Moon join the configuration, the men will cohabit with their mothers or aunts, and the women with their sons or nephews, but if the ☉ join the configuration the men will cohabit with their daughters or nieces, and the women with their fathers or uncles.

It must be here remarked, that Ptolemy wrote like an Egyptian, among whom such incestuous commerce was common: but, with the exception of the orientality of ♀, which may have some affinity with truth, the whole that is founded on the essential dignities of the planets is not worth attending to.

In modern astrology the lord of the 1st and the ☾ are directed to the lord of the 7th, or planets in the 7th, or to the planets in aspect with the ☾. It is entirely absurd so far as relates to nativities, but it may be found under the article "Horary Questions."

It is generally supposed, that the ☾ cadent, combust, under the Sunbeams, joined to ♄ or in a cadent house, or having ♄ more elevated, or in □ or ☍ to ♄ from cadent houses, or in ♊, ♍, ♌, or ♈, or ♑; are all signs of a single life, though the □ or ☍ of ♄ are reckoned very weak testimonies if there be no other. ♀ was also considered by Ptolemy and most others the same as the Moon, but this opinion cannot, I think, be correct. The Moon oriental of the Sun, or in the 10th, 11th, 12th, 4th, 5th, or 6th, house, denotes early marriage, the more so if the Moon be swift in motion. The time of marriage is generally predicted by directing the midheaven to the ☌, ⚹, □, or △, of ♀, or directing the ☉ to them, or by directing the ☾ to the same positions with the ☉ or ♂. Many direct them to the 7th or its lord, or the 7th to the lord of the 1st, or *vice versa:* but this though it may suit a horary question, can be of no use in nativities. For women these directions are made to the Sun instead of the Moon.

MARS. See Planets.

MASCULINE and FEMININE. There are few points in astrology more confused than the doctrine of the sexes of the planets, nor is it worth explaining in respect to its utility. Ptolemy says, the ☾ and ♀ are feminine because they are moist, and ♄, ♃, ♂, and the ☉, masculine because they are drying. ☿ sometimes dries and sometimes moistens, and is therefore sometimes masculine and sometimes feminine. They are also masculine when oriental and going before the Sun, and feminine when occidental and following it: they are also masculine when between the 1st and the 10th, and from the 7th to the 4th, and feminine in the other two quadrants. Here a planet may be masculine and feminine and masculine again all at one time. Again they are diurnal and nocturnal, and those that are diurnal are masculine, and those that are nocturnal feminine. Fortunately all the masculine planets are diurnal, except ♂, who being nocturnal is feminine, although in reality masculine. ☿ is diurnal and consequently masculine when oriental, and feminine when occidental.

Placidus divides them according to their active and passive qualities: those who possess active qualities, as heat and cold, are masculine; and those who rely more upon their passive qualities, as dryness and moisture, are feminine. Thus, the ☉ is masculine, because of his heat as he is more hot than dry. ♄ is masculine, by being more cold than dry. ♃ is masculine, by being more hot than moist. ♂ is feminine by being more dry than hot. ♀, feminine, by being more moist than hot. And the Moon is feminine for the same reason. According, therefore, to Ptolemy, a planet may be masculine, as Mars, because he is drying. and feminine at the same time, because he may be occidental and following the ☉; he may be also in an oriental quadrant, which makes him masculine again, and likewise feminine by being nocturnal all at once. As to Placidus, he is at issue with Ptolemy in this question (though he probably did not know it,) for he says, ♂ is feminine because his passive quality, dryness, exceeds his active quality, heat: whereas Ptolemy makes moisture the only passive quality that is feminine. Thus authors, by their formal, precise allegorical nonsense throw a science into confusion, and involve even themselves in their own labyrinths. Modern astrologers, too, with their usual sagacity, have rendered the confusion more confused, by discovering that a planet is diurnal, and of course masculine when in a diurnal nativity above the Earth, and in a nocturnal nativity under it; in short, when it is in the same hemisphere with the ☉. Of course, in an opposite condition it is nocturnal and feminine.

Although Ptolemy lays much stress in his quadripartite, on the masculine and feminine condition of a planet, the reader may rest assured the whole is an idle distinction, and no more founded in reason than his essential dignities. Placidus, as we have already shewn, differs from him in opinion, but this is not to be wondered at, when he differed so much in opinion with himself. I would advise the student to give himself no trouble about the sex of the planets, but to study their influence. Masculine and feminine distinctions are only useful in horary questions; which being wholly symbolical, a planet may be deemed masculine when in a masculine sign, and in oriental quadrants, and *vice versa.* If these two testimonies are opposite, that part of the question at least is not radical, and cannot be answered.

MARKAB, a violent star in the wing of Pegasus, in 21° of ♓ of the 2d magnitude, having the nature of ♂ and ☿. It is said to give honour and success attended with great dangers, and sufferings, and to threaten a violent death.

MASCULINE SIGNS are ♈, ♊, ♌, ♎, ♐, and ♒. Feminine signs are ♉, ♋, ♍, ♏, ♑ and ♓. Thus, the cold signs are masculine and the hot ones feminine.

MATUTINE, appearing in the morning. The stars are called matutine when they rise before the ☉ in the morning, until they arrive at their first station, where they become retrograde. The Moon is matutine until she has passed her first dichotome. They are supposed by Ptolemy to be in their first degree of orientality in this situation and very strong, except ♀ and ☿, who are there considered occidental and weak. They are also said to cause moisture when in this position. See "Oriental."

MEAN MOTION, when the diurnal motion of a planet is at a medium, neither fast nor slow. That of ♄, is 2′; ♃, 4′ 59″; ♂, 33′ 28″; the ☉, 59′ 8″; ♀, 59′ 8″; ☿, 59′ 8″; and the ☾, 13° 10′.

MEASURE OF TIME, the mode of measuring the time of an event by the arc of direction. Ptolemy recommends, after directing the midheaven by right ascension and the horoscope by oblique ascension, to allow a year for every degree of such distance, or five minutes for a month. Maginus, on the authority of Dr. Dee (who certainly was a good mathematician) recommends the arc of direction to be considered as right ascension, and measured according to the Sun's motion, by right ascension, at the time of birth. Placidus has a much more correct method, by adding the Sun's right ascension at the time of birth to the arc of direction, thereby converting the whole into right ascension, and finding in the ephemeris at what time the Sun arrives at the end of such arc, and allowing a year for a day, and so on in proportion. See Directions, and also Equation. Naibod recommends finding the distance by right or oblique ascension, and when the arc is discovered allow for every degree, 1 year, 5 days, 8 hours; and for every minute, 6 days, 4 hours. According to the following table.

NAIBOD'S TABLE OF TIME.

°	Y.	D.	H.	°	Y.	D.	H.	°	Y.	D.	H.
1	1	5	8	8	8	42	20	50	50	267	16
2	2	10	17	9	9	48	4	60	60	321	4
3	3	16	1	10	10	53	13	70	71	9	11
4	4	21	10	20	20	107	1	80	81	62	24
5	5	26	18	30	30	160	14	90	91	116	13
6	6	32	3	40	40	214	3	100	101	170	2
7	7	37	11								

By this table the measure of time for those who choose to use it, may be had for any number of degrees by adding them, if they are not to be found in the table. Thus, if the time were wanted for 26 degrees, add 6 years, 32 days, 3 hours, the time for 6 degrees, to 20 years, 107 days, 1 hour, the time for 20 degrees; the period will be 26 years, 39 days, 4 hours. The odd minutes must be equated at the rate of 6 days, 4 hours for each, and their time added to the rest.

MEDIUM CŒLI, the midheaven.

MEDUSA'S HEAD, Caput Algol: a violent fixed star of the 2d magnitude, of the nature of ♄ and ♃, in the constellation of Perseus, in the 24th degree of ♉, said when found with the ☾ to cause beheading. This is a very erroneous opinion, though supported by Placidus, who gives an instance of it in the nativity of Cardan,* who he affirms, was beheaded where he places this star in 20° of ♊, whether by mistake or design I know not, neither can it be near the ☾, for its declination is 40°.

MERCURY. See Planets.

MERIDIAN, a circle crossing the equator (from the poles) at right angles. Every place has its own meridian passing through its zenith where it forms the cusp of the midheaven or the ☉'s place at noon. From this to the horizon either way is the semediurnal arc of the ☉ or any star.

MERIDIONAL, southern.

METONIC, the lunar cycle of 19 years, so called from one Meton, an Athenian who invented it.

MIDHEAVEN, the south angle or cusp of the 10th.

MIND, QUALITIES OF THE, the disposition of any person is considered by Ptolemy from ☿ and the ☾, and the planets that have domal dignities in the signs, where they are, or what are vulgarly called their dispositors. ☿ governs the rational, and the ☾ the irrational or sensitive faculties. As these and their dispositors are posited in certain signs, or in respect to the ☉ and angles (by which is meant their oriental, occidental, matutine, or vespertine position,) so will the disposition of the native be.

If they are found in tropical or equinoctial signs, they make the mind more active, sharp and ingenious, ambitious and persevering.

If in double-boodied signs, they are crafty, subtle, unstable, deceitful, negligent, superficial characters; easily pleased, fond of music and women, and not to be relied on for anything.

If in fixed signs, they are just, plain, firm, upright, prudent, patient, steady, laborious, rigid, temperate and fixed in their purposes and pursuits, also malicious, contentions, rebellious, ambitious, and covetous.

If orientally configurated with the horoscope, namely, between the 1st and 10th or the 7th and 4th, they make the native open, candid, simple and without disguise, strong, ingenious and active.

*Cardan, having calculated his own nativity, is said to have starved himself to death, to verify his prediction.

If matutine or culminating, viz. between the 1st and 10th, or on the cusp of the latter, they are prudent, settled, thoughtful, constant and fit to be depended upon; fortunate in their endeavours, firm, rigid, penetrating, of strong mind and sound judgment, ardent and persevering.

Those stars rising in the beginning of the night, and occidental, (viz. those that ascend after sunset, and consequently in or near an opposition of the Sun), make the native wicked, unstable, weak, ambitious, bullying and boasting, yet dull, cowardly, mean, servile, and despicable.

Vespertine planets, viz. those between the 10th and 7th, or on the cusp of the 4th or near it, or ☿ and ♀ rising vespertine by day: namely, when at or near their greatest elongation, and rising or setting heliacally, make the native ingenious and prudent, not fond of labour, but more addicted to study and scientific pursuits and new inventions, good mathematicians, philosophers, and eminent in that which requires ready genius and mental exertion.

Planets having dominion in the places of ☿ and the ☾, being well posited, and free from affliction, and particularly when configurated in any manner to both ☿ and the ☾; give great mental endowments, and transcendant abilities.

If they are weak, or ill disposed, they give, according to their nature, imperfect and obscure ideas. They who are impressed by the malefics with evil dispositions, if a good aspect intervenes, have not the power to do the evil they otherwise would do, and even if they persevere, are so unfit for it that they are soon detected and punished.

Again, those whose dispositions are good through benefic aspects, if a malefic have also configuration to the place, will have an evil or hurtful impression mixed with the good, as being mean, covetous, hasty tempered, or meek and bashful, so as to merit censure, or meet with imposition or ill treatment.

♄ alone, having dominion over the mind by governing ☿ and the ☾, if his mundane position be angular or strong, makes the native obstinate yet fearful, laborious, envious, severe, and covetous; but if badly situated, sordid, mean spirited, ill-disposed, cowardly, envious, solitary, fretful, and apt to cry, laborious, melancholy, treacherous and slovenly. If he be configurated with ♃ in a good position, he makes the native well disposed, judicious, magnanimous, busy, and prudent; but if ill-disposed, foolish, cowardly yet violent, suspicious, superstitious, crafty, hypocritical, idle, austere, friendless, cautious and slow. If with ♂ well disposed, the native is laborious, firm, bold, turbulent and austere, full of contempt and insolence; seditious, rebellious, tyrannical, covetous malicious, proud, unyielding, insulting, inhuman, violently ambitious, implacable, curious, penetrating, active and invincible; able, commanding, fit for any undertaking, but extremely wicked.

If ♂ be ill-posited, the native will be a thief, murderer, and assassin: deeply rapacious, and inhuman, atheistical, sacreligious, lustful, luxurious, and every way wicked. If ♄ be configurated with ♀ well disposed, the native will be solitary, melancholy, envious, austere, unpleasant in company, superstitious and fanatical, grave, bashful, modest, ingenious, and faithful in attachment, but fretful, and jealous. If ♀ be ill disposed, they will be obscene, lustful, and filthy; vulgar in their pursuits and propensities, drunkards, impious, and fit for anything infamous, If ♄ be configurated with ☿ well posited, they will be ingenious, curious, studious, of good abilities, particularly in law or physic, careful, sober, industrious and successful; but of a bitter, ill-natured, captious disposition. If ☿ be ill-disposed, they will be malicious, cruel, treacherous, thieves, swindlers, forgers, pettifoggers, house-breakers, and every way base and infamous.

If ♃ alone have the dominion and be well posited, he makes the native honourable, open, just, magnanimous, and venerable, pious, courteous, and every way good and fortunate. If evil disposed, those qualities will be impressed on the mind more faintly; he will be more prodigal, fearful, proud, bashful, weak, and careless,

If he configurate with ♂ well situated, the native will be bold, proud, contentious, impetuous and insubordinate, hot headed, active, fond of fighting, magnanimous, and honourable; penetrating, judicious, courageous, and successful. If ♂ be ill placed, he will be cruel, seditious, arrogant, rapacious, rash, indiscreet desperate, factious, stubborn, unstable, lustful, faithless, dissatisfied and injudicious.

If he have familiarity with ♀ well disposed, the native is a person of taste and elegance, fond of pleasure, children, and beautiful objects, partial to music, active, kind, affable, cheerful, ingenious, liberal, and ambitious of love and admiration. If ♀ be ill-disposed, the native will be wholly sensual and addicted to every kind of pleasure, lust and dissipation; fond of dress, show, and pleasure; very lascivious, talkative, yet not evil disposed; affable, cheerful, and free, very effeminate, and generally handsome.

If he be in familiarity with ☿ well placed, he disposes to business, and all kinds of learning, poetry, oratory, and knowledge of every kind; the native is sober, kind, cheerful, affectionate, and wise. If ☿ be evil disposed, the native will be shallow, superficial, proud, stupid, trifling, enthusiastic, silly, and generally wrong.

If ♂ alone have dominion and be well placed, he makes the native bold, generous, brave, magnanimous, strong, confident, rash, contemptuous, angry, violent, desperate, and born to command. If ill-disposed, they are cruel, bloody, drunken, furious, headstrong, turbulent, rapacious, luxurious, athiestical, and desperately mischievous.

If he have familiarity with ♀ well posited, the native is cheerful, merry, fond of music, dancing and all kinds of amusement, simple, good humoured and friendly, but given to lust of every description, hasty tempered, jealous, and intemperate.

If ♀ be ill placed, they will be proud, mischievous, liars, drunkards, treacherous, perjured, rash, intemperate, very lascivious, adulterers, wholly debauched and infamous. If he have configuration with ☿ well posited, the native is bold, violent, laborious, crafty, ready to invent mischief, witty, quick, ingenious, treacherous, very active, eloquent and successful; good enough to those like himself, but mischievous to his enemies. If ☿ be be ill posited, they will be intemperate, cruel, liars, thieves, murderers, thieftakers, parricides, assassins, forgers, poisoners, bold, violent, and deeply wicked.

If ♀ alone have the dominion and be well placed, the native will be neat, delicate, elegant, and beautiful, fond of music, dancing, and amusement; cheerful, kind and happy, charitable and every way well disposed. They are not fond of labour, and inclined to be jealous. If ill disposed, they will be slothful, effeminate, lustful, timid, careless, obscure and infamous. If configurated with ☿ well placed, they will be learned, scientific, and judicious, eloquent, cheerful, fond of refined and delicate amusements, kindhearted, well-disposed, pleasing and courteous, magnanimous but given to contention where they think their rights are invaded, and if Ptolemy may be credited, addicted to unnatural practices. If ☿ be ill disposed, they will be treacherous, crafty, subtle, unstable, liars, slanderers, perjured, weak-minded, obstinate, effeminate, debauched, and notoriously infamous in all their propensities.

If ☿ alone have dominion and be well posited, they will be learned and scientific, great orators, logicians, mathematicians and philosophers, and generally well disposed. If ill placed, they will be foolish, stupid, liars, furious, trifling, thoughtless forgetful, covetous, knavish, deceitful and always doing wrong, through a defect in judgment.

To all those the ☾ contributes more or less according to her position. When in her greatest north or south latitude, she makes the native more crafty and changeable, but when in her nodes, more active and industrious. When in oriental quadrants or increasing in light, she makes the disposition more fixed, free, open, and ingenious, but when in occidental quadrants, or decreasing in light, they are more dull, unsettled, slow, cautious, and obscure.

The ☉, when angular, or in oriental quadrants, makes the native more just, industrious, honourable, and well disposed; but occidentally posited, or cadent, more abject, cruel, obstinate, laborious, obscure, and ill disposed.

The general qualities of ♄ are fear, melancholy, slowness, labour, solitariness, and a propensity to cry.

Of ♃, candour, gravity, greatness, magnanimity, security, boldness, goodness and love.

Of ♂, anger, rashness, desperation, courage, propensity to war or quarrels, roughness, obstinacy, theft, murder and rapine.

Of ♀, beauty, delicacy, good taste, fondness for music, dancing, pleasure and love, effeminacy, lust, debauchery, and dissipation.

Of ☿, learning, eloquence, wit and judgment, arts, sciences, and knowledge of every kind, genius, activity and invention: also dishonesty, fraud, theft, lying, unsteadiness, trick, and artifice. It is generally said, that ☿ with the ☉ makes the native fit for business, but when 20 or 25 degrees distant, more fit for learning. Others say, he renders the native more fit for business when in moveable signs, and dull when in watery signs. When afflicted, the native is said to be more shallow and divested of wisdom, however specious he may be in appearance. When retrograde, they are sceptical; and when swift they are unsettled and changeable; when under the sun-beams always busy in useless speculations, and inventions; but when above 17° distant, ingenious and judicious; when oriental, open and honest; when occidental, deceitful.

The greatest part of this exhibits a mass of confusion, or at least intricacy not easily elucidated. Indeed, the nature of the stars themselves and their various effects when combined, arising from so many opposite causes, will be ever in some degree incomprehensible to us. This is evident from the endless shades of dispositions, as well as countenance and feature, to be found in the

human race, insomuch that no two individuals are exactly alike
in mind or appearance

There is little reason to doubt but that the ☾ and ☿ have the
chief influence in forming the mind, but that their dispositors can
have any effect more than other planets is a very silly idea. Ptolemy is a very obscure author at most times, one cause of which is
his frequent allusions to opinions and technicalities very well understood at the time he wrote but now unknown. What he means by
planets ruling ☿ and the ☾, and being well posited, does not
clearly appear. In the list of these ruling stars he places ☿ himself, which is an absurdity, for he cannot be his own ruler. He
may possibly mean the dispositors of ☿ and the ☾ or planets in
aspect with them, but in either case, he can neither dispose of nor
aspect himself.

As to a star's being "in glory in respect to the ☉ and angles,"
we can only suppose he means oriental and angular, and yet these
seem but very inadequate causes for all these tremendous effects.
Stars rising in the beginning of the night are such as apply to
opposition of the Sun. I have endeavoured to give the best explanation possible of vespertine setting by day, which I conceive must
mean when ☿ and ♀ are in the higher part of their orbit in
respect to us, and appear in the morning before the ☉. They
thus set heliacally when the Sun rises, and this probably is what
Ptolemy calls vespertine settings, by day, though matutine settings would be the more proper term as they set in the morning.
Vespertine risings must be ☿ and ♀ rising heliacally in the evening.

The greatest part of this system is rendered unintelligible
through a mixture of obscurity and error: and the superstitious
remarks of modern astrologers have not contributed to render it
more intelligible. Even Ptolemy himself appears not to have
been any way master of the subject, and has certainly in many
cases asserted more than he could know from experience. The
whole therefore must be doubtful, and a new system founded
upon the basis of the old is absolutely wanted, in which the student must above all things shun the doctrine of lordships and
dispositors. How far matutine and vespertine, oriental and occidental, positions with respect to the Sun and quadrants may be
available, is not easy to determine, but I am certain their effects
cannot be so powerful as described. A planet angular is assuredly
powerful, but there is a great difference in the angles, and why a
planet should be more powerful succeedent than cadent (seeing
they are both at an equal distance from angles) is not easily

explained. There can be little doubt but that the configuration of the ☾ is the best aspect ☿ can have, he partakes of the disposition of every planet with whom he is familiar, and when in combustion, or retrograde, or under the sunbeams, the abilities of the native will be considerably impaired. When ☿ and the ☾ are in aspect with many planets the native will be very unsettled and unstable in disposition, resembling each by turns; but I have never observed that the nature of an aspect made much difference, whether a □ or ✶, except to one of the luminaries,

In modern astrology it is usual to judge of the mind of a native from the planets in the ascendant, and this at least appears correct, only their effect should be joined to that of ☿ and the ☾. If none be in the horoscope, the planets to which the ☾ applies, or if there be none such, those from which she separates are the significators of manners. The ☌, △, or ✶ of ☿ and the ☾, shews ingenuity and great ability: the □ shews wit, but often applied, it is said. to evil purposes; and the ☍ is said to denote a stubborn, wicked and seditious spirit.

☿ in ♉ or ♑, and cadent, retrograde, combust, or afflicted, makes the native rude, silly or stupid: but these debilities are enough without the aid of ♉ or ♑ to injure the intellect, though a good aspect of the ☾ from the midheaven, or probably from any angle, would in a considerable degree counterbalance it all. ☿ in ☌, ✶, or △ of ♄ is said to give sound judgment and a careful, constant wit; but I am certain the ☌ of ♄ would be productive of quite a contrary effect. ♃ in ☌, ✶, △, or indeed any aspect of ☿, causes honesty. ♂ gives confidence, and to this may be added extreme wickedness, if joined to ☿. The ☉ is said to cause pride when in any aspect, and this is probably the truth. ♀ gives pleasantness, elegance and sweetness, except counterbalanced by other planets. But the ☾ gives the most piercing wit and powerful abilities. The □ or ☍ of ♄ is said to cause an impediment in speech, but to do this the ☾ must be much afflicted. Any aspect of ♂ inclines to the study of medicine or surgery.

It is said, but I think without foundation, that the □ of ♂ or the ☉ to ☿, causes madness: as ☿, however, never can be even one sign distant from the ☉, the latter part of this observation is extremely ridiculous.

MINUTE, the sixtieth part of an hour in time, marked 1m.: or the sixtieth part of a degree in measure, and marked 1′.

MOVEABLE SIGNS, ♈, ♎, ♋, and ♑, so called because the weather is moveable or changeable when the ☉ is in them, and the disposition of the native whose ascendant they, or whose ☿ or ☾ they contain, is said to be the same.

MODUS RATIONALIS. The method of Regiomontanus for regulating the cusps of the intermediate houses between the angles in a figure, by dividing the ecliptic by the equator instead of the semiarc. It certainly is any thing but *rational*, for the cusps of all the houses except the 10th and 4th, can only be determined by oblique ascension. See "Figure."

MODERATORS, the ☉, ☾, 10th and 1st houses, and ⊕. They are so called because each is said to have its own mode of operating on the native according to its nature. Thus, the 10th operates differently from the 1st, the ☉ differently from the ☾, and the ⊕ differently from them all. Of the 5 moderators 4 only should be retained, for the ⊕ can have no effect in nativities.

MOISTURE, is said to abound when planets are matutine, when the ☾ is in her first quarter, and during the winter and the night.

MOON. See "Planets."

MOTION. The motion of a planet is either quick or slow, as it exceeds or falls short of its Mean Motion, for which see that article.

The following table will be found useful in calculating the hourly motion of a planet from its diurnal motion.

Pr. Day. Degrees or Minutes.	Pr. Hour. ′ ″ or ″ ‴		Pr. Day. Degrees or Minutes.	Pr. Hour. ′ ″ or ″ ‴		Pr. Day. Degrees or Minutes.	Pr. Hour. ′ ″ or ″ ‴	
1	2	30	21	52	30	41	102	30
2	5		22	55		42	105	
3	7	30	23	57	30	43	107	30
4	10		24	60		44	110	
5	12	30	25	62	30	45	112	30
6	15		26	65		46	115	
7	17	30	27	67	30	47	117	30
8	20		28	70		48	120	
9	22	30	29	72	30	49	122	30
10	25		30	75		50	125	
11	27	30	31	77	30	51	127	30
12	30		32	80		52	130	
13	32	30	33	82	30	53	132	30
14	35		34	85		54	135	
15	37	30	35	87	30	55	137	30

Pr. Day. Degrees or Minutes.	Pr. Hour. ' " " '''	Pr. Day. Degrees or Minutes.	Pr. Hour. ' " " '''	Pr. Day. Degrees or Minutes.	Pr. Hour. ' " " '''
16	40	36	90	56	140
17	42 30	37	92 30	57	142 30
18	45	38	95	58	145
19	47 30	39	97 30	59	147 30
20	50	40	100	60	150

EXAMPLE: Supposing ♄ to proceed at the rate of 7′ per day, his hourly motion would be 17″ 30‴ per hour, which, supposing the time required to be 7 hours, would, if multiplied by 7, give 122″ 30‴ for the arc he would describe during that time, which divided by 60 gives 2′ 2″ 30‴, but the seconds and thirds are of no consideration.

Again, if the ☾'s motion be 14° 34′ per day: for the 14° allow 35′ per hour, as the table directs, and for the 34′ allow 85″. The time being 7 hours, as before, multiply the 35′ by 7, it will give 245′, to which add 10′ more for the product of the 85″ multiplied by 7, and the sum will be 255′, which divided by 60 gives 4° 15′.

MUNDANE, in the world.

MUNDANE ASPECTS, distances in the world measured by the semiarc wholly independent of the zodiac. Thus, the distance of the 10th house from the 12th is a ✳ although perhaps not 50° of the zodiac distant. See "Directions."

MUNDANE PARALLELS, an equal distance of two planets from any angle. Thus, a planet on the cusp of the 9th is in mundane parallel to another on the cusp of the 11th, being at equal distances from the 10th. There are three kinds of mundane parallels: direct, where the significator remains fixed in his horary circle, and the promittor moves conversely; converse, where the promittor remains fixed in its horary circle and the significator moves conversely; and rapt, when both are carried away by what was called the rapt motion of the Primum Mobile so as to form parallels in their progress. All the mundane aspects were invented by Placidus, who, nevertheless, affirms, that they were known and referred to by Ptolemy, because the latter speaks of the ✳ of ♀, an aspect she never can form in the zodiac. So bigoted was Placidus to this mundane system, that, he says, he once actually rejected all the zodiacal aspects, though, by the manner in which he treats of the Thirty Nativities, he appears to have been soon reconciled to them again. For my own part, I have never found any thing in mundane aspects worth depending on; nor have I any opinion of their efficacy, and were I to direct to a promittor it should be in the zodiac. See Directions.

MUTE SIGNS, they are called dumb signs by the Arabians, and are said to have an effect on the native's speech, and cause dumbness, because the animals from whom they are named, viz. ♋, ♏, and ♓, have no voice. This is the very acme of ignorance and stupidity.

MUTILATED DEGREES, another silly distinction, of certain degrees supposed to cause lameness if they occupy the cusp of the ascendant; or if the ☾, lord of the ascendant, or the lord of the geniture be in them. They are from the 6th to the 10th degree of ♉; from the 9th to the 15th of ♋; the 18th, 27th and 28th of ♌; the 18th and 19th of ♏, the 1st, 7th, 8th, 18th, and 19th, of ♐, the 26th to the 29th of ♑; and the 18th and 19th of ♒.

NADIR, the point below the Earth directly opposite to the zenith.

NATIVITY, the birth, the instant the native draws breath, or rather that when the umbilical cord is divided. It also signifies a figure of heaven from the time of birth. See " Figure."

NATURAL DAY, the time of a complete revolution of the Earth on its axis.

NEBULÆ, clusters of stars that appear like clouds. When ascending, or with the ☾ at a birth, they are said to cause blindness or some occular defect, particularly when in an angle. Among these are included Præspe, the Pleiades, and even the Hyades.

NEOMENIUM, the change of the Moon.

NIGHT HOUSES, houses wherein planets are said to be stronger by night than by day. The night house of ♄, is ♑; of ♃, ♓; of ♂, ♏; of ♀, ♉; and of ☿, ♍. The ☉ and ☾ have but one house each, which serves them both by night and day.

NOCTURNAL ARC, the distance or space through which the Sun or a planet passes during the night. Also the time it takes in passing.

NOCTURNAL TRIPLICITIES. ♃ rules the fiery triplicity by night, ♂ the watery (both by day and night,) ☿ the airy and the ☾ the earthy. They are said to be stronger in these by night than by day. ♀ also rules the watery triplicity by day and the ☾ by night, in conjunction with ♂.

NOCTURNAL PLANETS, planets are said to be nocturnal when they excel in the passive qualities, moisture and dryness.

Thus, ♀ and the Moon are nocturnal, because they are moist, and ♂ because he is dry. The true reason why Ptolemy made ♂ nocturnal was because his heat and dryness should be opposed to the cold and moisture of the night so as to mitigate his noxious qualities. A planet is also said to be nocturnal when in a nocturnal nativity above the Earth.

NOCTURNAL SIGNS, ♉, ♋, ♍, ♏, ♑, and ♓, because they excel in dryness or moisture.

NODES, the point where a planet crosses the ecliptic out of of south into north latitude is called its north node, and where it crosses into south latitude its south node. The Moon's north node is called the Dragon's Head and marked ☊, and her south node the Dragon's Tail, and marked ☋. Their motion is retrograde, about 3′ pr. day.

NORTHERN SIGNS, ♈, ♉, ♊, ♋, ♌, ♍. They are also called commanding signs, because planets in them are said to command, and those in the opposite signs to obey.

OBEYING SIGNS, ♎, ♏, ♐, ♑, ♒, and ♓.

OBLIQUE ASCENSION, a part of the equator which rises obliquely in an oblique sphere, which is when one pole of the equator is elevated and the other depressed: of course, less of the equator ascends with northern signs and more with southern signs. This will make a difference between the right and oblique ascension, and the arc of this difference intercepted between the right and oblique ascension is called the ascensional difference. This, if subtracted from the right ascension in northern signs, or added to it in southern signs, will give the oblique ascension.

EXAMPLE:—Suppose ♃'s right ascension to be
   in ♋,   101° 54′
     His ascensional difference,   33   0
                                         —————

Being in a northern sign it must be subtracted,
    and the remainder will be the oblique ascension,   68° 54′
                                         —————

Had ♃ been in a southern sign the ascensional difference must have been added, and the sum would have been the oblique ascension.

Should it so happen that a star or degree has no declination north or south, the right ascension and oblique ascension are the same. The oblique ascension of any house may be found by adding 30° for every house to the left of the midheaven until it come to the 4th. Thus, 30° added to the right ascension of the 10th, will give the oblique ascension of the 11th; 60° added will give the oblique ascension of the 12th, &c.

OBLIQUE DESCENSION, a part of the equator descending obliquely in an oblique sphere in the same manner as the other ascends. A greater arc of the equator will descend with northern signs than with southern, and therefore the oblique descension may be found by adding the ascensional difference when a northern sign descends, and subtracting it when the sign has southern declination. The oblique descension of the cusp of any house may be found by subtracting 30° from the right ascension of the midheaven. Thus, if the right ascension of the midheaven be 221° 2′ the oblique descension of the 9th will be 191° 2′; of the 8th, 161° 2′; and of the 7th, 131° 2′. In fact, it is nothing after all but another name for oblique ascension: for if 30° be added for every house to the left of the midheaven, it will all come to the same thing.

OBLIQUE SPHERE, so called because all their ascensions and descensions are oblique, and all circles parallel to the equator are oblique to the horizon and form acute angles with it. This is caused by one of their poles being more raised and the other more depressed, according to their distance from the equator. All who inhabit between the poles and the equator live in an oblique sphere.

OCCIDENTAL, falling down, killing: western. See "Oriental."

OCCOURSES, or OCCURSORS, promittors.

OPPOSITION, when stars or places are diametrically opposite, or 180° distant, either in the world or the zodiac, it is reckoned a very evil aspect. See "Familiarities."

ORDER OF THE HOUSES. They are said to rank above each other as follows: 1st, 10th, 7th, 4th, 11th, 5th, 9th, 3d, 2d, 8th, 6th, and 12th.

ORB, the deferent of a planet, supposed by the ancients to fit into each other like the coats of an onion, and to carry the planets about with them. The word is now used to describe the distance at which a planet may operate from a partile aspect before it quite loses its effects. The orb of ♄ is said to be 9°; of ♃, 12°; ♂, 7°; ☉, 17°; ♀, 8°: ☿, 7°; and the ☾, 12°. Some only allow ♃ 9°, while others allow ♄ 12°; this extends to latitude as well as longitude. Stars of the first magnitude have 7° 30′ for their orbs; of the 2d, 5° 30′; of the 3d, 3° 40′; of the 4th, 1° 30′.

ORIENTAL. "Every one," says Placidus, "knows how largely and to what little purpose authors have treated of the orientality of the planets." This might well be the case, when the whole was unintelligible even to those authors themselves. Ptolemy, speaking of the masculine and femniine, says that planets "when oriental and going before the ☉ are masculine, and when occidental and following it they are feminine; also from the east to the midheaven, and from the west to the lower heaven they are masculine because oriental, and in the two other quadrants feminine because they are occidental." Here, therefore, we find that a planet is oriental when going before the Sun, and occidental when following it. This is called being oriental and occidental with respect to the Sun. They are also oriental in the south-east and north-west quadrants, and occidental in the south-west and north-east quadrants, and this is called being oriental and occidental in respect to the world. Now, upon this system a planet may be occidental and oriental at the same moment of time, for if it be in dexter ✱ to the Sun, it is oriental in respect to the Sun, and if in the south-west or north-east quadrant it will be occidental in the world. The words, therefore, "oriental" and "occidental," simply as such, have in themselves no signification whatever, except their relation to the ☉ or the world be specified. Again, if a planet going before the ☉ be oriental, every planet must be oriental until it reaches the opposition, for it certainly precedes the ☉ until then. Yet, in another place he says, "those quadrants preceding the Sun and the horoscope, and the quadrants opposite to them are oriental, and the rest are occidental." Here, then, we have another contradiction; for a planet is here discovered not to be oriental when preceding the ☉ after he has completed his first quadrature, but in the 2d quadrant until he arrive at the opposition, is actually occidental, although going before the ☉. When he has passed the opposition he again becomes oriental, although actually following the ☉, which Ptolemy has in the first instance affirmed to be occidental. Surely, when an author like Ptolemy founds his system almost wholly on the orientality and occidentality of the planets, he ought to be more consistent and intelligible.

The orientality of the ☉ is more easily comprehended, for as he cannot be oriental in respect to himself, he is only oriental in the south-east and north-west quadrants, and occidental in the opposite. The ☽ is oriental in respect to the ☉ when passing from the change to her first dichotome, and from the full to her second dichotome. In the other two quarters she is occidental, according to Ptolemy.

Although the planets are thus considered in a general manner, he in other places mentions the inferior planets as being stronger when occidental and vespertine. Placidus touches the matter as lightly as possible: he was obliged to notice it; but the truth is, he was himself ignorant of Ptolemy's meaning, and fully aware that it involved a contradiction which he could not unravel.

His doctrine throws no light whatever on the subject as it formerly stood, but it clearly demonstrates that he beheld it himself in its most natural point of view. He says " the planets have four respects to the ☉: first, from the ☌ to the first station, and in the ☾ towards her first dichotome; from the first station to the opposition, in the ☾ towards the full; from thence to the second station in the ☾ towards her second dichotome; and from thence to the ☌ again. This," he continues, " is a good reason why the three superiors are stronger when matutine from the ☉, and the three inferiors when they are vespertine, because they have then a greater degree of light, in which their influence consists, and then they are called *oriental*, but if otherwise *occidental*.

Here the truth breaks in upon us a little, though with a very faint light. For a matutine position only extends through one quarter of a planet's orbit; namely, that part of it which ascends between midnight and sunrise, and is therefore called matutine, because it rises in a morning before the ☉. In the same way, the vespertine quarter is that part of a planet's orbit which sets in the evening between sunset and midnight. Of the other two quarters Placidus has taken no notice whether they are oriental or occidental. If, however, his reason be just, and I believe it is, that a planet is deemed oriental when increasing in light, and occidental when decreasing, that half of the orbit entire must be oriental from the ☌ to the ☍, because it is then increasing in light, and the other half occidental because then its light is decreasing. Lilly says " ♄, ♃, and ♂, are oriental of the ☉ from the ☌ with him to the ☍, and occidental till they arrive at the ☌ again; for orientality is nothing but to rise before the ☉, and occidentality is to set after him, or to be seen above the horizon after the ☉ is set. ♀ and ☿ are oriental when in fewer degrees of the sign the ☉ is in, or when they are in the preceding sign, and occidental when they are in more degrees of the sign than the ☉ is, or when they are in the succeeding sign. The ☾ is oriental of the ☉ from the time of her ☌ to the ☍, and occidental from the ☍ to the ☌." The whole of this doctrine amounts to this, that a planet to be oriental must rise before the ☉, and of course set before him; and to be occidental must rise and set after him.

This is also the opinion of most modern astrologers, who always consider their planets as oriental or occidental of the ⊙ only.

The term oriental is generally derived from *oriens,* the east, and hence it is common to denominate a planet oriental when in the eastern part of the figure. Modern astrologers consider them oriental from the 4th eastward to the 10th. The word *oriens* itself is but a derivative from the Hebrew, and from this the term oriental, so far as relates to astronomy, seems to be derived, and it signifies, ' causing light.' The term *oriens,* or, ' brightness,' was derived from the same root, and applied to the east because the ⊙ and stars rose in that quarter.

The west was called *occidens* from *occido,* ' to kill,' because there the light was destroyed. Here we have the origin of oriental, which had no relation to the east, but merely signified, ' a causing' or ' increasing of light,' and undoubtedly applied to the increasing light of a planet until it arrived at its perigee, when its light decreasing in the same proportion, it was deemed occidendental or expiring. Of this original system of astrology Ptolemy must have been generally ignorant, as he only appears to have revived the system from what scanty materials he could collect of the old, which had probably perished with the rest of the learning, and even the language, of the Egyptians; hence his system is founded on certain planetary arrangements, for which he often found it difficult to assign a rational cause, and which frequently compelled him to have recourse to allegory and obscure unexplained dogmatisms to supply the defect.

What effect the increase or decrease of light may have on a planet must be proved by experience, for the orientality of planets being so very contradictory, has been little attended to by any astrologers. Placidus generally blinks the question, as he does in some other rules laid down by Ptolemy, which he was unable to comprehend and unwilling to contradict. Ptolemy himself just contrived to involve the matter in obscurity and paradox and there he left it.

The orientality of the planets, in my opinion, is merely their increase in light and their progress towards their perigee; and with respect to the oriental quarters in the south-east and north-west, they appear to have no foundation in reason, or in anything else but the imagination of Ptolemy. The three superiors will, therefore, of course be oriental when matutine, which matutine station will extend to the point of the perigee. The ☾, ☿, and ♀, will be oriental when vespertine and rising heliacally in the evening, because they are then increasing in light, and the two latter are in the lower part of their orbit, and consequently nearer to the Earth. Nevertheless, I would advise the student to examine seriously the rules laid down by Ptolemy, and try if it be possible to bring them to something like consistency before he finally rejects them. They form the chief basis of that extensive and generally received system, and ought to be well weighed before they are sacrificed to the opinion of any individual.

Orientality is generally meant with respect to the ☉, and is by modern astrologers considered a dignity of 2 degrees, though Ptolemy mentions nothing of the kind. ♀ and ☿ are considered oriental when to the west of the ☉, and ♄, ♃, or ♂, are oriental to the east of him. According to Ptolemy, it is a mark of great prosperity, if the ☉ be guarded by oriental stars and the ☾ by occidental, by which he appears to mean stars that are matutine, or going before the ☉, whether they be superior or inferior planets, but they must not be three signs distant from him. The ☾, on the contrary, should be followed, not preceded, and therefore they are called occidental only in respect to the ☾. I believe his only reason for forming such an opinion was, that the luminaries so guarded had the appearance of grandeur, and looked like princes attended by their retinue.

ORION'S FOOT, Rigel, a benevolent star of the first magnitude in the 15th degree of ♊, said to cause great honours and every degree of happiness when rising or culminating.

ORION'S RIGHT SHOULDER, Betelguese, a fixed star of the first magnitude in 26° of ♊, of the nature of ☿ and ♂, said to cause great martial honours and preferment.

ORION'S BELT, Cingula Orionis: three stars, from 21° to 24° of ♊, of the 2d magnitude, of the nature of ♃ and ♄. They are said to be fortunate.

ORION'S LEFT SHOULDER, Bellatrix, a star of the 2d magnitude, of the nature of ♂ and ☿, in the 19th degree of ♊, said to cause great military honours, attended by eventual loss, danger and ruin. It causes blindness by accidents when joined to the luminaries.

ORTIVE DIFFERENCE, the difference between the primary and secondary difference in directing the ☉ when found in the crepuscle. (See Directions.)

PARALLELS. There are two kinds of parallels: zodiacal and mundane. Zodiacal parallels are circles equidistant from the equator, namely, the beginning of ♈ and ♎, and consequently any two points of the zodiac having equal declination, whether of the same or the opposite kind, are in zodiacal parallel with each other. Thus, a star in 2° of ♐, another in 28° of ♑, another in 2° of ♊, and another in 28° of ♋, would all be in zodiacal parallel to each other, because they would all have the same declination in the number of degrees and minutes, viz: 20° 38.' The two first are called antiscions, because they have the same declination in number and name, viz; 20° 38' south declination; the others are also antiscions in the same way, as having 20° 38' north declination, but the two former are called contra antiscions to the two latter, because, although their declination is the same in number, it is different in name, one being north and the other south declination. Those having north declination are called commanding, and the southern, obeying: because the north being nearer our zenith must be most powerful. An antiscion is held by some to have the effect of a ✳ or △, and a contra antiscion that of a □ or ☍, but Placidus makes no such distinction.

Latitude makes a considerable difference in all antiscions. Thus, a star without latitude, in 22° of ♉, would have its antiscion in 8° of ♌, both of which have 18° 20' of north declination: but if such star had 5° of north latitude, its declination would be 23° 9' north, and therefore its antiscion would be in 10° of ♋. Its contra antiscions would be, of course, in the same degrees of the opposite signs. To find the antiscions of any star, recourse must be had to tables of declination.

Mundane parallels are taken from the angles of a figure in the same way as zodiacal parallels are taken from the equator, and are measured by the semiarcs of the planets. Thus, a star on the cusp of the 9th is in mundane parallel with another on the cusp of the 11th, because they are equidistant from the cusps of the 10th and 4th; and a star on the cusp of the 11th is in mundane parallel with another on the cusp of the 3d, because they are equidistant from the cusps of the 1st and 7th. Their opposite places are also taken in the same manner as the contra antiscions in the zodiac: so that two planets in parallel with any angle are really in parallel with all the four. For the method of finding parallels, see "Directions."

The effects of parallels are good or evil according to the nature of the planets composing them, and perhaps there is not any judgment more certain than that which is made from the effect of zodiacal parallels, which may be considered in every way the same in their effects as a ☌.

Placidus was the inventor of mundane parallels, and he appears to have relied much on their efficacy: but I have not yet been able to coincide with him in opinion. I would, however, recommend the student to examine them thoroughly before he comes to any final determination.

PARALLEL SPHERE, so called when the equator is parallel to its horizon. The polar inhabitants, if any, live always in this sphere. Their pole is their zenith. They have but one day in a year, one half of which is light and the other half darkness.

PARENTS. According to Ptolemy the ☉ and ♄ are significators of the father, and the ☾ and ♀ of the mother. If the luminaries are surrounded by the benefics, or the ☉ with ♄ and the ☾ with ♀, the parents will be splendid and fortunate; and the same when the ☉ is guarded by oriental stars, and the ☾ by occidental, that is, stars going before the ☉ and following the ☾. ♄ and ♀ oriental denote happiness.

If the luminaries are void of course and without a guard, the parents are poor, mean, and obscure, especially if ♄ and ♀ are not well configurated. If the lights are guarded, but not by those of the same condition, it shews but middling fortune, as if ♂ ascends to the ☉ (that is, matutine to the ☉) or ♄ to the ☾ (viz: following the ☾), because, if ♄ guard the Sun he is, although an infortune, the consignificator of the father, and therefore in this they are supposed to agree; but if he ascend to the ☾, he is no consignificator of the mother, and therefore operates as what he is, an infortune. If those guards of the lights have good aspect with the ⊕, the parents will be rich and prosperous; but if they have evil aspect, or if ♂ be the satellite to the ☉, or ♄ to the ☾, they will be liable to great losses and reverses of fortune.

If ♃ or ♀ have any configuration to the ☉ or ♄, or if ♄ be in good aspect with the ☉, or joined to him in an angle, or beholding him from angles, the father will have long life. If they are neither angular or succeedent, life will be short. If ♄ be in □ or ☍ to the ☉ and cadent, the father will be short lived, and subject to accidents. If ♄ □ or oppose the ☉ from the east or south angle, the father's life will be very short; but if from the west or north angle, or in their succeedents, the father will be sickly. If ♂ square or oppose the ☉ from angles or succeedents, the father will die suddenly, or be injured in his eyesight, but if he have evil aspect to ♄, he causes the father to be very diseased, and brings on fevers, wounds, burns, and death.

If ♃ be any way configurated to the ☾ or ♀, or the ☾ and ♀ in ☌, △, or ⚹, the mother will be long lived. But if ♂ or ♄ are joined to or in evil aspect with the ☾, in the 7th or 4th houses or their succeedents, the mother will be subject to many diseases; but if in the 1st or 10th, she will be very short lived. If ♂ afflict the

☾ when she is in the 1st or 10th, she will be liable to hurts in the eyes or sudden death; but if in the 7th or 4th, she will die by abortion, wounds, or burning. The ☾ in the 1st or 10th, afflicted by ♄, will cause the mother to be diseased, afflicted by fever, ague, consumption, &c. but in the other two angles, she will be filled with hysteric or nervous complaints. The signs containing the malefics are also to be considered. By day the ☉ and ♀ are the chief representatives of the father and mother, but by night ♄ and the ☾. He therefore directs a figure to be erected for the parents when more particularity is required, making the place of the ☉ by day and ♄ by night the degree ascending for the father, and the place of ♀ by day and the ☾ by night for the mother. There is much absurdity in this doctrine, and the chapter that treats of it is the most lame and ill-defined one in the whole book. A bare perusal of it will show that Ptolemy understood nothing of the matter, but inserted it merely from conjecture. From my own experience I can safely affirm, that neither ♄ nor ♀ are in way connected with the fate of the parents; nor can any judgment be formed of them from the condition of those planets. The luminaries do in some degree signify them, but I have no reason to suppose in any other way than that of general sympathy with the affairs of the native. If the lights are in good or evil condition, the native and every thing belonging to him will be the same.

PARS FORTUNÆ, the Part of Fortune.

PARTILE, an aspect is partile when it falls in the same degree and minute, both with respect to longitude and latitude. Thus, ♃ would be in partile ☌ of ♂, if they were both in 3° 4′ of ♌, and in partile △ of ♄, if the latter were in 3° 4′ of ♈. This can seldom happen, but a few minutes can make no difference. It is a perfect and powerful configuration, and in horary questions the business denoted is sure of completion and near at hand, especially if it be by application.

PART OF FORTUNE, an imaginary point in the heavens, supposed as a moderator to contain equal power with the luminaries, but which is really nothing but a phantom hatched in the figurative brain of Ptolemy, which has no influence whatever, except influence can arise out of nothing. It was a favourite maxim with that author to have every thing, as his grandmother might call it, "in apple-pie order:" hence the 12 signs were divided into 4 trigons, to suit the 4 elements; the planets were all accommodated among them with houses, triplicities, and exaltations, and the whole separated into fragments was divided among them for terms; they had their chariots, thrones, joys, sexes; three of them were diurnal and three nocturnal, and the odd one either or neither, as it suited him; they had oriental and occidental quarters assigned them; each of them had a note of music committed to his care, and, in short, the whole of the universe was parcelled out among them with an air of as much authority and importance as if Ptolemy had created it himself, and possessed a consequent knowledge of all its intricacies and bearings. Each planet had its wind, nations, animals, herbs, parts of the human frame, &c. allotted to it. The distribution certainly displayed much order, regularity and ingenuity, and only wanted truth and reason to render it complete.

Among other things it was observed that there was an ascending point in the heavens, and this they said belonged to the ☉. How they could imagine it belonged to the ☉ I have not the most distant idea, for the ascendant is a mundane point and has no more connexion with the ☉, except when he is there, than the most remote point in the heavens, nor can it have in any way more relation to the ☉ than to the ☾, or to any other planet. They found, however, by experience, that the horoscope was a point of some consequence (because there the stars first insert the effects of their *super terrene* rays in an animal), and this being so, it ought, they supposed, like everything else, to belong to something, and as the ☉ was the most glorious of the heavenly bodies, it must belong to him. The ☾, however, was also a planet of some consequence, and, in reality more so than the ☉ in the rapidity and power of her operations. It was necessary, therefore, that she should have a horoscope of some kind, for the sake of uniformity. There could be but one horoscope, and that being already disposed of, it became necessary to call some point a horoscope that was not one, and this is the point the ☾ is in when the Sun is ascending, and consequently in what is called his horoscope. "The ⊕," says Ptolemy, "is reckoned from the intermediate degrees between the luminaries, and has an equal number of degrees from the horoscope according to the succession of signs. Both by night and day, therefore, it is considered, that whatever proportional distance or configuration the Sun has to the horoscope, the ☾ has the same to the ⊕, that it may serve as a lunar horoscope.

The opinion of Placidus before he had seen that of Negusantius, was that the ⊕ moved on the path of the ☾'s latitude, and he was right, if anything can be called right that is fundamentally wrong: for as the Sun, having no latitude, is always in the ecliptic, therefore uniform with the horoscope according to the course of the ecliptic, so the ☽ should be uniform with the ⊕ according to the course of the ecliptic, the latter preserving the distance only of the ☽'s latitude from it. Negusantius invented another method, which is wholly unintelligible, though approved of by Placidus, which is that of giving the ⊕ the declination of the ☽, both in number and name, so that if the ☽ were in ♑ with 26° of south declination, and the ⊕ in ♋, the latter would have 26° of south declination also, which cannot fail to render the whole unintelligible. It is astonishing that Placidus could not see the cause of the mistake of Negusantius, and he would have seen it had he not been led away by the foolish doctrine of Ptolemy concerning aphetical places, which denied the ☽ to be hyleg because she was under the Earth. Now, there can be little doubt but that the ☽ is always hyleg wherever she may be, and here lay the mistake of Negusantius. He found death frequently to ensue when the anareta acquired the same declination with the ⊕, because this was the declination of the ☽, and what the ☽ suffered as hyleg was attributed to the ⊕. Now it is very certain, that, according to the rules both of Ptolemy and Placidus, the ⊕ cannot have uniformly the declination of the ☽, although the latter could not see the drift of his own theory, which is this, "The ⊕" he says, "is placed according to the ☽'s distance from the ☉, and, observe, whatever rays the Moon has to the Sun, for the latter should have the same as the ⊕ has to the horoscope. As the Moon is to the Sun so is the Part of Fortune to the horoscope, and as the Sun is to the horoscope so is the Moon to the Part of Fortune." Now, the Sun seldom has the declination of the horoscope, never, without he is in it, and consequently the ☽ should not have the declination of the Part of Fortune, except she be in it, else she cannot be to the Part of Fortune as the Sun is to the horoscope. So that we see the opinion of Negusantius is at variance with that of Placidus, which was certainly the same as that of Ptolemy. Whether Placidus changed his system when he embraced that of Negusantius we do not hear, but I often pity him when I reflect on his observation. ' I willingly confess," he says, "that I have with regard to the Part of Fortune laboured a long time, and have never yet been able to find any truth in it." This might well be the case when there was no truth in it, and it reminds me of a certain author, who says, "Some fools employ all their lives in writing nonsense, and others all theirs in trying to make sense of it."

It is here worthy of observation, that there can scarcely be a stronger proof of the truth of astrology than this. He could find truth in the planetary configurations, because their effects are founded on the immutable laws of nature, but when he came to investigate the effects of the ⊕ he could "find no truth in it," because there was none. When he received the new invention from Negusantius, who was another zealous disciple of Ptolemy, he approved of it much, and said it was perfectly agreeable to "rea-son and experience," though, in another place, when considering its dependance on the lunar parallels for its declination, he owns it wants the confirmation of "examples and experience." The method of bringing the anareta to the parallels of the Part of Fortune and the Moon both at the same time, he says "is truly ingen-ious" and so it is, for had not the effects of the Moon been ascribed to the Part of Fortune, he might have laboured at it all his life without finding "any truth in it." And after all, with all its agreeableness "to reason and experience," he appears to have made use of it but once, although many instances must have occured wherein the Part of Fortune was apheta. But except where its declination was made to suit the anaretic point, any judgment founded on it would be sure to fail.

The common way of taking the ⊕ is to add the sign, degree, and minute the ☾ is in to the sign, degree, and minute of the cusp of the horoscope, and from the sum subtract the place of the Sun, the remainder will be the place of the Part of Fortune.

EXAMPLE:—Suppose the cusp of the horoscope to be 7° 31′ of ♑, the ☾ in 8° 12′ of ♈, and the ☉ in 1° 45′ of ♈, I would know the place of the ⊕.

Place of the horoscope,	9s.	7°	31′
Place of the ☾,	0	8	12
Sum,	9	15	43
Place of the Sun,	0	1	45
Place of the ⊕,	9	13	58, or 13° 58′ of ♑.

When subtraction cannot be made, 12 signs must be added, or if more than 12 signs remain, 12 signs must be subtracted.

This method is, at all events, evidently incorrect; for the ☾'s place should always be taken with her latitude, which, supposing it in this case to be 1° 56′ north, it would make her declination 5° 7′ north, answering to 12° 55′ of ♈, which added to that of the horoscope, would make the sum 9s. 20° 26′, from which, when the Sun's place is subtracted as before, it would leave the place of the Part of Fortune 18° 41′ of ♑.

But this also would be incorrect, as it is mixing a zodiacal and mundane position together, and because the places of the luminaries are taken in the zodiac while that of the horoscope is taken in the world. The only true way, therefore, is to take the oblique ascension of the places instead of the places themselves, and work with them as before.

Oblique ascension of the horoscope,	311°	2′
Oblique ascension of the ☽ with lattitude in the pole of the horoscope, 51° 32′	0	27
	311	29
Oblique ascension of the Sun taken in the pole of the horoscope,	0	43
Oblique ascension of the ⊕,	310	46

If this be subtracted from the oblique ascension of the horoscope, it will give the oblique distance of the ⊕ from the horoscope, 0° 16′.

The method of Negusantius is, to subtract the oblique ascension of the Sun from that of the horoscope, and add the Moon's right ascension to the remainder, which will give the right ascension of the ⊕, which compared with the right ascension of the midheaven will give its distance from that angle; and this, again, compared with its semidiurnal arc, will give its distance from the horoscope, but it all comes to the same thing in the end as the other.

Oblique ascension of the horoscope,	311°	2′
Oblique ascension of the Sun in the pole of the horoscope,	0	43
	310	19
Right ascension of the Moon with latitude,	6	46
Right ascension of the Part of Fortune,	317	5
Right ascension of the midheaven,	221	2
Right distance of the ⊕ from the midheaven,	96	3

It must be here observed, that the ⊕ has the same declination as the Moon, and consequently its semidiurnal arc is the same. Now the Moon will have 5° north declination, and her semidiurnal arc will be 96° 19′, and that of the ⊕ will be the same.

Semidiurnal arc of the ⊕,	96°	19
Right distance of the ⊕ from the midheaven,	96	3
Oblique distance of the ⊕ from the horoscope,	0	16

When the right distance from the midheaven is greater than the semidiurnal arc, the ⊕ is under the Earth, and in that case its distance from the horoscope must be measured by its seminocturnal arc.

In the one instance given by Placidus, he directs it by direct motion, a kind of astrological bull, which signifies no motion at all, for the significator is supposed to remain fixed in its horary circle, waiting for the converse motion of the promittor. Whether or no it can be directed conversely, he says, reason and experience alone can determine.

The death of the child, wherein the Part of Fortune is supposed to have been hyleg, was caused by the Moon in the radix having the declination of ♄ and the □ of ♂. The effect of these aspects was such, that from the birth he was not expected to live, and he was drowned at 3 years old. 10° of ♎ were on the cusp of the 11th house, and 4° of ♏ on that of the 12th, and the Part of Fortune is said, by Placidus, to be about the middle of the 11th house; but where this middle was it is not easy to tell, for a little after he says, the ⊕ was about the beginning of ♏, which could be only 4° from the cusp of the 12th; a strange place to be called the middle of the 11th, but he wanted it, if possible, in both places, that it might catch the cosmical □ of ♄, and the ☍ of ♂, who was in 1° 26′ of ♉, without reflecting that while he was thus committing himself to uphold the credit of Ptolemy, he was losing his own. He observes, that at the hour the child died, ♂ transited the ☍ of the ⊕ by passing over the middle of the 5th house; but the ⊕ was not near the middle of the 11th, if it was at the beginning of ♏. What part of the zodiac ♂ transited he has not told us, but it was probably the □ of the Moon, which would be likely to cause such an effect, for I conceive that the Moon was hyleg, although near the cusp of the 3d; nor will all the crude formal dogmas of Ptolemy persuade me to the contrary. In his nativity of Philip the 3d, where, on the authority of Ptolemy, he makes the horoscope hyleg, there can be little doubt but the Moon, although in the 6th house, possessed a great share of hylegiacal influence. The direction of the horoscope to the □ of ♄ was apparently the more immediate cause of death, but the disease had been of 7 years standing, and originated in the Moon arriving at a parallel of the declination of ☿, which occasioned a violent flux of the humours from the head, and a bad state of health, which lasted without intermission until his death. This with the declination of ♄, which the Moon had at his nativity, was the real cause of his death; and the direction of the horoscope to the □ of ♄, if it had any effect (which I am not at present prepared to deny) only served to complete the catastrophe. The constitution was already broken by the lunar position and subsequent direction to ☿, and the Sun in the nativity had the declination of ♂ and was in zodiacal □ to the Moon, so that the luminaries mutually afflicted each other by the interchange of the evil effects of the two infortunes; and although they were both under the Earth, I have no doubt that they were both hylegiacal, and this, assisted by powerful secondary directions, might occasion death at the time, even without the assistance of the horoscope. The knowledge we possess of astral influence is very superficial, and although it is usual to expect some violent direction to terminate existence, it may often happen without, when those more remote causes that produce it are, as in this instance, extremely powerful. I have only made these observations to shew that there is a strong probability that the luminaries, and particularly the Moon, are at all times aphetical; that there is more probability of their being so than even the horoscope; that the doctrine of the ⊕ is wholly an absurdity; and that the effects ascribed to it may be traced chiefly to the Moon.

Some artists take the Part of Fortune differently in the night from what they do in the day, by reversing the rule, and adding the ☉'s place to the horoscope, and subtracting the Moon's place from it. It is all the same in horary questions, provided the artist steadily adhere to one system; but this was not the method used by Ptolemy.

The ⊕ enters a different quadrant about every 7 days. At the new moon, it is invariably in the ascendant, from thence it gradually removes through the 2d and 3d until the first dichotome, when it arrives at the cusp of the 4th; from thence it moves toward the 7th, where it arrives at the full of the Moon; at the 2d dichotome it occupies the cusp of the 10th, whence it passes to the ascendant at the ensuing change. A knowledge of this will be useful to correct any mistake that may occur in placing it.

The longitude and latitude of the ⊕ may, if required, be formed by trigonometry from its right ascension and declination, like that of a star.

PASSIVE STARS, the ☉ and ☾,

PASSIVE QUALITIES, moisture and dryness.

PERIGEE, that part of a planet's orbit where it is nearest to the Earth.

PERIHELION, the lower apsis of a planet, or that point of its ellipse where it is nearest to the Sun.

PEREGRINE. A peregrine planet is one posited in a sign where it has no essential dignity of any kind. It is reckoned a debility of 5 degrees. In questions of theft, a peregrine planet in an angle or the 2d house is the thief.

No planet is reckoned peregrine if it be in reception.

PERIODICAL LUNATION, the time required by the ☾ in returning to her own place, viz, 27*d*. 7*h*. 41*m*,

PHŒNON, terrible, cruel: a Greek name of ♄, but more applicable to ♂.

PISCES. See "Signs."

PLANETS. In all treatises of astrology only seven planets are considered, viz. Saturn (♄), Jupiter (♃), Mars (♂), the Sun (☉), Venus (♀), Mercury (☿), and the Moon (☾). Since then a new superior planet has been discovered, and named Ouranos, from the father of ♄, because its orbit includes that of ♄. It is marked ♅. Its appearance is white and shining, and not greatly unlike that of ☿. Whatever its influence may be, we are unacquainted with it at present, but, if any judgment may be formed from the colour of a planet, it does not appear very malignant. Some think it can have no power because its distance is so great, but if distance were an object in these cases, ♄'s effect would be much inferior to that of ♂ or ♃, whereas they are all considered as possessing an equal degree of influence. There are also four smaller planets, discovered between the orbits of ♂ and ♃, viz. Pallas (⚴), Ceres (⚳), Juno (⚵), and Vesta (⚶); but their effect can be but trifling, owing to their magnitude, which is very inconsiderable.

SATURN is the most distant of all the old planets: his orb was formerly supposed to be next to that of the fixed stars. He is of a dull, whitish, leaden obscure colour, and his motion is the slowest and his period the longest of all the rest, owing to his distance from the Sun. He is 29*y*. 167*d*. 5*h*. in finishing his revolution, which is the duration of his year.

He is considered a cold, dry, earthy, melancholy, masculine, malignant, diurnal, solitary planet, and the greater infortune.

When the body and mind of a native are formed by ♄, he will, it is said, be middle-sized, dark or pale complexion, with small black leering eyes, thick lips and nostrils, large ears; lean face, broad forehead and lowering aspect, dark or black hair, broad shoulders, small lean legs and thighs, and thin beard.

If well dignified, the native will be acute, penetrating and subtle; but austere, slow, and reserved; grave, close, and ungenerous; patient and laborious, covetous, and careful of what he gets, and constant both in attachment and hatred.

If ill-dignified, the native will be sordid, covetous, cowardly, and suspicious, envious, treacherous, stubborn and deeply malicious.

Without adhering too closely to these axioms, which are, perhaps, not quite well founded, the nature of ♄ is to make the native fearful, suspicious. covetous, reserved, melancholy, subject to fret, repine, and cry; they see everything through the worst mediums, and their vices are rather the effects of their fear and mistrust, and the natural result of the disappointments of a life that is seldom fortunate. This renders them often solitary, and glad to retire from the world, whom they equally fear and detest. They are not naturally inclined to be wicked, but are generally, like most people of slow parts, very laborious, chaste, and cool; very capable of strong and lasting attachment to those they think their friends, and malicious and unforgiving to their enemies.

On my own part, I do not in any way consider ♄ as the greater infortune: the malignancy of ♂ is ten times more tremendous than that of ♄, as may be seen by a discerning observer, when they are either of them in perigee, by comparing their effects. To know the effects of a planet in perigee no other should be in or near its perigee at the same time, else their influence will be so mixed as to entirely frustrate any attempt at considering each abstractedly.

If ♄ be oriental he is said to make the native more stout, tall and hairy than when he is occidental; if he have north latitude, they will be more strong, corpulent and boney, with much hair; but if with south latitude, more smooth and fleshy; if in his nodes, they will be very boney and muscular.

He is said to govern the bones, spleen, teeth, joints, and right ear, and those born under him are always said to have bad teeth, and to be very much afflicted with the toothache. He is also said to govern the memory.

His diseases are such as proceed from cold and obstructions, as melancholy, agues, all nervous diseases, epilepsy, black jaundice, tooth-ache, cold defluxions, catarrh, phthisis, atrophy, fistula, leprosy, palsy, apoplexy, dropsy, &c.

He is said to delight in the east, and to be friendly with the ☉,

♃, and ☿, and at enmity with ♂, ♀, and the ☾. Others say he is friendly with ♀, because his houses are in △ with hers; but the whole is absurd and nonsensical, and therefore not worth a dispute.

He is said to govern a number of countries, all of which may be found in Ptolemy: but the whole system is ridiculous, for he, like every other planet, will always govern those countries to whose zenith he is nearest, and it is the extreme of folly, to suppose that a star, which revolves in a certain circle in the course of twenty-four hours, should not equally govern every place within that circle according to its position. He is also said to govern a number of herbs and plants, all of which may be found in Culpepper by those who think them worth seeking.

His day-house is ♒, his night-house ♑; his exaltation is in 21° of ♎; he governs the airy triplicity by day; his greatest north latitude is 2° 48′, and greatest south latitude 2° 49′. He is considered retrograde 140 days, and stationary 5 days before and 5 days after. His orb or circle of influence extends 9°, some say 12°, but it is generally fixed at 10°. His mean motion is 2′ per day. His shortest year is 30, his mean year 43, his great year 57, which is said to be the longest time any one born under him can live. There is also his greatest year, 465: so that if a kingdom, city, or family, began under him, it will last this period of time, and no longer, which is foolish enough.

When he is oriental, he is said to cause cold and moisture, and when occidental, dryness.

His place in a nativity is unfortunate to the native as long as he lives, and therefore, among other things, he should never travel in that direction. His place in a revolution is said to be unfortunate for the ensuing year.

Lilly, who assigns angels to all the planets in imitation of the Arabians, says the name of the angel of ♄ is Casiel, or Captiel.

JUPITER is next in orbit to ♄, and is of a beautiful clear brightness. His period is 11y. 314d. 12h. 20m. 9s.

He is considered a hot, moist, airy, sanguine, masculine, beneficent, diurnal, social planet, the author of temperance, justice, and moderation, and is called the greater fortune.

When a native is born under his influence, he will be tall, well made, erect and free in his carriage, handsome, ruddy, robust, with a sober, commanding aspect, oval face, high forehead, full grey eyes, soft thick brown hair, short wide chest, long feet, and firm and frank in his manner.

If well dignified, he will be wise, magnanimous, affable, just and good, mild in manners, temperate, moderate, and inclined, they say, to religion.

If ill dignified, he will be indifferent and careless, of shallow abilities, easily led astray by fools, and a bigot in religion.

If oriental, the complexion will be more sanguine, eyes more full, and the body more corpulent, with a mark, they say, on the right foot. If occidental, the native will be more delicate and beautiful, somewhat shorter, with light brown hair near the temples and forehead.

The real character of ♃ is good nature, freedom, and a conscious confidence, openness, and a disposition that would feel a difficulty in doing or contriving to do wrong, and could never, under any circumstances, be a bad character. Being free from that nervous debility of mind so conspicuous in the natives of ♄, he has that prepossessing appearance which acquires universal confidence, as every one feels himself secure and happy in his society.

He is said to govern the lungs, reins, blood, and all the viscera, and his diseases are such as are seated in those parts, or that arise from plethoric habit, or corrupt blood.

He is said to delight in the north (but this is an Ægyptian story; because their fruitful winds, and clouds causing their inundations, come from thence), and to be friendly with all the planets except ♂.

His day-house is ♐, and his night-house ♓; his exaltation is in 15° of ♋, and he governs the fiery triplicity by night. His greatest north latitude is 1° 38′, and south 1° 40′. He is retrograde 120 days, and stationary 5 days before and 5 days after. His orb is said to be 9°, but Ptolemy and Placidus allow it to be 12°. His mean motion, 4′ 59″ pr. day. His least year is 12, his mean 45, and his great 79; his greatest year is 428.

When oriental he causes heat and moisture, and when occidental moisture only.

His place in a nativity is fortunate to the native all his life, and his place in the revolution fortunate for that year. He is said to govern the number 3. The name of his angel is Zadkiel.

MARS is the next planet in order to Jupiter, and performs his course in 1 y. 321d. 22h.

He is a hot, dry, fiery, choloric, feminine, nocturnal, malignant, violent planet, and is called the lesser infortune; though, when all his effects are considered, I deem him more injurious than ♄, and more certain in his operation.

He gives a strong well-set, but short body, boney, lean and

muscular; complexion red, rather than ruddy; sharp hazel eyes, violent countenance, some say round face, but this is seldom the case; light brown, flaxen or red hair, but this cannot be depended upon.

The disposition when he is well dignified is said to be fearless, violent, irascible and unsubmitting, fond of war and contention, but in other respects prudent, rational, and even generous and magnanimous.

If ill-dignified, the native is wholly destitute of any virtue, prone to violence, quarrels, treachery, robbery, murder, treason, and every species of cruelty and wickedness.

The real disposition of ♂ is anger, violence, and apparently an eager wish to be in quarrels and mischief, the countenance is extremely vicious and unbending, rude, unkind, ferocious and bitter. They expect and exact universal submission, and although often generous and magnanimous, they are never kind nor even sociable. Such dispositions, however, are seldom seen, as the aspects of other planets alter it materially. The greatest mark of the influence of ♂ is a general redness all over the face, of a dark, not rosy, hue, a tightness of feature, and a ferocious eye.

He is said to rule the gall, left ear, head, face, smell, imagination, reins, fundament, genitals and bladder; and his diseases are the small-pox, jaundice, fevers, measles, shingles, hot eruptions, carbuncles, diabetes, stranguary, burns, wounds and bruises, and all hot fiery diseases.

He is supposed to delight in the south by those who suffer from the pestilential heat of the south winds, but for this they should blame the ☉ not ♂. Others say he governs the west winds, and is friendly to all but the ☾. This friendliness of the planets is very great nonsense, and ♂ is friendly to nothing.

His day house is ♈, and his night house ♏. He is exalted in 28° of ♑, and rules the watery triplicity both by day and night. His greatest north latitude is said to be 4° 31', and south 6° 47' but he is very eccentric, and often has much greater latitude. He is retrograde 80 days, and stationary 2 or 3 days before and after.

His orb is 7° 30', his mean motion 31' 27'' pr. day. His least year is 15, his mean 40, his great year 66, and greatest 214.

When oriental he causes heat and dryness, and when occidental, dryness only. His place in a nativity or revolution is said to be very unfortunate.

The colour of ♂ is fiery, and when in perigee he appears like a flame, or bright spark, in the heavens. It is generally observed, that at this time the weather is warmer than is usual for the season, but this may arise from other causes, and although I have observed this warmth, I have also known it to freeze when ♂ was in perigee. It is certain, however, that murders are more frequent, and of a more atrocious nature, at the time when that planet is nearest the Earth; robberies and innumerable calamities mark the whole period of his retrogradation, particularly if ♃ be near his apogee at the same time, and when ♂ retires to his apogee they will gradually diminish, and if ♃ approach towards his perigee at the same time, the alteration will be still more remarkable. At the time of the murders of Marr and of Williamson, and also when Chennell murdered his own father at Godalmin, and Hussey destroyed Mr. Bird and his housekeeper at Greenwich, ♂ was in or near his perigee. When he is in ☌ with the ⊙ he is said to produce the same dreadful effects; but I suspect this to be an error. As his distance increases, his effects diminish, until nearly annihilated in the blaze of the Sun. His angel is called Samael.

Sol, or the ⊙, has no revolution, except round his own axis in about 25 days. He is considered temperately hot, dry, masculine, and diurnal; and when well dignified equal to one of the fortunes. He is said to be good or evil according to the planets in configuration with him, and when he is joined to a planet he destroys its power, and assumes its nature; but this does not seem justified by experience. He is always considered as malignant to the ☽ when in ☌ or ☍, and I believe the same when in her parallel of declination. With this exception, he seems to have little effect of his own in proportion to other planets, and fewer judgments are drawn from him than from any other except ☿. I scarcely know a stronger proof of the truth of Judicial Astrology than this, for were those judgments founded on whim and fancy I know of no celestial body so likely to attract our notice as the Sun, or one more calculated to receive the praise or censure of all the good or evil that occurs: but he seems like every other planet to have a distinct office assigned him, and to rule general more than particular events.

He is said to cause a large, boney, strong body; broad high forehead; light, sandy curling hair; piercing eye, and well made person; but one that will soon become bald.

If he be well dignified, the disposition is noble, generous, proud and magnanimous, yet humane and affable, a faithful friend and a generous enemy; one of few words, rather profuse and fond of magnificence.

If ill-dignified, the native is proud and mean, arrogant and submissive, a tyrant and a sycophant; talkative, empty, restless, troublesome, austere, uncharitable, and unfeeling.

The rule laid down here for judging the form of the body is merely taken from the sign ♌ ascending, and has nothing to do with the ☉ in particular. Every native is born under the ☉, for his influence is too powerful to be excluded from having the principal share in the formation of every one, but this power is general, and with little variation, except as the ☉ is more or less angular, or above or below the Earth; for the native generally possesses more confidence and freedom when the ☉ is angular and diurnal, than if cadent or nocturnal.

When in ♈, ♉, or ♊, he is said to be hot and moist; in ♋, ♌, or ♍, hot and dry; in ♎, ♏, or ♐, cold and dry; and in ♑, ♒, or ♓, cold and moist. This is only saying the seasons are so, and deserves no attention. He is said to delight in the east, and to cause east winds, but they do not inform us when or by what means.

He is also reported to govern the heart, back, arteries, right eye of a man, left eye of a woman, and the retentive faculty or memory. These are some of the ridiculous theories of astrology.

His diseases are supposed to be faintings, palpitation of the heart, weak sight, fever, disordered brain, cramp, foul breath, and all diseases of the mouth and throat, catarrhs, defluctions, &c. which means no more than that such diseases may be caught by a person overheating himself.

His house is ♌ both by day and night, his exaltation is in 19° of ♈, and he rules the fiery triplicity by day. He has never any latitude, being always in the ecliptic, and is never retrograde; but modern astrologers consider him as retrograde, when slow in motion. His orb is 17°. His mean motion is 59′ 8″. His least year is 19, his mean 69, his great year 120, and his greatest 461, though others say 1640. His swiftest motion is 61′ 6″.

He is said to be friendly to all the planets but ♄, His angel is called Michael.

VENUS is the next planet it rotation; she shines with a beautiful clear, pellucid, bluish light, sufficient at certain times to cast a sensible shadow, and superior to all others except the ☉ and ☾. Her period is 224*d.* 7*h.* She is generally considered cold and moist, but by others hot and moist, and if the observation of Placidus be correct, that a bluish lustre denotes heat, she must be warmer than ♃ himself. She is never above 48° distant from the Sun.

She is a feminine, nocturnal, temperate planet, and considered as the lesser fortune. If (as some have asserted) a beautiful brightness denotes beneficience in a planet, she ought to be the greater fortune, but experience does not prove her to be such, and although Ptolemy says that a ray of either ♃ or ♀ of any kind falling on the very anaretic point will preserve life, I should place little reliance on ♀ alone if ♃ did not assist. According to the opinions of most authors, she appears to be nearly as changeable as ☿, when with evil planets, and not unfrequently adds to their malignant qualities.

Those born under her are said to be elegantly formed, and extremely beautiful, with sparkling dark hazel or black eyes, round smooth face, light, or chestnut hair, dimples in the cheek or chin, a wandering eye denoting desire, sweet voice, and very engaging address.

If well dignified the temper is even, quiet, mild, kind, engaging and sweet, very merry and cheerful, neat, dressy, fond of music and every elegant amusement, and very much prone to venery, yet truly virtuous, but much inclined to be jealous.

If ill dignified the native will be lewd, profligate, shameless, and wholly abandoned and inclined to every species of lust and depravity.

If occidental, very handsome, though rather short and stout, but if oriental, tall and upright.

The general disposition derived from ♀ is mildness and goodness, and whatever defects may fall to the lot of the native, they are seldom great ones, and more the result of weakness and strong animal desires, than constitutional wickedness or a wish to do wrong.

She is said to govern the reins, spine, seminal vessels and their contents, the neck, throat, and breasts.

Her diseases are those of the back, loins, genitals, belly and womb, priapism, siphilis, hernia, impotency, and heart-burn.

She governs the south wind, and is friendly to all the planets but ♄. Her day house is ♎, and her night house ♉; her exaltation is in 27° of ♓, and she rules the earthy triplicity by day, her greatest north or south latitude is 9° 2'. Her orb is 8°. Her mean motion 59' 8''. Her least year is 15, her mean year 45, her great year 82, and her greatest 151. She is retrograde 42 days and stationary 2 days before and 2 days after.

When oriental she causes heat and moisture: occidental, moisture only. Her place in a nativity is reckoned fortunate by some, though others confine these local influences to the 3 superiors. Her angel is called Anael.

MERCURY is next to Venus, and appears when seen through a telescope of a bright, white, glistening colour, but more dull and leaden coloured to the eye. He performs his orbit in 87d. 23h. His greatest elongation from the ☉ is 28°.

He is considered as a cold, dry, earthy, melancholy planet, and is diurnal or noctuanal, masculine or feminine, good or bad, lucky or unlucky, according to those planets with whom he is configurated. When oriental, he is masculine, and when occidental feminine.

He gives a person a tall, straight, deep forehead; long straight nose, thin lips, narrow chin, and thin narrow face, little beard, long arms, hands, and fingers, thighs, legs, and feet. If he be oriental, they are shorter, and of a more sanguine complexion, but if occidental more lean and sallow.

If well-dignified, the mind is strong, active, and subtle, the memory strong, and the native is eager in pursuit of all kinds of knowledge, a good orator and very eloquent, witty and pleasing in conversation. If he be under the sunbeams, they are more qualified for trade than learning.

If ill-dignified, the native will be of a mean, shuffling, unprincipled character: a liar, thief, gambler, and tale-bearer; void of any kind of useful knowledge or ability, but very conceited.

He governs the brain, tongue, hands, feet and intellect. His diseases are consequently, madness, vertigo, apoplexy, convulsions, stammering, dumbness, stoppage or humour in the nose or head, stupidity, cough, and gout in the hands or feet.

He delights, they say, in the east, but causes such winds as are agreeable to the nature of such planets he is configurated with.

His day house is ♊, and his night house ♍, he is exalted in 15° of ♍, and governs the airy triplicity by day. His greatest north or south latitude is 3° 33'; he is retrograde 24 days, and stationary one day before and one day after. His orb is 7°; his mean motion 59' 8''; his year is 19, his mean year 69, his great year 120, and his greatest 461. He is friendly to all but ♂.

When oriental, he causes heat, and when occidental dryness. His angel is called Raphael.

LUNA, or the Moon, performs her synodical course, or the period between her conjunctions, in 29d. 12h. 44m. and her periodical course, or that wherein she traverses the entire circle of the zodiac, in 27d. 7h. 43m. Of this period she may be seen 26 days and a half.

She is a cold, moist, watery, phlegmatic, feminine, nocturnal planet, and fortunate or otherwise according to those with whom she is configurated, and is certainly in many respects the most powerful of them all, the ⊙ not even excepted.

She gives a full stature, fair pale complexion, round face, grey eyes, short arms, thick hands and feet, smooth corpulent and plegmatic body. If impeded by the ⊙ in an angle, she causes a blemish in the eye, and the same if near nebulæ or violent fixed stars, but if in a succeedent house the blemish will be near the eye. If combust, or approaching to a conjunction, the native will be short lived or sickly; but if separating, and ♃ aspect the place in any way, their health will improve; in this case, however, the eyes are generally weak, or out of order.

If well-dignified, the native will be mild, soft, kind, ingenious and polite, but timid and thoughtless, unsettled and fond of rambling about, yet peaceful and wholly averse to disputes or trouble of any kind.

If ill-dignified, idle, stupid, beggarly, mean and fond of drinking. If oriental, more tall, corpulent, and smooth: if occidental, lean, short, and ill-formed.

She governs, it is said, the brain, stomach, bowels, bladder, left eye of a man, and right eye of a woman. Her diseases are rheumatism, consumption, palsy, cholic, apoplexy, vertigo, lunacy scrofula, small-pox, dropsy, &c.

She produces such winds as proceed from the planet with whom she is configurated by application, and she is said to be friendly to all the planets but ♄ and ♂.

Her house is ♋ both by night and day; her exaltation is in 3° of ♉, and she rules the earthy triplicity by night, and also the watery, according to others. Her greatest north latitude is 5° 17', south 5° 12'. Her orb is 12° 30'; her mean motion is 13° 10' 36''. Her least year is 25, her mean year 66, her great year 108, and greatest 320. She is never retrograde, but is considered the same as retrograde when slow in motion.

From the new to the 1st dichotome she is considered hot and moist; from thence to the full, hot and dry; thence to the second dichotome, cold and dry; and from thence to the change, cold and moist. In her increase, she causes a full, fat, plump, tall, body; in her decrease, a short, low, squat stature. Gabriel is her angel.

Such is the strange mixture of truth and absurdity laid down by astrologers relative to the planets. The government of right and left ears and eyes would excite a laugh, were it not for the regret that a valuable science like this should be degraded by such stupidity. The from of the body is chiefly taken from the nature of the signs which are assigned to certain planets as houses, and consequently have no relation to the planets whatever.

By a planet's being ill or well dignified is meant, its being in its essential dignities, which, as I have already shewn, can have no effect. The true dignity of a planet consists in being angular, free from combustion, and in perigee: to which may be added, a near approach to our zenith. Whether a decrease in light and motion and being retrograde, are real debilities, I am not quite certain, any more than whether a planet may not be weaker when under the Earth. Orientality I do not comprehend any better than Ptolemy himself, and therefore can say little on the subject.

By a planet's ruling a native is frequently meant, its being lord of the ascendant, let it be posited where it may. The almuten is also reckoned by some as the lord of the geniture, and that it gives the disposition. Planets in the ascendant are likewise supposed to have a share in this endowment, as well as those planets that aspect the ⊙, ☾, and ☿. I believe firmly, that a planet ascending on or near the cusp of the horoscope, has a very powerful effect in forming both the body and mind of a native, and next to that, those that aspect ☿ and the ☾. Much depends on ☿ and the ☾ having aspect or position with each other; this is what I should call ruling a nativity. Whether the ⊙ has any effect from the particular aspects he receives, remains to be decided; but I believe his effects are regulated chiefly according to his position in the world.

The lord of the ascendant, except he be there, is not worth mentioning; nor can the almuten have any power that is founded on essential dignities. The nature of the sign on the cusp of the horoscope ought also to be attended to, though not quite in the way laid down by authors in general. Planets on a zodiacal parallel with ☿ and the ☾, particularly the latter, have likewise considerable influence in forming the mind.

The diseases occasioned by each planet are said to arise from that planet whose body or aspect arrives by direction first at the anaretic place, after the anareta has performed its office and destroyed life. If there be none such, that planet causes the disease which separated by body or aspect last from the anaretic place. Others say, that the diseases of the native are caused by those planets afflicting the ⊙, ☾, and horoscope, if they are malefics, or if the malefics and the luminaries have the same declination; but this cannot be the case with ♃ or ♀, for no aspect of theirs alone can cause disease. There is reason to suspect that most diseases owe their origin to the ☾, at least they are governed by her periods for some time, if acute, and even when chronic a manifest difference will be found about the quadratures and semi-quadratures. At the syziges they are not so manifest. except in the cases of lunatics, whose fluids, like those of the ocean, are more violently disturbed at the new and full.

In considering the natures of the planets, too much care cannot be taken to avoid error. Most of the doctrine handed down to us concerning them is full of absurdity, and even the benefic nature of ♃ is in some cases disputable. In all conjunctions of ♃ and ♄, instead of the former correcting the evil of the latter, he only increases it, and at those times a malignant influenza will be very prevalent, if their latitude does not differ considerably. In close conjunction with ♂ he also increases his malignity; but as ♂ is apt to differ in latitude, their effect is not so obvious. In perigee, or in zodiacal parallel, ♃ always lessens the evil of an infortune. In the horoscope, or having the same or opposite declination with the horoscope, he endows the native with a good constitution. ♂ in the horoscope near the cusp generally cuts life short, and the small-pox, if not prevented by previous inoculation, generally happens when he arrives at the horizon. This is a disease peculiar to ♂, and it will often happen by his zodiacal square to the horoscope. ♄, coming to the cusp of the horoscope, causes broken bones or dislocations, but these directions should, in my opinion at least, be all taken in the zodiac, and not in the world. As to the planetary angels, they are only mentioned here for the form's sake.

Lilly considers the Dragon's Head and Tail as planets in their effects, and denies the truth of the general opinion that the Head strengthens and the Tail weakens every planet to which they are joined. He says, he always found the Head to increase the power of a good planet, and weaken that of a bad one; and that the Tail doubled and trebled the power of an infortune; and when joined to a fortune the good promised by that fortune was unaccountably delayed by a variety of perverse accidents, and except the significator was angular and unusually strong the whole not unfrequently came to nothing. This is worth attending to in horary questions.

PLANETARY HOURS, See "Hours."

PLATIC, wide, a ray cast from one planet, not to another, but to some place within its orb. The usual way is to add the orbs of the aspecting planets together, and take the half for the orb of each, Thus, if ♂ be in 21° of ♓, and ♃ in 14° of ♏, they will be in platic $\triangle$, being only 7° distant. The orb of ♃ is 12°, and the orb of ♂ 7° 30′, making together 19° 30′, the half of which is 9° 45′ for the half of their orbs which is 2° 45′ more than their distance from the $\triangle$.

The orbs of the planets are said to be as follows:

♄, 10°; ♃, 12°; ♂, 7° 30′: the ☉, 17°; ♀, 8°; ☿, 7°; and the ☽ 12° 30′.

The fixed stars also have orbs of activity assigned to them; those of the 1st magnitude, 7° 30′; of the 2d, 5° 30′; of the 3d, 3° 40′; and of the 4th, 1° 30′. The platic aspect is considered not so strong as the partile, and always weak in proportion to its distance. The latitude should always be considered.

PLEIADES, the Seven Stars in the Bull's Neck, in 27° of ♉, all of which are of the 5th magnitude, except the middle star, which is of the 3d. They are said, when rising or with the luminaries, or when directed to the ascendant, to cause blindness, bad eyes, hurts in the face, sickness, disgrace, imprisonment, and every evil that can befall humanity.

POLE. See "Elevation."

POLE of the HOROSCOPE, the latitude of the country.

PONDEROUS PLANETS, ♄, ♃, and ♂, so called because they move slower than the rest.

POSITED, situated in any place.

PRÆSPE, a nebulous cluster in 5° of ♌, of the nature of ♂ and the ☽, said to cause blindness when ascending or joined to either of the luminaries, particularly when the conjunction is in an angle. They are also said to cause diseases, disgrace, and every calamity.

PRIMUM MOBILE, the first mover, the tenth sphere of the ancients. It was supposed to be beyond the sphere of the fixed stars, which was their ninth sphere, and by a motion of its own to whirl itself and all the subordinate spheres round the Earth every 24 hours.

PRINCIPAL PLACES, five places where the luminaries are said to have the most beneficial effects in a nativity. They are the 10th, 1st, 11th, 7th, and 9th houses.

PROCESS, the progression.

PROCYON. See "Dog."

PROFECTION, the progression.

PROGRESSION. See "Secondary Directions."

PROHIBITION, the same as frustration.

PROMITTOR, that which promises to fulfil some event. Thus, ♄ and ♂ are anaretic promittors, and promise to destroy the life of the native when the hyleg is directed to them. ♃ and ♀ are promittors of good when directions to them are fulfilled. In horary questions the planet signifying the event is the promittor, as in a question of marriage, the lord of the 7th is the promittor.

The following are the effects usually ascribed to promittors.

The Conjunction.

Of ♄ to the horoscope: sickness, coughs, catarrhs, agues, quartain and tertain, head-ache, melancholy, fear, consumptions, dullness, idleness, weakness, lassitude, ill humour, and a lethargic drowsiness; and danger, they say, of drowning, if the sign be watery, and a violent fixed star near the place.

Of ♃; good health, and a happy cheerful disposition; riches, favour, credit, and prosperity; preferment, and, if by direction, marriage. He is also said, if peregrine and in a fiery sign, to cause a slight fever; in a watery or airy sign, the measles or small-pox; and in an earthy sign, the scurvy; but these disasters are always accompanied by some benefit, sometimes an inheritance or gift, children, &c.

Of ♂ : danger by fevers, small-pox, measles, madness, eruptions of all kinds, pestilence, &c. and, in directions, danger by robbers, horses, iron, fire, or fire-arms, stones thrown: if in airy signs, by falls; if in fiery signs, by being burnt alive. It also causes imprisonment or danger to those who are prisoners, murder, bloody flux if in ♋ or ♏, and inflammation of the pleura, intestines, &c.

Of the ☉; it denotes dignity, office, preferment, with much anxiety, disease, pains in the head, and hurts in the right eye. In airy signs, blights in the eye; in fiery signs, fevers, ophthalmia; in watery signs, much rheum; in earthy signs, dim eyes, and humor in the head. They also say, it causes all the actions of a man's life to be made public, makes him waste his substance, and quarrel with his brethren and sisters.

Of ♀ : causes much happiness, courtship, marriage, dress, dancing, and dissipation, children and gifts. If she be in a watery sign, the native in such a direction, is apt, it is said, to turn drunkard, spendthrift, and debauched, and is afflicted with such diseases as are the natural consequences of such pursuits.

Of ☿ : it addicts the native to the study of letters and science, merchandise, and various employments. Directions of this kind generally bring the native to some new kind of study, employment, or profession, or improve the old one.

Of the ☾ : if she was weak in the radix or afflicted, it causes trouble both in body and mind, threatens drowning, and whether fortunate or unfortunate, causes sudden changes to good or evil, sometimes marriage, journeys, preferment, death of the mother, cholic, and other lunar diseases.

Of the ☊ : this is said to have the same effect as ♃, and the ☋ has the mixed effect of ♂ and ♄.

Of the ⊕; sudden fortune, the nature of which is denoted by the planets that aspect it, and the houses they are lords of. The power or weakness of its dispositors are also considered.

To the cusp of the 2d house: riches and moveable property.

To the cusp of the 3d house: visits to and from brethren, and short journeys for pleasure.

To the cusp of the 4th house: death.

To Arcturus or Deneb; good fortune, with many cares and anxieties, chiefly caused by the native's own folly.

To Spica, or The Crater: ecclesiastical preferment, or some very good fortune.

To Orion's Belt: legacies or inheritance, love or dissipation; it is also said to denote great gravity and austerity.

To Regulus: abundance of honour and wealth, favour of the great, victory over enemies, also scandal, and acute hot diseases.

To Procyon: military preferment, quarrels, lust and dissipation; waste and ruin; loss in trade, or by servants. It is said to denote an artful, crafty, dissembling person, who will acquire wealth by violence and rapine.

To the Lion's right Knee: great military preferment and riches.

To the south star in the Lion's Neck: great danger and loss; to a military officer it threatens mutiny and murder by his soldiers, and when such a direction occurs the native becomes violent and very intemperate, both in diet and disposition.

To Hydra's Heart, Alphard: great trouble about estates and buildings, with much anxiety and loss; the native is addicted to women and intemperance, which eventually brings him to disgrace and ruin.

To the Pleiades and Præspe; violent fevers, blindness of the left eye, wounds in the face and arms, ophthalmia, imprisonment, exile, violent lust, quarrels and mischief; and if the ☉ oppose the horoscope or ♂ at the same time, it denotes an untimely end.

To the Asselli: burning fevers, bad eyes, blindness in the left eye, injuries by beasts, quarrels, and slanders from low women or vulgar persons. They are said to give martial preferment.

These effects are the same, whether arising from position or direction, except that when they are so posited in a nativity, their effects are more durable than when they are brought to the body of a promittor by direction. The $\oplus$ and Ω and $\mathcal{B}$ are only imaginary points, and can have no effect whatever in nativities, although they may be very useful in horary questions, provided they do not cause confusion. As to the directing the cusps of the 2d, 3d, and 4th houses to the horoscope, it is absurdity itself, and not deserving of further notice.

The δ of $\hbar$ with the midheaven, causes disgrace and hatred of superiors, destroys preferment, and so vitiates the inclination of the native as to render him indolent, foolish, obstinate and mean; wholly undeserving of any one's regard, and accordingly he is ruined, and falls to rise no more. Sometimes it denotes an ignominious death, if there be symptoms of violent death in the figure, and it always renders him an object of hatred and contempt among his inferiors.

Of $2\!\!\!/$: gives great honour, profit and preferment, favour of the great, and extensive patronage. It benefits every one according to their capacity and condition in life.

Of δ : stirs up the resentment of great men, causes exile, imprisonment, hatred, secret injuries, dreadful losses by fire, thieves, treachery and fraud. Kings, from this direction or position, injure their subjects, and are dethroned and murdered by them in return. It, however, gives military honours, with much anguish and trouble, and where an untimely end is threatened in the radix, this shews the time and quality of the death.

Of the $\odot$: gives great honour and dignity, favour of the great, high preferment, and endows the native with honour and fidelity. It also renders the native proud and prodigal, and greatly expands his mind, endowing him with lofty conceptions, and a spirit of enterprise. It also denotes the prosperity of the parents, particularly of the mother of the native, and is likewise the forerunner of her death.

Of $\venus$: cheerfulness, joy and mirth, amusements, marriage, honour, profit, gain, love, respect, and preferment.

Of $\mercury$; fortune and success in dispatch of business; honour and profit by learning, sciences, or anything resulting from study and the use of letters; increase in business and fortune. Youths become apprentices, or men set up in business, scholars take degrees, &c. It also causes scandal and disgrace, according to the condition of $\mercury$.

Of the $\mathbb{C}$: much restlessness, and business, with good or evil result according to the condition of the Moon; marriage or friendship with women, and anything signified by the ☾ in the radix is now brought to perfection. Travelling, trade, office, dignity, and their opposites.

When the 11th house comes to the cusp of the 10th, it is said to give friendship and good offices.

When the 12th comes to its cusp, it causes enemies, imprisonment, and all the evils of the 12th; injury or loss by horses, oxen, &c.

If the horoscope reaches the midheaven, it gives great honour and esteem.

The ☊ and ☋ have the same nature always as ♃ or ♄ and ♂.

The ⊕ to the midheaven, gives, they say, great profit and increase of trade.

The ☌ of Capella or Antares with the midheaven, gives military or ecclesiastical connexions, and perhaps preferment in those departments, or at sea; but it is productive of waste, dissipation, envy, and trouble, for most honours gained by fixed stars are seldom durable.

Of Orion's right Shoulder, Betelguese; gives great military fortune, command and invention, it also assists in the perfection of arts and sciences, and causes ingenuity.

Of Aldebaran: improvement in fortune, ingenuity, military preferment, and favours from women, or military commanders.

Of Bellatrix, Orion's left shoulder: quarrels, disputes, hatred, infamy, fraudulent practices by the native or against him, forgery, swindling, coining, perjury, &c.

Of Rigel; great military command or ecclesiastical preferment, courage, magnanimity, anger, vexation, much gain acquired by much labour and anxiety of mind.

Of Canopus, or the Goats: the favour of some old gentleman, dignity, power, riches and fame.

Of Regulus, Sirius, and Arcturus: some high office under government, &c. giving great profit and reputation.

Of Arista: unexpected honour and preferment beyond the native's hopes or capacity, according to his situation in life. It is considere l the best of all the fixed stars.

Of the Pleiades: dangers, quarrels, rashness, murder, imprisonment, sometimes preferment, but such as always ends in evil.

Of Caput Algol: murder, manslaughter, sudden death, danger of beheading, the native is prone to murder and mischief. Lilly says he never knew an instance wherein it did not cause evil, whatever the condition of the native might be.

The Sun to the ☌ of ♄: trouble and sickness, diseases in the head, melancholy, fear, agues, weakness in the eyes, hurts in the right eye by blows or falls, injury from great men of saturnine dispositions, who will injure the native's fortune and reputation, and cause him much uneasiness. Great dangers in travelling by sea and land, and, some say, it denotes sickness and affliction to the father.

Of ♃; health, peace and plenty, preferment, honour, and favour of the great. In kingdoms it denotes the renewing of treaties, peace, just government, and the clergy respectable.

Of ♂ : acute diseases, fevers, head-aches, dim eyes, or blindness, wounds in the face, burns, scalds, hurts by iron; inconstancy, an evil mind both in the native and those he has dealings with, injury by robbers or great men, mischievous enemies, injuries by soldiers, mad dogs, horses, or ferocious animals, or large cattle. If a violent death be in the nativity, it is then at hand. In moist signs, it is said to cause the bloody flux. To kings it denotes murder, poison, treachery and rebellion. In a martial nativity, it gives preferment, and that generally to some post of danger.

Of ♀ ; music, plays, merry-making, veneral pleasures, courtship, marriage, and these events will be good or evil as ♀ is strong or weak in the radix. It gives increase of trade and property, and to kings it is said to denote marriage, or preferment to their children, In nativities, where ♀ is peregrine, it is said to cause dreadful debauchery.

Of ☿ : much business, mercantile enjoyments, literary undertakings, learning, literary contentions, embassies, danger of thieves, propensity to travel, law-suits, quarrels, and preferment, if the radix denote it. It also inclines the native to fresh studies, and to be constant to none.

Of the ☽ : sickness, pain of the head and stomach, griefs, blindness, especially if denoted by the radix. It inclines the native to travel, prodigality, waste, folly, rapine, theft, and inconstancy. If the native marries on this direction, the wife is proud and one that will usurp authority over him. It denotes journeys; and if the ☽ be strong, it may give preferment.

Of Rigel: boldness and insolence, faction, bloodshed, enemies and great misfortunes.

Of Antares: military honours, danger and treachery, fevers, hurts in the right eye, and some violence either suffered or committed.

Of Procyon: military preferment after great struggle and expense.

Of Cor Leonis: grandeur, preferment, violent disease, though not mortal, afflicting both the native and his father.

To Hercules' Head: the native acquires honour by wisdom or artifice, but is apt to suffer imprisonment for embezzling goods entrusted to him, lose his property, and suffer from a fever.

To Aldebaran: military honour and preferment, but loss of all in the end, with, perhaps, either life or fortune.

To Arista: eminent dignity and immense wealth, and it is said to denote great happiness both to the parents and children of the native; if the star culminate at the time, it denotes church and state preferment.

To the Bull's south Horn: military enterprises and stratagems, danger from deceit and ambushes.

To the Asselli: severe fever, danger of fire, disgrace, hanging, imprisonment, and many calamities.

To Præspe; murder, execution, banishment, danger of death from fire, iron, or stones, blindness, fever, flux, sharp diseases, wounds, stabs, and lawsuits. Lilly says, he knows most of this to be true from experience.

The ☉ directed to the cusps of any of the houses, is said to cause a certain series of events, suitable to the nature of those houses, which, therefore, it is useless to detail, and that these events will be good or evil according as the cusps of these houses are well or ill aspected, or according to the nature of the planets posited near them: but the whole is absurd, and not worth the artist's attention.

To the ⊕: profit. To the ☊, the same as to ♃, and to the ☋, the same as to ♄.

The ☌ of the ☾ with ♄ causes apoplexy, palsy, dropsy, gout, agues, and fevers; false accusations, loss of substance, great anguish, fear, melancholy, sorrow and affliction; loss of friends, deceit, consumptions, blindness, or bad eyes, &c.

With ♃: gives health, honour and riches, preferment, and success in all things.

With ♂: great sorrow, loss, and misfortunes; loss of sight, fevers, and eruptive diseases, siphilis, wounds, furious beasts, bites of dogs, quarrels, murder, especialy if ♂ be anareta, and if the conjunction happen in ♌ or near the Bull's Eye, or Antares, the disease will be pestilential.

With the ☉, when the ☽ is directed, it causes fevers (at which time, they say, the native will disclose all his former secrets,) changes, an unsettled life, great perplexity, bad eyes, also marriage. To kings it denotes success, to princes it shews honours or accession to the throne, and to merchants a decline in credit but not bankruptcy.

With ♀ : it causes joy and pleasure, and if a moist sign, drunkenness and all kinds of amusements; good health, marriage, courtship, and gifts. To kings, peace at home and abroad.

With ☿ : business, lying and dissimulation, eloquence, subtility, fraud, theft, lewdness, forgery, hard study and success. To a king it denotes negociations and treaties.

With the ☊, the same as ♃; to the ☋, the same as to ♄ or ♂; and to the ⊕, increase in property and substance.

To the horoscope: sickness; and to all the other houses, good or evil according to their signification and the familiarities they have with other planets or fixed stars.

To Rigel: injuries of life and fortune, and threatens, they say, death to the wife or mother; this is Lilly's opinion, who considered Rigel as a saturnine star, whereas it is more jovial, and is generally considered benevolent, and in nature similar to Arista.

To Arista: wealth and honour, from mercurial, venereal, or jovial persons.

To Hydra's Heart: lust, wantonness and profligacy; failures in projects, and ill fortune to the wife or mother.

To Bellatrix: lust, luxury, vain ambition, waste and ruin.

To the Left Hand of Ophiuchus: it denotes infamy and debauchery.

To the Left Shoulder of Bootes: preferment by indirect means, succeeded by disgrace and ruin.

To Attair: profit and preferment, marriage, children, &c.

To the nebulous star in the Dragon's Eye: blindness, wounds, quarrels, bruises, stabs, blows, kicks of horses, &c. This is all groundless, for the ☾ cannot come near that star.

To Antares: dignity with danger and suffering.

To Hercules: power, pride, sickness, and calamity.

The ⊕ directed to the ☌, □, or ☍ of ♄, denotes loss and ruin by theft, gaming, and sometimes by means imperceptible.

To the ✶ or △ of ♄ : increases fortune by building, mines, husbandry, legacies, old men, or maritime concerns, dealing in oxen or horses, grazing of cattle &c.

To the ☌, ✶, or ☍ of ♃: gain, success, and profit.

To the □ and ☍ of ♃: loss by religious persons of wealth, office, credit, &c. It also denotes lawsuits.

To the ☌, □, or ☍ of ♂: loss by thieves, soldiers, servants, gaming, fire, lawsuits, bad courses, &c.

To the ✶ or △ of ♂: wealth by dealing in iron, arms, miltary stores or horses, by sea, or by dealing in rabbits, goats, hogs, &c.

To the ☌ of the ☉: great waste, prodigality, and expensive living. Lilly says, he never knew the ☉ to bring an estate or property, but always to waste it.

To the ☐ or ☍ of ☉: loss by lawsuits, loss of office, &c.

To the ✶ or △ of ☉: gives great and eminent friends, honour and profit, but the whole will be spent or wasted.

To the ☌, ✶, or △ of ♀ : gifts from eminent ladies, wealth and honours, but what they produce will be wasted in dress &c.

To the ☐ or ☍ of ♀ : waste of property on women, which eventually leads to ruin,

To the ☌, ✶, or △ of ☿ : gain by contracts, learning, books, law, industry, wit, contrivance, and voyages.

To the ☐ or ☍ of ☿ : renders the native prone to defraud or to be defrauded, till he loses his all.

To the ☌, ✶, or △ of the ☽ : profit by women, and by the vulgar, by sea or land journeys.

To the ☐ or ☍ of the ☽ : loss in a similar way.

To the ☊ the same as to ♃, and to the ☋ the same as to ♂.

To Spica: great wealth and voluptuous propensities.

To Cor Leonis: riches and honours, but these will be of short duration.

To the South Scale the same as to ♂.

The ⊕ may also be directed to the cusps of the houses, according to their respective symbols: but the whole is groundless.

We are also directed to consider the term of a planet the same in its effects as the planet itself, and to be directed to promittors as such; but this is too absurd to merit any comment.

Of the Sextile and Trine.

The horoscope having the ✶ or △ of ♄, denotes favour from old men, gain by agriculture, gardening, mines, collieries, and all things relative to the Earth; legacies and inheritance. It is said to be a good time to let lands, or renew leases, build or speculate in saturnine employments.

Of ♃: great gain, riches and honours, health and friendship

Of ♂: martial employment or exercises, and preferment, also invention, impatience, anger and energy.

Of the ☉: health, honour, profit, friends, and happiness.

Of ♀ : pleasure, enjoyment, marriage, children and good fortune.

Of ☿ : gain and preferment by study and learning, literary encouragement, &c.

Of the ☾ : much business, health, and contentment, marriage, journeys, and children, particularly daughters.

The midheaven to the ✶ or △ of ♄, honour and esteem from old people, gravity and sobriety, gain by agriculture and other saturnine professions. If ♄ be in ♉ or ♑, it is all the better.

Of ♃ : the same as the ☌.

Of ♂ : disposes the native to warlike exercises, riding, hunting, and gives preferment in war, and gain by trade. To kings it is a fortunate time to declare war.

Of the ☉ : great honours and dignities, bounties, gifts from the great, and every degree of success, and happiness.

Of ♀ ; love of women, new dresses, furniture, armaments, &c.; health, marriage, children, and every degree of felicity.

Of ☿ : renders the native learned, eloquent, and fortunate in all mercurial undertakings.

Of the ☾ : great riches and prosperity, marriage to a rich or poor woman, according to the strength of the ☾, journeys, esteem and reputation.

The ☉ having the ✶ or △ of ♄, denotes honour and profit from old men, makes the native grave and severe, and like to gain wealth by husbandry, building, or an inheritance.

Of ♃ : sound judgment, honour, profit, preferment, and male children. But if ♃ be not radically strong the effect will be more weak and unavailing.

Of ♂ : friendship of martial men, preferment in arms, courage, magnanimity, military reputation, victory and travelling.

Of ♀ : reputation, office, dignity, love of women, marriage, children, health, easy and elegant manners.

The ✶ of ☿ in directions, gives much business with, it is said, little profit; propensity to travelling, with no good result; school or church preferment, dealing in books, &c.

Of the ☾ ; favour of great persons, many friends, a rich wife and honourable or diplomatic employment.

The ☾ to the ✶ or △ of ♄ : great and valuable connexions, gifts from old women, much esteem and veneration; profit from dealing with old people, or in saturnine commodities, as wool, lead, agricultural or horticultural productions, houses, &c.

Of ♃ : much the same as the ☌.

Of ♂ : boldness, pride, hatred, vigilance; oppression, martial pursuits, hunting, and riding. If ♂ be weak, he will drink, game, and waste his property. It generally shews increase of trade with success.

Of the ☉: honourable and profitable connexions, marriage, travel, much esteem, great success and preferment.

Of ♀ : pleasure and happiness, a good marriage, great favour with every one, and unbounded success if ♀ be strong.

Of ☿ : a propensity to learning, travelling, music and oratory; it also denotes incessant action, and a great propensity to trade.

Of the Square and Opposition.

The horoscope to the □ or ☍ of ♄, brings disease, death, chronic diseases, much melancholy, fear and nervous horrors; ruptures, flux, gout, cholic, fistulas, tumours in the legs, injuries in the privates; loss, disgrace, and ruin.

Of ♃: distempers, law-suits, enmity, and treachery; but not attended with any material loss.

Of ♂ : violent fevers, by being overheated, sudden misfortunes, or death; falls, wounds, burning, loss, false accusation, &c.; in a fiery sign, it causes inflammations, boils, pestilent eruptions, &c. While this direction lasts, persons should avoid all business or adventure as much as possible. In earthy signs it threatens murder; in airy signs, violent inflammations and eruptions; and in watery signs, violent fluxes, and drowning.

Of the ☉: diseases, ruin, sore eyes, oppression by great men, imprisonment, shipwreck, &c. The □ is not reckoned near so bad as the ☍.

Of ♀ : venereal disorders, lust and prostitution; quarrels with and ruin by women; love, madness, jealousy, and cockledom.

Of ☿ : vain and expensive attempts at learning, to no purpose: aversion to study, restlessness, law-suits, and vexations; fraud on all sides, injury by false witnesses, lying youths, libels, and sometimes trouble by writing books.

Of the ☽; disputes with the lower orders and low women, family strife, danger of drowning, anxiety, affronts, and ill-usage; robbery, disgrace, and a propensity to luxury and debauchery.

The midheaven to the □ or ☍ of ♄, causes disgrace, loss of office by some deceitful, mean, brutish people, chiefly the vulgar; it is said to cause all sorts of trouble, beggary, and ruin. To a king, breach of treaty, sedition and tumults among his subjects, and treachery among his servants.

Of ♃: enmity of judges and all great men, which will cause many troubles, but will not eventually injure the native materially. To a king it denotes disputes with his nobility and people, which will end to their credit and his disgrace.

Of ♂ : robbery, quarrels, imprisonment, and many evils; public accusation or death. To kings, loss of armies, deposition, broils with their subjects, armies to keep them in awe, &c.

Of the ☉: causes hatred and injury from great men, loss of trade, office, credit, substance, liberty, and life. It denotes bankruptcy and ruin, banishment, &c. To kings it denotes pride, which will end in many afflictions.

Of ♀ : scandal and disgrace by women, unsuccessful courtship, attended by scorn, delusion and contempt. To kings, disgrace from incontinence. It also denotes divorces, family broils, jealousy, loss of estate, jewels, &c. Marriages taking place when the midheaven is in ☍ to ♀, are soon succeeded by separation, according to Lilly, who says, that all such marriages are rash, and quickly repented of.

Of ☿ : great trouble, law-suits, literary disappointments, failure in all attempts at office or preferment, disgrace by false reports, libels, knavery, unjust witnesses and judges, anonymous letters, &c.

Of the ☽: hatred of the vulgar, disputes about women, profligacy, fornication, and waste of property; breaches between the native and his mother, wife, or mistress; condemnation by a judge or some great man; the evil will be durable according to the radical strength of the promittor and of the ☽ in that year's revolution.

The ☉ to the □ or ☍ of ♄ : it has much the same effect as the ☌, and it is foolishly affirmed, that this direction will kill the native's father, if he have but a slight direction of death in his own nativity.

Of ♃ : envy and hatred of lawyers, and other enemies, causing expense and loss of estate and character, all of which will be recovered again, if the geniture be not wholly unfortunate. To kings it denotes disputes with the nobility and people through their own illegal ambition.

Of ♂ : violent disease, bloodshot or inflamed eyes, blindness, wounds by fire, iron, hurts by machinery, robbery, and (if the ☉ be hyleg) murder, calenture, madness, &c. It is an evil direction in a climacterical year, or any other fatal direction or lunation.

Of ♀ : this can only be the square, for none but such men as old Parr can live to feel the effects of the ☍. The □ is said to denote barrenness, disappointment in marriage, lust, debauchery, and their natural consequences, disgrace, infamy and ruin.

Of ☿ : the □ of ☿ denotes infamy, false accusations, disgraceful conduct of the native, or his connexions: forgery, coining, swindling, loss of office and character, hatred, malice, robbery, and disappointment. As to the ☍, it is a direction that never can arrive.

Of the ☾: evils from great men, loss in fortune and trade, also in travelling; causes domestic quarrels, idleness, drunkenness, sickness, blindness, prostitution and debauchery, small-pox, fever, measles, worms, &c.

The ☽ to the □ or ☍ of ♄, causes hectic fevers, melancholy, nervous fear, loss by low clownish people or tenants, theft, &c. Family disputes and waste, quarrels with the wife, loss in every undertaking, trade, merchandise, &c. It often causes death, and always diseases.

Of ♃; difficulties, loss of office, disgrace, &c.; but the whole will be recovered, and his character restored. Injuries from religious men, magistrates, landlords, &c.

Of ♂: madness, robbery, syphilis, stone or gravel, hatred and disgrace by women, death of a good wife, or marriage to a bad one, all kinds of sickness, bad eyes, death, shipwreck, and every evil; wounds, kicks of horses, burning, &c.

Of the ☉: great danger and suffering, tumult and sedition, blindness, quarrels, injuries from superiors, fevers, fluxes, &c. Lilly says, the □ of the ☽ to the ☉ is of little importance, and therefore all this must be understood as the effects of the ☍. To kings it denotes loss of honour, deposition and death; and it is always the direction for a violent death, if it be so determined in the radix.

Of ♀ : fornication, adultery, and prostitution, attended of course by ruin and infamy; an unhappy marriage, venereal diseases, &c. To children it denotes the small-pox or measles; to women excessive menstrual discharges, &c.

Of ☿ : aversion to learning and study, or to those who apply themselves to either; ill usage from the vulgar, dishonesty and all its evil consequences; banishment, sentence of death, debt, ruin, delirium, madness, frauds by attorneys, unhappy lawsuits, &c.

These are said to be the general effects of promittors, whether the significators are so posited with them at the birth or brought to them afterwards by direction. For my own part, I think the greatest part of it to be a mass of superstition and absurdity, especially where it descends to minute particulars, which cannot be known. The effect of good or evil directions is to create a strong bias towards the persons, places, or other causes, that will most likely be productive of such events, which bias is generally too strong to be easily counteracted. It is a common observation, that one evil seldom comes alone; and this is the uniform effect of evil directions, transits, or lunations. When a direction is likely to terminate fatally, there will be a continual tendency to the causes, which will eventually produce such an effect; but this tendency, so far from being manifest and striking, is almost imperceptible to every one but such as are very acute observers, and the native is the least likely of all others to perceive it. As to directions to the ☊, ☋, ⊕, or the cusps of the houses, according to the supposed nature of such houses, the whole is false and absurd. They can only be useful in horary questions, where the mode of bringing up directions, is only counting the intermediate degrees between the significator and promittor, as may be seen in the article " Horary Questions."

The time the effects of a direction will endure, and the strength or weakness of their effects, are said to be according to the strength or weakness both of the significator and promittor; but this only respects the radix, for all promittors in directions are alike in strength, and the power and durability of their effects are in a great degree regulated by the strength or weakness of the luminaries at the nativity. If they are strong and free from affliction, subsequent evil directions will have less power and durability, and good ones will operate with double force; but if the significators be originally weak, or in bad positions, a trifling evil direction will have a very powerful effect, while a good direction is almost unavailing and quite transient. Much also depends on the present state of the heavens; for if the luminaries are in those places that harmonize with the radix, namely, the places of the fortunes, or those that are in good aspect with them, or that are inconjunct with the infortunes, or in good aspect with them: the effects of promittors will be much increased or diminished, according as their nature agrees with such positions. The revolution, also, for the year, ought to be consulted, as that is very powerful in its effects, if the luminaries harmonize, or disagree, with their radical positions; but where there is a mixture of testimonies, or the luminaries are inconjunct with the leading places in the radix, and have no particular radical declination, the revolution for such a year will have but little influence either way. Much depends on the lunations and more, I think, on a quadrate than on an embolismical lunation. Transits, also, have an effect: but I have not so high an opinion of ingresses as Placidus had. In addition to all these secondary causes, there is a maxim that astrologers should never forget, that a greater cause will always overcome a less. This may be seen in the seasons, when, from certain causes with which we are at present unacquainted, continued wet or dryness prevails, the lunations will be found not to have their usual effect, and all the changes they produce are of very short duration. If a man lives in a country where wars are seldom or never known, and the dispositions of the inhabitants are mild, symptoms of violent death in the radix can have little efficacy as such, whereas in those countries where wars are frequent, or in armies, very slight symptoms will cause a violent death, because the superior cause will overcome the inferior. Thus, animals resemble those by whom they are produced; children resemble their parents; men acquire propensities like those of the inhabitants of the countries where they are born, or like those among whom they are educated; aged people die of slight directions to promittors that would not have affected them while young; a child cannot be married when 3 or 4 years old, whatever direction may occur, &c, &c.; therefore, in ascertaining the effects of promittors we must always have respect to the greater and less causes, and avoid predicting impossibilities.

PROPER MOTION, the direct motion of a planet through the zodiac, so called in contradistinction to its diurnal motion from east to west.

PROROGATOR, the apheta.

PYROIS, a Greek name of ♂.

QUADRANTS, the four quarters of heaven. The two oriental quarters are from the 1st to the 10th, and from the 7th to the 4th. The two occidental quarters, from the 10th to the 7th, and from the 4th to the 1st. In the zodiac the oriental quarters are from the beginning of ♈ to the beginning of ♋, and from the beginning of ♎ to the beginning of ♑. The reverse are the occidental quadrants. The first quadrant is called, by modern astrologers, oriental, vernal, masculine, sanguine, and infantine. The second is called the meridian, estival, feminine, youthful, choleric quadrant. The third, the occidental, autumnal, masculine, melancholic, mature, cold, dry quadrant. The fourth, the northern, feminine, decrepit, wintry, phlegmatic quadrant.

QUADRATE LUNATIONS, every □, ☍, or ☌, of the ☉ and ☽. Their effects are good or evil according as they happen in good or evil aspect with the radical places of the fortunes or infortunes. See "Secondary Directions."

QUADRATURES, the ☽'s dichotomes.

QUARTILE, the square: a distance of 3 signs, or 90°, marked ☐. It is considered an evil aspect, but in a secondary degree.

QUERENT, the person who asks a horary question. His significator is generally the ascendant, its lord, the ☾, and planets in the ascendant.

QUESITED, that thing or person about which the querent inquires. The significator is various, according to the nature of the question.

QUINCUNX, a new aspect, containing 5 signs, or 150°. Ptolemy and most others consider it as inconjunct. It is the opposite point of the semisextile, and those who hold it to be an aspect, consider it a good one.

QUINTILE, another new aspect, reckoned beneficial. It is 72° or one fifth of the zodiac.

RADICAL, belonging to the radix. It is a term used in horary questions to signify that a question is fit, and may be resolved. It comes from radix, the radical figure of the querent's nativity, because it is supposed by many that the figure of a horary question must never be taken when the real figure of the querent's birth can be had; but if that time be not known, the figure erected to the time when the question is asked will, through the power of celestial sympathy, be the very figure of the querent's nativity. A horary question is called radical when the lord of the ascendant and the lord of the hour are of the same nature and triplicity. Thus, if ♂ be lord of the ascendant and of the hour, the question is radical. If he be lord of the hour, and ♋ or ♓ ascend, he is lord of the watery triplicity; or if ♌ ascend, he is of the same nature with its lord the ☉, as they are both hot and dry, and therefore the question in all these cases is radical. If 0° 0′ of any sign, or the 1st or 2d degree ascend (especially in signs of short ascension), the question is not considered radical, except the queent be very young, and his marks and appearance agree with the sign ascending.

If the 27th, 28th, or 29th degrees of a sign ascend, it is the same, except the person inquiring be of that age. In all questions, however, relative to the time when an event happens, as the moment of a decumbiture, a theft, &c., the degree is of no importance, because it is a certain, not a proposed, time.

The question is not supposed quite radical, when the ☾ is in 27°, or more, of a sign, particularly in ♊, ♏, or ♑; or when she is in the *via combusta*. It is also doubtful, when she is void of course, yet this can only relate to the matter inquired about, which will come to nothing, because her being void of course is itself a prediction. Some deem this no impediment when she is in ♉, ♋, ♐, or ♓.

The 7th house denotes the artist himself, and therefore, if the cusp be afflicted, or its lord combust, retrograde, or any way afflicted (except the question belong to the 7th house, for in that case it is a prediction,) the artist is likely to incur disgrace or censure, and therefore he had better decline it. ♄ in the 7th corrupts the judgment of the artist, or renders the whole issue unfortunate if the question belong to that house. If the lord of the 7th be in his fall, or in the term of an infortune, he is said to vitiate the judgment of the artist. If the lord of the ascendant be combust the querent is either a villain, or doomed to some great evil. If ♄ be ascending, and especially if he be retrograde, the question may be dropped, for no good can be the result. For further particulars, see "Horary Question."

RADICAL ELECTIONS, certain times chosen astrologically as being particularly fortunate for undertaking any particular business or enterprise. They are called radical as having for their basis the radix, or nativity. The revolutionary figure should also be erected, and judgment drawn equally from both. The application of the significator in the revolution to the points in the radix, and of those in the radix to the points in the revolution, must be considered, whether those significators or points be good or evil. If the revolution for the year oppose the radix, the year will be generally unfortunate in those matters wherein the ☍ consists: as, if the horoscope or luminaries be on the places of the infortunes in the radix, or in their square, opposition or declination, or if the ☾ be combust or otherwise unfortunate, in such a case, undertakings of any importance should be avoided for that year. In matters of great importance, the secondary directions and the ☾'s process are generally considered; but the most common way is to take the radical and revolutionary figures, and observe if any evil transit occurs, or is apylying in either, on the day in which any business is to be undertaken. The ☾ being combust, or going to the full at the time, is a bad symptom, and many planets retrograde, generally denote evil. Some, however, say, that the infortunes retrograde, is an additional proof of success; but, perhaps, this is of less importance either way than the application of the good or evil planets to the points in the radix, which I should always consider in preference to the revolutionary figure. The general way is to consider the lords of the 1st, 10th, and 11th, in the radix, or the lords of such houses as denote the business in hand, and see whether they are at that time free from affliction, angular, essentially dignified, or in any way well-conditioned, or in application to a good position; but this is making a horary question of it at once, which, if so, had better be done in the usual way. The luminaries in a radical election should be, if possible, in their radical places, or in △ or ✳ to them. If this in the radix be an evil aspect, some other should be chosen, free from that objection, yet having good aspect both with their own and each others places, and free from affliction of the radical infortunes, and, if possible, in ☌ or good aspect with the radical benefics. Places like these are difficult and sometimes impossible to be found where the radix is evil, which is the reason why such people are always unfortunate, as they seldom or never can have a good transit. The ☾ should never be combust at the time of any undertaking: but any other evil condition is of less consequence, provided she be well with the radix. It is said, the radical malefics should be cadent, if possible, and, at all events, not angular, and by the same rule, the radical benefics should be anything but cadent. The ascendant should, it is said, be the radical ascendant; but I am of opinion, that if the radical ascendant be an unfortunate sign, ♑ for instance, it should not ascend, and the same if it contain the body or evil aspect of malefics, or is configurated with afflicted luminaries, or perhaps containing violent fixed stars. Others say, the house denoting the thing undertaken should ascend, but this is founded on the modern system of converting every thing into a symbol, and can have no effect in any way. It is also said, the 10th and 11th in the radix should be free from affliction: but this is merely symbolical and of no consequence. An infortune, however, should not be in the radical 10th, or horoscope, if possible, though I think it would be of less consequence than is generally supposed. It is usual to have the radical and revolutionary significators applying to good aspect, or in mutual reception with each other, but the reception is of no consequence whatever, and the good aspect at the time of the undertaking is as little, provided all be right with the radix, and the luminaries, &c. were in harmony with each other at the time of the revolution.

If the radix be unfortunate, no strong election can be made, because an accidental good cannot prevail against a radical evil. By the same rule, no strong election can be made for evil where the radix is wholly good. Hence we perceive certain persons always unfortunate, while others continually flourish, owing to the weakness or strength of their respective nativities.

RADIX, the root, the radical figure of birth.

RAPT MOTION, the apparent diurnal motion of the heavens,

occasioned by the real diurnal motion of the Earth. It was called rapt, or forcibly carried away, because the stars were supposed to be forcibly carried round by the motion of the Primum Mobile.

RAPT PARALLELS, parellels formed by rapt motion, when two stars in their progress from east to west round the Earth form parallels, by arriving at equal distances from angles. See "Parallels."

RAYS. In the common acceptation of the word, a ray is a beam of light emanating from a star or luminous body; but in astrology it signifies, a beam of influence or sympathy, which accompanies such ray, and is supposed only to proceed from a planet. Thus, the doctrine that the fixed stars emit no rays, does not mean that they emit no light, but that they have no distant influence by aspect, but only operate with a planet when joined to it, or within from 7 to 2 degrees of its body, according to the magnitude of the fixed stars.

RECEPTION, one of the unmeaning refinements of modern astrology, signifying, two planets being posited in each others houses: as ♂ in ♉ and ♀ in ♈, which, they say, confers a dignity on them the same as if they were in their own houses, which it very well may do, for it is nothing. In horary questions, however, it is eminently useful as a symbol, and shews that the affair inquired after, will come to a happy termination, when the significators are in mutual reception. There is also reception by exaltation and triplicity, but they are seldom attended to, or considered of much efficacy. Lilly holds with reception in all the essential dignities, in which case the tripliciiy can only be according as it is diurnal; for the ☉ in ♐ by night would not have triplicity, nor would ♃ by day, because the ☉ governs the fiery triplicity by day only, and ♃ by night. In horary questions it is admitted in all the 5 essential dignities, of which the house is considered the strongest, and the face the weakest degree of reception.

RECTIFICATION, the method of bringing a nativity to its true time, as it is supposed that the inaccuracy of a clock or watch, or the mistake of those whose business it is to observe them, may cause an error in the time of birth, which requires rectification.

Several methods are recommended for this purpose, of which the oldest probably is the animoder of Ptolemy. This not being found effectual, almost every subsequent professor has invented one of his own with as little success. Beside the animoder of Ptolemy, we have the truitine of Hermes, the methods of Argol, Morin, Kepler, &c. &c. Placidus is wholly silent on the subject of Rectification, which is a proof he believed in none of them. Not one of his 30 nativities is rectified, although he seems very much to doubt the correctness of some of them.

The animoder of Ptolemy refers to the new or full moon preceding a nativity. If a new moon preceded, the degrees in which both the luminaries are at the birth must be taken; but if a full moon preceded, the degree of that luminary alone must be taken, which was above the Earth at the moment of delivery. The stars having dominion in those places (which dominion may be taken 5 ways, viz. triplicity, house, exaltation, term, and position or configuration) must be taken, and if there be more than one so dignified, that which has most dignities must be preferred, and the degree of the sign it was in at the time of birth will be the degree of the ascending sign on the cusp of the horoscope, if it be nearer to the horoscope than to the midheaven. If two or more planets have equal dignities, that which has the most partile configuration must be preferred. If they are all equally partile, that which has the best aspect to the conditionary luminary and the angles, must be preferred. If the chosen planet be nearer to the midheaven than to the horoscope, make the degree culminating the same in that sign which possesses the tenth, as the planet holds in the sign in which it is posited, and rectify the angles accordingly.

By the truitine of Hermes the ☽'s distance from the ascendant must be found in signs and degrees, if she be under the Earth, by subtracting the angle from it; but if above, her distance must be found from the 7th house in a similar manner. If subtraction cannot be made, 12 signs must be added to the ☾'s place.

Enter the following table with the remaining number in the column marked "☾'s Distance," and in the opposite columns, according to the month of birth, will be found a number of days, which must be added to the day of birth or subtracted from it, according as "add" or "sub." is marked above the column, and the sum or remainder will give the day of the month, in the month of conception. Should the year of birth be a leap-year, another day must be added. (See table on next page.)

If the birth was in January the conception was in April.

If February, in May.	If August, in November.
If March in June.	If September, in December.
If April, in July.	If October, in January.
If May, in August.	If November, in February.
If June, in September.	If December, in March.
If July, in October.	

When all this is found, get the ☾'s place on the same time of

THE TABLE.

Moon under the Earth.	Birth in Feb.	Birth in Jan. or Dec.	Birth in Apr. or Sept.	Birth in Mar. May. June July. Aug. Oct. Nov.	Moon above the Earth.	Birth in Feb.	Birth in Jan. or Dec.	Birth in Apr. or Sept.	Birth in Mar May June July Aug. Oct. Nov.
Moon's distance	add	add	add	sub.	Moon's distance	add	add	add	add
0s. 0°	3	2	1	0	6s. 0°	0	1	2	3
0 13	2	1	sub.	1	5 17	1	2	3	4
0 26	1	sub.	1	2	5 4	2	3	4	5
1 9	sub.	1	2	3	4 21	3	4	5	6
1 21	1	2	3	4	4 9	4	5	6	7
2 4	2	3	4	5	3 26	5	6	7	8
2 17	3	4	5	6	3 13	6	7	8	9
3 0	4	5	6	7	3 0	7	8	9	10
3 13	5	6	7	8	2 17	8	9	10	11
3 26	6	7	8	9	2 4	9	10	11	12
4 9	7	8	9	10	1 21	10	11	12	13
4 21	8	9	10	11	1 9	11	12	13	14
5 4	9	10	11	12	0 26	12	13	14	15
5 17	10	11	12	13	0 13	13	14	15	16
6 0	11	12	13	14	0 0	14	15	16	17

the day of conception as the birth was on, and make this the true degree and minute on the cusp of the horoscope.

It may also be done by subtracting the Sun's right ascension at the time of conception from its right ascension at the time of birth (taken in the table of houses opposite the ☽'s place, and adding 360°, if it cannot be done without), and if it be in time, or turned into time, the remainder will be the true hour and minute of the conception; and the degree and minute in which the ☽ was then in, is the minute ascending at the birth.

EXAMPLE:—Suppose the native to be born March the 22d, 1765, at 2 *h.* 40*m.* A. M: this is the estimate time.

I find the ☽ in 8° 12' of ♈, and 7° 31' of ♑ on the cusp of the horoscope.

☽'s place,	0s.	8°	12'
Add for subtraction,	12	0	0
	12	8	12
Cusp of the ascendant,	9	7	31
☽'s distance,	3	0	41

As the ☾ is under the Earth, I enter that column at 3*s* 0°, and under the column for March, I find 7 days to be subtracted, which gives the time of conception on the 15th of June preceding; and the ☾'s place on that day at 40m. after 2 o'clock in the morning, is the minute that, according to Hermes, should ascend at the birth. This certainly merits a trial, and, so far as my experience extends, I have little doubt but that this same sign ascends both at the conception and at the birth. It should be remarked, that this Hermes was not the Trismegistus of Egypt, all of whose works are lost, but a Christian author, who wrote in the second century.

Argol preferred rectifying by accidents: but his system is founded on wrong principles, for he attributes all accidents of the body to the horoscope, and all that relate to honour or disgrace to the midheaven. His method is as follows:

The time of the accident is to be converted into an arc of direction by Naibod's measure of time (though that of Placidus is by far the most rational), and then subtracting it from the promittor's right or oblique ascension, the remainder will be the right ascension of the midheaven, or oblique ascension of the horoscope. If it be the latter, subtract 90° from it, and the remainder will be the right ascension of the midheaven corrected. Find the difference between this and the right ascension of the midheaven at the supposed time of birth, and add or subtract it to or from the supposed time according as it is more or less, and the sum or remainder is the true time of birth required.

Kepler recommends making a table of the Sun's place for about 100 days after the birth, and to take as many days of the Sun's motion as there were years elapsed from the birth to the accident (allowing in proportion for the odd months, days, &c.), and find the Sun's place for that time, with its right ascension. Subtract this from the oblique ascension of the promittor that caused the accident, added to 270°. The remainder will be the right ascension of time corrected.

Then, having set the figure accordingly, find the difference between the Sun's place and his place at noon on the day of birth, but be careful it is the right noon, and the difference will be the ☉'s direction for the number of days required. For the odd days of the accident say, as 365*d*. 6*h*. are to the Sun's diurnal motion, so are the odd days to the odd minutes. Add these to the ☉'s direction above, and it will be the ☉'s true place at the birth.

If the accident belong to the 10th house, subtract the ☉'s right ascension (as found before) for the year and day of the accident from the promittor's right ascension (adding, as usual, 360°, if it cannot be done without), the remainder will be the right ascension of time corrected.

Morinus only differed from Argol in taking the latitude of the promittor, which Argol neglected.

Some, who cannot find any accident that can be traced to either of the angles, take the position of the luminaries to discover which of them might produce it, and when they have fixed on one, they direct it under its pole (for the estimate time) to the promittor which caused the accident, for an arc of direction. They then make a second supposition, working as before, and form another arc of direction. They then say, as the difference of these two arcs is to the difference of their two poles, so is the first difference between the first arc and the real time of accident to the difference between the estimate pole and the real pole of the luminary. From this real pole they find the real oblique ascension, or descension, of the luminary, and its distance from the midheaven, which will give the right ascension of the latter correct.

The shortest way, however, were a person inclined, to correct by accidents, would be to consider the time of the accident as a measure of time, and by subtracting the Sun's right ascension from it, the real arc would remain. It may be objected that the ☉'s right ascension would not be correct; but as the ☉ moves but two minutes and a half in an hour it could not differ materially in any reasonble space of time that could arise from a mistake, which could hardly exceed ten minutes, and never amount to even half an hour.

But the system of directing by accidents is very objectionable; for, in the present imperfect state of the science, nothing is more probable than that a wrong promittor, or significator, or both, might be taken. If Placidus be correct, we find there are several instances of the effects of aspects being delayed for years, until some secondary direction or transit causes it to appear, and therefore the time of accidents can hardly be called a criterion.

Another way, equally futile, is to erect the figure to the estimate time, and take that luminary which is in the center of the 1st, 10th, or 7th house, and bring it to the cusp, and that minute it was in should either ascend, culminate, or descend, at the moment of birth. If no such luminary be found, they must be brought to a parallel from angles, but if this cannot be done to suit the probable time, then ♃ or ♀ must be brought to a cusp, or parallel, in the same manner; and if their positions will not agree, let them be brought to a parallel with the conditionary luminary. If their position does not admit of this, either ♄ or ♂ must be taken in the same way; but in this case, their influence is so destructive that the native seldom arrives at maturity.

There is something very philosophical and ingenious in this contrivance; but as it pre-supposes, that some planet must either be on the cusp of an angle, or in parallel of angles, with some other at the moment of every birth, I fear it will not be justified by experience. The most probable cause of births is that sympathy between an infant and its parents, and as it is apt to acquire a likeness to one of them both in body and mind; that constitution of the heavens under which that person they most resemble was born must exist as near as circumstances will permit, and at this critical moment the child enters the world. Its resemblance will consequently be more or less striking, as the ambient more or less resembles that of the parent.

Upon the whole, the rectification of a nativity is very useless, and would never have been thought of, had it not been through the folly of professors in general, who, supposing they knew every thing, when, in fact, they knew almost nothing, were quite astonished when any of their predictions failed, and instead of attributing the failure to its true cause,—their own ignorance, they conceived some mistake must have happened in the time, and therefore set about rectifying the nativity, instead of their own blunders.

If the time of birth be taken at all, it is seldom considerably wrong, probably never ten minutes. This can make but small difference in the relative positions of the planets to each other. Even the ☾'s place would differ but 5 or 6 minutes, and probably the whole difference in the time of a direction would not exceed a month, and the artist who can bring his direction within three months of an accident will have no reason to complain. If the direction were to an angle, the inaccuracy would be much greater; but if angles be significators they will meet with a number of aspects which, when compared with the time of accidents, will be so exactly alike in error, that the true time cannot possibly be mistaken.

To bring two planets to a parallel from angles we are directed as follows:

1st, Subtract the right or oblique ascension of one from the other without latitude: it will give their distance from each other.

2d, Say, as the sum of their horary times is to their distance, so is the horary time of that planet which succeeds the other in the zodiac to the difference of their distances from the angle.

3d, Add this secondary distance to the place of the succeeding planet; the sum will be the cusp of the angle.

EXAMPLE:—Suppose the cusp of the 4th to be 13° 30′ of ♉, ♂ in 11° 29′ of ♉, and ♄ in 18° 15′ of ♉ : I would rectify by bringing them to a parallel from the 4th house, latitude 51° 32′.

Right ascension of ♄, without latitude,	45° 46′
Right ascension of ♂, without latitude,	39 2
Distance of ♄ from ♂,	6 44

The seminocturnal arc of ♂ is 69° 18′, and his horary time is 11° 36′. The horary time of ♄ is 11° 38′.

As the sum of their nocturnal horary time, 23° 14′, is to their distance, 6° 44′, so is the horary time of ♂, 11° 36′, to his secondary distance, 3° 21′. Add this to the place of ♂, 11° 29′ of ♉, and it will give 14° 50′ of ♉ for the cusp of the 4th house: to this all the other houses of the figure are to be rectified. There does not appear much correctness in this system, and it would be nearer the truth, as well as much easier, if, when the distance is found by ascension, the half of such distance were added to the place of the nearest planet. Thus the place of ♂ is nearer to the cusp of the 4th than that of ♄, and if 3° 22′ were added to 11° 29′ of ♉, the cusp of the 4th would be 14° 51′ of ♉, without any further trouble.

REFRANATION, is when two planets are approaching to any configuration, but before the configuration is quite completed, that planet which is overtaking the other, either by dexter or sinister aspect, becomes retrograde, and so refrains from completing the aspect. The business signified by such aspect, however close they may have been before the refranation, will wholly come to nothing.

RELIGION. ♄, ♂, or the ☋ in the 9th, or ♄ or ♂ in ♒ to the 9th, is said to make atheists, or violent sectarians, particularly if ♃ be combust, retrograde, cadent, or afflicted.

♃, ♀, or the ☊ in the 9th, shews true religion, as does also the ☉, ☿, or ⊕ there, in ✳ or △ to ♃ or ♀.

If no planets are there, the religion of the native is taken from the lord of the 9th and ♃. If neither of them be strong, angular, or well-dignified, or in reception with one of the lights, or with the lord of the 1st or planets therein, or in the ascendant, the native will be void of religion, and *vice versa*.

Others say, ♄ in the 9th shews zeal, chastity, and faith. The

☉ there, shews a good preacher. If the ☉ or ♃ have dignities in the 9th, or horoscope, and also in the places of ☿ and the ☾, the words of the native, they say, will be like oracles: this is all nonsense, like the greater part of modern astrology. Neither the houses nor stars have anything to do with religion merely as such any further than as it depends on the moral disposition of the native. The cause why the 9th house is supposed to be the house of religion originates in a term given to it by Ptolemy, who for some unknown reason, called it "the divinity."

RETROGRADE, when a planet appears to move backward in the ecliptic contrary to the order of the signs, and is denoted by an *R* marked next to such planet. All planets, except the ☉ and ☾, are retrograde from their first station to their second; the inferiors are retrograde in their inferior conjunction when they pass from one elongation to the other; but the superiors are retrograde when in opposition to the ☉ as they pass from their first to their second station, and all of them when retrograde are in or near their perigee.

In horary questions, it is reckoned one of the worst symptoms. Nothing signified by a retrograde planet can come to good, however good the planet itself, or its aspect, may be, but, with the exception of horary questions, I am not aware that a planet is weaker when retrograde than when direct. The planet is always the same, and the whole is an appearance caused by the relative motion of the Earth. The only cause I ever knew assigned is, that a planet is more powerful when most stationary in respect to the world, that is, when it is least affected by the diurnal motion, because then its rays, passing over the Earth more slowly, have time to operate with more force. This must always be the case when a planet is direct and swift in motion, because it then resists the diurnal motion, by moving in a contrary direction, whereas, when it is retrograde it rather increases the effect of the diurnal motion by moving zodiacally toward the west. Allowing, however, the truth of this hypothesis, the difference can be but trifling and would have a different effect from that usually assigned to retrogradation. Only the retrogradation of the benefics could injure a native, for a retrograde malefic would be rendered by it more innoxious, whereas it is always considered to be more mischievous when retrograde.

Placidus was of the opinion, that retrograde planets caused disease, and that those nativities and periods, wherein many planets were retrograde, would be very sickly. This may be so, because planets when retrograde are nearer to the Earth, and I have generally observed, that whatever good qualities they may possess, they are apt to disturb our atmosphere when in perigee, which will naturally cause distempers.

REVOLUTIONS, the time in which a star revolves round the Sun or the Earth. Thus, ♄ revolves round the Sun in nearly 30 years, and the ☾ round the Earth in a periodical lunation. The term, however, is chiefly applied to the annual period when the ☉ comes to his zodiacal place in a nativity, and for this point of time it is usual to erect a figure every year, and to judge of the events of that year from it. Some place such confidence in revolutionary figures as to deem them equal, if not superior, to the radix itself, and that an aspect in the revolution would nulify, or greatly alter, one in the nativity. The opinions of Ptolemy and Placidus are more rational; namely, that the places of planets in a revolution are only of importance as they respect their places in the radix. Of the truth of this I am fully persuaded; and there can be no doubt, that when there happens a remarkable coincidence between the revolution and the birth, it will cause striking events to occur in the native's life, for which no direction can be found in a nativity, and this alone demonstrates the error of rectifying by accidents. There is also reason to suspect, that the solar revolution, although the principal, is not the only one likely to produce such effects; but of this I am not so certain.

I shall here present the reader with a striking example, illustrative of this remarkable coincidence.

In the nativity of a certain person the planetary positions were as follows:

Plan.	♄	♃	♂	☉	♀	☿	☾
Signs.	♉	♑	♏	♈	♈	♈	♊
Long.	14° 42′	3° 21′	10° 16′R	15° 5′	19° 12′	18° 30′R	14° 12′

Revolution, 24 years after, exactly at noon.

Planets.	♄	♃	♂	☉	♀	☿	☾
Signs,	♓	♑	♋	♈	♈	♈	♈
Longitude,	12° 57′	12° 0′	5° 8′	15° 6′	21° 3′	17° 16′	13° 19′

Here we find ♄ in almost close ⚹ to his radical place, ♃ within orb of his radical position, ♂ in △ nearly to his, ♀ and ☿ nearly in their radical positions, and the ☾ near the ☉'s place and in ⚹ to her own. The ☉'s place is a minute distant, because I took it at noon.

There are few revolutions so closely resembling their radix, and the event was equally remarkable, for the native was married 2*h*. 50*m*. before the revolution took place. It is proper here to remark, that the arc of direction of the midheaven to the quintile of ♀ is 24° 3′, which, by Ptolemy's measure of time, of a degree for a year, gives 24*y*. 18*d*. for the period of marriage; whereas the time, as measured by Placidus, would be near 26 years: this is worth attending to.

What is called the annual revolution for the globe, is erected when the ☉ enters the first point of ♈, from a belief that the world was born or created when the ☉ was in that point; but this supposed effect of such ingress is equally ridiculous with the notion which produced it.

The usual mode of calculating events from revolutions, is to observe the sign ascending, and according to the house it occupied in the radix will be its effects, and also according to the planets or stars it contained. If the stars were all cadent in the radix, or peregrine, and in the revolution angular or domiciliated it denotes evil and *vice versa*. If they were all above the Earth in the one, and under the Earth in the other, it denotes the same. The planets are also supposed to produce effects corresponding to those radical houses and planetary places they are found in, at a revolution: as ☿, for instance, arriving at the radical position of ♂, makes the native quarrelsome, or causes him to enlist for a soldier, &c. The fortunes coming to the places of the infortunes helps them to do good, if they are so disposed, and restrains their evil, &c. Much of this doctrine is ridiculous; nevertheless, it contains some truth, and deserves the student's attention.

RICHES. Ptolemy says, the place of riches is the Part of Fortune, and their greatness and duration is to be esteemed by its dispositors, their strength, position, and the planets aspecting them. If they are strong, and particularly in good aspect with the luminaries, they cause great riches. As Ptolemy speaks in the plural number, he probably alludes to more lords than one, particularly as he speaks of those of the same condition, which must mean, several having dignity in the same sign, perhaps by house, exaltation, and triplicity. His words are as follows:

"We take what concerns property from that point called the Part of Fortune only, and accordingly we subtract from the horoscope the distance between the ☉ and ☾. This done, we take the lordships, and consider their strength and familiarity, and also the strength of those configurated with them, or elevated, whether they be of the same or opposite condition. Those having the government of the ⊕ being strong, produce great riches, particularly when the luminaries give testimony to them.

"♄ will cause riches by building, agriculture or navigation. ♃ by the bounty of others, or by offices of trust, or by church preferment. ♂ by warfare and military command. ♀ by friendship and bounty of women. ☿ by eloquence and attention to business.

"If ♄ be configurated to the ⊕ and ♃, they will cause riches by inheritance, particularly when angular and above the Earth, and ♃ being in a double bodied sign; for in that case they will be adopted, and thus become heirs, and if those of the same condition with the lords give testimony by dominion, this property will be theirs forever: but if those of a contrary condition be elevated above those places, or succeed to them, the property will not remain with them. The time must be taken from the respective significators, as they incline towards angles or succeedents.

To this modern astrologers have added, that those planets angular cause riches in youth; succeedent, in the middle of life; and cadent, in old age; and the nearer they are to the cusp of the house the sooner it will be. They also, with their usual consistency, affirm, that a planet oriental with respect to the ☉ or the world, will cause riches early in life; but if occidental, in old age; but these are also divided into four quarters; the orient orientality from the 1st to the 10th; the occident orientality from the 7th to the 4th; the orient occidentality from the 10th to the 7th; and occident occidentality from the 4th to the horoscope. There are also four quarters of oriental and occidental positions with the Sun, for which see "Oriental."

I should not have mentioned these modern opinions, had I not known that Ptolemy thought much of what he called the orientality of the planets, and therefore, although he has omitted to mention it here, it no doubt formed a part of what he calls the strength of those dispositors. I am obliged again to repeat, that lordships and disposition are nothing, and therefore the whole system is founded in error. Indeed, even if it were so, the whole would be a mass of indescribable confusion; for planets might be so posited with angular, cadent, and two kinds of oriental and occidental positions, as to signify both riches and poverty at the same moment of time. The doctrine of Ptolemy in this case is very unconnected and confused; he never comes directly to the point, and there can be no doubt, that the system was as unintelligible to himself as he made it to others. The moderns in some instances have come much nearer the truth, and could they have kept clear of houses and dignities, and Dragon's Tails, their opinions would have been worth attending to. Some of the best of them are as follow:

If many planets be strong in the geniture, particularly the luminaries and the three superiors, the native will be rich and respectable, and the same if the lights be angular and in good aspect with each other, particularly in the 10th, 11th, and 1st.

The luminaries afflicted or cadent, the ☾ combust or impeded by the ☉, all or most of the planets cadent and inconjunct, or in evil aspect, are signs of poverty, meanness and misery.

All or most of the planets under the Earth shew poverty, want, and many troubles in youth, especially if the lights be there and cadent; but if strong, and free from affliction, the native will improve in riches and happiness when old. Many retrograde planets are said to cause much poverty, sickness, and affliction.

The more nonsensical part must be added, not for its value, but to render the article complete.

The lord of the 2d retrograde, cadent, combust, peregrine, or in his detriment or fall, or any way afflicted, will always keep the native poor and in distress.

Planets in their houses, exaltations, or triplicities, particularly the lord of the 2d or the dispositors of the ⊕, the ☉ in his exaltation in △ to the ☾, ♃ or ♀ in the 2d or the lord of the 2d oriental, or increasing in number, light and motion, or the dispositors of the ⊕ in the same condition, or the ⊕ joined to the ☊, or to ♃ or ♀, or the ☊ in the 2d; are all said to be signs of riches and prosperity.

The dispositor of the ⊕ in the 8th, or the lord of the 2d there, or the lord of the 8th in the 2d; shew riches by legacies, if they are well dignified. If the significators of riches be in fixed signs, the property will be durable, and the same if a fortune be in the 2d; but if the ☋ be there, it will be lost; or if the significators be in moveable signs, it will be unstable. An infortune strong in the 2d, gives riches, but they will be got and kept with much labour and difficulty; and if weak, the native will always be poor.

If ♄ be in the 4th, strong, or in good aspect with a benefic, or with the lord of the 4th; or in reception with the luminaries, provided they are in good aspect with the 4th or its lord; the native will acquire a fortune by mines, quarries, &c.

The ☋ with any of the significators of substance, brings the whole to nothing.

The reader may be assured, that the best sign of riches, is for the luminaries to be angular in good aspect with each other, and one of them culminating, and in my judgement, this one should be ☽. The benefics angular, free from combustion, and in good aspect with the lights or joined to the ☽; all the planets above the Earth, and the benefics more angular than the malefics, and in good aspect with lights: are the best and truest signs of riches and good fortune. ♄ with the ☾, especially in an angle, is the worst of positions, and denotes utter poverty or ruin. The ☾ fortunate in the horoscope, is an excellent position; or if she culminate, or join with good fixed stars. Fixed stars also in the 10th or 1st, are all signs of riches or good fortune. Planets oriental of the ☉, or direct, or swift, gives riches in youth; but occidental, retrograde, or slow, not until old age. Directions have less or greater force as they concur with those times.

RIGEL. See "Orion's Foot."

RIGHT ASCENSION, any arc of the equator, reckoned from the beginning of ♈, and ending at that point which rises with any star or part of the ecliptic in a right sphere.

The longitude and latitude being taken the right ascension will be found in the common angle of meeting.

EXAMPLE:—Suppose the ☉ to be in 14° 30′ of ♓, I would find his right ascension. As the ☉ never has any latitude, I find the right ascension of 14° 0′ of ♓ to be 345° 16′: as 1° in ♓ gives only 56′ of right ascension, I take 28′ for the odd 30′, and this makes my right ascension complete, 345° 44′. When a planet has latitude, as they generally have, its right ascension may be found in the common angle of meeting of the longitude and latitude, by taking proportional parts in the case of fractions in the same manner as directed for the tables of declination.

RIGHT DESCENSION, an arc of the equator that descends with any star or point of the ecliptic: but this is only an unmeaning term, for the whole is right ascension from the first point of Aries to the first point of Aries again, including the whole circle of 360°.

RIGHT DISTANCE, the distance of any place from another by right ascension, and it is found by subtracting the right ascension of the preceding from that of the succeeding place, adding 360° if subtraction cannot be made without.

EXAMPLE:—Suppose 18° of ♒ to be on the cusp of the 10th, what is the right distance of 15° of ♈?

The right ascension of 18° of ♒ will be found in the table to be 320° 37′, and the right ascension of 15° of Aries, 13° 48′: add for subtraction 360°, the sum will be 373° 48', from which subtract 320° 30', it will leave the right distance, 53° 18'

RIGHT SPHERE, so called, because all the circles parallel to the equator make right angles with the horizon, and the celestial bodies ascend and descend direct; hence it is also called a direct sphere. The equator is always in its zenith, and the poles of the world in its horizon, and its days and nights are always equal. Those who inhabit the equatorial parts of the globe, have always a right sphere.

RUMINANT SIGNS, signs that ruminate, or chew the cud; ♈, ♉, and ♑. This in astrology may be called the very acme of the ridiculous, Because these three signs are called the ram, bull, and goat, animals that chew the cud, it has been asserted, that those born when the ☾ is in one of them will be apt to do the same, and some physicians have denied all medicines at those times, except vomits, because, they say, it would be thrown up again.

SAGITTARIUS. See "signs."

SATELLITES, attendants, or guards; a term applied in astronomy to those secondary planets or moons that revolve round the primary, as our moon, or those of ♄, ♃, and ♅. In astrology it signifies such planets as surround the luminaries within a certain distance, which is generally supposed to be 30° Placidus allows no limitation for distance but affirms every planet to be a satellite that in any way aspects the ☉ or ☾, because they dispose such luminary to operate throughout the whole life of the native according to the nature of such planet and aspect, whether good or evil. Ptolemy says, those guards must be either in the same sign with the luminaries, or in the following sign; and if the ☉ be guarded by oriental and the ☾ by occidental stars in this manner, the fortune of the native's father will be "glorious and splendid." Placidus appears either to have overlooked or to have misunderstood this passage, else he probably would have been of the same opinion, as it is, he is more correct; for Ptolemy probably was in this, as in many other things, guided wholly by fancy; supposing the luminaries when in that state to be surrounded by their guards and retinue, and when thus "gloriously and splendidly" equipped everything under their influence must be the same. Positions of this kind, however, are worthy of observation, for even imagination may lead to truth.

SATURN. See "Planets."

SCALES; the North Scale is a star of the 2d magnitude of the nature of ♃ and ♂, in the 17th degree of ♍, said to be of a benefic nature, and causing riches, honours, and happiness. The

South Scale is said to be of a violent nature, and productive of every species of disease and misfortune. It is of the nature of ♄ and ♀, and is posited in the 13th degree of ♏.

SCHEME. See "Figure."

SCORPIO. See "Signs."

SCORPION'S HEART, Antares, a violent fixed star, of the first magnitude, in the 8th degree of ♐, of the nature of ☿ and ♂, said to cause rashness, enterprise, violence and oppression, and productive of ultimate ruin and death.

SECONDARY DIRECTIONS, those daily configurations to the luminaries and angles that happen after birth, every day of which is reckoned for a year, 2 hours for a month, 30 minutes for a week, and 4 minutes for a day. Thus, whatever aspects take place in the first day of the native's life will develope their effects in the first year, those of the 2d day in the 2d year, and, consequently, if a person lives 50 years, his secondary direction for his fiftieth year will arise from those configurations which took place on the fiftieth day after his birth. Some, particularly the Egyptians, used to predict the events of a nativity wholly from the secondary directions, but Placidus was of opinion that they chiefly relate to the primary directions, whether good or evil, by accelerating or retarding their effects, and so fully was he persuaded of their efficacy, that he never calculated any event of importance with-out adding the secondary direction to it.

The general opinion concerning secondary directions is, that their effects will be in proportion to the strength or weakness of a nativity, because an accidental good cannot prevail against a positive evil, and *vice versa*. Indeed this is supposed to be the case even in primary directions, for where the radix denotes health and strength, a direction to a malefic will but produce a short or slight disease, unattended with danger, especially if the secondary direction does not concur.

The principal thing to be considered is the ☾ ; for on those days when she comes to the place or evil aspect, and, above all things, when she obtains the declination of the infortunes; the years corresponding to these days will be peculiarly unfortunate and dangerous; and where she acquires the position, good aspect, or declination of a benefic, they are equally fortunate, though with a bias in all cases to the nature of the radix, whether it be good or evil. Next to the ☾ the ☉ is to be considered, and in all cases of life or death, the hyleg must be observed; but I suspect that the ☾, whether what is called hyleg or not, will be found to have great weight on those occasions. We are also advised to form a judgment from the positions of the luminaries, or other planets, in the secondary direction, according as they respect the places of the angles in the radix.

As the luminaries in the secondary direction are considered with respect to the places and declinations of the fortunes, or infortunes. in the radix, so the luminaries in the radix are to be considered with respect to the fortunes or infortunes in the secondary direction, though, unless some considerable time has elapsed, these cannot have greatly changed their position.

The quadratures and syziges of the ☾ and her □, ☍, or ☌ with her own place, are all to be taken into the account, and judgment formed from them. The lights also must be considered as they are well or ill affected to each other in the secondary direction, as well as in the radix.

Progressions, called Processes, may also be considered as forming a part of the secondary directions. They are produced by synodical (or as Placidus calls them, embolismic) lunations, each of which is said to govern a year of the native in succession, every one of which commences at the moment the ☽ is exactly at the same distance from the ☉ as at the moment of birth. An embolismic lunation, therefore, has the same effect on the affairs of the native as a solar day, and the same judgment must be drawn from it, with this difference, that the process wholly belongs to the ☽ and her good and evil positions with the other stars, particularly at her quadratures and syziges. The Arabians had their annual and monthly progressions, by allowing 30° of the zodiac to every year and month; but this is as groundless as their other systems.

Ingresses are formed upon these secondary directions and processes, as well as upon the places of the primary directions; but they have no respect to the places of the nativity.

There are two kinds of ingresses, active, and passive. Active ingresses are those wherein the active stars operate by coming to the places of the significator; and passive ingresses are those wherein the passive stars come to the places of the promittors. By active stars are meant ♄, ♃, ♂, ♀, and ☿, and also the ☉ and ☾ when they acquire the nature of those stars and become promittors. Passive stars are the luminaries, because they remain passive, snd receive the good or evil communicated to them by the active stars. As to the active and passive ingresses, it is merely a distinction without a difference; for whether the promittor makes an ingress on the place of the significator, or the significator on that of the promittor, the effects are the same. The time of an ingress is on the day of death, or of any particular event or direction, whether good or evil, and they either accelerate or retard such events, as they agree with, or oppose it.

Transits are also a kind of ingresses, from which they differ alone in this respect, that they only operate on the points in the radix, and have nothing to do with any directions or processes. Indeed, they may all be called transits, for both ingresses and transits are the actual positions of the planets on the day of an event, whether they respect the places of the primary or secondary directions, or of the processes or the radix.

The chief thing, according to Placidus, to be considered, is the lunations or places of the ☽ last preceding the day of any event, whether it be a ☌, ☍, or □ to the ☉ in those places; for if either of the luminaries happen at such time to be on an evil place, it threatens disasters, diseases, murders, &c; but if on a good place, where the benefics or their good aspect is found, it denotes happiness and success, and this he says is found never to fail. For my own part, I am persuaded it never fails; but I cannot say so much for human judgment, which too often fails, owing, as Ptolemy justly observes, to the vast magnitude of the undertaking, where such numerous, opposite, and intricate points are left for our consideration.

By way of example, I shall here subjoin a specimen of the method of Placidus in calculating these directions, taken from his nativity of Charles the fifth, emperor of Germany.

The places in the radix were as follows:

Plan.	♄	♃	♂	☉	♀	☿	☽
Signs.	♉	♓	♉	♓	♓	♓	♑
Long.	17 37	7 20	24 40	14 30	26 40	19 36	6 45

Declinations:

♄, 15° 13′ N. ♃, 9° 37′ S. ♂, 19° 52′ N. ☉, 6° 8′ S. ♀, 2° 18′ S, ☿, 1° 51′ S. ☽, 25° 24′ S.

He lived 58 years and 7 months all but two days, and died from the effect of the ☽'s ☍ to ♄, according to Placidus, which she acquired by converse motion, the arc of direction for which when equated gives 58 days, answering to 58 years.

"I thus," says Placidus, "calculate the secondary directions for near 58 years, 7 months; for the 58 years I add 58 days to the time of the birth, and 14 hours for the 7 months, and I come to the 22d of April of the same year, (he was born on the 23d of February,) and the following is the position of the planets for the secondary direction.

Planets,	♄	♃	♂	☉	♀	☿	☽
Signs,	♉	♓	♊	♉	♊	♉	♓
Longitude	24° 11′	20° 28′	29° 19′	11° 36′	8° 4′	5° 45′	0° 0′
Latitude,	S 1 46	S 1 2	N 38		S 22	S 1 23	S 5 0

"The ☽, being in 4° of ♓ with 5° 0′ south latitude, has 14° 44′ of declination, which is the declination of ♄ both here and in the nativity, and on the day of death (as will be shewn presently) ♂ was in 4° 0′ of ♍ in partile ☍ to this place of the ☽. The ☉ in the secondary direction, 22d of April, had the parallel of ♄'s declination both on the day of birth and of death, and on the day of death he entered (from the ☍) the place of the ☽'s zodiacal square, and two days before he died there had been a lunation of the ☐ to the ☉ in those evil places. On the day of death the ☽ was in the last degree of ♑, with 4° 55′ south latitude, which gave her the same parallel of declination with ♂ in the secondary direction on the 22d of April; therefore, there was a mutual change of aspect between her and ♂, namely, an active and passive ingress to these motions on the day of death; an admirable proof of the truth of the calculation. The following are the planetary positions on the day of death.

Planets,	♄	♃	♂	☉	♀	☿	☽
Signs,	♉	♒	♍	♎	♌	♎	♑
Long.	24° 31′	2° 4′	4° 28′	7° 31′	29° 25′	17° 23′	29° 29′
Latitude,	S. 2 34	S. 0 51	N. 0 24			N. 0 42	S. 4 55

"I look for the process in this manner: 48 embolismic lunations are finished for the 48 years, in 4 years after the birth, all but 44 days, that is, 4 times 11; for, as we have said in its canon, that the ☽ finishes 12 embolismic lunations in 11 days less than a year, therefore, subtracting 44 days from the 23d of February, 1504 (he was born in 1500,) brings us back to the 10th of January, when the ☽ is posited in the 23d degree of ♏, at the same distance of 68° from the ☉ as she had at the nativity: thus the process is finished for 48 years. The other 10 embolismic lunations for the other 10 years brings us to the 31st of October, 1504, with the ☽ in 10° of ♍, and the ☉ in 18° of ♏. To preserve their distance correctly, for the remaining 6 months and 27 days to the day of death, add to this place of the ☾ six signs and 15 degrees for the 6 months, and 29° 30′ for the 27 days, and we come to 24° 30′ of ♈, where the ☾ is posited on the 18th of November, and the rest of the planets as follows:

"The Process.

Plan.	♄	♃	♂	☉	♀	☿	☾
Signs.	♌	♌	♐	♐	♐	♐	♈
Long.	3° 26′	16° 15′	14° 15′	6° 3′	13° 40′	24° 44′	24° 30′
Lat.	N. 0 11	N. 0 40	S. 0 2		N. 0 9	S. 0 40	

"On the day of death ♂ cast the □ to the place of the ☉ in the process; the ☾ had passed the place of her direction in the zodiac, but having arrived at 25° of ♈, she entered by ingress on the day of death the parallel of ♂'s declination, and came to the □ of this place of her progression when in 24° of ♑. She also applied in the progression to the □ of ♄.

Here we have the entire system laid down of calculating secondary directions. He first begins by allowing a day for a year, and 2 hours for a month, and makes a scheme of the planets' places for that time, which is the secondary direction.

He next finds the planets' places for the day of death, and compares the two together. Here he finds the ☾ on the fatal day in a parallel of ♄'s declination, which was the same both in the secondary direction and in the radix; or, as astrologers term it, both by ingress and transit; because, so far as it respects the secondary direction, it is called an ingress, and so far as it relates to the radix, a transit. There could not be a worse position than this. ♂, likewise, on the day of death made an active transit over the ☊ of the place of the ☾ in the radix, which was 4° of ♓, and ♂ transited 4° of ♍. The ☉ in the secondary direction had the same declination as ♄ had in the radix, and, what was extremely remarkable, ♄ on the day of death was within 20′ distance of his place in the secondary direction, and within 6° of his place in the radix. His declination at the three periods was nearly the same, and this was the ☉'s declination in the secondary direction. A striking instance here occurs of the truth of what I have already observed, that the lights are always in some way aphetical, whether they are above or under the Earth, and (although I am no friend to the doctrine of houses, or angles) I have much reason to suspect that the horoscope at the time of birth and in primary directions is the same, though it can have nothing to do with secondary directions, progressions, ingresses, or transits.

The ☉, also, on the day of death transited the □ of the ☾ in the radix, the latter being in 6° 45′ of ♑, and the ☉ in 7° 31′ of ♎. He had just left the sign ♍, where he had been in ☍ to the ☾'s place in the secondary direction, and to his own place in the radix. Placidus notices this with the design of shewing that one evil position succeeded another: but this is certainly making the most of everything, as Placidus always does on these occasions. The ☍ must have happened in the 4th degree of ♍ to the ☾'s secondary place, and to his own radical place in the 15th degree, both of which the ☉ had passed long before. The preceding □ of the ☉ and ☾ is deserving of attention. It had taken place two days before the day of death, when she was posited on her own place in the radix, and in the zodiacal □ of which the ☉ was found on the same fatal day. At the same time the ☾ acquired the declination of ♂ in the secondary direction, which is called a passive ingress, being made by the ☾, which is a passive planet; and thus there was a mutual change of aspect by ingress between the ☾ and ♂. First, the active ingress of ♂, who on the day of death came to the ☍ of the ☾'s place in the secondary direction; and, secondly, the passive ingress of the ☾, who entered on the day of death, the zodiacal parallel of ♂ in the secondary direction. All these are not only strong, but remarkable positions, and their strange coincidence on the day of death can hardly leave a doubt in the mind of any reflecting person, that they were the cause of it in a great degree, if not wholly, for I have little opinion of the converse direction of the ☾ to the mundane ☍ of ♄.

The next calculation relates to the procession of the ☾, by allowing an embolismic or synodical lunation, consisting of twenty-nine days and a half, for a year, and in a similar proportion for the odd days. When the ☾'s position is found for that period, the places of the planets are all likewise taken for the same point of time. This is also compared with the position on the day of death. ♂ on that day applies to the □ of the ☉ in the process; the Moon in the process had passed her zodiacal □ to her own place in the radix, so that no additional evil could happen in that respect; but on the day of death she made an ingress on the parallel of ♂'s declination in the process, and this at a time when she was in square to her own place in the process. Placidus also remarks, that she was applying in the process to the □ of ♄. This is a proof that he differed in opinion with those who imagine that a sign should be considered as a boundary, for here the Moon is in 24° 30′ of ♈, and ♄ in 3° 26′ of ♌, which according to modern notions, would have rendered her void of course to all but ☿. But Placidus knew that the zodiac is measured by distances, not by signs, and that the Moon was only eight degrees and a half distant from the zodiacal □ of ♄, to which she was applying. Here, again, is another strange agreement in position, though certainly not so striking as that which relates to the secondary direction.

I have dwelt more particularly on these operations, and have explained them twice over, because I am certain they merit the attention of the reader, and I wish them to be thoroughly comprehended. They shew the real, though minute, operations of the heavenly bodies on each other, and consequently on all things subjected to their influence, and at once demonstrate the necessity of close study, strict attention, long experience, acute observation, and rational conclusions. Any comment on the ignorance of those who decry those'truths, merely because they have read a few silly books about houses and dignities, and dragon's heads and tails, would be superfluous. No one who has not spent a considerable portion of his life in the pursuit of this kind of knowledge, can form any competent idea of its nature, and it would be as ridiculous to attach any importance to the opinion of a person who has not done this (however extensive his learning may be in other respects), as it would be for a mason to listen to a cobbler's opinion on the science of architecture. When a man wishes to explode any science, he should first learn it: for the student may rely on this as an infallible truth, that among all his opponents not one of them can bring up a direction, either primary or secondary, or calculate an ingress or transit, or even comprehend the meaning of the terms as applied to astrology.

SEMI, half.

SEMIARC, half a diurnal or nocturnal arc.

SEMICIRCLE, half a circle, 180 degrees.

SEMIDIURNAL ARC, half a diurnal arc. The time or distance of half the daily course of a star taken from its rising until it comes to the midheaven, or from the midheaven until it sets. It may be taken either in degrees and minutes, or in hours and minutes. If the semidiurnal arc be divided by six, it will give the diurnal horary time, of the star. If divided by three it will give its double horary time or space of its house by day. The semidiurnal arc of any star or point in the heavens is found by adding the ascensional difference of the star to 90°, if it have north declination; but if its declination be southern, the ascensional difference must be subtracted from 90°. It may also be found in tables of semidiurnal arcs. If the ascensional difference be in time, it may be found in time by subtracting the latter from six hours, or adding it, as before.

SEMINOCTURNAL ARC, half a nocturnal arc. The time or distance of half the nocturnal course of a star from the time of its setting until it comes to the lowest heaven, or from thence till it rises. Divided by six it will give the nocturnal horary time of the star, and divided by three, it will give its double horary time or space of its house by night. It is found by subtracting the star's ascensional difference from 90°, if the star has north declination, or by adding it to 90°, if the declination be south. If either the seminocturnal or semidiurnal arc of a star be known, the other may be found by subtracting that one known from 180°, and the remainder will be the other, or, if required in time, by subtracting it from twelve hours.

SEMIQUADRATE, one of Kepler's new aspects, containing a distance of a sign and a half, or 45 degrees in the zodiac, or the half of a semiarc in the world. It is the half of the □, and is said to be evil, because the square from whence it is derived is evil, but we have no evidence of the truth of this supposition, and we are also certain that the □ is of a neutralizing tendency, because it crosses two influences at right angles, which the semiquadrate does not. Placidus allows it to have no influence that is perfect of any kind, but supposes that at that distance a kind of operative power commences, which is not quite perfected until it reaches the ✳. One thing, however, is certain, that in general a most striking change takes place in the weather when the ☾ arrives within 6 or 7 degrees of her last semiquadrate, previous to the conjunction, and a similar change (though not so durable in its effects) when within the same distance of the first semiquadrate succeeding the conjunction. To the same cause also may be traced the two critical days of acute diseases so well known to physicians, namely the 4th and 7th, when the ☽ arrives at the semiquadrate and square of her position at the decumbiture. There is great reason to suspect, that the semiquadrate is a very powerful suspending position, as it at least suspends and often destroys the effects both of the square and conjunction. Indeed, it deserves more attention and investigation than it has hitherto received.

SEMIQUINTILE, half a quintile; one of Kepler's new aspects, containing 36° in the zodiac, or one-fifth of a diurnal or nocturnal arc in the world.   It is said to be good, because the quintile is good from whence it is derived, but it is not noticed by Placidus.

SEMISEXTILE, half a ✳; the distance of a sign, or 30° in the zodiac, and one third of a semiarc in the world.   It is said to be good by Kepler, but is not noticed by Placidus, though, for my own part, I think the effects both of the semisextile and the quincunx, which is its opposite point, are very manifest.

SEPARATION, when two planets having been in partile configuration are beginning to separate.   It is distinguished into simple and mutual. Simple separation is when the lighter planet pursues its course and separates from the other by excess of motion.   Mutual separation is when the heavy planet is retrograde, and consequently assists in the separation.   It is much weaker than application, for if the Moon separate from one planet and apply to another, she will be more affected by the latter.   The combustion of the Moon denotes sickness, but if the Moon separate from the Sun, there will be hopes of ultimate recovery in proportion to her distance; but if she apply, the danger is great.

In horary questions, applications and separations are of great importance.   The latter always denotes weakness, insufficiency, and declining influence or attachment.   Thus, in sickness, separating from an evil planet is a token of recovery; in marriage, it denotes the decline of affection in the party that separates, and if the separation be mutual, it is considered nearly the same as refranation.

SERVANTS.   The doctrine of Ptolemy concerning servants is so superficial as to plainly indicate he knew nothing of the matter.   " We take it," he says, "from the sign on the twelfth house, and from the stars in the geniture beholding that place either by conjunction or opposition, and chiefly when the rulers of that sign are configurated with the chief places of the geniture, or behold them with evil aspect."   That is whether the lord, or rather lords, of the 12th were well or ill configurated to the ascendant or midheaven.   If the aspect was good, they would be honest; if evil, dishonest.   This symbolical astrology can have no foundation so far as respects nativities.   The moderns, for reasons best known to themselves, make use of the 6th to signify servants, and say, that if the lord of the 6th be strong and well configurated to the lords of the 1st or 2d, or if either of these be lord of the 6th, or if the lords of the 1st and 6th be angular and in good aspect, or if any planet be in the 6th or 12th, in good aspect to the lord of the ascendant, or if a fortune be in the 6th, or if ☿ be lord of the 6th and strong, or if the ☊ be there, the servants of the native will be honest and well disposed towards him, and *vice versâ*. If the ☊ or ♄ or ♂ be there, or ☿ ill dignified, they will be rogues or thieves. The whole is too ridiculous to merit any attention. Those who keep servants will find their conduct of a piece with the rest of their fortune, whether good or evil, and if they wish to know any particular respecting them, it may be discovered by a horary question.

SESQUIQUADRATE, a new aspect of Kepler's, to which Placidus appears to attach some importance. It is a square and a half or 135° in the zodiac; and in the world it is a semiarc and a half. Its effect is considered evil, as it depends on the □ for its formation,

SESQUIQUINTILE, a quintile and a half, or three signs and eighteen degrees in the zodiac, or a whole semiarc and one fifth of another in the world. It is said to be good, because the quintile is good, on which it is founded.

SEXAGENARY TABLES, so called from *Sexaginta*, sixty; tables formed from the proportional parts of the number 60, so as to give the product of two sexagenary numbers, that are to be multiplied, or the quotient of the two to be divided.

SEXTILE (✳), an old aspect, when two planets are two signs or 60 degrees distant from each other. In the world it is two-thirds of a semiarc. It is also called a hexagon, and is supposed to be of the same nature as the △ (of which it is the half) but not so powerful.

SIGNIFICATOR. This term applies chiefly to the luminaries, which (particularly the Moon) are significative of the fortune of every native, who will be fortunate or otherwise according to their condition. The 1st and 10th houses are also deemed significators; the first governs in a considerable degree the health and life of the native, and the 10th his honour and prosperity. The ⊕ is also considered as a significator even of life in certain cases, but this appears quite inconsistent with reason, nor is it clear, to me at least, that the 10th house can operate as a significator except there are planets there at the moment of birth. In horary questions every house and its lord are significators of something, and the Moon is the general significator of a querent well as the ascendant and its lord. The 2d and its lord signify riches; the 3d, brethren, neighbours, &c. See "Horary Questions."

In directions the luminaries alone are considered significators, in contradistinction to ♄, ♃, ♂, ♀, and ☿, who are called promittors; though in certain cases the luminaries operate themselves as promittors. Whether the angles and ⊕ are considered as significators or promittors is of no great consequence, for they are taken in both capacities.

SIGNS,.every constellation or group of stars having a name is by some called a sign; but the principal of them all are the twelve which compose the zodiac, because the course of the ☉, called the the ecliptic, passes through them.

ARIES (♈), the first of them, is a vernal, hot, dry, fiery, cardinal, masculine, equinoctial, moveable, diurnal, eastern, commanding, northern, choleric, luxuriant, violent, four footed, fortunate, hoarse, bitter sign: of short ascension; the day house of ♂, and exaltation of the ☉.—Those born under it have a spare, dry, strong, body; piercing eye, long face, black eye-brows, long neck, thick shoulders, sallow or swarthy complexion, sandy or red hair, and the disposition is violent and intemperate.—It governs the head and face, and its diseases are the small-pox, measles, ringworms, shingles, epilespy, apoplexy, fevers, convulsions, palsy, megrims, baldness, and all diseases proceeding from heat and dryness. It is considered rather barren.—The countries under its influence are said to be to be Britain, France, Germany, Switzerland, Denmark, Less Poland, Syria, and Palestine, Naples, Capua, Ancona, Verona, Florence, Ferrara, Padua, Saragossa, Marseilles, Silesia, Burgundy, Utretch, Cracow, &c.—Its colours are white and red.—It denotes pasture-grounds for cattle, sandy hilly grounds, hiding places for thieves, and unfrequented places. In houses it denotes the covering, ceiling, or plastering: stables for small cattle, lands recently enclosed or ploughed, and lime or brick-kilns.

TAURUS (♉) is a vernal, cold, dry, earthy, melancholy, feminine, nocturnal, fixed, unfortunate, fourfooted, crooked, northern, commanding, hoarse sign; of short ascension: the night house of ♀ and exaltation of the ☽.—The native born under it will have a broad forehead, thick lips, dark curly hair; is dull and unfeeling, slow to anger and rather melancholy; but if once provoked, very malicious.—It governs the neck and throat, and its diseases are consumptions, scrofula, croup, melancholy, defluctions of rheum, putrid sore throat, quinsey, wens in the neck, &c. It is rather considered a fruitful sign, as belonging to ♀.—It governs Ireland, Great Poland, White Rnssia, Holland, Persia, Less Asia, the Archipelago, Mantua, Leipsic, Parma, and Nantz, Franconia, Lorraine, Sens, Bythynia, Cyprus, &c.—Its colours are red and citron. It denotes stables for horses, cow-houses, places for holding furniture of cattle, pasture-grounds at a distance from houses, grounds lately cleared of bushes and sowed with wheat, trees that are not far off, cellars and low rooms.

GEMINI (♊) is a vernal, airy, hot, moist, sanguine, masculine, northern, commanding, diurnal, western, double-bodied, human, barren, common, whole, changeable, speaking, fortunate, bicorporal, sweet sign; the day house of ☿ and exaltation of the ☊.— The native is tall and straight, fair, or according to others of a dark sanguine complexion, with long arms, but short fleshy hands and feet, dark hazle eyes, dark brown hair, quick sight, smart active look, and good understanding. It governs the arms and shoulders, and its diseases are brain-fevers, corrupt blood, fractures in the head, arms, &c. It is called a barren sign, because ☿ has no particular sex. It rules the south-west part of England, America, Flanders, Lombardy, Sardinia, Armenia, Lower Egypt, London, Versailles, Brabant, Wittenberg, Mentz, Bruges, Louvaine, Cordova, Nuremberg, &c. Its colours are red and white mixed. It denotes wainscot, plastering and walls, coffers, chests, barns, storehouses for corn, hills, mountains, and high places.

CANCER (♋) is an estival, cold, watery, moist phlegmatic, feminine, cardinal, tropical, northern, commanding, nocturnal, moveable, fruitful, weak, unfortunate, crooked, mute sign: of long ascension, the house of the ☽, and exaltation of ♃. The native is fair, but pale; short and small round face, brown hair, gray small eyes, and weak voice, the upper part of the body somewhat large; dull, effeminate constitution, and if a female, very prolific. It is a very fruitful sign, being the house of the ☽ and exaltation of ♃.—It governs the breast and stomach, and its diseases are short breath, bad appetite, coughs, consumptions, hoemoptoes, asthmas, inflammations of the lungs, stomach, and diaphragm, cancers, imposthumes, and dropsy.—It governs Scotland, Holland, Zealand, Burgundy, Africa, Algiers, Tunis, Tripoli, Constantinople, Amsterdam, Cadiz, Venice, Genoa, Magdebourg, York, St. Andrews, and New York.—Its colours are green and russet.—It denotes seas and great navigable rivers or canals, brooks, springs, wells, marshes, ditches, sedges, trenches, cisterns, sea banks, wash houses, and cellars.

LEO (♌) is a hot, dry, fiery, choleric, eastern, masculine, diurnal, northern, commanding, fixed, estival, brutish, barren, four-footed, broken, changeable, fortunate, strong, hoarse, bitter, violent sign; of long ascension; the diurnal and nocturnal house of the ☉.—The native has a large body, broad shoulders, austere countenance, large goggle eyes, dark yellow hair, strong coarse voice, oval ruddy countenance; of a high, resolute, haughty, ambitious temper; yet generous, and often free and courteous. The latter part of the sign makes the native weaker, his body more thin and small, and his hair rather flaxen. — It governs the the heart and back, and its diseases are pains in the back and ribs, convulsions, syncopes, fevers, pestilence, small-pox, measles, jaundice, and all hot diseases and inflammations. It is wholly barren, the ⊙ being barren.—It governs Italy, Bohemia, France, Sicily, Rome, Bristol, Cremona, Prague, Syracuse, Crotona, Ravenna, Philadelphia, &c.—Its colours are red and green.—It denotes haunts of wild beasts, woods, forests, dens and deserts, rocky and inaccessible places, castles, forts, parks, king's palaces, and fire-places in houses.

VIRGO ♍) is a cold, dry, earthy, melancholy, feminine, nocturnal, common, barren, human, speaking, changeable, estival, unfortunate, northern, commanding, sign; of long ascension; the night house and exaltation of ☿.—The native is well made, tall (Lilly says of a middle stature and no way handsome) and rather slender, but very compact and well made; has a dark ruddy complexion, roundish face, dark brown or black hair, small shrill voice; and is witty, ingenious and studious, but fickle-minded. If ☿ ascend in it, free from affliction, the native will be a great orator.—It governs the bowels, belly, spleen, and diaphragm, and its diseases are such as arise from wind, melancholy, illiac passion, dysentery, and all disorders of the intestines. It is wholly barren because of ☿.—It governs all Turkey both in Europe and Asia, Greece, Mesopotamia, Crete, Jerusalem, Croatia, Lower Silesia, Thoulouse, Paris, Lyons, Heidelburg, Padua, Basil, &c.— Its colour is black speckled with blue.—It denotes studies, libraries and book-cases, closets, dairys, cornfields, granaries, hayricks, malt-houses, storehouses of butter, cheese, or corn, and barns.

LIBRA (♎) is a hot, moist, airy, sanguine, western, diurnal, cardinal, equinoctial, moveable, masculine, human, speaking, whole, changeable, sweet, fortunate, autumnal, southern, obeying, sign; of long ascension; the day house of ♀, and exaltation of ♄.—The native is tall and elegantly made, with a round beautiful face, ruddy in youth, but inclined to pimples when old; light, yellow, auburn, or flaxen hair; blue eyes, sweet temper, and upright in principle. It is rather fruitful because of ♀.—It governs the reins, loins, and bladder, and its diseases are imposthumes and ulcers in those places, weakness, debility, tabis dorsalis, and the milder kinds of syphilis.—It governs Austria, Alsace, Savoy, Portugal, Livonia, India, Ethiopia, Lisbon, Vienna, Frankfort, Friburg,

Placentia, Antwerp, and Charlestown.—Its colour is black, crimson, or any dusky colour.—It denotes detached barns, outhouses, sawpits, or cooperages, inner chambers, attic stories, ground near windmills, mountain tops, sides of hills, chaces, commons, barren, stony, or sandy ground, and places having a pure, clear, sharp air.

SCORPIO (♏) is a cold, moist, watery, phlegmatic, feminine, autumnal, nocturnal, fixed, fruitful, mute, broken, unfortunate, strong, southern, obeying sign; of long ascension; the night house and joy of ♂.—The native is strong, corpulent, and robust; middle sized, dark complexion, brown curling hair, with thick neck and legs, and short body, hairy and coarse, active, but very reserved.—It governs the genitals, groin, bladder, and fundament, and its diseases are confirmed lues, and all the worst kind of syphilis, piles, fistulas, ruptures, scurvy, and urinal obstructions. It is the least fruitful of the watery signs because of ♂.—It governs Judea, Mauritania, Catalonia, Norway, West Silesia, Upper Bavaria, Barbary, Morocco, Valentia, Messina, and Frankfort on the Oder.—Its colour is brown.—It denotes places where vermin and reptiles breed, sinks, drains, quagmires, stinking pools, ruins near water, muddy swamps, marshes, gardens, orchards, vineyards, kitchens, larders, and wash-houses.

SAGITTARIUS (♐) is a hot, dry, fiery, choleric, masculine, diurnal, eastern, common, bicorporal, four-footed, changeable, autumnal, fortunate, bitter, half feral, southern, obeying, speaking, and half human half mute sign; of long ascension; the day house and joy of ♃, and exaltation of ☊.—The native is well formed, rather above the middle stature, ruddy complexion, handsome countenance, oval face, fine clear eyes, chestnut coloured hair, but apt to be bald, active, strong and intrepid. It is rather fruitful because of ♃.—It governs the thighs, and *os sacrum*, and its diseases are gout, rheumatism, fevers, falls, and broken bones.—It governs Arabia Felix, Spain, Hungary, Moravia, Liguria, Narbone, Cologne, Avignon, and Buda.—Its colour is light green or olive. It denotes stables for war horses, receptacles for great cattle, hills and high lands, any rising place, and the fire-places in upper rooms.

CAPRICORN (♑) is a cold, dry, earthy, melancholy, feminine, nocturnal, southern, obeying, weak, moveable, cardinal, tropical, domestic, four-footed, changeable, unfortunate, crooked, hoarse hyemal sign; the night house of ♄ and exaltation of ♂. It is rather barren because of ♂ and ♄.—The native is of a dry constitution, slender make with a long thin visage, thin beard, dark hair, long neck, narrow chin and breast, weak knees, and inclined to be crooked. The disposition is subtle, collected, witty, but changeable and at intervals melancholy, and the native is more disposed to be unfortunate, than those born under any other sign. The voice is generally weak, with a kind of whistling roughness. Lilly says the hair will sometimes be fair, when ♑ ascends, but always black when it descends.—It governs the knees and hams, and its diseases are sprains, dislocations, and broken limbs, melancholy, hysterics, cutaneous eruptions, &c.— The countries it governs are India, Macedonia, Thrace, and Greece in general, Mexico, Saxony, Muscovy, Wilna, Mecklinburgh, Brandenburgh, and Oxford. Colour black, or dark brown.—It denotes cow-houses, or receptacles for calves, tool-houses, or places for lumber or old wood, ship-store-houses, sheeppens, and fields, fallow or barren fields, thorny, bushy places, dunghills, or places for soil, dark corners near the ground or threshold, and low houses.

AQUARIES (♒) is a hot, moist, aerial, sanguine, masculine diurnal, western, fixed, human, rational, speaking, whole, fortunate, sweet, strong, hyemal, southern, obeying sign; the day house of ♄. It is more fruitful than barren.—The native is well set, robust, strong, healthy but not tall, with a long face, delicate complexion, clear but rather pale; sandy, or dark flaxen hair; hazel eyes, and of a good disposition. But if ♄ be in ♑ or ♒, the hair, Lilly says, will be dark, the complexion sanguine, and the teeth crooked. — It governs the legs and ankles, and its diseases are lameness, broken legs, gout, cramp, rheumatism, and foul blood. — The nations it governs are Arabia Petrea, Tartary, Russia, Denmark, Lower Sweden, Westphalia, Hamburgh, and Bremen.—Its colour is sky blue.—It denotes quarries of stone, or mines of metals, or any place recently dug up, hilly uneven grounds, vineyards, sources of springs or conduits, roofs and eaves of houses.

PISCES (♓) is a cold, moist, watery, phlegmatic, nocturnal, bicorporal, common, hyemal, effeminate, idle, sickly, broken, mute, unfortunate, crooked, southern, obeying, fruitful sign; the night house of ♃, and exaltation of ♀.—The native is short, pale, fleshy, crooked or stooping, thick, round shouldered, with brown hair, and the head bent downward.—It rules the feet and toes, and its diseases are all diseases in the feet, gout, lameness, ulcerous sores, and cold, moist distempers. It is the most fruitful of all the signs.—It governs Portugal, Spain, Egypt, Normandy, Galicia, Ratisbon, Calabria, and Compostella.—Its colour is white.—It denotes marshy grounds full of springs where water fowls

breed, rivers, and ponds full of fish, moats, water-mills, old her-
mitages, and those places in houses near where the water is, as
pumps, cisterns, or wells.

I have here given a description of the 12 signs according to the
best authors, although I am certain some part of it has no foundation whatever. The system is decidedly wrong; for by being
born under a sign signifies, according to them, its being on the
cusp of the ascendant, or containing either of the luminaries. A
native may therefore be born under three signs according to this
doctrine; for, the horoscope may be in one, the Sun in a second,
and the Moon in a third. This, were it true, would create confusion enough; for they might all be of opposite qualities, all of
which they say ought to be skillfully combined together. There
can be little doubt, that the sign ascending will much influence
the appearance and mind of the native, though not exactly according to the rules here laid down.

The diseases attributed to them are said to be caused by malefics
posited in them afflicting the horoscope or luminaries. An
instance of this we have in Placidus, where ♂ in ♓, the sign of
the feet, afflicting the ☾ with a mundane square, and ♄ in ♉ to
her from ♐, the sign of the thighs, while she was in the west
angle with her south node, caused the native to be born with his
feet inverted. General experience does not justify such an observation, and Placidus ought to have known better. Other authors
suppose those diseases, or rather a disposition to them, to exist in
such as are born when the horoscope is in such and such signs;
but this is not quite correct, because the diseases here laid down
are more formed from the planets supposed to have rule in such
signs than from the signs themselves. I would recommend the
greatest experience before an artist attempts to judge of diseases,
for they have many origins; though I think they chiefly depend
on the ☾. In horary questions or decumbitures they may be useful, provided they do not involve contradictions,

Lilly takes the appearance from the sign belonging to any person's ascendant, and the two signs containing its lord and the ☾.
The nature of these are to be mixed judiciously, and the greater
number of testimonies taken. He also takes the sign descending,
and thus renders the whole doctrine a mass of confusion; for such
a number of opposite testimonies may exist that nothing can be
made of them.

Diseases are taken from the signs on the ascendant and 6th,
but this rule, so far as my practice extends, is very erroneous.

The places denoted by a sign are those where any thing stolen or strayed is supposed to be secreted, according to the sign the significator of the thing is found in. Thus, if cattle be strayed and their significator be in ♏, they will be found near some stinking marshy place; or if a thing be stolen, it will be hid in a kitchen, or wash-house, or buried in a garden, orchard, &c.

In horary questions, signs containing planets have their signification considerably altered in respect to diseases, and the parts of the human body where they are situated, according to the planet which is posited in such sign, and its distance from the sign it governs, or what is called its house. If it be in its house, it affects the head; in the next following sign, the neck: in the sign following that, the arms and shoulders, &c. as will be shewn in the following table.

	♄	♃	♂	☉	♀	☿	☾
♈	Arms, shoulders, and breast	neck throat heart and belly.	Belly & head	Thighs	Reins & feet	Secrets & Legs	Knees & head
♉	Breast heart and back	Shoulders arms belly and neck	Reins & throat	Knees	Head & secrets	Thighs & feet	Legs & throat
♊	Heart back and belly	Breast reins and secrets	Secrets arms and breast	Legs & ankles	Throat & thighs	Knees & head	Feet shoulders and arms
♋	Belly reins and secrets	Heart secrets and thighs	Thighs and breast	Knees	Arms shoulders and knees	Eyes throat and legs	Head breast and stomach
♌	Secrets and reins	Belly thighs and knees	Knees heart and belly	Head	Breast heart and legs	Throat arms shoulders & feet	Throat stomach & heart
♍	Secrets thighs and feet	Reins and knees	Legs and belly	Throat	Stomach heart belly and feet	Head breast and heart	Arms shoulders and bowels
♎	Knees and thighs	Secrets legs head and eyes	Feet reins and secrets	Arms and should'rs	Head and intestines	Throat heart stomach & belly	Breast heart belly and reins
♏	Knees and thighs	Thighs and feet	Head secrets arms and thighs	Breast and heart	Throat reins and secrets	Shoulders arms bowels & back	Stomach heart belly and secrets
♐	Legs and feet	Knees head and thighs	Throat thighs arms & feet	Heart and belly	arms shoulders secr'ts and thighs	Breast heart reins and secrets	Back bowels and thighs
♑	Head and feet	Legs neck eyes and feet	arms shoulders knees and legs	Belly and back	Breast heart and thighs	Stomach heart and secrets	Reins thighs and knees
♒	Neck and Head	Feet arms shoulders and breast	Breast heart and legs	Reins and secrets	Heart and knees	Bowels heart and thighs	Secrets legs and ankles
♓	Arms shoulders and neck	Head breast and heart	Heart belly feet and ankles	Secrets and thighs	Belly and legs	Reins secrets knees and thighs	Thighs and feet

The whole is an Arabian system, and certainly must cause some confusion even in horary questions, where alone it can have any signification. As to nativities, it would be absurd to suppose it can be of the smallest efficacy. When these planets are near an azimene, pitted, or deficient degree of a sign, the disease or blemish is said to be stronger and more remarkable.

The countries they are said to govern, are wholly imaginary so far as relates to nativities. They are said to operate on such countries when the ☉ or ☽ is eclipsed in any of them, according to the condition of the luminaries, and on this foundation chiefly predictions are made in almanacs. This might be tolerated, but I am sorry to see a rational man like Placidus, affirming, that "the sign ♐ relates to Spain and its inhabitants." A silly observation like this casts a shadow over all his other accomplishments. Whatever may be the source of astral influence, it is at least uniform, it operates by its attraction and position, and a star whether fixed or erratic has the same influence in one country as another where its position and distance are the same. The famous prediction of April, 1807, respecting the Grand Seignor's deposition and death, has been much spoken of, and I sincerely wish it had been on good grounds. ♂ had been at that time long retrograde in ♍, the ascendant of Turkey, and was just then become direct in the beginning of the sign, so that he had to travel all through it again. His duration in that sign at that period was astonishing, for owing to his station being near its extremities, he had passed the whole of his perigee or a third of his period, in that sign only. According to the doctrine of Ptolemy, who says that ♍ has the disposing of Mesopotamia, Babylon, Assyria, Greece, Achaia, and Crete, the whole of the Grand Seignor's dominions are under its influence; and on the 28th of April ♄ opposed the ☉ from ♏, which is said to govern Syria, a part also of the Turkish dominion; the ☉ of course being in ♉, which is said to govern the whole of Turkey in Asia; the ☾ on the 1st of May came to the ☍ of ♂ in ♍; and where judgment is formed upon such principles, there could not be in appearance a more fatal position for the Turkish Empire. The ☉ being the significator of royalty, denoted the evil to fall there, and the event literally justified the prediction. But this is considering the stars as symbolical, rather than effectual, and converting the whole into a species of divination, or horary question, instead of accounting for these events from the immutable laws of nature. Did events so accounted for always take place, there would be no further room for argument, because facts must supersede every thing, but they do not; of numberless predictions founded on those principles scarce one in a century is fulfilled. There have been many striking events, not less important than this, concerning Turkey, that were never foreseen or hinted at, and it is therefore but just, when any prediction of this kind is fulfilled, to ascribe it to what it really is, the result of accident. That the fate of the Turkish Emperor was sealed by the position of ♂, there cannot be any doubt, but it probably would have been the same had he been in any other sign than ♍, so far as relates to the Turkish Empire, though probably no other sign might have so exactly suited his own nativity. ♂ had been long in perigee, producing incalculable evil; Spain, Portugal, and all Europe, were at that moment involved in calamities, much greater than any that could, or did befall Turkey, and the oppositions of the ☉ to ♄ and the ☾ to ♂ were not calculated to diminish them. The ☉ towards the conclusion of April had the declinations both of ♄ and ♂, and was far distant from those of the benefics and the ☽ on the last two days of April had the same declinations, and on the following day transited the ☍ of ♂ from Virgo. No position of the lights could have a more fatal tendency than this, or was ever more severely felt; Europe was already convulsed, and therefore, like a sick man, experienced the stroke more severely which shook it to its center. Other nations, though not in the same predicament, suffered proportionally, according to their internal situation, and Turkey only had a small sip out of the general cup of bitterness.

In describing those signs, I have frequently inserted a contradiction; as, for instance, where a sign is considered both northern and southern at the same time. This arises from the silly doctrine of triplicities; for a fiery sign is called northern because it belongs to the northern triplicity. All signs to the south of the equator are southern, and hence the sign ♐ is both northern and southern: northern by triplicity and southern by position. Again, the earthy triplicity is called southern, and therefore ♉ will be a northern sign from its position and a southern by triplicity. This is the way fools get entangled in their own absurdities.

SIGNS OF LONG ASCENSION, ♋, ♌, ♍, ♎, ♏, ♐, so called because they take longer time in ascending than the others. Ptolemy says a ✶ in a sign of long ascension will have the same effect as a □.

SIGNS OF SHORT ASCENSION, ♑, ♒, ♓, ♈, ♉, ♊, so called because they ascend in a shorter period of time than the others, from the diurnal motion of the Earth being when they ascend, nearly parallel with its orbit. A △ in a sign of short ascension is, according to Ptolemy, equal to a □ in its effect, but, long and short ascensions are only mundane, and not zodiacal positions; for all signs occupy the same distance in the ecliptic, and the stars can only operate on each other according to their zodiacal positions, let Placidus say what he will.

SIGNS OF VOICE, ♊, ♍, ♎, ♒, and the first part of ♐, because, it is said, if either of them ascend, and ☿ be strong, the native will be a good orator.

SINISTER ASPECTS, aspects to the left according to the course of the signs. Thus, a planet in ♈ will cast a sinister ⚹ to ♊. They are said to be weaker than dexter aspects; but this is all fancy. It was, however, a favourite opinion of Salmon, though he acknowledges in his Medical Synopsis, that the ancients thought differently.

SLOW OF COURSE, when a planet moves slower than its mean motion. It is considered a great debility, and it may be so in some cases of horary questions.

SOL (☉), the Sun.

SOLAR SEMICIRCLE, from ♌ to ♑, both included.

SOUTHERN SIGNS, ♎, ♏, ♐, ♑, ♒, and ♓, so called, because they are south of the equator. They are also called obeying signs, because a star in any of them would be weaker than another star in a northern sign having the same declination, because of the more powerful and commanding position of the latter.

SPEAKING SIGNS. See "Signs of Voice."

SPECULUM, a looking glass, a table so called, which should be made out for every nativity, containing the ascensions, semiarcs, latitudes, declinations, poles, ascensional difference, &c. &c. that the artist may always have them to refer to in bringing up directions, &c. The following is given as a specimen, and contains all the particulars which the author would require, except the crepusculine or obscure arcs of the ☉, had his position required it. But artists differ in their opinions, some requiring the horary time, terms, oblique ascensions or descensions under the pole of ☽ or ☉, or under their own poles, places of their antiscions, &c. &c. (See top of next page.)

SPHERE, a globe, the deferent of a planet was also called its sphere, and was what is called at present its orbit. Hence the Primum Mobile was called the 10th sphere.

SPICA VIRGINIS, Arista, a benevolent fixed star of the 1st magnitude, in 20° of ♎, of the nature of ♀ and ♂. It is said to be the most fortunate of all the fixed stars, and to ensure to the native every degree of success and happiness when it ascends, or

Form of a SPECULUM.

Planets.	*Latitudes.*	*Declinations.*	*Right Ascension, with latit'de*	*Ascensional difference.*	*Pole.*	*Oblique ascension in pole of the horosco'e.*	*Semi diurnal Arc.*	*Semi nocturnal Arc.*	*Oblique descension in the pole of the horosc'e*
	° ′	° ′	° ′	° ′	° ′	° ′	° ′	° ′	° ′
♅	0 46N.	14 1N	147 17	18 18	1 0		108 18		
♄	2 3S.	14 18N	42 51	18 43	19 30		108 43		61 34
♃	0 24N.	23 2S	273 39	32 26	13 0			122 26	241 13
♂	1 49N.	13 10S	218 26	17 8	22 30	235 34		107 8	
☉		5 58N	13 53	7 32	37 30		97 32		21 25
♀	1	6 30N	18 6	8 14	35 30		98 14		26 20
☿	2 42N.	9 39N	16 0	12 21	35 20		102 21		28 21
☾	4 52S.	17 38N	73 26	23 35	0 30	49 51	113 35		
⊕		17 38N	229 43	23 35	23 30	206 8		66 25	

Pole of the 3d, 5th, 9th, & 11th houses 23° 27′—Of the 2d, 8th, 6th, & 12th, 40° 48′.—Of the 1st & 7th, 51° 32′.

culminates, or is joined to either of the luminaries, or to a benefic in aspect to them.

SQUARE, the quartile aspect, containing a quadrant or right angle. It consists in the zodiac of 3 signs, and in the world of a whole semiarc. Its effect as an aspect is evil, though somewhat less than an opposition.

STATIONS, those parts in the orbit of a planet where it becomes either retrograde or direct, because it remains for a while there stationary before it changes its course. The first station is where they become retrograde, but in the ☾, who is never retrograde, it is called her first dichotome. The second station is after they have passed their perigee, and from retrogradation become direct. This in the ☾ is called her second dichotome. From these stations their orientality is reckoned. From their apogee to their first station they are called matutine, because they rise in the morning before the ☉, and are in their first degree of orientality. From the first station to the lower apsis or perigee, they are considered in their first degree of occidentality, and when near the ☍ to the ☉ are what Ptolemy calls, rising in the beginning of the night. At their perigee they again become oriental in the secondary degree, until they arrive at their second station, and from thence to their apogee or higher apsis they are in their last degree of occidentality. They are said to be moist, from the ☌ with the ☉ to the first station; warm, until they come to the ☍; dry, until they arrive at the 2d station; and cool, until they come to the solar ☌ again. (See "Oriental.")

This only relates to the superiors; for ♀ and ☿ are called oriental when vespertine or setting after the ☉ in the evening, because they are then increasing in light and coming nearer to the Earth, until they disappear in their lower conjunction with the ☉. When matutine or rising before the ☉ in the morning they are called occidental, as they are passing toward their higher conjunction and leaving the Earth.

STATIONARY, when a planet is in its station and appears to stand still. The lights are never stationary. ♄ is stationary 5 days; ♃, 5 days; ♂, 2 or 3 days; ♀, 2 days; and ☿ 1 day.

STELLIUM, a crowd of planets in an angle. Persons having this in their radix have at some period in the course of their lives prodigious good or ill fortune. So far as my observation extends, a stellium of 4 or 5 planets in any part of the radix always produces in the course of the native's existence some tremendous catastrophe.

STRENGTH. Planets are generally supposed to be strong when dignified either by house, exaltation, term, triplicity, or face, or by any accidental dignity; but these can have no signification whatever. Ptolemy is not very intelligible respecting essential dignities, but he appears to have considered them as qualities rather than strength. When he has occasion to refer to the latter, he appears to consider orientality, and angular or succeedent positions as the principal causes of strength; next to which is their being direct, swift, or increasing in motion. No doubt their being angular, especially in the midheaven, must be a very powerful position, but I think the perigee is the most powerful condition especially with north declination. As to the other degrees of strength, they are to me at least problematical.

STRONG SIGNS, ♌, ♏. and ♒, because they are said to give strong athletic bodies.

SUCCEEDENT. When houses succeed to or follow an angle they are called succeedent, and a planet posited in one of them is reckoned nearly as strong as in an angle. I cannot see any good reason for this, for their position and distance from the angle are the same in a succeedent as in a cadent house, and although they are advancing towards the angle, their power cannot rationally be considered from what they will be, but from what they are. The 11th, 5th, 2d, and 8th houses are all succeedent.

SUN. See "Planets."

SUPERIOR PLANETS, ♄, ♃, and ♂, so called because their

orbits are beyond those of ♀ and ☿. They are said to be more powerful in their effects than the inferiors.

SWEET SIGNS, ♊, ♎, and ♒, because the native is said to be of a sweet temper if born under one of these signs.

SWIFT IN MOTION, a planet is so called when it moves faster than its mean motion. It is deemed a very great fortitude, because its resists the effect of the diurnal motion.

SYMPATHY, a familiarity or attachment between two persons, arising from the similarity of the planetary positions in their respective figures. Ptolemy says, if the lights are in reception with each other, or at a distance of 17 degrees only, or if either of the lights are within that distance of the cusps of each other's horoscope or ⊕, there will be pure, sincere, and lasting friendship between the parties; but if only configurated to them by a △ or ✶, they cause slight attachments. When this attachment arises from the position of the lights only, it will be the result of choice and sincere affection; but if from any agreement with the Part of Fortune, it will be from motives of gain; and if from a familiarity with the horoscope, it will be from motives of pleasures or enjoyment.

Enmities and antipathies are said to arise from their being inconjunct or in evil aspect, and according as this happens with the lights, Part of Fortune, or the horoscope, the causes will be natural hatred, losses, and sufferings. The enmity will chiefly arise from that person who has most familiarity with the places and aspects of the other's nativity.

Slight friendships are formed by transits, when the lights or benefics in one radix come by direction to the places of the lights or benefics of the other radix, and will last until such direction be past.

Of the Part of Fortune and its supposed effects, I have no opinion, but I know from repeated experience, that a kind of attachment will take place between two persons whose nativities sympathise on account of most or all of the planets being posited in the same places, whether they be good or evil. The trine or sextile of the luminaries to each other in the zodiac, or their mutual position in each others places, or on those of ♃ or ♀, are the best signs of attachment and *vice versa*. The same planet in two person's horoscopes gives them the same manners and propensities. The infortunes in opposition to their own places cause continual quarrels. The fortunes on the places of the infortunes cause alternate enmity and attachment. If the ☉ and ☾, or the ☉ and ☿, or the ☾ and ☿, change places with each other, the attachment is not very strong. ♃ and ♄ in each others places, the natives form an attachment through covetousness. ♂ and ♀ in each others places, they are attached by lust and wickedness. If the ☉ or ♂ be in ☍ to ☿ or the ☾, they hate each other, and he that has ♂ will do the other a mischief. ♄ and ♂ in ☍, causes continual enmity.

I would particularly and seriously recommend the doctrine of sympathies to the student's attention, because it is founded on a sure basis, although but little understood. By way of throwing a little more light on this intricate subject I shall insert the observation of Placidus concerning the causes of the antipathy between Charles the 5th of Spain and Germany, and Francis the 1st of France.

"They originated," he says, "from their ascendants being nearly opposite within a few minutes: ♄ of Francis was on the ☉ of Charles (within about 4 degrees,) ♂ of Charles in □ to the ☾ of Francis, and ♂ of Francis in sesquiquadrate to the ☾ of Charles, ♄ in the 4th of Charles and the 10th of Francis, ♂ angular in Charles, and cadent in Francis, and in zodiacal square to each other, &c." These observations are worthy of attention, though I do not deem them of so much importance as Placidus did. The chief causes of sympathy that have fallen within my observation, are those wherein two nativities resembled each other by the planets possessing all or most of them the same zodiacal positions, though I think that the evil aspect of the malefics to the lights, or the ascension of opposite signs, are always productive of evil. The ☉ or ☾ in the same place in two nativities, is reckoned a sign of the most perfect agreement. It is said, that those parties never agree when the horoscope of the one is the same as the 6th, 8th, or 12th of the other. Many calculate friendship or enmity from the respective lords of the ascendants being friends or enemies to each other, but this is a groundless opinion.

SYNODICAL. See "Lunations."

SYZYGES, the new and full Moon, also the ☌ or ☍ of any two planets, and it is often used as a common term for familiarities of every description.

TABLE OF HOUSES. See "Figure."

TAURUS. See "Signs."

TEMPER See "Mind."

TEMPORAL HOURS, planetary hours.

TERM. Terms are certain degrees in a sign, supposed to possess the power of altering the nature of a planet to that of the planet in the term of which it is posited. Hence a malefic in the

term of ♃ or ♀ would lose much of its anaretic power and be
scarcely able to kill, and a benefic in the term of a malefic would
be rendered equally unable to save. This notion of terms (which
appears to me very ridiculous,) is of great antiquity; for Ptolemy
mentions two sets of terms, one Egyptian and the other Chaldean,
neither of which he approves, nor does he seem to know much
about the latter, for although he says he met with an old writing
containing the reason, order, and quantity of them, he has nowhere inserted it.

The order of the terms, as laid down by Ptolemy himself, is as
follows: Every star having two dignities in a sign, either by
house, exaltation or triplicity, has the first place whether benefic
or malefic; but, if it have but one dignity, however great that dignity may be, the malefics are always placed last. The highest of
all these essential dignities, according to Ptolemy, was the exaltation: next, the triplicity, and thirdly, the house; but the moderns
have thought proper to put the house first. The lord, therefore,
of the exaltation (if there were any) had the first choice if a benefic; next to him, the lord of the triplicity, if a benefic; and thirdly, the lord of the house. The ☉ and ☽, having no particular
qualities of their own, had no terms allotted them. If there were
no ruler having two testimonies in one sign, or in the other two
signs of the quadrant, then ♃ and ♀ had seven parts each; ♄ and
♂, five parts each; and there being then six parts remaining, they
were given to ☿, he being common to both sides of the question.
If any planet had two dignities in any sign in the quadrant, they
had a larger allowance of degrees given them, and the deficiency
was thrown upon ♄ or ♃, because of the slowness of their
motion. As the lights had no terms, the malefics made up in
some degree for the deficiency in other signs, by taking the first
parts in them. These are the rules laid down by Ptolemy, who
condemns the Egyptian terms, because they were not formed according to any known rule, and the Egyptian might have returned
the compliment, for his are not arranged according even to his
own rule. They are as shown in table on next page.

To those who can comprehend this nonsense of Ptolemy, the
table will be eminently useful. It is wholly unintelligible
to me nor am I less at a loss to discover how Placidus could con-
trive to reconcile them to the dictates of that reason he boasted of
having for his guide.

In whatever term a planet is posited, it denotes the persons signified by it to be of the disposition of the lord of that term, wheth-

er it be his own or any other, but has no reference to either wealth or poverty, or any condition in life.

Terms according to Ptolemy.

♈	♃ 6	♀ 8	☿ 7	♂ 5	♄ 4
♉	♀ 8	☿ 7	♃ 7	♄ 2	♂ 6
♊	☿ 7	♃ 6	♀ 7	♂ 6	♄ 4
♋	♂ 6	☿ ♃ 7	♃ ☿ 7	♀ 7	♄ 3
♌	♄ 6	☿ 7	♄ ♀ 6	♀ 6	♂ 5
♍	☿ 7	♀ 6	♃ 5	♄ 6	♂ 6
♎	♄ 6	♀ 5	☿ ♃ 8-5	♃ ☿ 5-8	♂ 6
♏	♂ 6	♀ ♃ 8-7	♃ ♀ 7-8	6	♄ 3
♐	♃ 8	♀ 6	☿ 5	♄ 6	♂ 5
♑	♀ 6	☿ 6	♃ 7	♄ ♂ 6	♂ 5
♒	♄ 6	☿ 6	♀ 8	♃ 5	♂ 5
♓	♀ 8	♃ 6	☿ 6	♂ 6-5	♄ 4-5

Terms according to the Egyptians.

♈	♃ 6	♀ 6	☿ 8	♂ 5	♄ 5
♉	♀ 8	☿ 6	♃ 8	♄ 5	♂ 3
♊	☿ 6	♃ 6	♀ 5	♂ 7	♄ 6
♋	♂ 7	♀ 6	☿ 6	♃ 7	♄ 4
♌	♃ 6	♀ 5	♄ 7	☿ 6	♂ 6
♍	☿ 7	♀ 10	♃ 4	♂ 7	♄ 2
♎	♄ 6	♀ 8	♃ 7	☿ 7	♂ 2
♏	♂ 7	♀ 4	☿ 8	♃ 5	♄ 6
♐	♃ 12	♀ 5	☿ 4	♄ 5	♂ 4
♑	☿ 7	♃ 7	♀ 8	♄ 4	♂ 4
♒	☿ 7	♀ 6	♃ 7	♂ 5	♄ 5
♓	♀ 12	♃ 4	☿ 3	♂ 9	♄ 2

TERMINUS VITÆ, the end of life, the fatal direction or directions, that inevitably kill.

TESTIMONY, a term used by Ptolemy to signify the mode of a planet's operation, which was either by having what he calls "rule in the place" alluded to, or casting an aspect to it.   Thus a planet would give testimony to ☿ or the ☾ by ruling them, that is, having dignity by exaltation, triplicity, house, or term, in that degree where they are posited; or by casting an aspect to it nearly partile.   Having testimony, or having two testimonies, &c. is having one or two of those dignities in any part specified.   In horary questions, every symbolical position or condition is called **a** testimony.

TETRAGONUS, the square aspect.

THEMA CŒLI, a figure of the heavens.

THRONES, any part of a sign where a planet has two or more testimonies, *i. e.* essential dignities, is called its throne, chariot, or any other foolish name that comes to hand. Thus ♄'s throne is in ♒ by house and triplicity; ♃ has his in ♐ the same; ♂, in ♏; ☉, in ♌; ♀, in ♉; ☿, in ♍ by house and exaltation; and the ☽, in ♋. But Ptolemy would not have fixed them thus, for he preferred exaltations to houses, and therefore ♄'s throne would have been in ♎, the ☉'s in ♈, and the ☾'s in ♉; for in his time she had no claim to the watery triplicity. The whole however, is nonsense, and therefore not worth a dispute.

TIME. See "Equation of Time."

TRADE or PROFESSION, according to Ptolemy it is taken from the star that makes oriental appearance next to the ☉, and the star which is in the midheaven; if the oriental star be in the midheaven or in aspect to it, that must be taken, particularly if the ☾ applies to it. If there be one oriental and another in the midheaven that must be taken which has the application of the ☾. If neither or both have her application, both of them must be taken, but the strongest must be preferred. If there be none oriental, nor in the midheaven, the planet having dominion in the midheaven must be taken. ♄ and ♃, however, he excludes from this prerogative, and only takes ♂, ♀, ☿, and the ☾, as significators of profession, although he allows ♄ and ♃ to coincide by testimony. ☿ makes writers, traders, scholars of every description, and all who get a living by any kind of learning. If ♄ give testimony to him, they will fill some ecclesiastical office, or agency for another. If ♃ give testimony, they will be painters, orators, and such as are employed among the great.

If ♀ be ruler of the profession, she disposes to dealing in perfumes, spices, sweetmeats, cordials, wines, medicines, drapery, paintings, dresses, dyeing of colours, &c. If ♄ give testimony to her, they will deal in charms, philtres, poisons, &c.; but these things are not so customary here as they were in Egypt. If ♃ give testimony to her, they will be knights-errant, champions, armour-bearers, and be be very prosperous through women.

If ♂ rule the profession and have any kind of configuration to the ☉, he disposes the natives to work at the fire, as cooks, founders, braziers, smiths, &c. but if he be with the ☉, they will be workers among wood or stone, or agriculturists. If ♄ give testimony to him, they will be butchers, sailors, nightmen, scavengers, feeders of beasts, cooks, or any that live by dirt or drudgery. If ♃ give testimony, they will be soldiers, tax-gatherers, innkeepers, &c.

If ☿ and ♀ be joint rulers, they make musicians, composers, poets, musical instrument makers, particularly if in mutual reception, for then they make actors, dancers, tumblers, and devote them to all kinds of music, painting, &c. If ♄ give testimony, they will deal in female dresses and ornaments. If ♃ give testimony, they will be lawyers, schoolmasters, and officers of state.

If ☿ and ♂ be joint rulers, they will be statuaries, makers of armour, surgeons, engravers, wrestlers, and addicted to knavish occupations, such as forgery, theft, thief-taking, &c. If ♄ give testimony, they will be thieves, murderers, plunderers, cattle-stealers, conjurors, and follow every kind of fraud, violence, and imposture.

If ♀ and ♂ are joint rulers, they become dyers, perfumers, tinmen, plumbers, gold and silversmiths, apothecaries, physicians, figure dancers, &c. If ♄ give testimony they will have some office in the church, or assist at funerals, as sextons, undertakers, &c. If ♃ give testimony, they will also have some religious employment, but more honourable.

If the ☾ govern the profession, and separate from the Sun and have familiarity with ☿, she makes astrologers, magicians, &c: but these are not fashionable callings at present.

These significators oriental or angular, make the profession great and powerful; but if occidental or cadent, weak and subordinate. If the benefics be stronger than the malefics the trade will be fortunate; but if the malefics be stronger than the lords of the profession, it will be mean, unprofitable, and uncertain. ♄ causes injury by apathy and inattention, and change of opinion. ♂, from too much forwardness and rashness.

The time of the increase or diminution of trade is taken from the places of the stars which cause the effect. If they are between the east and south angles, it will be in the early part of life; but if between the south and west angles, it will be in old age.

There appears to be some small portion of truth amongst this vast heap of rubbish of lordships and testimonies. I suspect that ☿ has some influence in this way, as well as a star in the midheaven. As to oriental stars, their effect must be proved by experience. The aspects to the 10th merit some consideration, and in fact every position should be carefully observed; for, in astrology, as in chemistry, of which it is a part, the truth can only be obtained by induction. As to the particular kinds of profession, as above described, they may be considered as mostly void of foundation. By the planet making oriental appearance is meant, that planet which rises next before the ☉, and I have seen some instances of the truth of this aphorism, though not enough to be depended on. There is reason to suppose, that ☿ and ♀ rule the profession, or at least the inclination, when they are next to the ☉, whether they rise before or after him, and probably other planets do the same.

TRANSITS, according to modern astrology, when a planet crosses a house or place of its lord in a nativity it is said to produce evil according to its nature and the nature of the place it transits. Thus, if the lord of the 8th, even if it be ♃, transit the cusp of the horoscope, it threatens death; if the lord of the 6th transit it, it denotes sickness; the lord of the 12th, imprisonment, or great troubles. It is the same with the other houses; for if the lords of the 8th, 6th, or 12th, transit the 2d, or place of its lord, it denotes loss; if the 3d or its lord, quarrels with brethren or neighbours; the 4th, loss of parents; the 5th, loss by gaming, or by children, &c. Lords of good houses are said to produce benefits by their transits, whether they be benefics or malefics. It is useless to dwell longer on these absurdities.

The transits of the ☾ are said to cause all the daily passing events of a man's life, as she transits the △, ✶, □, ☍, or ☌, of any particular house. ♄ and ♃ are held to be more powerful in their transits than the rest, and their effects last about a year.

I much suspect there is great power in transits, and I would recommend them particularly to the consideration of the artist, though not as they respect the houses or their lords, but as they respect the places of the lights or the angles. For the real use of transits, see "Secondary Directions." I have always observed those times to be most unfortunate to a native, when the luminaries are in ☌, □, or ☍, to the radical places of the infortunes, especially if they happen to square their own places at the same time, or if the preceding lunation was in an evil place. Some remarkably evil event is generally at hand when the ☉ is in ☍ and the ☾ in □ at the same time to a radical malefic.

TRANSLATION. Translation of the light and nature of a planet is when a planet separates from one that is slower than itself and overtakes another either by conjunction or aspect. In horary questions it is a good omen, if the aspect be good; but if by an evil aspect, it is said to denote evil or difficulty when the event comes to pass. Thus, if in a question of marriage a light planet translates the light of the lord of the 7th to the lord of the 1st, it is a good omen, if it be by good aspect, and denotes that a person answering the description of such translating planet will bring them together, and they will be eventually happy. If it be by evil aspect, it will be done either from ill motives, or will be attended with much trouble and disappointment.

TRAVELING. According to Ptolemy, the luminaries, and particularly the ☾, declining from angles and occidental, causes traveling. This must mean being in the 9th or 3d houses, for she is occidental and cadent in both these. I have reason to suspect there is some truth in this, which is too seldom the case in other matters. Sometimes he says ♂ occidental and declining from the midheaven when in □ or ☍ to the lights, will cause the same; and, if the ⊕ fall in traveling signs, the whole life and manners of the native will be foreign. What signs cause traveling I know not, but suppose he means the signs on the cusps of the 9th and 3d. If these signs be of one form, or the stars having rule in them be in signs of one form, the traveling will not be frequent; but if they are double bodied, or of two forms, the native will be always traveling. This is not only foolish, but unintelligible; for the sign may be of one form, and its lord in a sign of two forms. If the luminaries be in oriental quadrants the traveling will be south and east; but if in occidental quadrants, north or west. But how can this be, when the lights must be occidental, or the ☽ at least, to cause traveling at all, except he take it from the position of ♂ or ⊕? In that case, the native must always travel west or north, when the lights are in the 9th and 3d houses: for these are what he calls occidental quadrants.

If the benefics succeed to these places (meaning I suppose the 3d and 9th,) or are configurated with them, there will be much safety and profit in those journeys, but if the malefics behold or succeed, it will be dangerous and ruinous; but in all these configurations the strongest is to be preferred. Here he makes no distinction between the nature of the aspect, whether good or evil.

If ♃ or ♀ are rulers of those places, viz. those of the luminaries; the traveling will be safe and comfortable in every respect; and if ☿ be with them, meaning if he have dignities in the same places, there will be additional honour and profit attached to it. If ♄ and ♂ govern the lights, and especially if they oppose them, the traveling will be dangerous and unprofitable. If those planets are in watery signs, they will be shipwrecked, or lost in desert, uninhabited places; in fixed signs, they will suffer by contrary winds, or be injured by climbing of precipices; in cardinal signs, they will be sickly and in want of food; in human signs, they will suffer by thieves and banditti; and in earthy signs by wild beasts, or earthquakes. If ☿ have dignities there also, they will be injured by venemous reptiles or false accusations. The time of traveling, he says, must be ascertained by direction.

As to the Part of Fortune and the lordships, I have no opinion of them, and indeed the latter involves a contradiction, for if the benefics are configurated or succeed to the places, and the malefics have rule in them, and *vice versa*, what is to become of the traveler then? Neither can it be of any consequence what signs the evil planets are found in. Those whose births subject them to misfortunes are like those whose broken constitutions dispose them to disease. They are always out of order, because the slightest causes affect them. The luminaries cadent from the south or north angle, may be one cause of traveling, but there are other causes which are not yet discovered. The planet Mars cadent in like manner is not, I think, productive of any such effect. I know a person who had Mars near the cusp of his 3d, who all his life had the greatest aversion to traveling, was seldom three miles and never thirty miles from the place of his birth. Neither is the position of the lights indicative of the direction in which the native will travel, for I know one who had them both in his 3d, who went abroad but once, and that was for many years, to the East Indies; yet, according to Ptolemy, he ought to have traveled west or north, this being what he terms an occidental quadrant. Even allowing the modern system to be true, that it is a north-east quadrant, he ought to have traveled to Russia instead of the East Indies. It was a favorite maxim with Ptolemy, to account for every thing in some way or other, right or wrong, but it is probable the direction of journeys only depend on common circumstances, and not on any planetary position.

TRIGON. See "Triplicity."

TRIGONOCRATORS, rulers of trigons. The ☉ and ♃ rule the fiery; ♀ and ☽, the earthy; ♄ and ☿, the airy, and ♂ alone, the watery, though the moderns have united ♀ and the ☾ with him in the watery triplicity.

TRIGONOMETRICAL CALCULATIONS, the method of performing astrological calculations by trigonometry, wherein the use of logarithms will be found indispensably necessary. It is useless here to enter any farther into the principles of trigonometry than is necessary to the subject we are upon, and it is therefore only requisite to observe, that tables of logarithms, sines, tangents, and secants, as referred to here, are those used with the Nautical Ephemeris, and may be had of almost any bookseller.

Problem. 1st.—The longitude of a star, without latitude, being given to find its declination in the ecliptic.

Rule, Add the sine of 23° 28′ to the sine of the star's distance from the nearest equinoctial point, the sum, less radius, will be the sine of the star's declination.

Example: Suppose the ☉ in 27° 36′ of ♈, what is his declination?

The first point of ♈ is the nearest equinoctial point to where the ☉ is, his distance from it is 27° 36′, the logarithmic sine of which will be found in the table (in the common angle of 27 degrees and 36 minutes) to be 9.66585. Add to this the logarithm 9.60011, belonging to the tropical sine, 23° 28′, less radius, and it will give the logarithm 9.26596, which will be found to answer to the sine of 10° 38′, which is the ☉'s declination.

Problem 2d.—The declination of a star without latitude being given, to find its longitude in the ecliptic.

This problem is evidently the reverse of the former, for if the tropical sine, 23° 28′, be subtracted from the sine of the declination, the remainder will be the longitude required. It is usual, however, to work as much as possible by addition, and the arithmetical complement of a logarithm being added, has the same effect as if the logarithm itself were subtracted, we therefore add the arithmetical complement of the tropical sine, as found in problem 1st, to the sine of the declination, and the sum will be the sine of the longitude required. Example:

Logarithm of the declination,	9.26596
Arith. comp. of the tropical sine,	0.39989
Logarithm of the longitude,	9.66585, equal to 27° 36′

of ♈.

Problem 3d.—The longitude and latitude of a star given, to find its declination.

Rule. *1st,* Add the tangent of 23° 28′ to the sine of the longitudinal distance from the nearest equinoctial point, the sum, less radius, will be the tangent of the 1st angle.

2d, If the latitude and longitude have the same denomination, namely, if the latitude be north and the star in a northern sign, or south and the star in a southern sign, the latitude must be sub-

tracted from 90°. But if the latitude and longitude are of different denominations, the latitude must be added to 90°. Subtract
the 1st angle from the sum or remainder, and it will give the
amount of the 2d angle.

3d, As the cosine of the 1st angle is to the cosine of the 2d
angle, so is the cosine of 23° 28′ to the sine of the required declination.

The declination will have the same denomination as the sign in
which the star is, north or south, provided it be greater than the
latitude. But if it be less than the latitude, and the latitude be of
an opposite denomination to the sign, the declination will have
the same denomination as the latitude.

Example: Suppose ♃ to be in 3° 21′ of ♑, with 0° 24′ north
latitude, what will be his declination?

The nearest equinoctial point is ♈, from which ♃ is distant
86° 39′.

Sine of 86° 39′,　　　　　　　　　　9.99926
Add the tangent of 23° 28′,　　　　　9.63761
_____

It gives the tangent of the 1st angle, 9.63687, equal to 23°
26′. As the latitude and longitude are of opposite denominations,
I add the 24′ to 90°, which gives 90° 24′, from which I subtract
the 1st angle, 23° 26′, leaving a remainder of 66° 58′, which is the
2d angle.

As the cosine of the 1st angle, 23° 26′ (of which I take the
arith. comp. for the sake of addition)　0.03738
is to the cosine of the 2d angle, 66° 58′　9.59247
so is the cosine of 23° 28′,　　　　　　9.96251
_____

to the sine of the required declination, 9.59236, which is equal
to 23° 2′ of south declination, as ♃ is in a southern sign. Had
this declination been less than the latitude, it would have been
north, because the latitude is north, and of a different denomination from the longitude.

Problem 4th.—The right ascension and declination of a star
being given, to find its longitude.

Rule 1*st*, Add the sine of the right ascension to the cotangent of
the declination, the sum, rejecting radius, will be the cotangent
of the first angle, which will be north or south according to the
declination.

2d, Call the obliquity of the ecliptic south, if the right ascension be in the first six signs, or north if in the last six signs, and

subtract it from the 1st angle, or the first angle from it, according to which is the most, the remainder will be the second angle, and south or north accordingly.

3d, Add the arithmetical complement of the cosine of the 1st angle, the cosine of the 2d angle, and the tangent of the right ascension together, their sum, rejecting radius, will be the tangent of the longitude, which will be north or south according to the right ascension, except the 2d angle be above 90°, in which case the quantity found of the same kind as the right ascension must be subtracted from 360°.

Example: Suppose the right ascension of ♃ to be 273° 39′ (this subtracted from 360° will be 86° 21′ from the nearest equinoctial point) his declination, 23° 2′ south, obliquity of the ecliptic 23° 28′, what is his longitude?

Sine of ♃'s right ascension, 86° 21′,	9.99911
Cotangent of his declination, 23° 2′,	10.37145
Cotangent of the 1st angle, 23° 4′ south,	10.37056

The obliquity of the ecliptic being in southern

signs, is north,	23° 28′
Subtract the 1st angle, south,	23 4
2d angle, north,	0 24

Cosine of the 1st angle, 23° 4′, arith. comp.	0.03619
Cosine of the 2d angle, 0° 24′,	9.99999
Tangent of the right ascension, 86° 21′,	11.19524
Tangent of the longitude, 86° 39′,	11.23142

The latitude of the same star may be found by adding the sine of the longitude and the tangent of the 2d angle together, the sum, rejecting radius, will be the tangent of the latitude.

Sine of the longitude, 86° 39′	9.99925
Tangent of the 2d angle, 0° 24′, north,	7.84394
Tangent of the latitude, 0° 24′,	7.84319

The latitude is always of the same kind as the 2d Angle, which here being north the latitude is also north.

If the longitude should come out near 0° or near 180°, the operation must be changed by substituting the tangent and cosine of the longitude, instead of its sine. The operation will then stand thus: add the tangent of the longitude, the cosine of the longitude, and the tangent of the 2d angle together, rejecting a double radius, or 20.00000, the remainder will be the tangent of the latitude.

The longitude must always be taken from the nearest equinoctial point, and, of course, the right ascension must be taken in the same way. Therefore, if the right ascension exceed 90°, it must be subtracted from 180°, and the remainder used as right ascension, because it is its distance in right ascension from ♎. In this case, the longitude, when found, will be, for the same reason, its longitudinal distance from ♎, and therefore it must be subtracted from 180° to give its longitudinal distance from ♈. If the right ascension be above 180°, the 180° must be taken from it, and the remainder will be the right ascension from ♎. The longitude, when found, will be the longitudinal distance from ♎. If the right ascension be above 270°, it must be subtracted from 360°, and the remainder used as right ascension, which is its distance from ♈ south of the equator. When the longitude is found, it must be subtracted from 180°, which will give the longitudinal distance from ♎; or if subtracted from 360° it will give the distance from ♈.

Problem 5th.—To find the ascensional difference from the declination.

Rule. Add the tangent of the latitude of the place to the tangent of a star's declination, the sum will be the sine of the ascensional difference.

Example: What is the ascensional difference of ♃ in the latitude of 51° 32′ with 23° 2′ declination.

Tangent of 51° 32′,   10.09991

Tangent of 23° 2′,   9.62855

Sine of ascensional difference required,   9.72846, or 32° 21′.

N. B. If the tangent of the declination be added to the tangent of the pole of a star, it will give the tangent of the ascensional difference of that star under its pole.

Problem 6th—To find the right ascension of a star, not having latitude.

Rule.—Add the cosine of its longitudinal distance from the nearest equinoctial point to the arithmetical complement of the cosine of its declination, the sum will be the cosine of its right ascension from the equinoctial point, from which the longitudinal distance was taken. The arc thus found will, if the star be in ♈ ♉, or Ⅱ, be the right ascension, but if it be in ♋, ♌, or ♍, it must be subtracted from 180°; if in ♎, ♏, or ♐, 180° must be added to it; and if in ♑, ♒, or ♓, the arc found must be subtracted from 360°.

Example: Suppose the ☉ to be in 15° 6′ of ♈, with 5° 58′ of declination, I would know his right ascension?

Arithmetical complement of the cosine of the declination, 5° 58′,	0.00236
Cosine of its longitudinal distance from the first point of ♈, 15° 6′,	9.98474

Cosine of the Sun's right ascension,   9.98710

equal to 13° 53′, which, as the Sun is in ♈, is the true right ascension required.

Problem 7th.—To find the right ascension of a star, having latitude.

Rule. As the cosine of the star's declination is to the cosine of its longitudinal distance from the nearest equinoctial point, so is the cosine of its latitude to the cosine of the right ascension required.

Example: Suppose ♃ to be in 3° 21′ of ♑, with 23° 2′ of declination, and 0° 24′ of latitude, what will be his right ascension?

As the cosine of ♃'s declination (arith. comp.) 23° 2′,	0.03608
is to the cosine of his longitudinal distance from the first point of ♈, 86° 39′,	8.76667
so is the cosine of his latitude, 0° 24′,	9.99998

to the cosine of his right ascension from that point, 86° 21′,	8.80273

Subtract the 86° 21′ from 360°, ♃ being in ♑ it will leave a remainder of 273° 39′, which is the true right ascension of ♃.

If, however, the star be in the beginning of ♈ with great north latitude, or in the beginning of ♎ with great south latitude, the above method will not give the right ascension correctly, and therefore the proportion must be altered as follows.

As radius is to the sine of the star's longitudinal distance so is the cotangent of the latitude to the tangent of the first arc.

This first arc, when found, must be subtracted from the ecliptical difference, 23° 28′, and the remainder will be the second arc.

As the sine of the first arc is to the sine of the second arc, so is the tangent of the longitudinal distance to the tangent of the right ascension, from that point from whence it was taken, which, being regulated as before directed, will give the true right ascension. But the first rule will answer very well if the star be 2° distant from the first point of ♈, or ♎.

When the ascensional difference and right ascension are obtained the semiarcs and oblique ascension or descension will be found in the usual way, as directed under the head of those articles; the oblique ascension, by subtracting the ascensional difference from the right ascension, if the declination be north, or adding it if south; and the oblique descension, by adding the ascensional difference, if the declination be north, or subtracting it if south; if the star have no declination it has only right ascension.

The semidiurnal arc will be found by adding the ascensional difference to 90°, if the declination be north, or subtracting it if south; and the seminocturnal arc by subtracting the ascensional difference from 90°, if the declination be north, or by adding it if south.

Problem 8th.—To find the point of the ecliptic on the cusp of the midheaven for any given time.

Rule. 1*st*, Add the time from the last noon to the Sun's right ascension in time, the sum will be the right ascension of the midheaven in time. This must be turned into degrees and minutes.

2*d*, Add the cotangent of the right ascension from the nearest equinox to the cosine of 23° 28′, the sum will be the cotangent of the longitude from the said nearest equinoctial point.

Example: Suppose the right ascension of the midheaven to be 72° 38′, what point of the ecliptic should culminate?

Cotangent of 72° 38′ (its distance in right as-
cension from Aries,)   9.49519
            Cosine of 23° 28′,   9.96250
                                                          _____
        Cotangent of the longitude from ♈, 74° 0′   9.45769
Equal to 14° of ♊ (see plate 3, fig1.)

When the star is in ♈, ♉, or ♊, this gives the longitude from ♈; if in ♋, ♌, or ♍, subtract the arc so found from 90°, it gives the longitude from ♋; if in ♎, ♏, or ♐, it gives the longitude from ♎ without subtraction; and if in ♑, ♒, or ♓, by subtracting it from 90° it gives the longitude from ♑.

Problem 9th.—To find what point of the ecliptic occupies the cusp of any house, except the 10th or 4tn.

Rule. Add 30° to the right ascension of the midheaven for every house, according to its distance from the midheaven eastward, the sum will be the oblique ascension of such house (namely, 30° for the 11th, 60° for the 12th, 90° for the horoscope, 120° for the 2d, and 150° for the 3d.) Thus, if the right ascension of the midheaven be 72° 38', the oblique ascension of the 11th will be 102° 38'; of the 12th, 132° 38'; of the horoscope, 162° 38'; of the 2d, 192° 38'; and of the 3d, 222° 38') :

2d, To the cosine of the oblique ascension of the house, taken from the nearest equinoctial point, add the cotangent of the pole of the house, the sum will be the cotangent of the first arc.

3d, If the cusp of the house be nearest to Aries add to the first arc 23° 28', but if nearest to Libra subtract 23° 28' from it; the sum or remainder will be the second arc.

4th, As the cosine of the 2d arc is to the cosine of the 1st arc, so is the tangent of the oblique ascension of the house to the tangent of its longitude from Aries or Libra; for if the 2d angle be less than 90° the longitude must be reckoned from the same equinoctial point the oblique ascension was taken from, but if more than 90° from the other point.

Example: What point of the ecliptic should occupy the cusp of the 11th house, the right ascension of the midheaven being 72° 38'?

Cosine of the oblique ascension of the 11th,
   102° 38', or 77° 22', from ♎,   9.33987
Cotangent of the pole of the 11th, 23° 27'   10.36274

Cotangent of the 1st arc,   63° 14',   9.70261
Being the nearest to ♎ subtract   23   28

           Second arc,   39 46
As the cosine of the 2d arc, 39° 46', (arith comp.)   0.11427
   is to the cosine of the 1st arc, 63° 14',   9.65355
so is the tangent of the oblique ascension, 77° 22',   10.64949

to the tangent of its longitude, 69° 4',   10.41731

As the 2d arc is less than 90° the longitude must be taken from ♎, from whence the oblique ascension was taken, it is therefore 69° 4' distant from ♎, and as it lies between that sign and the first point of ♋, it must be subtracted from 90°, and it will give 20° 56' of ♋ for the cusp of the the 11th house. The cusps of the other 4 houses, viz. the 12th, 1st, 2d, and 3d, may be found the same way, by means of their respective poles, and adding 30° to each for its oblique ascension. The cusps of the other six houses are of course in opposite signs, degrees, and minutes.

Example: In the 12th house of the same figure, its oblique ascension will be nearer to ♎ by 30°, so that its oblique ascension will be distant from that point only 47° 22′.

Cosine of 47° 22′, its distance from ♎,   9.83078
The pole of the 12th is 40° 48′, the co-
    tangent of which is   10.06390

               Cotangent of the 1st arc,   9.89468   51° 53′ 1st arc
                                                  23 28

As cosine of 2d arc   28° 25′,   0.05576   28 25 2d arc
is to cosine of 1st arc,   51 53   9.79047
so is tangent of dist.   47 22,   10.03592

to the tangent of long. 37° 19′,   9.88215

This is its distance from ♎, which subtracted from 90°, gives the distance from ♋, of 52° 41′, or 22° 41′ of ♌, for the cusp of the 12th house.

The longitude of the horoscope may be had the same way, but as we have it correct to a minute in the table of houses, we shall proceed to the 2d house.

By taking 60° of oblique ascension away for the difference between the oblique distance of the 12th and 2d houses we bring it 60° nearer to Libra, or, to speak more properly, we pass Libra, for our distance of the 12th from Libra was but 47° 22′ of oblique ascension, which subtracted from 60°, will make our distance from Libra, 12° 38′, on the other side, the cosine of
    which is,   9.98935
Cotangent of the pole of the 2d house,
    40° 48′,   10.06390

         Cotangent of the 1st arc,   10.05325   41° 30′ 1st arc
                                                  23 28

                                                  18   2 2d arc
As the A. C. of the cosine of the 2d arc, 18° 2′,   0.02184
is to the cosine of the 1st arc, 41° 30′,   9.87445
so is the tangent of this dist. 12 38,   9.35051

to the tangent of longitude, 10° 1′,   9.24680,
  which, without any alteration, is 10° 1′ of Libra.

For the 3d house we add 30° to the oblique distance, 12° 38′ from Libra, and it will give 42° 38′, the cosine

    of which is,   9.86670

The pole of the 3d house is 23° 27′, the

    cotangent of which is   10.36274

    Cotangent of the 1st arc,   10.22944 1st arc, 30° 31′

                                        23 28

As the cosine of the 2d arc, 7° 3′ 0.00330 2d arc, 7 3

is to the cosine of the 1st arc, 30 31 9.93524

so is the tangent of the dist. 12 38 9.96408

to the tangent of longitude, 38 42 9.90362, which is 38° 42′ distant from Libra, or 8° 42′ of ♏. The opposite houses have of course the same degrees and minutes of the opposite signs.

Problem 10*th.*—To find the pole of a star, or house, in any figure.

Rule. 1*st*, As the semiarc of the star or point is to 90°, so is its right distance from the 10th or 4th house (according as it may be situated) to the difference between its circle of position and that of the meridian, which difference, subtracted from its right distance, will give its ascensional difference under its own pole.

2*d*, To the sine of this ascensional difference add the cotangent of its declination, the sum will be the tangent of its pole.

Example: Suppose the seminocturnal arc of ♃ to be 122° 26′, his right distance from the 4th, 21° 1′, and his declination 23° 2′, what will be his polar elevation (commonly called his pole)?

Here we may use the proportional logarithms, which are contained in the same book as the logarithms of sines, tangents, and secants.

As the S. N. A. of ♃, 122° 26′ (proportional logarithm),   1674

is to 90° (pro. log.)   3010

so is his right distance from the 4th, 21° 1′ (pro. log.)   9327

                                                      1.2337

                                                      1674

to the distance between its circle of position from

    the 4th, which is equal to 15° 27′   1.0663

Subtract this 15° 27′ from the right distance, 21° 1′ it will give the ascensional difference of ♃ under his pole, 5° 34′.

To the sine of the ascensional diff. of ♃, 5° 34′, 8.98678
add the cotangent of ♃'s declination,   23 2 , 10.37145

the sum is the tangent of ♃'s pole,   12 51 , 9.35823

When the polar elevation of any house is wanted, its semiarc and declination will be those of the ☉, when he is posited in that point.

The arithmetical complement of these proportional logarithms may be found by subtracting the logarithm from 10.000, which will enable the operator to perform the whole by addition. At the tops of the columns of these logarithms the value is placed in degrees and minutes, leaving the left hand column for the seconds, but they may be made to answer to any sexagenary proportion. For instance, the logarithm of ♃'s S. N. A., 122° 26′, is the logarithm of 2° 2′ 6″, but by considering every minute as a degree, the operation will be the same.

Problem 11*th.*—To find the degree of the ☉'s depression.

Rule. 1*st,* The difference between the right ascension in time of the midheaven and the ☉'s ☍, is the horary angle.

2*d,* With this horary angle enter Douwes' Latitude Tables (which constitute the 16th set in the above mentioned Nautical Tables) and take the logarithm rising which corresponds with its quantity.

3*d,* To this logarithm rising add the cosine of the latitude of the place, and the cosine of the ☉'s declination.

4*th,* Their sum (rejecting all the tens in the index) will be the logarithm of a natural number (to be found in table 18 according to the usual rules.

5th, This number, subtracted from the natural sine of the Sun's meridian altitude (found in table 17th,) will give the natural sine of the altitude of the ☉'s ☍, which is of course the sine of the Sun's depression.

Example: Suppose the right ascension of the ☉'s opposite point to be 5*h.* 39*m*; right ascension of the midheaven, 11*h.* 54*m.*, the ☉'s declination, 23° 23′ : and the latitude of the country, 44°; what is the degree of the ☉'s depression?

Right ascension of the midheaven,   11*h.* 54*m.*
Right ascension of the Sun's opposite point, 5 39

       The horary angle will be 6 15
The logarithm rising of which is   5,02750

Cosine of the Sun's declination, 23° 23'   9.96278
Cosine of the latitude of the country, 44°,   9.85693

it gives the logarithm,   4.84721

(The value, or natural number of this logarithm must be sought for in table 18, called Logarithms of Numbers, as follows:

The nearest less logarithm to it is 84720, the natural number of which, in the left hand column, is 703, and the figure at the top of the column where the logarithm is, being 4, this figure is added, and it makes the natural number 7034. The difference between the nearest less logarithm and the real logarithm is 1, and the difference between the nearest less logarithm and the next greater is 6. Add a cypher to the 1, it makes it 10 (for as only one figure is wanted, only one cypher can be added,) and divide by the 6. It does not go twice, though very near, and therefore a 1 or a 2 may be added, for the difference is nothing, and the natural number will be 70342, for it must have the same number of figures as the decimal parts of its logarithm. All this has nothing to do with the problem or the example, and to those who understand the method of working by logarithms it is wholly useless, but I have inserted it merely for the sake of those who do not, to prevent them from being lost and confused.)

The natural number of the logarithm is 70342.

We now find the altitude of the ☉'s opposite point by adding the difference of latitude between the pole of the country and 90° to the ☉'s declination. As the latitude of the country is 44° the difference will be   46° 0'
                  Sun's declination,   23 23

        Altitude of the ☉'s opposition,   69 23   the natural sine of which is   93596, as may be found in the table of natural sines.

Subtract the natural number,   70342

It gives the natural sine of 13° 27', 23254, which is the degree of the Sun's depression, and as it does not extend to 18°, is a proof that it is within the crepusculine circles; whereas, had it been more than 18°. the Sun would have been in the obscure arc, or beyond the bounds of the crepuscle.

Problem 12*th.*—To find the extent of the crepusculine and obscure arcs without tables.

Rule. 1*st*, Add the difference of the latitude of the country from 90°, and the difference of the ☉'s declination from 90°, to the distance of the crepusculine circle from the zenith, and take half their sum.

2*d*, Subtract the difference of latitude from this half and take the sine of the remainder. Subtract also the difference of the declination from the half sum, and take the sine of its remainder.

3*d*, Add the logarithms of both these sines to the arithmetical complements of the sines of the difference of latitude and the difference of declination, and take half of the sum of the logarithm produced, of which no part of the index must be rejected.

4*th*, Find the sine of this half and double it, reduce it to time and subtract is from 12*h*., the remainder is the time when the twilight begins. Subtract this from the time of sunrise, it gives the distance of time between the beginning of twilight and sunrise, which being turned into degrees and minutes, will give the distance of the crepusculine are.

If the crepusculine arc be subtracted from the seminocturnal arc, the remainder will be the obscure arc.

Example: Suppose the ☉'s declination to be 42′ north, in the latitude of 51° 32′, what will be his crepusculine and obscure arcs?

As the crepusculine circles always extend to 18° below the horizon, the crepusculine circle of the ☉ must be distant from the zenith, 108° 0′

Difference of latitude between 51° 32′ and 90°, 38 28

Difference of the ☉'s declination from 90°, 89 18

Sum, 235 46

The half of which is 117° 53′.

Subtract from this half sum the difference of declination, 89° 18 , the remainder will be 28° 35′, the sine logarithm
of which is 9.67982

The difference of latitude subtracted from the same half sum leaves 79° 25′, which will give the sine logarithm 9.99254

Arith. comp. of the sine of the diff. of dec. 89° 18′, 0.00003

Arith. comp. of the sine of the diff. of lat. 38° 28′, 0.20616

2)19.87855

The half of which is the sine of 60° 24′, 9.93927
which multiplied by 2

gives 120 48, equal to 8*h*. 3*m*.

which subtracted from 12*h*. 0*m*. gives 3*h*. 57*m*., which, subtracted from the time of sunrising, which is 5*h*. 52*m*., leaves 1*h*. 55*m*. for the Sun's crepusculine arc, and this subtracted from the Sun's seminocturnal arc, 6° 53′, leaves 3*h*. 58*m*. for the space of the Sun's obscure arc.

Problem 13th.—To direct the ☉ in the crepuscle to the aspect of a star.

Rule. 1*st*, Add the difference between the ☉'s depression and 90°, the difference between the latitude of the country and 90°, and the difference between the declination of the place of the aspect and 90°, all three together, and take half their sum.

2*d*, Subtract from this half sum the difference of latitude, and take the sine of the remainder. Subtract the difference also of the declination, and take the sine in like manner.

3*d*, Add the logarithms of both these sines to the sine arithmetical complements of the two differences in latitude and declination (without rejecting radius) and divide the logarithm by 2.

4*th*, Find the sine of this half and double it, and subtract it from the seminocturnal arc of the place of the aspect, the remainder will be the secondary distance, which, when subtracted from the ☉'s primary distance from the horoscope (taken by oblique ascension) will give the ortive difference, which added to the common arc of direction will give the true arc.

Example: Suppose ♄ to be in 2° 24′ of ♐, I would direct the ☉ as posited in problem 11th to the □ of that planet. The direction falls of course in 2° 24′ of ♓.

Difference of the ☉'s depression 13° 27′ from 90°	76°	33′
Difference of latitude between 44° and 90°,	46	0
Difference of declination between 10° 39′ (2° 24′ ♓) and 90°,	79	21
Sum	201	54

the half of which is 100° 57′.

Subtract the diff. of declination, 79° 21′, the remainder will be 21° 36′ and its sine,	9.56599
Sub. the diff. of lat. in like manner, its sine will be	9.89693
Sine arithmetical comp. of the diff. of declination,	0.00755
Sine arithmetical comp. of the diff. of latitude,	0.14307
	2)19.61354

9.80677

Sine of 39° 51′

which multiplied by   2

___

gives   79 42, which subtracted from the seminocturnal arc of the aspect, 100° 27′, leaves the secondary distance, 20° 45′.

This is taken from the nativity of Cardinal Farnese, in Placidus, where the oblique ascension of the horoscope is 268° 35′, and by subtracting it from the ☉'s oblique ascension, 289° 32′, there remains his distance from the horoscope, 20° 57′. Subtract from this the secondary distance, 20° 45′, there remains for the ortive difference, 0° 12′, which, as the secondary distance is less than the primary, must be added to the common arc of direction, 55° 18′, the true arc of direction will be 55° 30′.

Placidus, who did nothing of this kind trignonometrically, has brought up this direction in a very slovenly way in other respects. He made the Sun's depression only 13° instead of 13° 27′, and he took the secondary distance from 2° of ♓ instead of 2° 24′. He likewise takes the ☉'s primary distance in the tables at 20° 14′ instead of 20° 57′, affirming the difference to be of little or no consequence, and when all these defects are added to the natural inaccuracy of the crepusculine tables, it is not surprising that the ortive difference should be only 12′ instead of 1° 54′, as Placidus makes it. This, however, is no impeachment of his candour, for by lengthening the arc of direction it weakened his own system of crepusculine positions.

Those who can work by trigonometry, according to the problems here laid down, will find their operations more correct than they possibly can be by referring to tables, provided they take their logarithms right. In finding the crepusculine circle or obscure arc, it is infinitely more perfect than the crepusculine tables; and in finding the pole of a planet or house or working with it when it is found, it is indispensibly necessary, for by this means the pole may be taken and used even to a minute, a circumstance wholly neglected by Placidus, and indeed most others, who think if they take the pole of a planet to an even degree it is sufficient. I would therefore advise the operator, if he be not already acquainted with trigonometry and the use of logarithms, to become so as soon as possible, for he can never calculate to any degree of exactness without it.

TRIMORION, the distance of 3 signs, or the square aspect. This distance may, it is said, in certain cases, give 120° of direction and not more (though I never knew an instance of it), and as the direction to the □ of the anareta, they suppose, is sure to kill, those wise-acres have therefore limited the utmost extent of human life, since the flood, to 120 years, which they call the Trimorion.

TRINE (△) a distance of 4 signs, or 120°, in the zodiac. In the world it is the whole of a semiarc and a third of another. It is reckoned the best aspect of the whole, though I own I have some doubts about this. The △ in signs of short ascension will kill, according to Ptolemy, if it comes from ♄ or ♂, because it is in his opinion equal to a □. See "Aspects."

TRIPLICITY, a fourth part of the zodiac, forming an equilateral triangle; or, a triangle of equal sides; it being composed of three signs, each of which are at equal distance from the other. These triangles are called Trigons. The first trigon is composed of ♈, ♌, and ♐, and is therefore called the fiery triplicity. ♂ is lord of ♈; the ☉, of ♌; and ♃, of ♐, but ♂, being an enemy to the ☉, is excluded and deprived of having any share in the government, which devolves on the ☉ and ♃ as lords of this triplicity, the former of whom rules it by day and the latter by night. The 2d trignon contains ♉, ♍, and ♑, which being three feminine signs, are committed to the care of ♀ and the ☾, viz. ♀ by day and the ☾ by night. The 3d trigon contains ♊, ♎, and ♒, and is ruled by ♄ and ☿, ♄ by day and ☿ by night. The 4th trigon is formed of ♋, ♏, and ♓, 3 feminine signs, and is ruled by ♂, because he is a feminine planet, though the ☾ by night and ♀ by day have a share in its government.

The fiery trigon is northern because of ♃, who is said to govern the north, because he brought the Egyptians fruitful showers from that quarter. It would be no bad policy, were the Europeans to assign him the government of the south, which would enable him to accommodate them in a similar way. This trigon is also north-west, from the mixture of ♂, who although outlawed, took the liberty of introducing the west wind among them and it is also south-west, because ♂ is feminine and the south is feminine.

The earthy trigon is called southern, being under the petticoat government of ♀ and the ☾, who contrived between them to exclude ♄ and ☿, for what reason we are not informed. It is south, because ♀, they say, brings south winds, and east, because ♄ brings east winds.

The 3d trigon is chiefly eastern, because ♄ brought east winds, and persuaded ☿ to do the same. It is also north-east, because, it is said, ♃ claimed a share in it on account of his affinity to ♄, being both diurnal planets.

The 4th trigon is westerly, because governed by ♂, who delighted in the west winds, because they scorched the Egyptians, and it is also south-west, because of ♀ having a share in it, and governing the south winds.

The stupid childish absurdity of all this requires no comment, only just to observe, that the doctrine of countries and cities being governed by certain signs and planets is founded on this folly alone, and is consequently not deserving the smallest attention.

In horary questions a planet in its triplicity denotes a respectable person, who has a sufficiency of every thing, and is quite comfortable.

TROPICAL SIGNS, ♋ and ♑, so called because they limit the course of the ☉.

TRUITINE OF HERMES. See "Rectification."

TRUE MOMENT OF BIRTH, that wherein the child becomes independent of the mother, and the lungs are inflated.

VENUS. See "Planets."

VERTICAL, directly over head.

VESPERTINE, the reverse of matutine: when a planet sets in the evening after the ☉. It is reckoned the same kind of dignity in an inferior planet as a matutine position is in a superior planet, because they are then descending to the lowest part of their orb, increasing in light. and approaching nearer to the Earth.

VIA COMBUSTA, the combust way: the last half of ♎ and the whole of ♏, though others say, the first 15 degrees of ♏, so called from several violent fixed stars, which, they say, render that place extremely unfortunate, particularly to the ☾, who suffers there as much as during an eclipse.

VIOLENT SIGNS, those that are the houses or exaltations of the malefics, viz. ♈, ♎, ♏, ♑, and ♒. Also those signs are called violent where there are any remarkably violent fixed stars, as ♉ for Caput Algol, &c.

VIRGO. See "Signs."

VOID OF COURSE, when a planet forms no aspect during the remainder of its course through the sign where it is posited. It is only a distinction in horary questions, and signifies that the business denoted by such a significator will come to no good conclusion. Placidus never considers the sign to make any difference in an aspect, but always calculates them as if the zodiac were not divided into signs.

UNDER THE SUNBEAMS, when a planet is not 17 degrees from the ☉. It is reckoned four debilities. In horary questions it is reckoned fear, trouble, and oppression, but not so bad as combustion.

UNFORTUNATE SIGNS, ♉, ♋, ♍, ♏, ♑, and ♓. The natives are said to be unfortunate in the general tendency of the events of their lives. The most unfortunate of them all is ♑.

WATERY SIGNS, ♋, ♏, and ♓.

WATERY TRIPLICITY, the triplicity formed of the three watery signs.

WEAK SIGNS, ♋, ♑, and ♓. The natives are said to be weak in frame and less robust than if born under any other sign.

WHALE'S JAW, Menkar, a star of the 2d magnitude, of the nature of ♄, in 12 degrees of ♉, said to cause sickness when united to the luminaries, and when in the midheaven disgrace, ruin, and great affliction.

WEATHER. The methods made use of in judging of weather are several. It is usual to erect a figure for the ☉'s ingress into the four cardinal signs ♈, ♋, ♎, and ♑, and prognosticate according as the ☉ and planets are posited. The last ☌ or ☍ also of the luminaries is to be considered, and what signs it happened in, whether heat or cold, dryness or moisture, predominated, and what kind of fixed stars were near them.

The ☌ of ♄ and ♃ in fiery signs, or near fixed stars of the same nature, produce heat and dryness in summer, and mitigate the cold in winter, for sometimes both before and after the ☌. In watery signs it causes rains and floods; in earthy signs, extreme cold; and in airy signs, wind and tempest.

If ♄ have higher latitude than ♃, terrible diseases or influenza prevail, but if ♃'s latitude be more northern the evil will be greatly mitigated. Some say the evil or good will prevail according as ♄ or ♃ are essentially dignified above each other. This weather is said to be renewed every time they come to a ⚹, ☐, △, or ☍, until the next ☌. In all their aspects they generally stir up tempests and rain. In the spring, from watery signs, they produce moist air and rain; in summer, thunder and hail; in autumn, wind and rain; and in winter, dark, thick, cloudy weather.

♂ in ☌, ☐, or ☍ of ♄ causes, in spring, wind, rain and thunder; in summer, thunder and hail; in autumn, heavy rains; in winter, warm, thick, cloudy weather.

☉ in ☌, ☐, or ☍ of ♄ causes a dark, cloudy spring; hail, thunder, and cold in summer; rain and cold in autumn; and clouds, snow, and frost in winter.

♀ in ☌, □, or ☍ of ♄ generally causes cold rain in spring; sudden, hasty showers in summer; cold and wet in autumn; and snow or sleet in winter.

☿ in ☌, □, or ☍ of ♄ brings drought in fiery signs; rain in moist signs; wind in airy signs; and cold, dry air in earthy signs. In spring wind and rain; in summer wind and sharp showers; in autumn wind and clouds; in winter wind and snow.

☾ in ☌, □, or ☍ of ♄ in moist signs gives cold cloudy weather; in airy signs, or ♐ or ♑, cold; in dry signs, a sharp air, and frost in winter. They generally cause cloudy, rainy weather. In spring they cause a foggy moist air; in summer, a moist, cool air, but if ♂ or ☿ aspect them, they cause thunder or hail; in autumn, cloudy cool air; and in winter, clouds and snow with excessive cold.

The ☌, □, or ☍ of ♂ with ♃, in fiery signs, causes great heat; in watery signs, thunder and rain. In spring, wind and thick clouds; in summer, heat and thunder: in autumn, tempestuous weather; and in winter, a temperate air with little cold. If ♃ have higher latitude or declination than ♂ at these times, it causes general fertility: but if ♂ be more northern, it causes pestilential air and much evil. If they are near violent fixed stars, as Atair, Arcturus, the bright star in the Crown, Cauda Delphini, &c. they cause thunder, hail, and wind.

☉ in ☌, □, or ☍ of ♃ gives serene weather and salubrious winds in spring and autumn; in summer, thunder; and in winter, warmth.

♀ in ☌, □, or ☍ of ♃ causes fine, serene, temperate air; but if in watery signs, gentle showers, and in all cases fine fertile seasons.

☿ in □, ☌, or ☍ of ♃ causes wind and rain. In fiery signs, warm wind, and dryness; in airy signs fine weather; in moist signs, very gentle showers; and in earthy signs, fine, temperate weather, but they generally cause brisk, winds; in spring and autumn, they cause hail; and in winter, snow.

☾ in ☌, □, or ☍ of ♃ causes general mildness, gentle winds and serene air; in fiery signs, more warm and dry; in watery signs, gentle showers; and in airy and earthy signs, fine weather.

☉ in ☌, □, or ☍ of ♂ in fiery signs causes much heat and dryness; in watery signs, thunder, rain and hail; in airy signs, violent winds,; and in earthy signs, thick cloudy weather. In spring and autumn, great dryness; in summer, great heat; and in winter, warm weather for the season.

♀ in ☌, □, or ☍ of ♂ in watery signs gives much rain both in spring and autumn; in summer, warm showers; in winter snow, but without much cold.

☿ in ☌, □, or ☍ of ♂ causes snow in winter and spring; in summer, hail-storms and thunder; and in autumn, the same, with high winds. In fiery signs they give great heat, and in earthy signs much dryness.

☾ in ☌, □, or ☍ of ♂ causes rain when in moist signs, but in fiery signs dryness, with red windy clouds, and sometimes rain. In summer, hail, lightning, and corruscations, and at all times, a warm, pestilential, unwholesome air.

The ☉ and ♀ in ☌ produce rain at all times of the year.

The ☉ and ☿ joined in airy signs cause winds; in watery signs, rain; in fiery signs, heat, and pestilential winds; and in earthy signs, cold dry weather.

The ☉ and ☾ at the ☌, □. and ☍, generally produce such weather as is congenial to the planets giving testimony. In watery signs they give rain; in airy signs, wind; and in earthy or fiery signs, fair weather.

The ☌, semi✳, and ✳ of ♀ and ☿ cause winds and rain, or if in winter, snow, particularly if they keep pace with each other so as to prolong the aspect.

When ♄ passes out of one sign into another, the weather becomes unsettled and turbulent, and ♂ produces the same effect, only with a greater degree of warmth.

♂ in Cancer with north latitude, brings warm weather, with rain and wind, and if in aspect with ♄, ♀, or ☿, makes the atmosphere very unwholesome. When near the Hyades he causes wind and rain; near the Pleiades, he makes the weather cloudy; with Atair and Frons Scorpio, cold rain or snow; and when he rises or sets with Atair, Arcturus, Occulus Taurus, Cauda Delphini, Procyon, Sirius, the bright star in the Crown, Orion, Regulus, the Hyades, Antares, Spica, &c. he causes a windy and tempestuous or sultry obnoxious air.

The ☉ setting with Regulus causes west winds; with the Pleiades north-east winds; with Arcturus, south winds. Rising with the Pleiades, he brings the east wind; with the Asselli, thunder-storms; with Atair, Caput Algol, and the Goat's Tail, snow; with Orion or Aldebaran, wind and thunder-storms; with Deneb, Cor Hydra, the Crown, Frons Scorpio, or Orion, cloudy weather. When he sets with Lyra, cold, rainy weather; with the Pleiades.

mild showers; with Regulus, thunder-storms; with Sirius, great
heat, thunder-storms, and corruscations; with Orion or Aldebaran, stormy, wet weather; with stars of the nature of ♄, cold rain
or snow; of the nature of ♃, serene weather; with those of the
nature of ♂, thunder; and with those of the nature of ♀, mist
and rain.

♄ with Caput Algol gives cold rain; with the Pleiades, stormy
weather, rain and snow; with Orion or Arcturus, wind and rain;
with Spica, thunder-showers; with the Dolphin, Crown, Goat's
Tail, or the Harp, cloudy, wet weather, and sometimes snow;
with Præspe and the Hyades, wind, thunder, and rain; with Cor
Leonis, thunder-storms; and with Sirius, tempests, thunder, and
lightning.

♃ with Regulus gives fine weather, and mild even in winter.
With the Lion's Neck, winds; with the Goat's Tail, showers;
with Frons Scorpio, cold weather, rain or snow: with Arcturus,
violent winds, and thunder-storms; with the Eagle, cold rains
or snow; with Orion, the Hyades, Regulus, or Sirius, great
heat.

♀ in the first decade of ♋, or with the Pleiades, Hyades, or the
Asselli, causes rain.

☿ with the Pleiades, causes mild wind and rain; with Atair,
cold rains or snow: with Orion, Hyades, Sirius, and Regulus,
wind, rain and thunder; with the Goat's Tail, windy rain, or
snow; with the Back and Neck of the Lion, moist wind; with
Deneb, Spica, Lyra, &c. it causes a sudden change from fair
weather to wind, or rain.

☽ in a fiery sign causes north-west winds; in an earthy, south-
east; in a watery, south-west, in an airy sign, north-east.

♄, ♃, ♂, or ☿, with Arcturus, cause high winds; but if at the
matutine setting of the Dolphin there will be rain, there will be
none at the rising of Arcturus. The Hyades at the rising and setting cause wind and rain, especially if ♂ and ☿ give testimony.
The rising of the Hyades causes rain. The matutine rising of
Sirius causes great heat and unwholesome air. Orion's Belt rising cosmically makes a turbid atmosphere. The Crown, setting,
or Sirius and the Eagle rising acronycally, cause tempests. Regulus setting causes north wind and sometimes rain. The Dolphin
setting, causes wind and snow. Vindemiatrix setting causes a
north-east wind. The Ram's Horn rising causes wind and snow.
Arcturus rising acronycally causes tempests. The Pleiades rising
brings north winds. Sirius setting acronycally causes south-east
or north-east winds. The matutine setting of the Hyades causes

south winds and rain. The vespertine setting of the Pleiades causes a mild south wind, passing round to the west. The rising of the Succulæ brings rain. Orion rising brings the west wind. The Eagle setting matutine brings south wind and great heat; Arcturus and the Succulæ setting in like manner, causes rain, wind and snow.

These are the rules by which almanac makers put down the changes of weather, and every year's experience proves how seldom they are verified. This is because they attribute effects to the planets and fixed stars which belong to the luminaries alone. When the ☉ arrives at ♌ the Earth has been extremely heated during his progress through Cancer, and this accumulated heat operating in conjunction with his own natural power, causes all those effects attributed to the matutine rising of Sirius. The truth of this may be fully experienced in cold wet summers, when by the interposition of clouds and excessive rain the Earth has not acquired that degree of heat necessary to produce such effects. The matutine position of the Dog Star then is productive of no such influence, and even the Asselli, so much dreaded, lose their burning power. The Hyades have been blamed for causing those heavy rains and storms which result from the breaking up of the winter season as the Sun proceeds northward, and poor Orion lost his good character (if he ever had one) through a similar mistake. So far as relates to my own observation, all changes of consequence proceed from the Sun and Moon. On the third day after the ☌ a change may be expected, but it is seldom of long duration. On the day the ☽ forms her first dichotome, another change may be expected, but it seldom lasts above a day, especially when the weather has a strong bias in any particular way. Rain, however, that has lasted a week, will frequently clear up on that day, and not return till the end of the lunation. Changes sometimes happen at the △ and the ☍, but very seldom, particularly the latter, for which I own it is difficult to account. The water is affected in a similar way at the full as at the change, yet the weather seldom manifests any alteration. The ☽'s second dichotome makes little variation in the weather that can be depended upon, but on the third day after she has passed it, a most striking difference may always be observed. For the most part, the temperature of the air is materially altered, the wind frequently changes, rainy weather becomes fair, or fair weather rainy. If rain continues, it will be much increased, or come from a different quarter; and if fair weather continues, as it sometimes will when the wind remains fixed in the east, a turbid, cloudy substance will be

seen rising in the west on the day in question, which after a seemingly hard struggle to gain the ascendency, will gradually dissolve.
Severe frosts generally break on this day, but when they remain,
are attended by an excessive fall of snow.

WHOLE SIGNS, ♊, ♎, and ♒. Those born under these are
said to be strong, robust, and not so liable to accidents.

ZENITH, the point directly over head. Thus, every place has
its own zenith, and the nearer the planets are to that zenith the
more powerful is their operation.

ZIGIATUS, a very foolish name given by some silly astrologers to any person born under ♎, who, they say, will be apt to
commit suicide, because when Libra ascends, ♉ will be on or
near the cusp of the 8th house, and thus the lady of the ascendant,
♀, being also lady of the 8th, the person will somehow or other be
the cause of their own death. The opinion was Ptolemy's originally,
but he not giving his reasons, Pontanus, as above explains it for
him. This probably was not Ptolemy's reason, else the same
thing might have been said of those born under ♈, who would by
the same rule have ♏ for their 8th, and ♂ would be lord of both.

ZODIAC, a kind of circle or rather belt, 12 degrees broad, with
the ecliptic passing through the middle of it. It contains the 12
signs of the ecliptic, all of which being animals, it takes its name
from them. Modern astronomers consider it as 18 degrees broad,
on account of the extensive latitude of ♂ and ♀.

ZODICAL ASPECTS, aspects measured by the degrees of the
zodiac. In this case the promittor's place is taken without latitude, instead of which the latitude is taken which the significator
will have when it arrives at the place where the aspect is formed.

ZODIACAL PARALLELS. See "Parallels"

THE END.